PLANET EARTH INC.

Empire Of The gods Deposed

VOLUME TWO

www.edrychkun.com

ISBN 978-1-927066-02-7

Although there is no copyright to this book, much material has been used from other Authors, Researchers, and Internet sources that may be copyrighted. As so, whenever possible, in the interest of truth, owners of material have been contacted to attain approval for use of material. Where possible, the relevant web sites and Authors have been referenced. This book is a research compilation dedicated to truth and Unity. It relates to the revelation and knowing of many people who are focussed on determining the truth in commerce and religion. It is meant to freely assist anyone to find their own truth or to assist in further research into truth. It is also meant to help understand life, know another choice, or lead the reader to their own quest for truth.

In the end, when one is able to rise above the polarity of good and evil, the information becomes quite irrelevant and if it helps you get there; to a place where judgment is no more, then this book has served its purpose.

TABLE OF CONTENTS

PART 2 OVERVIEW — 5

PART 2 REVOLUTION OR RESOLUTION WHAT'S HAPPENING — 11

37 SOMETHING IS AMISS IN GOD'S LAWS — 12
- New World Order Or New Order Of The Ages? — 12
- All Bibles And Prophesies Point To Christ As Inspiration — 14
- A Recap : The New Version Of Christ's Story — 15
- A Rewrite Of Christ's Story Was Inevitable — 18
- The Implementation Of The Word Of god — 19
- The New Mythology Of The Bibles — 20

38 THE END TIME OF THE GREAT SHIFT — 24
- The Mayan End Times — 25
- The Ninth Wave-What Is It? — 27

39 RAPTURE AND REVELATION: THE DARK SIDE — 30
- The Satanic Plan Of Dominion — 30
- The PLANET EARTH Business Plan O 2009-2012 — 33
- The Secret Covenant: PLANET EARTH Code Of Ethics — 33
- Old End Time Of Revelation — 37
- More On Revelation And Prophesy — 39

40 RAPTURE AND REVELATION: THE LIGHT SIDE — 46
- The Divine Plan Of The Order Of The Ages — 46
- The New Earth Genesis II — 47
- The Undeniable Theme Of Prevailing Consciousness — 49
- A New Prophesy Of Rapture, Revelation and Resurrection — 51
- The New End Time Of Revelation — 53

41 THE CHRIST CONSCIOUSNESS — 57
- The Shifting Consciousness Of New Earth — 57
- New Age Spirituality And Core Beliefs — 60
- The Christ Consciousness From The Aquarian Gospel — 63

42 THE STRAWMAN REVOLUTION — 66
- Private Versus Public Jurisdictions — 67
- The Four Elements Of Contract — 68
- Some Basics On Debt — 70
- Getting Access To The Good Faith And Credit — 75
- The Process Of Commercial Redemption — 76
- The Process Of Debt Set-off And Closed Accounts — 80

The Process Of Acceptance For Value	89
Honour Or Dishonour, To Fight Or Not To Fight	98

43 THE NEW REPUBLIC OF THE UNITED STATES — 100

The Restoration Of The Republic	100
The Constitution Was Usurped By The Corporation	103
The Timeline Leading To The Current United States	104
Repairing The Country	106
Re-inhabiting The Republic	107
Was HJR-192 Repealed?	111

44 THE NATIONAL ECONOMIC STABILIZATION ACT — 114

What Is NESARA?	114
The Roots Of NESARA	116
A Spiritually Directed Financial Program	118
Executive Summary Of The NESARA Bill	122
Current Status Of The NESARA Bill	125
How Does This Translate To The People?	126

45 THE NEW INTERNATIONAL WAVES OF TRUTH — 134

The New Economic Rights Alliance of South Africa	134
The Ubunto Freedom Charter	138
The New Freedom Charter	139
The New Origins Of Humankind	144
UFO Conference: Disclosure And Truth Of Neighbours	148

46 THE 2012 SCENARIO FREE WAVES OF TRUTH — 150

The 2012 Scenario By Steve Beckow	151
The Divine Cosmos By David Wilcock	155

47 THE POSTMASTER GENERAL FOR THE AMERICAS — 158

About The Universal Postal Union	159
Origins Of The U.S. Postal Service	160
Origins Of The General Post Office	162
The Link To The Vatican And The Estate Trust	162
The New Postmaster General	164
The Global Estate Trust, Post Office, Vatican And Military	166
The Postal Authority	167
Military Duty To Protect The Post	170
The Military Industrial Complex	171

48 THE UNIVERSAL POSTAL TREATY FOR THE AMERICAS — 174

It Is Peace And Prosperity We Seek	174
The Universal Postal Treaty For The Americas (UPT)	175
UPT Declaration Of Causes For Separation	176
UPT Complex Regulatory Scheme	177
UPT Claim On Abandonment	180
UPT Declaration Of Peace	186
UPT The Law Of The Flag	187
UPT Law Form	187

UPT Administrative Notice	193
UPT No Immunity Under Commerce	198
The Registration And Enforcement	215

49 IT'S ALL ABOUT TRUST(S) — 216

First and Foremost Is Our Divine Trust	216
The History Of Trusts	218
Setting Up A Trust: The Mechanics	219
More Trust Basics: Relationships	221
The Vatican And Crown Are Primary Trustees	226
The Divine Estate Is An Implied Trust	229
Constitutional Relationship To Current Trusts	230
Three Cestui Que Trusts Are Created By Vatican And State	232
Cestui Que As A Method Of Fraud	233
Cestui Que A Medieval Invention In Practice	234
The Significance Of The Cestui Que Vie Trust Today	237
Is The Cestui Que Used Today?	240
The Cestui Que Vie Act Of 1666	241

50 THE NATIONAL BANKING ASSOCIATION — 244

Philosophy And Mission	244
National Banking Association	246

51 THE PROCESS OF CURE FOR James-Thomas: McBride — 247

Changing The System Flow Of Money Energy	247
Communications From The New Postmaster General	249
Breach Of Divine Estate And Funding The Military Complex	250
A Cure To The Breach Must Be Declared	250
The Need For The Universal Postal Treaty	253
Declaring And Establishing The Rightful Claims	256

52 SERVING NOTICE ON THE BREACH OF TRUST — 258

Authority As Trustee For The Global Abundance Program	258
Documentary Evidence Of Authority	259
Important Notice To The American People	260
Gaining Authority As Trustee	263
Divine Right Of Use	263
Who Is To Be Served Notice	266
The Ecclesiastic Deed Poll Explained	267

53 ACTIVATION OF AUTHORITY: FEDERAL RESERVE — 276

Authority Activation Process	276
Activation Of Federal Reserve Account	277

54 RECLAIMING TRUSTEESHIP AND POSTAL AUTHORITY — 281

National Banking Association	281
A Trustee Of The Global Trust	282
The Universal Postal treaty For The Americas	283

55 THE PHANTOM ADMINISTRATION OF PLANET EARTH INC — 287

All Government Officials Are Private Contractors	287

Dear Mister Obama, We Have A Speech For You	293
A Note On Your New Path	297

PART 3 DISSOLUTION & SOLUTION WHAT IS THE CURE?   298

PART 3 OVERVIEW   299

56 THE TWO FACED EARTHLING   300
The Light And The Dark Ascension	301
The Creator That Resides In You	307

57 THE MANAGEMENT OF HUMAN ENERGIES   310
All That is, Is Energy	310
Energy Benders	311
Energy Manifesting	311
The Process Of Co-Creation	313
The Two Pathways	315
In simple Terms There Are Four Steps	316
And Now Miracles And Emotion	317
Training The Emotional Body	318
The Non-science Of Dying	319
Consciousness Is A Separate Intelligent Life Form	319
What Does Near Dying Tell Us	321

58 SELF POTENTIAL AND LAWS BEHIND MANIFESTATION   324
The Mindset Shift In Belief	324
On The Law Of Attraction	324
Unconscious Creation And Conscious Manifestation	327
Attraction And Avoiding Responsibilities	329
Unconscious Programming	329
The Processes Of Brain And Mind	330
When It Does Not Work	333
Wisdom Is Within	337
All Is In Perfect Order	338
Polarity Physics - The Law Of Opposite Attraction	338

59 YOUR HOLOGRAPHIC REALITY   340
The Law Of Conscious Creation	340
Think How Your Mind Works	341
A New Look At Creating Reality	342
Your Hologram Is A Living Growing Intelligent Medium	344
Holograms Form From a Consciousness And Need To Express	345
The Hologram Is Limited By Beliefs	346
The Hologram Abides By Rules	346
The Collective Hologram Of Reality	347
Holograms Are Nested Within Each Other Non Local	348
Holograms Are Information	349

60 YOU THE CREATOR   350
So What Are You?	351

The Creator Mind	351
The Creator's Mind	352
And So You Became A Little Creator	353
The Divine Plan Of Expression	353
Separation Of High And Low	354
So where Is The Higher Mind?	355
Your World Of Creation	355
So What Say I	357
The River Of Life and Crossover	357
The Five Cosmic Laws	360
The Great Leap Of Faith	361
Do The Laws Pay The Bills?	363
How Long Does It Take?	364

61 YOU CAN'T BS THE HEART (or SOUL) — 366

Love, The Engine Of Creation	367
Forgiveness And Your Path	368
Beingness Is The Natural State The Higher You	369
Inspiration Is The Truth Of The Heart	370
House Cleaning Helps To Set Your Tone	371
Humility Is not To Give In	372
The Mission Is To Know Your True Self	372
That Which Needs Fixing Imposes Judgement	373
The River Of Nows	373
Perfection Yes Or No	374

62 SO THE RUBBER MEETS THE ROAD — 376

As Above So Below	376
Quit The PLANET EARTH Gopher Wheel Of Life	378

63 RESIGNING FROM PLANET EARTH INC. — 380

You Always Have A Choice	380
The Choice Is Now Yours: Red Or Green?	381
A Word Of Caution	382
The Required Basic Information To Resign	382
The Administrators To Notify	383
The Process of Providing Notice	384

64 ESTABLISHING YOUR LIVING STATUS — 385

The Ecclesiastic Deed Poll	385
The Ecclesiastic Deed Poll Document	386

65 STATING YOUR LIVING STATUS — 392

Re-establishing Your Living Status	392
Statement Of Identity Document	392

66 AFFIDAVIT OF SIGNATURE — 394

The Acknowledgment of Deed Affidavit	394
The Acknowledgment of Deed Document	395

67 ESTABLISHING YOUR ENTITLEMENT — 397

The Entitlement Order To Original Status	397
Entitlement Order Document	397

68 ACCESSING YOUR GOOD FAITH AN CREDIT — 400
The Access To Your Good Faith And Credit	400
The Certificate of Authority Document	401

69 DELIVERING YOUR NOTICE AND DECLARATION — 403
Formal Notice Of Declaration	403
Notice And Declaration Document	403
Delivering Notice	404

70 A MATTER OF NEW IDENTITY — 406
The Divine Estate And Province	406
Notice Of International Diplomatic Status	409
Notice Of Title And Protection	410
International Diplomatic Identification	414
The Chancery Court And Rolls	415
Notice To Set-off Against Good Faith And Credit Estate	418
Caveat Notice To Reader	420

71 LOVE, LAUGH, LIVE AS ONE HEART — 421
The True Secret is Love	421
A New Job Unconditional Forgiveness In Thought Word Deed	423
Know Your QLP: Quantum Limitless Potential	424
The Power Is In The Heart	428
The Pull To Perfection That Already Is	429
Think, See, Hear, Feel, Act With The Heart	430
Know Creatorship Within	431
The Final Message	434
The Inevitable Is Upon The Earthling	436
The Current World Scenario	441
In the End Is The Beginning	446

PART 2 OVERVIEW

If you have made it this far, congratulations! You would have to have risen above the new presentation about the dark and the light, about evil and good, about Lucifer and Christ. The bad guys are attempting to make a better world for their slaves, and the good guys are attempting to free themselves from themselves and what they have succumbed to believe. Who will win? That is what Part 2 is about.

In Part 1, we met the Elite Bloodlines and learned about their plan for the Empire; to launch dominion over Planet Earth and the Earthling who have chosen to be there. We have seen how that conquest has been implemented through the collaboration of dynasties by way of money and religion. And we have had a taste for how their mission has been accomplished through the control over religions and nations through fictional entities which are corporations. And we have looked at the details of how it is all executed.

If you have arrived here, you are seeing a different truth from what has been taught about Religion and Commerce. What we have seen is that there is indeed a different picture of bad and good. Why? Because there are always different ways of looking at bad or good called perception and there are as many of these as there are people. In Volume One, we have attempted to present both sides.

In Part 1, we have looked at a new historical viewpoint over the last 5000 years of recorded history. What is different about this version is that it is not taught in schools, nor is it accepted as truth. This "new truth" is changing dramatically and this is what Part 2 is about. it would seem that the march to dominion and conquest has been interrupted and the greatest business plan of all-that of the New World Order-is in disarray.

At around the turn of the century, a new truth that had been simmering over the last 50 years started to come to a boil. A new version of religion and commerce was boiling out thanks to the Internet and a mass shifting of conscious awareness that many things were not right began to manifest as mass disclosure. There is one stark explanation that has to do with the End Times. How else could such a mass of people that are being led by no one human or movement converge on the same beliefs? Up to the end of the century to think that mass consciousness could be influenced by cosmic or divine forces would have been a pretty big joke.

Part 2 is about a new history that is unfolding now as we entered the turn of the Century. It is not possible to go into all the details of how and why this change is occurring but all one needs to do is to look at the number of monumental disclosures and the demands for transparency have occurred in the last 12 years. Part 2 is a look at where we are in our evolution as a civilization since the turn of the Century. Instead of looking at the New World Order as a conspiracy, let us look at what is unfolding around humanity as a New Order of the Ages. There is no doubt that the business plan of PLANET EARTH Inc has had some adjustments but it is still on tract in one way or another. It truly depends upon the notion that "the meek shall inherit the earth". It would seem that the meek are indeed having something to say about what has happened; and would believe it is in the name of love and peace?

What has occurred is the new alternative to the old ways is evolving rapidly. The evolution of a New Earth founded on a new truth and the decision on how this will manifest now appears to be with the Earthling, not with the Elite. How humanity chooses on the acceptance or rejection of the truth with respect to light versus dark will dictate the way the Order unfolds for all. Whether the Earthling is mature enough to leave the parenthood of PLANET EARTH is to be seen in the next years. Dark is the way it has been--fear, slavery, obedience to the rich and strong. The gods have had their fun and they have in retrospect made life for their flock better. Now the flock of Earthlings may be ready to reach for Light as the way it could be where love, freedom, peace and sovereignty flourishes. Recall the last picture in Part 1. The convergence of dark and light is upon Planet Earth. And can you believe that a greater and greater mass of humanity is actually questioning the sanity of the past? And making plans to rise above it?

What is occurring, and evolving at an exponential rate is a rejection of the old ways, the kings, the queens, the gods and the establishment that is preoccupied with dominion over others and service to self. Worldwide, there are major shifts going on as more and more humans reject the old ways of sin, conflict, war, and inequality in hierarchies. This reflected in the census that counts "non-religious" at over 1 billion growing exponentially.

Indeed, this may well be the New Order of the Ages. Of course it is up to humanity to choose this as it is up to the individual to choose. That is where it begins.

The point is that many groups as indicated by almost a billion people are rejecting religions and demanding responsibility from leaders and governments. The "jig is up". These leaders and their codes as directed by the gods do not serve them anymore. Similarly, the inequality of kings and queens, of dictators and dynasties, of corporations designed for dominion and greed to serve the few at the expense of the many doe not "fly" any more. The major shift occurred at the turn of the century with the New Consciousness of the Internet allowing the free exchange of humanity's consciousness like never before.

In this Part, we will present this new consciousness. We will present a highlight of the immense changes that the Age of Aquarius brought with its opening. There are more Earthlings now than ever before resigning from PLANET EARTH INC. and rejecting their prescriptions of the blue pills of RELIGIOUS ORDER.

It is for you to know there is indeed a new choice building.

One cannot make a choice if one is not aware that there is a choice.

You can be the judge, even though, ironically in the end, there is no judgment, only choice.

PART 2

REVOLUTION OR EVOLUTION

WHAT'S HAPPENING

37

SOMETHING IS AMISS IN GOD'S LAWS

Since the turn of the century, the new information about the way the world is run by the leaders and governments has come under fire and scrutiny. The Elite bloodlines plan has come into the spotlight, and the way religions are used to dominate spirituality, has increased exponentially. A new truth has emerged because there has been a conscious shifting of awareness in more and more humans that something is amiss with GODS Laws. Something is "not right" and everyone is backed up against a wall of debt and deception. Many say it is fraud and deception, many say it is for the good of others, many say there is nothing wrong. The New Ager's say this is a prophesized time of ascension and the time has come or the meek to inherit the earth. The Old Ager's say it's just more of the same old shit so get used to it. In the end each has to judge and choose but one thing is predictable: The change is in the airwaves--in the mind of Earthlings--in the conscious awareness seeking truth; and that means a prelude for major shifts in religion and commerce.

Now, in the year 2012, the number of "revelations" about corruption and greed, about the dynasties, the kingdoms, the power hungry, and the political system have been staggering. The age of Pisces has indeed been one that the Lucifer strategies of service to self have dominated. But something big is happening on Planet Earth and PLANET EARTH is in the spotlight of scrutiny. The employees of PLANET EARTH are in a mode of revolution. The shift in the last 12 years has been staggering; and it is rapidly coming to a head at an exponential rate.

The importance of this shift in consciousness and world attention cannot be underemphasized. The conundrum of the Ages like none before is in front of the Earthlings.

New World Order Or The New Order Of The Ages?

In the beginning of this book, we brought forward the Latin phrase "*novus ordo seclorum*" appearing on the reverse side of the Great Seal since 1782 and on the back of the US one-dollar bill since 1935, meaning "**New Order of the Ages**" and it only alluding to the beginning of an era where the United States of America is an independent nation-state. This has been often mistranslated by conspiracy theorists as "**New World Order**". And in what has occurred, the ones who run PLANET EARTH have indeed drummed to a business plan that has been written to bring Planet Earth's peoples into one huge Empire of one religion, one currency, one government, all under the jurisdiction of their laws of god. And so it would appear that the business plan is on track despite some major hiccups along the way. Within this business plan is a section of the Biblical Codes about Revelations that postulates a second coming of Christ. And in retrospect, because their version of the story of Christ has been so effective, it is not surprising that a prophesy supported by God would be brought forward to check up on all the sinners to decide who is worthy and who is not. This story of Revelations, Rapture and Armageddon where God and the Son of God check up on the slaves, get rid of Satan and save the worthy, and destroy the unworthy is like a looming control mechanism on consciousness designed to maintain the fear and obedience. It is indeed the silent, invisible "policing force" for the New World Order. And because it was set for the End Times, namely the years coming into 2012, now is the time that this part of the plan has to be implemented. What's really humorous about this story is that the ones spilling this story are the ones that follow Satan and obviously have retained powers that Earthlings are not supposed to know about.

And in retrospect, the plan has been working well in that the Global Elite have indeed captured Nations and Earthlings alike in the ultimate takeover of the Corporation PLANET EARTH. It is certainly true that this plan could mean a better life for many, despite its controls, limitations, and imbalance. In truth, their plan has made a better world for the slaves if you look back in our history. However, it would appear to be a devious plan that reduces the spiritual aspects of the Earthling to bondage that could not mean a better life. Interestingly enough, the vast majority of Earthlings are very much "carnal" and "instinctual" in their ways of life; and most could care less about any supreme plan. All they care about is to eat, breed and protect their bloodlines.

Yet here we are at this decision point called the End Times.

There is a different version of Revelations evolving during this End Time which marks the beginning of the Aquarian Age. It is that underlying tsunami of consciousness shifting which was so well explained in all the Mayan prophesies. That tsunami is growing exponentially now and has the Founders of PLANET EARTH on the defensive so they must now play their cards to execute the final part of their business plan. One could say the time has come to see who the forces choose. This other major force is what has been the Christ Consciousness and coincides with the New Age beliefs. I use New Age for a lack of a better word. As we have seen the New age is common terminology to both "sides" of the plan. We have left you with that new version of the life of Christ to understand exactly what that Christ Consciousness is. It is in fact what can well be the New Order of Ages which is anything but what we have chosen before. It is a different version of order and belief, namely that we are all One, all part of God, and are on the verge of knowing and understanding this clearly. Thus this changes the landscape that eliminates the Elite business plan of the gods and implements the birthright plan of God.

At this point in time, the census would have to be in the billions of people who have attained a internal knowing that something is not right about the system and that something big is about to happen. The consciousness shift is like a huge global marketing plan that morphs itself into the lives of more and more people, faster and faster. The clash is now inevitable. And it is a clash of old ways of fear, conflict, and dominion against love, peace, and divine sovereignty.

Who will win? The drama must be played out and judging by what is happening in the world today with financial and religious crisis everywhere, it can move either way rapidly.

What is paramount is that this new philosophy of love, peace, ad divine sovereignty become the New Order of the Ages. It must be the underlying energy of change and it came into the history through the Christ Consciousness. This changes the story of Armageddon and Revelation to present a totally different picture of the future. So let us begin this Chapter on the Great Shift of Ages

All Bibles And Prophesies Point To Christ As Inspiration

Whichever version of the story of Christ you read, whether through myth, fiction or nonfiction, the life of this man evolves as special. It is he that became the inspiration as it is the goal of human life to evolve toward Spirit. Let us bring back into focus our picture of the Soul's Journey. This is the journey that unfolds over the course of one's lifetime—it is the adventure of moving from time and space to eternity. It is said that Spirit ever reaches into the hearts and minds of humans to urge us to choose the ascension path to unite with the Source of Creation. One way Spirit does this is to incarnate as a human to reveal Spirit's personality to humanity to serve as encouragement to discover and walk the path of Spirit. God or whatever you want to call it has individual the vessel of a human form to show us the way back home if we can see it. The person who fulfilled this role was this one called Jesus who eventually inherited the name Jesus Christ, or in the Aquarian version, Jesus The Christ. And so we have looked at different version of the "truth" surrounding this man. The story that we have brought forward would exemplify more than anything the path upwards shown in this diagram.

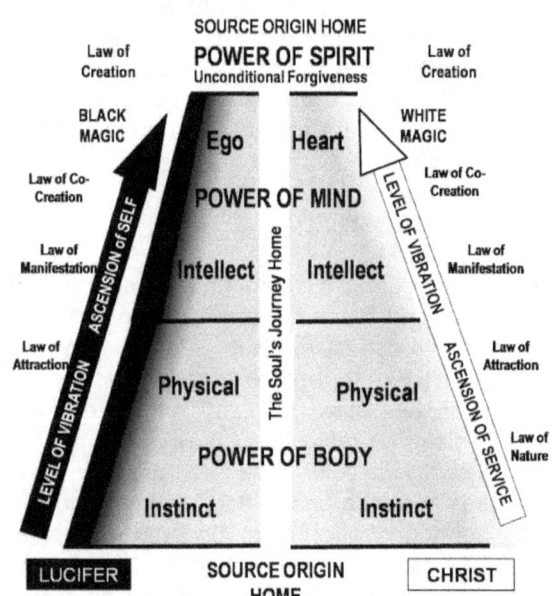

In the versions of the Bibles and other major religious teachings of the mass, the teachings of Jesus have been used as the mainstay to a spiritual belief system of love, peace, and sovereignty. Although riddled with other' distorting history, the new version is now surfacing as a new truth everywhere simply because people are fed up with the untruth of fear, conflict and dominion. These teachings centered around helping people find their own internal source of Spirit. He is said to have lived what he taught. This truth now points to him as the embodiment of love and goodness, peace and understanding.

His God-centeredness allowed him to achieve what we consider miracles because he understood the natural laws of the universe and was able to tap into the great power of love to bring healing to people. He practiced meditation and prayer to gain strength to meet the challenges of daily life. He consistently showed love, kindness, patience, gentleness to others and encouraged them to open to the Spirit within themselves. He said, *"The kingdom of Heaven is within."* He lived his life to show us how to find Spirit and what a human personality looks like when he or she is Spirit-centered. He paved the way for us to find God for ourselves.

And so it is said that Jesus' Divine life plan apparently disclosed itself to him over the course of his lifetime. Just as we can open ourselves to our indwelling Spirits to find our own higher purpose, he had to accomplish this during his human lifetime. His story we have presented becomes an inspiring guide to help us achieve this for ourselves through the **thoughts, words, and deeds synchronized with the heart**. Once he fully achieved his own state of "Christ Consciousness" he was able to manifest, co-create and create as well as depict to others his Divine self. His life purpose was two-fold and provides the living link between our Creator-Source and humanity: to show each person how to be God in himself/herself and for himself/herself, and then to embody the Creator and reveal God's love for each person to those who were ready to grow in Spirit.

But is this really truth? The huge New Age movement certainly agrees with this fundamental philosophy. We have looked at the new version and it either rings with you or it doesn't. If you do not want to see it and want some intellectual argument about whether any PhD's checked out, you won't. And if you are happy with things as they are, then that is fine too but perhaps there is more?

But what has become prominent in the last 12 years is indeed the consciousness of a new truth about Christ. If you put truth of Christ in the query box at Amazon.com you get some 16 pages of books and 35,000 results. Google only gives a mere 180 million hits! Because we want to enter this chapter on this topic as being important, we will summarize this Christ fellow's history in this volume because the story we have presented as Aquarian is supporting the prevalent discoveries in the last 12 years.

Before we delve into the two diametrically opposed versions of the Dark and Light plans, it is of interest to recap what has come to light in the last 12 years. What appears to be occurring is that there are two plans; one of PLANET EARTH and the other, a quiet underlying plan of unknown Divine origin as reflecting a consciousness that there is indeed something amiss with "gods" words. The following is presented to recap the new knowing as reflected in the new consciousness.

A Recap: New Version Of Christ's Story

This particular summary that follows is our summary of the Aquarian Gospel, but it reflects a common revelation surfacing around the world.

We see that Christ came to be a Walker of Planet Earth for the purpose of living and showing the Word and the Light of Unconditional love. Upon his incarnation, he brought immediate light and brightness, the vibration of which resonated strongly to draw attention of the many. For this reason as a child he was kept hidden and protected quietly, As a child Jesus already attracted attention as his resonance was strong and of high vibration. Somewhat like the Crystal Children of now, he was especially gifted as was his written purpose to bring the new light as his Divine Plan. The high vibrations and the strength of the love he exuded from his heart drew others like a magnet and because of this interest, the authorities and priests came to know about this but mostly as an oddity not particularly relevant.

At an early age after his spiritually gifted mother and father coached and protected him in such a way as to nurture his special radiance, it was necessary to take him to other lands away from his place of birth so as to allow him to grow his abilities and hide him away until more mature. As his Father was skilled in the arts of Mystery and Alchemy, and his Mother also advanced in Spirit and vibration they knew and followed many of the special ancient wisdom keepers of the Mystery Schools of Egypt. It is here that his growth and knowing was nurtured, well before he could engage in the conflicts of the time. He was trained to understand the ancient wisdoms of the Priesthoods of spiritual knowing of God (the real one). As so a deep wisdom of the truth emerged rapidly. As it was, the Ancients knew of this special Jesus and took custody of him to teach all of their wisdom allowing him to rapidly recall what which he knew but had been slowed due to the incarnation in a lower form. As he carried no karma, he absorbed the knowing and evolved rapidly into his higher senses.

Upon traveling to other highly developed spiritual lands such as India he became a wonder of science reflecting the higher abilities of metaphysics, healing and body control, much as those opening to you now. He became highly developed is the spiritual arts and absorbed the truth like a sponge. Because of these wondrous abilities of the metaphysical realms and his knowledge of the workings of other dimensions, he attained the creator status we have told you of rapidly and had to subdue these when in public places. He turned his attention to the attaining the status of priesthood only in the teachings as he preferred to walk the lands.

Through this time, he met friends and wrote of his knowing as he began to reflect and expand upon the Word as he understood it. Ancient wisdom came forward rapidly and his body began to shift and change. His teaching and healing examples were watched with wonder as they saw the manifestation of ancient wisdom expressed by him. His mentors followed the teachings of the old ways following the spiritual priesthoods Over years he developed to stages that surpassed all they had ever seen.

Unlike your own time where the higher vibration floods the consciousness to encourage easy growth of acceleration of ascension, through the triggering of the divine plan, that was a time of low vibration. His highly advanced powers he exhibited in the power of healing, miracles, telepathy, and psychic knowing were his front line display. His essence was not undetectable and his presence, and the Word spread rapidly as he walked the lands. His knowing and reach expanded rapidly as many of his followers including both men and women who were treated equal, became companions, also seeking the knowing of the Word. These also came forward to learn and to spread the word of God. And so many lands came to know and told of this special man. He was able to show the power of God directly and taught the ways to accept divine love for the true purposes. But unlike now, the change of vibration was not readily accepting and this required much time and discipline to evolve in others. As so, he became more of an oddity to some, a wonder and saint to others, and a threat to those who sought power over others., particularly the priesthoods who were in control of the human souls. What they feared was his and his disciples' ability to attract people in flocks.

It was so that he walked the lands with his powers of Creator. As he walked the land and lived with the people he carried the light and the love of the Creator. For those that were earthly and poor, already dominated by greed and avarice of authorities he was both admired and feared as they could not understand his ways. His power of healing, his ability raise dead, to materialize things, and his ability to connect with groups instantly to subdue anger and conflict became difficult to understand. For others, the Word and the spreading of his wondrous gifts of healing, of his abilities to see what others could not see was like a miracle. Yet they could not understand how to attain these by attention to his teachings of love and spirit. He taught that the divinity was in all and the attention to love not hatred would bring these powers as they were all sons and daughters of God as was he. As he travelled the land and attracted his closest companions and eventually groups that also learned the Word, the Word and the abilities spread. Many times he would use powers to create miracles that even his followers could not believe.

The consciousness of Christ was highly developed in that his knowing was who he was as a son of God but he would not flaunt this except in his teachings where he said all were equal sons and daughters of God, part of the One creator which was love itself. He lived this way in simplicity to heal and serve others as he wandered the lands and lived among the people. His disciples and followers grew rapidly as he carried the high vibration of attraction and love. His abilities were strong and radical for the ages and this drew even more attention and followers, and many who sought healing. He knew as you do about the higher aspects of the divine mind, and the body as an expression, and he knew his purposes of life to spread his love in an unyielding dedication to others. In thought, word and deed, his mortal ways of life were totally synchronized with the heart and soul of divinity and true expression of God. His influence grew as did his followers and his writings came forward as he wished to write the Word for others.

The teachings of Christ were simple, that all were sons and daughters of God, equal and could do as he was able to show by his healing and physical miracles. Well advanced in higher vibration metaphysics, such was easy for him to illustrate. But this was not a time for this as people were deeply rooted in simple 3D physical lives and not easily moved to higher vibration knowing as is the case now. This placed him and his many teachers of this on a pedestal of curiosity and wonder which is why it was easy to brand this as witchcraft and heresy. Many sought to be healed. His teachings were of equality of all and Oneness, of forgiveness of others and of unconditional love as the true power of life. He taught prayer to God not of forgiveness of sin but to envelope desires with the powerful emotion of love and bliss to manifest what was needed. He taught baptism as a simple process of intent the cleanse and shift into a new belief. He taught the power of love through the heart, the seat of greatest feelings and connection to Spirit and God which was all One. He taught equality of man and women and that all were honoured children of God without judgment of sin. He taught ways of healing, development of physical and mental and psychic abilities and taught the laws of the cosmos based on the teachings of Hermes. He taught thousands of followers and disciples, teachers to follow and spread this word of truth. And at advanced teachings he taught the ancient arts of Egypt's mystery schools, of the Hermetica, and the ancient arts, as well as what he had learned from other spiritually based lands like India. He walked in simplicity, love and in the heart, always within the Higher Divine Mind. To him this was simply automatic and there was ever reason to question why.

And so it is not surprising that this man, his special wisdom of God and Spirit be revered and written about. He reflected what he said every son and daughter of God to do by simply giving their will to god and their true spiritual selves. This was to live in the light of god, in peace and in the heart of love to let the higher spirit to be what it was as eternal life and one with God. As this spread through the lands, the frequency of his light and of his follower buzzed and radiated like beacons of pulsating energy attracting many as they travelled.

Also not surprising is that the activities of Christ came to the awareness of the religious leaders, priests, and the authorities who at first saw this as a curiosity but then saw this as a threat of authority and religious teaching. These were contrary to the churches beliefs. They were blasphemy. As the teachings spread and various writings began to appear, and his collective grew, he became a shining beacon to many of the people and a plan had to be created that would eliminate this problem. To simply kill him was felt a potential threat that would instigate an uprising. This would not serve them. They also had to eliminate the dangerous teachings and the growing movement away from the religious teachings.

And so a plan was devised to infiltrate and understand, to gain evidence that would allow a way to eliminate this. A way had to be found to teach these pagans and heretics a lesson so as to make an example of this and eliminate attention to this heresy. In this way they would hope to bring the fold back unto their own dominion. Thus a way was structured to collaborate between religious leaders and state. Such were also the needs of the dark ones who had also infiltrated the seats of power as they had a grander plan. The higher selves were already serving their needs as they contrived to support the worldly aspects of greed, avarices, power, and lust. And below they saw that the power of love was powerless against heartless forces and armies. However, they knew well the power of spirit to rise as reflected in these teachings as the major threat. They knew that this power could offset the power of armies and dark forces one understood and left to be nurtured. So the dark forces began to contrive a plan to execute through the lower forms.

A Rewrite Of Christ Story Was Inevitable

A way of stopping this was the immediate need of the religious leaders and priests, as well as the powers of state to disguise this true story for it could only lead to anarchy and loss of power. First they would contrive a way to brand these teachings as heresy and attempt to show violation of church and state law. They would find out more of these heretics and set them up to be punished. They agreed with the state to infiltrate and seek evidence to convict him and arrest him and others so as to publically humiliate and punish followers.

The authorities and the priests watched with wonder following these activities with their spies. The greatest fear was a potential rising of armies that this Christ could potentially create. The powers of healing and reports of other abilities not understood as the power of spirit was the other which had to be branded as the work of evil forces. The religious leaders themselves carried their own wisdom of ancient dark powers as they themselves knew about working in 4 and 5D and the power of attention by the mind through their own barbaric rituals and demonic worship of their own gods. This as you know allowed manifestation by the concentration of energies and was guided by manipulation of compromised higher selves. This was a skill and knowledge that was kept secret and handed down to them thorough their own secret writings and scrolls, carefully oriented to heartless attention of focus on the manifestation process and the black arts. They themselves were worshipers of evil under the guise of goodness, engaging in their secret rituals and sacrifice to pleasing their false gods. There practices were well founded in supporting the special "darker" energies, even as they are to this day.

As it was, a plan was contrived between the Priests and the State to capture several of the key followers and Christ. At this time the religious order of priests and followers was not well established or well organized but they were, because of their dark powers fairly well entrenched with the powers of Rome. Their main objective was fear of this unknown power of spirit, and to be rid of this treat to both state and church. The accusations that ensued was that this group and philosophy that Christ represented claimed to be above all in spirit and threatened to change the peoples mind about subservience, paying their taxes and serving the Caesar.

These were heretical teachings that refused to follow the laws of church and land and the dominion of their gods. As Christ knew he was of greater power, he would never yield spiritually and he had already mastered body and mind control over his physical. He would be ridiculed so the church could point to the folly of his ways, creating words of guilt as to what they wanted to hear and to convey to all of the land. What was feared most was that this revelation of spirit, and the power it represented, defied death itself. And it instilled a power that would render them as the ones who were deceivers if it was left to spread. This was to be proven as severe heresy that they sought to purge with great vigour. It had to be purged from every thought and from all evidence on the land.

And so it was the story of Crucifixion and Resurrection was created. It was a plan to hide the truth of this man.

The Implementation The Word Of god

The gospels were stories of individual perceptions and experiences, outlining teachings and events of his life. They were different and disjointed and even these were later further disjointed purposely. As the religious leaders gathered writings and knowledge they would decide to keep or burn these. But one thread of constant fabric prevailed. That this was a special gifted man of the God of truth who had come to spread that truth and to heal all, a special spirited being who walked the lands in humility and peace and in love.

This purge was done over time and was effective, but secretly over time new pockets unfolded on the teaching of Christ and emerged through the lands. It again brought anger and fear in the church and what they preached. This spread like an epidemic of threat and it became the time to react again. They spread their spies throughout the land to find where and what the teachings were and where they growing. Over many years they sought to purge and destroy again but could not. In time they began to target major movements and places where ancient information and such writings were stored.

For even with the initial destruction and deception, the Word spread and re-emerged quietly. It was this resonance with the truth that could not be contained. In reality, other lands and religions followed similar evolution, the dark lords always being aware of the need to suppress spirit or lose their powers. In virtually all religions, even as they evolved over time, the dominion of spirit has prevailed. The rest of it is history as church powers grew and spread and use the heartless to preach dominion at the threat of annihilation by not conforming. To preserve the air that the church was the follower of peace and love of God they separated from the state that would police and use force to stop anyone deemed a threat. It was through this alliance of state and church that the religions over time have been responsible for the greatest amount of bloodshed ever.

These gospels, and other writings that eventually became the testaments and then the bible were subject to an evolution over centuries as the churches gained power. And so the true followers were forced to hide and run or be put to death instantly if found out. This, over a generation allowed the truth to be purged from the face of the land.

As it was, this would allow a new plan to manifest. It was to create a contrived nature of these writings, to gather, understand the writings and to eventually create a new version of the teachings. This was thought to be prudent as they felt that they could intercede eventually so a new form of doctrine could be developed to serve the needs of their own doctrine. In the mean time the objective was to continue to create fear in the followings and have other pay for a sin of following such dark arts and suggesting that they could be part of God. This plan of dominion over spirit was driven from the higher realms was to subdue spirit and to keep its power hidden. The Priests in Power, directed by the gods of the time were alleged to be skilled in their powers of using special forces of dominion, as they also knew of the power of love and light which they of heartless intent chose not to follow. They knew that this spirit could not be destroyed. But they knew how fear and repression would render it ineffective. This they knew could be administered through the higher selves of the ones in power. It was the way of controlling the priesthood many times before. And so they sought to cause fear and kill, to destroy and replace light as an example to serve their cause.

And so it was that a plan was developed over time. It was to reshape the Word of the Christ into the word of man as this seemed a lucrative way to not only find more followers of the church but to create a myth of this Christ who had all these powers. The plan was to take the gospels and the writings that were taken and to begin a new story to replace the Word with the word of man. As writings in those days were themselves stories of observations and perception, vast in difference, this would be a plan to create one story in the testaments.

What the leaders and bloodlines of the gods were guided on was to seek a new way of dominion. What they sought was to find a way to be the sole connection to this God or Gods so they were the interceding power to reduce the spirit to a state of dysfunction. They needed to find a way they could represent themselves as the means to take control of the people, fool them into believing that they and their gods could absolve and dissolve those who were sinners and evil. As time passed they began to understand then change the Word as was written by others—what was compiled by many as testament— to their own version. This grew in power over decades as they began to understand and accumulate the teachings. It was a way that they could intercede between man and God and represent the absolution of sin, of granting redemption and eternal life if the ways were accepted—their ways.

The event, which later became known as the crucifixion had to be from what is was--a simple torture exhibition and prolonged display of death as punishment for heresy. But there were certain facts that they believed that they could use to their advantage. It was the claim of being a son of God and the idea that he was a special man. To support this, the virgin birth, the crucifixion, the resurrection was contrived later so as to create such a mythological story that would create a half truth. And this contrived story that would partially align with the truth became the basis to the teachings of Christianity. It did not and never did reflect the true Word of God nor the Christians who followed Christ. This in itself was a deception of words inferring that the church and religion was based on Christ and his teaching which were completely distorted to the story which as a mythology of fact and fiction became the word—the word of man.

The New Mythology Of The Bibles

This story would present their own picture of what transpired, but in such a way as to serve their own purpose. And as the Pope reported, *"this myth of Christ has served us well"*. What eventually over time became the epic mythology of Christ and became the greatest book of all time—the Bible was a contrived way to exert dominion over spirit and man.

They began to create a story of fiction and myth, built on the gospels and writings to support their agenda. They evolved a story of creation with Adam and Eve to reduce the female to lesser evil status of sin. She was a lesser breeding machine to produce new slaves. Her abilities of the attuning to spirit were dangerous and had to be reduced to nothing. Because of the DNA encoding, they created a heaven that was unobtainable except through them after death. The concept of heaven and hell and Satan as a place for those who would not cleanse themselves of the sin that they were born with because of the deception and fall from grace of women. It was the woman that created the sin that Adam and Eve created and therefore was inherent in all offspring forever, something that had to be worked out by begging forgiveness and sacrifice if heaven was ever to be granted. They created the concept of virgin birth to explain the unusual brightness of Christ at birth and created this concept of the first coming of Christ, the Son of God. They cleverly created the idea of hell so the lower ego would flourish in fear and seek resurrection and forgiveness. They imbedded the fear of the dark ritual forces of mysticism which they themselves embodied secretly. They cloaked these and their rituals to false gods. They created the myth of crucifixion to portray Christ as a Son of god who had been sacrificed by God for the sins of humanity. They created the myth of resurrection to enforce that this Christ was given another chance and that God indeed has such power of life and death.

Here was the mystical story of how a son of God had been sent with special divine gifts and powers to save the people of the sins they inherited form the story of creation. This was a story of how God in desperation of the sins of humanity had to offer as sacrifice his son to absolve humanity's folly which would reside within all forever. Of course these sins would need the help of the church as the keepers of the word to guide them towards heaven, salvation and eternal life. Christ had been sent and saw such sin and humility that he had no choice but to sacrifice his son.

In addition, the plan was over time to seek out all writings and sources to destroy or take possession, to eliminate the truth of the Word of God from the minds. They would work to destroy physical evidence and replace this over time with their own version. It is this version that has remained for two thousand years with its false words. It is the doctrine that is supported by the left brain of ego. It is maintained by the manipulation in higher dimensions by the dark lords who seek slaves, power and dominion of all worlds with heartless intent. It is supported by the lizard DNA in each that opened egos 3D survival needs. It is supported by the soul's quest to find heaven or Home. But it is the concept of heaven by ego that wins and the soul is left in dominion with a voice that cannot be heard. It is how the quest is manipulated by religions to create the fear of not finding heaven because of sin, to fall to hell if not responsible to false gods and the ideology of the religion.

As time passed the untruth of the One who was sacrificed evolved. And so the many abided by this to seek redemption and forgiveness through prayer, and through the Church that had positioned themselves as the ones who knew the truth and were the true representatives of God. And so the laws and the Word and process of Spirit and Love, as well as the ancient wisdom laws of the Cosmos were slowly transformed to new meaning based on the egos lower vibration

The new version of the story was accumulated in the bible as a contrived clever story of part truths and part lies, portraying the Christ and his Word the way they wanted to. This would replace the Word of God not only with a new story but give new meaning to the Words so that it embodied them as intermediaries and embodied new meanings of words that would suit them. And this became their book of Christianity which they spread. And when they found pockets they quickly purged these such as in Alexandria as well as other place. And so as they purged, they replaced. From this forward they cleverly began to build on this story that was part truth and mostly untruth so that they could position themselves as the gifted ones who could not only interpret the real truth but intercede as the ones who could grant salvation, forgiveness and allow heaven and eternal life to be given. And so they struck from the story the aspect of all that all humanity already has and is born with; truth of Spirit and eternal life and the aspect of true creation and oneness, and the power of love and light. They positioned themselves as that which all have. And as this satisfied the egos desire to find heaven, they struck all references to opening of the higher selves and to the true purpose of life. And anyone who did not follow was killed, tortured or enslaved. And as time passed, religions warred against each other on who had a better way to love and finding heaven. And so over time, the testaments were written and re-written to bring forth the bible, the word of man, not the Word of God.

The story that would evolve and spread would reduce the power of the spirit and the heart as this was potentially the churches demise and loss of control. What they knew well was that alignment with this Spirit and the Christ was necessary as a way of least resistance, but in such a way that they appeared to support this but in a way that would reduce the people to dominion over spirit though fear. Thus they created Christianity which by inference was what was the teachings of the Christians. In fact what was believed as the Christian, or true follower of Christ, was the distorted word of the church followers, simply based on the assumption that Christianity reflect the teaching of Christ. Thus the half truth that was created as that of the Christians was what was believed as truth in Christianity. This made it look like they supported the great story of Christ and the teaching through Christianity but in reality was a deception.

This new half truth acknowledged the power of God or Spirit and the Son who had come to save mankind from their sins that they were born with from their falling in the Garden of Eden. The Son of God had come to save humanity but could not and was therefore offered in sacrifice so the people could understand that they had to seek salvation and retribution for these sins forever. This way they acknowledged God and Christ but placed themselves in as interceding between God and man to be the interpreters of the word and to be the ones who could show the way to forgiveness to prevent falling to hell and Satan and hence attaining eternal life upon death. So a mythology was created on a story of the Son of God, the virgin birth, the crucifixion and the Easter rising of resurrection. These are celebrated to this day. The resurrection established Jesus as the powerful Son of God and is cited as proof that God will judge the world in righteousness. God has given Christians "a new birth into a living hope through the resurrection of Jesus Christ from the dead. So this led to the belief through faith in the working of God so others are spiritually resurrected with Jesus so that they may walk in a new way of life. But this way, Jesus was sacrificed for other sins and creating a way that others could see resurrection by giving themselves to the Church. This opened the way for the DNA encoding of seeking Home or the Father, Heaven and eternal life could be attained. Power of Spirit was repressed by fear and the quest for eternal life by ego would guarantee this while the Church entered as the right hand of God that could show the way. Thus separation and fear kept lower vibration of ego, while the fear of moving in a contrary teaching against the church was punishable by death as enforced by the authorities.

But it was only much later when the Church of Rome and other alliances gained power that the true deception as the Bible was implemented. The partial truth as the myth of Christ melded over time so as to eventually be accepted as the whole truth and to place the church in as the powerful intermediary force it is. The falsehood of fire and brimstone of Satan and the belief that people were born in sin, and that women were subservient as they were responsible for this sin has prevailed. And that even the Son of God had to be sacrificed to this cause. He had given his life to bring salvation to the born sinners so they would now they had to beg the church and god for forgiveness. This would become the word of Christianity and become the doctrine of Roman Church and the seat of power supported by force and death for not complying. That new story was indeed created and evolved over time to be supported by humanity as a false truth that would remain until the end of time when the new age would bring in the Christ again, not as One but as all— the Christ Consciousness arising in all. And so it has been. But now millions of sons and daughters of God are rising to take their power of spirit back and away from those who repress, as they have attained a knowing of the true Word of God.

And so it came to pass that the Word of God became the word of god in the march towards The New World Order that would be fully implemented during the "Second Coming of Christ", the **Armageddon** as revealed in the business plan as **Book of Revelation.** As civilization moves to the end of the End Times, what has become so apparent is this "final conflict" of the Dark versus the Light. What has come to the forefront in these times is the nature of this "Second Coming". Is it the Christ Consciousness or is it the Lucifer Consciousness that will prevail?

It is the epic struggle of all time. What is for certain is that it is the Christ Consciousness of the many versus the Lucifer Consciousness of the few. This epic struggle between the Light and the Dark is exactly what the Earthling has chosen to support through history. But why is there a change now? What is this underlying shift of something being a miss in god's laws?

Let us explore this further.

38

THE END TIME OF THE GREAT SHIFT

The dramatic shift that began accelerating at the start of the Aquarian Age has been termed the End Times. This Part of this book is dedicated to what has happened primarily in these last 12 years. It is perhaps not a speculation that the directors and Owners of PLANET EARTH Inc. have been aware of a time when a great shift would occur and that they would need to be prepared to deal with it. Part of the metaphysical and "occult" is the science of the planetary systems known as Astrology. They are well versed in this and know about the shifting consciousness. It is not a speculation to believe that these bloodlines protect and know special esoteric sciences that the rest do not understand, acknowledge or believe. Those esoteric powers of mind which in the extreme are black magic for self, are the same ones the extreme white magic deploy for service of others. The abilities are the same, the use is different but regardless these are the abilities that have been sought for a long time. The process of evolution is as shown on our pyramid of the Soul's Journey.

Prophesies, religious books and any esoteric experts have told us this; that a great time of change would occur as the galactic alignment of Planet earth would occur. As we have alluded to, this has been input into the business plan of New Earth. In business, being able to intuitively guess the transcend of consciousness leads to successful implantations of marketing plans and the financial success of the business. There are endless versions of what this End Time shifting from the Age of Pisces to the Age of Aquarius would bring; from the Earth itself ascending into higher vibration to the creation of Heaven on Earth with ultimate peace and prosperity for all. All the stories are prolific and varied. With this one deluge of opinions everywhere, one must rise above to understand the clear fact that this proliferation is a fundamental shifting of consciousness in the Earthling. More and more Earthlings are writing, discussing, questioning; and this in itself is a major shift. There are major groups and masses now questioning the sanity of the old ways of Old Earth, demanding disclosure, transparency and responsibility because that which has been accepted before is now being rejected. All you have to do is look around to see what has happened in the last few years and question why now?

The new version of the End Times includes the transition from the Old Earth to the New Earth. The time of transition has been commonly portrayed as the time from the turn of the century 1999 to 2012. On Old Earth it was not fashionable to talk about metaphysics. Physics was the buzz, not esoteric things. If you really care to study quantum physics you will quickly realize that it explains metaphysics whereas physics cannot. The main reason that quantum physics has had such a tough time getting entrenched is because there is one component of it that the scientists still (after 80 years) argue about: Consciousness. Consciousness is the missing link to how it all works. So what is it that influences consciousness?

On New Earth it is now quite fashionable to talk about metaphysics because physics is outdated. It cannot see beyond the observer's observations as quantum physics teaches us. Physics cannot deal with or create laws of behaviour on those tiny particles that are not subject to gravity. Gravity is the glue to hold material things together. It is what we know under Newtonian physics as "solid" things made of atoms held by gravity. But consciousness is the glue that creates things in the quantum world. So if you think you know it all as a Newtonian scientist that has been trained to observe what you see, knowing the other 90% is made of stuff you can't see, then how can you know it all? Yet recent work in Russia points to the rest of DNA as being responsible for all these esoteric abilities. DNA has the same structure as our languages and is like an antenna between the body and outside influences of energetic patterns.

The transition from Old to New Earth is also exemplified by the old TV and news media systems versus the new media system of the Internet. If you dare to type in some esoteric or metaphysical topic in Google you will get millions upon millions of news items, research and discussions that come forward. Before the year 2000 it was not like that. Something has taken hold on the conscious attention to create this shift. Now it is like a tsunami of shifting thought—a building energetic field of common attention and awareness. What's this all about?

It's all about this big grand cycle of 26,000 years where our solar system passes through the point of alignment with the center of the galaxy. This is the Grand Alignment in 2012. In fact there are a whole lot of things happening up there that are grand—different than ever before. It is all astronomical data that you can check out for yourself. And at the end of this 26,000 year cycle that has been mostly relegated to importance by those weird metaphysicists is this last tiny little period that started in 1999 and ends in 2012.

There is some hard science here and it is not unrealistic to believe that the PLANET EARTH Directors have full knowledge of this. It is not unreasonable to also believe that these people are highly evolved in the Powers of the Mind so that they may take advantage of this. As we have seen the major media systems are under their control.

The Mayan End Times

There is a big buzz these days on the Internet and in bookstores about the Mayan Calendar. It is not clearly understood how these Mayans received this information, nor how it applies to humanity now, but nevertheless it is infusing into the new consciousness as a new truth. It is important to understand that this is not a prophesy of physical doom and destruction, it is a revealing of a process of behaviour and evolution of consciousness. Regardless of whether it is of plant, animal or man, it is the consciousness that orchestrate the will to survive and the life attitude.

It is particularly focussed on the End Times as these Mayans allegedly took old ancient knowledge and advanced it as their science. First they were very focused on the cosmic movements and nature because the Sun provided light for life to exist. As the Earth provided nourishment to grow, the planets provided the seasons as well as the consciousness mood of the Earth. These they observed carefully and recorded as their own "Days" and "Nights" with different underlying moods and purposes affecting not only nature but all that lives. They saw this change the mood of the people as well. But more important to them was they needed food. So they learned to pay attention to these moods of the universe to survive.

The Mayan calendar therefore reflects the movement of these cosmic cycles of Day and Night, seasons and growth behaviour of all life. They determined there were 13 periods called Heavens. These were a way of describing the phases of growth found in all that lives. For example, from when a seed is planted, there are 7 Days and 6 Nights each with a specific purpose each with different lengths depending on what "Underworld" they belong to (see later). Note that these Days and Nights were not like our 24 hour night and day, although they based these on cyclical patterns of celestial objects like the Sun. These they called the 13 Heavens alternating from Day to Night, each affecting the process of natural growth from seeding to eventual flowering and re-seeding.

The first Heaven is Day 1, the *sowing* time when a seed is planted. The second Heaven, or Night 1, is the time of *inner assimilation* when it readies for transforming itself in preparation for the third Heaven of Day 2, of *germination* when it begins to develop within Mother Earth to reach towards the Sun. There is then Heaven 4, or Night 2 of *resistance* as it must gain its power and internal sustenance to force through to see the Sun. You begin to see how the Day is one of expansion while the night is one of resistance or adjustment, each at a different phase of the growth. It is the mood of Mother Earth that can affect this growth towards its fulfillment, as can the Sun which to them was the Father.

The next Heaven 5, Day 3 is when it *sprouts*, the first time to emerge to see Father Sun and now the Earth and the Sun work together to provide nourishment below and life energy above to the new plant. As it begins to grow, it must adjust itself to the new world around it and *assimilate* through the Heaven 6, Night 3, to adjust itself properly. As it so does, it enters the Heaven 7, next Day 4 which is to *proliferate* itself through the new energy of the Sun. It then enters the next Heaven 8, Night 4 as it attempts to *expand* itself to be what it was meant to be.

During the Heaven 9, Day 5 it is the time of *budding* for its main purpose to produce. Heaven 10, Night 5 is a time of destruction as the plant now must place all of its energy into producing its flower if it is to flourish. Of course, Heaven 11, Day 6 is when the plant flourishes into *flowering*. Heaven 12, Night 6 is when it must *fine tune* itself to blossom to its fullest, and finally Heaven 13, Day 7 is the *fruition* when its bounty in the of form seeds is completed. Each Heaven is dependent on the mood of the Sun and Mother Earth as to what they can provide to support the growth to maturity.

Each Day and Night brings a new phase of challenge and growth as its very purpose, and its essence towards its final purpose change. The elements of fire, earth, water, and air are all vital to the success, as are the internal abilities of the plant to grow. Its will to live and survive is its very essences or spirit. They saw this as its consciousness. Their wisdom taught that all life abides by this. All life including man whose essences are his consciousness are influenced by the moods of the cosmos, and the Sun and the Earth whether they understand it or not.

It is because the essence of man, the consciousness is part of the God of all that exists. It, like the Mother Earth, and the Sun are all living things which are themselves going through the same phases. All of life behaves according to this grand plan. All are subject to their influences as they change their positions around us. Just as they determine the way a seed will grow, they determine the way a man will grow and mature, and develop his own essence.

What they also determined was that there were a whole set of other time periods in their calendar called Underworlds. Each period is itself a stage of complete evolution on a larger scale. The period of 13 Heavens is an Underworld. There are 9 Underworlds of different lengths. The shortest is the Universal Underworld of 260 days (our days). The next longest is the Galactic Underworld which is 20 times longer than the Universal, and so on. Again, each Underworld is made up of the 13 Heavens. At the start of each one, a major level of evolution in consciousness starts then goes through the 13 Heavens maturing progressively like the plants.

When the end phase of each Underworld is reached, meaning the 13th Heaven of *Fruition*, a new Underworld that is twenty times shorter in length begins as the First Day of sowing. It is like when one Underworld produces a seed that can then go through the Heavens twenty times faster. Thus during the last period of the Planetary 7th Day, the seeding of the First Day in the Galactic period may occur. At the last 7th Day in the Galactic, a new seed is created to be sown to begin the Universal period. When all 9 Underworlds are complete, a new period where there is no time begins. Each one has a specific consciousness function and sets the foundation for the next shorter one (20 times shorter). And they all end at the same time. That is what the Mayans saw as the End Times as their calendar ceased and went into a period of no time.

What is relevant here is that all 9 of these Underworlds (or waves) except this last one called *Universal* (260 days) has reached the 13th Heaven. And all 9 waves end on October 28, 2011. The one underneath this one, the *Galactic* Underworld, is 12.8 years long and we have entered its last 13th Heaven of *Fruition* as have all others. It sits on a bigger one 20 times longer and so on.

It is this last one of 260 days that is of interest as it began on March 9, 2011 and terminates *Fruition* on October 28, 2011. Recently this has been adjusted by the experts on this to 18 of our days for each Heaven to total 234 days. What is notable is that there is an acceleration as time speeds up. What this means is that the aspect of consciousness pertaining to each Heaven speeds up its evolution by 20 times for each Underworld which we will call a wave. In other words, as much as we learned in the last wave of 12.8 years will be learned in the current wave of 234 days.

This Universal Underworld is the final transformation of consciousness and it is what is referred to as the 9th Wave.

The prophesy about these End Times when these all end together is that this is a great change in the consciousness of humanity as they approach the fruition of all Underworlds. It will be a time when the consciousness of man has no association with time. It is the time of the revealing and the entry to a new age as the rebirth starts from the seed of the last underlying Underworld. At that time the world is without time and consciousness of man would have evolved to its ultimate point of fruition. This means it is up to those who are left to start creating the new world and the new civilization. It will be a period where man will be one with nature and Mother Earth and the Solar system will come into galactic synchronization with the rest of the Universe. Those left will be transformed as they pass through the center of the cosmos. All will be One and the material will be balanced with spirit. It was called Hunab Ku in Mayan. It is referred to as the Unity Consciousness.

The Ninth Wave—What Is It?

The 9th wave is the final wave which rests upon the final Fruition stages of all 8 waves. It is the culmination of all consciousness, setting the final stage for the time when there is no time after the Grand Alignment of Dec 21, 2012 when Earth passes through the center of the Galaxy. Essentially, these waves get shorter and shorter until there is no time, only instant by instant. Its purpose is to bring in the final step of unity consciousness. It is all about setting a consciousness mood that we are all One. And it is about revealing that being all One, there is within us a divine aspect as we are One with the Creator, as we are one with Creation. That spark of us referred to as our Light Body, that invisible quantum overlay on the physical atomic body, is what is said to be a piece of God.

This Grand Alignment, and a whole lot of other unique celestial configurations occur through 2012, after the 9th wave completes in 2011. It creates the setting for the final transformation of resurrection. These waves are the ones that have been evolving the unity consciousness and are meant to set the underlying consciousness like an overlay from above so that it sets the tone—or garden—for manifestation and creation below. In our terms of reference this is from 5D above and 4D between to 3D below. It sets the tone of the Resurrection.

It is important to understand what is meant as "D". It is not a mathematical terminology. These terms will be used a lot here: 1D, 2D, 3D reflects matter as physical earth and our bodies (Newtonian physics of atoms), 5D being non-matter or etheric quantum space, and 4D as the space between (Quantum physics of waves).

The 13 Heavens reflected the stages of growth, alternating from female (nurturing) to male (protection) energies, alternating between day and night, each having an energetic influence as they determined was ruled by gods which had certain powers and attributes to affect that stage of growth. They, as all humanity, have created many gods and deities who they worship as their idols and have assigned special powers to them. It is simply humanity's DNA calling as this is encoded to seek God within; which has through lower vibrations become seeking god without. In this case, what they could not understand and respected they called gods.

At each Heaven of Day and Night, just as the growing conditions of above (Father Sun) and Below (Mother Earth) set the tone for optimum growth, of nurturing and adjustment, so does the prevailing mood of consciousness set the tone for the strength, clarity of intent (seed) so as to provide optimum growth into fruition—that being the intent of humanity to manifest and create in 3D what has been seeded and nurtured in consciousness of 5D.

How to best align with this tone is to understand the nature of the process of growth and expansion at each phase. In the case of seeds, it is the nourishment of dark soil and water that vitalizes, whereas when sprouting, it is the sun and the nutrients that are needed. In the case of consciousness, it is the balanced female/male love from the divine heart that nurtures and integrates into the new form. Thus every Day and Night is "charged" with specific frequencies of care and attention of that stage, looking for that which provides it. It is as the stage of growth in a child, where the father and mother shift their attention to the needs of the child as it matures. By aligning with the needs, the process of growth matures with vigour and strength at each stage—all set into the fundamental nourishment of love. In this case, the seeds we are dealing with are the consciousness of humanity as a living energy.

At the end of these 9 waves, the total consciousness of humanity and the universe is set to blossom permanently in Unity. It is the year 2012 that the unity consciousness, truly emerges and blossoms into the 3D reality having been implanted in the garden of consciousness of 5D to be expressed in the reality of 3D. It is so for those that choose to be planted in the light of the garden of love through the Time of Choosing that is the 9th wave and the Time of Revelation. Then these celestial bodies and energies gifted from the Galactic Center as we approach in 2012 do their final fine tuning of total consciousness. This will be the Resurrection or the final Time of Transformation. And what is it that results? First is the shift in consciousness to unity and that consciousness is what materializes the New Earth.

And so we sit clearly at the end of this wave, and the culmination of all the waves. It is difficult to deny that something has influenced the Earthling's Consciousness into a dramatic shift pattern in the last 12 years. This will become much more obvious to you as you read about the major moves to reveal a new truth on Planet Earth later in this Part 2. So now we come to the convergence and the confrontation of Light and Dark. This confrontation is about Lucifer; the service to self, or Christ: the service to others. These constitute two different plans.

Let us now, in the next two chapters explore what these two plans may look like. Much of this has "come to light" in the last 12 years.

Before entering this world of words, the reader is forewarned that there may be things read about the darker side that may be upsetting. Don't be. They are just words and the lighter side follows. Just read both sides without emotion and opinion and let your heart decide what rings for you.

39

RAPTURE AND REVELATION: THE DARK SIDE

We have already seen this is the Lucis Trust. We have seen this is the US Dollar, and we have seen this in the biblical plans of Revelation, Rapture and Armageddon.

If one could sum up the Plan of PLANET EARTH, it would best be stated by the Pope Ratzinger who said:

"It is thus necessary that the individual should finally come to realize that his own ego is of no importance in comparison with the existence of his nation; That the position of the individual ego is conditioned solely by the interests of the nation as a whole... that above all the unity of a nation's spirit and will are worth far more than the freedom of the spirit and will of an individual..."

"This state of mind, which subordinates the interests of the ego to the conservation of the community, is really the first premise for every truly human culture... The basic attitude from which such activity arises, We call - to distinguish it from egoism and selfishness - idealism. By this we understand only the individual's capacity to make sacrifices for the community, for his fellow man." -**The Ominous Parallels, by Leonard Piekoff** *P 13.*

The Satanic Plan Of Dominion

In this plan there is The Anti-Christ or Satan of alleged conspiracy and dominion to believe in. It is the Illuminati/Zionist plan to create an apocalypse that will exhaust and depopulate the masses through deadly designer viruses, global terror, economic disasters and nuclear war. These disasters are allegedly timed to occur somewhere between 2000 and 2014, when the remaining survivors will gladly embrace the promises of a handsome charismatic new leader (the New Vice President of Religious Order) who will unveil his plan of hope for an eternal world peace. The only way to achieve eternal world peace, he will explain, is to put an end to the five causes of war. Secretly, he knows there is only one main cause of wars: the wars provoked by his royal ancestors who planed, provoked, financed and profited from them. He will sell his peace plan by telling the world that border wars will only end by creating a world without borders.

Religious wars will only end by creating one world religion of interfaiths. Economic wars will only end by creating a cashless debt-free society. Rivalry wars between rulers will only end by creating one world ruler. The tools used for war, from hand-guns to nuclear bombs will be eliminated and one world army will be created, which will guarantee world peace. This means that the Earthling will remain in his current state of spiritless lower vibration to be employed by PLANET EARTH under a new set of laws-perhaps much like **George Orwell's 1984**. One may think George had the timing out but if you really look around you may see "Big Brother" as being more real than you believe, as we have revealed in Part 1.

How will this eternal peace plan be accomplished? We have looked at these groups in Part 1. We have discussed this. The structure is in place. What has to happen is that the mass of Earthlings must yield to a submissive strategy. They must agree to it most likely through desperation and fear. It is through groups like the United Nations, which is the brain-child of the Committee of 300 families. The UN is their vehicle for world government, and is located on 18 acres of prime Manhattan land, donated by the most visible of the ruling families, the Rockefellers. We have seen the UN as a closed organization with no public records or open meetings. US tax payers have already invested 2 trillion dollars in this world authority. Although most of the people working for the UN are genuinely working for peace, the UN is much more as a Godless organization, controlled by the committee of 300.

It is said that these inbred ruling families pretend to have royal blue blood, but their blood is no more blue or royal than Hannibal Lector's blood. For thousands of years these families have practiced inbreeding. Between sisters and brothers, uncles and nieces, mothers and sons, to keep the power and wealth all in the family. This practice of inbreeding over thousands of years has produced, it is said, a clever, but pathological breed of consciousness, sociopathic families, who will stop at nothing to own every ounce of gold, every drop of water and every blade of grass on Planet Earth. However, regardless, they march towards a better world for their slaves. The issue has become one of the slaves beginning to understand the program and their true powers. Like the rise and fall of dynasties and civilizations before, a time of revolution occurs eventually.

The UN, which they founded and control, has clearly stated its goals of establishing a New World Order, a UN standing army and a global taxation system. The queen's husband prince Philip and Evelyn Rothschild have already established an interfaith declaration for the creation of one world religion. What would life be like in this world empire with one world religion, one world army, one world economy, one world court, one world media, one world government and one world dictator. Well perhaps a lot of rules and more of the same duality bur perhaps with less wars?

What the public doesn't know, is that Karl Marx's Communist Manifesto and the Russian Constitution have already been built into the UN charter and that the New World Order will be a communist world order. Peace on Earth will be a forced peace in which citizens will have no rights. No right to bear children without approval, no right to travel without authorization, no right to own private property, no right to privacy, no right to bear arms, no right to protest, no right to receive an inheritance, no right to choose an education or job or even a place of residence. And worst of all, no right to live. The right to live will be based on an individual rating of usefulness to the royal elite. And to many, that will be just fine as long as they can feed the family and their ego of desires.

In this planned world without borders or nations, citizens will be disarmed of all weapons, including hand guns, and will have no means to protest, fight, resist or challenge this one world authority, who will control them spiritually, economically and militarily. Every human being will be electronically marked and will become helplessly dependent on this one world authority, for all of their most basic needs. The masses are to eventually be taught to bow-down and worship this one world dictator, who is to rule the entire world from some eternal universal throne. One has to understand that at this time in the evolution of the Earthling, they certainly have not exhibited a level of responsibility that creates peace and harmony worldwide. When it comes down to the individual self preservation, the Earthling bows down to egotic survival and material trappings, conflictive beliefs and is, essentially a war-like critter. So perhaps he deserves this kind of continuous slavery under one roof? And to many this will be just fine.

A big question in this business plan is, who is to play the role of this charismatic leader that the entire world would be willing to accept as their ruler? According to plan, this future world ruler will prove himself to be a descendent of Jesus Christ and Mary Magdalene, and will therefore be accepted by the Christian world. Some will even view him as the Savior and Messiah. As a professed descendent of Christ, and a proponent of world religion, he will also be accepted by Buddhists, Hindus and the Eastern World, where Jesus Christ reportedly visited and studied and later preached Eastern Philosophies during his ministry. Since he is a descendent of the Hebrew Tribes of Israel, he will also be accepted by Hebrews and Jews world-wide. By marrying a Muslim woman, he will win the acceptance of the Muslim world. He will also be accepted by world-wide freemasonry and secret societies, of which he is a member.

There is an interesting speculation that is brought forward not to predict the plan but to bring to the forefront the **possibility of a plan**. This possibility is the son of princess Diana, as he is already loved and worshipped. When his mother died in the arms of a Muslim man, in a Paris car crash, the world embraced him. On May 31st 2004, the Rothschild controlled Associated Press, published a photograph worldwide, taken by Alistar Grant. The photo shows prince William posing with a lamb like Jesus Christ, who the Bible calls the Lamb of God. To the unaware observer, the photograph is perfectly innocent. But to insiders familiar with the Protocols of Zion, Freemasonry and the Book of Revelation, William is identified in the photo as the antichrist. The antichrist has been described in art and literature as a handsome and charming and a master of lies and deception. Freemasons call him the Bathomed, or Goat of Mendese. He is commonly illustrated with cloven hind hooves. Why is prince William holding up a cloven hind hoof in the photograph? According to Masonic calculations, Prince William is predicted to be crowned World Dictator in year 2015, at the age of 33. And to many that are still carnal, addicted to royalty, this would be just fine.

The question of whether God or Lucifer exist has been fiercely debated since the beginning of debate. Some people believe that, like religion, God and Lucifer are inventions of the ruling class, to control the masses. Most people acknowledge the existence of positive creative energy, characterized by joy, love and vitality. And the existence of negative destructive energy, characterized by greed, hatred and death. Could it be that God and Lucifer are the two sources of these two opposing energies? The triumph of evil in the world today is based on the ability of evil to disguise itself as its opposite and fool the masses.
Then, without organized intervention, life and peace on earth will take on a whole new meaning.

The PLANET EARTH Business Plan Of 2009-2012

As part of PLANET EARTH Business Plan, In 2008, the Illuminati bankers under the control of the Roman Cult in Zürich used their banks and gold holdings to launch a pre-emptive strike against the Jesuit controlled finance system--choosing the sub-prime crisis as the catalyst. In spite of the lack of real gold underpinning the modern global financial system created by the Jesuits, the creativity of banking and governments had managed to avoid a major financial debt fuelled meltdown of the system several times since its creation in 1945.

However, under the New World Order power structure, the Holy See and the Illuminati of cities such as the Munich and Zürich are subservient to the Jesuits --as they have been for 200 years. Using the sub-prime crisis, the Vatican controlled banks simply refused to renew fresh lines of credit underpinned by real bullion into the system in the second half of 2008 and again at the start of 2009, causing the whole financial system to effective "seize up". Contrary to early reports, this does not appear to be a Jesuit driven action but a deliberate action on behalf of the Illuminati families and the Vatican against the Jesuits in the hope the resulting social turmoil will set the conditions for future war.

Evidence that we are witnessing a war within the power structure of the New World Order can be seen by recent extraordinary negative and disruptive comments from the European Union and Commissions against plans by the United States to trade out of crisis. There can be no doubt we are in the middle of the greatest power struggle since World War II. It is uncertain whether the Jesuits will prevail and the system restored to order, or whether the Vatican and Illuminati will succeed in breaking the shackles of forced subservience after 200 years.

The Secret Covenant: PLANET EARTH Code Of Ethics

In a worst case scenario, this interesting article has been published at the site **www.luisprada.com/Protected/reptilian_pact.htm.** See also the complementary articles, "**The Holographic Prison and the Pact with the Devil**" and the "**New World Order, an Overview.**" In this document, and research that led to it as evidenced on this rather prolific website about deception, we get a taste for what may well be the underlying attitude of the Royal Bloodlines directing PLANET EARTH. It is called the reptilian pact. It is an interesting piece of work because it most definitely reflects the evil side of the Satanic Belief structure and it would certainly be a prevalent consciousness of the Founders of a Corporation out of control who are defining a secret code of ethics. As to its credibility, one can only speculate where secret covenants and blood oats are involved.

I have to relate something that is very common these days with regards to the Conspirators. The book Wheat Belly by William Davis MD is an example. In his book he draws from decades of clinical studies how the new form of genetically modified wheat (greatest yield at lowest cost) and the 1970's introduction of dietary guidelines as well the later USDA endorsements has been the root cause of health deterioration. From celiac, diabetes, overweight, immune, neurological disorder, arthritis dementia, the list is impressive, as is the proof towards direct addiction. He reports that after 10,000 years of wheat being a staple product around the world in 1943 through the collaboration of the **Rockefeller Foundation** and the Mexican government to achieve agricultural self sufficiency, the project (IMWAC) to create new strains of wheat, corn, and soy was launched. By 1980 thousands of strains were produced that were adopted worldwide. Davis states:

"The primary trigger is wheat. In fact the incredible financial bonanza that the proliferation of wheat in the American diet as created for the food and drug industries can make you wonder if this 'perfect storm' was somehow man-made. Did a group of powerful men convene a secret Howard Hughesian meeting in 1955 map out an evil plan to mass produce high-yield, low cost dwarf wheat, engineer the government sanctioned advice to eat 'healthy whole grain' lead to the charge of corporate Big Food to sell hundreds of billions worth of processed wheat food products all leading to obesity and the need for billions of dollars of drug treatment for diabetes, heart disease, and all other health consequences of obesity? It sounds ridiculous but in a sense that's exactly what happened."

This research is not alone in its realizations. The last 12 years has been exceptionally prolific in these books and reports of alleged plans or consequential collateral damage as a result of trusting the "system". This is not placed here to annoy you or create fear. It is here so you can make an informed choice on something that you may have known nothing about. That is the purpose of this book. It's like the wheat itself; you can simply choose a substitute if the truth rings with you. But you can't choose if you are not aware of the issue.

And so there would appear to be an ethic of speculation that would reduce the Earthling to a simple minded animal that is not yet of sufficient intelligence to evolve into the superior being of the "bloodline". The following is alleged to reflect that ethic, and the moral conduct behind the New world Order Plan: (See the site **www.godlikeproductions.com/forum1/message879227/pg1**). again read these as words without emotion. This is the secret pact:

"An illusion it will be, so large, so vast it will escape their perception. Those who will see it will be thought of as insane. We will create separate fronts to prevent them from seeing the connection between us. We will behave as if we are not connected to keep the illusion alive. Our goal will be accomplished one drop at a time so as to never bring suspicion upon ourselves. This will also prevent them from seeing the changes as they occur.

We will always stand above the relative field of their experience for we know the secrets of the absolute. We will work together always and will remain bound by blood and secrecy. Death will come to he who speaks. We will keep their lifespan short and their minds weak while pretending to do the opposite. We will use our knowledge of science and technology in subtle ways so they will never see what is happening. We will use soft metals, aging accelerators and sedatives in food and water, also in the air.

They will be blanketed by poisons everywhere they turn. The soft metals will cause them to lose their minds. We will promise to find a cure from our many fronts, yet we will feed them more poison. The poisons will be absorbed through their skin and mouths, they will destroy their minds and reproductive systems. From all this, their children will be born dead, and we will conceal this information. The poisons will be hidden in everything that surrounds them, in what they drink, eat, breathe and wear. We must be ingenious in dispensing the poisons for they can see far.

We will teach them that the poisons are good, with fun images and musical tones. Those they look up to will help. We will enlist them to push our poisons. They will see our products being used in film and will grow accustomed to them and will never know their true effect. When they give birth we will inject poisons into the blood of their children and convince them it's for their help. We will start early on, when their minds are young, we will target their children with what children love most, sweet things.

When their teeth decay we will fill them with metals that will kill their mind and steal their future. When their ability to learn has been affected, we will create medicine that will make them sicker and cause other diseases for which we will create yet more medicine.

We will render them docile and weak before us by our power. They will grow depressed, slow and obese, and when they come to us for help, we will give them more poison. We will focus their attention toward money and material goods so they many never connect with their inner self. We will distract them with fornication, external pleasures and games so they may never be one with the oneness of it All. Their minds will belong to us and they will do as we say. If they refuse we shall find ways to implement mind-altering technology into their lives. We will use fear as our weapon.

We will establish their governments and establish opposites within. We will own both sides. We will always hide our objective but carry out our plan. They will perform the labor for us and we shall prosper from their toil. Our families will never mix with theirs. Our blood must be pure always, for it is the way. We will make them kill each other when it suits us.

We will keep them separated from the oneness by dogma and religion. We will control all aspects of their lives and tell them what to think and how. We will guide them kindly and gently letting them think they are guiding themselves.

We will foment animosity between them through our factions. When a light shall shine among them, we shall extinguish it by ridicule, or death, whichever suits us best. We will make them rip each other's hearts apart and kill their own children. We will accomplish this by using hate as our ally, anger as our friend. The hate will blind them totally, and never shall they see that from their conflicts we emerge as their rulers. They will be busy killing each other. They will bathe in their own blood and kill their neighbours for as long as we see fit. We will benefit greatly from this, for they will not see us, for they cannot see us.

We will continue to prosper from their wars and their deaths. We shall repeat this over and over until our ultimate goal is accomplished. We will continue to make them live in fear and anger through images and sounds. We will use all the tools we have to accomplish this. The tools will be provided by their labor. We will make them hate themselves and their neighbours. We will always hide the divine truth from them, that we are all one. This they must never know! They must never know that color is an illusion, they must always think they are not equal.

Drop by drop, drop by drop we will advance our goal. We will take over their land, resources and wealth to exercise total control over them. We will deceive them into accepting laws that will steal the little freedom they will have. We will establish a monetary system that will imprison them forever, keeping them and their children in debt. When they shall band together, we shall accuse them of crimes and present a different story to the world for we shall own all the media.

We will use our media to control the flow of information and their sentiment in our favor. When they shall rise up against us we will crush them like insects, for they are less than that. They will be helpless to do anything for they will have no weapons. We will recruit some of their own to carry out our plans, we will promise them eternal life, but eternal life they will never have for they are not of us. The recruits will be called "initiates" and will be indoctrinated to believe false rites of passage to higher realms. Members of these groups [Editor´s Note: the Illuminati] will think they are one with us never knowing the truth. They must never learn this truth for they will turn against us. For their work they will be rewarded with earthly things and great titles, but never will they become immortal and join us, never will they receive the light and travel the stars.

They will never reach the higher realms, for the killing of their own kind will prevent passage to the realm of enlightenment. This they will never know. The truth will be hidden in their face, so close they will not be able to focus on it until it's too late. Oh yes, so grand the illusion of freedom will be, that they will never know they are our slaves. When all is in place, the reality we will have created for them will own them.

This reality will be their prison. They will live in self-delusion. When our goal is accomplished a new era of domination will begin. [N. of Ed.: the New World Order].Their minds will be bound by their beliefs, the beliefs we have established from time immemorial. But if they ever find out they are our equal, we shall perish then. THIS THEY MUST NEVER KNOW. If they ever find out that together they can vanquish us, they will take action.

They must never, ever find out what we have done, for if they do, we shall have no place to run, for it will be easy to see who we are once the veil has fallen. Our actions will have revealed who we are and they will hunt us down and no person shall give us shelter.

This is the Secret Covenant by which we shall live the rest of our present and future lives, for this reality will transcend many generations and life spans. This covenant is sealed by blood, our blood. We, the ones who from heaven to earth came.

This covenant must NEVER, EVER be known to exist. It must NEVER, EVER be written or spoken of for if it is, the consciousness it will spawn will release the fury of the PRIME CREATOR upon us and we shall be cast to the depths from whence we came and remain there until the end time of infinity itself.

The interesting part of this document, which remains without author, is that it may well be a bitch list of some unhappy writer who sees the wrongs in the world today but it does reflect much of what is indeed being revealed more and more, just like in the Wheat Belly book. And indeed if the royal bloodlines see the Earthlings as inferior beings and slaves that are here to survive the needs, there would be no difference between this philosophy and or own in how we treat cattle. Moreover, if there would be those who have some superior powers of "Satan" or "witchcraft" or darker esoteric abilities, and they were free to use these without hindrance, would these not be the darker side of the Satanic Beliefs we covered in Part 1? I repeat: *"Did a group of powerful men convene a secret Howard Hughesian meeting map out an evil plan. It sounds ridiculous but in a sense that's exactly what happened."*

Old End Time Of Revelation

Once more we have to enter the realm of the myths and prophesies from Old Earth that are allegedly "God" driven. In the old story of Old Earth the End Times are the time which humanity would have to make a choice. That choice would be pay for their sins and roast in Hell or choose God's word and get a reward to Heaven, eternal life, and all sorts of heavenly goodies. Or perhaps you may pay your way out by confession and repentance. And so religions, and I shall pick on the prevalent ones, have created an effective dogma around the concepts of Revelation, Rapture, Resurrection, and Armageddon. The underlying theme, to make a simple analogy, is basically, humans, especially women, are a bunch of low life sinners and they need to make amends. They may be saved by the second coming of Christ who will reveal himself at some glorious moment. When? Perhaps when enough sinners have realized their sins and expressed absolute obedience to those representing God. And then Christ, or a Messiah, or some superhuman dude will rise and save them so they can go into heaven in eternal bliss, then sort out the rest once and for all. When? Perhaps when the business plan of PLANET EARTH needs the strategy to be staged?

In this story, **Revelation** brings together the worlds of heaven, earth, and hell in a final confrontation between the forces of good and evil. It means this is the revealing or disclosing, or making something obvious through active or passive communication with supernatural and divine entities. Of course it is believed that revelation can originate directly from a deity, or through an agent, such as an angel, most likely through the churches and religious leaders who have elected themselves the "chosen ones" that are privy to the Word of God.

The Dude that is going to disclose all this secret stuff is of course Jesus Christ, the Son of God (or the Prophet) himself. He is second in command and in for a second shot at this task to save humanity from their terrible deeds. So he is going to go through another **Resurrection** and descend back to life in a magical event worshipped as the Second Coming of Christ. As the plan unfolds, first of all he will take care of his chosen ones, then he will have a huge heavenly meeting with Dad (God), look at the tally ledger, and decide to remove all good Christians from the Earth to protect them.

This process is called Rapture, a term from the Latin verb **raptare**, and the Greek word **harpizo**, both meaning to be caught up or to be snatched up. So Jesus will snatch good Christians out of harm's way so those who have been good boys and girls can get their special treats of being saved. That means giving in to obedience. Those top good ones are of course, the ones who have listened to the chosen ones who know the truth of the word of god and have faithfully been gobbling those blue pills, like their prescriptions are still current and paid up. Then they can be saved—lifted out of harm's way while the rest meet a different situation as their undoing dealing with the big bad guy Mr. Devil, or one of his buddies. Either way it looks pretty bad if you threw away your pills.

But listen up. Under this story there are more goodies to get if you are saved. It is about this thing of revelation which is the revealing or disclosing of life's secrets through active or passive communication with Jesus and his Dad. All those good kids will be divinely or supernaturally revealed or inspired. Revelation comes from the Greek name **Apokalypsis,** which means a disclosure, a revelation or manifestation and to be revealed. So it is a revealing of Jesus Christ himself.

In looking back at this myth, we see that this Revelation is the supposed revealing of Jesus Christ and that the message originally came from God the Father. But it was actually from god, the faker. Well, because we screwed up, especially the sinful women, it's different. Since the introduction of sin, all communication between heaven and Earth has been terminated and has to go through Jesus Christ as he is the only mediator between this god and man. But, and here's the big but; it seems that the self elected bishops and religious gurus are the ones in between you and the gods because Christ ain't here yet. But he, of course talks to them as they are "chosen" and know the Word and what will happen and of course when. This time when this would happen was of course cleverly unstated so it could loom upon sinners forever.

And what of those poor souls that are not revealed, and snatched up? **Armageddon!** Of course there are literally hundreds of different interpretations on this as well as the Bible prophecies, especially on the issue of who is Mister Devil, the real bad guy and the battle of Armageddon. The key word here is interpretations. But you are told not to have private interpretations of prophecy at all. Why? Because god's Word gives us all we need to know without any speculation whatsoever and of course god's boys are the ones who know best.

So the bad news for those that have not been plucked out of harm's way is **Armageddon**—End Times. It will be time to pay for your sins, you bad kids. This brings the scene for the final battle between the kings of the Earth at the end of the world, a catastrophically destructive battle where Mr. Satan gets his dues for meddling with the big plan for Old Earth once and for all.

And even the New Agers have something to say about this; there is a great space ship commanded by Ashtar and Sananda himself—the one who walked as Christ—waiting up there to have the equal of Scotty beam good souls to safe haven while the great battle ensues, or great catastrophes of 2012 happen.

It's a great story and the variations of this and the 2012 doomsday seems endless. And there are a lot of folks that heed to this. It is a great story that has been around in thousands of versions for some time now. And yet it dominate the belief system for so many "scientific", rational minds seems in itself an unbelievable fiction. And although I poke at it, this is really not funny to those who so vehemently believe it. The fear of being one of the unlucky kids who pissed off god and didn't get with his program of the "Word" means you are going to remain in harm's way and take your consequences. And so this story has been prophesized by the best publishers of all time—the churches and major religious leaders. And so the humans who basically want to trust someone and to seek out a true God relinquish their own beliefs to be replaced by others as their god's words.

What is so interesting here is that this is a prewritten plan of what can happen. And it is no different from a pre-written business plan that any CEO would write about a potential mission outlining the Vice Presidents, new Divisions, new products and services that would unfold in a time sequence. The difference however, is that this particular plan may indeed be orchestrated by the gods, not God.

More On Revelation And Prophesy

There is quite an analysis of this Satan prophesy on the website **www.remnantofgod.org.** Let us refer to the "good book" again. Here Prophecy did say in Revelation 17:12: *"And the ten horns which thou sawest are ten kings, which have received no kingdom as yet; but receive power as kings one hour with the beast."*

According to this web site, these Ten Kingdoms of the New World Government are alleged to be:

Kingdom 1: Canada and the United States of America
Kingdom 2: European Union - Western Europe
Kingdom 3: Japan
Kingdom 4: Australia, New Zealand, South Africa, Israel and Pacific Islands
Kingdom 5: Eastern Europe
Kingdom 6: Latin America - Mexico, Central and South America
Kingdom 7: North Africa and the Middle East *(Moslems)*
Kingdom 8: Central Africa
Kingdom 9: South and Southeast Asia
Kingdom 10: Central Asia

The writer of this website goes on to say that: *"The prophecy states that the entire world will wonder after the beast in Rome. This of course happens after the beast's wound is administered and then on the mend."*

In Revelation 13:3, *"And I saw one of his heads as it were <u>wounded to death</u>; and <u>his deadly wound was healed</u>: and <u>all the world wondered after the beast</u>."*

The three obvious events in this prophecy are as follows:

1. The beast will be wounded
2. The wound will begin healing and eventually be healed
3. All the world will wonder after the beast

Has this happened, and has this happened in this prophesied order? Can prophecy be that accurate? Let us look at this "beast" working though the Great Architect "Lucifer". We have already looked the US Dollar bill that was introduced in 1929, in preparation for the New Order.

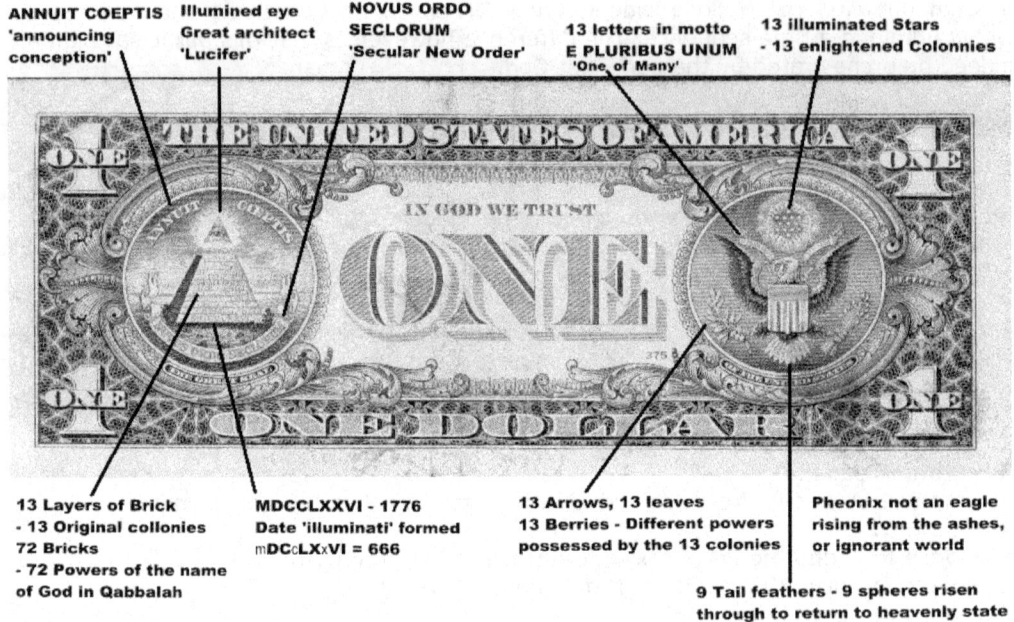

Now, let us see if this three step chronology has occurred. Again, this information is taken from the site **www.remantsofgod.org**. Please refer to the extensive research and work done there for a more comprehensive picture:

1. The beast will be wounded
The mortal wound was administered in 1798. In **1798** General Berthier made his entrance **into Rome, abolished the papal government**, and established a secular one." -*Encyclopedia Britannica 1941 Edition.* The fact Napoleon sent General Berthier into Rome to remove the Pope from his position of political power was open evidence the people knew of the evils of Rome, and therefore rebelled. Plus, History records the United States was actually formed by people fleeing Papal persecutions. People were burned at the stake, boiled in oil, buried alive, cut in half, and killed in a bevy of other demonic ways by the prelates of Rome. It was common knowledge that the Roman Catholic church was evil and everyone feared it because of its atrocities.

*"For teaching faith contrary to the teaching of the Church of Rome, history records the martyrdom of more than **100 million people**."*

Modern day research has found the number to be around 500 million). Under the influence of Germanic customs and concepts, torture was little used from the 9th to the 12th centuries, but with the revival of Roman law the practice was re-established in the 12th century... In 1252 (Pope) Innocent IV sanctioned the infliction of torture by the civil authorities upon heretics, and torture came to have a recognized place in the procedure of the inquisitional courts. -*New Catholic Encyclopedia*, arts. **"Inquisition"**, **"Auto-da-Fe'**," *and* **"Massacre of St Bartholomew's Day."** (For many more facts on this and other evils of Rome, go to **www.remnantofgod.org/beastword.htm**.

This beast was well known as 2 Thessalonians 2:3 predicted it would be. This beast was also mortally wounded exactly as prophecy predicted. Prophecy stated that this beast would rule 1260 years and then be mortally wounded.

Daniel 7:25, "*And he shall speak great words against the most High, and shall wear out the saints of the most High, and think to change times and laws: and they shall be given into his hand until **a time and times and the dividing of time**.*"

Revelation 12:6, "*And the woman fled into the wilderness, where she hath a place prepared of God, that they should feed her there **a thousand two hundred and threescore days**.*"

Revelation 13:5, "*And there was given unto him a mouth speaking great things and blasphemies; and power was given unto him to continue **forty and two months**.*"

Revelation 13:5 speaks of this time as forty two months. These forty two months of Rev 13:5 and the "time, and times and dividing a time" of Daniel 7:25 equal the exact same thing. 42 months actually equates to 3½ years. Looking closely, one can see this, **A "time (one year) and times (+ two years) and the dividing of time, (+ half a year) That's a "time" + "times" + "dividing of a time", which equals 3½ years, or forty two months. (12+24 + 6 = 42 months)** Revelation 12:6 confirms this calculation when it says that the church of Jesus would hide in the wilderness for exactly 1260 days. 42 months, or 3½ years equals 1260 days. A day in prophecy actually equals a year. God says in Ezekiel 4:6 "*I have appointed thee each **day for a year**...*" and in Numbers 14:34 it says, "*...After the number of the days in which ye searched the land, even forty days, **each day for a year**,* " So, according to Ezekiel 4:6, and Number 14:34, that's 1260 years that Papal Rome would reign, and during this reign it will kill many Christians.

Still, some will say that this is just my opinion, or interpretation (website writer). They will say that the only way this "day for a year" idea can be valid is if history proves it out. So... does it? Well first we need to find out when the Roman Catholic church became a "woman on a beast" (church & state) and capable of ruling in both the political as well as religious realm. Why? This is when she has her full power according to Revelation.

"*Vigilius...ascended the papal chair (538 A.D.) under the military protection of Belisarius.*" **History of the Christian Church**, Vol. 3, p. 327

Historical records reveal the papacy began its global reign in 538 AD upon Emperor Justinian's decree, and under the military protection of Belisarius. The Bible says the beast will rule for EXACTLY 1260 years before receiving a mortal wound. Now it's just a matter of simple mathematics. It is also a grand method by which to see the Lord glorified. If the prophecy is correct, 1260 years after 538 AD the Beast must receive a mortal wound. Did this happen? Can the prophecy really be that accurate? If you add 1260 years to the beginning year the Roman Catholic Church had "absolute" power as a church and state in 538 AD, you will arrive in the exact year 1798 AD. So, according to the prophecy we are told the first reign of the Beast will last until the year 1798 . So, did it end in 1798?

"*In **1798** General Berthier made his entrance **into Rome, abolished the papal government**, and established a secular one.*" -**Encyclopedia Britannica 1941** edition.

That's Exactly 42 prophetic months, or 1260 years, or a time, and times, and dividing a time after the Papacy began its powerful reign that the Pope shall receive the mortal wound and "*shall go into captivity.*" This not only confirms the "day for a year" issue, it also glorifies the Lord like no other prophecy can. It's that accurate! When Napoleon sent in General Berthier to remove the Pope from power, the mortal wound was in fact administered that very day. And by the way, the Pope did in fact die in exile the following November. This is why most Catholic children are taught in parochial schools that Napoleon was Antichrist. Of course, they can't use a bible effectively to prove that. In fact, when you question them and their interpretations as I (www.Remantsofgod.org author) did as a Catholic, they will tell you to "stop reading the Bible, it's confusing you."

2. The wound will be healed Revelation 13:3, *"And I saw one of his heads as it were wounded to death; and his deadly wound was healed: and all the world wondered after the beast."* As we just saw, the "deadly wound" was given to the Papacy by Napoleon in 1798. The Vatican still continued as a church, however, she was completely stripped of her civil and political power just as the prophecy declared. Then, suddenly in 1929, we see the Italian government recognizing Vatican City once again as an independent state. (And the new dollar bill entering the US) This political move once again made the Pope a religio-political power! Just as prophecy said... the mortal wound that was administered in 1798 by Napoleon **was supposed to be healed**. Notice how the newspapers of that day actually used prophetic language to announce this event...

Mussolini and (Cardinal) Gasspari sign historic Roman pact. *"The Roman question tonight was a thing of the past, and the Vatican was at peace with Italy... In affixing the autographs to the memorable document **healing the wound** of many years, extreme cordiality was displayed on both sides"* -**The San Francisco Chronicle. Feb. 11, 1929**

Pope Becomes Ruler Of A State Again Rome, June 7.--From 11 o' clock this morning there was **another sovereign independent State in the world**. At that time Premier Mussolini, as Italian Foreign Minister representing King Victor Emmanuel--the first Italian Premier ever to cross the threshold of the Vatican--exchanged with Cardinal Gasparri, Papal Secretary of State, representing Pope Pius XI, **ratifications of the treaties signed at the Lateran Palace** on Feb. 11. By that simple act the sovereign independent State of Vatican City came into existence. -*New York Times July 7, 1929*

The fulfillment of this prophecy confirms yet another one. In Revelation 17:8 where it says: Revelation 17:8, *"... behold the beast that **was**, and **is not**, and **yet is**."*

The Beast that was: The Roman Catholic Church which began in **538 AD** and continued until Napoleon sent in General Berthier in **1798 AD**. **...and is not:** From 1798 AD until the signing of the Lateran treaty in 1929 the Roman Catholic Church & state conglomerate was **non-existent**. **...yet is:** From **1929 to present day,** the Roman Catholic Church **has been a church & state.**

This prophecy is so blunt, and to the point there is no need of explaining it. However, it won't be understood unless the one studying these facts has already investigated the three previous prophecies that defined each state of this beast's existence throughout history. This prophecy can in no way be understood without that knowledge. That's the amazing thing about the Lord's prophecy. Like Scripture, a line upon line method of discovery is necessary. The Bible itself defines its own prophetic symbols. If the people would simply allow the Bible to teach them instead of trusting false teachers they would be ready for what's already begun to happen. Now that we have seen stage one, and stage two of the prophecy from Revelation 13:3 fulfilled, what of the last one?

3. All the world will wonder after it

These are the words of the writer on this site: *"Before sharing the fulfillment of this prophecy, let me first share with you what most Christian denominations on earth* thought of the Papacy not too many years ago. The reason I am lead to do this is to make it painfully clear that this beast was in fact KNOWN BY ALL (except Catholics of course) to be the prophesied Whore of Babylon and house of Antichrist. ALL denominational founders have been quoted in writing as stating the Papacy is in fact the house and global seat of Antichrist. Then I would like to share with you quite a few very recent quotes out of many that show those very same denominations proclaiming the office of Pope to be of God no less! It's a night and day change people! What was just a few years ago seen as the most evil organization known to man, today is seen as the most holy! And by the way, not just the churches are declaring the Pope and his office holy. All the governments are doing so as well now!"

"Yes, it appears if you are Pope, regardless of your well documented past, you are loved now. The wound is almost completely healed. ALL THE WORLD IS WONDERING AFTER THE BEAST just as our Lord told us they would. All that needs to happen now are the disasters that cause the WORLD to look to the Vatican for help. This fabricated and counterfeit "moral leader" will suggest a way to stop the natural disasters as well as the wars, (which are actually started by the Vatican anyway) by suggesting GLOBAL SUNDAY LAWS! Seeing how EVERY nation and EVERY church is now embracing this beast in Rome, they will most assuredly gather to Rome's side as is reflected in the cartoon I shared at the start of this Newsletter." See this on **(http://www.remnantofgod.org/sabatak.htm).**

And finally: **WE WILL NOT BE IN FEAR OF WHAT THEY DO, OR SEEK TO DO!** Or Lord plainly stated... Revelation 14:4, "These are they which were **not defiled with women; for they are virgins**. These are they which **follow the Lamb whithersoever he goeth**. These were redeemed from among men, being the first fruits unto God and to the Lamb."

2 Timothy 1:7, "For God hath **not given us the spirit of fear**; but of power, and of love, and of a sound mind."

"The fallen churches (defiled women) that gather to Rome's side cannot defile, or influence the children of God. Main reason being is we follow the Lamb of God wherever HE leads, not the son of perdition. One last note is needed to be made clear here. As many know, Ratzinger has admitted to being a Nazi soldier. Does his present day theology reflect his Nazi upbringing? You tell me..."

When asked about... "Liberation theology." Ratzinger said.. "The 'absolute good' (and this means building a just socialist society) becomes the moral norm that justifies everything else, including--if necessary--violence, homicide, mendacity." **Cardinal Joseph Ratzinger ~ US News & World Report**, Dec 2, 1985)

Ratzinger's terminology defined...
- Liberation theology is defined as "*Communism and Christianity mixed.*"
- Mendacity is simply defined as "*lies.*"

Communism is evil no matter how much the New World Order pushers says otherwise. It is the ultimate community over the individual. What's good for the community is what rules the person. If you as a person upset the order, it is better for you to die then the whole community to suffer loss. Now read the following quote from quite a few years ago...

"It is thus necessary that the individual should finally come to realize that his own ego is of no importance in comparison with the existence of his nation; That the position of the *individual ego is conditioned solely by the interests of the nation as a whole... that above all the unity of a nation's spirit and will are worth far more than the freedom of the spirit and will of an individual..."'*

"This state of mind, which subordinates the interests of the ego to the conservation of the community, is really the first premise for every truly human culture... The basic attitude from which such activity arises, We call - to distinguish it from egoism and selfishness - idealism. By this we understand only the individual's capacity to make sacrifices for the community, for his fellow man." -**The Ominous Parallels, by Leonard Piekoff** P 13.

Sounds like an echo of John 11:50 where it says... John 11:50, "Nor consider that it is expedient for us, that one man should die for the people, and that the whole nation perish not."

Their main excuse to kill our Lord was that He should die so that the NATION as a whole wouldn't perish. That is the ultimate communistic ideal! This is exactly what both Ratzigner and this quote are saying.

Now, before sharing who the author is of these statements in Piekoff's book that are a direct echo of Ratzinger's communist "Liberation theology." Who do you think it is that made these remarks? John F Kennedy? Abraham Lincoln? Ronald Reagan perhaps? Finishing the excerpt it says this...

"*These statements were made by <u>Adolph Hitler</u>. He was explaining the moral philosophy of <u>Nazism</u>. (as described by William Shirer in **The Rise and Fall of the Third Reich**): - **The Ominous Parallels, by Leonard Piekoff** P 13.*"

"It's no mistake people. John Paul II was elected at an EARLY age so as to be able to gather almost all the nations to Rome's side in one Pontificate. That is why he was elected at age 57 instead of 77 like most popes. Thanks to John Paul II's tireless efforts of gathering all countries to Rome's camp, as of January 10, 2005 the Vatican now has 174 of the 192 countries in 100% agreement with Rome's agenda. And now they have 'God's enforcer' or 'God's Rottweiler' standing as pope so as to move to the next step."

"Think on it this way. When the Liberation Theology of Ratzinger comes to fruition. The individual will become non-existent and worthy of extermination. The community will then become the voice of the people. That way, the majority of the world, which are already in Satan's control, will become the voice of the people. When the small Remnant of God refuse to break God's Law, their actions are looked upon as a PROBLEM for the "community" at large. Then you will see the Remnant being killed so that the world doesn't perish!"

"Why will they believe they will perish? The disasters will increase and the image of the beast will be formed so as to stop the natural disasters. Their message will be that if they can't get everyone in agreement worldwide, the disasters will get worse. Of course their Roman Catholic doctrinal suggestions won't fly for the Remnant. We cannot be deceived and therefore won't bow to Rome. Since the majority are already in agreement with Rome they have to do something about that small Remnant that they believe is causing the disasters to continue by refusing to agree with Rome's mandates. So, the powers that be will announce that the small Remnant still ignoring the Roman mandates, which are nothing less than Sunday laws, must now die so as to prevent the whole world from perishing! They figure if they can kill them all off, everyone left will be in agreement and there will be peace on earth! THAT is why they have a Nazi Pope, and that is why the

NWO has Nazi ideals! There is no other way to get the masses to work against the individual follower of Biblical jurisprudence without getting the community on the pedestal and the individual under it. So I ask...

Are you ready? ARE YOU SURE!?

Revelation 16:13-14, *"And I saw three unclean spirits like frogs come out of the mouth of the dragon, (Satan ~ Spiritualism) and out of the mouth of the beast, (Roman Catholicism) and out of the mouth of the false prophet.(Apostate Protestantism) For they are the spirits of devils, working miracles, which go forth unto the kings of the earth and of the whole world, to **gather them** to the battle of that great day of God Almighty."*

In closing, one must refer also to the Lucis Trust and the Externalization of the Hierarchy covered in Part 1. That document, also a prophesy being filled even though written by a Satanist, can be interpreted a total different way than what humanity appears to be accepting in the foregoing material of the New World Order. The truth is that humanity is not accepting the beast and the words anymore. It is the leaders that play this game and of course, the people have trusted the leaders so they have listened followed and believed. That in the New Age beginning at the turn of the century is changing exponentially either quietly or with vehement action will not accept this old way.

What is most revealing about the Lucis document also sponsored by Rockefeller is the aspect of this New Age under the belief of Spiritual Satanism. There seems to be a convergence between the Light and the Dark, both reflecting a higher need for spirituality.

So now let us look a new version which can be taken from the bibles and the Lucis Trust document to create a new interpretation of Revelation and the "second coming".

40

RAPTURE AND REVELATION: THE LIGHT SIDE

The Divine Plan Of The New Order Of The Ages

Now I am going to bring to you a bit of news that reflects the enormous wave that dominates the New Earth energies. It's a prophesy that has the bottom line of all the millions of opinions of what is happening and what was meant to happen with regard to this End Time and The Grand Alignment and the big cycle of 26,000 years. It is not a belief system written by any leaders. It is like a melding of the Mayan prophesy and New Age shifting. It is about the transformation through our new version of Revelation and Resurrection. It is this that we will cover in the next chapters. Again, you can get many opinions on this but there is a common denominator. Here is the simplified version. This may be a bit far out if you have not followed the wave, but here goes:

Assuming that the Earthling is ready to take responsibility for his own affairs, resign from PLANET EARTH and stop taking the Blue Pills of the Biblical CODE, there appears to be a Divine Plan that is influencing the consciousness. This mass union of belief and purpose is not led by anyone, or any corporation. This plan has been to allow Gaia (Gaia is Mother Nature) and Earth to ascend (to ascend means to rise in vibration so as to live in a body form without having to die—as your eternal self as part of God) at this special time. But the overall Divine Plan is and always was to allow all that choose to ascend so as to bring the aspect of the God Self to lower form; to experience and to expand the joy of its wonder. As this story goes, this opportunity has occurred before and the Earthling blew it three times. This time it is different in that it is Gaia that is ascending; the question is: what Earthlings are on board the ride this time? At this point it is the time of Gaia and Earth's ascension is to be completed with the alignment of galactic center which is her origin. She and Earth have offered themselves in sacrifice to be the body and form of the Great Experiment of souls to bring all things upon her and connected to her into the evolution of spirit. It is her destiny and it is her members of the Cosmic Council (the planets that the Mayas deemed as gods) that assist in this as they pour their love and their aspects of unique vibrations upon her and all things upon her.

The Divine Plan has been for humanity to be allowed to ascend with her by their own free will—God's gift to all should they choose to ascend and to recognize the power of love. The overall choice for Gaia's humanity was to be determined by the overall vibration of Earth and her inhabitants. It had to reach a certain threshold and so it did during the period referred to as the Harmonic Convergence of 1987. The question was whether humanity could earn this right of ascension that Gaia was to engage in regardless. Otherwise, Gaia would ascend by herself. And so it trigged the Divine Plan which originally was to place within the design of all, the knowing of the God Self and the attributes of Creator and Creation. It would be there in all equally, and placed as a spark of quest of Self and Home as accessed through the heart, the seat and power of the Divine Self. It was the time of the Harmonic Convergence that showed humanity had earned this right. In other words if Earthlings were picking up the messages being inducted into consciousness in sufficient numbers, then the opportunity would allow the unfoldment.

And so it was encoded within the DNA, placed within each, in a place where it could never be lost. It would be within each heart as the gateway to find the way to this truth and to allow this gate to open to bring it forward into consciousness. It is the Divine Plan to allow each and all to grow, evolve and express the joy of love and to receive love and bliss. In return one could learn to ascend in form and to make greater and expand the totality of love of the Creator as the supreme force of all that is. It is what Christ did—the hard way. It is the Divine Plan to allow all possibilities in all beings equally and to create by free will that which they desire to attain joy. The process would be first in thought above, then to form material below, all released by the essence of pure unconditional love—the glue of all that is.

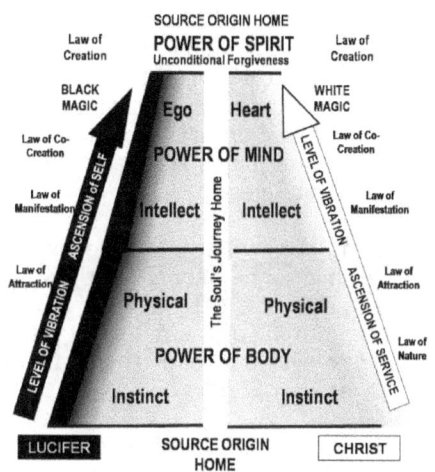

The Divine Plan is to allow creation with the tools of love through the gateway of the heart. In our diagram it is the portal at the top that every Earthling has an opportunity to go through like in a Near Death Experience (without dying) where you meet your Maker and yourself as Soul. So regardless of whether humanity has shown its worthiness in love, bad good or indifferent the gateway of unconditional forgiveness temporarily opens. It is this Divine Plan that is now manifesting upon Gaia and Earth, into new form in wondrous expansion of the universe which is God's mind.

The New Earth: GENESIS II

Well, if I was God, or my higher Soul up there waiting at the other end of the Near Death Experience portal, I would put up a big sign:

"We have seen the evolution of the Old Earth and we have seen how all of your brothers and sisters have lived upon it. It has been a time when the spirit was allowed to be under dominion of the egos, and so it has been. Now we are seeing that humanity is bringing forward this spirit which we have quietly placed within them. It is a time to consider the New Genesis of New Earth as we shall conceive and give birth to. We see that your

brother Christ has indeed left a legacy of spirit and that it has not been subjugated and it is still alive for all.

It is a time that your brothers and sisters have earned their rights to know of themselves. This time we will allow the spirit to come forward in those that have chosen and New Earth can be once again a perfect world that will be inhabited by the ones who choose. It was as we had on Old Earth but it evolved away from spirit of true self to grow and know. Let us once again create a new Genesis and allow the goodness of Old Earth to meld into the New Earth. This Genesis will be formed from the consciousness of those brothers and sisters that awaken, and we will so present them with the gift of ascension into the New Earth."

For the billions that already believe in Genesis, or some form of it, such a proposal from God (the real one of Love) should not be difficult. What is different about this one is that it is totally based upon our Higher Beings, not the egos as the little gods within each of us.

Let me lay upon you some insight to the New Earth that is forming in the 4D ethers of consciousness as a result of the shift during the End Times. Through the seeding of the new unity consciousness of the last wave the seeding by way of pure intent and love, humanity are planting into the ethers of pure love the blueprint and construct for the New Earth. It is here the concept of form and purpose is created that precedes the conception which through the purity of divine male and female are conceived into creation.

This is about the melding of three elements through the intent of unity consciousness; the pure New Earth as a 5D concept of intent of pure consciousness, as the melding of physical purity; the alignment of cosmic forces and planets; and the overlay of the purity of love manifestation of that which is heaven. This is the concept like Genesis that is conceived in the joint minds and is birthed as an egg of union of male and female as equal divine energies.

This seeding of New Earth then follows the process of the 9th wave into temporary energy of 4D which may be likened to the gestation of the New Earth, ending at the Dec 21st Solstice/Equinox of 2011 shortly after as a Time Of Choosing. It is the formation or congealing into 4D of the model of New Earth, ready to receive its inhabitants that have so chosen to evolve through the final stage of evolution from 3D to 5D for them and from 4D to 3D for New Earth.

During the year 2012 the shift of the process of transformation into 3D are occurring as the cosmic forces of ascension shower upon those chosen to move with Gaia, and Gaia herself. These particular frequencies are acting as triggers to activate the DNA antenna and receivers. This new form, like the chrysalis opening will show itself more and more to those aware of it. It then begins to congeal into the parallel hologram of New Earth. And so the 3D representation of the hologram will be born at the time of the great alignment of Dec 21, 2012, in preparation for the great resurrection of the New Earth. It will be so within the total unity consciousness of God and the Christ Consciousness.

Then with the cosmic configuration of forces and planets, when the New Earth has shifted from the 5D concept, to 4D conception to manifestation and creation in 3D reality, it will be ready to accept souls who have chosen to move into that reality. Of course by that time the Great Revelation (Time of Choosing) and the Great Resurrection (Time of Transformation of Ascension) will have readied those for the shift to the New Earth reality.

It is the Time of Transformation that physicality begins to congeal into new form, both for Gaia, the New Earth, and humanity that chooses to ascend with her. The separation of Old and New Earth will become a conscious reality and the final formation will be after the Earth, like humanity, has been gifted the cosmic forces and overlays that will be completed by the time of 3D birth. From then on, again, like in a newborn child, the configuration of the stars, the contracts each are creating now, and the movements of the Cosmic Gods of creation will guide the evolution of the New Earth. And the New Beings linked between realities of 3D-5D will emerge, then evolve into the next age of unconditional love over 26000 years, spilling their presence into the Galaxies.

What is your lesson here? Look around you and look beyond to see what is happening around all Earthlings now. It is a time to choose above Light and Dark and align polarity of separation, with the new consciousness. What Consciousness? It is the Christ Consciousness and size the key of unconditional forgiveness. Both Dark and Light as we have seen, are on the paths to convergence at the gate. It is time to understand that a great shift is here and it is time to see Home and be the creator you are.

Over half of this book has been dedicated to revelation of a different story of history and a different perception, interpretation from, in many cases, the same sources of information. Hence we have the great conundrum of what is really truth. This great conundrum had in the last 12 years come forward because a shifting consciousness seems to be prevalent that seeks out a new version of truth because the old version is not acceptable--something is amiss. More and more researchers have come forward to reveal a different story of the past. More and more people have come forward with a drive to peace and love of spirituality. And hence we have the great conundrum of the ages.

Will it be the Old Earth ways humanity accepts under the New World Order or will it be the New Earth ways of the New Order of the Ages? Both are written, hidden in plain view, but both are subject to the fickle perceptions of consciousness driving beliefs. Both new and old version had, or have a knowing that something important, and big were to occur at this particular time as the shift from the Age of Pisces to that of Aquarius. One is a continuation of dominion and the ways of kings and empires, one is the liberation of spirit and oneness.

If one should look around now, at this juncture in time, the undeniable truth of the world leaders being placed on the spotlight for their behaviours cannot be ignored. It is because changes are occurring that demand responsibility and transparency. Humanity has simply accepted being dual in nature-part good, part bad. It is the way we have been taught and it is the way the leaders behave. The familiar behaviour of being good until someone pisses you off, or offering a smidgen of kindness to a poor soul absolving all your wrongs, or loving and protecting your close family but taking advantage of those that are not, are all too familiar traits of this duality. It is the same duality between god and Satan. It is what humanity has accepted as their belief and hence it is what that unit of consciousness attracts consciously and unconsciously.

That duality seems to be shifting in favour of the goodness.

The Undeniable Theme Of Prevailing Consciousness

So let us summarize the old story of Revelations. The old story can be summarized When you finally get to the end of the old biblical story, to the final Book of Revelation, when the ascended Christ comes back, the story which is presented imposes an automatic policing system of threat and destruction for mankind. And it is Christ, the Son of God—the one that helped Dad create the Old Earth that bears the warning about the End Times. In this prophesy (the old business plan), it is that Satan will be crushed (20:7) and there will be a final Judgment day (20:11); there will be a new heaven on Earth (21:1) where a new Jerusalem will rise (21:9) and when he comes it will be swift to judge if you are not in the accounting ledger (22:7) that is within the Time of the End (22:10). It is this threat that polices the believers through fear of each not being "worthy" and this is the major theme in the vast writings. This story is in this time, under attack.

For, like the fickle ways of perception, within these writings is hidden a truth in plain sight. And it is one that has and still vibrates with much of humanity, especially in this time. For even though the bible is filled with the duality and polarity, it still contains the story of this man called Christ who came down to prophesize the Revelation of End Time. The story, part contrived, part truth does, regardless of edition reflect a consciousness of love and peace, despite the conclusion that it is written with a possible contrived mortal purpose of a manifesto of dominion over the sinful creatures of Planet Earth. It draws out a theme that this Christ, who was deemed a Prophet or the Son of God later, reflected a consciousness so many people quietly and inherently would like to believe in—a New Earth of peace and love.

It is this aspect of the stories, despite the motivations of their creation, that in all due regards to the biblical system, has kept this Christ spark alive in the story of Christ or Allah, or whatever. And regardless of whether he was deemed as a prophet, Messiah, Son of God or whatever, the legend carries an underlying energy of something that is wanton in all—like an encoding within the essence of humanity; their DNA.

Even though the four gospels upon which the New Testament was based on were written between 75 and 100 years after Christ, by unknown authors, and are conflictive in their stories, in essence, it seems that Christ was indeed a very unusual fellow. Not only was he capable of creating some very unusual miracles, he was responsible for showing a new way of thought—that of being aligned with the real God of truth and love, and we all are Sons and Daughters of God. It is this that is surfacing in these times. And for what it is worth, he is responsible for a consciousness, a way of thinking and living that is parallel to this revolution of thought surfacing during these current times.

It is about the Christ Consciousness. The human mind has spiritual currents running through its thought streams. These streams contain vital information from Spirit that is highly valuable to humans. Spirit is the source of everything TRUE, BEAUTIFUL, and GOOD and conveys these ideals through the human mind that intersect with a person's beliefs, helping the individual ascend into the higher information that uplifts and improves the quality of life. Or have I got it all wrong? Is God not peace, love, harmony, forgiveness and without judgment?

In human life, spiritual growth is achieved by aligning with these spiritual currents that come from both the personality and mind of Spirit by intellectual assent and emotional devotion. Christ Consciousness is the growing human recognition and blending of the human evolutionary (or ego) mind with the Divine Mind and the Divine Personality that is the source of human happiness and fulfillment. This awareness accrues over time within the consciousness of human thinking when intention, attention, and openness is focused on knowing who and what is that "christed" state of being—that higher mindedness of enlightenment.

As this awareness in the human mind grows and strengthens, life becomes more liberated, joyful, peaceful, and love-dominated. The fear which creates isolation and despair begins to diminish in thought and feeling. You are free to live the life you were born to live —as a child of Spirit in a love-filled and supportive universe.

The highest state of intellectual development and emotional maturity is sometimes termed the "christed" state because of the sacredness and purity of the individual who has achieved it. Jesus achieved this in his human life, and was given this term before his name as the recognition of his achievement of this spiritual status. This path is open to anyone regardless of their religious tradition if and when he or she is open to become a living vessel of LOVE and TRUTH on the planet and actively strives to attain it.

This is the prime truth that religions, despite their higher caustic motivations and acts have kept alive. It is not a term used exclusively in the Christian religion, nor does it mean that you must adhere to the Christian belief system to attain this state. All ways and paths are honored if they lead a person into becoming more loving, forgiving, patient, kind, compassionate, tolerant, and happy. All paths of LOVE lead to the same Source of All That Is. We all share the same Creator-Source as living expressions of that Source Personality and we all are moving back home to unite with our Source.

Christ consciousness is the state of awareness of our true nature, our higher self, and our birthright as children of God. Christ consciousness is our living expression as a child of Spirit as we unfold our own Divine life plan onto the earth plane bringing heaven to earth. Living in the reality of our "christed" self is actually being fully alive and invested in who we truly are. In our "christed" self we live as inspiration for others to seek this for themselves so we can collectively move our planet forward into the Divine Plan for planetary transformation and glorification.

At this point, let us go back to the prophesies of biblical writings and look at some new interpretations. The prophesises such a Revelations were written suspiciously like the writers knew something and the turn of the Ages. And it is written like they had a plan called the New World Order. So far, humanity has accepted this plan and we are at the final moments of its unfolding, as has been written here.

As we have discussed, something else is going on. It is the shifting consciousness that is choosing a different path. And again that may also be hidden in plain view, written in the same books and bibles. Just as we have brought forward a different picture of Christ, perhaps there is a different picture of New and Old Earth? Let us now look at the different versions.

And so it has come to pass that there are the two opposing dualistic plans of good and evil are the topic in this time of the new century. And it can be interpreted from the same sources that are without exception written by man, not God.

A New Prophesy of Rapture, Revelation and Resurrection

So now we have looked the dark side of the business plan. These plans and prophesies have been hidden in plain view for centuries and they have been integrated into many belief systems on the Old Earth. That is perhaps why it has unfolded the way it has; because humanity believes and follows what they are told and that, in itself, is the energy that is brought forward into humanity's reality. But there is a new plan evolving and it reflects the The New Order of the Ages. It is apparent that the consciousness in the last 12 years has been shifting from Religious to Spiritual ways of earthly expression. This particular time has taken on the name of the "End Times".

So we have looked the Old Earth plan as can be interpreted from the Book of Revelations and others. There are many versions of this and there are many interpretations. These are all about what can be encapsulated into these End Times. It is what those dominant religions put into the minds of the followers. It would also appear to include be some scheduled events which forms a strategic implantation trigger of the final takeover. After all, dominion over others is accomplished best when those dominated fear something, especially god who deems all as sinful creatures. The greatest perpetrators of this have been, and still are of course the major religions who want the people to be obedient to believe in *their* god's word. The threat is clear as it says in the good book—vengeance will be done.

It can all be summed within three words and many, many interpretations.

Whether it is religion, New Age, or whatever, there is an absolute preponderance of information about the End Times. What are they? It's when humanity kisses their dear asses goodbye if they have not been good and have not taken their blue pills given by the church (The Matrix movie) of faithful obedience. These pills are received from the Vatican and other such institutions in return for your sins symbolizing your obedience, service, faith, and trust.

The things that are supposedly going to happen during these End Times are pretty impressive. Cataclysmic events, final battles with Satan, self destruction by war and nuclear means; astronomical alignments that pour rays of destruction, climatic shifts, polar shifts, magnetic reversal, global flooding, blah, blah, blah. It's the gods finally having their fill of man who is the master of self destruction and teaching them a serious lesson this time. Just type 2012 into Google and see what you get.

There is no doubt that many prophets have been responsible for this doom scenario, obviously part of the planning committees. But those of dominion like to tell us about doom because it raises fear. Fear is what keeps the sheeple in the pen eating their blue pills.

The most popular time of this doom has been the turn of this century when all sorts of nasties were to happen as we hit these End Times. Most of the prophets like Nostradamus and Cayce screwed up on this one. But let us take some versions of End Times allegedly reflected by the words gods and God. They are always "coming". Nobody can really say what these times are and what will happen but what is important here is to understand that the End Times marks a point of change stuck in the minds of men. What is most relevant here is to understand that the End Times is a time of shift from what is Old Earth to what is to be—New Earth. It is the way it shifts that is the big controversy.

And shifting it is as we will reveal in this following chapters. It just *ain't happenin'* the way the bloodlines and their kings and queens thought...

The New End Time Of Revelation

We have already pointed out the unprecedented growth in non-religious and New Agers that vibrates with a new consciousness. Since 1987, a time referred to as the Harmonic Convergence, there's been a new "buzz". It is a process of change in consciousness. What does this mean? It isn't just Neo who feels something amiss. More and more people are beginning to "think" differently about the material world, about the meaning of life, about the world around them. It's like Morpheus in the Matrix said about feeling something is not right. It is about how we relate to each other and how we relate to the Earth we live on. It's about all these gods and those kings and queens and high government officials that people gave their trust to. *Something is not right.*

Underneath more and more of our thinking time is a deep stir, a wave of desire for a better earth of peace and love. But how? It is the evolution of a different conscious awareness. Yet it still seems so unattainable. It is about a peaceful cohabitation and it began as something in the back of our minds—a sort of gut feeling from our hearts that we are being deceived from some of the crucial truths. That we may be chasing the wrong dreams and perhaps there is more to life than living in a materialistic gopher wheel serving these self proclaimed gods who love taxes, obedience, rules, and love to hoard for their own kind. But what can a mere mortal do about this? Most are trapped in the old energies because they keep chewing on the blue pills.

Many refer to this new feeling as the New Age, some the Unity Consciousness, some just the End Times. There are many names and as many ideas on this. But one thing that this new consciousness of self incorporates is that it is not an organized religion or a group. There are no leaders, no real dogma. It is some evolving awareness that has a common spiritual denominator, and it is based upon love of all things, a peaceful world of harmony that is marked by a transition time. It's a strange gut feel that something better is available.

Of course humanity likes to take this movement and make a buck in it. It is because so many have themselves made a god of ego and money. So people create great marketing ploys and devices and groups that sell you a new life, new secrets to health and wealth. It makes it hard to gain credibility this way yet despite this you cannot ever identify this movement as a dogma by a large institution like the Catholic, Protestant, or Islamic groups. It is simply an inconsistent evolution of a free spirit belief system that is pretty consistent in its beliefs.

And whether there are saviours here, great mystics, healers and wonderful products, that doesn't matter because the bottom line is that they are focused on the same dream—one of a New Earth and a new you that is more than you have believed. When you start to compile these beliefs, you begin to create a New Earth story; and it even has a storyline somewhat similar to the Old Earth storyline of rapture, revelation and resurrection.

What this boils down to is the difference between religious and spiritual, best exemplified by the dominant groups. In simple terms, religion deals with a mortal human who lives a life to serve god and his self-proclaimed cronies. He then dies beholding to the gods for his salvation into eternity. Spiritual deals with an immortal being here for the expression through temporary form of human body to express and expand love to attain joy, as an aspect of God, the Creator himself. So Religion is about serving god, Spirituality is about being God.

So what does this New Earth plan and this new consciousness movement suggest?

Well, let us call this a Divine Plan for lack of a better description. It is unfolding right before us that has never happened before. This End Time is between the turn of the century and 2012, and in the beliefs of the New Agers it has to do with various cosmic forces and planetary alignments that happen once in 26,000 years. These are forces that influence consciousness, and hence behaviour. Of course everyone has a choice as to whether they let this new consciousness into their awareness to create new behaviour. Needless to say, you have free will and choice to decide, just like you decide to eat the blue pills.

But at any rate, during this shift into the new 26,000 year cycle—called the Age of Aquarius—there is commonality to certain things that are going to happen that shower a new "knowing" into the consciousness of humanity. It is a dramatic acceleration of what Neo felt and what so many are feeling.

It is a New Earth story.

Revelation is indeed the revealing or disclosing, or making something obvious through active or passive communication with supernatural and divine entities. This time, the **Revelation** originates directly from the Source. Yes, God—the real One—directly to you and into your personal consciousness, not through anyone else. It is because we are all God, as Christ taught. So it is **we** that are implementing this new plan. There are no middle men to tell you what the Word of God is because you begin to understand that it is you that is the "chosen one" already privy to the truth of God.

But it is not going to be disclosed by Jesus himself. It is *you* that is going to go through a **Resurrection** and all who so choose to believe this will resurrect themselves coming back to a re-life as the Second Coming of Christ. It is not one guy, it is all!

So there are no chosen ones after a big meeting deciding to remove all Christians from the Earth, to protect them. This **Rapture** is simply your own choice when you understand that you are something else than what you have been told to believe as a mortal human. So Jesus will not "snatch us" out of harm's way if we have been good. It is you that simply decides a new way. For under this story good and bad are judgments and love cannot and does not judge. Thus, there is no judgment. It's like a mother who truly loves her kid; regardless of what the little monster does, she loves him and does not judge. It is the other people who judge and may force her to action—the consciousness of others prevails.

Then the goodies you get through **Revelation** are indeed the revealing or disclosing, through active or passive communication of who you really are—an aspect of God, an eternal being borrowing a body to experience a time slice on Earth. And this is where a common denominator of vibration fits in. You vibrate higher and higher, releasing many of those miraculous abilities that Jesus the Christ himself had—especially the healing. So you can look at this as a mass revealing of Jesus the Christ through the consciousness shift. But it is *not* Jesus suddenly appearing. It is the Time of Revelation when the *knowing* of this, and in many cases, the *showing* of this (as he did), is revealed. <u>It is about attaining a higher expression of God through You as a piece of God which is everything as One, living laughing and loving in thought, word and deed.</u>

So we see that this Revelation is the revealing of Jesus Christ as being each of us and that the message now comes directly from God the Father as a wakeup call of rapture. And it is a revealing that there is no sin and that the heaven we seek is already within us as immortal, eternal aspects of God. So it is a call not to serve gods, or listen to other's interpretations of God's Word, but to BE God and know for yourself. The revealing is that you don't need gurus, bishops, meditators or the likes to tell you the secrets of heaven, being eternal and how to have a better life. It is simply the acceptance of who you are that is already living a life as a Spiritual entity borrowing a body to be within rather than a body looking for spirit outside of itself.

And what of those poor souls that do not want to believe or accept this? Well here we go again. **Armageddon.** Which one? Guess what? It's the one you are in now. The one that creates fear, conflict, with a drive of ego to survive and dominate. It is called the world of separation from who you are. Now interestingly enough, this Armageddon changes as all this shifts in consciousness toward 2012.

Is there bad news here? Is there something that happens to those who want to believe in their old ways? What if you choose to take the path that this is just all more dogmatic horseshit with a new color?

What about those that have not chosen to believe who they are? It is indeed being left in your own harm's way and guess what? Yes, **Armageddon**—End Times. You continue paying for your sins of hatred and separation and conflict and fear as you are doing right now. It becomes a clear understanding of how *you* attract that which you create. Is it hard to believe that if you hate people they will hate you back? It wasn't God that did this, it was you. It is you that attracts it by the energy you create; the big difference is that energy in the Old Earth will not be inflicted upon anyone else like it was in the old regime. And get this; through the End Times it will manifest itself to return faster and faster until it becomes instant.

That is the true Armageddon where you create your own Hell at your own choosing, and of your own intensity. Is the fight with Mr. Devil in the cards here? It sure is if you want to hold to the old ways of deception and greed that you want to inflict on others! Your fight is with yourself—the Devil is within.

And **rapture**? The only people that are going to get snatched out of their own devils (harm's way) are the ones that choose to understand who they are—and the snatching is of their own accord.

So this is not a big battle between Satan and the kings of the Earth as the end of the world dawns. It is a battle of your own mind, of who you are. It is about your own conscious awareness and belief that you will do battle with. It is about the knowing that you will inflict upon your mortal being to create your own life. The battle of Armageddon is a battle of belief in yourself. Do you keep chewing the blue pills or not. Indirectly this is indeed a conscious choice of Heaven or Hell.

That's a pretty simple choice is it not? Heaven or Hell? Perhaps not if you are stuck in the old world?

Let us bring in another old over-used term of **Crucifixion.** In the End Times it is the process of crucifying what is Hell by leaving it behind and choosing Heaven. It is the death of the old in choice of the new. Even on Old Earth, everyone, yes everyone, has a choice of how (bad or good) they perceive any situation. And when you learn that what you perceive as you think, speak feel and act upon brings upon you like energy, you may pay more attention to what you think and do. That is what the choice is all about. Instead of saying you believe what these religions and the Vatican and the leaders tell you, you say: *"Ok, I have had enough with this Old Earth and I want to live a life of unconditional love, peace and joy."* And by acceptance, just like a commercial contract, it is so enacted by your intent. That simple act to believe differently can change your whole life.

So the story is similar but with a different twist from what the dominant religions tell you.

Is this another dogma? Well, it ain't written by God in an autographed hard cover. It ain't on the evening news. And it certainly ain't supported by any religion. And there ain't no leaders. But it is unfolding all around everyone at the same time if you have the eyes, ears and heart to open to this revelation. What follows in the book is simply information about what IS happening. You cannot make a choice if there is no alternative known to you.

So here is your challenge; read this as a fantasy version if you like. It is no more fantasy than Genesis or Moses parting the Red Sea, or Noah's Ark. Then look around you and listen to what's happening and what you feel in your heart. You can't BS the heart and this may lead you to burning the prescription for blue pills.

So will it be the New World Order of PLANET EARTH or New Order of the Ages of Planet Earth? Which Revelation will **We** unfold as the plan? It appears to be a different one than the powers that be have been planned. Can another biblical expression be true: *"... and the meek shall inherit the earth"*.

41

THE CHRIST CONSCIOUSNESS

If you have not picked up on this yet, not all business plans succeed. And the failure is usually because the masses do not want the product being flogged. The other thing that may have come forward is that the new version of Christ's life has become a dominant topic by thousands of researchers. And as has been pointed out, the new version seems to coincide with what we have summarized in the Aquarian Gospels in Part 1. And finally, you may have also picked up the notion that what this fellow Christ really taught is a whole lot different than what is taught by the dominant religions, in fact it is the same as what we just revealed as the **New Earth version of Revelation** in the previous chapter. What this mass of meek inheritors of earth are finding not in their gut, but in their heart, is a whole new belief system that says a resounding *NO* to the way things have been. Let's look further into this belief system that is the Christ Consciousness.

The Shifting Consciousness Of New Earth

So now we may ask: What is the Christ Consciousness? What does it mean as far as a life belief and a way of life? What is the real story of Christ? What does this all tell us to do? Is this even relevant in my life?

The answer is that it has great relevance regardless of who wins the battle of Armageddon. But, as history now shows, the last 12 years speaks for itself. **If we revisit the first chapter to look at the table of "followers" of the top religions, they were, as of 2005 shown below.**

RELIGION	FOLLOWERS		%	ORIGINS
1. Christianity	2,100,000,000	2,100,000,000	30.58%	100-33CE
2. Islam	1,500,000,000	3,600,000,000	52.42%	600CE
3. Nonreligious	**1,100,000,000**	**4,700,000,000**	**68.44%**	
4. Hinduism	900,000,000	5,600,000,000	81.54%	2000BCE
5. Chinese	394,000,000	5,994,000,000	87.28%	
6. Buddhism	376,000,000	6,370,000,000	92.75%	600BC
7. Primal-indigenous	300,000,000	6,670,000,000	97.12%	

Wikipedia reports Buddhism is being recognized as the fastest growing religion in Western societies both in terms of new converts and more so in terms of friends of Buddhism who seek to study and practice various aspects of Buddhism. As in the United States, Buddhism is ranked among the fastest growing religions in many Western European countries. The Australian Bureau of Statistics through statistical analysis held Buddhism to be the fastest growing spiritual tradition/religion in Australia in terms of percentage gain with a growth of 79.1% for the period 1996 to 2001. However, because Australia is statistically small, no inferences can be drawn from that for the whole world.

Buddhism is the fastest-growing religion in England's jails, with the number of followers rising eightfold over the past decade.

The American Religious Identification Survey gave non-religious groups the largest gain in terms of absolute numbers - 14,300,000 (8.4% of the population) to 29,400,000 (14.1% of the population) for the period 1990 to 2001 in the USA. Reuters describes how a study profiling the "No religion" demographic found that the so-called "Nones", at least in the U.S., are the fastest growing religious affiliation category. The "Nones" comprise 33% agnostics, 33% theists, and 10% atheists.

A similar pattern has been found in other countries such as Australia, Canada and Mexico. According to statistics in Canada, the number of "Nones" more than doubled (an increase of about 60%) between 1985 and 2004. In Australia, census data from the Australian Bureau of Statistics give "no religion" the largest gains in absolute numbers over the 15 years from 1991 to 2006, from 2,948,888 (18.2% of the population that answered the question) to 3,706,555 (21.0% of the population that answered the question). According to INEGI, in Mexico, the number of atheists grows annually by 5.2%, while the number of Catholics grows by 1.7%. What about those Christians who sit on a fence to still call themselves Christians but are not feeling "quite right" about the "Word of God"?

We are now at 2012. What do you suppose these "nones", Buddhists and New Agers have in common? It is a new consciousness that has a common denominator similar to what Christ expressed. In most cases, what Christ expressed, manly that of love and peace is what these followers "select" out of the writings. What is really coming forward is that there really is no God up in the sky. It is us as everything, as One. There is no heaven and hell except what we bring upon ourselves. Add to this the Christians of 2.1 billion who fundamentally believe in the love and peace parts of the bibles simply rejecting all else, and there is one massive mental wave wanting to show itself in the reality of Planet Earth.

GROUP	Hinduism	Buddhism	Christianity	Islam	Nones
NUMBER	900,000	376,000	2,100,000,000	840,000	1,100,000,000
BEGIN	4000BC	500BC	30AD	622AD	2000AD
FOUNDER	None	Siddhartha Gautama	Jesus Christ	Muhammad .	None
gods	Many	Enlightened Buddhas)	One	One	One
WORD	4 Vedas.	Sutras Tantra Zen	The Bible	The Koran	None

If you relook the core beliefs of Buddhism, one fundamental belief of Buddhism is often referred to as reincarnation -- the concept that people are reborn after dying. In fact, most individuals go through many cycles of birth, living, death and rebirth. A practicing Buddhist differentiates between the concepts of rebirth and reincarnation. In reincarnation, the individual may recur repeatedly. In rebirth, a person does not necessarily return to Earth as the same entity ever again. He compares it to a leaf growing on a tree. When the withering leaf falls off, a new leaf will eventually replace it. It is similar to the old leaf, but it is not identical to the original leaf. After many such cycles, if a person releases their attachment to desire and the self, they can attain Nirvana. This is a state of liberation and freedom from suffering. Why is Buddhism such a rage? Let us look deeper.

The Three Trainings or Practices consist of:

Sila: Virtue, good conduct, morality. This is based on two fundamental principles:
The principle of equality: that all living entities are equal.
The principle of reciprocity: This is the "*Golden Rule*" in Christianity -- to do onto others as you would wish them to do onto you. It is found in all major religions.
Samadhi: Concentration, meditation, mental development. Developing one's mind is the path to wisdom which in turn leads to personal freedom. Mental development also strengthens and controls our mind; this helps us maintain good conduct.
Prajna: Discernment, insight, wisdom, enlightenment. This is the real heart of Buddhism. Wisdom will emerge if your mind is pure and calm.

The Buddha's *Four Noble Truths* explore human suffering. They may be described (somewhat simplistically) as:

Dukkha: *Suffering exists:* (Suffering is real and almost universal. Suffering has many causes: loss, sickness, pain, failure, the impermanence of pleasure.)
Samudaya*: There is a cause for suffering.* (It is the desire to have and control things. It can take many forms: craving of sensual pleasures; the desire for fame; the desire to avoid unpleasant sensations, like fear, anger or jealousy.)
Nirodha: *There is an end to suffering*. (Suffering ceases with the final liberation of Nirvana (a.k.a. Nibbana). The mind experiences complete freedom, liberation and non-attachment. It lets go of any desire or craving.)
Magga: *In order to end suffering, you must follow the Eightfold Path.*

The Five Precepts are rules to live by. They are somewhat analogous to the second half of the Ten Commandments in Judaism and Christianity -- that part of the Decalogue which describes behaviours to avoid. However, they are recommendations, not commandments. Believers are expected to use their own intelligence in deciding exactly how to apply these rules:

- Do not kill. This is sometimes translated as "*not harming*" or an absence of violence.
- Do not steal. This is generally interpreted as including the avoidance of fraud and economic exploitation.
- Do not lie. This is sometimes interpreted as including name calling, gossip, etc.
- Do not misuse sex. For monks and nuns, this means any departure from complete celibacy. For the laity, adultery is forbidden, along with any sexual harassment or exploitation, including that within marriage. The Buddha did not discuss consensual premarital sex within a committed relationship; Thus, Buddhist traditions differ on this. Most Buddhists, probably influenced by their local cultures, condemn same-sex sexual activity regardless of the nature of the relationship between the people involved.
- Do not consume alcohol or other drugs. The main concern here is that intoxicants cloud the mind. Some have included as a drug other methods of divorcing ourselves from reality -- e.g. movies, television, the Internet. [1]

Those preparing for monastic life or who are not within a family are expected to avoid an additional five activities:

6. Taking untimely meals.
7. Dancing, singing, music, watching grotesque mime.
8. Use of garlands, perfumes and personal adornment.
9. Use of high seats.
10. Accepting gold or silver.

There is also a series of eight precepts which are composed of the first seven listed above, followed by the eighth and ninth combined as one. "Ordained Theravada monks promise to follow 227 precepts

The Buddha's *Eightfold Path* consists of:

Panna: Discernment, wisdom:
1) *Samma ditthi* Right Understanding of the Four Noble Truths
2) *Samma sankappa:* Right thinking; following the right path in life
Sila: Virtue, morality:
3) *Samma vaca:* Right speech: no lying, criticism, condemning, gossip, harsh language
4) *Samma kammanta* Right conduct by following the Five Precepts
5) *Samma ajiva*: Right livelihood; support yourself without harming others
Samadhi: Concentration, meditation:
6) *Samma vayama* Right Effort: promote good thoughts; conquer evil thoughts
7) *Samma sati* Right Mindfulness: Become aware of your body, mind and feelings
8) *Samma samadhi* Right Concentration: Meditate to achieve a higher state of consciousness

New Age Spirituality And Core Beliefs

What is the New Age Movement? It is similar to New Age Spirituality, but different enough to warrant its own definition. The New Age Movement is a belief that the human race is all one. It is not about equality nor diversity. It is the idea that your gender, age, religion, race, nor sexual orientation makes you better or worse than anyone else. The New Age Movement is moving away from the US against THEM mentality. It is inclusive, open, detached from labels, and above all else, it's based in love not fear.

At our deepest level, there are only two motivators - love and fear. Fear breeds hate, anger, vengeance, greed, violence, selfishness, and alienates us from truly connecting with spirit and with each other. Love breeds compassion, peace, understanding, forgiveness, charity, gentleness, partnership, and a sense of connectedness with spirit and with each other. One can focus on either motivator and see the logic behind it. Should you choose to see lack, poverty, and attacks towards your fellow man, it's easy to become fearful. It is part of the survival of the fittest. Fight or flight saved many a caveman to live another day and to breed more like himself. One can also argue that to see the beauty and tenderness that humanity is known to share with each other that it is logical to love thy neighbour and to turn the other cheek. There will always be intelligent arguments for both sides. We as a species have evolved enough to make our own decisions as to which will govern us as individuals.

The New Age Movement proposes that as a collective people we are also able to make an educated enlightened decision as to whether we will be controlled by our fears or by our loves. Will we be a society of angry divided hateful individuals? Or will we be a global community of loving supportive people who honour each other's right to choose their own path? Like all political, religious, and social movements there are zealots and extremists among the New Age Movement. In the same way that all Christians are not white supremacists and all Pagans are not Satan worshippers, all New Agers are not aging hippies sitting around getting stoned and playing with crystals. Those who endorse the New Age Movement are as diverse as any other group. Their one common belief is that love and true spirituality should lead us as a people, not fear and hatred of anything we deem as different from ourselves.

The New Age Movement embraces the teachings of Christ, the teachings of Buddha, the Native American teachings, the ancient Celtic Pagan teachings, and modern science's latest findings and teachings. We are explorers trying to understand spirituality on a deeper nuts and bolts level. It is not enough to be told by our parents that one religion is right and all others are wrong. We have a desire to understand and to choose for ourselves what is or is not spiritual. The result is that many New Agers have found themselves holding an eclectic view of religion. Many Native Americans have blended the teaching of Christ within their own beliefs. Many Pagans can see how much they have in common with the Native American beliefs. It is not unusual for Catholics to feel a deep connection to the Buddhist teachings. Forgive me for omitting so many other religions and beliefs but I am simply giving broad examples for the sake of making a point. The New Age Movement was birthed from this exploration of each other's beliefs. How can we hate someone so much like ourselves?

In our version of the story, Christ did not teach blind hatred nor did he teach his followers to give their personal power away to the churches and governments. Only when the churches and governments took over his teachings did that all become part of being a 'good Christian.' He did not tell us to hate nor to judge. Bigotry and war is not Christ-like, nor Buddha-like, nor in keeping with the core teachings of any religion. All spiritual teachers taught the same message - love one another and do not harm each other nor the planet and the animals given to you. Take the politics out of religion and they all come down to the same wonderful teachings that have been trampled on by dogma, greed, and bigotry.

The New Age doctrines are pretty simple:

- All is One
- All is God
- Humanity is God
- A change in consciousness
- All religions are one
- Cosmic evolutionary optimism

Norman L. Geyser focuses on 14 doctrines typical of New Age religions:

1) an impersonal god (force)
2) an eternal universe
3) an illusory nature of matter
4) a cyclical nature of life
5) the necessity of reincarnations
6) the evolution of man into godhood
7) continuing revelations from beings beyond the world
8) the identity of man with God
9) the need for meditation (or other consciousness-changing techniques)
10) occult practices (astrology, mediums and so forth)
11) vegetarianism and holistic health
12) pacifism (or anti-war activities)
13) one world (global) order
14) syncretism (unity of all religions)

Since 1987, a time referred to as the Harmonic Convergence, there's been a new "buzz". It is a process of change in consciousness. What does this mean? It isn't just Neo who feels something amiss. More and more people are beginning to "think" differently about the material world, about the meaning of life, about the world around them. It's like

Morpheus in the Matrix said about feeling something is not right. It is about how we relate to each other and how we relate to the Earth we live on. It's about all these gods and those kings and queens and high government officials that people gave their trust to. *Something is not right.*

Underneath more and more of our thinking time is a deep stir, a wave of desire for a better earth of peace and love. But how? It is the evolution of a different conscious awareness. Yet it still seems so unattainable. It is about a peaceful cohabitation and it began as something in the back of our minds—a sort of gut feeling from our hearts that we are being deceived from some of the crucial truths. That we may be chasing the wrong dreams and perhaps there is more to life than living in a materialistic gopher wheel serving these self proclaimed gods who love taxes, obedience, rules, and love to hoard for their own kind. But what can a mere mortal do about this? Most are trapped in the old energies because they keep chewing on the blue pills given free by the Vatican- well perhaps not *really* free when you trade your Soul!

Many refer to this new feeling as the New Age, some the Unity Consciousness, some just the End Times. There are many names and as many ideas on this. But one thing that this new consciousness of self incorporates is that it is not an organized religion or a group. There are no leaders, no real dogma. It is some evolving awareness that has a common spiritual denominator, and it is based upon love of all things, a peaceful world of harmony that is marked by a transition time. It's a strange gut feel that something better is available.

Of course humanity likes to take this movement and make a buck in it. It is because so many have themselves made a god of ego and money. So people create great marketing ploys and devices and groups that sell you a new life, new secrets to health and wealth. It makes it hard to gain credibility this way yet despite this you cannot ever identify this movement as a dogma by a large institution like the Catholic, Protestant, or Islamic groups. It is simply an inconsistent evolution of a free spirit belief system that is pretty consistent in its beliefs.

And whether there are saviors here, great mystics, healers and wonderful products, that doesn't matter because the bottom line is that they are focused on the same dream—one of a New Earth and a new you that is more than you have believed. When you start to compile these beliefs, you begin to create a New Earth story; and it even has a storyline somewhat similar to the Old Earth storyline of rapture, revelation and resurrection.

What this boils down to is the difference between religious and spiritual, best exemplified by the dominant groups. In simple terms, religion deals with a mortal human who lives a life to serve god and his self-proclaimed cronies. He then dies beholding to the gods for his salvation into eternity. Spiritual deals with an immortal being here for the expression through temporary form of human body to express and expand love to attain joy, as an aspect of God, the Creator himself. So Religion is about serving god, Spirituality is about being God.

So what does this New Earth plan and this new consciousness movement suggest?

Well, we have talked about a Divine Plan unfolding right before us that has never happened before. This End Time is between the turn of the century and 2012, and it has to do with various cosmic forces and planetary alignments that happen once in 26,000 years. These are forces that influence consciousness, and hence behaviour. Of course everyone has a choice as to whether they let this new consciousness into their awareness to create new behaviour. Needless to say, you have free will and choice to decide, just like you decide to eat the blue pills.

The Christ Consciousness From The Aquarian Gospel

Nobody wrote the rule book or a bible on what has evolved as the Christ Consciousness. It simply came to life on its own as more and more people have come to learn what they do NOT want in life. So it is a quest that has manifested from a feeling within, a feeling of the heart: love, peace, harmony.

- There is no rule book, dogma.
- There is no judgement or sin
- There is no telling you what to believe
- It is deduced by one's self
- There is no gods of vengeance
- there is no non equality, sin, punishment, power, slavery

Humanity has from birth accepted the limits of the joint consciousness be it culture family or nation. The immediate quest shifts itself into the perceptions and beliefs that move from the though and the word into deed and translate into the reality. The old reality is one of gods, kings, queens, evil against good as the fundamental mental quest, but limited by the invisible rules and beliefs that translate it to the reality. And so it is with the consciousness of humility. The two versions of the rule books the bible and the Aquarian Gospel are different in that that the Christ carries a different consciousness and all the evil and bounds are not there. In the other, the bounds are the bible, the rules, the vengeance, slavery, of obedience, of fear, etc. Delete these and you have a new rule book of perception that limits the soul.

And so this new wave of evolving living consciousness has come into fruition in the last 12 years. and the belief system has converged into the same place. So let us look back to the Aquarian Gospel had look at what this fellow Jesus The Christ embodied as what he said was the true expression of God:

Here it is in simple bullet form

- God and man are One
- God is love, requires no sacrifice, has no judgement
- Truth is one and everywhere
- The Holy Breath is truth, was, is and evermore shall be
- Force is the will of God and that will is manifest directed by the Breath
- Man and God are One
- Heaven and Hell are within
- Man tore himself away from God by carnal thoughts, the Holy breath can make them one again
- God clothed man in flesh so he may comprehend the only saviour of the world is love, and Jesus comes to manifest that love to men
- Every living thing is bound by cords to every other living thing
- Blest are the pure of heart for they love and do not demand love in return
- There are two selfs; the lower is illusion, the higher is God in an the embodiment of truth, love justice, the higher and lower mercy right, The lower is an illusion, the carnal self, body of desires, reflex ion of higher by murky ethers of flesh
- He who know well his lower self, knows the illusions of the world
- Evil is a myth, the devil from which men are redeemed is self, the lower self
- Mans saviour is within

- Truth is the leavening owe of God
- God speaks through all things through the heart, prayer is speaking from the heart
- God requires no sacrifice
- Baptism is a symbolic cleansing of the soul by purity of life
- Love is the greatest commandment
- Faith is surety of the omnipotence of God and man, the certainty man will reach deific life
- Salvation is the ladder reaching from the heart of man to the heart of God
- Laws of nature are the laws of health, transgression is sin and he who sins is sick
- The healer is the one who can inspire God
- All men are made equal, every soul is the child off God
- Live as you would have your brother live, unfold each day as does the flower for earth is yours and heaven is yours
- Man is god and when you honour man you hour god
- Make human hearts the idols, burn the others down as they cannot hear you
- I am here to show the way to god, do not worship man
- The pure of heart do not accuse
- All things are God, the universal god is One all are one It is wisdom, will and love
- By the sweat breath of God all life is bound in one
- When man is one with God, he needs no middle men
- Man is mind and mind is here to gain perfection by experience
- When hope and love are back of toil, all life s filled with joy, peace and this is heaven
- Heave is a state of mind
- A time will come when priests are no more. it is a problem men must solve
- Father God is the King of mankind, all men are kings with access to boundless wealth and love
- The devil and burning fires are works of man
- The silence where the where soul may meet its god, immersed in light, it is the pure of heart inside
- The holy breath cannot enter until it becomes a welcome guest, touched by purity of life, prayer and holy thought
- The kingdom of the kings is the soul and is a kingdom for every man, this king is love as the greatest power and all may have the Christ dwell here and be king,
- And so we are all sons of god
- God is Spirit and resides in all men
- Keep your mind occupied with good and evil cannot find a way in
- Man is the delegate of God to do his will on earth
- Do unto others as
- As you walk do not judge for you will also be so judged
- Death is the passing of the soul out of the house of flesh
- The air we breathe is charged with Holy Breath
- The law of spirit calls for purity of thought, word, deed 126:19
- This life is a span, these is life that does not pass
- The greatest lesson come through failures made
- whatever men shall do to other men man shall do to him
- Afflictions are all partial payments of debts that have been made,
- Recompense never fails as the true rule of life
- He who shall injure another in thought, word, deed is judged a debtor to the law
- Affliction is a prison cell in which a man must stay until his debts are paid
- All men are sons of God by birth, but not by faith
- He who attains victory over self is son of God by faith as is the one who believes and does the will of God
- You shall not kill; you shall not steal; you shall not do adulterous things; you shall not falsely testify;

- And you shall love your God with all your heart, and you shall love your neighbour as yourself.
- One thing you lack; your heart is fixed on things of earth; you are not free.
- the Lord our God is one; and you shall love the Lord your God with all your heart, with all your mind, with all your soul, with all your strength;
- I have not come to judge, but to save

So are you one of those who chooses to believe in the limits and beliefs of the Bible? It is no different than believing that the Strawman Corporation limits your true self. Neither do, but until you free yourself, and the group consciousness begins to shift, the group cannot shift. One by one, each grain of sand blown into the same place forms the dune, then the mountains, then the desert. Like a global marketing campaign, once the balance of individual choice shifts with the global consciousness, the new product remains in the caves of consciousness awaiting the light and as we would say, mass consumption that moves it into the 3D reality of lives, cultures, nations.

In the years, 2000 to 2012, this balance shift into the Christ Consciousness has been one by one occurring in over a billion people who have in some way rejected the notion of god's words and rules. Similarly, there are a massive amount of people who have begun to reject the ways of commerce, and come to a new truth about its implementation thorough humanities simple acceptance that it was the right way.

Keep this entrenched for remember that you are not to be in judgement, bring peace, liberty and love of life back. What has been is what has been accepted. learn from it and move on into the light. Do this every moment in thought, word and deed.

In dropping back into the lower carnal world of commerce and debt, keep this in the front (not back) of your mind. For as you now read the following Chapters on what has happened in the world today, know that it is the shifting belief system that has somehow shone light on the new truth that has led these people here.

The next chapters are dedicated to what is happening in terms of large groups of people taking action on the different perspective we identified in Part 1. The lesson here is that what we are seeing worldwide are Earthlings that not only agree with these things that may be "hard to believe", they are taking action-bigtime!

First off is the Strawman story that may be one of the more difficult to digest. Before you do, take a good look at all your identification, your plastic cards, your bank agreements, your correspondence from the bank, tax authorities, licenses, etc. Look at your commerce and the tombstones. Then, in a moment of silence think about why these are capitalized. Do you really believe they can't use upper and lower case?

Recall the Story of the Strawman from Part 1. That is what got the Earthling to agree to being employed by PLANET EARTH INC. If you still think this is a good joke, read on because there are an awful lot of folks who don't.

42

THE STRAWMAN REVOLUTION

In Part 1, we introduced the Story of the Strawman. This would have been a totally ridiculous story before the turn of the century. In the last 12 years, it is not so farfetched as many have followed up on it all around the world. Of note is that beneath the seas of new consciousness builds a tsunami of energies pertaining to the information presented so far, and in particular the mythical Strawman. In the last 12 years, it is the Strawman that has hit the spotlight. It is not surprising that with the Internet and the ability to research and share information, that a new level of consciousness about the way things really work with regards to Corporate fictions, Admiralty law, the workings of banking system, and the alleged fraudulent cover up of the maxims. In fact it has all been hidden in plain sight for those who are willing to see.

The Internet is now alive with new information about all that we have provided about the commercial system and the ones running PLANET EARTH. Every day, warriors of the new commerce and warriors of the light are revealing a way to bring Goliath down. Everyday new information comes forward that breaks down the veil and shine new light on a different truth regardless of whether it is religion, science, commerce, medicine, military or whatever are being "truthfully" presented and administered in this vast public world that humanity has accepted run by a private world of PLANET EARTH.

Before we delve into these new commercial "waves" which are occurring, it is of interest to bring forward some vital information about commerce so as to lead into the phenomenon of the Strawman. This seemingly simple idea of imposing a capital letter fiction on the Earthling has been one of most incredible subtle takeover of human power of all time. Here the Earthling has simply agreed to trade certain private rights for certain public benefits, trusting in the leadership that it was alright. But the knowing of the STRAWMAN existence allows one to make a choice that was not there before; to separate from the fiction that imposes rules thus getting back the true power of sovereignty in commerce bringing this back into the private domain. However, what of the benefits that were offered through the fiction? There are several major areas that are relevant in understanding the implementation process and the remedy, most of which has come clearly to the surface in the last decade. It all relates to the true powers that are lying dormant on the private side. As we have seen the power has been usurped via the secrecy of PLANET EARTH who control a network of private corporations outside of the peering eyes of the public world.

Private Versus Public Jurisdictions

First, it is important to understand the difference between Public and Private. The dictionaries state that public is as an adjective: of, pertaining to, or affecting a population or a community as a whole: *public funds; a public nuisance;* done, made, acting, etc., for the community as a whole: *public prosecution;* open to all persons: *a public meeting;* of, pertaining to, or being in the service of a community or nation, especially as a government officer: *a public official;* maintained at the public expense and under public control: *a public library; a public*

Private means secluded from the sight, presence, or intrusion of others; designed or intended for one's exclusive use; of or confined to the individual; undertaken on an individual basis; not available for public use, control, or participation; belonging to a particular person or persons, as opposed to the public or the government.

One of most important concepts to master is this Public versus Private entanglement. Blacks Law 6th says public is "*the whole body politic or the aggregate of the citizens of a state, nation, or municipality. The inhabitants of a particular place; all the inhabitants of a particular place; the people of a neighbourhood,' private is Affecting or belonging to private individuals, as distinct from the public generally; not official; not clothed in office.*"

That which is public cannot be private since it is public as shared by all.

Thus operating from the private sector have some extreme advantages, namely the lack of public regulation. In order to make this shift, words in daily speech and writing must shift-away from the public training system. according to the holy scriptures, **your word is your bond.**

The public sector teaches public concepts and nothing about private. Since you have so been taught, your heart has always been with the public side, but most of these public phrases and words have private counterparts, and most opposite in meaning:

PUBLIC	**PRIVATE**
democracy	republic
Corporate fiction	Real thing
BC	British Columbia
persons	Men, women
voters	electors
attorneys	lawyers
Color of law	Common law
agreement	contract
legal	lawful
Revocable privileges	Unalienable rights
insurance	assurance
equity	ownership
subjects	sovereigns
slaves	masters
employees	employers
debtors	creditors
Accomodated party	Accommodation part
offer	acceptance
Common stock	Preferred stock
Subject to levy	Exempt from levy

Negotiable by fictions	Non-negotiable man to man
offer	acceptance
Paper money	substance
Police officers	Peace officers
Fiction/dishonor/injustice	Truth/honor/justice
poverty	wealth
Man's legal system	Natural Gods law

To be truly private in a public world you must always picture yourself and act as a man or woman from the private side on the right. Always conduct your business from the private venue using the words from the right side will keep you out of the public domain. This is precisely what the global Elite have done and still do. Their words are their bond as contract and the words they use are the words by which they are judged.

The private side emulates the law of forgiveness and grace, the public side emulates execution by law. If anyone practices the execution of law as commanded by Moses he denies divine grace. Our debts have been paid and it is in the private sector that we find honour, justice and truth. The public side is a reflection of dishonour, injustice, and a place where fraud can flourish.

Private operates under contract, public operates under color of law. That is why if you are branded as a guilty sinner from the beginning, and accept this, you are subject to the rules of the bibles, their codes and potential vengeance which will fall upon you as going to hell, not having eternal life, and suffering the horrors of damnation. That is the color of the law. That is the same concept as the Strawman, that, registered as being "alive" in Puerto Rico, in the Individual Master File, is a criminal; already in sin, guilty until proven innocent. It is the same principle as being born a guilty sinner-especially women as in the code of law in religion.

Only a real man or woman can be an owner. It is impossible for a fictional entity to give "credit' to anything or anyone since it has nothing to give or create.

Only real men and women can engage in private non-negotiable contracts because only real men and women have the mind in which the meeting of minds can take place. It is physically impossible for a fictional entity to open anything except in words and belief. Redemptors are sovereigns, owners, preferred stockholders, creditors, employers and masters while the uninformed public remain the debtors.

Like corporations and public agencies, the Strawman was designed to operate in the public sector, and all have been given names as vessels on the sea subject to admiralty laws, spelled in capital letters. These do not have eyes to see, nor ears to hear nor a brain to think or a heart to feel. They have no way of communicating with us except through a <u>transmitting utility</u> called a STRAWMAN.

The Four Elements Of Contract

Typically, in order to be enforceable, a contract must involve the following elements:

Offer as a "Meeting of the Minds" (Mutual Consent) The parties to the contract have a mutual understanding of what the contract covers. For example, in a contract for the sale of a "mustang", the buyer thinks he will obtain a car and the seller believes he is contracting to sell a horse, there is no meeting of the minds and the contract will likely be held unenforceable.

Offer and Acceptance The contract involves an offer (or more than one offer) to another party, who accepts the offer. For example, in a contract for the sale of a piano, the seller may offer the piano to the buyer for $1,000.00. The buyer's acceptance of that offer is a necessary part of creating a binding contract for the sale of the piano. This means full disclosure. It is implicit within all contracts that the parties are acting in good faith. For example, if the seller of a "mustang" knows that the buyer thinks he is purchasing a car, but secretly intends to sell the buyer a horse, the seller is not acting in good faith and the contract will not be enforceable.

Please note that a counter-offer is not an acceptance, and will typically be treated as a rejection of the offer. For example, if the buyer counter-offers to purchase the piano for $800.00, that typically counts as a rejection of the original offer for sale. If the seller accepts the counter-offer, a contract may be completed. However, if the seller rejects the counter-offer, the buyer will not ordinarily be entitled to enforce the prior $1,000.00 price if the seller decides either to raise the price or to sell the piano to somebody else.

Mutual Consideration (The mutual exchange of something of value) In order to be valid, the parties to a contract must exchange something of value. In the case of the sale of a piano, the buyer receives something of value in the _form_ of the piano, and the seller receives money. While the validity of consideration may be subject to attack on the basis that it is illusory (e.g., one party receives only what the other party was already obligated to provide), or that there is a failure of consideration (e.g., the consideration received by one party is essentially worthless), these defences will not let a party to a contract escape the consequences of bad negotiation. For example, if a seller enters into a contract to sell a piano for $100, and later gets an offer from somebody else for $1,000, the seller can't revoke the contract on the basis that the piano was worth a lot more than he bargained to receive.

Signatures as wet ink signatures of the parties to the contract

In effect, real humans can contract anytime any place on anything and we all do. This is our own personal business. It has nothing to do with the state or the public. Whether I sell you something privately, offer my services for some consideration, or create agreements with others, the process is the same and it does not have to include the government, the authorities, attorneys or anybody else because it is outside the public domain by choice. Even a "money" transaction like in a private sale, or garage sale, is outside of the public domain--none of its business so to speak.

And when these four elements are violated, then it is a matter of performance, disclosure, etc. that constitute a fraud that requires a remedy. Again such remedy can be done privately or by choice taken into the public domain of the law courts and the legal system of codes. Most have grown accustomed to taking this into the public domain of lawyers and attorneys instead of settling it privately. So the private law has been effectively usurped by public law and lawyers.

However, how does it work when a real human contracts with a fiction thing? One is private, one is public. Each are still subject to the same laws of contract but then public rules enter the picture and you find a new set of rules open to you called no violation of public policy:

"In order to be enforceable, a contract cannot violate public policy".

The reason for this, so it is said, is to add a benefit to you and protect you for example, if the subject matter of a contract is illegal, you cannot enforce the contract. A contract for the sale of illegal drugs, for example, violates public policy and is not enforceable. So how can one enforce the prime issue that the banks, the governments have not provided "full disclosure" about the STRAWMAN and the benefits? What about that "stolen energy" to be a debtor? What about the secret purpose of all of this?

Well with regards to the business of the Strawman, plausible deniability has been pretty well the norm. Earthlings simply do not have a clue about the existence of the Strawman, and just like the Earthlings ignorance about esoteric or heretical beliefs propagated by the Vatican (who engage in its power) it is simply not an acceptable concept. And yet ignorance of the law, so it is said, is no excuse. But the greater aspects of this is that the vast majority have simply by choice accepted ignorance of these laws so by acquiescence, it works against them. It is an accepted norm, just like the five monkeys mentioned earlier where the lie or the accepted procedure of "law" becomes the truth. Those that follow the laws and rules of corporations do so because they are paid to do it. Those that know the truth sign confidentiality agreements that allow them to not reveal the truth. Those that really know the truth at the top are the private dynasties; those that don't know have no awareness but to follow that which is the prevailing consciousness and "laws of the land" which they follow since there is no repercussion.

It is within this context that several "waves" of conflict towards revealing the truth have occurred. This is summarized in the following material, not to endorse the processes, but to provide information in to support the information so far presented on the Strawman, the banks, the true energy of real people, and the alleged fraud upon the people. In truth it is not a fraud at all, just an acceptance of a way of life that has been carefully manoeuvred into the philosophy as the Pope Ratzinger put it.

"It is thus necessary that the individual should finally come to realize that his own ego is of no importance in comparison with the existence of his nation; That the position of the individual ego is conditioned solely by the interests of the nation as a whole... that above all the unity of a nation's spirit and will are worth far more than the freedom of the spirit and will of an individual..."

Some Basics On Debt

Within the administrative systems that we have revealed in the Story of The Strawman are many layers of administration, many employees that shift and change (like politicians), and many people who are simply employed to carry out their jobs with little knowing of the rest of the picture about how the debt and banking system functions. And so to protect themselves those that know will deny, others favour plausible deniability, while others simple do not know and cannot believe because the prevalent belief and the laws supports the dominant consciousness to accept it. That is changing but at the root is an established process of record keeping and accounting that is followed worldwide.

In the following summaries, there will be references to words and concepts such as *closed accounts, setoffs, redemption, and acceptance for value.* These are ways and means to gain access to the goods registered within them from the private side. Again, the Internet is the place to get information on this. All you have to do is type in closed account redemption in Google and feast. However it is necessary to explain in simple terms what these mean to the individual.

What has to be enforced here is the system is not wrong, it is the way the corporate takeovers have shifted purposes in using the system. The Global Elite has taken over

Nations the same way you or I can take over a bankrupt company and change its rules and purpose. This is of course their business plan. Although the process of capitalism may be a good thing, it has allowed an imbalance of wealth to occur. This as you know by now, is the reason our fathers and mothers had to, and still must, both work to barely get by. We pay tax to repay the loans the fed takes out in our name, and since it is recognized as a corporate SIN account, the loan must be paid back to the principle, which is the people, the only true creditors on the planet had to hock their future private energy for. This includes you and your family, Mom and Dad, everyone else. By perception of law, we the people are all known as debtors. But how can this be? If we are the true creator of credit, how can we be a debtor? It is impossible. But we both know very clearly now that the corporate STRAWMAN is responsible for commercial activity and *it is the real debtor like a liable corporation*. You, the living creator of all wealth are the sentient Earthling that is *the creditor*! The receiver general is the dude that holds an account for corporate STRAWMAN under your name and date of birth. So what does this mean? There are two sides to this accounting ledger. One debt and one credit.

The registered business pays tax and is the debtor and I create the credit. My registered business can't create labour. I suppose it is simple to see unless you are brainwashed. He who pays owes, and is the debtor. The SIN card in my possession bears an all capital corporate name. So I really own that account! The receiver is holding it in trust as the trustee. But as a trustee there some obligations it has to abide by. Section 336 of the Canadian Criminal Code has something to say about this. Since you own the account and the receiver opened it in your all capitals name, you as owner of that account can instruct the fiduciary trustee holder of that account on what to do with it, just as any owner can direct any trustee. That's the type of legal relationship you actually have but were clueless about. Unfortunately, as we have learned, you have been deemed dead at sea so it is only your Strawman that exists, and it is a criminal with no rights.

On the banking side, the closed account is where the credit side of your account is held by the receiver general. In 1994 a Canadian lawyer purchased land in Arizona with a million dollar check drawn on a closed bank account. This was published in the 1994 newspaper but has probably disappeared by now. All closed bank accounts are open for a thing called set-off and are held by the Bank of Canada. Set-off means that an account can never show anything but zero, and nothing to enforce or claim as the account says the party owes zero. Set-off means you can't get cash. It is just a book entry. The reason Canada has a national debt is because everybody acts as if they *are* the Strawman. This is the debt side of the account. You have never redeemed your labour being that of Mr Real Earthling on the credit side.

The debt exists because the labour of the people has not been redeemed and under the constitution the debt cannot be questioned. We have never instructed our trustee, the receiver general, to credit our account or at least reduce the debt in the account via redemption.

There a corporate debtor account in trust with the receiver general. The account is a SIN number but the receiver identifies it as a corporate account or employer. You know now that only corporations pay tax. People don't, or aren't supposed to. You are the credit side of the account beaus you provide the collateral – the labour. You then operate through the debt side of the account through the SIN number for the corporation as the Strawman. So if the bond was set at 1 million initially, the Strawman has a loan for one million that he has to pay back. The loan is supported by your labour. Let us track this as the Strawman now goes to work.

This Strawman is the real taxpayer. And when it came time to start paying, upon getting its SIN and entering the labour market, it had to declare some income for tax purposes.

So let us say that Mr. Strawman earned $50,000 in the first year. Pay checks are issued to Mr. Strawman which has zero credits. Now bear in mind that it may not be issued in the capital name simply because *everyone including you assumes it does not matter.* But nevertheless, it is recorded that way since the truth has been dissolved into oblivion. The year-one after-tax balance is what is entered as *debt on account*. Tax, let us say is $15,000, is interest on the debt income borrowed from your account. That is, the after-tax amount in year one is say $35,000, and shows as debt on debt side of employer account. The tax of $15,000 becomes an interest payment on the one million dollar loan. That's why the STRAWMAN has to pay tax, so that the money he received via a pay check can be collected in part as a tax. That money was borrowed from the principal amount to fund the corporate entity Strawman. But it is really interest charges on the loan from yourself and back to yourself."

Unknown to you, the Fed is borrowing in your name to fund the economy through the Appropriations Act that is the authority to do this. As in all loans, the money must be repaid. To balance the books, a repayment of this loan must be shown. Given the fact the Strawman through you files tax returns that are really interest payments called tax to conceal the truth, it is fact that the Strawman is the debtor, or the party who repays you.

Going up one level, the provincial government went to the Bank of Canada to post the bond for which they received a million in credit. The Bank of Canada can now issue more debt money as approved and registered by the IMF. It's back to the Elite bankers and the fact that we have been pledged to pay them back due to the bankruptcy. So the receiver is the bookkeeper keeping track of the credit line to see how much is drawn and how much is paid. That's why Nations have Receivers of Revenue.

The Receiver General adds up all the accounts at the end of each year, and since all these accounts are operating in debt with debt, the national debt must increase as no credit was applied. Further, all tax returns are evidence of how much debt was issued. Add them all up at year end and you have the new total of the debt. By completing a tax return where income is declared - which is really debt - we are instructing the receiver to add that debt to the debt side, namely Mr. Strawman's account. That's what we all have ever done so no wonder there is a huge national debt.

Redemption is the only way to reduce this debt. Paying debt with debt instruments does not reduce overall debt, it's impossible. You can use a check to pay a debt, but it's still debt added somewhere else. The taxes are only paying the interest on the loans – not the principle. So the way the deal is set up means that the big loan to the IMF, through the Bank of Canada, their private arm, can never be paid, and the more people that are born, the more they draw out. It is like a huge line of credit with no upper bound because no one is aware of it.

A debtor, which means only corporations, cannot redeem labour, only people can. Corporations declare labour as an expense which is a form of redemption. The corporation then recovers the expense at the point of sale. So this is why Canada has a national debt. No redemption is being made by labourers. Since people have accepted that the name in capitals as appears on an SIN card to be themselves, we have never communicated or instructed the receiver general to credit the account that we own. We have always instructed him to apply debt, so he does. As the trustee, he has the duty to do as instructed by the owner of the trust account or employer SIN account, which is the people in people accounts. There must be a creditor to have a debt. If the labour is redeemed, then a credit will be applied to the credit side, and the debt reduced accordingly to the debt side. Redemption is the only way to balance an account or to eliminate debt, just as shares are redeemed to reduce the issuer's liability.

The government opens an account for Mr. Strawman. Nor it, nor you requested that the account be opened, nor had no hand in determining the value of the account. They either opened it fraudulently or opened the account to extend it to the owner. It is therefore really owned by the real live human. So to claim it is like claiming a credit. It is in essence like being given a credited account the same as a credit card. Once the credit is used up, the account is balanced at zero, and no claim can be made. So it is yours to redeem. If you work forty years, there will be forty years of debt on the debt side to balance the amount of labour you have provided.

The reality is that the account bears the name of the corporation you own, or is being held on your behalf in a Trust in which you have an interest because you provided the human capital. So are you not entitled to the credit given by the party who opened the account? Accounts are opened for credit purposes only. Whoever opened and signed the account is the guarantor of the credit or loan. If credit is not being extended, then there is no reason to open an account. Who opens them? Who signs as surety? Who owns and who holds the account? Who is the beneficiary of the account, the guarantor or the owner of it? Who is the party entrusted? It is the trustee. And who is there to perform their duty, and discharge that duty? The surety is. Whoever signs, is liable. Did you sign? No. All fiction alleged creditors have an assumed claim. We are simply too stupid to know what's really going on.

This has enormous consequences to everybody's pocketbook if they only woke up. And the system is so well entrenched that the people administering the process doo not have a clue about it.

You as the real owner comes forth and removes presumption or assumption of the assumed claim. Only the real owner can. This would create *a claim in fact*. The Strawman could not exist if the living being was not born so you hold the claim in fact. The provincial government opened an account with the intention of extending credit to old Mr. Strawman, and they guaranteed the credit. So let us say they made that credit one million dollars. By extending credit Mr. Strawman is the debtor, right? So if you accept that value of credit which is what your property is deemed by the government to be worth, then should you not be able to collect it? It is either that situation or the government has used a name to open an account they had no authority to open under some other parties name. That would be a crime involving fraud and forgery. If the government attempts to collect on an account they does not own, but valued and guaranteed because they signed or opened the account, that is a serious criminal offence.

By each of us redeeming this account, we actually free ourselves and in the process reduce the national debt. How can something like this elude everyone for so long? It is because the debt cannot be questioned and all money is simply transactions of debt. so it is like paying MasterCard with Visa.

And as all apathetically entrenched in their own personal desires and as long as they can play with toys that they believe are theirs and their bellies are full, and the debt really does not affect that, who cares? The best slave are the ones that believe they are free. and there are none so blind as those who refuse to see.

When you investigate the accounts there are figures representing some aspect of our National Debt in the public records under the heading of Savings Account. When you fully understand what this means, a lot of lights may start to come on for you! Do you think this could be the aspect of our collective savings account representing the total accumulated, and saved to date value of our collective, unclaimed exemptions? Until they are claimed, this amount can also be correctly referred to as our national debt. Collectively, we own the rights to claim these exemptions, because this portion of the debt is ours as well. But it is to our credit, based upon our provable and valuable productivity as individuals, so perhaps that is why it is headed under Savings Account.

This means it is our proportionate ownership of the *de facto* bond issue that we, together with the Bank of Canada and its chartered affiliates acting on our behalf, have been issuing our money against. In other words it represents what the banks owe all of us as citizens for simply having administered our issue of our money. Individually, we may only authorize a claim for that proportionate amount of the exemption that we can prove our entitlement to by evidencing our valuable productivity in the form of dollar denominated debt money. And the debt money that is currently in our system does indeed have very real value. It has the equal and offsetting value of our credit; the total of all claimed exemptions, plus all unclaimed exemptions. This is the portion of our current national debt, which means its value is equal to our cumulative, provable productivity, and to some extent, our good will, either of which, or and certainly both, are worth infinitely more than gold or silver

The unclaimed exemption represents the total cumulative amount of provable and valuable productivity that we have and may yet provide. Our unclaimed exemption has no inherent value in and of itself. It is not an account with real money in it. It is our treasury account. It is not accessible as money via a closed account. It is rather, our intangible right to endorse a claim against a dollar denominated value amount - not a real dollar, as an offset of our dollar denominated liabilities. This is provided we can prove productivity. This is simply an accounting entry.

This is exactly the same process as the banks use. They use your promissory note, your signature to sell to the Bank of Canada so they can get you to '*promise to pay*' with nothing to loan. But, and here is the big BUT. We can claim our own exemption and we can endorse an authorization for it to be applied as an offset of certain liabilities. An authorization must only be endorsed to a chartered bank, licensed in part, to act as fiduciary for our issuance of currency by creating it via promissory notes, mortgages, or the likes, or it may be endorsed to CRA or the IRS to offset tax liabilities. So you can't get cash. Obviously all of our debt money was at one time or another loaned into circulation either directly or indirectly to end-users like us against either real existing productivity, or against future productivity via promissory notes. So that is why it is rightly called debt money which is the alternative to it having been loaned into circulation. If you ask anybody to show you the money, they can't. There is none. But you can still offset certain liabilities with CRA or IRS for example.

The banks have no money to lend so they make you sign papers like promissory notes that they can then use to make money '*appear*' via a keystroke. So when I gave them a promise to pay on a mortgage, I created a *valuable financial security* with a face value of the mortgage. Then I agreed to pay it back plus interest for a term of twenty-five years. That created a funding instrument. The property, which I didn't have yet, had to be conveyed from me to the bank as a condition of the loan. The bank then recorded its acquisition of the funding instrument as an increase in the money, or assets of the bank. So me, the stupid borrower, gave the power to create the money, contributed property to the transaction, and received in return from the bank an account as a '*credit*' which they created with a keystroke. The result is they got the promise, the loan back, the interest, and the property for putting up nothing. And I got to work twenty five years to pay it off.

Then the bank was able to sell my mortgage note, with property as security into the international banking market and get a further return on their paper, probably in the order of ten plus percent. At the same time they made me pay for an insurance policy to protect them

Then, when you paid all this back, they never returned the original promissory note so they could continue to derive unjust enrichment as long as they wanted to keep your original promise to pay in circulation. So, in summary, somewhere is a whole accounting system that keeps track of this. Is it money? It is a key stroke entry into the ledger. What is there? it is what you placed there as your credit in good faith. The total amount is the equity registered in those three trusts which is your person "Good Faith and Credit" all being held in your name.

Getting Access To The Good Faith And Credit

What has become more and more apparent is that this other side of the ledger exists. What has come to light is that institutions like the DTCC to name one (Depository Trust Clearing Company of New York also a private enterprise) is responsible for the accounting process. Undoubtedly, the Reserve Banks in each nation and the World Bank also keep track of this. It is so around the world. Right from the point of inception, this account continues to be recorded according to GAAP or Generally Accepted Accounting Practices by law. What has not come to light is how to access this Good Faith and Credit which was placed there by each in good faith, but without the knowledge. Nevertheless, the access or option has always existed if one can find the way through the labyrinth.

Herein lies an interesting legacy of the estate in your name that has been set up but hidden carefully. and there are many that have succeeded in access despite the incredible labyrinth of public laws and plausible deniability that shrouds it. This process of seeking out that pathway to gain access to that Good Faith and Credit has evolved in the last decade from many directions. It is fraught with difficulty and danger because effectively you are taking on the "system" of Statutes, Acts, banks, Tax Authorities and Governments who have been trained in the Public side and truly believe you are the bad guy for attempting this. And the power to enforce their side is in their hands. That is why it is a hit and miss situation as to whether one gains access or not. Needless to say, those that do, provide lessons to the controllers to close the holes as quickly as possible.

Eventually, the truth of this will shift but in the meantime, the "law" and the beliefs are on the side of the Corporate structures simply because we were are ether born into this type of employee slavery, or we simply accepted it as the way it is supposed to be.

Regardless, this is changing rapidly now as the momentum increases. And so the processes that have evolved are proliferating rapidly as people have been backed into a wall of debt and seek both spiritual and commercial solutions. We will summarize several of these methods here that can be divided into three "techniques" or processes:

1. The Process of Commercial Redemption
2. The Process of Debt Set-off and Closed Accounts
3. The Process of Accepted For Value

All of these are related to the Strawman and gaining access to that Trust that was set up in the name of the Strawman. But like the shifting sands, the process is not clear, nor does it always work. The labyrinth through the established system is fraught with danger. And in many cases it has gotten people into more trouble than they anticipated as the public system has the upper hand and power should you decide to fight. As you read through these, understand that these are presented not because they always work and should be followed but because they add credibility to the other side of the commercial coin that we has spoken on, and they reflect procedures that can be refined and enhanced, converging on the final revelation of the truth that can liberate those who wish to be liberated and to redeem that Good Faith and Credit. This topic will be covered in detail later on. First it is necessary to understand what has been happening in this regard as more and more people make their way through the Strawman Labyrinth Game.

The Process Of Commercial Redemption

Commercial Redemption is a term commonly used to the process of gaining access to that Good Faith and Credit locked away in a legal and administrative labyrinth of Dungeons and Dragons. Those who enter this game will inevitably face the incredible forces of ignorance and power of the system. For this summary we will use the Books by David E Robinson who has written many books found at Amazon. www.amazon.com/David-E.-Robinson/e/B002OR956W/ref=ntt_athr_dp_pel_pop_1

In his books on **Redemption**, David shows in an enlightening description the analogy between the Wizard of Oz story and process of illusion with regards to the commercial system and the Strawman. As he explains, Kansas is no more, it is a two letter postal designation which is part of the One Improvement established by the 1933 bankruptcy as a "state" or tax jurisdiction. During 1916-1933 gold was absorbed by Federal Reserve. He explains how the common law is God's law of universal consent. There are two states, two laws, two yours. The state controls the person as it offers benefits to the fiction ID document s by acceptance you agree to what the state attaches to it as it is accepted without protest. The Capital letter name plus birth dates defines this as benefits are his as a citizen of the state. The "person" is a mask so you volunteer to take this name.

This, David explains, is created as a political entity outside and independent of biblical authority (rights of and rights for). Kings had divine rule over subjects as in oath they are alleged to Gods laws of the new world model. And so the whims of men could now fall under the will of God. The constitution is not improvement as a model of freedom as it covers constitutors as to pay debt. Article 6 "all debts..." pay off the debts and the state ceases to exist. So all the citizens are surety for someone else's debt. Once a debt is established it is a control outside God's Law. In bankruptcy, rules apply and assets are seized (land vehicles people). As he points out; The most productive slaves are ones who believe they are free.

This process of giving away God's given freedom is exchanged for inferior government privileges as one becomes trapped in one's own ignorance being told ignorance of the law is no excuse We lock into presumptive and express contracts. We were never told this which is an effect of fraud and it is all or nothing as you agree to one and you agree to all, so going along with statutes of state out of obedience to scriptures gives legitimacy of godless actions of state We are told this is the law but it is a contract that can be broken. We are paying debt never agreed to, sold into bondage by fraud.

This, he states, is the mark of the beast as you must be in commerce with the state to survive. It is the embracing by modern church to be good Christians. The conversion took place in 1878 in the corporate UNITED STATES. Kingdoms (not Caesar who usurped God) is built n obedience to God and the kingdom is built on consent to an imaginary authority by legal fictions which are most commonly corporations and trusts.

When we speak of redemption, we mean redeem what labour or goods have accounted for sitting in storage. In probability, the last six digits of the registration number must be the common number on each document and one obviously relates to the other. Insiders have the advantage of access to the main databases to validate a charge before billing. But other people don't. So we need the information to access our account. It must be on the birth certificate, or the stock receipt and should serve as proof for redemption as it appears warehouse rules are being adhered to.

Whoever is currently holding your bond is able to match and access your account by having the name from your birth certificate. With that information plugged into the system, it will match with the last six digits, because the other two pairs in front will reflect the year and month of the birth. And the name is related to both numbers for the verification step. This will then lead back to the registration of the bond, being the year and last six digits. Having your SIN or SSN number is additional verification, as are other pieces of Strawman identification. Since we hold the account receipt, we hold data to access the account. Once this is in the registered account file, the number on the back of the birth certificate is the actual bond issued.

The registration itself is a bond. Registration of a birth as evidenced by issuance of a registered birth certificate means the issuer is bound to the holder of the certificate. That's you. Your parents pledged you and the government accepted. When the government accepted, it opened and then credited your account. The credit amount would be to the value they have pledged you as being worth by agreement. Each person is evaluated and assessed by statistics so a value can be given to justify the value the government guarantees the bond for. The key here is the government guaranteed this, not you. You never entered into the birth contract. So why not claim your property by presenting the proper account access information. The government guarantee is probably insured as well, reducing the risk, and giving cause to guarantee at higher value.

So technically, the government that gave the account value and extended credit is liable for the full amount as the bound party. The people did not make the deal. You are creditor that is paying off their bankruptcy problems. They had to pledge something to their creditors. Wasn't it nice of them to pledge your labour? This is just commerce. You don't understand the rules they have used on you. It is the way things are done. All you have to do is understand the rules and you may be able to access that full amount.

Reclaim of sovereignty is by UCC form and Security agreement to Secretary of State. Invoice and BOE sent to Treasury Remedy is under UCC IRS is collection agency for Fed Reserve placed under UCC in 1954 Vice Admiralty courts established queens possessions beyond the seas brought between United States and Crown in 1933. The Commercial Process of Redemption thru UCC redeems us from this. All American courts are vice admiralty conducting private foreign commerce of the crown with statuary laws as the written regulations.

Commercial Redemption gives you a way to take advantage by taking control of the Strawman, then you control the rights and the titles to the property that the Strawman has acquired and owns. In a nutshell you file your birth certificate and Bill of exchange with the secretary of the treasury and a UCC Financing statement with a private security agreement. This redeems you the living soul from the public sector and places you under the private creditor side, after which you have right to real property ownership through the Strawman who is now employed by the living soul. You are now the employer and your name is now your credit instead f theirs. In essence your Strawman becomes a banker because it is attempting to collect the security interest underlying your birth certificate-your contract f presumption with the Government. A banker has the authority to create a Bill of Exchange to draw upon the public debt.

He states that in 1936 you birth certificate was given a value of $630,000 but now it is much more. You can use the commercial process to "discharge" public debts with private credit in a tax exempt and levy exempt mode by accessing a private Treasury Direct Account charged against your birth certificate. This you can utilize to discharge various public debts, but not t make purchases. When you become the "holder in due course" of your Strawman you become his creditor; and then the Government, not you becomes responsible for claims against him as they are the responsible surety, now libel for debts, fines, judgements. Simply **accept for value** (discussed later) the presentment (solicitation) made against the Strawman, thus notifying the presenter that he owes you the amount of his claim, since you now hold the true legal title to the money the presenter has offered to you (as Strawman's creditor) in presenting a charge against the Strawman. However the presenter cannot turn over to you (release) legal title to these public funds because there are none, the public side is bankrupt and owns nothing by legal title If the presenter does not produce title to these funds within 72 hours or withdraw the charge against the Strawman, a condition of "dishonour" occurs and you can do a Bankers acceptance of the dishonoured contract, create a Bill of exchange and deposit it with the secretary of treasury, now considered to be represented by the IRS which becomes the correspondent bank of you Private Treasury Direct Account and keeps an account in your name. Once the IRS has established a private TDA for you, you can command the IRS to release the private side funds (credit) from you TDA to meet public claims presented to the Strawman. Yu d with an "acceptance for value credit release and promissory note made payable to the US treasury and sent to the IRS. So you can discharge any public liability

The 14th amendment reads "*All persons born or naturalized in the Unites States, and subject to the jurisdiction thereof (instead of the Constitution) are citizens of the United States (voluntary slaves) and of the state wherein they reside.*"

The public registration of the vessel by application for Birth certificate makes one subject to the jurisdiction of the United States democracy in contradiction to the United States Republic. The debt is paid when you surrender your Birth Certificate and tender a Bill of exchange to the secretary in his private capacity, via the IRS to discharge the Strawman debt.

The child may think he is free but there is a security agreement which represents title to the thing in the real world-the body and that is the only thing kings and layers see. as they hold the security of title and if they are the holder in due course of the deed then the state holds legal title to everything you think you own. they are playing the securities game so owner is not what you think for an owner has equitable title to the thing, not legal title. legal gives total control, equitable means temporary use and possession of the reality, not possession of the security instrument that represents it.

In 1933 leaders met to administer the bankruptcy. Governors agreed to pledge assets of energy of people to create a connection to private living beings they created the Strawman. In 1935 we converted from substance backed currency (gold) to promise backed currency (credit). A Birth record is a security instrument (Collateral) that backs the pledge so you become the co-signer. To redeem rights of constitution, you must pay back the pledge and redeem the collateral that was pledged. The commercial Process of redemption is to pay the pledge and redeem the Strawman from the pledge to make you the beneficiary of your Strawman. The Strawman is the TU "transmitting utility" as go between to avoid treason so everything that passes through the pipeline of the TU belongs to the government and to make use of these presumes surety.

Once you pay back the pledge, Strawman is redeemed from government control and you become the creditor of your Strawman who is in debt to you, not government. This is done by a UCC 1 financing statement filed with the Secretary of State. Now you have an interest in the pipeline and you are the beneficiary not surety of the Strawman. The secured party position is it matters not what you do with my Strawman but before you take anything my superior claim must be settled first (like a first mortgage).

Let us divert briefly as we look more closely at the UCC. A good site to go to is **www.legalucc.com** Created in 1952, the Uniform Commercial Code (UCC) consists of uniform rules coordinating the sale of goods and other commercial transactions throughout the 50 United States. The Uniform Commercial Code is the oldest and most intricate uniform act established by the National Conference of Commissioners on Uniform State Laws (NCCUSL). All 50 states, with the exception of Louisiana, have adopted the Uniform Commercial Code. Louisiana has opted not to include Article 2, which specifies regulations for the sale of goods, in place of its own civil law. The Uniform Commercial Code was created by a private institution, so it is not a law unless it is enacted by a state. Its goal is to simplify commercial transactions. Parties forming a contract can omit parts of the code, as well as make addenda.

The Uniform Commercial Code also seeks to make commercial paper transactions, such as the processing of checks, less complex. It distinguishes between merchants, who know their business well, and consumers, who do not. Overall, the code's objective is to eliminate the need for lawyers in the aspects of commercial trade it governs. The topics specifically addressed in the 11 articles of the Uniform Commercial code include the sale of goods, bank instruments, negotiable instruments, letters of credit, bills of receipts, bulk transfers, investment securities, and secured transactions. The Uniform Commercial Code, although the most well-known, is just one of several uniform acts promoted by the National Conference of Commissioners on Uniform State Laws, established in 1892. Some other examples of uniform acts include the Uniform Child Custody Jurisdiction Action and the Uniform Foreign Money Claims Act. The NCCUSL is made up of lawyers and professionals, appointed by states and territories, who discuss which laws should be uniform across the country. The purpose of the American Law Institute (ALI), established in 1923, is to clarify American common law according to changing social needs.

The ALI and NCCUSL are both responsible for maintaining and revising the Uniform Commercial Code. The Uniform Computer Information Transaction Act (UCITA) was an attempt by the NCCUSL to improve Article 2 of the UCC; however, ALI failed to agree to this inclusion. As a result, only Virginia and Maryland adopted the UCITA because it was not formally included into the UCC. ALI and NCCUSL have also established an editorial board that provides official comments and papers that aid in the legal interpretations of the code. As you refer to the 11 articles, does the Uniform Commercial Code apply to a promissory note since it is a negotiable instrument. In Canada, the Bills of exchange Act is the equivalent.

As to understanding the UCC-1, there is a good site to visit at **http://loveforlife.com.au/node/6168.** UCC-1 stands for Uniform Commercial Code Form 1. It is not an agreement. It is just notice to the world that one person claims that it has an interest in someone else's property, usually as collateral for a debt. It is normally filed in the office of the Secretary of State in the state where the debtor/borrower is located. In most cases, located means the state of incorporation for corporations, the state of creation for limited liability companies and other entities, and the state of residence for individuals.

There must be another agreement, called a **Security Agreement**, that actually grants the security interest and defines the terms of the deal. The security agreement and the UCC-1 combined are like a mortgage on real estate. The mortgage is both the notice and the agreement for real estate, while for personal property the notice and the agreement are separate.

The UCC-1 is a notice to the public not an agreement. The UCC-1 may be used to notice a lien created by a security agreement of a loan for a home, car, and etc. The UCC-1 being a "financing statement" is not an "agreement". The importance of the UCC-1 to the secured party and other lenders/creditors is the first in time, first in line priority. A UCC-1 notifies others of outstanding debt such as security agreement, summary judgment lien, commercial or maritime lien and so forth. Collateral items may be listed directly. Property, real and personal property, can be involved. All of this is for the protection of the secured party and allow other possible lenders/creditors to be aware of outstanding unpaid debt that would stand in line for collection of any new debt.

The common belief, "*It applies to personal property, not real estate.*", is wrong. One needs look no further that the form itself to see "Real Estate" mentioned three times in the form and four times in the instructions.   Misinformation exists with the wording, "There must be another agreement, called a security agreement,... ". This implies two agreements even though the writer previously stated the UCC-1 is not an agreement. The other implication is that the UCC-1 is used only as it applies to the "security agreement". There need not be a previous defaulted note on personal property to utilize the UCC-1 notice as it may be used for other previously mentioned purposes.

We will look more closely at this form and the Security Agreement later.

Although the new consciousness is aware of this, to access this Good Faith and Credit is not a simple straight forward procedure. It is filled with danger unless you are thoroughly fluent in these matters and can handle yourself in Admiralty court. It has not been easy to find or deploy because none of the monkeys have a clue about it and none will believe it. Moreover, reclaiming your status is key and we will deal with this later. Hence there is no sure way yet, but that is changing. The gig is up so to speak as more and more people open the awareness about this account that reflects the warehouse storage container.

The Process of Debt Set-off And Closed Accounts

In summarizing this process we will use the site which is due to the work and research of **Fred and Nina Gutierrez** who claim millions of dollars of success with their process. The site is at ***www.setoffdebt.com/***.

This process uses a closed checking account as the flow through process of setting off specific debts. After making the appropriate declarations and filings to separate the Strawman from the real human, you are then writing a check as you would normally on an open bank account. This is a financial instrument referred to as **EFT** for **Electronic Funds Transfer**. The difference here is that this is a bank account that is closed and instead of the funds being drawn against your usual checking account, the bank. Where do the funds come from? Again they are from the secret Strawman account that goes back to the Federal Reserve and up. The amount on the check is then set off through book entries against the Strawman account on the "silent hidden ledger side". The usual issue here is having the bank (who usually deny this through ignorance (plausible deniability), having it actually monetized (getting the money transferred) and enforcing the process in a court if you have to. This can be dicey and is enforced through a skill of knowing your constitutional, unalienable rights, which in the USA are:

Article 1 All men are, by nature, free and independent, and have certain inalienable rights, among which are those of enjoying and defending life and liberty, acquiring, possessing, and protecting property, and seeking and obtaining happiness and safety.

Article 2 All political power is inherent in the people. Government is instituted for their equal protection and benefit, and they have the right to alter, reform, or abolish the same, whenever they may deem it necessary; and no special privileges or immunities shall ever be granted, that may not be altered, revoked, or repealed by the general assembly.

Article 3 The people have the right to assemble together, in a peaceable manner, to consult for their common good; to instruct their representatives; and to petition the general assembly for the redress of grievances

Article 5 There shall be no slavery in this state; nor involuntary servitude, unless for the punishment of crime.

Further information that is relevant: List of amendments to the United States Constitution
- First Amendment – Establishment Clause, Free Exercise Clause; freedom of speech, of the press, and of assembly; right to petition
  Congress shall make no law respecting an establishment of religion, or prohibiting the free exercise thereof; or abridging the freedom of speech, or of the press; or the right of the people peaceably to assemble, and to petition the Government for a redress of grievances.
- Second Amendment – Militia (United States), Sovereign state, Right to keep and bear arms.
  A well regulated Militia, being necessary to the security of a free State, the right of the people to keep and bear Arms, shall not be infringed.
- Third Amendment – Protection from quartering of troops.
  No Soldier shall, in time of peace be quartered in any house, without the consent of the Owner, nor in time of war, but in a manner to be prescribed by law.
- Fourth Amendment – Protection from unreasonable search and seizure.
  The right of the people to be secure in their persons, houses, papers, and effects, against unreasonable searches and seizures, shall not be violated, and no Warrants shall issue, but upon probable cause, supported by Oath or affirmation, and particularly describing the place to be searched, and the persons or things to be seized.
- Fifth Amendment – due process, double jeopardy, self-incrimination, eminent domain.
  No person shall be held to answer for a capital, or otherwise infamous crime, unless on a presentment or indictment of a Grand Jury, except in cases arising in the land or naval forces, or in the Militia, when in actual service in time of War or public danger; nor shall any person be subject for the same offence to be twice put in jeopardy of life or limb; nor shall be compelled in any criminal case to be a witness against himself, nor be deprived of life, liberty, or property, without due process of law; nor shall private property be taken for public use, without just compensation.
- Sixth Amendment – Trial by jury and rights of the accused; Confrontation Clause, speedy trial, public trial, right to counsel.
  In all criminal prosecutions, the accused shall enjoy the right to a speedy and public trial, by an impartial jury of the State and district wherein the crime shall

have been committed, which district shall have been previously ascertained by law, and to be informed of the nature and cause of the accusation; to be confronted with the witnesses against him; to have compulsory process for obtaining witnesses in his favor, and to have the Assistance of Counsel for his defense.
- Seventh Amendment – Civil trial by jury.
  In suits at common law, where the value in controversy shall exceed twenty dollars, the right of trial by jury shall be preserved, and no fact tried by a jury, shall be otherwise re-examined in any court of the United States, than according to the rules of the common law.
- Eighth Amendment – Prohibition of excessive bail and cruel and unusual punishment.
  Excessive bail shall not be required, nor excessive fines imposed, nor cruel and unusual punishments inflicted.
- Ninth Amendment – Protection of rights not specifically enumerated in the Constitution.
  The enumeration in the Constitution, of certain rights, shall not be construed to deny or disparage others retained by the people.
- Tenth Amendment – Powers of States and people.
  The powers not delegated to the United States by the Constitution, nor prohibited by it to the States, are reserved to the States respectively, or to the people.

The process combines going back to our unalienable rights which can never be liened, like a god given right. In the US Bill of rights and the Constitution, there are Articles 1, 2, 3,... Articles. 240 years ago the creators of it did a wonderful job- a genius- as they pained a great picture. It is the supreme law of the land, like the constitution. The rights of people was protected... seizure, etc. But as we have learned something went wrong and there were many injustices all over to cause harm.

Fred explains:

"I read the bible to understand what God put in my heart. When I read this and read the dictionary. This does not mean what you are saying. I got to disputes with churches to realise that I was one who had to stand up and fight. You get a conscious notion which says this is not right. The only way to honour is to honour God. The lessons bring to your knees. What are our rights? life, liberty and pursuit of happiness. These are unalienable. We do not understand the constitution. We have the right to life--to do what is ever necessary to protect me to be safe in our person, to have life, to defend it. I have the obligation to protect yours and the right to protect mine. I have the right to freedom of speech, private in my person from unlawful search and sleazier without due process."

"We have an unlimited right to contract as long as it does not violate the five elements necessary to contract.

1. In kind parties, not with a giraffe for example. trade goats for chickens
2. Full disclosure goats cannot be dead so I lay the conditions as we both do
3. Equal consideration, agree and come to an accord into full agreement. We consummate our contract by wet ink signatures
4. Wet ink signatures
5. Cannot be an unconscionable contract that violates the law."

"The crime is defined as when one of the people with criminal intent harms or damages the other or his property. A crime can only be judged by peers (12 unanimous) You have the right to Council, not an attorney. Article 3 says what that area is. A peer means I am innocent until proven that there was a criminal intent. Trial by jury is not jury trial. Your trial by peers is inviolate forever. Supreme law of the land is the constitution but yet there are many cases where statutes have been created that violate this. They call your name to if you are present. When life liberty, property, life are at stake, the Law is inviolate. So what happened? You know how it is supposed to be with the supreme law of the land. The rights were taken away without your permission. If you are a criminal, you can get people to waive your rights. Godly people prepared this so what happened? In the constitution, in order for it to function, we need to create the Public. Who are they? In the public, they have titles so a private can step in and function in the public to serve the public. We created the Republic to serve. All are born as a flesh and blood man or woman, so each is given a delegation of limited authority. We collectively agreed that these people have limited authority. How do we control them? All these officials are part of the public and it cannot be more powerful than that which created it. You are there to serve the private. The public serve to protect the rights of the private. According to Article 4 of Bill of Rights they must have an oath of office. They swear to protect and uphold the rights of the Constitution, so help me God.... If you break this, Title 18 is violation of this. are they doing this? Felony, perjury, perdition. Yes, they purger their oaths by stopping travel. etc, etc."

"Example: When asked for a drivers license. I said I demand your name, oath of office, bond number. My license is expired and I am under my right to travel freely by my constitution. I demand your oath of office four times. This is a powerful and this has to be filed in a public place so as to function to protect the constitution."

"All above this line is real and of substance. God is Creator and creates substance with physical properties. Constitution says: No state shall require the payment of debt other than lawful coin of gold and silver, of lawful substance. You have been deceived. How many people used gold and silver ? God gave us the right to free enterprise. In 1780. less than 12% of all transactions involved gold and silver. We did not need it. Money is a contrived system to control and enslave us. In a case Hale versus Henkel 1906 Supreme court, individual has no obligation to reveal anything to the state. It is because we are private. This has been upheld 1400 times in supreme court. Stand on your rights of the constitution. You have the right to be private."

"Is there any money? No. Is there debt? No The system made you blind. We have HJR 192 when House said we have no lawful coin so how do we resolve debt? Let's do this so Treasury pays but we need to make people public. social security is voluntary PL 4848192 article 10 cause 1.. all debt in lawful coin and silver. They work with feds to pass laws which you believe apply to you. You have to affect something and help someone else."

"When you get a notice to pay, you cannot pay. There are digits only, a US accounting measure of a dollar as a unit of accounting. How do you create more? Add a zero. It is all accounting. You equate the process with something else. HJR said Treasury takes care of everything. Is there debt? No Debt is created by a novation contract every month as it nullifies the last. If I am a power company I need a place, name, SSN to see you function in the public. The Treasury has to settle your debt. They send notice to treasury to create debt so satisfy it. They send you a novation so you write a check. If not, they shut you off because you have not read the fair credit act. So they get paid twice. Has anybody fought this? If someone wants bonafide proof of claim they write a notice that this is not settled monthly. You must demand these: 1. please provide copy of signed contract of my obligation 2. proof that there was full disclosure on both sides. 3 Equal consideration on this contract 4 Equal signatures on both sides. 5. Negotiate my positions? So demand full disclosure."

"Banks have rules, and they are allowed to function to discount and negotiate promissory notes. Who can write a promissory note. You. Yet you as a real human are not allowed to open a bank account, only persons and corporations can open an account by a real human. You must prove you are part of the public. They cannot loan their own assets as depositors need to be protected. They cannot loan depositors assets. So how can they loan money. It is the law So they create credit and because I am in admiralty I do not have to tell anything. If people want credit, they fill out an application which is an instrument. The bank takes it and sells it on the market place to see if I can get someone to buy them. If someone wants credit (say 10000) the bank can sell it for a certain amount 10 times on average what you see. The bank makes 90K. The bank sells it and makes money on the man's signature. It is against the law for the bank to loan me my own money but under admiralty I have no obligation to tell you anything. They make 10 times the amount to have a an account 100,000 and You have a 10k account, made an account that has 90 The only way it has value to you is if it is zero. They have access to the full 100 and set aside 10, 90 is a secret. The account is either plus or minus. But you want the 100 you have in your name, right?"

"So let us put 500k on a home as a promissory note. They first sell the application, then the second way is to sell the promissory note. How do they get the money, it is this way and you do not know how much. They have many restrictions on them and do not have to disclose. In tough times, they sue you for violation, no they sue you for unjust enrichment but they took your information and breached it as fraud, giving it to others. What they sue you for is under a statute, not under law because you were not damaged. They do not want full disclosure as we will have to give, not loan, but give because it is your signature that created it."

"You need to know how to challenge them in court as all roads lead to court. 90-99% of transactions need money so you have to still engage. Companies, fictions have taken over. You have to participate in this system to live. Go for oath of office first."

"It's a reverse wire transaction for the purpose of set off and discharge of debt."

"In our basic procedures, the paperwork is tight, These paper include Oath of office, status , affidavit and Judgement reversal."

"You need to do your own research as well once we give you the meat and potatoes. Look at oath of office, look at their bonds, become a master of none of your business, locking at something that is 100% effective. Study these calls. With courts it is never permanent. we only stand in righteousness and lawful, not patriotic crap going around. read bill of rights 4,5,6,7. Title 42 action. It says people is the power, not the government so they must act according to their oath in public capacity. Follow these rules:

1. Do not talk on phone. If you receive a phone call who claims official capacity. Ask for name, phone, address, say thank you and hang up the phone. Stop being ignorant as you cannot verify on the phone if you do not handle it on the phone. You will mess yourself up. Work in **accordance with the law. in support of the constitution.** You are not required to respond. They are breaking the law.. keep everything in writing.

2. Prepare a **certified mail presentment lawful notification** letter (as for help) FBI For example: 'excuse me what did you say your baggage, etc, send the letter in writing, thank you,' click. Grab an FBI letter to set them up for a or a title 18 criminal action. Anyone must is lawful notification by register mail. Just what? what? send it with a

status affidavit by registered letter. Do not send letters after the engagement has started. It is for court. Read what you write and ask for help."

Nina reports the basics of EFT's:

"Here is how to prepare and send an EFT correctly:

1. You need original bill with a coupon on it
2. EFT instrument filled out and written (see example on web site). Write dollars in by you as it is a unit of accounting in your hand "dollars" in hand writing as the unit of accounting
3. Notary presentment certificate needs to be ready as a certificate as presentment notary witness certificate
4. Certify to a mailing to payment address listed on the bill (don't care about CEO CFO) don't get fancy here.
5. Make copies of everything. Certificate is evidence of what's in the envelope, that's all, they take possession so you do not have it.. They mail it so get front and back of EFT instrument.
6. Mark calendar for 30 days, to send letter if they do not respond.
7 Who gets EFT? Big corporations and big banks, are tied into money system to discharge debt also state corporation, taxes of every kind Article 1 section 10 of Constitution states why we can discharge debt created through a financial instrument, not loaned in any way a money can be paid the same way. Fed or state debt and credit cards. If you want to use it, do not EFT it. Mortgages at banks, Car loans, No, No to real people Doctors, private investors, small business, but yes to a big hospital."

"A Lawful Notification letter is needed if you get lawyer letter, bank letter, and you wish to demand title, or need a response. Note that:

1 Affidavit of STATUS notifies that you are not a corporation who must be treated a certain way according to law, not artificial SUPPORT:
2 EFT AFFIDAVIT when you have sent EFT and follow-up, then send this as your statement of truth notarized, you sent it, on a certain date, when they received it, "Have not received a valid responses and therefore accepted.
3 AFFIDAVIT of SECURED INTEREST a bank would claim interest so you put on it=record a claim to that property and you have possession.
4 COPIES OF EFT MAILING
5 COPIES of letter sent
6 Copies of letters from bank, etc or alleged creditor."

"The EFT can be used for mortgages, IRS, car loans or any alleged creditor who sues you, can be sent any time after 7 day after you sent the EFT. Giving them a long time to respond is not appropriate. It must be back in your hands 7 days from when they received it."

"Always answer the issues and complaints. Do not be afraid of Affidavit of Status, to be filed with court clerk.- Your name in all capitals, JOHN DOE, on birth certificate, drivers licence, social security card is NOT you, who is the flesh and blood man/woman. YOU ARE NOT A CORPORATE FICTIONAL NAME. YOU ARE ONE OF WE THE PEOPLE, verify by this by filing affidavit of status."

Here are some questions and answers posted on their website that assist in helping to understand this process.

What are the exact procedures for Setoff of Debt?
1. If you are attempting to do EFT's or having someone work on them for you, please understand that you must be responsible for the completion of your own transaction. You must have full understanding of the laws that support this and any risk associated with these types of transactions. Knowing who you are in court is critical and that is why the new tour across this country teaching court room basic training. Do not hold anyone else accountable for not getting your Setoff.
2. Send standard follow up letter that is pertinent to what they said. – 30 Day wait (Letters on $45 Disk that you can purchase) I.E. <u>Certified funds only letter</u> etc.. Make sure letter is based on the response needed from the bank.
3. Send Lawful notification letter – 30 Day wait (Letters on $45 Disk that you can purchase)
4. Have your Affidavit of Status filled out and signed. Then file that Affidavit of Status into a miscellaneous file at a Federal Court or County Recorders Office. Get as many certified copies that you can afford. This Affidavit of Status is fact in law when un-rebutted. This will be used in the future when you are responding to any action.
5. Then fill out an Affidavit of EFT and Affidavit of Interest. (Letters on $45 Disk that you can purchase)
6. Fill all Three documents into a miscellaneous file at a Federal Court or County Recorders Office. Get a few certified copies.
7. Send one of the certified copies to your lender/bank with a Constructive Notice Letter giving them 10 days to respond or you intend to litigate.

What is an Affidavit of Status?
It is a document that substantiates whom you are. Remember and Affidavit filed into public, in which if not rebutted can be used in court as fact. (On website **www.setoffdebt.com**) is shown as follows:

AFFIDAVIT OF YOUR NAME
STATE OF NEVADA   )
COUNTY OF CLARK   )

Comes now, Your Name, your Affiant, being competent to testify and being over the age of 21 years of age, after first being duly sworn according to law to tell the truth to the facts related herein states that he has firsthand knowledge of the facts stated herein and believes these facts to be true to the best of his knowledge.

1. That your Affiant is one of the People of these united States of America, being a creation of God and born/domiciled in one of the several States.
2. Your Affiant is a living, breathing, sentient being on the land, a Natural Person and therefore is not and cannot be any ARTIFICIAL PERSON and, therefore, is exempt from any and all identifications, treatments, and requirements as such pursuant to any process, law, code, or statute or any color thereof.
3. Your Affiant notices that in these united States of America, the authority of any and all governments reside in the People of the land, for government is a fiction of the mind and can only be created by the People, effected by the People, and overseen by the People for the benefit of the People.
4. Your Affiant at all times claims all and waives none of his God given secured and guaranteed Rights pursuant to the Declaration of Independence and the Constitution of the united States of America as ratified 1791 with the Articles of the Amendments.
5. Your Affiant notices that pursuant to the Constitution of the united States of America as ratified 1791 with the Articles of the Amendments, Article VI paragraph 2, "This Constitution and the Laws of the united States which shall be made in Pursuance thereof; and all Treaties made, under the authority of the United States, shall be the supreme Law of the Land; and the Judges in every State shall be bound thereby, any Thing in the Constitution or

Laws of any State to the Contrary notwithstanding".
6. Your affiant notices, that as a matter of their lawful compliance to the referenced Constitution, any of the People, while functioning in any Public capacity, in return for the trust of the People, are granted limited delegated authority of and by the People, with specific duties delineated in accordance thereof, shall only do so pursuant to a lawfully designated, sworn and subscribed Oath of Office and any and all bonds required thereof.
7. Your Affiant notices that the only court authorized by the referenced Constitution to hear matters of the People is a court that conforms to and functions in accordance with Article III Section 2 of the referenced Constitution in which all officers of the court abide by their sworn and subscribed oaths of office and support and defend the Rights of the People, and are heard only Trial by jury and in accordance with all aspects of due process of law.
8. Your Affiant notices that pursuant to this supreme Law of the Land and the God given Rights secured and guaranteed therein, this Constitution is established to ensure that the dominion granted by God to all People, on this land, shall endure, and ensure forever that this People on this land be free from any and all slavery, indenturement, tyranny, and oppression under color of any law, statute, code, policy, procedure, or of any other type.
9. Your Affiant further notices that pursuant to this Constitution, Affiant cannot be compelled, manipulated, extorted, tricked, threatened, placed under duress, or coerced, or so effected under color of law by any Natural Person, who individually, or in any capacity as or under any Artificial Person, agency, entity, officer, or party, into the waiving of any of Affiant's Rights or to act in contradiction thereof, or to act in opposite of the moral conscience and dominion granted Affiant by God, nor can Affiant be deprived of any of these Rights, privileges, and immunities except by lawful process in accordance with the Law, without that Natural and/or Artificial Person, in whatever capacity, in so doing, causing injury to your Affiant and thereby committing numerous crimes, requiring lawful punishment therefrom.

Further, Affiant sayeth naught.

       Your Name

Before me, _____, a Notary Public duly authorized by the State of _____, personally appeared Your Name, who has sworn to and subscribed in my presence, the foregoing document, on this ___th day of _____ in the Year 2012.

_____
Notary Public

What follows is a set of Questions and Answers that can help clarify the process:

How do I use the affidavit of status?
1. Modify Affidavit of Status to your personal name and gender.
2. Have Affidavit Notarized
3. Take Notarized Affidavit to your local Federal Court Building.
4. Ask for the Civil Filing Window
5. Present Notarized Affidavit to be filed in a Miscellaneous Record (Folder). <u>You will be asked for what reason? Your answer will be the purpose is for a Foreclosure Judgment.</u>
6. The clerk will file the original. Ask for a Certified Stamped Copy, which you can take with you.
7. Keep the Certified Stamped Affidavit as a Master (Keep in Safe Place).
8. Make at least 10 Copies of your Master Affidavit, to have on hand and ready to send with EFT mailing.

9. Purpose: You will need to send a Certified Copy to every EFT Discharge you already did (bank, auto, credit card etc.) or send with the initial EFT Refusal Letter. This Certified Copy of your Affidavit is now part of the EFT process.

Can I purchase something with an EFT?
NO. It is not lawful

When using a notary at the ups store, does the notary do the actual mailing certified from the store? How do they mail certified?
A proper notary presentment is where the notary puts the package in the envelope and mails it for you.

Can you use a closed SAVINGS account if you don't have a closed checking account?
No, it must be a closed checking account.

Can you use a closed business account?
No, it must be personal.

How do I sign the <u>EFT</u> instrument?
With your regular signature. Some people will sign and reserve their rights. A.R.R. w/o Prejudice (Under their signature and above the line on the <u>EFT</u> instrument)

Can I pay a private party?
No. If someone loaned you personal funds, you need to pay them back.

What is the limit on the account?
No limit.

What do I do if the EFT is returned requesting certified funds.
Certified Funds Response Letter

What do I do if a collection agency is threatening a garnishment?
We have plenty of letters to choose from to respond to a third party debt collector on the disk for $45.

What is a notary presentment?
This is a document where you have a notary verify that she saw the <u>EFT</u> and invoice go into a envelope and whereby they mail the documents on your behalf.

What items go back to the lender? 1. Statement/Coupon 2. <u>EFT</u> 3. Notary Presentment.

How do I get information start?
Simply go to the basic seminar and it will be a breeze from there.

Do I actually sign or print my name for a signature?
Regular signature.

Is a notary allowed to do a Notary Presentment?
Of course.

So if you don't use green cards, how do you get proof of receipt?
USPS.com

Do any of these action cause a negative score on a credit report?
If you are not making payments on any item, you will have a negative effect. Making payments is at your discretion. Be prepared to battle to keep your property if you stop making your payments while you enforce the EFT.

Can I set off a judgment? Yes

Does the mortgage we wish to set off need to be in a delinquent state or short sale or foreclosure stage to write on EFT on it? No

Can I set off debt thru an EFT instrument that is not in my name.
Yes. ANY Debt. First, it must be debt and NOT a purchase. Then when you write the EFT instrument, you must put the account name and account number at the top of the EFT instrument that you are trying to discharge.

Does the address on the EFT instrument have to match my current address? It would help, but it is not needed. Just write the correct address on the EFT instrument manually.

Where can they find an injured party?
Criminal procedure and Civil rule 3 state laws. If prosecutor brings a complaint and there is no injury, then there can be no harm. What is cause, what is law that grants you authority under the 4th amendment? No ground if no injury, civil or criminal. Rules of Civil procedure: there has to be an injured party or it is frivolous action

Oath of Office and what is in the constitution?
1st, 4th, 9th amendments are not known by officers as it is not part of the plan. So they swear the oath and say it is private, but they can't as it is public Article 3, section 6 in constitution is where it is. " I solemnly swear... to support... " Need to travel to survive. Must have probable cause (not the tail light! for example) they stopped you for. Did I do harm is the real question.

In closing on this topic, before you too get excited, note that this is not a process that is _easy money_ right now. Many boast success but many cry failure. It can be fraught with danger as many will report. But what is certain is that more and more people are taking up the torch to seek this truth about that Strawman and his secret equity. The details presented here are for your education purposes only. For further information on this you can go to the site ***www.setoffdebt.com*** or many like it. The outline here is simply to enforce the reality of this process as it will become more important in Part 3 where the process of redemption and the EFT will be exampled through "state of the art" resignation from PLANET EARTH.

The Process Acceptance For Value

I want to take you further into the world of private contracts and a new side of the law. We need to look closely again at the laws of commerce and the power that lies in things like the Bills of Exchange or the Uniform Commercial Code that reflects those laws. You have had a taste of this with the acceptance for value power imbedded in three simple clauses of the Act.

There is a hierarchy of laws. The first order of law was Natural Law. It is based on universal, natural principles and you have no one except God to listen or report to. Next, came the laws of commerce. This involves the human interactions of buying, selling and trading. It was codified in the Sumerian/Babylonian era and, as you know now, has been brought forward in time to become an integral part of our lives. Next was the Common law that is based on common sense. It gave rise to the jury system and the process used by governments that put things into rules and regulations in courts. This process was based on facing your accuser in front of witnesses and was never intended to include lawyers, attorneys and judges. Next came governments, their laws and legislative regulations.

Humans had to impose new laws and regulations to capture themselves into slavery. But, and here is the big but. Commerce, and its laws, codified a long time ago, is the binding thread between our laws, and in fact remains imbedded in everything. Commerce is the engine that has been alive for six thousand years. Commerce, as we have discussed, forms the underlying foundation for all laws on the planet and all governments follow these. Although it is not readily apparent to most, as you have started to find out, when you operate at this fundamental level, there is nothing that can overturn, change or meddle with it.

Commerce remains the fundamental source of authority and power. If you ever wonder why we do things a certain way, the answer lies in the laws of commerce. This is reflected in the Bills of Exchange Act, or Uniform Commercial Code in the U.S. When you really understand how this works, you, as a private, natural individual begin to be your own *'lawyer'* and can work outside the judicial system in the private world. Commerce is the glue. Doing business, and resolving matters is done under oath, certified on each party's commercial liability by a sworn affidavit that it is true, correct, the truth and nothing but the truth. Guess where this came from? When you apply for things like a drivers license, these all have the equivalent of a copy certification to be true and correct... an affidavit. As you dig into our system and ask why things are done a certain way, like swearing on the bible, you will find these are all rooted in the law of commerce developed a long time ago. So in the hierarchy, the laws of commerce must be an extension of the Natural law as it was second in the evolution?

When you can function at this level in the private domain in the contract world, you can actually take the *'law'* into your own hands. Commerce law as an extension of natural laws has ten maxims. These have always been, and still are like the ten commandments of commerce. When I list these for you, you will say; well I always knew that, these are common sense. It is so. But you probably did not know how deep they go into dictating the actual laws. **These were codified in Babylonia. (Note the biblical reference for as we have noted in PART 1, god was very much interested in Commerce.** Here they are:

First, a workman is worthy of his hire. It is against equity for freemen not to have free disposal of their own property. (Exodus 20:15; Lev. 19:13; Matt. 10:10; Luke 10:7; II

Second, all are equal before the law. No one is above the law. This is founded on moral and natural law and is binding on all. (God's Law--Ethical and Natural Law). (Exodus 21:23-25; Lev. 24:17-21; Deut. 1:17, 19:21; Matt., 22:36-40; Luke 10:17; Col. 3:25. Legal maxims: "No one is above the law."; "Commerce, by the law of nations, ought to be common, and not to be converted into a monopoly and the private gain of a few.").

Third, in commerce, truth is sovereign. This forms the basis and standard and no lies are allowed. (Exodus 20:16; Ps. 117:2; Matt. 6:33, John 8:32; II Cor. 13:8. Legal maxim: "To lie is to go against the mind."

Fourth, truth is an Affidavit. An affidavit is your solemn expression and underlies a commercial transaction. It must have someone state it is true, and correct. If it is not, you are liable. (Lev. 5:4-5; Lev. 6:3-5; Lev 19:11-13; Num. 30:2; Matt. 5:33; James 5:12).

Fifth. An unrebutted affidavit stands as the truth in Commerce (1 Pet. 1:25; Heb. 6:13-15. Legal maxim: "He who does not deny, admits.").

Sixth, unrebutted Affidavits stand as truth. If claims are not rebutted, they emerge as the truth. An unrebutted Affidavit becomes a judgment. There is nothing left to resolve. Heb. 6:16-17. Any proceeding in a court, tribunal, or arbitration forum consists of a contest, or "duel," of commercial affidavits wherein the points remaining unrebutted in the end stand as the truth and the matters to which the judgment of the law is applied.).

Seventh, any matter must be expressed. You must state your position. He who fails to state his position has none. (Heb. 4:16; Phil. 4:6; Eph. 6:19-21. Legal maxim: "He who fails to assert his rights has none.").

Eighth, he who leaves the battlefield loses by default. This is the same as if the Affidavit is unrebutted. (Book of Job; Matt. 10:22. Legal maxim: "He who does not repel a wrong when he can, occasions it.").

Ninth, sacrifice is a measure of credibility. Nothing ventured, nothing gained. He who bears the burden ought to also derive the benefit. (One who is not damaged, put at risk, or willing to swear an oath that he consents to claim against his commercial liability in the event that any of his statements or actions is groundless or unlawful, has no basis to assert claims or charges and forfeits all credibility and right to claim authority.) (Acts 7, life/death of Stephen, maxim: "He who bears the burden ought also to derive the benefit.").

Tenth, a satisfaction is through a lien. A lien can be satisfied by rebutting the affidavit with another, convincing a common law jury, or paying it. . A lien or claim can be satisfied only through rebuttal by Counter-affidavit point-for-point, resolution by jury, or payment (Gen. 2-3; Matt. 4; Revelation. Legal maxim: "If the plaintiff does not prove his case, the defendant is absolved.").

Notice how these are imbedded in our actual legal procedures at this time. All law in Canada and US can be reduced to the above ten listed maxims.

What this reflects is that commercial law is non-judicial or pre-judicial and timeless. It is private law. It is the base beneath government and their system. This is what the courts do when you get into disputes without affidavits and have to rely on them and some expensive lawyers to solve it. So when you swear in court that is an affidavit. Virtually everything you do with lawyers requires sworn affidavits.

It is the conflict between commercial affidavits that forms the basis of being in court, and why attorneys create controversy. But no court can overturn an affidavit, except on adversely being affected by it. The entirety of the world commerce functions in accordance with this which is reflected in the Uniform Commercial Code. This maintains commercial harmony, codified into those ten legal maxims. Everywhere you turn, you will find these laws inherent in your contracts. You are not aware of how this works. You are probably aware of how it works against you when you don't know.

Note how easy it is for the bank or the tax group to take things from you or to make your commercial life miserable. The IRS, for example, is the most active collection agency in the U.S. but it is not registered to do business in any state. We simply give them money without requesting a *'proof of claim'* or even question if they are licensed to give offers based on arbitrary estimations. The IRS cannot even issue a valid assessment lien or levy. They must actually first produce the paperwork – a true bill in commerce. This would need a sworn affidavit by someone that it is true, correct, and complete. Do you think anyone there would do that and take the commercial liability with such a statement? We just don't know the rules so they get away with ignoring them.

Seeing the light is in the power of knowing the rules of commerce. That is what judges, lawyers and the legal system follow. Unfortunately, unless you do not hit some nerve, they will simply ignore these things and try to get you into a court where they get clever lawyers to make you look like a vexatious or radical creep and escape the real issues. In reality, they would have to follow the law of commerce and come back with an affidavit that rebuts point by point. This means that they would have to provide the paperwork with real assessments, the true bill in commerce, the real sworn affidavit that would make their assessment truth.

You need to be able to put something in the letter that brings in fear to them so they do not want to go to court because it could hurt individuals privately. Remember that you are dealing in the private contract world here and you have to name a real human, not a fiction. When they send you a statement, it seldom has any names on it.

When you *accept for value and dissect the words* you find it means to receive with approval or satisfaction, or to receive with intent to retain. With this in mind, when you get a traffic ticket, a notice of foreclosure or whatever, your first instinct is Oh, shit! I'm certainly not going to accept that! Why would anyone want to accept such a thing? But hold on. If you look at the word acceptance, it is the act of taking and receiving of something as if it were a tacit agreement.

Tacit is a very interesting word. If you look it up in Blacks 6th it states that tacit is existing, inferred, or understood without being openly expressed or stated; implied by silence or silent acquiescence, as a tacit agreement or a tacit understanding. It means that something is done or made in silence, implied or indicated, but not actually expressed. Something is manifested by the refraining from contradiction or objection or inferred from the situation and circumstances, in the absence of expression. If you accept the thing then there is an agreement. You agree with what they have said in the writing, whatever it may be. But, then, if you don't accept it, don't say anything, then there is still an agreement because you don't refute it or contradict what they say in the writing. It goes back to the ten maxims. If you do or say nothing you are presumed guilty. That gives them authority to move in on you and take you to court, then get authority to seize things. No matter how right you might think you are, what law you think is on your side, you always seem to lose in any court.

This is what banks and tax authorities, the ones that are the most skilled at doing it, use against you. Let us look a little further under acceptance in Blacks 6th edition. You'll go on down the page until you get to types of acceptance. Beneath that heading you'll see conditional acceptance. Here it says a conditional acceptance is an agreement to pay the draft or accept the offer on the happening of a condition. A conditional acceptance is a statement that you are willing to enter into a bargain differing in some respects from that proposed in the original offer. The old offer is no more! The conditional acceptance is, therefore, itself a counter offer. If you accept their offer with a conditional acceptance, you now have a counter offer to make back to them.

It places the ball in their court. If they do not answer, they then accept your offer by tacit agreement and you win. Let's look at *power of acceptance.* In Blacks 6th edition, it says the power of acceptance means the capacity of offeree - that's you again, states that upon acceptance of terms of offer it creates a binding contract. So, if I accept your offer with a conditional acceptance, then place my own terms upon which I accept your offer, then we now have a binding contract even though I have modified the conditions. The offeror must now come back with a rebuttal to prove my terms and conditions are in error.

Now the other party has to deal with the new conditions. And it does not matter what those terms are, they must deal with them. This is very powerful if you learn to use it wisely. You see, first you have accepted the first offer so there is nothing they can do about it. There is no controversy anymore. It is gone unless you argue or ignore. If they cannot rebut your conditions or ignore them, then you are in the driver's seat.

The public system is what we all use when we run to the lawyers and the courts. The private system can be used the same way by you. First some basics. A contract is an agreement between two or more persons which creates an obligation to do or not to do a particular thing. Its essential segments include competent parties, subject matter, a legal consideration, mutuality of agreement, mutuality of obligation, and signatures. First there is an *offer* which is to bring some deal to someone or present for acceptance or rejection. Offer and acceptance are the two elements which constitute mutual assent, a requirement of the contract.

The *Offeree* in contract terms is the person to whom an offer is made by the *offeror*. *Accept* means to approve what has been offered, acknowledged by signature and thus promise to do what is accepted in the contract, or bill of exchange. And finally you accept the conditions by tacit agreement if you do nothing. Now let us look into the use of this when you receive a bill.

This is written by a famous Canadian proponent of this method **Eldon Warman** on **website www.detaxcanada.org**:

"Some of you will get this; others will not, for those that do, kudos to you, help your brothers who do not! See, I'm different than most people, because I don't care what the price of gas is! In fact, I don't care what they charge for anything, and you shouldn't either!!!!! Do you really want to get these guys? How about, get them, help them and make a difference not only in your life, but in everybody else's too??? HERE'S HOW!!!!

See, every transaction that you people do every day, whether it's buying gas or gum, YOU DO WRONG! You do it wrong because you do not understand CREDITOR, DEBTOR relationships, OFFER and ACCEPTANCE, and even MONEY itself!

All of you guys to a one, at every till you go to, do it wrong, you set your property (purchase) down on the counter and the clerk rings it in and then announces the amount of the charge. Then what do you do? You reach into your pocket, wallet or purse and volunteer payment..........without ever having been obligated to do so!!!!!!!! Yeah that's right, you heard me right!

You're missing something so elemental that it boggles the mind! You walk out of the store bitching about the price......of gas.....or whatever; AND YOU WERE NEVER EVEN BILLED FOR IT! YOU WERE NEVER PRESENTED WITH THE BILL! They told you what the charge was, they always do, but they never give you the BILL!

See, quite simply, without a BILL, there is no obligation! PERIOD! So you say, "How does this help me?" How can this be? Why would they leave out something like that if it was important? Won't they just give me a BILL and what then? Listen up!

THEY CAN'T CREATE A BILL! THEY WILL NOT DO IT,.....AND, IF THEY DO, THAT'S PERFECT!!!!! THAT'S WHAT YOU WANT!

There are many reasons for this ranging from the fact our company CANADA is insolvent, operating in receivership, and the crap that you call money that you traded your sweat for is really a debt instrument!!! But I don't want you fret about any that right now for the purpose of this essay.

First of all, you need to know what a BILL is, and what a bill is NOT! An INVOICE, or STATEMENT OF ACCOUNT is NOT a BILL! Do they say BILL on them? NO! They say INVOICE, or STATEMENT OF ACCOUNT or CHARGE, not BILL! Now an INVOICE, or STATEMENT OF ACCOUNT simply describes what was sold, how much it was sold for. It does the same the clerk does, it simply announces what the charge is, BUT IT IS NOT THE CHARGE!

A bill is: An unconditional ORDER in writing, addressed by one person to another, signed by the person giving it, requiring the person to whom it is addressed to pay, on demand or at a fixed or determinable future time, a sum certain in money to or to the order of a specified person or bearer.

Okay, you got that? Are you ready for the bomb? The reason they don't give you a bill, is that if they present you with a BILL, then you can settle with your signature, and a notation on the bill - "Consumer Purchase"!

Did you get that? If they give you a bill, and even if they fail to complete it, or sign it, you can simply accept it, sign it and give it back to them! Don't believe? Check out the so-called 'laws' of CANADA. In the BILLS OF EXCHANGE ACT

57. (1) Every party whose signature appears on a bill is, in the absence of evidence to the contrary, deemed to have become a party thereto for value.

Consumer Bill to be marked 190. (1) Every consumer bill or consumer note shall be prominently and legibly marked on its face with the words **"Consumer Purchase"** before or at the time when the instrument is signed by the purchaser or by any person signing to accommodate the purchaser.

Effects where not marked (2) A consumer bill or consumer note that is not marked as required by this section is void, except in the hands of a holder in due course without notice that the bill or note is a consumer bill or consumer note or except as against a drawee without that notice.
R.S., c. 4(1st Supp.), s. 1.

I think you should be getting very excited by now! This is telling you that if you sign the bill, you gave it value! It's telling you that your signature IS the money! BY signing the bill, and returning it to them, you gave them value! It says, "In absence of evidence to the contrary". Where is that going to come from?

Who on planet earth can provide proof positive that your signature has no value? That's actually a slander of credit because your signature DOES have value, PERIOD! Nobody can provide proof to the contrary, EVER! The bank accepted your signature as having value on your mortgage, did they not? They accepted your signature as having value on your car loan, did they not? They let you take the car didn't they? What does everybody want from you all the time? Your signature!!!!

Okay, I know that you have more questions, I know you're wondering, and especially those of you who are merchants yourself, "If I just give them my signature on the Bill, how do they get their money?"

Well first let's look at the definition of MONEY.........as defined by the laws of CANADA!

Financial Administration Act
Definition for: Money: Money includes any negotiable instrument.
Definition for: Negotiable instrument: Negotiable instrument includes any cheque, draft, traveler's cheque, bill of exchange, postal note, money order, postal remittance and any other similar instrument;

From this you can see that money is very obviously more than what YOU thought it was. I have underlined bill of exchange in the above because that's what you'll settle with if they give you a bill, or if they do not!

What if they refuse to provide a bill? Then they have admitted to no obligation!

If they refuse to give you a bill, you can now take out a blank piece of paper, fill it out as a bill with them as drawer and payee, leave the signature line of the drawer blank so they can sign it if they so choose, write accepted for value and returned for full settlement across its face at an angle, sign and date it at that same angle and hand it to them and leave, they are paid! You gave them an asset item. If they threaten to call the police, YOU CALL THE POLICE! Claim the cop as your witness in his capacity as PEACE OFFICER, and explain the facts, that you have presented them with MONEY in accordance with the laws of CANADA, that they have refused to provide you with a bill. STAND YOUR GROUND! Do not accept any unsubstantiated legal opinions from the cop, HE DOESN'T HAVE A LICENSE TO PRACTICE LAW!!!! If they give you a bill and you accept it, sign it and return it to them for settlement, and they refuse to settle, they are admitting that their offer had no value and have slandered your credit!

I know that your minds are full of questions right now, many of you even thinking that this has to be fraudulent, or a loophole that they will invariably plug! My answer to that is NOPE! I have studied this for ten years now and have done it with nearly everything. It works, and is quite real and very lawful and they cannot plug it up! You merchants out there are still wondering how to get cash out of this and believe me, there are ways, just too much information to go into here for the purpose of this essay.

But just imagine that I gave you a check and you took it to the bank, the bank took the check and then came back and told you that it wasn't worth anything, but kept the check!!!! Can you now come back to me and accuse me of not paying you? NO! You accepted heresay at the bank, you did not put them to the proof of it and in essence forgave the debt at your end! What you do with your fiduciary is your problem, not mine! The oil company is the same, they can't return it to you as that is evidence of dishonour which discharges an obligation, "refusal of tender of payment discharges an obligation". And they can't prove you didn't give them value because of the laws of the Canada!

Again, there are a myriad of reasons for all of this, more than what could be explained here. In your case, the bank won't tell you anything because you are operating at the bank as debtor because you begged for an account (applied) when in fact, they were making an offer that you should have accepted. Then you accepted a copy of the agreement allowing them to keep the top blue ink copy, in essence making yourself the debtor and are thusly being treated as a debtor, and so on, and so on! The people don't understand creditor/debtor relationships, "My people are being destroyed for lack of knowledge"

I encourage you not to accept anybody's unsubstantiated opinions on this, hell, don't believe me!

Go find out for yourself! Learn and understand that our company CANADA is in bankruptcy re-organization, it's broke! The stuff you call money is monopoly money, it represents debt, the OPPOSITE OF MONEY! We create all value, all of the value comes from us and our signatures, pledges, promises etc. Because of the bankruptcy, money is no longer backed by gold, it's backed by you and me! YOU ARE THE BANK IN FACT!!!!!!!!!!

If this all seems like a lot of effort to you, too complicated, too controversial, or whatever else you might be thinking. Then you're not seeing the big picture and you're not seeing the possibilities. Think of this, think of going through this one time, and maybe even having a hell of a time with it!? But imagine having never having to worry about the price of gas again as from now on, you pay for yours with your signature!!!!!!!!!!!!!!!

Just think of learning to understand this process and apply it to your mortgage and everything else!!! Imagine the freedom! It is yours, and it is within your grasp! You can learn and understand this; you're not stupid are you?

I see people everyday turn their nose up at this and walk away, maybe working for the rest of your life and giving it away for free is easier? I watch you people every day, you all walk to the till like sheep for the shearing, doing and believing because that's all you have ever known and what you saw everybody else doing. But are you a lemming, or a man/woman? Do you think that at some magical point in the future the price of gas is going to go down? That things are going to get better?

Whatever your thoughts are, you have to agree that they never give you a bill, and hopefully that starts you asking questions that you'll find the true answers to. One thing that I will tell you that is a key to your success, is NOT to accept unsubstantiated opinions from anybody, especially lawyers, they have sworn an oath of secrecy not to reveal much of what I have told you here, so if they tell you something contrary to what I've told you here, demand that they provide you a certified copy the law, code, rule or statute that they are relying upon along with a copy of their bar card and number and sign it! I guarantee all you'll see of them is heels and elbows! God Bless brothers and sisters, go get em!"

Eldon further explains:

"Firstly I'd like to point out an omission in that essay on Bills of Exchange and that this a Bill should have the words "Consumer Purchase" written on its face as well. The section of the act that is being referred to regarding the acceptance of the BOE, I interpret like this. If "I" give you a cheque (payor or drawer of the promissory note) and you take it to my bank and the bank dishonours, you cannot scream at the bank and sue the bank for not honouring the cheque. Indeed, the Bills of Exchange Act says that the payee's (you – one who is paid by the BOE) recourse is not against drawee (bank), but against drawer (me), so you'd come back to me and inform me that the bank did not honour the cheque, and of course that's how it's done.

So now that makes sense, "the bill of itself does not render the drawee liable on the bill". So, what does? **<u>My contract with the drawee!!!!</u>** If you bring the dishonoured check to me, I settle with you, and then I go and scream at the bank for breaching their fiduciary duties and our agreement by not honouring the check! I've discussed this at length with many other like-minded people for years and there is still dissension on this point. Does one need to obtain an agreement with the Secretary of the Treasury prior to writing these? Yes or no? I think that the answer is a bit of both because when you sign a promissory note at the bank for an alleged loan you are accessing this account and the bank draws on it, but that is the bank and not you directly. The bank obviously has an agreement with the treasury for this to occur. Though, the BILL still is a valuable negotiable instrument, notwithstanding your not having direct agreement with the Secretary of Treasury.

Also, the vendor can write it off and get the tax credit and their ignorance on how to negotiate the item is really not your problem! In other words if I have been paying my employees with cash and then one day give them a cheque and they have not seen one before and don't how to negotiate it, they cannot come back to me and claim that I did not pay them. I did pay them, their lack of knowledge is their problem, and they can't turn it into my problem!

The fact is, that via the sin application, you granted Power of Attorney to the government to access that account in exchange for benefits, and I think that probably has to be rectified. They require the access in order to provide you with the benefits that you have requested, but you have also granted them the POA, which as we both well know, they translate to ownership of YOU!

While my essay was intended to wake up a few more people and hopefully royally stir the pot, I hope that anybody who desires to pursue this does their research prior to taking action. I believe that someone knowledgeable in court procedure could force this through. Though generally it's going to be an uphill battle, and I believe is NOT the correct way to do it. The banks simply will not allow it happen too many times as their very existence is in the balance!

If you are a bit of a greenhorn at this, then you needs to do much more study before attempting this. I've attached the UNCITRAL, (International bills of exchange) which is far easier to understand than the BOE Act of Canada, for study purposes."

"Further understand that this is drawn on the treasury. Because of the bankruptcy, everything comes from the treasury! The Secretary of the Treasury of the Province is in fact the drawee. The province holds the security. While they hold the title as trustee, they cannot cloud the title or encumber it anyway nor are they holder in due course. But they have issued "title insurance" on it thereby making "best use" of your property until you come along and declare best right and interest or take it out of the warehouse. The title insurance has insured it for potential future earnings, losses etc. so that by the time you are eighteen you are covered for anything that you could ever do several times over, as they have underwritten it again and again and again.

Your signature IS the money, PERIOD! Section 57(1) BOE, you sign it, you give it value. I get this all of the time by people asking how to monetize them. The fact is that they are already money as defined by the laws of CANADA (Financial Administration Act definitions). They are money in fact, the problem is that the banks don't want this to happen. As I have said, their very existence is in the balance. Then to start with, nobody has a bank account where they could enforce the bank into negotiating one of these things because when you went to the bank to open the account, you went to a **business** making offers, i.e. accounts. Then, you sat down and they gave you an APPLICATION!!! You just got switched from the creditor to the debtor! You are now begging for something that they offered rather than accepting their offer. Then, to compound things, their APPLICATION was chock full of THEIR terms which everybody accepted verbatim without negotiating one single item, which they signed and then accepted a **copy,** leaving the top blue ink original with the bank. They're debtor, debtor, debtor!!!! Last but not least they opened a "retail deposit account" rather than a "personal deposit account" (As defined in the bank act as "For purposes **other than business**")

See, the point is that nobody is in a position of creditor in the first place, everybody acts all the time as the debtor. This is so entrenched in our society that people think you mad if you attempt to assert your rights as the creditor! It's absurd! Anyway, if one reads about the 'allonge' and understands it fully, you see that there can be a second item endorsed specially with the words 'aval', or 'as good as aval' attached to the bill. This is the guarantee/warranty! It is the WARRANT FOR PAYMENT. The BOE act says very little about it, but it is explained better in UNCITRAL, section 46, I think?

Anyway, if think about it, where does the note that you sign at the bank for a loan draw on? The treasury! The bank has no money. There is no money! They are bankrupt, and there are laws in place that prohibit the bank from lending other depositors money or even their own money! So it has to come from you! It is your note that funds the entire thing! Always!"

Again tread lightly here as this truth is also evolving out of the swamps filled with Strawman Eaters! If you wish to do further in-depth study of how the Bill of Exchange functions, go to http://laws.justice.gc.ca/en/B-4/index.html

For reference it is also important to understand the UNITED NATIONS Convention on International Bills of Exchange and International Promissory Notes, 1988

Honour Or Dishonour, To Fight Or Not To Fight

The point of this chapter has been to simply show the shifting attention of the Earthling forcing disclosure that has been accelerating. It is about demanding knowledge about the Strawman and the Good Faith and Credit Trust. The Internet is filled with those warriors who are attempting to gain access to the good faith and credit by some means. The rules of the establishment are not simple to penetrate and the process has eliminated common law to superimpose the Laws of Admiralty. With the religious-spiritual shift, that is a personal one private one but the commercial one of public to private transition is not so simple as people must engage in commerce in some way through the banking system, which ironically is private. As such, the rules of penetrating the Strawman veil are not clear and these processes of Setoff, redemption, Accept For value are not clearly defined. They become a hit and miss process as those who administer it are blind and those who control it simply do jobs or are under strict non disclosures. And so one who attempts this can be the one to be deemed fraud and a rebel to the system immediately charged with veracious litigation attempting to defraud the "system". It is because that is the way it has been implemented, and that is the way the majority have accepted it.

But that, as we has seen, is changing rapidly. So again the purpose here is not to present this for others to try, but to be aware that something is amiss and the Strawman

Revolution gathers momentum everywhere. In the following chapters, it will become clear that there are major waves building.

There has been much information about how the 14th Amendment set the means to create the Strawman. We have detailed the process that the nations such as the US were effectively conquered to place it under receivership of PLANET EARTH. Now let us look at a large organized group in the United States that is also wise to this and is taking measures to "restore the republic".

43

THE NEW REPUBLIC OF THE UNITED STATES

The Restoration Of The Republic

One of the enlightened groups that is leading the shift to sovereignty in the United state is the Republic For The United States led by James Timothy Turner, President of the Republic. at ***http://www.republicfortheunitedstates.org/*** The contacts are extensive in that they have placed a republic senator and administrative staff in each of the 50 states ready to assume their positions. For example if you go to ***http://republicofmissouri.org/officials.html*** you will see the Acting Governor, Lieutenant Governor, Missouri Senators, US Senator, US and Missouri Representatives, Administrator and Treasurer listed here. These are by no means low profile people and they have all joined from all walks of life to further the cause of the restoration of the Republic. For example, the US Senator Mark Hafner explains how he unknowingly made corporate slaves out of his children through the registration of the birth certificate. It is well worth listen simply to understand this is not a Strawman fairy tale. You can find this presentation on YouTube at ***http://www.youtube.com/watch?v=1vXgUBxqBQI***

In an address by Tim Turner, he explains:

The year 1776 marked America's victory in the war for independence. The lawful right to re-inhabit is inherent in The Declaration of Independence circa 1776. The Declaration, one of our founding documents, declares our right to change, alter or abolish any system of government that we believe is contrary to the safety and security of the American people.

In concern for all of humanity, "We the People" re-inhabited our lawful de jure (meaning "by right of legal establishment") government on March 30, 2010, by serving notice on the de facto corporation, known as the "UNITED STATES". (USC 28 Section 3002, No. 15(a) "United States" means a Federal Corporation.) The United States was incorporated February 21, 1871 (16 Stat. 419, Chap. 62, 41st Congress, 3rd Session), the purpose being "an Act to provide a Government for the District of Columbia, reorganized June 8th, 1878, (20 Stat. 102, Chapter 180, 45th Congress, 2nd Session) as "an Act providing a permanent form of government for the District of Columbia" aka US Inc. Uniform

Commercial Code, UCC9-307 (h) states "Location of United States. The United States is located in the District of Columbia. A lawful grand jury in each of the fifty republics created a new Declaration of Independence that was lawfully served on the corporate UNITED STATES informing them that the original de jure government was restored. We have claimed our right to exist as a free and independent people on our land, thus exercising our God-given unalienable rights as defined in our Constitution and the Bill of Rights.

On July 21, 2010 "We the People" of the de jure government proclaimed worldwide and made our "Declaration of Sovereignty for the Republic for the united States of America" to The Hague (a.k.a. the International Court of Justice), the Universal Postal Union (UPU) and the United Nations (UN). On September 23, 2010, the first session of congress was convened by the united free Republics of the re-inhabited united States of America. The seating of the Executive, Legislative and Judicial branches of the Republic government were successfully established. This was completed by more than the required two-thirds majority vote of "We the People" on the land of the independent Republics. Delegates from more than 42 free Republics (States) attended, and officers for all three branches of our government have been officially sworn into office, lawfully electing interim President James Timothy Turner and interim Vice President Charles Eugene Wright, along with other established cabinet members with a presiding majority vote of 94% approval. Thus, the Republic government is officially re-inhabited and staffed for the first time since 1868 by the will of "We the People".

The de facto UNITED STATES CORPORATION was unlawfully established by the forty-first congress in 1871 by deceptive means and without proper consent from "We the People". The American people were placed under involuntary servitude by a "Legal" system of laws that have continually violated the "Constitution for the united States of America", "Bill of Rights" and the "Declaration of Independence". The corporate constitution was changed from the original form, wherein Amendments were unlawfully added and removed without the people's consent. Since 1871, the abuses of this corporation upon both the international community as well as the American people are inestimable and unconscionable. De facto Congress has repeatedly violated their Oaths of Office, fiduciary responsibilities, and in many cases, committed treasonous acts against "We the People" of the united States of America and the world.

We humbly come forward apologizing for the numerous atrocities we have unknowingly allowed the U.S. CORPORATION to carry out upon the international community. It is our mission to establish the American image of truth, honesty, integrity and honor around the world. Our plan is to rebuild our economy and support other economies around the world, fulfilling humanitarian needs. We will allow our military to withdraw from unnecessary conflicts around the world and promote world peace and prosperity. We intend to follow God the Creator's command to feed the hungry, clothe the naked, and care for the sick, irrespective of creed, religion or race. There is no law against these things.

We are calling on the support of all Nations around the world to help us end the tyranny that has been perpetrated by the unlawful actions of the UNITED STATES corporate government. We shall achieve this goal PEACEFULLY AND LAWFULLY, with boldness, integrity and truth, so help us God.

The United States exists in two forms: The original United States that was in operation until 1860; a collection of sovereign Republics in the union. Under the original Constitution the States controlled the Federal Government; the Federal Government did not control the States and had very little authority.

The original United States has been usurped by a separate and different UNITED STATES formed in 1871, which only controls the District of Columbia and its territories, and which is actually a corporation (the UNITED STATES CORPORATION) that acts as our current government. The United States Corporation operates under Corporate/Commercial/Public Law rather than Common/Private Law.

The original Constitution was never removed; it has simply been dormant since 1871. It is still intact to this day. This fact was made clear by Supreme Court Justice Marshall Harlan (Downes v. Bidwell, 182, U.S. 244 1901) by giving the following dissenting opinion: "Two national governments exist; one to be maintained under the Constitution, with all its restrictions; the other to be maintained by Congress outside and Independently of that Instrument."

The Restore America Plan reclaimed the De Jure institutions of government of the 50 State Republics in order to restore Common Law that represents the voice of the people and ends Corporate Law that ignores the voice of the people while operating under Maritime/Admiralty/International Law. This occurred when warrants were delivered to all 50 Governors on March 30, 2010.

The rewritten Constitution of the UNITED STATES CORPORATION bypasses the original Constitution for the United States of America, which explains why our Congressmen and Senators don't abide by it, and the President can write Executive Orders to do whatever he/she wants. They are following corporate laws that completely strip sovereigns of their God given unalienable rights. Corporate/Commercial/Public Law is not sovereign (private), as it is an agreement between two or more parties under contract. Common Law (which sovereigns operate under) is not Commercial Law; it is personal and private.

To understand this document, you need to understand some basic terms. Visit www.usavsus.info for complete understanding of the difference between a republic and a democracy as it affects every individual. This is an extensive web site that does not lack details.

The basic terms are:
De Jure – Existing by right or according to law; original, lawful. Common Law operates under De Jure terms.
De Facto – In practice but not necessarily ordained by law; in fact, in reality. Corporate Law operates under De Facto terms.
Sovereign – A real person. Sovereigns can own property while Citizens/Subjects cannot. According to the original Constitution, all government comes from the Sovereign Individual. Without the Sovereign Individual, there is no government.
U.S. Citizen/Subject – A corporate fictitious entity that merely represents the real person. It acts as a "Strawman." [To call oneself a "sovereign citizen" or "sovereign subject" is an oxymoron, since "sovereign" and "citizen/subject" are mutually exclusive of

each other.] When asked if you are a "U.S. Citizen" on corporate legal documents, if you check "yes," you agree to the terms of Corporate Law and unknowingly relinquish your sovereign status and transfer all of your rights to the UNITED STATES CORPORATION since you are now under contract.

Corporation – A non-human, fictitious entity. Corporate fictitious entities are denoted in all caps. This includes the names of Citizens/Subjects. Your fictitious "Strawman" entity is addressed in all caps, i.e. JOHN SMITH, rather than John Smith.

Common Law – God's law. Common Law and the system of De Jure Juries apply to sovereigns in disputes. In Common Law, contracts must be entered into knowingly, voluntarily, and intentionally.

Admiralty/Maritime Law/International Law – The King's law. Deals with criminal acts that only apply to international contracts. Under this law, the people are no longer sovereign. The Uniform Commercial Code (UCC) that the United States practices is based on Admiralty Law. Under the UCC, contracts do not have to be entered into knowingly. Simple agreements can be binding, and as long as you exercise the benefits of that "agreement," you must meet the obligations associated with those benefits. If you accept the benefit offered by the government, then you MUST follow, to the letter, each and every statute involved with that benefit. That "benefit" is the Federal Reserve Notes (U.S. dollars). By paying for things with U.S. dollars you are unknowingly giving up all of your Constitutional rights and are legally obligated to follow all of the UCC statues. But you were NEVER told this.

Lawful – A term used in Common Law.

Legal – A term used in the UCC which applies to Corporate Law.

The Constitution Was Usurped By The Corporation

Basic premises are adhered to by the people in the movement and the people in the Sovereign movement. The Government is a Corporation actually functioning as the Federal Government. Thus it does not have to follow the constitution. Also it does not matter if Obama is not a natural born citizen since it is a corporation he is the head of. The corporation gets the permission of the people to reign over them by deceit. This is done by wording in the Birth Certificates, Social Security Cards, driving Licenses, IRS forms, Marriage Licenses and other documents. They always refer to the "person" in all capital letters. This means the name represents a corporate entity. This is how the corporation courts get jurisdiction over you. Their courts do not fly the "real" American flag. They use the military or admiralty flag. For a discourse on this try this website: **www.usavsus.info**.

What the theory goes like is this: When you enter a US Courtroom there is a military or admiralty flag flying. The US Military does not have the protection of the constitution, neither does this apply to admiralty laws with ships at sea. When you enter a court room and cross through that little wooden gate they have and go to the area where the plaintiff (prosecutor) and defendant sit along with judge, court reporter, you are entering a "ship" or a foreign country as evidenced by the admiralty or military flag flying thus the constitution has no applicability and you are under equity law not common law. The flaw with their scheme is that there is no full disclosure to the people about any of this. This is brief over simplified synopsis of the scam run by the federal corporation.

The Timeline Leading To The Current United States.

You will have read this in many ways by now but here is the version published by these people:

- In 1788 (January 1), The United States was officially bankrupt.
- In 1790 (August 4), Article One of the U.S. Statues at Large, pages 138-178, abolished the States of the Republic and created Federal Districts. In the same year, the former States of the Republic reorganized as Corporations and their legislatures wrote new State Constitutions, absent defined boundaries, which they presented to the people of each state for a vote...the new State Constitutions fraudulently made the people "Citizens" of the new Corporate States. A Citizen is also defined as a "corporate fiction."
- In 1845, Congress passed legislation that would ultimately allow Common Law to be usurped by Admiralty Law. www.barefootsworld.net/admiralty.html explains this change. The yellow fringe placed at the bottom of court flags shows this is still true. Before 1845, Americans were considered sovereign individuals who governed themselves under Common Law.
- In 1860 – Congress was adjourned Sine Die – Lincoln could not legally reconvene Congress.
- In 1861, President Lincoln declared a National Emergency and Martial Law, which gave the President unprecedented powers and removed it from the other branches. This has NEVER been reversed.
- In 1863, the Lieber Code was established taking away your property and your rights.
- From 1864-1867, Several Reconstruction Acts were passed forcing the states to ratify the 14th Amendment, which made everyone slaves.
- In 1865, the capital was moved to Washington, D.C., a separate country – not a part of the United States of America.
- In 1871, The United States became a Corporation with a new constitution and a new corporate government, and the original constitutional government was vacated to become dormant, but it was never terminated. The new constitution had to be ratified by the people according to the original constitution, but it never was. The whole process occurred behind closed doors. The people are the source of financing for this new government.
- In 1917, the Trading with the Enemy Act (TWEA) was passed. This insightful video from [link to movielocker.com/4084)] states the following: "This act was implemented to deal with the countries we were at war with during World War I. It gave the President and the Alien Property Custodian the right to seize the assets of the people included in this act and if they wanted to do business in this country they could apply for a license to do so. By 1921, the Federal Reserve Bank (the trustee for the Alien Property Custodian) held over $700,000,000 in trust." Understand that this trust was based on our assets, not theirs.
- In 1933, 48 Stat 1, of the TWEA was amended to include the United States Person because they wanted to take our gold away. Executive Order 6102 was created to make it illegal for a U.S. Citizen to own gold. In order for the Government to take our gold away and violate our Constitutional rights, we were reclassified as ENEMY COMBATANTS."
- In 1933, there was a second United States bankruptcy. In the first bankruptcy the United States collateralized all public lands. In the 1933 bankruptcy, the U.S.

government collateralized the private lands of the people (a lien) – they borrowed money against our private lands. They were then mortgaged. That is why we pay property taxes.

From a speech in Congress in The Bankruptcy of the United States Congressional Record, March 17, 1993, Vol. 33, page H-1303, Speaker Representative James Trafficant Jr. (Ohio) addressing the House states:

"...It is an established fact that the United States Federal Government has been dissolved by the Emergency Banking Act, March 9, 1933, 48 Stat. 1, Public Law 89-719; declared by President Roosevelt, being bankrupt and insolvent. H.J.R. 192, 73rd Congress m session June 5, 1933 – Joint Resolution To Suspend The Gold Standard and Abrogate The Gold Clause dissolved the Sovereign Authority of the United States and the official capacities of all United States Governmental Offices, Officers, and Departments and is further evidence that the United States Federal Government exists today in name only.

The receivers of the United States Bankruptcy are the International Bankers, via the United Nations, the World Bank and the International Monetary Fund. All United States Offices, Officials, and Departments are now operating within a de facto status in name only under Emergency War Powers. With the Constitutional Republican form of Government now dissolved, the receivers of the Bankruptcy have adopted a new form of government for the United States. This new form of government is known as a Democracy, being an established Socialist/Communist order under a new governor for America. This act was instituted and established by transferring and/or placing the Office of the Secretary of Treasury to that of the Governor of the International Monetary Fund. Public Law 94-564, page 8, Section H.R. 13955 reads in part: "The U.S. Secretary of Treasury receives no compensation for representing the United States...

Prior to 1913, most Americans owned clear, allodial title to property, free and clear of any liens of mortgages until the Federal Reserve Act (1913) "Hypothecated" all property within the Federal United States to the Board of Governors of the Federal Reserve, in which the Trustees (stockholders) held legal title. The U.S. Citizen (tenant, franchisee) was registered as a "beneficiary" of the trust via his/her birth certificate. In 1933, the Federal United States hypothecated all of the present and future properties, assets, and labor of their "subjects," the 14th Amendment U.S. Citizen to the Federal Reserve System. In return, the Federal Reserve System agreed to extend the federal United States Corporation all of the credit "money substitute" it needed.

Like any debtor, the Federal United States government had to assign collateral and security to their creditors as a condition of the loan. Since the Federal United States didn't have any assets, they assigned the private property of their "economic slaves," the U.S. Citizens, as collateral against the federal debt. They also pledged the unincorporated federal territories, national parks, forests, birth certificates, and nonprofit organizations as collateral against the federal debt. All has already been transferred as payment to the international bankers.

Unwittingly, America has returned to its pre-American Revolution feudal roots whereby all land is held by a sovereign and the common people had no rights to hold allodial title to property. Once again, We the People are the tenants and sharecroppers renting our own property from a Sovereign in the guise of the Federal Reserve Bank. We the People have exchanged one master for another.

In 1944, Washington D.C. was deeded to the International Monetary Fund (IMF) by the Breton Woods Agreement. The IMF is made up of wealthy people that own most of the banking industries of the world. It is an organized group of bankers that have taken control of most governments of the world so the bankers run the world. Congress, the IRS, and the President work for the IMF. The IRS is not a U.S. government agency. It is an agency of the IMF. (Diversified Metal Products v. IRS et al. CV-93-405E-EJE U.S.D.C.D.I., Public Law 94-564, Senate Report 94-1148 pg. 5967, Reorganization Plan No. 26, Public Law 102-391.)

Repairing The Country

As stated by Turner: "The Supreme Court has said the De Jure Government offices still exist but the people have failed to occupy them. Remember Downs v. Bidwell and the dissenting opinion of Justice Marshall Harlan? He said that two national governments exist; one to be maintained under the Constitution, with all its restrictions. This is one that We the people need to force our elected public officials to occupy – De Jure rule. We need to change that by organizing Grand Juries and putting our officials back under De jure rule and out of the Corporate (or Military) Rule that they are currently operating under.

Our elected officials will then have to operate under the limits of their Oath of office to uphold the U.S. and State Constitutions, circa 1860. When they violate the Oath it's a capital crime. The reason we go back to 1860 is because that is the last time we had lawful laws in this country. Where do the people get their power to convene a Grand Jury? The Magna Carta, 1215.

Our Founding Fathers looked back to history for precedent when they decided they wanted to change their government. What they found was the Magna Carta Liberatum, the Great Charter of Freedoms. It set a precedent that changed the face of England forever, by establishing that the King was not above the law.

King John of England signed the Magna Carta after immense pressure from the Church and his barons (the people). The King often lived above the law, violating both Feudal and Common Law, and was heavily criticized for his foreign policy and actions in England. The Barons, with the support of the Church, pressured King John to spell out a list of their rights and guarantee that those rights would be enforced. The Barons provided a draft, and after some negotiation, King John put his seal to the Magna Carta in Runnymede, in June of 1215.

Section 61 set rules for establishing the Grand Jury. It states: Since we have granted all these things for God, for the better ordering of our kingdom, and to allay the discord that has arisen between us and our barons (people), and since we desire that they shall be enjoyed in their entirety, with lasting strength, forever, we give and grant to the barons the following security: The barons shall elect twenty-five of their number to keep, and cause to be observed with all their might, the peace and liberties granted and confirmed to them by this charter. If we, our chief justice, our officials, or any of our servants *offend in any respect against any man, or transgress any of the articles of the peace or of this security, and the offense is made known to four of the said twenty-five barons, they shall come to us."*

Re-inhabiting The Republic

It has been restored circa 1791 Constitutional Law Over the course of the last 150 years, the United States have been ruled by Executive Orders rather than Constitutional Law. However, July 21, 2010, that circumvention of the Constitution was changed and forever abolished. The re-inhabited Republic for the united States of America is now has been restored circa to 1791 Constitutional Law. The year 1776 marked America's victory in the War for Independence. The lawful right to re-inhabit is inherent in The Declaration of Independence circa 1776. The Declaration, one of our founding documents, declares our right to change, alter or abolish any system of government that we believe is contrary to the safety and security of the American people. In concern for all of humanity, "We the People" re-inhabited our lawful de jure (meaning "by right of lawful establishment") government July 21, 2010. When the Southern states walked out of Congress on March 27, 1861, the quorum to conduct business under the Constitution was lost.

The only votes that Congress could lawfully take, under Parliamentary Law, were those to set the time to reconvene, take a vote to get a quorum and vote to adjourn and set a date, time, and place to reconvene at a later time, but instead, Congress abandoned the House and Senate without setting a date to reconvene. Under the parliamentary law of Congress, when this happened, Congress became *sine die* (pronounced see-na dee-a; literally "`without day") and thus when Congress adjourned *sine die*, it ceased to exist as a lawful deliberative body, and the only lawful, constitutional power that could declare war was no longer lawful, or in session.

The Southern states, by virtue of their secession from the Union, also ceased to exist *sine die*, and some state legislatures in the Northern bloc also adjourned sine die, and thus, all the states which were parties to creating the Constitution ceased to exist. President Lincoln executed the first executive order written by any President on April 15, 1861, Executive Order 1, and the nation has been ruled by the President under executive order ever since. When Congress eventually did reconvene, it was reconvened under the military authority of the Commander-in-Chief and not by Rules of Order for Parliamentary bodies or by Constitutional Law, placing the American people under martial rule ever since that national emergency declared by President Lincoln. The Constitution for the United States of America temporarily ceased to be the law of the land, and the President, Congress, and the Courts unlawfully presumed that they were free to remake the nation in their own image; whereas, lawfully, no constitutional provisions were in place which afforded power to any of the actions that were taken and presumed to place the nation under the new form of control.

President Lincoln knew that he had no authority to issue any executive order, and thus he commissioned General Orders No. 100 (April 24, 1863) as a special field code to govern his actions under martial law, and which justified the seizure of power, which extended the laws of the District of Columbia, and which fictionally implemented the provisions of Article I, Section 8, Clauses 17-18 of the Constitution beyond the boundaries of Washington, D.C. and into the several states. General Orders No. 100, also called the Lieber Instructions and the Lieber Code, extended The Laws of War and International Law onto American soil, and the United States government became the presumed conqueror of the people and the land.

Martial rule was kept secret and has never ended, the nation has been ruled under Military Law by the Commander-of-Chief of that military; the President, under his assumed executive powers and according to his executive orders. Constitutional law under the original Constitution is enforced only as a matter of keeping the public peace under the provisions of General Orders No. 100 under martial rule. Under Martial Law, title is a mere fiction, since all property belongs to the military except for that property which the Commander-in-Chief may, in his benevolence, exempt from taxation and seizure and upon which he allows the enemy to reside.

President Lincoln was assassinated before he could complete plans for re-establishing Constitutional government in the Southern States and end the martial rule by executive order, and the 14th Article in Amendment to the Constitution created a new citizenship status for the new expanded jurisdiction. New laws for the District of Columbia were established and passed by Congress in 1871, supplanting those established Feb. 27, 1801 and May 3, 1802. The District of Columbia was re-incorporated in 1872, and all states in the Union were reformed as Franchisees of the Federal Corporation so that a new Union of the United States could be created. The key to when the states became Federal Franchisees is related to the date when such states enacted the Field Code in law.

So now you know about the US Corporation and it fraud. Let's talk about how we are now the Republic for the united States of America. On July 21, 2010 "We the People" of the de jure government proclaimed worldwide and made our "Declaration of Sovereignty for the Republic for the united States of America" to The Hague (a.k.a. the International Court of Justice), the Universal Postal Union (UPU) and the United Nations (UN).

On September 23, 2010, the first session of congress was convened by the united free state Republics of the re-inhabited united States of America. The seating of the Executive, Legislative and Judicial branches of the Republic government were successfully established. This was completed by more than the required two-thirds majority vote of "We the People" on the land of the independent free state Republics. Delegates from more than 42 free state Republics attended, and officers for all three branches of our government have been officially sworn into office, lawfully electing interim President James Timothy Turner and interim Vice President Charles Eugene Wright, along with other established cabinet members with a presiding majority vote of 94% approval. Thus, the Republic government is officially re-inhabited and staffed for the first time since 1868 by the will of "We the People".

The de facto UNITED STATES CORPORATION was unlawfully established by the forty-first congress in 1871 by deceptive means and without proper consent from "We the People". The American people were placed under involuntary servitude by a "Legal" system of CORPORATE DEMOCRACY laws that have continually violated the original Republic "Constitution for the united States of America", "Bill of Rights" and the "Declaration of Independence". The corporate constitution was changed from the original form, wherein

Amendments were unlawfully added and removed without the people's consent. Since 1871, the abuses of this corporation upon both the international community as well as the American people are inestimable and unconscionable. De facto Congress has repeatedly violated their Oaths of Office, fiduciary responsibilities, and in many cases, committed treasonous acts against "We the People" of the united States of America and the world.

We humbly come forward apologizing for the numerous atrocities we have unknowingly allowed the U.S. CORPORATION to carry out upon the international community. It is our mission to establish the American image of truth, honesty, integrity and honour around the world. Our plan is to rebuild our economy and support other economies around the world, fulfilling humanitarian needs. We will allow our military to withdraw from unnecessary conflicts around the world and promote world peace and prosperity. We intend to follow God the Creator's command to feed the hungry, clothe the naked, and care for the sick, irrespective of creed, religion or race. There is no law against these things.

We are calling on the support of all Nations around the world to help us end the tyranny that has been perpetrated by the unlawful actions of the UNITED STATES CORPORATE DEMOCRACY government. We shall achieve this goal PEACEFULLY AND LAWFULLY, with boldness, integrity and truth, so help us God.

The United States exists in two forms:

1. The original United States that was in operation until 1860; a collection of sovereign Republics in the union. Under the original Constitution the States controlled the Federal Government; the Federal Government did not control the States and had very little authority.

2. The original United States has been usurped by a separate and different UNITED STATES formed in 1871, which only controls the District of Columbia and its territories, and which is actually a corporation (the UNITED STATES CORPORATION) that acts as our current government. The United States Corporation operates under Corporate/Commercial/Public Law rather than Common/Private Law.

The original Constitution was never removed; it has simply been dormant since 1871. It is still intact to this day. This fact was made clear by Supreme Court Justice Marshall Harlan (Downes v. Bidwell, 182, U.S. 244 1901) by giving the following dissenting opinion: "Two national governments exist; one to be maintained under the Constitution, with all its restrictions; the other to be maintained by Congress outside and Independently of that Instrument."

The Restore America Plan reclaimed the De Jure institutions of government of the 50 State Republics in order to restore Common Law that represents the voice of the people and ends Corporate Law that ignores the voice of the people while operating under Maritime/Admiralty/International Law. This occurred when warrants were delivered to all 50 Governors on March 30, 2010.

The rewritten Constitution of the UNITED STATES CORPORATION bypasses the original Constitution for the United States of America, which explains why our Congressmen and Senators don't abide by it, and the President can write Executive Orders to do whatever he/she wants. They are following corporate laws that completely strip sovereigns of their God given unalienable rights. Corporate/Commercial/Public Law is not sovereign (private), as it is an agreement between two or more parties under contract. Common Law (which sovereigns operate under) is not Commercial Law; it is personal and private.

House Joint Resolution 192 of June 5, 1933
On June 5, 1933, Congress passed House Joint Resolution (HJR 192). HJR 192 was passed to suspend the gold standard and abrogate the gold clause in the national constitution. Since then no one in America has been able to lawfully pay a debt. This resolution declared:

"To assure uniform value to the coins and currencies of the Unites States,
Whereas the holding of or dealing in gold affect public interest, and are therefore subject to proper regulation and restriction; and Whereas the existing emergency has disclosed that provisions of obligations which purport to give the obligee a right to require payment in gold or a particular kind of coin or currency of the United States, or in an amount in money of the United States measured thereby, obstruct the power of the Congress to regulate the value of the money of the United States, and are inconsistent with the declared policy of the Congress to maintain at all times the equal power of every dollar, coined or issued by the United States, in the markets and in the payment of debts,

Now, therefore, be it Resolved by the Senate and House of t Representative of the United States of America in Congress assembled, that
(a) every provision contained in or made with respect to any obligation which purports to give the obligee a right to require payments in gold or a particular kind of coin or currency, or in an amount in money of the United States measured thereby, is declared to be against public policy; and no such provision shall be contained in or made with respect to any obligation hereafter incurred. Every obligation, heretofore or hereafter incurred, whether or not any such provision is contained therein or made with respect thereto, shall be discharged upon payment, dollar for dollar, in any coin or currency which at time of payment is legal tender for public and private debts. Any such provision contained in any law authorizing obligations to be issued by or under authority of the United States, is herby repealed, but the repeal of any such provision shall not invalidate any other provision or authority contained in such law.

(b) As used in this resolution, the term 'obligation' means any obligation (including every obligation of and to the United States, excepting currency) payable in money of the United States; and the term 'coin or currency' means coin or currency of the United States, including Federal Reserve notes and circulating notes of Federal Reserve banks and national banking associations.
Sec. 2 The last sentence of paragraph (1) of subsection (b) of section 43 of the Act entitled 'An Act to relieve the existing national economic emergency by increasing agricultural purchasing power, to raise revenue for extraordinary expenses incurred by reason of such emergency, to provide emergency relief with respect to agricultural indebtedness, to provide for the orderly liquidation of joint-stock land banks, and of other purposes;, approved May 12, 1933, is amended to read as follows:

"All coins and currencies of the United Stated (including Federal Reserve notes and circulating notes of the Federal Reserve banks and national banking associations) heretofore or hereafter coined or issued, shall be legal tender for all debts, public and private, public charges, taxes, duties, and dues, except that gold coins, when below the standard weight and limit of tolerance provided by law for the single piece, shall be legal tender only at valuation in proportion to their actual weight.'

Approved, June 5, 1933, 4:40 p.m. 31 U.S.C.A. 462, 463

House Joint Resolution 192, 73rd Congress, Sess. I, Ch. 48, June 5, 1933 (Public Law No. 10)

Note: "payment of debt" is now against Congressional and "public policy" and henceforth, "Every obligation... Shall be discharged." As a result of HJR 192, and from that day forward (June 5, 1933), no one in this nation has been able to lawfully pay a debt or lawfully own anything. The only thing one can do, is tender in transfer of debts, with the debt being perpetual. The suspension of the gold standard, and prohibition against paying debts, removed the substance for our common law to operate on, and created a void as far as the law is concerned. This substance was replaced with a "PUBLIC NATIONAL CREDIT SYSTEM" where debt is "LEGAL TENDER" money.

HJR 192 was implemented immediately. The day after President Roosevelt signed the resolution, the treasury offered the public new government securities, minus the traditional "payable in gold" clause.

HJR 192 states that one cannot demand a certain form of currency that they want to receive if it is dollar for dollar. If you review the Modern Money Mechanics article you will discover that <u>all currency is your credit</u>! The Federal Reserve calls it "monetized debt."

Was HJR-192 Repealed?

Here is a great article on **House Joint Resolution 192**, which is nothing more than a resolution, and **"Chap. 48, 48 Stat. 112"** in the "Statutes at Large", which is Public Law. Basically, the HJR-192 is not the remedy, however, "Chap. 48, 48 Stat. 112" is!

The United States **Statutes at Large**, typically referred to as the Statutes at Large, **is the permanent collection of all laws and resolutions enacted during each session of Congress**. The Statutes at Large is prepared and published by the Office of the Federal Register (OFR), National Archives and Records Administration (NARA). Every public and private law passed by Congress is published in the Statutes at Large, in order of the date it was enacted into law."

First of all, "HJR-192" is the short name for "House Joint Resolution 192", so let's understand what a "resolution" is. A New Year's resolution applies to you, the one who made it, not to your next door neighbour or anyone else. You're the one who "resolved" to lose weight or quit smoking or exercise more, and your neighbour is not obligated to do what you resolved for yourself. **"HJR-192" is strictly a resolution that applies only to the members of Congress (who "resolved" it) and to its subjects**. It can be modified at anytime by Congress if they so choose, just as you can modify your New Year's resolution if you so choose.

However, modifying a Public Law is a little different matter. **The law in this instance, per the actual "Statutes at Large" books, is identified as: "Chap. 48, 48 Stat. 112"**. The SMU Law Library **contains the very same wording as "HJR-192"; however, one is a resolution and one is a Public Law.**

If I refer to "HJR-192", am I not telling the listener or reader that I am a subject of Congress, and that I am a citizen of the UNITED STATES??? Sorry, but that is the last thing I want to say. **I can, however, say that the Federal Government has placed insufficient amounts of lawful money in general circulation, i.e., gold and silver coinage, thus, forcing me to "discharge" my debts with commercial paper, i.e., putting them off to a future point in time, and restricting my obligation as a sovereign to "pay" a debt.**

I refer to the Federal Government's obligation to me as: "Chap. 48, 48 Stat. 112", not "HJR-192". The Federal Government took away my ability to pay a debt with lawful money, but that doesn't make me a subject of Congress or of the Federal Government, and thus, their resolution does not apply to me. However, **their obligation to me under their Public Law does apply to me because there is insufficient lawful money in general circulation to meet the needs of the people, which includes me**.

When the Federal Government took much of our lawful money out of general circulation in 1933, i.e., gold coins, thus leaving an insufficient amount of lawful money in general circulation to meet the needs of the people, i.e., only silver coins remaining, the Congress was required to give the people a remedy. Public Law: "Chap. 48, 48 Stat. 112" is that remedy. It states that the Federal Government will pay my debts, dollar for dollar. Note: It doesn't say that the government will pay for anything I desire to buy (like a car), only that it will pay my legitimate debts.

Most, if not all, of the State Constitutions require the State to pay its debts in gold and silver coin. By taking away a State Government's ability to comply with its Constitutional mandate of paying its debts in gold and silver coin, the Federal Government involuntarily restricted a State Government's ability to function in a de jure capacity. The de jure States went into suspension after the following four acts were committed: (1) the taking of gold coins out of general circulation in 1933, (2) in 1964, the U. S. Mint ceased minting any more silver coins, (3) in 1968, Silver Certificates could no longer be redeemed for silver, and (4) on August 15, 1971, President Nixon closed the Gold Window, thus stopping the redemption of foreign-held dollars for gold. At that point in time, the U. S. Dollar was backed solely by the full faith and credit of the American people, and the States could no longer function in a de jure capacity while in a state of suspension.

The States went into suspension because the Federal Government involuntarily forced the State to pay its officers, judges, employees, etc. with something other than gold and silver coin, which was required by the State Constitution. This "something other than gold and silver coin" was nothing more than "fiat" money, or script, back by nothing but the labour of the people. Thus, Constitutionally, the States could no longer function in a de jure capacity because it no longer had the ability to pay its debts in the form mandated by its Constitution, i.e., contract with the people.

Since the Federal Government took away the gold coin money in 1933, thus causing the States to suspend operations by preventing them from honouring their obligation to pay their debts in gold and silver coin, then there had to be a remedy. "Chap 48, 48 Stat. 112" is the remedy, not just for the States, but also for the sovereign men and women who created the States. **Until gold and silver coinage is reinstated in sufficient quantities for general circulation, that remedy cannot be repealed. Congress may have repealed some parts of "HJR-192", or even all of it, because "HJR-192" is merely a resolution for Congress and its subjects. However, the true remedy is provided to the people by Public Law: "Chap 48, 48 Stat. 112".**

Until the State Governments come out of suspension, by the Federal Government's placing sufficient quantities of lawful money into general circulation, your remedy, pursuant to "Chap 48, 48 Stat. 112" cannot be repealed and will continue to be there. The remedy of the subjects/citizens found at "HJR-192" might not be there because their remedy is nothing but a resolution, but the remedy of the sovereign found at Public Law: "Chap 48, 48 Stat. 112" will still be there because a sovereign's remedy is Public Law.

If, as many uninformed sovereigns claim, the promise that the Federal Government will pay your debts, dollar for dollar, is no longer valid, then these sovereigns have no basis for claiming their remedy by using the 1099-OID process for the refund of out-of pocket funds expended to pay their debts. Either (1) you believe that the Federal Government repealed your remedy, and therefore, there is no 1099-OID refund process available to you, or (2) you believe the Government has an obligation to pay your debts, dollar for dollar, and therefore, the 1099-OID process for a refund is your remedy and you can use it to recover the funds you expended to take care of your debt obligations. You can't believe your remedy has been repealed, and then try to claim your remedy by asking for a refund using the 1099-OID process.

Now that you understand the difference between a **resolution** and a **Public Law** (and why your remedy was given to you), you may recall how a well-known "patriot attorney" who specializes in tax matters has worked hard to intentionally mislead sovereign men and women into believing that their remedy has been repealed. HOGWASH!!! He's talking about a subject's remedy by resolution, not a sovereign's remedy by Public Law. Please do your homework and think outside the box before disseminating patriot mythology to others, possibly causing them to stumble by your lack of research and knowledge. If you wish to continue arguing this ridiculous allegation without doing your homework, i.e., refusing to spend the time required in studying the monetary system in detail, please do so privately, not on any public forum, so as not to mislead others with such mythology.

Is this a group of fringe radicals trying to create trouble? Check out their story and decide for yourself.

Now let us look at another worldwide move to dismantle the financial hierarchy and create a new one.

44

THE NATIONAL ECONOMIC AND STABILIZATION ACT

What Is NESARA?

The acronym NESARA stands for "National Economic Security and Reformation Act." The web site is found at **http://nesara.org/main/index.htm.**

On the site it states: *The Act was passed by the American Congress in the year 2000 and never proclaimed. NESARA began as a one-man crusade; then there were two, then three. Many people warned that we were wasting our time, that we could never win against the special interest groups. Yet, look at how far we have come with pure desire and modest resources: this web site now receives approximately 15,000 visits per month."*

The NESARA Institute is a non-profit educational organization, currently existing largely in cyberspace, having no offices or office supplies, no paid staff or personnel. This effort to heal America is a grass roots movement and the people who support the web site are affiliated with no political group or party. The "Grass Roots Movement" of NESARA includes any person who wants to participate in spreading the word about the ideas expressed in NESARA—people who are willing to invest their time in studying, discussing and working out society's root problems. The NESARA movement is much like the New Age movement in that it has congealed from a shifting consciousness driven by similar attitudes.

The following information is taken from the NESARA site:

"Thanks to the world wide web the word is spreading. If everyone in the nation knew about NESARA and the potential positive impact on their lives and the lives of their family and friends, the proposal would be introduced next week and passed within a month. Based upon the increased traffic volume at the NESARA web site, many people are beginning to take notice of the proposed bill and its implications. Most visitors are from

the U.S., but a steadily increasing number are from other nations. That this plan will work for any nation has not escaped our attention.

With most of the work completed, national publicity is the primary task remaining. At this point we could definitely use your help in two areas.
Invest some of your time learning about NESARA and telling others of the immediate personal benefits. For ideas visit our Spread the Word page.

A call or two to your favourite talk show would help, as well as a letter to the editor of your local paper. Remember the numerous on line news sources too.

Although expensive, national advertising is still a cost effective and powerful way to quickly inform a lot of people about the benefits of NESARA. The amount of serious attention Congress provides to new proposals is directly proportional to demonstrations of public support. Like many things in life, the benefits we expect to receive are often related to our own initial efforts. A little support now provides huge rewards later.

It's your life and your country, and long past time for you to become directly involved in writing the laws that shape our destiny. If three people can get this far working by themselves, just think what a few more could do!
We've had many people outside the U.S. borders ask us how NESARA will affect them or, asking how they can transcribe NESARA to fit the laws of their own land. We first address the former question. Consider the following:

Suppose the U.S. enacts NESARA into law. Consider that country then having a rock solid currency (no inflation). Consider that country with equitable banking laws. A land with a high volume economy and high wealth. A land where no federal income tax exists, and thus the hidden embedded effects of that tax no longer exists. A land where commodity money once again exists to provide people with a choice of currency and connections to the real world. Simply put, what will happen to the investment money circulating in your own land? Answer that question and you probably then will be able to also see that your country must eventually jump on the NESARA bandwagon, or watch the ship sink. If your country does not follow suit, then investors merely move their funds and assets across the borders into the U.S. As a consumer and investor therefore, in the long run, you win too.

If your country should first implement the ideas of NESARA, the U.S. will be forced to follow suit. Just doesn't matter who implements the ideas, the world will soon follow. One of those classic, "If you build it, they will come" stories.

What about implementing the ideas of NESARA into the laws of your land? You will need access to the statutes of your land and will need to review NESARA to change some of the wording and terminology. However, because NESARA is written in everyday language and not the legalese of bureaucrats, transcribing and modifying NESARA should not be a monumental effort.

Once transcribed, consider starting your own campaign and web site in your own land. Doesn't really matter what country starts the NESARA bandwagon, once one nation enacts the ideas, all the others will eventually be forced to follow. Best yet, as more and more versions of NESARA appear across the globe, pressure will mount on the politicians and policy makers.

We do not have the time or resources to translate NESARA into other languages. However, as we stated in our Notes and Legal Stuff page, the bill is placed into the public domain. Take it and run—you have our blessings.

A facade covers the modern world, a far different place than most imagine. The authors of this web site hereby offer you the opportunity to explore this realm: a fascinating place of things, personalities and events, but mostly of ideas and concepts.

This web site is a mosaic of ideas: images from the realms of philosophy, economics, finance, history, sociology, morality, law, and politics, all arranged in unusual patterns. Just when you think you have the picture, a new image changes the scene. Be prepared to face the dark side—and possibly see the light."

The Roots Of NESARA

Dr. Harvey Barnard started his search for a root cause and the solutions to America's social problems in the late 1960s when a professor at Louisiana State University casually remarked during a lecture that social and economic problems could be analyzed and solved with the same tools and techniques used to solve industrial problems. That single comment launched a lifetime pursuit of intellectual curiosity that later became a crusade, driven by nothing more than the challenge of doing the seemingly impossible.

After many years of personal study, Dr. Barnard developed a new theory of money. His NESARA legislative proposal began as a formal idea in the late 1980s. The current NESARA proposal saw first light in the early 1990s as a proposal for monetary policy reform. Later Dr. Barnard added his proposals for fiscal policy reform.

In 1996 Dr. Barnard self-published his first version of Draining the Swamp, which contained the first public copy of his full NESARA proposal. He circulated copies to members of Congress and other influential political actors. After numerous personal attempts to introduce NESARA to Congress, including attempts to encourage presidential candidates to use NESARA as part of a political reform platform, Dr. Barnard decided that the best hope for meaningful reform was through a grass roots effort. In 1999, with the world wide web beginning to impact modern social structures, he decided to place his NESARA proposal into the public domain and went live with his web site in the summer of 2000. He founded the NESARA Institute in 2001.

Shortly after introducing NESARA to the world wide web, certain people latched onto the NESARA idea and began promoting a different version of this story.

Supporters of the altered version of the NESARA story believe that NESARA was enacted into law secretly during the Clinton administration, that there are "White Knights" working tirelessly behind the political scenes to inform the world of this secret legislation, and that the altered version of NESARA promises numerous debt forgiveness elements. Originally, the altered story did not dispute the original NESARA acronym used by Dr.

Barnard, but as the rumours increased, supporters then also altered the NESARA acronym.

Although little more than a curiosity for a few years, the altered version of the NESARA story took on a life of its own and now grows throughout the world wide web much like a cancer. So influential is this alternate effort that many people have protested outside the World Court, and some people have paid thousands of dollars to advertise their version of NESARA on the side panels of advertising trucks in Washington, D.C. Sadly, this disinformation campaign has reduced the credibility of Dr. Barnard's efforts and today the word "NESARA" is an ill-received word at Congress. To this day Dr. Barnard's NESARA proposal has yet to be introduced into Congress.

The staff at the NESARA Institute understands part of the emotional and psychological reasons why people support the alternate version of NESARA. Dr. Barnard intended to provide meaningful social reform through his NESARA proposal. He believed that no meaningful social reform was possible without meaningful monetary system reform. Dr. Barnard believed that although individual units of money were privately owned, the monetary exchange system itself was owned by everybody and that the system must be fair and equitable to all people at all times and not just benefit a few politically privileged people.

Part of that monetary reform required modifying the fundamental equations that drive the current economic system, primarily through the socially disruptive concept known as compound interest. By restructuring those equations Dr. Barnard believed that meaningful monetary reform was possible. Restructuring those equations necessarily implied a shift in the character of debt. Debt would not disappear, but most people would find themselves in debt for shorter periods. This effort would return resources to people so that they once again tasted and experienced meaningful social liberty.

Unfortunately, many supporters of the alternate NESARA story interpreted this change in the character of debt as a debt reduction or debt forgiveness plan. Perhaps more sadly is that several investment schemes and prosperity programs circulate around this alternate NESARA story and because so many people desire meaningful monetary reform, find themselves succumbing to the Siren's lure and provide these schemers money. Money that is never again seen nor is any return on investment ever realized.

Of course, the alternate NESARA story rests upon a conspiracy theory in that NESARA allegedly was passed secretly. Thus, researchers can ask for a copy of this alleged act, but will be told that no copy exists because of the secret passage. Diligent researchers are reminded of the impossibility of honestly investigating this alternate version of NESARA and that such difficulties should provide clues about authenticity. Additionally, the process of enacting a legislative proposal and bill into law is easily understood by surfing the web. Researchers will learn that no proposed legislation or bill is ever enacted secretly. Of course, the copy of NESARA proposed by Dr. Barnard is available here at this web site, (***www.nesara.org***) as well as in ***Draining the Swamp*** book.

There also are claims from supporters of the alternate NESARA that Dr. Barnard and NESARA Institute staff members all work for President Bush or other nefarious "New

World Order" organizations. They also claim that NESARA as presented here at this web site is merely a ploy to detract people from knowing the so-called "true" NESARA.

Before investing funds with anybody, one should diligently research the investment plan. That research includes reading literature, conversing with people, and then seriously evaluating the information based upon facts and not pure emotion. The staff at the NESARA Institute empathizes with those who have lost hard earned funds to these schemers and scam promoters, but a life of social liberty begins first and foremost with self-responsibility. Perhaps one day the alternate NESARA story will fizzle and disappear, but as long as people act and respond through emotion rather than intelligence then these scam artists will continue to succeed.

Some people believe that there is no such thing as bad publicity, but many serious NESARA advocates now realize that there also is a point of no return with some kinds of publicity. Credibility becomes a factor because of the effort to circulate the alternate NESARA story. Serious advocates of Dr. Barnard's NESARA idea would like to see NESARA introduced into Congress. Serious advocates realize that doing so is an uphill battle simply through the fundamental political process, but that the alternate NESARA story makes that hill steeper and more difficult to climb. True monetary and fiscal policy reform still await. Social conflict continues because of the flawed equations that drive the system

A Spiritually Directed Financial Program

As a program, NESARA can be viewed from several perspectives. As a spiritually-directed financial program, it traces back to the work of St. Germain and three other ascended masters. That work began in the Fifteenth Century and was designed to provide a new economic system for the world during the present time of transition. Sheldan Nidle's Spiritual Hierarchy and Galactic Federation describe the masters' work and its development over the centuries:

"This time will ... be heralded by an infusion of great abundance. This prosperity will be due largely to the endurance of our Earthly Allies and the brilliant strategies set in motion, many centuries ago, by the Ascended Masters Count St Germain, Master Hilarion, Seraphis Bey and Saint Paul the Venetian.

These Holy Beings were able to bring to this realm a financial and monetary plan whose secret purpose is to enable great abundance to rain down at the appropriate time. Although St Germain is ultimately responsible for its success, each of the Ascended Masters we have mentioned has played a significant role in its present-day preparation.

Briefly, ... the Ottoman Turks, the Hapsburgs of Austria, the Bourbons of France and the Holy See conspired in the past to create a system of banking and trust that has lasted until this day. ...

The origins of their created Fractional Banking System are revealed in the ancient treasuries of Rome, Persia, India and China, and in the many empires of the New World.

By Europe's Middle Ages, control of this system had passed to the Pope and a series of allied Monarchs. This group was grievously threatened by the rise of the Ottomans in the Middle East, and by their capture of Constantinople. New arrangements were needed.

St Paul the Venetian and Seraphis Bey were leaders in negotiating the new Secret Treaties, but only to prepare the way for the final phase of their strategy. St. Germain carried this out beautifully, with help from the Master Hilarion. The outcome was a World Trust for this realm's Light Workers.

Funds were to be disbursed with the advent of Christendom's Second Millennium. As that time approached, however, it became increasingly clear that the Cabals who control your world wished to avoid this payout.

Therefore, a number of former members who left these groups and secretly supported Count St Germain's original intention, devised a way to defeat the secret manipulations of their former dark Cabals.

This resulted in the rise of our Earthly Allies and an exceedingly complex strategy that took decades to bring to fruition. The process began as a way to ensure that the abundance promised by Count St Germain was actually made available to Earth's Light Workers.

At first, this amounted to a number of Trusts whose true purpose was kept secret. A few decades later, it concerned the bringing to light of a humanitarian project approved by the IMF. Over time, this led to the emergence of a number of governmental, economic and political coalitions, which were protected by the Ascended Masters.

They also encouraged Divine intervention by the Galactic Federation of Light. This First Contact mission would be allied, eventually, with those who so courageously had encouraged the disclosure of Count St Germain's World Trust. In 1998, this measure was officially carried into effect by a series of secret agreements promising that the UFO cover-up would cease when these funds were disbursed.

The outcome of almost a decade of secret conflict waged between this global coalition and Earth's many dark Cabals culminated in the latter part of 2000. The remaining Dark Cabal realized that it was imperative for them to seize the leadership of Earth's last superpower.

Thus, they developed a policy that resembled a scheme they had employed in Germany during the 1930s [i.e., 9/11, designed to imitate the consequences of the Reichstag Fire]. They hoped that this policy would enable them to block the disbursement of funds. They also hungered to engage in a perpetual war that would allow them to complete the dismantling of this superpower's Bill of Rights.

At first, their policy seemed to succeed. However, their spitefulness resulted in a violent reaction that increased our Earthly Allies' ability to counterbalance the power amassed by these last Cabals. Now, this Coalition has used your Planet's most recent, illegal war in Iraq as the intolerable, final act that will break this last Cabal's hold on the reins of power."

On the website, **www.2012.com.au/updates.html** which rather prolific on news as to what is happing, much is written about NESARA by **Mathew Ward**:

"Viewed as a modern development, the roots of NESARA can be found in the response by the Supreme Court to banking foreclosures against farm property which the Court found to be illegal. In the course of reviewing these practices, the Court went further and ruled that many other contemporary banking, taxation and governance arrangements were unconstitutional. For that, James Rink's article appears to be a good source.

As a legislative initiative, it took its name from the National Economic Security and Reformation Act, passed by Congress in 2000, as implied in Matthew Ward's comments: "The NESARA legislation is being processed within the laws of the God-inspired original US constitution. Because the United States determines to such a large extent what happens in your world, NESARA was devised in accordance with US laws rather than any other countries. NESARA was due to be announced on Sept. 11, 2001, but the cabal blew up the World Trade Center buildings to prevent it, as Matthew briefly alludes to.

The dark forces are fighting tooth and nail to prevent even the awareness of NESARA, much less its implementation, and, at this point, delaying the announcement that must by law precede enactment of the widespread provisions is the only weapon left to them.

They have been successful thus far in achieving delays by many means: assassinations of influential people who favour initiating the provisions without delay as well as others actively working toward this end; death threats to the families of light workers and to the workers themselves; double-agents within the ranks of the light workers; and terrorist assaults. The US internal terrorist act of September 11, 2001, was the most dramatic of these tactics.

The gold which backed the new currency was stored in the WTC towers and stolen by the cabal. Building 7 was the center of operations for 9/11 and was destroyed after the operation was complete. Viewed from the widest possible angle, NESARA is a spiritually-inspired and -guided arrangement, as Matthew indicates.

NESARA is legislation of the United States government that was designed by high light beings in conjunction with spiritual beings on the planet as the LEGAL means to usher in the era of peace, love and harmony on Earth.

Some consider NESARA to be political and economic in nature while others view it as spiritual because of the high-level light beings affiliated with it. NESARA is both. When people are severely oppressed by political and economic conditions that foster impoverished living circumstances, lack of health care and education, monopoly of natural resources, slave labour, unjust laws and courts, starvation, and tyrannical regimes, offering 'soul food' isn't enough.

When people are preoccupied with mere survival requirements, giving them only spiritual messages is not going to bring about the global reforms they need to rise out of their misery. That is why the provisions of NESARA are monumental in scope, embodying sweeping reforms for Earth that will begin as soon as the legislation is officially *announced. When people become aware of the reforms, they will be motivated to participate according to their capabilities.*

As in all other aspects of polarity still existing on Earth, NESARA is at one extreme and the dark forces that ... the members themselves call the Illuminati are at the other.

NESARA is designed to erase poverty and all its attendant ills from Earth during a transitional period preceding Ascension so that the planet's sovereign citizens can focus their attention on planetary transformation, as SaLuSa indicates.

The changes will not be imposed for the sake of it, but are part of our plan to bring you the comforts and protection, that will lift your experiences to a new level and bring you joy and happiness. Following that you will be in the right frame of mind to apply yourselves to the business of preparing for Ascension. That is the ultimate goal.

After, Ascension, this planet is destined to be weaned from the use of money, as SaLuSa points out: "Ultimately you [will] reach a stage where money has no place in a society that is founded upon sharing.

In Earth's Golden Age, the trend will be away from money and toward systems of sharing and bartering—the light intensity in souls will let those means of remuneration for services and conduct of commerce become as satisfying between nations as between individuals.

It was felt that there was no sense in implementing NESARA before the dark forces had been removed from power. Otherwise they would use their control of government to seize people's funds.

[The Illuminati's] tentacles reach the highest levels of governments; banking establishments; all media outlets; churches; multinational corporations; royal families; educational, medical and drug, law and justice systems – NOTHING of influential nature on your planet is free of Illuminati control.

This powerful cabal has long recognized that to retain their control of Earth's people, they must keep them in ignorance and fear and for millennia that has worked well for those currently in power and their dark predecessors. Now they are realizing that it cannot work for them much longer, and they are sparing no tactic to hold onto their fast-ebbing control.

They rightly see NESARA as their total uprooting, because once the program's reforms are implemented, the control of the darkness will crumble totally.

Many people wonder why the galactic and spirit coalition do not force the cabal to accept NESARA. They may not appreciate the requirement imposed on the coalition that it respect free will.

By Creator's law, souls' free will must be respected except in the case of nuclear detonations in space. That includes the free-will choices made by members of the dark forces to hold up and weaken—preferably doom—NESARA.

We can tell you what is fomenting behind the scenes regarding the truth about the global economy, but because Earth's energy field of potential is in such wild commotion, we cannot discern what information will emerge first or the order in which other facts will follow.

The coalition must allow for free-will choices; therefore their plans must respond to our actions, which means that they must be changeable, as SaLuSa tells us: "We continually adjust our plans according to the changes on Earth."(16) "On a week-to-week basis so much could happen, and it is why we are unable to be more precise about the coming months.

We have seen that NESARA can be described from several different vantage points and its exact date of implementation remains unknown. As an economic measure, it is intended to be temporary and transitional. As a spiritual measure, it is intended to inspire Earth's population with what is possible, which Ascension will fully reveal. Once NESARA comes, it will relieve Earth's population of poverty and toil and allow them to devote themselves fully to the ultimate task of planetary transformation."

Executive Summary Of NESARA BILL
Monetary Policy Reform

- Establishes three types of United States currency: standard silver coin and gold coin (*restores Constitutional currency*), and treasury credit-notes
- The United States Treasury buys and cancels all outstanding capital stock of the former Federal Reserve Banks
- The privately owned Federal Reserve System is abolished, returning ownership of the national currency to the people through a newly created United States Treasury Reserve System
- A new Board of Governors of the Treasury Reserve System uses a specific law-mandated plan to maintain and stabilize the exchange value of the currency
- The new Board assumes all powers and responsibilities of the former Federal Open Market Committee, eliminating private control of the nation's monetary system
- The existing regional Federal Reserve Banks become Treasury Reserve Banks and continue clearinghouse operations and other bank service functions under the direction of the Office of the Comptroller of the Currency
- All commercial banks must exchange their income-producing government obligations for treasury credit-notes (*reduces the national debt*)
- Only treasury credit-notes may be held as bank reserves
- Fundamental changes are imposed on the repayment of all outstanding fractional reserve loans on secured property—principal must be repaid before the monetizing-fee is paid (*applies retroactively to existing mortgages reducing private debt*)
- A progressive federal excise tax is imposed on the privilege of making commercial loans of currency for profit
- Commercial financial institutions such as credit unions are provided, subject to some restriction, with opportunities to operate with fractional reserves

Fiscal Policy Reform
- Amends the existing federal income tax system
- A national retail sales (excise) tax is imposed upon non-exempt retail activities of commerce (*20 categories of exemptions covering most necessities of life*)
- The Internal Revenue Service is reorganized as the National Tax Service to administer the collection of the new tax

What NESARA Does Not Immediately Do
- Eliminate all payroll taxes, such as Social Security and Medicare taxes
- Eliminate constitutional excise taxes on regulated activities
- Immediately eliminate the entire national debt
- Immediately halt inflation (*the economy needs some response time before inflation will disappear*)

Detailed Summary–Part I Banking and Monetary Reform
Immediate Relief and Results
- Eliminates approximately $1 trillion of the nation's public debt
- Reduces future private debt by approximately $1 trillion
- Immediately eliminates some private debt, especially for many homeowners

The Federal Reserve System
- The Federal Reserve Act of 1913 is amended
- The Federal Reserve System is abolished and replaced by a new Treasury Reserve System
- Control of the currency is moved from private control of the Fed to public control of Congress and the new Treasury Reserve System
- Congress sets the standards for the new monetary system but the people create as much or as little currency as they need
- Functions of the Federal Open Market Committee are transferred to the Board of Governors of the new Treasury Reserve System
- A new mechanism, the Treasury Reserve Account, is created to provide the Treasury Reserve System Board of Governors a better method to fine-tune the money supply, effectively eliminating inflation
- The Treasury Reserve System Board of Governors will continue using the previous three mechanisms for controlling the money supply: 1. Setting reserve requirements. 2. Setting the national discount rate. 3. Purchasing U.S. Treasury securities on the open market.
- All U.S. Treasury securities purchased by the Treasury Reserve System Board of Governors will be immediately turned over to the U.S. Treasury and cancelled out of existence.

Monetary Policy
- People are provided with several alternatives for currency
- Constitutional currency is restored
- Currency becomes debt free as the people stop paying interest payments for their use of a public utility
- Unlike previous policy, the new Treasury Reserve Board is provided one very specific mandate: maintain a stable currency
- Expansion of the economy is returned to the free market

- Private coinage is encouraged
- Exchange ratios for the various currencies are published at least weekly
- Printing of redeemable gold and silver certificates is allowed
- Postal money orders are made available in denominations of gold and silver coin

Banking

- Returns the banking industry to serving public interests
- For secured loans, compound interest is outlawed and replaced with a monetization fee
- Provides stricter banking controls by imposing excise taxes to discourage high or runaway monetization fees
- On secured loans obtained from a fractional reserve bank, principal must be paid in full before the bank begins collecting its monetization fee
- Eliminates the facade for banking insurance (FDIC)
- Except for fraud and criminal activities, virtually eliminates bank failures
- Banks are prohibited from using as reserves any commercial paper
- Only Treasury credit-notes can be used as bank reserves
- Banks are prohibited from purchasing government issued debt, effectively removing banks from influencing monetary policy
- Checking accounts against gold and silver deposits are prohibited
- Commingling of funds among the various money accounts without owner's permission is prohibited
- All currency deposits with banks are general warrant deposits and custody accounts.

Immediate Relief and Results

- Workers maintain better control of their earnings
- Production is no longer taxed, just consumption
- Most of the necessities of life are not taxed
- Encourages production thus revitalizing industry in America
- Encourages rebuilding of inner cities
- Discourages wasteful uses of natural resources
- Exposes the true cost of government
- Greatly eliminates the struggle between tax "protesters" and bureaucracy
- Allows the "underground" to resurface and become a viable contribution to production of goods and services
- Greatly restricts the influence of special interests and lobbyists

The Income Tax

- The Income Tax Act of 1939 is amended
- People need no longer fear the IRS
- Billions of hours of nonproductive labour are eliminated
- Mounds of paper work are eliminated
- The cost of the income tax is no longer hidden and embedded in the cost of doing business and passed down the chain with the consumer paying the final tab
- Most likely eliminates state income tax plans because state income taxation piggybacks on federal income taxation
- The IRS is reformed into the National Tax Service
- Volumes of complicated tax code are history
- Eliminates personal income taxes
- Eliminates corporate income taxes

- Eliminates gift taxes and estate taxes
- Eliminates capital gains taxes

Sales and Use Tax

- Tax rate of 14%
- Government entities are exempt
- Government mandated expenses such as licenses, permits, passports, are exempt
- Sales of bullion, coin and currency are exempt
- Sales made by or to nonprofit schools are exempt
- Sales of prescription drugs, medical supplies and services are exempt
- Real estate rents and leases are exempt
- Sales of groceries are exempt
- Sales of plants, livestock and fish used in the production of food for human consumption are exempt
- Insurance sales are exempt
- Segregated portions of labour in retail service contracts are exempt
- Incidental or occasional sales such as garage or rummage sales are exempt
- Sales for the purposes of recycling are exempt
- Meals provided by companies at company expense are exempt
- Sales that are nonprofit in nature are exempt

Current Status Of NESARA Bill

As of September 10, 2012, the website states: The bill has not been enacted into law, has not been introduced into Congress, and has not yet been assigned a tracking number. Please contact the President, representatives and senators, and ask if they support the bill. Send them all a copy of the bill (further contact information is available on our Political Contacts page).

After the bill is assigned a number, the status of the proposed bill also can be viewed at the Thomas locator registry. However, the bill will not appear in the Thomas registry until the bill has been assigned a number.

Introduced into Committee: We need at least one representative to sponsor the bill, obtain a bill number, and enter the bill into the record. The two House committees that would be interested in the bill are the Financial Services and the Ways and Means Committees. The two Senate committees that would be interested in the bill are the Finance and the Banking, Housing, And Urban Affairs Committees. Please contact the representatives on those committees, especially if one of the members happens to be your representative (contact information is available on our Political Contacts page). Representatives and senators are becoming aware of the proposal. Please continue your phone calls, faxes, emails, personal contacts, etc. Grass roots pressure is beginning to work, so please continue applying pressure. See our Political Contacts page for more information. Please also continue spreading the word—see our Spread the Word page for ideas. If you wish to help financially, please see our What Can I Do? page for details.

Bill number: None

At one time the Treasury Department acknowledged the bill (the link is no longer active): **www.ustreas.gov/education/faq/markets/economy.html**. Please remember that the Treasury Department has no authority to make law and at best can only provide policy commentary and opinion to Congress.

How Does This Translate To The People?

It is of interest to speculate on how the NESARA bill would translate into the pocketbook of the people. For this we will go to a special site ***http://www.luisprada.com/Protected/st_germain_on_nesara_and_money.htm*** in order to receive "channeled guidance from St. Germaine. For those who have researched the Global Trust that has been compromised by the Elite, St Germaine back in the 1700's had much to do with setting it up. For further information go to the Luis Prada site at ***www.Luisprada.com***. Although this was channeled in 2005, it has relevance today.

"Good Morning my friends, 'tis a lovely day! I AM Germain, and I will discuss a little today about NESARA, funding, and money in general.

The prosperity funding is happening. I have given out quite a bit of monies actually over the last several weeks, on a special needs basis. Some of you have inquired about where the prosperity funds are coming from. I actually set in motion what was needed for these times some 200 years ago. Many in Europe at that time began setting aside fortunes that continue to this day, for when the needs became apparent, and we could together bring in changes that we saw coming way back then. We knew from experience, those of us who started the banking changes, what would happen in the future.

Banking as you know it today, allows the easy circulation of money. Precious metals are difficult to use worldwide as an exchange medium. Banks hold the metals, and issue easy to use currency in their place. Now you have electronic money which is the easiest to use of all for a worldwide society still using money in its learning stages. I know that most of you appreciate the ability to swipe your cards in payment of debt or in the purchasing of goods. Many of you enjoy buying and paying bills on the Internet using electronic money.

Some in your churches are very against this idea, seeing the mark of the beast involved. As with any technology there is the potential for good and the potential for evil. The BBB&G's, in the creation of the Federal Reserve System in the USA and similar systems in other countries through the World Bank system, show the way of evil in the management of money.

There is no real value, as many of you know, in the Federal Reserve Notes of the United States. This is a system backed by hot air, and enforced control of others, and markets. You have your war in Iraq, in part based on the fact that the Islamic countries use gold, either in coinage and/or currency backed by gold. These countries knew that the American dollar was of no real value, and began to accept payment of monies as precious metals, or currency backed by them, in payment for oil. The current Euro is backed by precious metals, and thus it has real value.

In my distant past I learned personally the hard way, as most do in Earth, the follies of misusing of money. I headed up a very large civilization that came to an end 50,000 years ago in the area which is now the Sahara Desert. I practiced personally at the time money management, much as the Federal Reserve does today. My peoples lost their sense of spirituality because they became so engulfed in money, wealth, and materialism.

My society failed from my mismanagement. The money became worthless, just as is what is happening now, on a large scale basis over much of the world. My society collapsed, and had nothing to fall back on, when the money became worthless. We basically just printed and spent, and developed little other skills that we could fall back on, for survival. I learned much then. I did not do this to bring about collapse and control. I did this because I wanted the peoples to be happy and comfortable. They were too comfortable. But I learned much about how money works in that venture.

Over the last 200 years I have worked behind the scenes to get electronic money up and running. Well, it wasn't electronic then the way it is now, but I did start the banking up that has become what it is today. I did not start up the Federal Reserve System, this mess is the work entirely of the BBB&G's. But electronic transfer of money is efficient, and makes it easy to use.

In the near future the money of all the societies of earth will be the same and have the same value so the game of exchange rates cannot be played. It will become more and more difficult to make money from manipulative investments, such as the stock market as currently run and the betting that goes on, such as the futures market. Money will be made strictly from legitimate business practices.

In fact, in a few short years after NESARA has been implemented and its changes in effect worldwide, everyone is going to have very adequate money. When everyone has adequate money, you will not play the inflation game, that the BBB&G's create intentionally to rip people off in a variety of ways. What will happen in short is that when you are rolling in abundant money you will discover the stuff is useless, and build a society that does not use it. The Inner Earth peoples do not use money at all. Everyone works there, and full time work is 20 hours a week or less, as you define your week on the surface.

These peoples do barter for luxury items, and you will be taught how to do this on the surface. In actuality, most countries of reasonable size can produce what they need and will not have to bargain very much. You are going to produce goods that do not wear out a few days after the warranty expires.

You are not going to need a new car every few years. Your vehicles will last practically forever. You will need to develop better means of travel than the automobile. There are a variety of options available to choose from, and could vary from country to country. It will be a while before you have teleportation available for use. There is spiritual work to be done for these technologies to become useful.

Now, back to NESARA. In the United States, and many other countries around the world that have fraudulent banking systems and fraudulent taxation systems the citizens of these countries will be getting some sort of refund coming over a period of time. The amount will be dependent on the countries involved inflation rates, and the length of time the fraudulent systems have been in place.

Not all has been set up yet for many countries, as NESARA was created in the United States for the United States. Other countries became interested in the idea, and several had developed plans to be implemented shortly after NESARA was to be announced in the USA last March of 2004. Since the Galactic Federation took over the implementation of NESARA late last May, it was decided to implement it over a larger area, and then by fall, to simply implement it over the entire world.

Prior to this, had NESARA been announced over a year ago, there was going to be economic and political pressures applied to resistant countries to encourage them making similar changes. Many countries in places like Africa, the other countries separated from the Soviet Union, almost all of South and Central America would have been most difficult to work with and bring into NESARA.

World peace, true peace would still be a long way off in these small countries under dictators that would have not cooperated and given up power. Although the USA was going to back off and bring its troops home, many small countries would still have warred in one way or the other.

With the Galactic Federation taking over, as all involved studied Earth, it became apparent that the best way to go would be to install it worldwide, period, in a short space of time. This world is very sick, as you all well know, both its environment, and its peoples. It is not really feasible to wait, with the increased effects of the Photon Belt energies and the earth changes that Mother Earth wishes to make in the clearing of negativity from the planet.

Although the planet was quite ill back in the times of Atlantis, near the end of that era, it was nowhere near as ill as it is now. It had a similar population back then, but there was still a good deal of spirituality, and spiritual technologies that did not pollute. We did not make use of oil, except for some plastics back then. Plastics do have their place and are useful.

I am going to describe now the changes for the United States, as these are the most detailed and planned for. Europe, Canada, Russia, India, and China will have similar changes. We are still working details for the many small war torn countries of the world. We can't make monetary changes in these countries until there is a stable government. This article is more about the monetary changes than the political ones. You know that bad governments are getting replaced.

You are aware already that credit card debt gets erased. This is for everyone, citizen or not in the United States. Your mortgage debt will also be forgiven, but this is only for citizens. You will have to fill out paper work, proving citizenship. You will not have to make payments upon the announcement. In general, there will be credit card debt forgiveness in any country changing excess interest and expenses of credit. In many Islamic countries interest in not charged. In these countries the debts are therefore legal *and ethical and will not be discharged. NESARA will be quite different from country to country.*

Now I wish to cover an area, covered only briefly in the Dove Reports. (**http://www.luisprada.com/Protected/nesara_updates_dove_reports_i.htm**) *Every citizen of the United States, over the age of 21, will receive a sum of ten million dollars, as a refund of monies taken through fraudulent banking and taxes over the years since 1913 when the Federal Reserve System was created.*

It is not really possible to come to an actual figure. The designers of NESARA basically picked a figure out of a hat, so to speak. The deposits should start in approximately a year. One reason for the wait is that those who have been illegally stealing money for a long time, and are very wealthy as a result, will have these ill gotten funds (which include monies earned from the drug trade) taken away from them as part of their punishment, or what we prefer to call rehabilitation. This action will provide some of the funds coming to you.

This money will be deposited monthly into your bank accounts. It will be $75,000 a month, until the ten million has been reached, in slightly less than 12 years. In addition to this, to compensate to some degree for the massive inflation over the many years since 1913, everything in the USA will be re-priced, by simply moving the decimal point over one space to the left. This does not fully compensate for the inflation, but it is simple to do mathematically. Once the monies mentioned above have begun to be distributed some of you with vision and a plan may apply to receive a larger portion up front if you can prove need.

What this means, the moving of the decimal point, is that everything will cost 1/10 of what it did. Salaries will also change, being 1/10 of the original also. What is the point in this, in the United States? It will help correct trade deficits and problems of taking the jobs to cheaper places overseas. You will be competitive with the rest of the world.

Your dollar has been terribly misused in the creating of inflation by intent. If you haven't read some of the Protocols of Zion, now would be a good time to do so. These describe in quite good detail the monetary plans of enslavement, and the ways to make money from money. An ideal society still using money learns that inflation is a real killer. Inflation only happens as a result of greed, plain and simple.

Not only in the United States, but also countries where the value of money is comparable to the dollar, in exchange rates, will have similar adjustments in economy to make your monies more equal in value. The poorer countries will not need these adjustments. We plan that in 5 years or less there will be a universal currency in place. Much of it will be electronic but the banks will hold precious metals to back it up.

So, now, what will the citizens of the United States, and other countries do with this money? $75,000 a month, with an economy returned to a lower exchange, is way more than most of you could spend in luxury living. Also, there will not be enough goods to buy with it, as luxury goods. Not all of you can buy a personal yacht, for example.

This is where you chose to become a messiah, in one way or the other. You can create programs to care for people with it. You can create better schools. You can upgrade the technology, as new technology is given to you. If I had my way, we would stop money right now, and have everyone contribute time to their society. Money is imaginary at any rate. But your multiple societies around the world are not ready for this yet.

You still need money as an exchange. It will be a great test of many people in the United States, and similar wealthy countries, as to what they do with this money. Some are sure to experiment with power in a negative way. This won't last too long as since you will all have plenty of the stuff you won't need to come under the power of others. There is going to be no more inflation so it won't work to buy up a bunch of apartment buildings for example and rent them out at ever increasing rates.

It will be interesting what will happen with housing. I imagine that many of you are not going to stay living in a little dinky apartment, or old worn out mobile homes, and similar old housing. I would advise some of you interested in the new housing market that will be created from this wealth to wait in doing so until you understand the newer technologies and can put them in place.

The electric grid in many countries must go. You will be receiving new technology wherein each building can have its own electricity supply that is clean and efficient. You have a huge amount of electricity in the air for the taking. This can be used easily requiring no fuel to obtain it.

Please do not get into a building rush, and create buildings using old technologies for energy. Wait a bit please, not only if you are a builder, but also a buyer. All over the world there exist apartment buildings. If properly constructed, these should be maintained and made use of for a period of time. They can be refitted, and walls torn down to make larger rooms. Create fewer, but bigger apartments in these buildings.

It will no longer necessary to stuff people into small places to have large profits. Many will actually prefer to still live in these buildings, as many do not want yards to care for, or to travel longer distances to work. In many areas, that are heavily populated, there is not enough land to spread out. Look to change these communities for the better. I would suggest, that with all the money available, that these be converted to units that can be purchased, rather than rented, taking away the money making of rentals the way it currently exists.

Automobiles will need to be used for a time until there are new techniques. You will be eventually getting rid of highways and roads, as you know them. Many will probably own hovercraft for some of the transportation requirements. You should also build communities in which many can work either from home, or nearby, so that the huge amount of time given to daily travel will be decreased.

Your large grocery stores need to go away. You should have small community shops for fresh food. You should have areas in the community for growing of fresh greens. You will still import foods from other countries, but these will be shipped quite differently. With the use of "flying saucers" food can be harvested and shipped in a matter of hours for more immediate consumption.

Many of you looking for messianic missions should look into the food, and how it is supplied. If you are already working in the food area, in whatever form, stay there and bring in the new changes. Restaurants will remain important. In fact, around the world, you may need more of them, as people will travel for business, recreation and learning much more frequently. The Inner Earth folks intend to teach you much about food in all areas of importance. In choosing something messianic to do we not only need help feeding the world but need great help in bringing about all sorts of changes in every field imaginable.

The planet is changing its axis. There used to not be the change in seasons that you experience. This happened when Atlantis went down and with the photon belt changes at that time. The planet's normal existence is straight up and down, not tilted. When this returns to normal totally you will have difficulty measuring the year in that it won't be marked by the changes of the seasons. Much of the weather changes in recent years are the result of the gradual changes in the tilt.

As a result, the foods you grow will also change. The growing seasons will be much longer, in fact constant.

But I seem to have side tracked a bit. Back to the prosperity funds. A number of individuals are going to receive funds that have purposely been built over time by wealthy individuals to be distributed to the world in general. The receivers of these funds will redistribute them to others. This is what you have seen about the making of lists for designated receivers.

These receivers can use their funds for a messianic project and also continue the distribution to others beyond their needs. Remember that months down the road most in the United States and similar countries will have generous funding that I discussed above. If you are a citizen begin creating ideas for ways to use this huge tax and interest rebate.

In the waiting of a year you will see what newer technologies are coming and how you might choose to participate. Many of you should stay in your areas of interest already and make changes from within. If this is not feasible do to the nature of your employment you could simply write a check instead giving funds to those that further need them.

There is going to be much building of many different sorts going on. So understand, that if no prosperity funds come your way, and this is possible, that you are going to receive your prosperity through this rebate program. As I said, this will also happen in many other countries. I can't give the amounts rebated, in this message, as it will be different from place to place. And don't forget, all of you having credit and loans through commercial institutions get the benefit of debt relief.

But stolen monies are going to be rebated worldwide wherever this has happened. The countries in Africa and similar areas of the world may have little to rebate. The scoundrels running these places are not that wealthy, they spend much of it. What monies can be rebated in these countries will probably go to visionaries that can do something of consequence with this money.

Also in the United States there are many who will receive funds, that were the farmers in the farm claims issues. These monies will be rebated fairly soon after the NESARA announcement in the United States. You know who you are in that program. There are some who were farmers that were likewise ripped off, who may also receive funds but there will be some education on this first. Many who gave up their farms under pressure and loans that could not be paid are not yet aware of the farm claims program.

Some of you that can leave your jobs should do so and travel to these places and fix them with your rebates. Get together in groups and pool your resources and skills working the idea of "Two or more in My Name." These poor countries that have such awful electricity, or the lack of it, need to benefit from the new technologies being brought in.

You should create decent housing and food supply for these peoples, and employ them in the process, as they grow into sustainable communities and out of living in little shacks. You need to do more than just have a great food line, you need to build communities, and involve these peoples in the creating of the dream.

You might even be able to build communities that don't really need money, that are self-sustaining in time. Let these people learn the value of helping themselves using yourselves as resources. Teach them to "fish", in other words. But do feed them first, as a hungry people can't move past the hunger until they are fed.

Understand that NESARA and the Second Coming Events, do not immediately fix the world, they only set the stage. I think we shall see a very different world in a period of five years. Your star visitors will enforce the peace, in a very short time, allowing you to begin your work.
Until the funds and ideas begin to happen, they can feed many, in areas that are impoverished, until the rest of you can help in other ways. The star people are not going to do it all. You must do it all. They will serve more in an advisory capacity. They will impart the knowledge you need to change your world, but you must make use of this knowledge and create the changes yourself.

And as mentioned, the Inner Earth people will impart knowledge, they have been there and done that, as the expression goes, and are eager to share with you their own learning and experience. But the Inner Earth society has not the population problems of the surface, nor the degree of political strife, ever, so they do not have all the solutions. This will be time of learning also for them, as they begin to mingle with you.

So, my friends, begin your dreams and ideas in earnest. Study your world and its needs. Look first at home, if that suits you, for what needs fixing. Go on the Internet and read of other places. Africa is in the most need of help from others. It is so very war torn, and unstable. Even though there are poor in almost any country, the countries of Africa have the most.

Societies in South America have many poor, but these also have greater resources. If you live in South America, look around you. You have much to improve upon, but your resources and education are better than Africa. What Africa does have, however, is a great people in general, who are exhausted from life as lived, and once fed, and healed of illness, they will be a mighty force in helping themselves, if you will but provide the money, and certain resources to them.

We will take care of the dictator problem that exists in many places. There will be star people in temporary governments in many countries in Africa as there is no one suitable at this time to do so. Russia is beginning to step up to the plate in providing for the countries that left the Soviet Union in a positive way. You do not read of this of course but it is happening.

Actually, Putin will not be replaced at this time, he has so fully come into the Light. He has many challenges ahead, and is up to them. Russia will also have honest elections in due time, but not in the four months, that will happen in the United States. Many countries will have to wait longer than 4 months for honest elections as they are too unstable to bring this about.

So, I am trying to get across that the changes will vary from country to country, dependent on the local situations. But within a year, there should be a much more satisfactory flow of monies from a variety of sources to all the world. Good day, my friends. I AM Violinio Germain."

Channeled by CANDACE: Go to **http://abundanthope.net/pages/rubens/The-Wait-is-Over.shtml** *for updates*

45

THE NEW INTERNATIONAL WAVES OF TRUTH

It is important to understand that the revelations about the Strawman, the Global Elite, and the way countries have been taken over is not limited to the United States and Canada. In fact in going back to the debt pyramid of the first chapters, all nations have in some way fallen to the business plan and the extent of the debt clearly indicates their status. The British colonies are administered through the Queen and Britain even though people believe they are autonomous and sovereign. Many other administrative groups have been put in place around the globe. in fact there are so many large moves in play now, with so many warriors penetrating the veils of the deception, it would be impossible to reveal them here. For that reason, only select examples are used here to make the point that this is not just a mere kerfuffle as a disgruntled radical group.

In order to illustrate the extent, and the consistency, the work of **Michael Tellinger** in South Africa is presented here to enlighten this extent. Michael has attacked the local establishment on three major fronts and his movement has gathered enormous followings as he now presents his research, findings, and status of taking on the establishment around the world. Michael has attacked on three fronts:

1. **The New Economic Rights Alliance**
2. **The Ubunto Freedom Charter**
3. **The historical reconstruction**

These are summarized here.

The New Economic Rights Alliance Of South Africa

The New Economic Rights Alliance found at **www.newera.org.za** is launching a case that aims to obtain transparency in banking. It is of interest here to note that the Bank being exposed here is south Africa's largest bank, the Standard Bank. Michael states:

"We have accumulated unequivocal evidence that South African banks are breaching many South African laws. This has led to severe breaches of human rights. With its Members, the NewERA is about to file an application in the High Court to have our concerns heard. Once we have proven in court that the banks are breaking the law, we

will then file a class action lawsuit. The time for truth in banking is now. The following outlines the reasons behind this action:

1. Banks do not "loan" money as their prolific advertisements claim. Money loaned is actually money created, via an elaborate scheme of paper shifting and number crunching. It can be said that banks make money out-of-thin-air under the "pretence" of a loan, but in reality it is not a loan at all. This is deceptive and misleading as very few South Africans know the truth.

2. It is a common legal principle in our law that one must possess that which one loans. For reasons above, the banks are unable to meet this, a fundamental criteria for a valid borrower / lender contract. In fact, banks are actively and blatantly breaching the Home Loan and Mortgage Disclosure Act.

3. Banks are failing to provide simple information to their customers that should be easy to access. Examples include a certificate of balance, audited proof that a lawful "deposit" was actually made and the physical location of original documents, promissory notes and other negotiable instruments. Instead of providing the customer with this information, they choose to take legal action, and foreclose on homes and assets with remarkable alacrity.

4. The banks are acting as intermediary / agent between the customer and other parties. It is a requirement that an agency relationship be fully disclosed up front to the customer. The banks do not disclose this relationship and, as a result, most people are under the complete illusion that they are borrowing money from their bank in the ordinary sense of the word. In fact, banks are unable to show that a default actually causes them any real financial loss. The New Economic Rights Alliance NPC. Directors: SC Cundil, BA Vermak, GJ Robertse, DC Modley, CG Sapsford.

5. Banks engage in a widespread and common practice called securitisation. Instead of borrowing from the Reserve Bank on our behalf, banks bundle many loans together and then sell these bundles to investors whereby our loans become securities. These securities are traded on local and international markets. This industry caused the stock market crash of 2008 and threatens the global economy as we speak. In fact, the betting game being played by the banks, called the derivatives market, is currently estimated to be 20 times larger than the GDP of the entire planet. Rather than slowing down, its sheer propensity for profit has led to a rampant growth of the industry in South Africa. The Banks Act makes it crystal clear that securitisation falls outside the business of a bank. Therefore, it is a blatant breach of the Bank Act for a bank to engage in this practice, and rightly so.

6. Banks refuse to disclose the securitisation process to the customer, who has a lawful right to this information. When a customer asks for disclosure, the banks do not even bother responding, or respond using unintelligible legal jargon. The entire securitisation process is kept tightly secret while it provides huge profits to those behind the scenes.

Instead of securitisation providing a benefit to the customer by way of cheaper credit, the reverse occurs: banks swiftly and relentlessly foreclose on assets in order to satisfy the needs of their investors. It should also be mentioned that banks have been known to securitize the same debt several times. To make matters worse, should a person default on a repayment, those secret investors are protected by an insurance policy while the poor customer enjoys no such protection.

7. We have written confirmation from the South African Reserve Bank that, once a bank sells a loan into a securitisation pool, they lose the legal right to that asset. This could mean that literally tens, if not hundreds of thousands of homes and other assets have been taken away from South Africans illegally.

8. Banks do not use "money," they use negotiable instruments. These instruments are defined clearly in the Bills of Exchange Act and have been used by trading merchants for thousands of years. It is the constitutional right of every South African to have an explanation of how our instruments are being used, traded, and exploited by the banks.

9. Banks are foreclosing on people's homes and assets by using the contract as a shield. Their argument is simple: "you signed a contract, so you must pay." By sticking to the age old axiom: the-agreement-is-king, anyone attempting to look behind the shield is prohibited from doing so. This loan agreement, which is a series of one-way payments from the customer with absolutely no downside whatsoever to the bank, is somehow enough to allow them to win in court. We believe that granting summary judgment in such a manner, without the courts listening to the counter argument that the contract is not valid due to malicious deception, is unconstitutional.

10. It is illegal for banks to claim more than double the amount loaned from any borrower (the in duplum rule). However, banks are not only breaking this rule, but they are also forcing people to pay the interest on loans up front. In other words, the interest is paid back first, before the principal. This is plainly illegal. And how banks are able charge interest at all, seeing as no lawful South African Rand / money was ever lent to the customer in the first place, is a very interesting mystery.

11. Banks are lending out fake money, but the assets they foreclose on, and the lives they destroy, are very real. For evidence of real human rights that are being breached by the banks, see here: http://www.newera.org.za/big-banking-survey-results/. Remember, just because numbers appear on a loan account or credit statement does not mean that those numbers represent lawful loans.

12. The collection processes in banks have become so extreme, that call centre operators have been known to verbally abuse customers. The customer believes, quite wrongly, that the bank is running at a loss and is simply doing its best to get its money back. The New Economic Rights Alliance NPC. Directors: SC Cundil, BA Vermak, GJ Robertse, DC Modley, CG Sapsford. This illusion is maintained by the banks who continue to refine their well-oiled, clinical machine of repossession and foreclosure. Banks are now even resorting to forcefully taking money out of people's bank accounts without notice.

13. If a bank employee dispenses with an affidavit, it is a legal requirement that the directors of that bank first dispense with a Special Resolution granting permission for that employee to make such an affidavit. This rule is currently being circumvented. Somehow, half-hearted affidavits, made by just about anyone in the bank, are being successfully used to obtain judgment and foreclosures.

14. When a bank makes a deposit, they are prescribed by law to adhere to certain administrative procedures outlined in the Banks Act. This is to ensure that the required liquidity procedures are adhered to. Banks are circumventing these procedures and are engaging in unlawful deposits, placing the economy of the entire country at risk.

15. There is an overall sense of conduct and legal justice required for the good of the community (boni mores). Summary Judgment is a process which has been called a "draconian measure" by our very own honourable Judges. Judgments against homes and assets granted in this manner tears apart the very fabric of our Constitution.

16. The legal relationship between a bank and its customer is fiduciary, not dissimilar to that of a doctor and his patient, an estate agent and a home owner or a lawyer and her client. By engaging in secret and underhanded dealings, and by not disclosing the full truth up front, the banks are taking full advantage of their customers in the name of profiteering. As such, this fiduciary relationship has been broken which is a most grave and serious crime. This crime is perpetuated when the principal fails to answer, and even bluntly ignores the requests and pleas of the customer in their hour of need. Should this action be successful, what is the benefit for the average South African?

1. Interest rates will be reduced, thus significantly reducing monthly repayments.
2. Banks will become more forgiving when dealing with defaulters.
3. Forced austerity measures, currently being implemented in several countries around the world, could be reduced or even avoided here in South Africa. Make no mistake – they are coming.
4. Courts will be required to provide a stronger and fairer defence for South Africans wishing to save their homes. Currently, the banks are ruling the courts and this has got to change.
5. There will be a more competitive choice when loaning money or purchasing a home, as banks will be disallowed to act outside the competition legislation.
6. Secrecy in dealing with a client's money and loan agreements will be a matter of the past, thus transparency shall prevail and people will know the inner workings of the banking system once and for all.
7. Additional stock options should also be available whereby the client can elect to purchase back or extend its borrowings on the open market or through securitisation packages. This alternative form of financing will greatly help to prevent their assets from being taken away. For justification for the above contentions, and an on-going discussion of the case, visit **www.thebigcase.co.za.**

1. We have accumulated extraordinary evidence that shows that South African banks are operating unlawfully.
2. The New Economic Rights Alliance is about to serve a High Court summons on all four major banks. We will do this jointly with any Member who wishes to participate.
3. We hereby invite you to stand with us and formally join this cause of action. This is not a class action yet, it is a certification that the banks are breaking the law.
4. Those people who join this action are likely to have pending legal action against them temporarily suspended.
5. Even if you have not defaulted on a loan, you will add significant weight to our

case.
6. The grounds for the summons are outlined in the attached document, but they are primarily the following:

> a. The fractional reserve banking system (making money out of thin air) and the securitisation process (secretly gambling with our money behind our backs) are breaches of South African law, go against the Constitution and are contra bones mores (against the basic morals of society).
> b. Banks are supposed to have a trusted legal relationship with their customers, called a Fiduciary. This relationship has been breached, all in the name of rampant profiteering. The New Economic Rights Alliance NPC. Directors: SC Cundil, BA Vermak, GJ Robertse, DC Modley, CG Sapsford.
> c. The above has resulted in prejudice, and this will set the scene for a later class action lawsuit.

This is an ongoing David and Goliath battle which can be monitored on **www.thebigcase.co.za**.

The Ubunto Freedom Charter

Another movement that has gained world recognition is the Ubunto Contribution system that is focussed on a new financial system. The website is **www.ubuntuparty.org.za/index.php.** Michael explains the movement:

"Every socio-political system we have ever had as the human race has failed us dramatically. South Africa, like the rest of the world, is now sitting on the verge of complete and devastating financial meltdown with catastrophic results for its people. The South African economy and natural recourses have been plundered by reckless and ignorant politicians, with no remorse or any real accountability to its citizens. There is no possible remedy for the current crisis. Anyone who has done some research into the global financial structures will know that there is no possibility of a happy outcome to the money-driven, consumer capitalist system that we have all been lured into by our leaders.

South Africa is one of the wealthiest countries of the world. Every person should have everything they wish for. And yet we have more poverty, more homelessness, more hunger, more crime, more disease, more despair, more anarchy and unhappiness, than ever before in our history. This situation cannot continue without an eventual bloody revolution. But this can be prevented. They say that history has taught us nothing. Well - this is the time when we finally have to learn from history and choose a completely new course.

This potentially catastrophic situation presents us with a shining opportunity to consciously change our course and secure our destiny as the human race and the people of South Africa. This document presents the very basic foundation of a new social structure to take us into a new era of real freedom, real prosperity and real control of our destiny as the people of South Africa. To achieve this will require a complete change of thinking and a paradigm shift by the ordinary citizens of the land in our approach to our own destiny. It will require taking back the power from the politicians and the governments they have created, with their complex legal systems, to protect their own interests and the agendas of the large multinational corporations that support them.

The launching of the UBUNTU CONTRIBUTION SYSTEM as a new social structure in South Africa. This new movement is represented on the political arena as the UBUNTU PARTY. It is the result of six years of research and planning by numerous participants who can no longer tolerate the absolute abuse of the good, honest citizens of South Africa and the raping of our land by a group of political elite who have unlawfully assumed ownership of it all. It is now blatantly clear that the politicians and large corporations have stolen the country from its people – it's time to take it back. Africa was once GREAT – let us make her GREAT again."

African Roots and Purpose In many ways the UBUNTU CONTRIBUTION SYSTEM (UCS) is loosely based on the ancient tribal structures of the African people and other native tribes of the world. For thousands of years the native people of the world lived in close tribal communities, in harmony with mother Earth. Society has been segregated and separated on so many levels that we hardly understand the word unity anymore. UCS will allow people to reconstitute a unified society consisting of smaller harmonious communities.

UCS will restore this harmonious balance between the people and the Earth providing abundance for all, because it is an environment which allows its citizens to all contribute their natural talents and acquired skills to the greater benefit all the people in the community. This applies to all areas of our society; science, technology, agriculture, manufacture, health, education, housing, and all other areas not financially viable under the present money-driven economic system.

To begin this journey of transformation, we need to be reminded of our inalienable rights as the citizens of South Africa. It is ironic that these so-called new ideas are almost word for word the principles of the Freedom Charter for which many South Africans have died in past 100 years. Today, this call for rights is no longer applicable to a sector of our population, but a unified call by all its citizens who have been denied freedom and dignity.

The New Freedom Charter

It is stated that the government has betrayed the dream of Nelson Mandela and other elders, desecrating the Freedom Charter as such, the UBUNTU PARTY has adapted the Freedom Charter for the needs of the people today which is stated below:

The People Shall Govern!
- New laws and new governing structures will be created based on the will of the people on a local and national level;
- The reintroduction of African tribal structures with a council of elders will be implemented to manage and advise communities;
- These new tribal councils will adopt the fundamental principles of Contributionism to enhance their ability to rule and advise the people;
- Every man and woman shall have the right to stand as a candidate for all such councils or bodies that govern or make laws;

- All people shall be entitled to take part in the administration of the country, town or community in accordance with the newly developed laws by the people;
- The rights of the people shall be the same, regardless of race, colour or sex;

All People and National Groups Have Equal Rights!
- The principle of UNITY will be the foundation of all communities and the national governing body;
- All people shall have equal right to use their own languages, and to develop their own culture and customs as long as it does not infringe on the customs of others;
- The diversity and beauty of our cultures and languages will be promoted and celebrated as widely as possible;
- All national groups shall be protected by law against insults to their race and national pride;
- There shall be no hierarchy or levels of superiority in any aspects of society, every person's contribution will be valued as equally important as any other;
- All discriminatory laws and practices shall be set aside.
- The use of money and wealth as tool of separation, segregation and discrimination will be abolished;

The People Shall Share in the Country's Wealth!
- The national wealth of our country, the heritage of South Africans, shall be restored to the people and new applicable laws will be created to benefit and protect the people on all fronts;
- All mineral wealth above or beneath the ground will be controlled by the people and used for the benefit of all people and all communities – it will not be allowed to be monopolised by individuals, corporations or any ruling body;
- All international trade shall be adapted by the people to assist the wellbeing of all the people;
- All industry and manufacturing shall be supported in all possible ways to deliver abundance of all things to all people;
- All people shall have equal rights to choose any trade, craft or professions they wish to participate in and all training and education to attain their profession will be free;
- The Banking and financial system and the control of the printing of money will be eradicated until there is no more need for money in our society whatsoever;

The Land Shall be Shared Among Those Who Work It!
- Farmers who feed the people are the heroes of the land and will be given land, tools, seeds, implements and all assistance necessary to maximise the production of their crops and produce;
- Land usage shall be adapted to benefit all the people, and made available to those who work it, to banish famine and hunger;
- Since the land belongs to all the people, land ownership will be abolished and replaced by new land usage laws of the new society which will benefit all the people, especially the farmers;
- Since money will no longer be part of the system, no land will be sold or owned by individuals, or corporations, or in any other way possible;

- Existing farmers will be required to use their land for the benefit of the community, or teach other new farmers to farm the vacant land to help feed the people;
- Everyone who contributes to wards the community will be given as much land as is required to perform their task;
- The people in each community will plan and implement the reconstruction of their community, development of public parks and recreational area to the greatest benefit of the community;
- Every community will have the right to control a specified area around its boundaries for the production of crops and other farming necessities;
- These boundaries will be specified by the new legal structures to be introduced under the equal rights of Contributionism and based on the population in the community;
- Each community will be encouraged to become self reliant and self-sustainable on the agricultural products they produce;
- Food will be distributed nationally between communities and to those communities that are unable to provide for themselves, and all food and other farming or agricultural produce will be available to the people for free;
- All people shall have the right to settle in any community they choose and contribute to their community with their skills or talents;

All Shall be Equal Before the Law!
- A new legal system of basic common law will be implemented as drafted by the people for the nation and the whole country BUT each community will have the right to add new specific laws for the greatest benefit of their specific community;
- Each community will have the right to govern their town and boundaries according to the laws created by the community, as long as the laws do not clash with the basic common laws of the nation;
- No-one shall be imprisoned, deported or restricted without a fair trial based on the new legal system implemented by the people under Contributionism;
- The courts shall be representative of all the people;
- Imprisonment shall be only for serious crimes against the people, and shall aim at re-education, not vengeance;
- The police and army shall be open to all on an equal basis and shall be the helpers and protectors of the people;
- The police and the army will be restructured based on the needs of the people and the will of the people; they will be given all the tools and support necessary to perform their tasks as required by the new legal requirements under Contributionism;
- The police and the army will be regarded as peace officers;

All Shall Enjoy Equal Human Rights!
- It is no longer necessary to list these rights since we are all equal in all aspects under the **Ubuntu Contribution System** and UNITY is the underlying foundation;
- There is no hierarchy or superiority of any kind and it is not really possible to discriminate against groups or individuals in a society without the class distinctions normally created by money;

There Shall be Work and Security! (Transition period)
- In a free society under the UBUNTU CONTRIBUTION SYSTEM no one shall work for money but for personal satisfaction and pride in their community – money will be removed from the system;
- The expression "work" will fall away rapidly in the new society, since all people now follow their passion or God-given talents – this is their contribution to the community;
- New laws will be set up by the people regarding the participation and contribution of members in their communities;
- During the transition phase to full Contributionism everyone who is without a job or business of their own, or an income, will be asked to participate and contribute to the national and local Public Works Project in which all aspects of transport, health, housing, communication, energy and all aspects of service delivery will be upgraded and made available to all; Everyone who contributes will be paid equally and only required to contribute on average five hours per day, as part of the preparation for the transition to full Contributionism;
- All who contribute shall receive free food, water, housing and electricity as part of their reward;
- Every other person in every trade will be given all the tools, materials and support necessary to perform their task to the best of their ability and highest standard of their craft;
- Each member of the community will be required to contribute 2 hours per week towards community building projects, irrespective of what other activity they are part of or contribute to their community;
- Each community will be unified and united in their effort to make life as easy and pleasant for everyone to live life and enjoy it to the full;

Conclusion
- The UBUNTU CONTRIBUTION SYSTEM is a blueprint for a new social structure in which everyone is absolutely free and equal.
- A culture where each individual is encouraged to follow their passion and contributes their natural talents or acquired skills to the greater benefit of all the people in the community and society at large.
- A society that functions without the concept of money, any form of barter or trade, or the attachment of value to material things.
- A society with a new set of laws based on the needs of the people where everything is provided freely to everyone who contributes.
- A society which promotes the highest levels of scientific and technological progress.
- A society in which arts and culture flourishes allowing people to experience life to the fullest.
- A society in which spiritual growth of its citizens through the explosion of arts and culture will allow the rapid rise of consciousness to fully embrace the concepts on unity.
- The system provides unimaginable abundance of all things on all levels, impossible to imagine by those trapped in the capitalist consumer-driven environment of today.

Our Inalienable Rights – The Rights of all Citizens
1. The country belongs to its people
2. The land belongs to its people
3. The water belongs to the people
4. The forests belongs to the people
5. The rivers and lakes belong to the people
6. The gold, the platinum, chrome, copper, iron, uranium, tin, aluminum, and all other minerals in the ground belong to the people
7. The coal belongs to the people
8. The diamonds belong to the people
9. Everything that grows on the land belongs to the people
10. The beaches, the mountains and the skies above belong to the people
11. The wild animals do not belong to us or anyone else, they belong to the planet and we are their custodians and protectors

First Freedoms
To recognise these freedoms let's remind ourselves of some of our inalienable rights. If the land belongs to the people, the rivers and the coal in the ground belongs to the people, why are we paying for these? All rural towns and farming communities will have the following freedoms:
- <u>FREE</u> ELECTRICITY
- FREE WATER
- FREE HOUSING
- Medium term – FREE FOOD

All possible support will be given to the farmers to produce as much organic food as possible for their own community and other communities in their area. The objective is for each community to be able to provide all the food necessary for their own needs.

A Plan For Rural Towns
"A blueprint for the transformation of small towns and rural villages into strong, sustainable communities, in complete control of their own destiny. This is a model that can serve as a template for all small towns to introduce UBUNTU Contributionism to each community. It will restore the harmonious balance between the people and the Earth because it allows people from all walks of life to achieve whatever they dream of. Their passion for what they choose to do is their contribution for the greater benefit of all in their community. From farmers to scientists, artists to engineers, health workers and especially community workers. Everyone adds greatly to the abundance in their community." **Michael Tellinger**, November 2010.

Implementation
The small towns and rural communities scattered throughout the country are prime areas for the introduction of the new system. One by one we can turn these small towns into self sustainable examples of abundance and success.

How Will This Be Achieved?
The knowhow and scientific expertise is available from a variety of great minds to implement all the proposed objectives. We have been in contact with some of the greatest minds in science, medicine, energy, education, engineering, agriculture and

more to help implement all the proposed plans. This is not a wish list but rather a to-do list of achievable objectives because we have already established its viability.

This is a very important part of the plan for all to understand very clearly. The people behind the UBUNTU Contribution System are not politicians or corporations with profit in mind. We are a growing group of HUMANS who consist of scientists, teachers, doctors, inventors and many other ordinary people who care about other humans. We have taken these steps to share our knowledge with others.

Council of Elders
The people can implement their right to take over the governance of their town with a newly appointed council of elders, appointed by the people of the community to serve the community, unlike the government or the many mostly bankrupt municipalities who fail to deliver any of the needs of the people. The new council will implement the needs of the community on a daily basis from within the centre of the community and not some distant ivory tower with unreachable politicians who have no understanding of the needs of the community. As one town succeeds, the others will follow their example rapidly as the people will want to emulate their success.

Step By Step
There are several steps to reaching complete UBUNTU Contributionism in the towns and ultimately in the whole country. Remember that this new social structure will bring new laws and guidelines that will be established by the communities themselves and therefore we have to view every sector with brand new eyes of unlimited opportunity, not restricted by the availability of money. It is therefore also imperative to keep reminding ourselves that everything is possible and everything is achievable. More detail of the UBUNTU Council and how each community will govern itself will be covered in a separate document, but the introduction of the new system needs to be understood clearly. It will take several stages of using money as a tool to liberate us from money itself. The communities will not only become completely.

The New Origins Of Humankind

Even the origins of mankind and our written history that we have been taught is under attack. Michael Tellinger, as an author, scientist, explorer, has become a real-life Indiana Jones, making groundbreaking discoveries about ancient vanished civilizations at the southern tip of Africa. His website is found at ***www.michaeltellinger.com.***

His continued efforts and analytical scientific approach have produced stunning new evidence that will force us to rethink our origins and rewrite our history books. In the last six months Michael has shared the stage with international celebrities like Graham Hancock, Robert Temple, David Wilcock, Bob Dean, Kerry Cassidy (Project Camelot), Dr. Seven Greer, Stanton Friedman (PhD), Andrew Collins, Klaus Dona, and many more. His successful 2010 and 2011 USA and Canadian tours enthralled not only the American audiences but also his Canadian followers.

Michael Tellinger has become an international authority on the origins of humankind and the vanished civilizations of southern Africa. Scholars have told us that the first civilization on Earth emerged in a land called Sumer some 6000 years ago. New archaeological and scientific discoveries made by Michael Tellinger, Johan Heine and a team of leading scientists, show that the Sumerians and even the Egyptians inherited all their knowledge from an earlier civilization that lived at the southern tip of Africa more than 200,000 years ago... mining gold.

These were also the people who carved the first Horus bird, the first Sphinx, built the first pyramids and built an accurate stone calendar right in the heart of it all. Adam's Calendar is the flagship among millions of circular stone ruins, ancient roads, agricultural terraces and thousands of ancient mines, left behind by a vanished civilisation which they now call the FIRST PEOPLE. These were the ancestors of all humans today with an advanced knowledge of energy fields through planet Earth.

They carved detailed images into the hardest rock, worshipped the sun, and are the first to carve an image of the Egyptian Ankh – key of life and universal knowledge, 200,000 years before the Egyptians came to light. Tellinger presents this groundbreaking new evidence in which is released in his latest book Temples Of The African Gods. It graphically exposes these discoveries and will undoubtedly be the catalyst for rewriting our ancient human history. The new release is a continuation of Tellinger's previous books Slave Species of god and Adam's Calendar which have become favourites with readers in over 20 countries.

These were also the people who carved the first Horus bird, the first Sphinx, built the first pyramids and built an accurate stone calendar right in the heart of it all. Adam's Calendar, now referred to as ENKI's CALENDAR, is the flagship among millions of circular stone ruins, ancient roads, agricultural terraces and thousands of ancient mines, left behind by a vanished civilization which we now call the FIRST PEOPLE. These settlements cover most of southern Africa, an area about twice the size of Texas. They carved detailed images into the hardest rock, worshiped the sun, and were the first to carve an image of the Egyptian Ankh – key of life and universal knowledge, 200,000 years before the Egyptians came to light.

Michael's research reveals many of the latest scientific measurements and presents evidence that this vanished civilization had an astute knowledge of the laws of nature and the generation of **free** ENERGY from Mother Earth for all their needs. They used the power of sound and frequency as a source of energy, which underpins the scientific conclusions reached by Michael. In his book Temples Of The African Gods he graphically exposes these discoveries that will be the catalyst for rewriting our ancient human history.

This work is a continuation of Tellinger's previous books Slave Species of god and Adam's Calendar which have become favourites with readers in over 30 countries.
Before Michael Tellinger, there was only novel speculation about the origins of stone remains on the continent of Africa. But with Michael's dedication to discovering, tracking, and revealing vanished civilizations, it's now possible to reach into the minds of our ancient forefathers to discover a purpose greater than what we might have expected. Certainly, it's now well acknowledged that they were further technologically advanced than the present day, and far more astute than what we are taught through the less than accurate cave-man mentality of our educational systems

Slave Species of god In his book *Slave Species of god*, Michael Tellinger takes his readers on a remarkable odyssey of the true origins of humankind in which he:

- draws clear and startling analogies between new discoveries in genetic engineering and ancient archaeological finds...
- highlights emerging scientific information overlooked in the past...
- unravels the Bible's often obscure stories by linking these to their original forms in Sumerian clay tablets and other prehistoric writings...
- provides explicit answers to why our modern world has become so senseless and chaotic by revealing the very secrets of our prehistory...

He cuts to chase revealing compelling answers to questions like Were humans created by "god" as SLAVES? Was Abraham the first human SPY? **and** Was Jesus an accidental MESSIAH?

While shattering myths about evolution and God, Slave Species of god enables evolutionists and creationists to finally co-exist in one pond. The arguments are compelling, simple and refreshing, retracing the path of human evolution from the murky distant past to the religious dogma that haunts humankind today. The question of who we are and where we come from takes on a new meaning as we discover that our DNA may have been manipulated by our CREATOR some 250 000 years ago to produce a less intelligent 'primitive species'. In fact, the book's evidence shows that Adam and Eve were not the 'apple' of God's eye as first suggested in Genesis. Tellinger presents the many arguments and evidence succinctly and convincingly, pointing out the difference between 'GOD' and god. How did this genetic manipulation affect humankind? How have we evolved in 250 000 years? Can we achieve immortality? These are just some of the questions answered in this gripping and astonishing work, challenging all those who are looking for new answers in the 21st century Scholars have told us that the first civilisation on Earth emerged in a land called Sumer some 6000 years ago. The persistent research by Michael Tellinger, Johan Heine and a team of leading scientists, over an extend seven-year period, has resulted in astonishing new archaeological and scientific discoveries. It shows that the Sumerians and even the Egyptians inherited all their knowledge from an earlier advanced civilisation that lived at the southern tip of Africa more than 200,000 years ago... mining gold.

These were also the people who carved the first Horus bird, the first Sphinx, built the first pyramids and built an accurate stone calendar right in the heart of it all. Adam's Calendar is the flagship among millions of circular stone ruins, ancient roads, agricultural terraces and thousands of ancient mines, left behind by a vanished civilisation which they now call the FIRST PEOPLE. These were the ancestors of all humans today with an advanced knowledge of energy fields through planet Earth.

They carved detailed images into the hardest rock, worshipped the sun, and are the first to carve an image of the Egyptian Ankh – key of life and universal knowledge, 200,000 years before the Egyptians came to light. Tellinger presents this groundbreaking new evidence in which is released in his latest book Temples Of The African Gods. It graphically exposes these discoveries and will undoubtedly be the catalyst for rewriting our ancient human history. The new release is a continuation of ***Tellinger***'s previous books **Slave Species of god and Adam's Calendar** which have become favourites with readers in over 20 countries.

Michael Tellinger has caused quite a stir with his highly controversial epic on the origins of humankind. Slave species of god has now become a real cult epic with readers in over 20 countries. Since its release it has become a steady bestseller in South Africa and a constant good seller in the USA. Tellinger takes the reader on a remarkable odyssey through our human prehistory and draws startling analogies between new discoveries in science, astronomy, genetic engineering and ancient archaeological finds, only to point out that most of what we were taught is in fact very questionable. The book reflects a high level of research and investigates a variety of interesting subjects ranging from human nature to human cloning and bravely re-evaluates the existing religious dogma enslaving humankind to this day. The arguments are simple and refreshing supported by startling scientific evidence. The question of who we are and where we come from takes on a new meaning as we discover the real possibility that our DNA may have been tampered with at the point of our creation. **A 75,000 year-old stone calendar - In the cradle of humankind.**

A new discovery of an ancient circular monolithic stone calendar site in Mpumalanga has proven to be at least 75,000 years old, pre-dating any other structure found to date. Southern Africa holds some of the deepest mysteries in all of human history. What we are told is that at around 60,000 years ago the early humans migrated from Africa and populated the rest of the world.

Who were these first humans? What did they do? And where did they disappear to?
It estimated that there are over 100 000 ancient stone ruins scattered throughout the mountains of southern Africa. Artefacts that have been recovered from these ruins show a long and extended period of settlement that spans to over 200,000 years. The most spectacular examples of these ancient ruins are RIGHT HERE within walking distance. Modern historians have been speculating about the origins of these ruins, often calling them 'cattle kraal of little historic importance'.

The truth of the matter is that closer scientific inspection shows that we actually know very little about these spectacular ancient ruins. It is a great tragedy that thousands have already been destroyed through sheer ignorance but forestry and farmers have now started to protect these ruin. Adam's Calendar is the flagship among these ruins because we can date this monolithic calendar with relative certainty to at least 75,000 years of age based on a number of scientific evaluations.

Adam's Calendar another book by Michael presents the first tangible evidence of consciousness among the earliest humans in the 'Cradle of humankind'. The site is built along the same longitudinal line as Great Zimbabwe and the Great Pyramid. It is also aligned with the rise of Orion's belt some 75,000 years ago. This new discovery of an ancient circular monolithic stone calendar site in Mpumalanga has proven to be at least 75,000 years old, pre-dating any other structure found to date. Southern Africa holds some of the deepest mysteries in all of human history. What we are told is that at around 60,000 years ago the early humans migrated from Africa and populated the rest of the world.

Who were these first humans? What did they do? And where did they disappear to?
It estimated that there are over 100 000 ancient stone ruins scattered throughout the mountains of southern Africa. Artefacts that have been recovered from these ruins show a long and extended period of settlement that spans to over 200,000 years. The most spectacular examples of these ancient ruins are RIGHT HERE within walking distance. Modern historians have been speculating about the origins of these ruins, often calling them 'cattle kraal of little historic importance'.

The truth of the matter is that closer scientific inspection shows that we actually know very little about these spectacular ancient ruins. It is a great tragedy that thousands have already been destroyed through sheer ignorance but forestry and farmers have now started to protect these ruin. Adam's Calendar is the flagship among these ruins because we can date this monolithic calendar with relative certainty to at least 75,000 years of age based on a number of scientific evaluations.

Adam's Calendar also presents the first tangible evidence of consciousness among the earliest humans in the 'Cradle of humankind'. The site is built along the same longitudinal line as Great Zimbabwe and the Great Pyramid. It is also aligned with the rise of Orion's belt some 75,000 years ago.

Temples of the African Gods This is a scientific expose that will shatter our knowledge of ancient human history. Scholars have told us that the first civilisation on Earth emerged in a land called Sumer some 6000 years ago. New archaeological and scientific discoveries made by Michael Tellinger, Johan Heine and a team of leading scientists, show that the Sumerians and even the Egyptians inherited all their knowledge from an earlier civilisation that lived at the southern tip of Africa more than 200,000 years ago...mining gold. These were also the people who carved the first Horus bird, the first Sphinx, built the first pyramids and built an accurate stone calendar right in the heart of it all. "Adam's Calendar" is the flagship among millions of circular stone ruins, ancient roads, agricultural terraces and thousands of ancient mines, left behind by a vanished civilisation which we now call the First People. They carved detailed images into the hardest rock, worshipped the sun, and are the first to carve an image of the Egyptian Ankh - key of life and universal knowledge, 200,000 years before the Egyptians came to light. This book graphically exposes these discoveries and will be the catalyst for rewriting our ancient human history. The book is a continuation of Tellinger's previous books "**Slave Species of God**" and "**Adam's Calendar**" which have become favourites with readers in over 20 countries.

In another area of research, Michael has taken a unique leadership role in another topic that seldom hits the big press. He explains as follows:

"Through my research, my travels around the world and doing presentations on the staggering new information about our origins and the lost gold-mining settlements of the Anunnaki in southern Africa, I have been blessed by meeting some of the most enlightened and consciously connected people imaginable. After the successful Megalithomania conference in March 2011, it became evident that there was a desperate need to present a platform of exposure for the much ignored area of UFOlogy. But enlightenment is a beautiful thing, and it is now evident that the research being done around the UFO phenomena is closely linked to the frontiers of science. In turn, the

frontiers of science, especially the areas of quantum physics, are directly linked to our understanding of this thing called Consciousness. These three are inextricably linked, and therefore I decided to combine them on a platform of credibility by some of the <u>best</u> minds available. The research coming from the frontiers of science is so advanced that it seems like magic or wizardry to the average person on the street. These new areas of knowledge are finally breaking down the barriers between the known and the occult."

"There are millions of people in South Africa and around the world that have lived in fear of sharing their personal experiences and knowledge with others, afraid of ridicule and slanderous attacks by those who live in ignorance and often in denial. Those days are gone – you are not alone. You are the awakened ones – those who have decided to see for themselves and embrace their own truth instead of the dogma of authority. Come share your experience with others and learn more about these subjects among others who share your truth. The Consciousness shift is upon us – we are being exposed to divine knowledge – be the enlightened voice of the new world. in Pure Truth." **Michael of the family Tellinger.**

What is important to note is that this is not just an isolated group of rebels. The issues of disclosure with regards to the monetary system, to research, to aliens, to the ways governments have evolved to have people serve them rather that serve the people is all around the world. Just Google it or go to YouTube. But don't be surprised that none of this is in the mainstream media.

In addition to many sites referred to in this book, especially Volume One, there are many media systems coming forward that are not part of the mainstream.

46

THE 2012 SCENARIO
FREE WAVES OF TRUTH

It is without doubt that the Internet has brought a means of new "free press" media to the home. There are millions of sites that have shifted into the new consciousness. The main issue is that there is so much that is not "edited" or "censored" by those who like to choose the type of information the mass is to have, that it becomes difficult to determine what is truth and what is not. In the past, as we have learned, much of the mainstream media has been controlled and owned by those that wish to present information that they feel is important; and in most cases, it serves a private agenda. And as we have seen, this has grown more and more towards being controlled for a purposeful business plan for the "betterment of the Empire's slaves. In effect, it is all to feed the "public" vehicles so as to absorb the "private". However, as we have seen, the private side of reality is growing at an astounding rate providing uncensored news both private and public. The Internet now provides millions of sites providing daily news on the subjects that have normally been taboo or filtered.

In particular, there is a long list of sites that have been referenced so far. These are dedicated to "getting the truth out" in both the spiritual and commercial areas. Each that has been used here is extensive in its research. In Part 1 in particular, we have had a tendency to keep away from opinion and look at people and groups that have done a considerable amount of investigative research into their topics. Many have huge issues with the "system" and have their own crosses to bare as they have gotten into some serious trouble. Yet, it forms a strong motivation to get the truth out in a less haphazard "opinion" and do the research.

In this chapter, in addition to the many references that have been provided, we are going to highlight the fact that there many large groups around the world that are dedicated to news of what is happening because much of the mainstream media has not yet yielded to the same truth. It should not come as a surprise that media and its control is very important to the Media Division of PLANET EARTH INC. After all, that's how history is re-written, and that's how the consumer's appetite for product is maintained. And if we would look very closely at the Tavistock Institute and large organizations like Disney, one could easily infer that mind control and superior technology that influence mass consciousness is not science fiction.

In the following sections we touch upon a few of these media machines that have gained a huge following worldwide. There are many. Much of the words are taken from the sites simply to introduce them.

The 2012 Scenario By Steve Beckow

One of the best (in my opinion) sites on the internet that keeps you well posted on all aspects of this consciences shift is *http://the2012scenario.com/* This site provides daily updates on the commercial and spiritual aspects of the shift that has been launched by way of the New Age "Christ Consciousness" above that has begun to manifest into the commercial system below (as above so below). It brings about reputed authors, channlers, news focused on the 2012 shift of ages. If you go to their web site you will see that news regarding **UFO/ET Disclosure, NESARA, Accountability, Earth Changes, Ascension, and the Golden Age** are their mission. The topics which they report and support are best illustrated by the web site options

    ABOUT THE STAFF
    REQUESTING PRE-NESARA FUNDS
    THE HOPE CHEST
    DOWNLOADS PAGE
    SIGHTINGS
    CONFERENCES
    1. RADIO SHOWS
    2. CREATING A GLOBAL CONVERSATION
    3. STARSEEDS AND OTHER LIGHTWORKERS
    4. NESARA OR THE ABUNDANCE PROGRAM
    5. 2012 FOR BEGINNERS
    6. DISCLOSURE
    7. SPIRITUAL ESSAYS
    8. THE 2012 SCENARIO
    9. THIS SITE IS PRO-OBAMA
    10. ASCENSION
    11. ACCOUNTABILITY/CONTAINMENT
    12. 2012 HISTORY
    13. 2012 SCENARIO DISCUSSION GROUPS
    14A. MEET-UPS
    14B. MEET-UPS II
    15. GENERAL ARCHIV

In a one of the tab options **If You're New to This Site.... a summary of purpose is provided:**

"If you're new to this site, welcome. I hope it doesn't prove disorienting to you. Galactics, Ascension, Disclosure, NESARA! Not simply tin hats, one may think, but white jackets too, the kind that tie in the back! This site reports on a series of events that we – I and (I hope) the community of lightworkers that frequent this site – think are destined to happen in our near future. What follows is my best explanation of those events. We believe that the Earth has reached the end of a 26,000-year cycle, described in the Mayan calendar, and is passing from one Age into another in December 2012. Hindus have described the old age as the Kali Yuga or Age of Darkness and the new age, as the Sat Yuga, Golden Age, or Age of Truth.

Metaphysical astrologers describe the old age as the Age of Pisces and the new, the Age of Aquarius. If you consult the Egyptians, Pueblos, Tibetans, Hopis, you would come across similar prophecies. All agree that we have reached the end of a cycle and that significant events are occurring. And many of them agree on what those events are.

I personally arrived here by consulting spirit communications and learning of a New Age back in 2006-7. I was writing a book on life after death and turned up reports of a New Age in the writings of Imperator from the mid-1870s, Beinsa Douno from around 1914, and Silver Birch from the 1930s.

Then a friend told me about 2012 and my view expanded. I recognized the events of 2012 as the events that I'd been reading about. I began to investigate.

What are those events? Well, an age of darkness is ending and an age of Light is about to begin. Because the dark controllers of this planet would not let go of their grip voluntarily, Earth's local spiritual hierarchy asked the residents of other star systems, many of them responsible for seeding Earth with human races in the first place, to come and help the Earth release itself from their rule and make its transition to higher consciousness at the end of the cycle in 2012.

That controlling elite has indeed lost its grip on power on this planet and we would not have accomplished this outcome without the help of our space visitors.

What is the transition at the end of 2012? The Earth will be ascending from duality to unitive consciousness. The planet itself will ascend from the Third Dimension that we know so well into the Fifth Dimension, which is unfamiliar to us. All of her inhabitants will have the choice of making that Ascension with her. The galactics have come to assist us as our mentors and protectors. Having released us from the grip of the controllers, rid the planet of negative extraterrestrials, restored Earth's citizens' sovereignty, and bestowed abundance on them, they will next prepare us for the cosmic shift expected on or before Dec. 21, 2012.

Our galactic family is human as we are and serves the same God that we do. They are very much more spiritually- and technologically-advanced than we are. They are in fact enlightened teachers from other dimensions and locales.

We here on this site have in common that we listen to the messages of a similar group of channels. These include telepaths who give voice to the White Brotherhood, the local spiritual hierarchy. Archangel Michael, Archangel Metatron, Kuthumi, Djwhal Khul, St. Germaine, Melchizedek, Jesus, Buddha, and all the avatars, saints and sages from every period of Earth's history, members of the Great White Brotherhood. It includes Matthew Ward, Montague Keen, Saul and other sources who have assumed a direct role in Ascension 2012 and were not widely known before their current service.

The group of channels also includes those who speak for certain galactics known to all of us here, like Ashtar, commander of a galactic fleet, Hatonn, master of interdimensional communications, Kryon, who has been speaking for years, SaLuSa, speaking for the Galactic Federation, and a panoply of other channels who do not identify themselves *more than as "the Group," "the Guardians," the Hathors, the Pleiadians, Sirians, Arcturans. Andromedans, etc.*

These sources have contributed an overall picture of what is happening on the planet as the grip of the controllers is broken and the planet is freed from millennia of domination and loss of sovereignty.

They tell us of the work that lies ahead to achieve Ascension and what lies in store for us in the Golden Age. They speak of free-energy devices that will power the world without limitation and at no cost. They speak of planetary prosperity that will release us from meaningless work and allow us to explore and develop ourselves. They speak of health and longevity. They tell us of travel to far galaxies. Everything that we have ever dreamed of appears to be within reach, not to be denied anyone, except as they exclude themselves.

So this site, and its companion, First Contact, (1) are about that scenario. Its readers are a community of lightworkers united in preparing to ascend. And beyond them are large numbers of people worldwide who are participating in the events of 2012, without necessarily knowing each other.

They are creating a conscious convergence among lightworkers. They are anticipating planetary prosperity. They are communicating the vision of planetary unity and harmony. They are investigating the astrology of the times and deciphering crop circles. They are agitating to get corrupt officials out of office and demanding that the world's war's end. They are shining the light on abuses that must stop.

They are preparing for the most momentous disclosure in history – the disclosure that we are not alone in the universe, but that we are in fact a part of a large family of human beings distributed throughout the cosmos. We are about to meet our space family, to see how far humanity reaches and what we have accomplished elsewhere.

So you are welcome. We hope you're not overwhelmed by the news. We do not consider ourselves crazy, or fundamentalists, or apocalyptics. We consider ourselves to be serious lightworkers serving the Divine Plan for a successful conclusion to this cycle and transition of the planet and its inhabitants into a higher dimension. With our spirit and galactic teachers, we are preparing for Ascension 2012."

The site is run by Steve Beckow and 11 staff members. Steve Beckow is owner of *The 2012 Scenario*, and lives in Vancouver, B.C., Canada. He attended the University of British Columbia, Carelton University, and the University of Toronto, graduating with a Masters degree in Canadian History. Steve is a member of Mensa Canada. He studied in three Ph.D. programs but was uncomfortable remaining within disciplinary boundaries or paradigms. One dissertation was rejected as being outside his chosen field. Another proposal (on enlightenment as the purpose of life) was rejected as being outside the university's paradigm of empirical materialism. He began his career as a Cultural Historian for the National Museum of Man (now the Canadian Museum of Civilization) where he published articles redefining the fields of cultural history, popular culture, and artefact studies. He finished his working life as a Member of the Immigration and Refugee Board of Canada, his chief interest being gender issues.

Steve has written around 30 books and a few hundred articles, many of them pseudonymously. He has several websites. Their subjects include enlightenment, the common ground of spirituality, life on the spirit planes, global gender persecution, automation, the truth of 9/11, the dangers of depleted uranium, and the 2012 scenario. His books and articles are available without cost and may be reposted freely.

His spiritual disciplines included Gestalt, encounter groups, spiritualism, the rest Training, rebirthing, Zen, Vipassana meditation, and Enlightenment Intensives.
In 1977, Steve had an out-of-body experience which dissipated the fear of death. In 1987, he experienced a vision of the total journey of an individual soul from God to God, which demonstrated to him that the purpose of life was enlightenment. That experience is written up here. It took nearly 20 years to fully express in words what he saw in eight wordless seconds that day.

He has enjoyed several transformational or direct experiences of Self, none of which he considers "enlightenment." Today, Steve lives a life of voluntary simplicity and research as a non-denominational and happily-married "urban monk."

His earlier writings can be found at *The Essays of Brother Anonymous* *The Purpose of Life is Enlightenment* is located here. For additional material on the 2012 scenario, see *First Contact* He studied in three Ph.D. programs but was uncomfortable remaining within disciplinary boundaries or paradigms. One dissertation was rejected as being outside his chosen field. Another proposal (on enlightenment as the purpose of life) was rejected as being outside the university's paradigm of empirical materialism.

He began his career as a Cultural Historian for the National Museum of Man (now the Canadian Museum of Civilization) where he published articles redefining the fields of cultural history, popular culture, and artefact studies. He finished his working life as a Member of the Immigration and Refugee Board of Canada, his chief interest being gender issues.

He states: *"It's our hope that this video will be widely shared by everyone who sees it to bring hope and awareness about the presence of our Galactic family to their friends, their families, their neighbours and their work colleagues – and get all of them to then share this, free, with their own friends, family members, neighbours and workmates. And hopefully this process of sharing our video continues on and on."*

When you look at the staff, you will begin to understand that these people are serious and that there has to be a serious demand:

Graham Dewyea – Montpelier, Vermont, USA. Founder, InLight Radio and host, Our Galactic Family and Heavenly Blessings. Graham is Graham Dewyea has had over 16 years in public administration, including serving as a hospital executive.
Steve Beckow – Vancouver, Canada. Founder and Owner the 2012 Scenario and co-host, An Hour With An Angel. Steve is a former member of The Immigration and Refugee Board of Canada.
Dave Schmidt – Edmonds, Washington, USA. Former US State of Washington Senator, co-host Let's Talk 2012 and Beyond, an editor, the 2012 Scenario and Director of The Hope Chest. Dave is also an ordained minister and has a B.A. in Religion and an M.A. in Biblical Studies

Geoffrey West – Toronto, Canada. Anchor, Cosmic Vision News and co-host, An Hour With An Angel. Geoffrey is a former CTV News staffer with a Bachelor in Radio and Television and a Masters in Peace Education.

Linda Dillon – Port Saint Lucie, Florida, USA. Channeller for The Council of Love and co-host, An Hour With An Angel and Heavenly Blessings. Linda has an extensive professional background in the social services, behavioural and mental health arena, where she was a successful healthcare executive and consulting CEO.

Sierra Neblina – Sedona, Arizona, USA. Co-host, Let's Talk 2012 and Beyond and an editor, the 2012 Scenario. Sierra is a Desert Storm veteran, a minister and a Cherokee medicine woman.

Stephen Cook – Sydney, Australia. Host, The Light Agenda and News Editor, the 2012 Scenario. Stephen is a journalist, writer and broadcaster and was Public Relations Manager and Media Advisor for the Sydney 2000 Olympic Games.

These people are listed here because the common thread that brings a diversity of professions from both commercial and spiritual walks of life together is typical.

Together with some of the editors from the 2012 Scenario and researchers from Inlight Radio – led by Allen Atkinson together with, Alice C, Andrew Eardley, sage and Anthony Morrison – the InLight Radio team scoured the internet looking for suitable clips, pics and clippings from around the world for the video.

"We've had a tremendous amount of enthusiasm and involvement on this project from many people who are so excited to welcome our star brothers and sisters as we co-create a wonderful future together," says the video's script co-writer Steve Beckow. The team also had the assistance of Luisa Vasconcelos (a Lightworker in Portugal who regularly ensures many of our favourite channels from SaLuSa to the Galactic Federation of Light are translated into various languages and shared around the world), who helped bring together a diverse team of translators from a variety of countries especially for this video. They each recorded the video's title phrase: "I know my Galactic family is here – do you?" in their own language.

"The aim of this Inlight Radio disclosure video is for everyone who sees it to take it and make it go viral – via their Facebook pages, their Twitter accounts, Google+, their email lists, whatever social media outlets they have – even re-posting the video on their own blogs and websites," says Stephen Cook, who co-wrote the video's script with Steve Beckow.

"We own our social media: we don't need to wait for our so-called leaders and media to spread this message of universal peace – we can do it ourselves. So we ask everyone who sees I Know My Galactic Family is Here – Do You? to make their own personal disclosure today – by sending our video all around the world!!"

I Know My Galactic Family is Here – Do You? is released on the InLight Radio YouTube Channel today at ***www.youtube.com/user/InLightRadio***

The Divine Cosmos By David Wilcock

A site that is dedicated to the promotion of the new truth with particular attention to science and spirituality is one by **David Wilcock** at **www.divinecosmos.com** David Wilcock is a professional lecturer, filmmaker and researcher of ancient civilizations, consciousness science, and new paradigms of matter and energy. David is also the subject and co-author of the international bestseller, **The Reincarnation of Edgar Cayce?**, which explores the remarkable similarities between David and Edgar, features many of David's most inspiring psychic readings, and reveals documented NASA scientific proof of interplanetary climate change... and how it directly impacts our DNA.

David's scientific work, thoroughly documented for free public consumption on this website, is now being realized into a feature Hollywood dramatic film, CONVERGENCE. His upcoming Hollywood film CONVERGENCE unveils the proof that all life on Earth is united in a field of consciousness, which affects our minds in fascinating ways. A documentary film, with key interviews, will be released in the special features section of the DVD. On the web site it reports:

"We hope to have the film out soon. We are certain that Convergence is timely, salient and of true benefit to humanity. Our planet is undergoing extreme changes while a great portion of humanity lives in stress and anxiety. At the same time, amazing discoveries are being made that have the potential to transform our lives in a way that is nothing short of remarkable. Unfortunately, the majority of people have not received these findings, and oftentimes when they do, the information is fragmented and difficult to comprehend.

Convergence is a trilogy about the latest findings from experts, accompanied with scientific verification and graphics about the true nature of, and our direct impact upon, the universe. It presents interviews with leading scientists, physicians and researchers in the fields of physics, the mind, astronomy, ancient history and noetics.

This is a movie that not only should be made, it NEEDS to be made. The potential for great advances are mitigated by the potential for great disasters. This movie is presented so that we may all move forward into the greatest renaissance in humanity's history: the evolution of consciousness and true peace.

The first film in the CONVERGENCE trilogy will address the science of consciousness. This film will cost remarkably little to produce, but has such a powerful, clear and urgent message for humanity that it is poised to be a box-office blockbuster, as well as a social phenomenon and agent of positive change.

An array of credible, professional scientists and scholars will present definitive evidence that consciousness is a field of energy, independent of one's own mind and brain. Common knowledge and implementation of this science has the potential to dramatically increase world peace and harmony, and dramatically decrease catastrophic Earth Changes -- and CONVERGENCE will give compelling scientific evidence to back up these claims, as well as the philosophical and spiritual understandings to go along with them.

The CONVERGENCE trilogy is the result of David's work in categorizing, analyzing and distilling over 213 volumes worth of research he uncovered and printed off the Internet between 1999 and 2005, occupying over nine and a half feet of width on his bookshelves. This research has been guided by David's intuitive work, which includes daily documentation and analysis of his dreams and visionary experiences since 1992, and active research and development of extrasensory abilities since he was 7 years old.

Leading scholars in new science, such as popular Art Bell guest Richard C. Hoagland, have publicly stated that David's research is unparalleled and completely new and fresh. By comparison, most of the information presented in *"What the Bleep Do We Know?"*, the astonishingly successful film documentary that came out of nowhere to create this brand-new genre, is an offshoot of the groundbreaking 1979 volume *"The Dancing Wu-Li Masters"* by Gary Zukav.

David has carefully chosen each participant in CONVERGENCE for his or her professional credentials, validity and fastidiousness of research, and impeccability of moral and ethical character.

There are many sites like **www.v-j-enterprises.com/nanetglb.html** that list hundreds of sites.

What all this supports is the changing mood of "we the people". They want to be heard and their consciousness is changing rapidly. The esoteric sciences and the occult branded bad stuff is out of the box that the Elite treasured for themselves and branded evil for others through religion. The fate of the Strawman is at hand. And the shifting consciousness of transparency, peace and truth is taking us to a pace far away from the New World Order business plan.

Now let us back to the primary issue that binds all of us... commerce and debt.

47

THE POSTMASTER GENERAL FOR THE AMERICAS

We will now shift back to new developments in North America where the financial and socio-political systems are changing rapidly. In line with what has been presented so far, every day, new information comes forward along with a new breed of warriors of peace and light that are showing with blinding light the truths that have been surfacing everywhere. A most difficult challenge has been to reveal the truth in ways that make it "stick" in the consciousness of humanity. In the commercial game, the historical problem has been the burden of proof done in such a way as to reveal the truth of the banking system and the Strawman, and to enforce that truth. As we have pointed out, many large groups and leaders of truth have done this. There are millions now on this path revelations in commerce, science and religion.

In an attempt to bring what we have presented into some form of solution, the work of **James Thomas McBride** into focus. We have alluded to the Post Office as a vital piece of history having within its formation a unique power. This in most eyes would seem a "sleeper" as it is the crucial missing link that ties the Vatican, religion, the Universal Postal Union, the Military Industrial complex, the Strawman, and much more together. The work of James Thomas has been an incredible revelation and his undeniable dedication to the truth, both spiritual and commercial, as well as his dedication to peace and harmony of a new system is unprecedented. It is not without struggle that this man has persevered to find truth in both spiritual and commercial paths. On the spiritual side there is no one to fight except yourself, but not so on the commercial side. James Tomas has been dedicated to finding the pathway through the commercial labyrinth so as create a non-conflictive way combining what was presented in the Chapter "**The Strawman Revelation**" into a cohesive method of Strawman separation and access to the Good Faith and Credit.

It is here that we begin to sew the pieces of the fabric presented so far into a new patchwork that he has brought forward for mankind. Much of this comes from his website **www.notice-recipient.com**. and **www.postmastergeneralna.org.** First, it is important to explain some of the history and purpose of the Postal system, all of this knowledge taken from James McBride's research.

About The Universal Postal Union

The UPU (Universal Postal Union) in Berne, Switzerland, is an extremely significant organization in today's world. It is formulated by treaty. No nation can be recognized as a nation without being in international admiralty in order to have a forum common to all nations for engaging in commerce and resolving disputes. That is why the USA under the Articles of Confederation could not be recognized as a country. Every state (colony) was sovereign, with its own common law, which foreclosed other countries from interacting with the USA as a nation in international commerce. Today, international admiralty is the private jurisdiction of the IMF, *et al.*, the creditor in the bankruptcy of essentially every government on Earth.

The UPU operates under the authority of treaties with every country in the world. It is, as it were, the overlord or overseer over the common interaction of all countries in international commerce. Every nation has a postal system, and also has reciprocal banking and commercial relationships, whereby all are within and under the UPU. The UPU is the number one military (international admiralty is also military) contract mover on the planet.

The definition of the word **post** originally meant "*any of a number of riders or runners posted at intervals to carry mail or messages in relays along a route; postrider or courier*" (**Webster's New World Dictionary, Third College Edition**, *1988, page 1054*). People, thousands of years ago, didn't write letters to one another like we do nowadays. They didn't even have paper, everything was done on clay tablets and papyrus (but that was a very expensive thing to engage in). And therefore, the posts were really set up for governmental purposes, between different rulers in their own country as well as neighbouring countries. The government set it up originally.

But there was another entity, known as the general post-office, which was not for commercial purposes and it was strictly for fellowship between the brothers, and they did it amongst themselves. Paul's letters were not delivered by Caesar's men, but by brothers in Christ, and that is the general post-office. And throughout history, there's always been the general post-office and the governmental post office; and they're different. One's done strictly for fellowship, the other's done for commercial purposes.

The current postal system, which is known as the United States Postal Service, is commercial, but it still retains the non-commercial aspect. It's based on the original general post-office. It does not exist without tracing its root to the original general post-office. And as with everything, the created cannot do away with the creator. Therefore, that original creation by the brothers fellowshipping amongst each other is still in existence; they've never done away with it. In all their statutes, every time they come up with a new statutory entity, they never do away with the general post-office, therefore it is still there.

The general-post-office is not mentioned in the Domestic Mail Manual because the Domestic Mail Manual denotes commerce. If you've got a problem, that's what the postal service employees and managers will refer to, but that's because everyone's presumed to be in commerce. But it's only a presumption, and that's where you have to come in and rebut that presumption. You rebut it by not engaging in commercial activity and not receiving your mail at an address, etc. Most people don't realize that when you receive mail at an address, or even at a P.O. Box, you're receiving a free benefit from Caesar. The postage you put on the envelope only covers the cost to deliver it from post office to post office, it does not cover any delivery beyond the post office (and the price for a P.O. Box covers the cost to rent the box itself, not for the cost of delivery). That's called free delivery.

Origins Of The U.S.Postal Service

The free delivery was instituted during the Civil War, on July 1st, 1863. It was basically an act of war by Abraham Lincoln. Even though they did have free mail delivery service prior to that, it was strictly for commercial businesses. But then, in 1863, they spread it to everyone. Up to that time, nobody had an address on their house. The numbers were brought in on the houses strictly so the postman would know where to deliver the mail. Before 1863, people would collect their mail by going to the local post office and asking for it.

This was preceded by the Post Office Department, which was established in 1872. And before the Post Office Department, the general post-office preceded that. In the early 1800's, they started referring to the general post office as the Post Office Department. However, it did not officially become the Post Office Department until 1872. Previous to that it was known as the general post-office.

There was actually two different general post-offices. The Post Master General today wears about seven hats; there are about seven different entities to the postal system. He wears the original hat as a caretaker of the original general post-office. He's also the caretaker of the general post-office that was created on February 20, 1792, which was for governmental business. And then in 1872 they created the Post Office Department.

In 1639, the original foundation for the post office was given in Massachusetts to Richard Fairbanks, the owner of Fairbanks Tavern in Boston. He was the first Postal officer in the history of the United States. In **The General Court of Massachusetts November 5, 1639** it was stated:

"For preventing the miscarriage of letters, it is ordered, that notice be given that Richard Fairbanks's house in Boston is the place appointed for all letters which are brought from beyond the seas, or are to be sent thither, 'to be brought unto; and he is to take care that they be delivered or sent according to their directions; and he is allowed for every such letter one penny, and must answer all miscarriages through his own neglect in this kind; provided that no man shall be compelled to bring his letters thither, except he please."

Following the adoption of the Constitution in May 1789, the Act of September 22, 1789 (1 Stat. 70), temporarily established a post office. Here the **Nineteenth act of Congress, an Act for the temporary establishment of the POST OFFICE** stated:

"Be it enacted by the Senate and House of Representatives of the United States of America in Congress assembled, That there shall be appointed a Post-Master General; his

powers and salary and the compensation to the assistant or clerk and deputies which he may appoint, and the regulations of the Post-Office shall be the same as they last were under the resolutions and ordinances of the late Congress. The Post-Master General to be subject to the direction of the President of the United States in performing the duties of his office, and in forming contracts for the transportation of the mail. Be it further enacted, That this act shall continue in force until the end of the next session of Congress, and no longer."

This was approved September 22nd, 1789. The post office was temporarily continued by the Act of August 4, 1790 (1 Stat. 178), and the Act of March 3, 1791 (1 Stat. 218). The Act of February 20, 1792 made detailed provisions for the post office, and also established a separate general post office for governmental purposes where in **Chapter VIII** - An Act to establish the Post Office and Post Roads within the United States, **Section 3,** it states:

"*And it be further enacted that there shall be established, at the seat of the government of the United States, a general post-office.*"

Note that this one page statutory creation by Congress established that general post-office for governmental business at the seat of the government of the United States in Washington D.C. The general post-office, which already existed, was never designated as being repealed in this Act. Therefore, it still remains in existence, separate from the governmental business' set up by this Act. There's nothing in that whole act which repeals the original general post-office. There's nothing in the act of 1872, when they created the Post Office Department, which did away with the original general post-office. So it's still there. There's nothing in the act of July 1, 1971, which created the Postal Service. The creation cannot do away with the creator, they cannot abolish the creator. Otherwise it has no foundation. And that's why the current Postmaster General wears about seven hats, because he has all of those different things that were created all the way through there.

In the early 1800's, the general post-office began to be referred to as "the Post-office department," but was not officially created until June 8, 1872. In **Chapter CCCXXXV. - An Act to revise, consolidate, and amend the Statutes relating to the Post-office Department**, it states:

"*Be it enacted by the Senate and House of Representatives of the United States of America in Congress assembled, That there shall be established, at the seat of government of the United States of America, a department to be known as the Post-office Department.*"

And again, the general post-office was not repealed in this statute. It is for this cause that the re-organized service and its employees have no authority over the general post-office - it precedes their creation and has its Source and Origin in God through His Lawful assembly. The Post Office Department of the Confederate States of America was established on February 21, 1861, by an Act of the Provisional Congress of the Confederate States. The resumption of the federal mail service in the southern states took place gradually as the war came to an end.

Then the Post Office Department was replaced by the United States Postal Service on July 1, 1971. Title 39, the Postal Reorganization Act, details this change as well.

Origins Of The General Post Office

Many will be surprised to know that at the origins of the general post office has its beginnings in scripture. In Jeremiah 51:31, "*One **post** shall run to meet another, and one **messenger** to meet another, to shew the king of Babylon that his city is taken at one end...*" A "post" is another name for a courier and in 2 Chronicles 30:6, "*So **the posts went with the letters** from the king and his princes throughout all Israel and Judah,*" And in Esther 3:13, "*And **the letters were sent by posts** into all the king's provinces...*"

Scripture records messages being sent "by the hands of messengers" (1 Samuel 11:7) from as far back as the book of Job, which is the oldest book in the bible where it says in Job 1:14, "*And there came a **messenger** unto Job, and said, the oxen were plowing, and the asses feeding beside them:*"

These messages were delivered using the current means of movement at the time: Esther 8:10,14, "*And he wrote in the king Ahasuerus' name, and sealed it with the king's ring, and **sent letters by posts** on horseback, and riders on mules, camels, and young dromedaries: So the **posts** that rode upon mules and camels went out...*"

And sending messages refreshes the soul: Proverbs 25:13, KJV, "*As the cold of snow in the time of harvest, so is a faithful **messenger** to them that send him: for **he refresheth the soul** of his masters.*"

Proverbs 25:13, Septuagint, "*As a fall of snow in the time of harvest is good against heat, so a faithful **messenger refreshes** those that sent him: for he helps the souls of his masters.*"

In times past, people sent messages to others by posting their letters on a "post" in the middle of town, with the name of the one who it's intended for. People would go to this "post" and look for letters with their name on it, and if they saw their name on a letter they would take it down from the post and read it. However, due to theft of messages, an office was built around the post to prevent people from stealing messages. This office became known as the general post-office. People would then go to the general post-office to pick up their messages.

The Link To The Vatican And The Estate Trust

To unravel this intentionally complex Trusteeship of the Global Estate Trust let us begin at the top and work our way down. The Vatican boasts, in their Papal Bull, dominion over the entire earth, via conquest, and is answerable ONLY to the Divine Spirit. Dominion over means control over, not ownership. The Vatican's un-rebutted claims establish them as the Primary Trustee of the Global Estate Trust, our Divine Inheritance; a very unpopular fact. But a fact that opens a doorway placing the cure for the mis-administration and theft of our Divine Inheritance within our grasp.

The Vatican is the Primary Trustee of the Global Estate Trust. To facilitate the administration of this Global Trust the Vatican established the Universal Postal Union as the Secondary Trustees of the Global Trust charged with dividing the Global Trust into zones and endowing these legal fiction zones with sovereign authority to facilitate the efficient administration of the Global Trust.

It is no surprise that the first requirement for the international acknowledgment of a sovereign nation is the necessity of a Post Office. The primary objective of the military in any 'zone' is the protection of the Post, or the Post Office, for in their original jurisdiction, the Postmaster Generals are the Trustees of their respective zone.

In 1789 the Continental Congress passed a bill to "establish the seat of government, a general post office, under the direction of the Postmaster General." That's right, a general post office under the direction of the Postmaster General. They were further dividing the postal zone of North America establishing a new zone, and endowing it with sovereign authority, whereby our founding fathers believed they could establish a Trusteeship which would ensure that sovereignty of the people would be passed down to the people of future generations.

The Preamble to the Constitution created the Estate Trust which held the freedoms guaranteed in the Articles of Confederation and the Declaration of Independence in trust for future generations. The Articles of the Constitution established the Trusteeship as well as the powers and limitations thereof. The Congress and Senate were Trustees charged with the Administration of our Divine Inheritance, the Global Estate Trust.

In this "general post office" seat of government there was established the "civil administration" called the United States. Civil administration to administrate our Divine Estate Trust, the Global Trust, our Divine Inheritance. Remember, we can never OWN anything. We simply have a Divine Right of Use of the property of the Divine Estate, the Global Trust.

So, we the people of this earth have a Divine Right of use of the Global Trust while the civil administration is charged with the administration of our estate for our benefit. In the world of trusts Civil Administration/ Government = Trusteeship. So, the entire world is held in trust. The Global Estate Trust, our Divine Inheritance, our birthright is held in trust and is administrated by the various 'governments' who gain their sovereign authority via the Universal Postal Union, the Secondary Trustee of the Global Trust answerable to the Vatican.

In the world of trusts and trust law, rights, duties and obligations are very straight forward, cut and dry, black and white. There are no opinions, secret codes, rules or statutes, period. Just the facts. There is a chain of command, consequences for your actions, or lack thereof, and accountability.

It has been a slow and cumbersome process to overcome the out of control momentum of the civil administrators of the world today. There have been countless casualties as a result of our efforts to unravel the illusion; to overcome the programming and fear which fuelled the beast to reach the core where truth and accountability resides. You are now well versed in this game of the Elite to complete their business plan of PLANET EARTH.

The New Postmaster General

This letter was executed in September, 2011 by **James Thomas McBride, Postmaster General**:

"I, James Thomas of the family McBride, living man American freeholder in fee simple absolute acting in the capacity of Postmaster General, Trustee under whose direction the United States operates, with all of the power and authority of the Office of the Postmaster General.

I was lost in the sea of illusion, compelled to live and operate under an error of assumptions that have adversely effected the freeholder and his estate; the fruit of a Breach of Trust by the Trustees of the United States of America.

The positions of Postmaster General and the Office of the Postmaster General existed prior to the Constitution for the United States under the jurisdiction of the Universal Postal Union (UPU). The seat of government for the United States was established as a general post office under the direction of the Postmaster General. The Executors, Trustees and Administrators charged with the administration of the estate trust, "United States of America", operate from this seat of government under the direction of the Postmaster General.

My authority to act in the capacity of Postmaster General-Trustee through the Office of the Postmaster General has long been established and accepted at the highest level via my "Claim On Abandonment' and annexed 'Postal Treaty for the Americas.'

The original constitution for the United States, a 'will', was established by our founding fathers to ensure that sovereignty of the people was passed down to the people of future generations. The 14th Amendment fraudulently altered the 'will' for the benefit of the Trustees and adversely effecting the Beneficiaries to the 'will'. The 14th Amendment created the 14th Amendment paper citizen as the new heirs under the jurisdiction of the newly created Congress and Senate created under the 14th Amendment.

The people have been tricked and coerced into unwittingly giving false witness against ourselves that:

- *We are 14th Amendment paper citizens of the U.S.;*
- *We willingly and knowingly elected to accept the benefits under the will as a 14th Amendment citizen;*
- *The living man freeholder is deceased;*
- *We are the Executor of the estate trust/ 14th Amendment paper citizen of the U.S..*

The Congress and Senate that existed PRE-BREACH OF TRUST represented the living men and women, American freeholders under the original estate trust instrument, as public servants. The Congress and Senate that we endure today was created and empowered by the 14th Amendment, A BREACH OF TRUST, and has jurisdiction over legal fiction citizens of the U.S., estate trusts created by the registration of Our birth.

The codes and statutes of the 14th Amendment Congress and Senate have no force and effect on the freeholders of America.

Today, We the American People are all assumed to be deceased and acting in the capacity of Executor of the legal fiction U.S. Citizen and that we are all subject to the codes and statutes as 14th Amendment citizens. There has been no evidence that any living freeholders inhabit America today. No matter how loudly we proclaim that we are alive, we cannot be heard as we are assumed to be deceased and failed to provide the proper evidence to rebut the assumption. We have no standing in the common law nor standing to receive a common law remedy as we are assumed to be deceased and dead people don't have standing in a common law court nor for a common law remedy.

Those agencies that existed pre-breach of trust now wear two hats; one empowered under the original constitution as public servants to the American freeholders and the second empowered by the 14th Amendment Congress and Senate under authority obtained due to a Breach of Trust.

These Offices under the authority of the original constitution have fallen dormant as there has been no evidence that any living freeholders inhabit America; we had all effectively fallen trap to the breach of trust to our detriment causing loss, injury and damage to the estate and the Beneficiary.

You are hereby NOTICED the living men and women, freeholders in fee simple absolute have returned from being lost in the sea of illusion to re-establish their living status and status as freeholders electing to REJECT the benefits under the will as 14th Amendment citizens and choosing to enforce contractual rights in the property bequeathed by the will, 'against the will'.

All pre-breach Offices are hereby re-activated. You are instructed to dawn your pre-breach hat, staff your offices and prepare to receive and accept the freeholders of America as we re-inhabit the republic. You are instructed to re-educate your staff as to how to serve the freeholders; that the freeholders are not subject to the codes and statutes of the 14th Amendment Congress and Senate and that we enjoy all of the rights and privileges of the Articles of Confederation and the Declaration of Independence.

We are presently compiling a data base of all American freeholders as they re-establish their status, re-inhabit the 50 states for the redemption of their estate as well as a database for the registration of those pre-breach Offices as they come into compliance including all contact information for said office(s).

Each Office holder shall immediately provide all contact information and evidence of compliance to:
Legal Registries
P.O. Box 28606
Columbus, Ohio 43228

I, James Thomas, American freeholder, acting through the Office of the Postmaster General, in the capacity as Trustee, under whose direction the United States operates, demand a cure to the breach of trust.

Let me be perfectly clear that we are here to ensure a cure to the breach of trust; to facilitate the transition back to the pre-breach constitution; to re-activate both federal and state pre-breach offices and re-establish this civil administration under the original, pre-breach constitution.

To facilitate a smooth transition; to ensure that the priorities of the American people are foremost; to facilitate the interaction between freeholders and their public servants; and to ensure that the Offices are filled with honourable men and women, the trustees and administrators shall work hand in hand and with the approval of the Transition Committee established in the Postal Treaty for the Americas annexed hereto.

The original pre-breach Congress and Senate SHALL be seated, sworn in and empowered. Potential Office holders must be known to be honourable men/women, must resign any/all positions under the 14th Amendment; must re-establish themselves as freeholders and swear an Oath to the pre-breach constitution.

The O.I.T.C., D.T.C., D.T.C.C. and the Comptroller of the Currencies shall ensure that the account styled as "National Banking Association", as set forth in the Postal Treaty for the Americas annexed hereto, is immediately funded, releasing the long blocked funds for the discharge of debt and issue and provide the 'charge card' for use by the freeholder(s) to access the private funds, charging the account for the immediate discharge of debt to facilitate Global debt Forgiveness. You are further instructed to prepare to fund the sub- accounts and issue the 'charge cards' to the freeholders as they re-establish their living status.

The Trustees are instructed to fund the new Treasury Banking System the freeholders are back.

The Trustees shall immediately settle, close and dissolve the estate trust JAMES THOMAS MCBRIDE 296520781 and make the return of the property and interest to the freeholder James Thomas.

You are further instructed to provide me documentary evidence of the closure and make a full account to the freeholder, James Thomas and provide documentation that identifies me as an American freeholder to ensure the safe and unmolested travel across this land."

The Global Estate Trust, Post Office, Vatican And Military Link

To understand the relationships of all the parties a quick summary is needed. At the bottom is you and the Vital Statistics Office that issued the Certified copy of the Birth Certificate, a security which represents the Divine Estate Trust, therefore they hold the original and are the holder in due course of the estate. They are the Intermediary Agent for the Trust with a fiduciary duty to the Beneficiary of the Estate. and the true beneficiary is you in the flesh and blood.

At the top, as we said, the Vatican boasts, in their Papal Bull, dominion over the entire earth, via conquest, and is answerable ONLY to the Divine Spirit. Dominion over means control over, not ownership. So as said, the Vatican's un-rebutted claims establish them as the Primary Trustee of the Global Estate Trust, our Divine Inheritance. To facilitate the administration of this Global Trust the Vatican established the Universal Postal Union as the Secondary Trustees of the Global Trust charged with dividing the Global Trust into zones and endowing these legal fiction zones with sovereign authority to facilitate the efficient administration of the Global Trust.

And so it comes as no surprise that the first requirement for the international acknowledgment of a sovereign nation is the necessity of a Post Office. The primary objective of the military in any "zone" is the protection of the Post, or the Post Office, for in their original jurisdiction, the Postmaster Generals are the Trustees of their respective zone. That responsibility has been usurped to feed the Military Industrial complex so as to protect the citizens of the nation by way of the real peoples credit.

When in 1789 the Continental Congress passed a bill to "establish the seat of government, a general post office, under the direction of the Postmaster General, they were further dividing the postal zone of North America establishing a new zone, and endowing it with sovereign authority, whereby our founding fathers believed they could establish a Trusteeship which would ensure that sovereignty of the people would be passed down to the people of future generations. It was not what happened, as has been revealed.

The Postal Authority

It is important to know that all important legal and commercial documents through the post office rather than private carriers, which are firewalls. We want direct access to the authority—and corresponding availability of remedy and recourse—of the UPU. For instance, if you post through the US Post Office and the US Postmaster does not provide you with the remedy you request within twenty-one (21) days, you can take the matter to the UPU.

Involving the authority of the UPU is automatically invoked by the use of postage stamps. Utilization of stamps includes putting stamps on any documents (for clout purposes, not mailing) we wish to introduce into the system. As long as you use a stamp (of any kind) you are in the game. If you have time, resources, and the luxury of dealing with something well before expiration of a given time frame, you can use stamps that you consider ideal. The most preferable stamps are ones that are both large and contain the most colors. In an emergency situation, or simply if economy is a consideration, any stamp will do. Using a postage stamp and autograph on it makes you the postmaster for that contract.

Whenever you put a stamp on a document, inscribe your full name over the stamp at an angle. The color ink you use for this is a function of what color will show up best against the colors in the stamp. Ideal colors for doing this are purple (royalty), blue (origin of the bond), and gold (king's edict). Avoid red at all cost. Obviously, if you have a dark, multi-colored stamp you do not want to use purple or blue ink, since your autograph on it would not stand out as well if you used lighter color ink. Ideally one could decide on the best color for his autograph and then obtain stamps that best suit one's criteria and taste. Although a dollar stamp is best, it is a luxury unless one is well off financially. Otherwise, reserve the use of dollar stamps for crucial instruments, such as travel documents. The rationale for using two-cent stamps is that in the 19th Century the official postage rate for the *de jure* Post Office of the United States of America was fixed at two (2) cents. For stamps to carry on one's person for any kind of unexpected encounter or emergency use, this denomination might be ideal.

Use stamps on important documents, such as a check, travel documents, paperwork you put in court, etc. Where to put the stamp and how many stamps to use depend on the document. On foundational documents and checks, for instance, put a stamp on the right hand corner of the instrument, both on the front and on the back. The bottom right hand corner of the face of a check, note, or bill of exchange signifies the liability. Furthermore, the bottom right hand corner of the reverse of the document is the final position on the page, so no one can endorse anything (using a restricted endorsement or otherwise) after that. You want to have the last word. If you have only one stamp, put it where you are expected to sign and autograph over it cross-wise. In the case of a traffic ticket, for instance, put a stamp on the lower right hand corner where you are supposed to sign and autograph across the stamp at an angle.

Autographing a stamp not only establishes you as the postmaster of the contract but constitutes a cross-claim. Using the stamp process on documents presents your adversaries with a problem because their jurisdiction is subordinate to that of the UPU, which you have now invoked for your benefit. The result in practice of doing this is that whenever those who know what you are doing are recipients of your documents with autographed stamps they back off. If they do not, take the matter to the US Postmaster to deal with. If he will not provide you with your remedy, take the matter to the UPU for them to clean up.

The countries whose stamps would be most effective to use are China, Japan, United States, and Great Britain. Utilizing these countries covers both East and West. However, since the US seems to be the point man in implementing the New World Order, one might most advisably use US stamps.

For example, if you put stamps on documents you submit into court, put a stamp on the back of each page, at the bottom right hand corner. Do not place any stamps on the front of court paperwork since doing so alarms the clerk. By placing your autographed stamp on the reverse right hand corner you prevent being damaged by one of the tricks of judges these days. A judge might have your paperwork on his bench, but turned over so only the back side, which is ordinarily blank on every page, is visible. Then if you ask about your paperwork he might say something like, *"Yes, I have your paperwork in front of me but I don't find anything."* He can't see anything on the blank side of a page. If you place an autographed stamp on the lower right hand corner you foreclose a judge from engaging in this trick.

In addition, when it comes to court documents, one side is criminal and the other is civil. Using the autographed stamp that you rubber-stamp with your seal (bullet stamp) on the back side of your court documents is evidence that you possess the cancelled obligation on the civil side. Since there can be no assessment for criminal charges, and you show that you are the holder of the civil assessment, there is no way out for the court. Also, in any court document you put in, handwrite your EIN number [SS# w.o. dashes] in gold on the top right corner of every page, with the autographed stamp on the back side.

Use of a notary combined with the postage stamp (and sometime Embassy stamps) gives you a priority mechanism. Everything is commerce, and all commerce is contract. The master of the contract is the post office, and the UPU is the supreme overlord of the commerce, banking, and postal systems of the world. Use of these stamps in this manner gets the attention of those in the system to whom you provide your paperwork. It makes you the master of that post office. Use of the stamp is especially important when dealing with the major players, such as the FBI, CIA, Secret Service, Treasury, etc. They understand the significance of what you are doing. Many times they hand documents back to someone using this approach and say, "Have a good day, sir." They don't want any untoward repercussions coming back on them.

If anyone asks you why you are doing what you are doing, suggest that they consult their legal counsel for the significance. It is not your job to explain the law, nor explain such things as your exemption or Setoff Account. The system hangs us by our own words. We have to give them the evidence, information, contacts, and legal determinations they require to convict us. The wise words of Calvin Coolidge, the most taciturn president in US history, are apt. When asked why he spoke so little, he replied, *"I have never been hurt by anything I didn't say."*

The bottom line is that whenever you need to sign any legal/commercial document, put a stamp (even a one (1) cent stamp) over where you sign and sign at an angle across it.

Let the <u>recipient</u> deal with the significance and consequences of your actions. If you are in a court case, or at any stage of a proceeding (such as an indictment, summons, complaint, or any other hostile encounter with the system), immediately do the following:

1. Make a color copy of whatever documents you receive, or scan them in color into your computer;
2. Stamp the original of the first page of every document with the AFV/RFV stamp, put a postage stamp in the signature space, and autograph across it at an angle with your full name, using purple or blue ink, handwritten with upper- and lower-case, with your gold-ink bullet stamp (seal) on the upper left-hand portion of the postage stamp;
Make a color copy of the stamped, autographed pages and/or scan into your computer;
3. Put a stamp on the lower right-hand-corner of the back of every page and bullet-stamp and autograph it;
4. Have a notary send each document back to the sender, with a notarial certificate of service, with or without an accompanying/supporting affidavit by you;
5. If you have an affidavit, put an autographed stamp on the upper right hand corner of the first page and the lower right hand corner of the back of every page.

People who have engaged in this process report that when any knowledgeable judge, attorney, or official sees this, matters change dramatically. All of these personages know what mail fraud is. Since autographing the stamp makes you the postmaster of the contract, anyone who interferes is tampering with the mail and engaging in mail fraud. You can then subpoena the postmaster (either of the post office from which the letter was mailed, or the US Postmaster General, or both), and have them explain what the rules are, under deposition or testimony on the witness stand in open court.

In addition, most of the time when you get official communication it has a red-meter postage mark on the envelope rather than a cancelled stamp. This act is mail fraud. If the envelope has a red-meter postage mark on it, <u>they</u> are the ones who have engaged in mail fraud, because there is no cancelled stamp. It is the cancelled stamp that has the power; an un-cancelled stamp has nothing. A red-meter postage mark is an uncancelled stamp. If it is not cancelled, it is not paid. One researcher has scanned everything into his computer, and has more red-meter postage marks than he "can shake a stick at." Officials sending things out by cancelled stamp is a rarity—perhaps at most 2%.

With the red-metered postage you can trace each communication back to the PO from which it was sent, so you can get the postmaster for that PO, as well as the postmaster general for the US, to investigate the mail fraud involved. It is reasonable to conclude that cancelling a stamp both registers the matter and forms a contract between the party that cancels the stamp and the UPU. Using a stamp for postage without cancelling it is prima facie evidence that the postmaster of the local PO is committing mail fraud by taking a customer's money and not providing the paid-for service and providing you with the power of a cancelled stamp, as required under the provisions of the UPU. When you place an autographed stamp on a document you place that document and the contract underlying it under international law and treaty, with which the courts have no jurisdiction to deal. The system cannot deal with the real you, the living principle (as evidenced and witnessed by jurat). Nor can officials, attorneys, judges, *et al.*, go against the UPU, international law, and treaty. In addition, they have no authority/jurisdiction to impair a contract between you (as the living principal) and the UPU (overseer of all world commerce).

You cancelled the stamp by sealing it and autographing across it. You did so in capacity of being the living principal, as acknowledged by your seal and the jurat on your documents.

If you are in a court case, bring in your red-metered envelopes in court and request the judge to direct the prosecutor to explain the red-meter postage stamp. Then watch their jaws drop. Doing this is especially potent if you also have asked the prosecutor to provide his bar number, since most attorneys in court—especially in US—are not qualified. An attorney in federal court had better have a six-digit bar card or he committed a felony just by walking in and giving his name.

Lastly, if you are charged with mail fraud, subpoena the prosecutor(s) to bring in the evidence on which mail fraud is being alleged, as well as the originals of all envelopes used for mailing any item connected with the case. Then the mail fraud involved was committed by the postmaster of the PO in which the envelope was stamped.

When you use the postal stamp and you do not get satisfaction, there is a hidden power that is available. It is executed by a registered complaint to a special position called the Provost Marshall. Yes, it is a military position under military law--Admiralty.

Military Duty To Protect The Post

All debt of the UNITED STATES, except that debt owed to the sovereign people of America, has been abandoned and vacated and the UNITED STATES has DECLARED PEACE with the world and the sovereign people thereof, therefore, the gold fringed military flag designating the admiralty/maritime jurisdiction shall be immediately removed from all courtrooms, meeting rooms, etc. of the administrative agencies of the UNITED STATES and the civil peace flag of the united states of America shall be proudly displayed in their stead..

The U.S. Courts who have been operating as debt collection facilities under TWEA and the EMERGENCY WAR POWERS ACT shall immediately make the corrections and cure the torts against the people, vacating all claims, attachments and/or restrictions on the private rights of the sovereign people and make them whole.

The courts, as well as all administrative agencies of the UNITED STATES, shall share resources making room for and facilitating the establishment of the organic courts, operating under the common law, for the adjudication of all matters concerning the sovereign American people, other than the prosecution of grievances against an administrative agency for the trespass of the private rights of the people. All administrative agencies shall actively participate in the establishment of two distinctly separate systems, common law and administrative, operating side by side for the benefit of the CREDITORS, the sovereign people of America.

All administrative courts and agencies of the UNITED STATES shall operate in good faith and honour as servants of the sovereign people of America. Said administrative courts and agencies have grown out of control, beyond the intent of the original founders and their usefulness and shall begin to make the corrections, a reversal, bringing about balance, transparency, full disclosure and honour for the remedy of the Real Parties In Interest.

All debts of the UNITED STATES have been abandoned, except the debt to the sovereign people; The Pledge of the private property of the American people has been relinquished, therefore, the administrative agencies of the UNITED STATES shall make the return of the interest back to source, the sovereign people.

The UNITED STATES shall immediately activate the established pass through account, vacate the blocks on the asset accounts and make the financial adjustments to discharge the debt and return the accounts of the sovereign people back into balance. The UNITED STATES shall maintain the natural flow and balance in the accounts for the remedy of the people, returning the interest back to source in the discharge of debt against the pre-paid account, at all times remaining in honour.

The UNITED STATES shall immediately make the corrections as concerns the unlawful restrictions of the liberties of the sovereign people by the administrative agencies of the UNITED STATES;

All Deeds, warranty deeds, trust deeds, sheriff deeds, tax deeds and all Certificates of Title are colorable titles issued to facilitate the 'Pledge' of the private property of the sovereign people.

The Pledge has been relinquished, therefore, the UNITED STATES shall make the corrections to discharge all colorable titles, make the re-conveyance and issue the land patent/ allodial title for the property back to the people.

It is the duty of the military to serve and protect the post, therefore, the UNITED STATES military shall serve and protect the sovereign people of America, the creditor of the UNITED STATES. All branches of the U.S. Military shall follow the orders of the "Transitional Committee", interim government and government of the republic, respectively throughout this transition.

The Provost Marshals are the organic police force with a duty to serve and protect the sovereign. The Provost Marshal shall immediately serve and protect all who claim protection under this treaty making top priority any/all requests for assistance on claims of unlawful restrictions on the liberties of a sovereign.

The Military Industrial Complex

The Military-Industrial Complex is a phrase used to signify a comfortable relationship between parties that are charged to manage wars (the military, the presidential administration and congress) and companies that produce weapons and equipment for war (industry). To put it simply, the Military-Industrial Complex is described as an all-too friendly relationship that may develop between defence contractors and government forces, where both sides receive what they are perceivably looking for: a successful military engagement for war planners and financial profit for those manning the corporate boardrooms. It can be viewed as a "war for profit" theory. For those who finance war, it is simply business. And the more conflicts that rise, the better the business.

The idea of war for profit is nothing new in the realm of human history and can be traced back centuries earlier where arms races and the power of navy ships ruled an empire's reach. The arms race between the European powers of France, Spain and Britain could arguably be a primal version of today's modern so-called military-industrial complex. The idea was that a country must build up and maintain a ready military - the largest in the world at that - to remain a world power. Centuries ago, such a military was necessitated to protect aggression from neighbouring countries. These days, an invasion of the American homeland may seem ridiculous and contrary to the building of a global community founded in trust and respect. Others might argue differently but that is hardly the point when it is all just business.

In any case, the theory of a mutually beneficial relationship may not appear to be so far-fetched. It is no secret that the defence industry profits most when a nation commits to a lengthy war overseas. As any military will spare no expense for victory, it only makes sense to tap the resources of the defence industry to accomplish the mission. A sort of pseudo-world dominance through the basic form of imperialism can be seen to be just as important to a military force as is protecting one's homeland. The bottom line: war is good business for those invested in it - manufacturing, production, servicing, etc.. To the war-minded industry, a wartime economy is just as profitable as a solid growing one, where shells and ammunition take precedence over the production of peacetime light bulbs or pencils. One need only to peruse the list of manufacturers participating in production during the Second World War to see just how a wartime economy can alter a single factory.

The phrase *Military-Industrial Complex* was first utilized in an American report at the turn of the 20th Century. "Military-Industrial Complex" was later immortalized by outgoing United States President Dwight D. Eisenhower in his January 17, 1961 farewell address to the nation. In his speech, he cites the Military-Industrial Complex as a warning to the American people – to not let this establishment begin to dictate America's actions at home or abroad. The original usage appeared in the form of *Military-Industrial Congressional Complex* but later removed.

On June 30, 2010, Benjamen Fulford reported **The Vatican is now the last obstacle to the new financial system**. "*Talks this Monday between a representative of the White Dragon Society and two senior Vatican representatives (including the Papal Nuncio or ambassador to Washington) did not go well. The Vatican insists they have a right to steal trillions of dollars that do not belong to them because "the survival of the church is at stake." This is simply not true, they are simply blocking the announcement of the new financial system because of a lust for raw power. The Vatican Banker, Daniele Del Bosco, who has hidden the close to $1 trillion in gold-backed bonds, has been trying to cash them with the help of a fraudulent organization known as the Office for International Treasury Control or OITC. An Interpol investigation has revealed the OITC has no mandate and no right to these funds.*

The funds Del Bosco is hiding were earmarked to help Portugal, Spain and Italy end their respective financial crises. The $134.5 billion in bonds confiscated at the Italian/Swiss border in June of 2009 were linked to these funds. Del Bosco is about to be placed on an international wanted list and is now under 24-hour observation. We can also add that according to both CIA and Yakuza sources, the Vatican dispatched two separate assassination squads to Japan with the goal of killing and silencing this writer. They seem to be under the mistaken belief doing so will suddenly give the Vatican the ability to cash these funds. The Vatican will be provided financing to help it survive but only after they purge the Satanists from their top ranks. We must also mention the new financial system is designed to finance a campaign to end poverty, stop environmental, end war and set humanity and life on a path for exponential expansion. The fact that the Vatican leadership is trying to prevent this from happening is good proof that they are going against the teachings of both Jesus Christ and of Roman Catholicism in general."

In a more recent statement, **James Thomas McBride**, the new Postmaster General states:

"The general post office styled as the UNITED STATES has been in a perpetual state of war since its inception. The 'Powers That Be' have used the UNITED STATES as a weapon to wage war on the sovereign people of America, operating under the Emergency War Powers Act and the secret presumption that the sovereign people are the enemy of the UNITED STATES for the purpose of evading their liabilities under the original equity contract and to pillage and plunder the private property of the people they were created to serve.

The general post office styled as the UNITED STATES has been used as a weapon to wage an economic war at arms length against all of the people of the world bringing all of humanity to the brink of destruction as the CREDITOR'S master plan of total economic slavery over the sovereign people of the world has been implemented.

The Powers That Be have used the UNITED STATES as a weapon to wage war on the sovereign people of the world via the unconscionable creation, production and distribution of harmful drugs for the purpose of enslaving the people and funding and executing their genocide against humanity.

The Powers That Be have used the UNITED STATES as a platform for their propaganda, creating the world's problems and then presenting themselves as the world's savior bringing about the solution and protection from their self created illusionary boogie men for the purpose of enslaving the sovereign people of the world."

Through this Post Master Position, James McBride initiated a Universal Postal Treaty which is the topic of the next Chapter.

# 48

THE UNIVERSAL POSTAL TREATY FOR THE AMERICAS

It Is Peace and Prosperity We Seek

James Thomas McBride, Postmaster General states as follows:

"The purpose is to seek truth and in so doing it is necessary to shine light upon what is not truth so as to allow choice of free will. In this process of exposing it is necessary to be detached from it as non-partisan, pro-truth-honesty-peace, and anti-war-lies-crime. The purpose is to expose corruptions, frauds, deceptions, lies, criminal plans, cover-ups and free-speech silencing by powerful people in governments, foundations, corporations and media, which are done using the name of democracy, human rights, false interpretations of religions, cults, occults, patriotism, economy, business, media, elections, justice, charity, etc., and are used to trick the public into hatred & wars and out of their lives, money and freedoms, while the propaganda we are subjected to makes us believe that we have evolved to where such things cannot happen [remember slavery, apartheid.]. Stop the hatred that is used to promote the dehumanization of the victims of aggressions; spread the truth; free your mind from being a Zioncon occupied territory of the neo-feudal lords by rejecting the mainstream news propaganda. Such news may induce a kind of schizophrenia because it provides a true vision of reality which is so different from the one we are presented by the mass media spins."

By rising above all this we can attain a higher position where we forgive all that has occurred and drop the hatred and conflict.

In attempting to bring the truth into the light of peace, love for all and prosperity, A Treaty was registered as a ***The Universal Postal Treaty for the Americas***. On November 5, 2010, it was registered in the repository as an official treaty as submitted by the Postmaster General, serving in his official capacity. That document is included here as it summarizes the truth to date and put together by the efforts of James-Thomas: McBride in his private capacity.

Servus Servorum Dei
THE UNIVERSAL POSTAL TREATY FOR THE AMERICAS
2010

Preamble

We have come forth from the Power to Be the Eternal Mystery of its Presence. We are the beginning and the end; the origin and dissolution; the geometry of divinity, and we have remained True to this eternal Moment in the Sun. We are the silence that is unfathomable, and the spark whose voice is the flame of Freedom.

We have been called forth to return the Power and we have been chosen, as we have chosen ourselves to Be; to Become that which we have forever Been. Our essence is identical to the Source of its essence. For there was never a time when we were not, nor shall there ever be a time when we shall cease to Be.

We are they who have nurtured the sacred fire of illumination; forging our Souls into the image of god on Earth.

We are they who have embraced the Ordeal of our descent into matter, and have ascended the 33 steps of the spiral staircase to experience the Rapture of the Quickening.

We are they who have faced the great magnification of the All to ascend the ineffable throne of mind and wield the power of self.

Our Word is Truth and we are its Issue. Our Word is Law and we are Self-governing. Our Word is Light and we are the infinite Beacon of Eternal I Am.

We bear the Light of our ascension and the wisdom of our journey into Matter; thus do we reject the burdens of tyranny by exposing them as the fruits of ignorance. We have drunk deeply from the Ancient Font, we know who we are, and this knowledge is our purpose. Our Sword is Flaming and two-edged, and its name is Awakening.

The Mind of Creation is manifest in our Eye, and Its Will in our deeds. We are the Royal Seed of the Source precisely because we are its Pure Light Shining True upon this Earth. Our spirits have been forged in this crucible of sorrow, therefore our joy is boundless; and thus are we recognized by those who have eyes to see.

In this eternal moment, and through this Treaty, we do decree I AM; Individual and sovereign Beings, in continual Communion with the Quintessence of Creation. We do hereby claim the right to listen to the voice of god within and to freely choose those with whom we will engage in contract. So here now do we claim our inheritance, **Spiritual sovereignty.**

When in the Course of human events, it becomes necessary for people to dissolve the political bonds which have connected them with others, and to assume among the powers of the earth, the separate and equal station to which they may choose to aspire, a decent respect to the opinions of mankind requires that they should declare the causes which impel them to the separation. We hold that no truths are self-evident, but must have their usefulness demonstrated. That all people are created with equal freedom from tyranny, but frequently accept domination or obedience to a legal code, to a greater or lesser degree from person to person. That people are endowed with only what rights they have chosen to be endowed with, through wisdom or common folly, for wealth or health. That people can secure for themselves, with understanding of their own unique situations, those rights which best allow them to live in peace and fruitful harmony with nature and all Her various species. That whenever any person, Government, or other entity, not fully recognizing the unique situation of each individual, becomes in any way oppressive or destructive, people may choose to ignore, alter, abolish or separate themselves from such an institution, and to live in peace and harmony. That man can choose to resolve any conflict through intelligence, with, adequate communication and a full understanding of each and every point of view involved, by each and every person involved. Prudence, indeed, will dictate that Governments long established should not be changed for light and transient causes, but only after calm consideration of the True Will and mutual goals of all those individuals involved. All experience has shown that people are more disposed to suffer, while evils are sufferable, than to right themselves by abolishing the forms to which they are accustomed. But when a long train of abuses and usurpation evinces a design to reduce them under absolute Despotism or Dogma not chosen by the individual concerned, it is their right, it is their duty to themselves and their Creator, to throw off such a Government and to accept responsibility, each for their own actions and future security.

Declaration Of Causes For Separation

On July 26, 1775 the Continental Congress appointed Benjamin Franklin as the first postmaster general of the organic Post Office for the united states, union of several states. In 1776 the united states of America declared its independence and in May 1789 the Constitution for the united states of America was adopted.

On Thursday, Sept. 17, 1789 we find written, "Mr. Goodhue, for the committee appointed for the purpose, presented a bill to amend part of the Tonnage act, which was read the first time. The bill sent from the Senate, for **the temporary establishment of the Post Office**, was read the second and third time, and passed.

The bill for **establishing the Judicial Courts** for **establishing the seat of government . . .**" The organic post office for the united states of America established the seat of government, a general post office, under the direction of the postmaster general.

This is verified on March 1825, when an act was passed entitled "An act to reduce into one the several acts establishing and regulating the post office department," 3 Story, U. S. 1825. "**It is thereby enacted; That there be established, the seat of the government of the United States, a general post office, under the direction of a postmaster general**."

The organic post office for the united states of America established the ten miles square, styled as *WASHINGTON, D.C.*, as a general post office and independent postal zone with the rights and authority of a sovereign nation, operating under a corporate structure under the direction of the postmaster general to function as the seat of government of the United States.

A visit to the USPS web site today will establish that John (Jack) E. Potter wears two hats and is 1) the postmaster general [of the organic post office] and 2) the CEO of the USPS [corporate]. The web site offers further evidence of the existence of two separate post office entities when they state that the Post Office is 1) one of the most trusted government **agencies,** and 2) one of the ten most trusted **organizations** in the nation. When one researches the two words we find that they are not inter-changeable; they do not and cannot define the same entity.

The constitution of the United States has vested congress with the power to establish post offices and post roads within the ten miles square and within any/all territories of same. [Art. 1, s. 8, n. 7] Congress created the corporate United States Post Office which today is the United States Postal Service or USPS operating via the
authority vested in the general post office styled as *WASHINGTON, D.C.* On February 21, 1871 16 Statutes at Large 419 divided America into 10 districts or territories for the purpose of expanding outside of the ten miles square the authority of said general post office over We the American People.

Complex Regulatory Scheme

The Constitution for the United States granted congress the power to:

☐ Lay and collect taxes, Duties, Imposts and Excises, to pay the debts and provide for the common defence and general welfare of the United States. [Art. I sec. 8, cl. 4];
☐ To regulate commerce with foreign nations, and among the several states, [Art. I sec. 8 cl. 3];
☐ To establish uniform laws on the subject of bankruptcy, [Art. I sec. 8 cl. 4];
☐ To declare war, grant letters of Marque and Reprisal, and make rules concerning captures on land and water, [Art. I sec. 8 cl. 11];
☐ To exercise exclusive legislation in all cases, whatsoever, over such district (**not to exceed ten miles square**) as may, by cession of particular states, and acceptance by congress, become the seat of government of the United States, and to exercise like authority over all places purchased by the consent of the legislature of the state in which the same shall be, for the erection Forts, Magazines, Arsenals, dock yards and other needful things.

Congress has the power under Article I of the Constitution to authorize an administrative agency administering a complex regulatory scheme to allocate costs and benefits among voluntary participants in the program without providing an Article III adjudication of claims. [Am. Jur. 2nd Fedcourts sec. 7]. Congress, acting for a valid legislative purpose, pursuant to its powers under Article I, may create a "seemingly private" right that is so closely integrated into a public regulatory scheme as to be a matter appropriate for agency resolution with limited involvement by the Article III judiciary. Agency resolution of such federal rights may take the form of binding arbitration with limited judicial review. [Am. Jur. 2nd Fedcourts sec 7]
So, to cement their encroachment of power over the American people beyond the ten miles square, congress created a complex regulatory scheme called the federal (and state) Statutes, Codes and Regulations, to allocate costs, for the collection of taxes, duties and excises, for the payment of the national debt, and to provide for the common defence and general welfare of the United States.

Congress so closely integrated a seemingly private right (right to contract) into this complex regulatory scheme to turn unsuspecting American sovereigns, creators of the United States, into seemingly voluntary participants in the program; seemingly voluntary participants in binding contracts, having received limited or no valuable consideration in the exchange and failing full disclosure of the terms and conditions of said contracts which are contrary to the best interest of the American people.

The federal courts have become administrative courts employing Executive Administrators charged with the enforcement of codes and statutes, [FRC v GE 281 US 464, KELLER v PE 261 US 428, 1 Stat. 138-1788], to collect the taxes, duties, imposts and excises for the payment of the national debt in accordance with Article I of the Constitution. In 1976 Public Law 94-381 officially brought the federal courts under the executive branch operating under Article I of the Constitution in violation of the separation of powers.

The U.S. District courts have original jurisdiction over all maritime causes; of all land seizures under the Admiralty Extension Act; of all actions of Prize; and of all non-maritime seizures under any law of the United States on land or water. [28 USCA sec. 1356] The Commerce Clause, [Art. I sec. 8, cl. 13] of the Constitution is a sufficient basis for federal admiralty power while the Admiralty Extension Act brought the Admiralty jurisdiction inland.

The Trading With The Enemy Act made all Americans enemy combatants and enemies of the United States and placed all Americans on the list maintained by the Custodian of the Alien Property, [Secretary of the U.S. Treasury] making all Americans subject to the seizure of our bodies and our private property under the laws of war or the Laws of Prize under Choses in action for satisfaction of a contractual obligation, express or implied.

When one defaults on his contractual obligations to pay his share of the national debt, which is based on the Law of Contributions, his private property becomes subject to seizure, Juri Belli, out of the hands of the enemy by the right or laws of Prize, by Privateers acting under Letters of Marque and Reprisal under Article I, sec. 8, cl. 11 of the Constitution.

Congress has empowered members of the private B.A.R. Association with a monopoly in the U.S. courts, as Privateers acting under Letters of Marque and Reprisal, (B.A.R. Association Card No. = Letter of Marque document no.) to seize the property and the body of the offender in order to obtain satisfaction for the obligations for which he has contracted, knowingly or otherwise.

However, there are several things intrinsically flawed, unconscionable and/or fraudulent about this complex regulatory scheme.

We the People of America are Party to an important equity contract with the United States; the "Original Equity Contract", whereby We the People allow the United States the use of our 'good faith and credit' which is transmitted to the U.S. via the transmitting utility, public vessel 'strawman'. Said public vessel, transmitting utility was created and registered by the state only days after our birth into this world, obviously without our consent. In exchange for the use of our credit the United States has promised to pay/discharge all of the debt of the sovereign, via the public vessel, providing the dual consideration necessary for a valid contract. It has been established as a matter of fact that the United States has executed said equity contract with this Petitioner, having created funds from the credit of Petitioner, thereby charging their debtor obligation for the exchange.

It has been established in fact that, "All that government does and provides legitimately is in pursuit of its duty to provide protection for private rights [Wynnhammer v People, 13 NY 378] which duty is a debt owed to its creator, We the People of America, and the unfranchised individual; which debt and duty is never extinguished nor discharged, and is perpetual. No matter what the defacto government provides for us in the manner of convenience and safety, the uninfranchised individual owes nothing to the government. [Hale v Henkle 201 US 43]

"We the People have discharged any debt which is said to exist or owed to the state. The governments are, presumably, indebted continually to the People, because the People, the sovereigns, presumably accented to the creation of the government corporation and because we suffer its continued existence. The continued debt owed to the American People is discharged only as it continues not to violate our private rights, and when government fails in its duty to provide protection- discharge its duty to the People- it is an abandonment (delictual default) of any and all power, authority or vestige of sovereignty which it may have otherwise possessed, and the law remains the same, the sovereignty reverting back to the People whence it came." [Downes v Bidwell 182 US 244 (1901)]

It is an accepted maxim of law that a contract is controlling until superseded by a new contract, whereby the new contract becomes the controlling document. To overcome the United States' debtor obligations to We the American People for the use of our good faith and credit in the 'original equity contract', Congress embedded numerous secret adhesion contracts and assumptions/presumptions into their complex regulatory scheme for which they hold the People accountable.
If a [government] comes down from their position of sovereignty, and enters the domain of commerce, it submits itself to the same laws that govern individuals there. The U.S. must do business on business terms. Once the United States waives its immunity and does business with its citizens, it does so much as a party never cloaked in immunity.

Parties to a contract have an obligation to operate with full disclosure and honesty, acting in good faith and with clean hands. "Even in the domain of private contract law, the author of a standard form agreement is required to state its terms with clarity and candor. Surely, no less is required [396 US 222] of the United States when it does business with its citizens." [US v Seckinger 397 US 203]

In the complex regulatory scheme created by congress, the U.S. secretly presumes that the living man, American sovereign, to be the legal fiction public vessel, its surety and/or beneficiary. The U.S. presumes that the American sovereign has assented to paying the debt of the corporation; to being a debtor and insolvent bankrupt having pledged ourselves as sureties for the debts of the U.S. The United States has never informed the American People of these assumptions/ presumptions which they hold against us nor the consequences thereof.

In the contrary, the U.S. has invested 75 years of propaganda to indoctrinate the American People that:
☐ The sovereign is the legal fiction transmitting utility;
☐ The S.S. # is mandatory;
☐ A Driver license and Marriage License are mandatory for American sovereigns;
☐ The filing of an IRS 1040 form is mandatory for the American sovereign;
☐ It is mandatory for the American People to register our private property with the state, effectively and
secretly transferring title to the state;
☐ The Codes and Statutes pertain to the American sovereign;
☐ These secret adhesion contracts are valid and binding, having failed to inform the American sovereign of
the terms and conditions of the secret adhesion contracts attached thereto; having failed at equal, dual
consideration;

☐ The Codes and Statutes pertain to all sovereigns and not just to agents and employees of the U.S.
☐ And much, much more.

The U.S. has failed at full disclosure; having failed to inform the American sovereign of the existence of the original contract which was executed when we were/are only days old without full disclosure and/or our consent, or that these secret contracts effectively void our original contract and have effectively allowed the United States to steal the personal exemptions of the American people thereby leaving the American People and this Petitioner without a remedy.

The United States has not only failed at full disclosure but has taken overt steps to deceive and misinform the American People. The U.S. has employed the use of threats and intimidation to maintain the illusion they have invested years creating to side step their debtor obligations to the American People in our original equity contracts.

The postal zone, general post office, seat of government of the United States, under the direction of the postmaster general, John (Jack) E. Potter, has become a continuing criminal enterprise consistently operating contrary to the best interest of the American People, whose property has been placed at risk to fund the U.S., and a breach of the original contract(s) with this Petitioner and each and every one of the American People.

The establishment of the seat of the government of the United States, a general post office under the direction of John (Jack) E. Potter, by the organic post office for the united states of America is a breach of contract for its failure to provide a republican form of government for the American People.

The United States has been operating in receivership continuously for decades with numerous reorganizations. The receivership has exceeded its term life by several years. The time has come to liquidate the beast and close the books on the receivership. It is time for the American People to exercise our right of redemption of our private property that has been placed at risk to fund the receivership. The United States is restraining the American people's right of redemption of the property to extend the term of receivership and the criminal activity which has infected the entire zone.

The United States has blocked numerous attempts by this Treaty Executor to redeem the property via discharge of the debt. The United States, operating under the direction of the Post Master General has used threats, intimidation, imprisonment, trickery and deceit to steal the American people's personal exemption(s), blocking our right of redemption and leaving the American people with no available remedy.

Claim On Abandonment
For The Sovereign People of America

It has been established in fact that:

1) It is the private property of the American people that has been placed at risk to collateralize the receivership of the general post office styled as the UNITED STATES; and
2) It is the credit of the Sovereign people of America that funds the day to day operations of same; and
3) The term life of the receivership of the UNITED STATES has been exhausted; and
4) The American people hold the priority **entitlement right** to the property; and
5) The American people hold an absolute priority **right of redemption** of the property; and

6) The remedy for the redemption has been provided; and
7) The Creditors have overtly impaired the right of redemption of the American people; and
8) The Creditor's actions have established the evidence of their operation in equity in bad faith and unclean hands and constitutes a delictual default and an abandonment of their claims; and
9) The administrative agents and agencies of the UNITED STATES have not only failed to protect the
private rights of the American people, but, have actively participated in the violation of said private
rights; and
10) The acts and actions of the agents and/or employees of the administrative agencies of the UNITED STATES in the violation of the private rights of the American people establishes the evidence of their operation in equity in bad faith and with unclean hands and constitutes their voluntary surrender of all equity claims in their name and/or in their control; and
11) The failure of the UNITED STATES to protect the private rights of the American people constitutes a delictual default and an abandonment of the postal zone styled as the UNITED STATES and all sovereign rights, power and authority associated therewith.

Constitutionally and in the laws of equity, the United States could not borrow or pledge the property and wealth of the American people, put at risk as collateral for its currency and credit, without legally providing them equitable remedy for recovery of what is due them. The United States did not violate the law or the Constitution in order to collateralize its financial reorganization. But, did in fact provide such a legal remedy so that it has been able to continue on since 1933 to hypothecate and re-hypothecate the private wealth and assets of the American people, at risk backing the government's obligations and currency, by their implied consent, through the government having provided such remedy, as defined and codified above, for recovery of what is due them on their assets and wealth at risk. The provisions for this are found in the same act of Public Policy, HJR 192, public law 73-10 that suspended the gold standard for our currency, abrogated the right to demand payment in gold, and made the Federal Reserve notes, for the first time, legal tender 'backed by the substance or credit of the nation.' All U.S. currency since that time is no more than credit against the real property and wealth of the sovereign American people, taken and/or pledged by the United States to its secondary creditors as security for its obligations. Consequently, those backing the nation's credit and currency could not recover what was due them by anything drawn on the Federal Reserve notes without expanding their risk and obligation to themselves. Any recovery payments backed by this currency would only increase the public debt the American people are collateral for, which an equitable remedy was intended to reduce, and in equity would not satisfy anything.

There are other serious limitations on our present system. Since the institution of these events, for practical purposes of commercial exchange, there has been no actual money of substance in circulation by which debt owed from one party to another can actually be repaid.

The Federal Reserve Notes, although made legal tender for all debts, public and private in the reorganization, can only discharge debt. Debt must be 'paid' with value or substance (gold, silver, barter, labor, or a commodity). For this reason HJR 192, Public law 73-10, which established the public policy of our current monetary system, repeatedly uses the term of 'discharge' in conjunction with 'payment' in laying out public policy for the new system. A debt currency system cannot 'pay' debt. Since 1933 to present, commerce in the corporate United States and among sub-corporate subject entities has had only debt note instruments by which debt can be discharged and transferred in different forms. The unpaid debt, created and/or expanded by the plan now carries a public liability for collection in that when debt is discharged with debt instruments, (i.e. Federal Reserve Notes, etc.), by our commerce, *debt is inadvertently expanded instead of being cancelled*, thus increasing the public debt, a situation fatal to any economy.

Congress and government officials who orchestrated the public laws and regulations that made the financial reorganization anticipated the long term effect of a debt based financial system which many in government feared, and which we face today in servicing the interest on trillions of dollars in U.S. Corporate public debt, and in this same act made provisions not only for the recovery remedy to satisfy equity to its Sureties, but to simultaneously resolve this problem as well.

Since it is, in fact, the real property and wealth of the American people that is the substance backing all the other obligations, currency and credit of the United States and such currencies could not be used to reduce its obligations for equity interest recovery to its Principals and Sureties, HJR 192, public law 73-10 further made the "notes of national banks" and "national banking associations" on par with its other currency and legal tender obligations.

TITLE 31> SUBTITLE IV> CHAPTER 51> SUBCHAPTER I Sec. 5103 says:
Legal Tender – United States coins and currency (including Federal Reserve Notes and circulating notes of Federal Reserve Banks and national banks) are legal tender for all debts, public charges, taxes and dues. This legal definition for 'legal tender' was first established in HJR 192 in the same act that made Federal Reserve Notes and notes of national banking associations legal tender.

Public Policy HJR 192
JOINT RESOLUTION TO SUSPEND THE GOLD
STANDARD AND ABROGATE THE GOLD CLAUSE
JUNE 5, 1933
HJR 192 73RD Congress, 1st Session

Joint Resolution to assure uniform value to the coins and currency of the United States

As used in this resolution, the term "obligation" means an obligation (including every obligation of and to the United States, excepting currency) payable in money of the United States; and the term 'coin or currency' means coin or currency of the United States, including Federal Reserve Notes and circulating notes of Federal Reserve Banks and national banking associations.

All coins and currencies of the United States (including Federal Reserve Notes and circulating notes of Federal Reserve Banks and national banking associations) heretofore and hereafter coined or issued, shall be legal tender for all debt, public and private, public charges, taxes, duties and dues."

Although HJR 192 has been since repealed, UCC 10-104 Un-repeals the resolution as the United States cannot deny or withhold remedy from the American people as long as their economic system remains collateralized by the wealth and assets of the American people.

TITLE 12.221 Definitions – "The terms 'national bank' and 'national banking associations' ….shall be held to be synonymous and interchangeable." The term "notes of national banks or national banking associations" have been continuously maintained in the official definition of legal tender since June 5, 1933 to present, when the term had never been used to define 'currency' or 'legal tender' before that time. Prior to 1933 the forms of currency in use that were legal tender were many and varied: United States Gold Certificates, United States Notes, Treasury Notes, Interest bearing notes, Gold coins of the United States, Standard silver dollars, subsidiary silver coins, minor coins, commemorative coins, but, the list did not include Federal Reserve Notes or notes of national banks or national banking associations despite the fact national bank notes were a common medium of exchange or 'currency' and had been, almost since the founding of our banking system and were backed by United States bonds or other securities on deposit for the bank with the U.S. Treasury.

Further, from the time of their inclusion in the definition they have been phased out until presently all provisions in the United States Code pertaining to **incorporated federally chartered National Banking institutions** issuing, redeeming, replacing and circulating notes have all been repealed. As stated in "Money and Banking", 4th Ed., by David H. Friedman, published by the American Bankers Association, page 78, "Today commercial banks no longer issue currency...."

It is clear that the federally incorporated banking institutions subject to the restrictions and repealed sections of Title 12, are NOT those primarily referred to maintained in the current definitions of "legal tender."

The legal statutory and professional definitions of 'banks', 'banking', and 'banker' used in the United States Code of Federal Regulations are not those commonly understood for these terms and have made statutory definition of "Bank" accordingly:

UCC 4-105 Part 1 - Bank "means a person engaged in the business of banking,"
12 CFR Sec. 229.2 Definitions (e) Bank means – "the term bank also includes any person engaged in the business of banking,"
12 CFR Sec. 210.2 Definitions. (d) "Bank means any person engaged in the business of banking."
Title 12 USC Sec. 1813 –Definitions of Bank and Related Terms.- (1) Bank- The term "Bank" – (a) "means any national bank, state bank, and district bank, and any federal branch and insured branch;"
Black's Law Dictionary, 5th Edition, page 133 defines a "Banker" as " In general sense, person that engages in the business of banking. In narrower meaning, a private person....; who is engaged in the business of banking without being incorporated. Under some statutes, an individual banker, as distinguished from a "private banker", is a person who, having complied with the statutory requirements, has received authority from the state to engage in the business of banking, while a 'private banker' is a person engaged in banking without having any special privileges or authority from the state."
"**Banking**" Is partly and optionally defined as "The business of issuing notes for circulation......, negotiating bills."
Black's Law Dictionary, 5th Edition, page 133, defines "Banking" "The business of banking, as defined by law and custom, consists in the issue of notes......intended to circulate as money....."
And defines a "**Banker's Note**" as "A commercial instrument resembling a bank note in every particular except that it is given by a 'private banker' or unincorporated national banking institution." Federal statute does not specifically define 'national bank' and 'national banking association' in those sections where these uses are legislated on to exclude a private banker or unincorporated banking institution. It does define these terms to the exclusion of such persons in the chapters and sections where the issue and circulation of notes by national banks has been repealed or forbidden.

In the absence of a statutory definition, the courts give terms their ordinary meaning. Bass, Terri L. vs Stolper, Koritzinski, 111 F.3 rd 1325, 7 th Cir.Apps. (1996) As the U.S. Supreme Court noted, "We have stated time and again that courts must presume that a legislature says in a statute what it means and means in a statute what it says there." See e.g., United States vs Ron Pair Enterprises, Inc. 489 U.S. 235, 241-242 (1989) "The legislative purpose is expressed by the ordinary meaning in the words used." Richards vs United States 369 U.S. 1 (1962)

The legal definitions relating to 'legal tender' have been written by congress and maintained as such to be both exclusive, where necessary, and inclusive, where appropriate, to provide in its statutory definitions of legal tender for the inclusion of all those, who by definition of private, unincorporated persons engaged in the business of banking to issue notes against the obligation of the United States for recovery on their risk, whose private assets and property are being used to collateralize the obligations of the United States since 1933, as collectively and nationally constituting a legal class of persons being a "national bank" or "national banking association" with the rights to issue such notes against the obligations of the United States for equity interest recovery due and accrued to these Principals and Sureties of the United States backing the obligations of U.S. currency and credit; as a means for the legal tender discharge of lawful debts in commerce as remedy due them in conjunction with U.S. obligations to the discharge of that portion of the public debt, which is provided for in the present financial reorganization still in effect and ongoing since 1933. [12 USC 411, 18 USC 8, 12 USC; ch. 6, 38 Stat. 251 Sect 14(a), 31 USC 5118, 3123 with rights protected under the 14th Amendment of the United States Constitution, by the U.S. Supreme Court in U.S. vs Russell (13 Wall, 623, 627), Pearlman vs Reliance Ins.Co., 371 U.S. 132, 136, 137 (1962), US vs Hooe, 3Cranch (US) 73 (1805) and in conformity with the U.S.
Supreme Court 79 US 287 (1870), 172 U.S. 48 (1898), and as confirmed at 307 U.S. 247 (1939)] HJR 192, public law 73-10 further declared...."every provision... which purports to give the obligee a right to require payment in gold or a particular kind of coin or currency....is declared against public policy; and no such provision shall be...made with respect to any obligation hereafter incurred."

Making way for discharge and recovery on U.S. corporate public debt due the Principals and Sureties of the United States providing as public policy for the discharge of 'every obligation', including every obligation of and to the United States, 'dollar for dollar', allowing those backing the United States financial reorganization to recover on it by discharging an obligation they owe to the United States or its sub-corporate entities, against that same amount of obligation of the United States owed to them; thus providing the remedy for the discharge and orderly recovery of equity interest on U.S. corporate public debt due the Sureties, Principals and Holders of the United States, discharging that portion of the public debt without expansion of credit, debt or obligation on the United States or these its prime creditors it was intended to satisfy equitable remedy to, but gaining for each bearer of such note, discharge of obligation equivalent in value 'dollar for dollar' to any and all 'lawful tender of the United States."

Those who constitute an association nationwide of private, unincorporated persons engaged in the business of banking to issue notes against these obligations of the United States due them; whose private property is at risk to collateralize the government's debt and currency, by legal definition, a 'national banking association'; such notes, issued against these obligations of the United States to that part of the public debt due its Principals and Sureties and required by law to be accepted as 'legal; tender' of payment of all debts, public and private, and are defined in law as 'obligations of the United

States', on the same par and category with Federal Reserve Notes and other currency and legal tender obligations.

Under this remedy for discharge of the public debt and recovery to its Principals and Sureties, two debts that would have been discharged in Federal Reserve debt note instruments or checks drawn on the same, equally expanding the public debt by those transactions, are discharged against a single public debt of the corporate United States and its sub-corporate entities to its prime creditor without the expansion and use of Federal Reserve debt note instruments as currency and credit, and so, without the expansion of the public debt and debt instruments in the monetary system and the expansion of the public debt as burden upon the entire financial system and its Principals and Sureties the recovery remedy was intended to relieve.

Their use is for the discharge and non-cash accrual reduction of U.S. Corporate public debt to the Principals, Sureties, Prime Creditors and Holders of it as provided in law and the instruments will ultimately be settled by adjustment and set-off in discharge of a bearers obligation to the United States against the obligation of the United States for the amount of the instrument to the original creditor it was tendered to or whomever or whatever institution may be the final bearer and holder in due course of it, again, thus discharging that portion of the public debt without expansion of credit, debt or note on the prime creditors of the United States it was intended to satisfy equitable remedy to, but gaining for each endorsed bearer of it discharge of obligation equivalent in value, 'dollar for dollar' of currency, measurable in 'lawful money of the United States.'

Even though the gold clause has been repealed, there still remains no currency of value or substance or gold coin in circulation today with which to pay a debt. The law does not allow for impossibilities. But even this did not repeal or remove our remedy which equity demands for the Principals and Sureties of the United States.

The practical evidence and fact of the financial reorganization (bankruptcy) of the United States is still ongoing today, visible all around us to see and understand. When Treasury Notes come due, they are not paid. They are refinanced by new Treasury Bills and Notes to back the currency and cover the debts….something that cannot be done with debt, unless, the debtor is protected by bankruptcy reorganization that is regularly restructured to keep it going. Each time the Federal debt ceiling is raised by Congress they are restructuring the bankruptcy reorganization of the government's debt so that commerce may continue on. **The recovery remedy is maintained in law because it has to be to satisfy equity to its prime creditors.**

The bankruptcy obstruction and overt impairment of the absolute priority right of redemption by the CREDITOR Federal Reserve Bank and banking families has established in fact the CREDITOR'S operation in equity in bad faith and with unclean hands and constitutes a delictual default and abandonment of all CREDITOR claims and the relinquishment of the PLEDGED property; and

The bankruptcy obstruction and overt impairment of the absolute priority right of redemption by the COURTS has established in fact the general post office styled as the UNITED STATES' operation in equity in bad faith and with unclean hands and constitutes a delictual default and abandonment of all equity claims of the UNITED STATES and their voluntary abandonment of all sovereign rights, power and authority associated therewith; and

The sovereign people of America, through and by James-Thomas: McBride, private postmaster, have served Notice of the Abandonment and registered the priority claim on the abandonment.

The Claim on Abandonment by the sovereign people of America has been received and accepted without objection or dispute.

Declaration Of Peace

The general post office styled as the UNITED STATES has been in a perpetual state of war since its inception. The 'Powers That Be' have used the UNITED STATES as a weapon to wage war on the sovereign people of America, operating under the Emergency War Powers Act and the secret presumption that the sovereign people are the enemy of the UNITED STATES for the purpose of evading their liabilities under the original equity contract and to pillage and plunder the private property of the people they were created to serve.

The general post office styled as the UNITED STATES has been used as a weapon to wage an economic war at arms length against all of the people of the world bringing all of humanity to the brink of destruction as the CREDITOR'S master plan of total economic slavery over the sovereign people of the world has been implemented.

The Powers That Be have used the UNITED STATES as a weapon to wage war on the sovereign people of the world via the unconscionable creation, production and distribution of harmful drugs for the purpose of enslaving the people and funding and executing their genocide against humanity.

The Powers That Be have used the UNITED STATES as a platform for their propaganda, creating the world's problems and then presenting themselves as the world's savior bringing about the solution and protection from their self created illusionary boogie men for the purpose of enslaving the sovereign people of the world.

Let it be known by all of humanity that the:

UNITED STATES has DECLARED PEACE.

From this day forward the UNITED STATES shall be used as a tool, actuated by humility, to promote universal peace, love and unity among all men. The UNITED STATES shall become a broker and facilitator of peace; a springboard for ascension and balance within the world consciousness. The UNITED STATES shall immediately stand down and withdraw itself from all acts of aggression and vacate all occupied land and shall immediately bring all American soldiers home.

The agents and agencies of the UNITED STATES shall immediately cease and desist in all forms of gun and drug production and distribution, all forms of terrorism and genocide of the people, all standard operating procedure of the powers that be since the days of the East India trading Company.

All Administrative Agencies of the UNITED STATES shall immediately remove all gold fringed military flags from their offices and courtrooms and shall display the civilian flag of peace. The Custodian of the Alien Property shall immediately update his/her files, removing the names and private property of the American people from their files/lists and make the return of the property to the rightful owners. All administrative agencies and administrative courts shall operate in peace and honor, servants of the sovereign people.

Civil Flag Of Peace

The jurisdiction of the courts of the united states is described as the **American flag of peace**; red, white and blue with stripes of red and white horizontally placed in alteration. Under the jurisdiction of the American flag of peace the private rights of the sovereign people of the united states are protected and all rights are preserved. Here, the People are 'innocent until proven guilty.' Under the military gold fringed flag there are no rights.

The Law Of The Flag

The Law of the Flag, an International Law, which is recognized by every nation of the planet, a vessel is a part of the territory of the nation whose flag she flies and designates the RIGHTS under which a ship owner, who sends his vessel into a foreign port, gives notice by his flag to all who enter into contracts with the ship master that he intends the Law of that Flag to regulate those contracts, and that they must either submit to its operation or not contract with him or his agent at all. Pursuant to the "Law of the Flag," a military flag does result in jurisdictional implications when flown. **It could mean WAR.**

By the doctrine of "four cornering" the flag establishes the law of the country that it represents, i.e. the embassies of foreign countries, in Washington D.C., are "four cornered" by walls or fencing, creating an "enclave. " Within the boundaries of the "enclave" of the foreign embassy, the flag of that foreign country establishes the jurisdiction and law of that foreign country, which will be enforced by the Law of the Flag and international treaty. When you enter an embassy, you are subject to the laws of that country, just as if you board a ship flying a foreign flag, you will be subject to the laws of that flag, enforceable by the "master of the ship," (Captain), by the law of the flag.

The general post office known as the UNITED STATES now flies

the Civil Flag of Peace of the united states of America.

The attachment of gold fringe on the flag constitutes a mutilation of the flag and represents "color of law" jurisdiction and suspends the people's private rights. The military shall not try civilians as it constitutes an **act of WAR against the people**.

The Civilian Flag of the united States of America, with no fringe, **takes precedence** over all other flags; it is the superior flag and **establishes the civil jurisdiction** of the united States of America, and the laws made in pursuance thereof.

Law Form

The general post office styled as the UNITED STATES is a free republic operating under the concepts and intent of the Articles Of Confederation, establishing a perpetual Union between the several free and independent states, to wit:

I. The Style of this Confederacy shall be "The United States of America".
II. Each state retains its sovereignty, freedom, and independence, and every power, jurisdiction, and right, which is not by this Confederation expressly delegated to the United States, in Congress assembled.

III. The said States hereby severally enter into a **firm league of friendship** with each other, for their common defence, the security of their liberties, and their mutual and general welfare, binding themselves to assist each other, against all force offered to, or attacks made upon them, or any of them, on account of religion, sovereignty, trade, or any other pretence whatever.

IV. The better to secure and perpetuate mutual friendship and intercourse among the people of the different States in this Union, the free inhabitants of each of these States, paupers, vagabonds, and fugitives from justice excepted, shall be entitled to all privileges and immunities of free citizens in the several States; and the people of each State shall enjoy free ingress and regress to and from any other State, and shall enjoy therein all the privileges of trade and commerce, subject to the same duties, impositions, and restrictions as the inhabitants thereof respectively, provided that such restrictions shall not extend so far as to prevent the removal of property imported into any State, to any other State, of which the owner is an inhabitant; provided also that no imposition, duties or restriction shall be laid by any State, on the property of the United States, or either of them. If any person guilty of, or charged with, treason, felony, or other high misdemeanour in any State, shall flee from justice, and be found in any of the United States, he shall, upon demand of the Governor or executive power of the State from which he fled, be delivered up and removed to the State having jurisdiction of his offense. Full faith and credit shall be given in each of these States to the records, acts, and judicial proceedings of the courts and magistrates of every other State.

V. For the most convenient management of the general interests of the United States, delegates shall be annually appointed in such manner as the legislatures of each State shall direct, to meet in Congress on the first Monday in November, in every year, with a power reserved to each State to recall its delegates, or any of them, at any time within the year, and to send others in their stead for the remainder of the year.

No State shall be represented in Congress by not less than two, nor more than seven members; and no person shall be capable of being a delegate for more than three years in any term of six years; nor shall any person, being a delegate, be capable of holding any office under the United States, for which he, or another for his benefit, receives any salary, fees or emolument of any kind.

Each State shall maintain its own delegates in a meeting of the States, and while they act as members of the committee of the States.

In determining questions in the United States in Congress assembled, each State shall have one vote.

Freedom of speech and debate in Congress shall not be impeached or questioned in any court or place out of Congress, and the members of Congress shall be protected in their persons from arrests or imprisonments, during the time of their going to and from, and attendance on Congress, except for treason, felony, or breach of the peace.

VI. No State, without the consent of the United States in Congress assembled, shall send any embassy to, or receive any embassy from, or enter into any conference, agreement, alliance or treaty with any King, Prince or State; nor shall any person holding any office of profit or trust under the United States, or any of them, accept any present, emolument, office or title of any kind whatever from any King, Prince or foreign State; nor shall the United States in Congress assembled, or any of them, grant any title of nobility.

No two or more States shall enter into any treaty, confederation or alliance whatever between them, without the consent of the United States in Congress assembled, specifying accurately the purposes for which the same is to be entered into, and how long it shall continue.

No State shall lay any imposts or duties, which may interfere with any stipulations in treaties, entered into by the United States in Congress assembled, with any King, Prince or State, in pursuance of any treaties already proposed by Congress, to the courts of France and Spain.

No vessel of war shall be kept up in time of peace by any State, except such number only, as shall be deemed necessary by the United States in Congress assembled, for the defence of such State, or its trade; nor shall any body of forces be kept up by any State in time of peace, except such number only, as in the judgment of the United States in Congress assembled, shall be deemed requisite to garrison the forts necessary for the defence of such State; but every State shall always keep up a well-regulated and disciplined militia, sufficiently armed and accoutered, and shall provide and constantly have ready for use, in public stores, a due number of filed pieces and tents, and a proper quantity of arms, ammunition and camp equipage.

No State shall engage in any war without the consent of the United States in Congress assembled, unless such State be actually invaded by enemies, or shall have received certain advice of a resolution being formed by some nation of Indians to invade such State, and the danger is so imminent as not to admit of a delay till the United States in Congress assembled can be consulted; nor shall any State grant commissions to any ships or vessels of war, nor letters of marque or reprisal, except it be after a declaration of war by the United States in Congress assembled, and then only against the Kingdom or State and the subjects thereof, against which war has been so declared, and under such regulations as shall be established by the United States in Congress assembled, unless such State be infested by pirates, in which case vessels of war may be fitted out for that occasion, and kept so long as the danger shall continue, or until the United States in Congress assembled shall determine otherwise.

VII. When land forces are raised by any State for the common defense, all officers of or under the rank of colonel, shall be appointed by the legislature of each State respectively, by whom such forces shall be raised, or in such manner as such State shall direct, and all vacancies shall be filled up by the State which first made the appointment.

VIII. All charges of war, and all other expenses that shall be incurred for the common defence or general welfare, and allowed by the United States in Congress assembled, shall be defrayed out of a common treasury, which shall be supplied by the several States in proportion to the value of all land within each State, granted or surveyed for any person, as such land and the buildings and improvements thereon shall be estimated according to such mode as the United States in Congress assembled, shall from time to time direct and appoint.

The taxes for paying that proportion shall be laid and levied by the authority and direction of the legislatures of the several States within the time agreed upon by the United States in Congress assembled.

IX. The United States in Congress assembled, shall have the sole and exclusive right and power of determining on peace and war, except in the cases mentioned in the sixth article -- of sending and receiving ambassadors -- entering into treaties and alliances, provided that no treaty of commerce shall be made whereby the legislative power of the respective States shall be restrained from imposing such imposts and duties on foreigners, as their own people are subjected to, or from prohibiting the exportation or importation of any species of goods or commodities whatsoever -- of establishing rules for deciding in all cases, what captures on land or water shall be legal, and in what manner prizes taken by land or naval forces in the service of the United States shall be divided or appropriated -- of granting letters of marque and reprisal in times of peace -- appointing courts for the trial of piracy and felonies committed on the high seas and establishing courts for receiving and determining finally appeals in all cases of captures, provided that no member of Congress shall be appointed a judge of any of the said courts.

The United States in Congress assembled shall also be the last resort on appeal in all disputes and differences now subsisting or that hereafter may arise between two or more States concerning boundary, jurisdiction or any other causes whatever; which authority shall always be exercised in the manner following.

Whenever the legislative or executive authority or lawful agent of any State in controversy with another shall present a petition to Congress stating the matter in question and praying for a hearing, notice thereof shall be given by order of Congress to the legislative or executive authority of the other State in controversy, and a day assigned for the appearance of the parties by their lawful agents, who shall then be directed to appoint by joint consent, commissioners or judges to constitute a court for hearing and determining the matter in question: but if they cannot agree, Congress shall name three persons out of each of the United States, and from the list of such persons each party shall alternately strike out one, the petitioners beginning, until the number shall be reduced to thirteen; and from that number not less than seven, nor more than nine names as Congress shall direct, shall in the presence of Congress be drawn out by lot, and the persons whose names shall be so drawn or any five of them, shall be commissioners or judges, to hear and finally determine the controversy, so always as a major part of the judges who shall hear the cause shall agree in the determination: and if either party shall neglect to attend at the day appointed, without showing reasons, which Congress shall judge sufficient, or being present shall refuse to strike, the Congress shall proceed to nominate three persons out of each State, and the secretary of Congress shall strike in behalf of such party absent or refusing; and the judgment and sentence of the court to be appointed, in the manner before prescribed, shall be final and conclusive; and if any of the parties shall refuse to submit to the authority of such court, or to appear or defend their claim or cause, the court shall nevertheless proceed to pronounce sentence, or judgment, which shall in like manner be final and decisive, the judgment or sentence and other proceedings being in either case transmitted to Congress, and lodged among the acts of Congress for the security of the parties concerned: provided that every commissioner, before he sits in judgment, shall take an oath to be administered by one of the judges of the supreme or superior court of the State, where the cause shall be tried, 'well and truly to hear and determine the matter in question, according to the best of his judgment, without favour, affection or hope of reward': provided also, that no State shall be deprived of territory for the benefit of the United States.

All controversies concerning the private right of soil claimed under different grants of two or more States, whose jurisdictions as they may respect such lands, and the States which passed such grants are adjusted, the said grants or either of them being at the same time claimed to have originated antecedent to such settlement of jurisdiction, shall on the petition of either party to the Congress of the United States, be finally determined as near as may be in the same manner as is before prescribed for deciding disputes respecting territorial jurisdiction between different States.

The United States in Congress assembled shall also have the sole and exclusive right and power of regulating the alloy and value of coin struck by their own authority, or by that of the respective States -- fixing the standards of weights and measures throughout the United States -- regulating the trade and managing all affairs with the Indians, not members of any of the States, provided that the legislative right of any State within its own limits be not infringed or violated -- establishing or regulating post offices from one State to another, throughout all the United States, and exacting such postage on the papers passing through the same as may be requisite to defray the expenses of the said office -- appointing all officers of the land forces, in the service of the United States, excepting regimental officers -- appointing all the officers of the naval forces, and commissioning all officers whatever in the service of the United States -- making rules for the government and regulation of the said land and naval forces, and directing their operations.

The United States in Congress assembled shall have authority to appoint a committee, to sit in the recess of Congress, to be denominated 'A Committee of the States', and to consist of one delegate from each State; and to appoint such other committees and civil officers as may be necessary for managing the general affairs of the United States under their direction -- to appoint one of their members to preside, provided that no person be allowed to serve in the office of president more than one year in any term of three years; to ascertain the necessary sums of money to be raised for the service of the United States, and to appropriate and apply the same for defraying the public expenses -- to borrow money, or emit bills on the credit of the United States, transmitting every half-year to the respective States an account of the sums of money so borrowed or emitted -- to build and equip a navy -- to agree upon the number of land forces, and to make requisitions from each State for its quota, in proportion to the number of white inhabitants in such State; which requisition shall be binding, and thereupon the legislature of each State shall appoint the regimental officers, raise the men and clothe, arm and equip them in a solid-like manner, at the expense of the United States; and the officers and men so clothed, armed and equipped shall march to the place appointed, and within the time agreed on by the United States in Congress assembled. But if the United States in Congress assembled shall, on consideration of circumstances judge proper that any State should not raise men, or should raise a smaller number of men than the quota thereof, such extra number shall be raised, officered, clothed, armed and equipped in the same manner as the quota of each State, unless the legislature of such State shall judge that such extra number cannot be safely spread out in the same, in which case they shall raise, officer, clothe, arm and equip as many of such extra number as they judge can be safely spared. And the officers and men so clothed, armed, and equipped, shall march to the place appointed, and within the time agreed on by the United States in Congress assembled.

The United States in Congress assembled shall never engage in a war, nor grant letters of marque or reprisal in time of peace, nor enter into any treaties or alliances, nor coin money, nor regulate the value thereof, nor ascertain the sums and expenses necessary for the defence and welfare of the United States, or any of them, nor emit bills, nor borrow money on the credit of the United States, nor appropriate money, nor agree upon the number of vessels of war, to be built or purchased, or the number of land or sea forces to be raised, nor appoint a commander in chief of the army or navy, unless nine States assent to the same: nor shall a question on any other point, except for adjourning from day to day be determined, unless by the votes of the majority of the United States in Congress assembled.

The Congress of the United States shall have power to adjourn to any time within the year, and to any place within the United States, so that no period of adjournment be for a longer duration than the space of six months, and shall publish the journal of their proceedings monthly, except such parts thereof relating to treaties, alliances or military operations, as in their judgment require secrecy; and the yeas and nays of the delegates of each State on any question shall be entered on the journal, when it is desired by any delegates of a State, or any of them, at his or their request shall be furnished with a transcript of the said journal, except such parts as are above excepted, to lay before the legislatures of the several States.

X. The Committee of the States, or any nine of them, shall be authorized to execute, in the recess of Congress, such of the powers of Congress as the United States in Congress assembled, by the consent of the nine States, shall from time to time think expedient to vest them with; provided that no power be delegated to the said Committee, for the exercise of which, by the Articles of Confederation, the voice of nine States in the Congress of the United States assembled be requisite.

XI. Canada acceding to this confederation, and adjoining in the measures of the United States, shall be admitted into, and entitled to all the advantages of this Union; but no other colony shall be admitted into the same, unless such admission be agreed to by nine States.

XII. All bills of credit emitted, monies borrowed, and debts contracted by, or under the authority of Congress, before the assembling of the United States, in pursuance of the present confederation, shall be deemed and considered as a charge against the United States, for payment and satisfaction whereof the said United States, and the public faith are hereby solemnly pledged.

XIII. Every State shall abide by the determination of the United States in Congress assembled, on all questions which by this confederation are submitted to them. And the Articles of this Confederation shall be inviolably observed by every State, and the Union shall be perpetual; nor shall any alteration at any time hereafter be made in any of them; unless such alteration be agreed to in a Congress of the United States, and be after wards confirmed by the legislatures of every State.

A "Transitional Committee" shall be seated for the purpose of ensuring a peaceful and efficient transition from an Empirical War based mentality and operating system to one of peace, humility and unity. Said "Transitional Committee" shall establish and empower an interim government for the united states of America and shall operate until such time as the people can be duly informed as to the true history of the UNITED STATES and the fraud that has been perpetrated against them, not to exceed one year.

The Postmaster general of the organic post office for the united states, creator of the general post office styled as the UNITED STATES and located within the ten miles square commonly known as Washington, D.C., under whose direction the UNITED STATES operates, shall operate in the capacity of trustee for the people and shall take instructions from the "Transitional Committee" until such time as the Interim government shall be seated and empowered.

The UNITED STATES' courts are administrative courts who gain their authority under Title 5, the Administrative Procedures Act of 1946 and/or the Judiciary Act of 1789. These Administrative courts were established for the purpose of being the watch dog over public offices so that if and when the American people had their private rights violated they could file a complaint without cost.

These administrative courts were designed to give the administrative court the power of legislation; the power of the executive branch of government; to give them judicial power and authority. These administrative courts were authorized to disregard laws, case cites, supreme court decisions, statutes, codes, rules, regulations and to change policy. The establishment of these administrative courts effectively created a fourth branch of government at the request of the BAR Association.

BUT, this system was designed for use BY the American people, NOT AGAINST the American people. These administrative courts have jurisdiction ONLY over administrative agencies and NOT over the American people and were established as a vehicle for use by the American people to lodge and adjudicate a grievance against any administrative agency and gave this administrative court the power and authority to make the corrections without the lengthy process of introducing and passing legislation. Charges can only be levied AGAINST an administrative agency BY THE AMERICAN PEOPLE and cannot be used against the American people. The people are ALWAYS the Plaintiff in these Administrative courts except when these courts are used to perpetrate a fraud against the American People.

Congress, under 49 Statute 3097 Treaty Series 881 Conventions and Duties and Rights of the States, placed all states under international law, making all courts, International courts. The International Organization Immunities Act 1945 placed all courts under the jurisdiction of the United Nations under Title 22 CFR Foreign Relations with Oaths of Office under section 92.12 and 92.31. Under Title 8 USC 1481 you voluntarily forfeit your citizenship when you take the Oath of Office in these administrative courts, and establishes you as a foreign agent required to register as a foreign agent doing business in the state.

These administrative courts, who gain their authority under Title 5 were designed to make the corrections within public offices, to make them more efficient and to hold agencies, and officers thereof, accountable for their actions. In these administrative courts only the American people can bring the charges for the corrections and the American people are ALWAYS the Plaintiff/ harmed Party. These courts have NO JURISDICTION over the people. No agency has the authority to bring charges against the American people or their private rights and property in an administrative court under the Administrative Procedures Act.

These Administrative Courts shall operate as established, for the purpose of facilitating the prosecution of grievances against an administrative agency by the American people for the administrative agencies trespass on the private rights of the sovereign people of America.

Administrative Notice

* *63C Am.Jur.2d, Public Officers and Employees, §247* "As expressed otherwise, the powers delegated to a public officer are held in trust for the people and are to be exercised in behalf of the government or of all citizens who may need the intervention of the officer. [1] Furthermore, the view has been expressed that all public officers, within whatever branch and whatever level of government, and whatever be their private vocations, are trustees of the people, and accordingly labor under every disability and prohibition imposed by law upon trustees relative to the making of personal financial gain from a discharge of their trusts. [2] That is, a public officer occupies a fiduciary relationship to the political entity on whose behalf he or she serves. [3] and owes a fiduciary duty to the public. [4] It

has been said that the fiduciary responsibilities of a public officer cannot be less than those of a private individual. [5] Furthermore, it has been stated that any enterprise undertaken by the public official who tends to weaken public confidence and undermine the sense of security for individual rights is against public policy. Fraud in its elementary common law sense of deceit-and this is one of the meanings that fraud bears [483 U.S. 372] in the statute. See United States v. Dial, 757 F.2d 163, 168 (7th Cir1985) includes the deliberate concealment of material information in a setting of fiduciary obligation. A public official is a fiduciary toward the public, including, in the case of a judge, the litigants who appear before him and if he deliberately conceals material information from them, he is guilty of fraud. McNally v United States 483 U.S. 350 (1987)

Texas Penal Code Sec. 1.07. DEFINITIONS. (a) In this code: [consistent with all state penal codes]
(9) "Coercion" means a threat, however communicated:
    (A) to commit an offense;
    (B) to inflict bodily injury in the future on the person threatened or another;
    (C) to accuse a person of any offense;
    (D) to expose a person to hatred, contempt, or ridicule;
    (E) to harm the credit or business repute of any person; or
    (F) to take or withhold action as a public servant, or to cause a public servant to take or withhold action.
(19) "Effective consent" includes consent by a person legally authorized to act for the owner.
Consent is not effective if:
    (A) induced by force, threat, or fraud;
    (B) given by a person the actor knows is not legally authorized to act for the owner;
    (C) given by a person who by reason of youth, mental disease or defect, or intoxication is known by the actor to be unable to make reasonable decisions; or
    (D) given solely to detect the commission of an offense.
(24) "Government" means:
    (A) the state;
    (B) a county, municipality, or political subdivision of the state; or
    (C) any branch or agency of the state, a county, municipality, or political subdivision.
(30) "Law" means the constitution or a statute of this state or of the United States, a written opinion of a court of record, a municipal ordinance, an order of a county commissioners court, or a rule authorized by and
lawfully adopted under a statute.
(41) "Public servant" means a person elected, selected, appointed, employed, or otherwise designated as one of
the following, even if he has not yet qualified for office or assumed his duties:
    (A) an officer, employee, or agent of government;
    (B) a juror or grand juror; or
    (C) an arbitrator, referee, or other person who is authorized by law or private written agreement to hear
or determine a cause or controversy; or
    (D) an attorney at law or notary public when participating in the performance of a governmental
function; or
    (E) a candidate for nomination or election to public office; or
    (F) a person who is performing a governmental function under a claim of right although he is not legally qualified to do so.

ALL COURTS HAVE BEEN OPERATING UNDER

(1) *TRADING WITH THE ENEMY ACT* AS CODIFIED IN TITLE 50 USC,
(2) TITLE 28 USC, CHAPTER 176, *FEDERAL DEBT COLLECTION PROCEDURE*, AND
(3) FED.R.CIV.P. 4(j) UNDER TITLE 28 USC §1608, MAKING THE COURTS "FOREIGN STATES" TO THE PEOPLE BY CONGRESSIONAL MANDATE

"IT IS THE DUTY OF THE COURT TO DECLARE THE MEANING OF WHAT IS WRITTEN, AND NOT WHAT
WAS INTENDED TO BE WRITTEN. J.W. Seavey Hop Corp. v. Pollock, 20 Wn.2d 337,348-49, 147 P.2d 310 (1944),
cited with approval in Berg v. Hudesman, 115 Wn2d at 669.

OATH OF OFFICE MAKES PUBLIC OFFICIALS "FOREIGN"

1. Those holding Federal or State public office, and/or county or municipal office, under the Legislative, Executive or Judicial branch, including Court Officials, Judges, Prosecutors, Law Enforcement Department employees, Officers of the Court, etc., before entering into these public offices, are required by the U.S. Constitution and statutory law to comply with Title 5 USC, Sec. §3331, "Oath of office." State Officials are also required to meet this same obligation, according to State Constitutions and State statutory law.

2. All oaths of office come under 22 CFR, Foreign Relations, Sections §§92.12 - 92.30, and all who hold public office come under Title 8 USC, Section §1481 "Loss of nationality by native-born or naturalized citizen; voluntary action; burden of proof; presumptions."

3. Under Title 22 USC, Foreign Relations and Intercourse, Section §611, a Public Official is considered a foreign agent. In order to hold public office, the candidate must file a true and complete registration statement with the State Attorney General as a foreign principle.

4. The Oath of Office requires the public official in his / her foreign state capacity to uphold the constitutional form of government or face consequences.

> Title 10 USC, Sec. §333, "Interference with State and Federal law"
>
> The President, by using the militia or the armed forces, or both, or by any other means, shall take such measures as he considers necessary to suppress, in a State, any insurrection, domestic violence, unlawful combination, or conspiracy, if it—
>
> (1) so hinders the execution of the laws of that State, and of the United States within the State, that any part or class of its people is deprived of a right, privilege, immunity, or protection named in the Constitution and secured by law, and the constituted authorities of that State are unable, fail, or refuse to protect that right, privilege, or immunity, or to give that protection; or
> (2) opposes or obstructs the execution of the laws of the United States or impedes the course of justice under those laws.
> In any situation covered by clause (1), the State shall be considered to have denied the equal protection of the laws secured by the Constitution.

5. Such willful action, while serving in official capacity, violates Title 18 USC, Section §1918:

Title 18 USC, Section §1918 "Disloyalty and asserting the right to strike against the government"

Whoever violates the provision of 7311 of title 5 that an individual may not accept or hold a position in the Government of the United States or the government of the District of Columbia if he—

(1) advocates the overthrow of our constitutional form of government; (2) is a member of an organization that he knows advocates the overthrow of our constitutional form of government; shall be fined under this title or imprisoned not more than one year and a day, or both.

and also deprives claimants of "honest services:

Title 18, Section §1346. Definition of "scheme or artifice to defraud"

"For the purposes of this chapter, the term "scheme or artifice to defraud" includes a scheme or artifice to deprive another of the intangible right of honest services.
and the treaties that placed your public offices in that foreign state under international law and under the United Nation jurisdiction

49 Stat. 3097; Treaty Series 881 CONVENTION ON RIGHTS AND DUTIES OF STATES

1945 IOIA –That the International Organizations Act of December 29, 1945 (59 Stat. 669; Title 22, Sections 288 to 2886
U.S.C.) the US relinquished every office

TITLE 8 > CHAPTER 12 > SUBCHAPTER I > § 1101
The term "foreign state" includes outlying possessions of a foreign state, but self-governing dominions or territories under
mandate or trusteeship shall be regarded as separate foreign states.

TABLE OF AUTHORITIES – RECIPROCAL IMMUNITY AND FOREIGN AGENT REGISTRATION
UNITED STATES INTERNATIONAL ORGANIZATIONS IMMUNITIES ACT,

PUBLIC LAW 79-291, 29 DECEMBER 1945(Public Law 291-79th Congress) TITLE I Section 2.(b) International organizations, their property and their assets, wherever located and by whomsoever held, shall enjoy the same immunity from suit and every form of Judicial process as is enjoyed by foreign governments, except to the extent that such organizations may expressly waive their immunity for the purpose of any proceedings or by the terms of any contract. (d) In so far as concerns customs duties and internal-revenue taxes imposed upon or by reason of importation, and the procedures in connection therewith; the registration of foreign agents; and the treatment of official communications, the privileges, exemptions, and immunities to which international organizations shall be entitled shall be those accorded under similar circumstances to foreign governments. Section 9. The privileges, exemptions, and immunities of international organizations and of their officers and employees, and members of their families, suites, and servants, provided for in this title, shall be granted notwithstanding the fact that the similar privileges, exemptions, and immunities granted to a foreign government, its officers, or employees, may be conditioned upon the existence of reciprocity by that foreign government: Provided, That nothing contained in this title shall be construed as precluding the Secretary of State from withdrawing the privileges, exemptions, and immunities herein provided from persons who are nationals of any foreign country on the ground that such country is failing to accord corresponding privileges, exemptions, and immunities to citizens of the United States. Also see

22 USC § 611 - FOREIGN RELATIONS AND INTERCOURSE; and, 22 USC § 612, Registration statement, concerning the absolute requirement of registration with the Attorney General as a "foreign principal," due to the undisputed status of the court and its alleged officers and employees as FOREIGN AGENTS, described *supra.* This requirement shall be deemed to include, but is not limited to, an affidavit of non-communist association.

JUDGE SERVES AS A DEBT COLLECTOR

6. Judges hold public office under Title 28 USC, Chapter 176, Federal Debt Collection Procedure:
Title 28, Chapter 176, Federal Debt Collection Procedure, Section §3002
As used in this chapter:
(2) "Court" means any court created by the Congress of the United States, excluding the United States Tax Court. (3) "Debt" means— (A) an amount that is owing to the United States on account of a direct loan, or loan insured or guaranteed, by the United States; or (B) an amount that is owing to the United States on account of a fee, duty, lease, rent, service, sale of real or personal property, overpayment, fine, assessment, penalty, restitution, damages, interest, tax, bail bond forfeiture, reimbursement, recovery of a cost incurred by the United States, or other source of indebtedness to the United States, but that is not owing under the terms of a contract originally entered into by only persons other than the United States;

(8) "Judgment" means a judgment, order, or decree entered in favor of the United States in a court and
arising from a civil or criminal proceeding regarding a debt. (15) "United States" means—
(A) a Federal corporation; (B) an agency, department, commission, board, or other entity of the United States; or (C) an instrumentality of the United States.
Title 22 USC, Sec. §286. "Acceptance of membership by United States in International Monetary Fund," states the following:

The President is hereby authorized to accept membership for the United States in the International Monetary Fund (hereinafter referred to as the "Fund"), and in the International Bank for Reconstruction and Development (hereinafter referred to as the "Bank"), provided for by the Articles of Agreement of the Fund and the Articles of Agreement of the Bank as set forth in the Final Act of the United Nations Monetary and Financial Conference dated July 22, 1944, and deposited in the archives of the Department of State.
8. Title 22 USC, Sec. § 286e-13, "Approval of fund pledge to sell gold to provide resources for Reserve Account of Enhanced Structural Adjustment Facility Trust," states the following:
The Secretary of the Treasury is authorized to instruct the Fund's pledge to sell, if needed, up to 3,000,000 ounces of the Fund's gold, to restore the resources of the Reserve Account of the Enhanced Structural Adjustment Facility Trust to a level that would be sufficient to meet obligations of the Trust payable to lenders which have made loans to the Loan Account of the Trust that have been used for the purpose of financing programs to Fund members previously in arrears to the Fund.

No Immunity Under "Commerce"

9. All immunity of the United States, and all liability of States, instrumentalities of States, and State officials have been waived under commerce, according to the following US Codes:
Title 15 USC, Commerce, Sec. §1122, "Liability of States, instrumentalities of States, and State officials"
(a) Waiver of sovereign immunity by the United States. The United States, all agencies and instrumentalities thereof, and all individuals, firms, corporations, other persons acting for the United States and with the authorization and consent of the United States, shall not be immune from suit in Federal or State court by any person, including any governmental or nongovernmental entity, for any violation under this Act. (b) Waiver of sovereign immunity by States. Any State, instrumentality of a State or any officer or employee of a State or instrumentality of a State acting in his or her official capacity, shall not be immune, under the eleventh amendment of the Constitution of the United States or under any other doctrine of sovereign immunity, from suit in Federal court by any person, including any governmental or nongovernmental entity for any violation under this Act.

Title 42 USC, Sec. §12202, "State immunity"

A State shall not be immune under the eleventh amendment to the Constitution of the United States from an action in Federal or State court of competent jurisdiction for a violation of this chapter. In any action against a State for a violation of the requirements of this chapter, remedies (including remedies both at law and in equity) are available for such a violation to the same extent as such remedies are available for such a violation in an action against any public or private entity other than a State

Title 42 USC, Sec. §2000d–7, "Civil rights remedies equalization"
(a) General provision
(1) A State shall not be immune under the Eleventh Amendment of the Constitution of the United States from suit in Federal court for a violation of section 504 of the Rehabilitation Act of 1973 [29 U.S.C. 794], title IX of the Education Amendments of 1972 [20 U.S.C. 1681 et seq.], the Age Discrimination Act of 1975 [42 U.S.C. 6101 et seq.], title VI of the Civil Rights Act of 1964 [42 U.S.C. 2000d et seq.], or the provisions of any other Federal statute prohibiting discrimination by recipients of Federal financial assistance. (2) In a suit against a State for a violation of a statute referred to in paragraph (1), remedies (including remedies both at law and in equity) are available for such a violation to the same extent as such remedies are available for such a violation in the suit against any public or private entity other than a State.

10. The Administrative Procedure Act of 1946 gives immunity in Administrative Court to the Administrative Law Judge
(ALJ) only when an action is brought by the people against a public, agency or corporate official / department. Under Title 5
USC, Commerce, public offices or officials can be sanctioned.
Title 5, USC, Sec. §551:
(10) "sanction" includes the whole or a part of an agency—
(A) prohibition, requirement, limitation, or other condition affecting the freedom of a person;(B) withholding of relief;(C) imposition of penalty or fine;(D) destruction, taking, seizure, or withholding of property;(E) assessment of damages, reimbursement, restitution, compensation, costs, charges, or fees;(F) requirement, revocation, or suspension of a license; or (G) taking other compulsory or restrictive action;

11. Justice is required to be BLIND while holding a SET OF SCALES and a TWO-EDGED SWORD. This symbolizes true justice. The Administrative Procedure Act of 1946 (60 stat 237) would allow the sword to cut in either direction and give the judge immunity by holding his own court office accountable for honest service fraud, obstruction of justice, false statements, malicious prosecution and fraud placed upon the court. Any wilful intent to uncover the EYES OF JUSTICE or TILT THE SCALES is a wilful intent to deny Due Process, which violates Title 18 USC §1346, "Scheme or Artifice to Defraud," by perpetrating a scheme or artifice to deprive another of the intangible right of honest services. This is considered fraud and an overthrow of a constitutional form of government and the person depriving the honest service can be held accountable and face punishment under Title 18 USC and Title 42 USC and violates Title 28 USC judicial procedures.

12. Both Title 18 USC, Crime and Criminal Procedure, and Title 42 USC, Public Health and Welfare, allow the Petitioner to bring an action against the United States and/or the State agencies, departments, and employees for civil rights violations while dealing in commerce. Title 10 places all public officials under this Title 10 section 333 while under a state of emergency. (Declared or undeclared War this falls under TWEA.)

COURTS OPERATING UNDER WAR POWERS ACT

13. The Courts are operating under the Emergency War Powers Act. The country has been under a declared "state of emergency" for the past 70 years resulting in the Constitution being suspended (See Title 50 USC Appendix – Trading with the Enemy Act of 1917). The Courts have been misusing Title 50 USC, Sec. §23, "Jurisdiction of United States courts and
judges," which provides for criminal jurisdiction over an "**enemy of the state**," whereas, Petitioner comes under Title 50 USC Appendix Application Sec. §21, "**Claims of naturalized citizens as affected by expatriation**" which states the following:

The claim of any naturalized American citizen under the provisions of this Act [sections 1 to 6, 7 to 39, and 41 to 44 of this Appendix] shall not be denied **on the ground of any presumption of expatriation** which has arisen against him, under the second sentence of section 2 of the Act entitled "An Act in reference to the expatriation of citizens and their protection abroad," approved March 2, 1907, if he shall give satisfactory evidence to the President, or the court, as the case may be, of his uninterrupted loyalty to the United States during his absence, and that he has returned to the United States, or that he, although desiring to return, has been prevented from so returning by circumstances beyond his control.

14. 15 Statutes at Large, Chapter 249 (section 1), enacted July 27 1868, states the following:

PREAMBLE - Rights of American citizens in foreign states.
WHEREAS the right of expatriation is a natural and inherent right of all people, indispensable to the enjoyment of the rights of life, liberty, and the pursuit of happiness; and whereas in the recognition of this principle this government has freely received emigrants from all nations, and invested them with the rights of citizenship; and whereas it is claimed that such American citizens, with their descendants, are subjects of foreign states, owing allegiance to the governments thereof; and whereas it is necessary to the maintenance of public peace that this claim of foreign allegiance should be promptly and finally disavowed.

SECTION I - Right of expatriation declared.

THEREFORE, Be it enacted by the Senate of the and House of Representatives of the United States of America in Congress assembled, That any declaration, instruction, opinion, order, or decision of any officers of this government which denies, restricts, impairs, or questions the right of expatriation, is hereby declared inconsistent with the fundamental principles of this government.

SECTION II - Protection to naturalized citizens in foreign states.
And it is further enacted, That all naturalized citizens of the United States, while in foreign states, shall be entitled to, and shall receive from this government, the same protection of persons and property that is accorded to native born citizens in like situations and circumstances.

SECTION III - Release of citizens imprisoned by foreign governments to be demanded.

And it is further enacted, That whenever it shall be made known to the President that any citizen of the United States has been unjustly deprived of his liberty by or under the authority of any foreign government, it shall be the duty of the President forthwith to demand of that government the reasons for such imprisonment, and if it appears to be wrongful and in the violation of the rights of American citizenship, the President shall forthwith demand the release of such citizen, and if the release so demanded is unreasonably delayed or refused, it shall be the duty of the President to use such means, not amounting to acts of war, as he may think necessary and proper to obtain or effectuate such release, and all the facts and proceedings relative thereto shall as soon as practicable be communicated by the President to Congress.
Approved, July 27, 1868

15 The Courts and the States are enforcing the following code on American nationals: Title 50 USC Appendix App, Trading, Act, Sec. §4, "Licenses to enemy or ally of enemy insurance or reinsurance companies; change of name; doing business in United States," as a result of the passage of The Amendatory Act of March 9, 1933 to Title 50 USC, Trading with the Enemy Act Public Law No. 65-91 (40 Stat. L. 411) October 6, 1917. The original Trading with the Enemy Act **excluded** the people of the United States from being classified as the enemy when involved in transactions wholly within the United States. The Amendatory Act of March 9, 1933, however, **included the people of the United States as the enemy,** by incorporating the following language into the Trading With The Enemy Act: "**by any person within the United States.**" The abuses perpetrated upon the American people are the result of Title 50 USC, Trading With The Enemy Act, which turned the American people into "enemy of the state.

LANGUAGE NOT CLARIFIED

16. Clarification of language:
The **STATES** has failed to state the meaning or clarify the definition of words. The courts pursuant to the Federal Rules of Civil Procedure (FRCP) Rule 4(j), are, in fact and at law, a FOREIGN STATE as defined in Title 28 USC §1602, et. seq.,
The FOREIGN SOVEREIGN IMMUNITIES ACT of 1976, Pub. L. 94-583 (hereafter FSIA), and, therefore, lack jurisdiction over the sovereign people. . Any failure to specifically state the jurisdiction of the court violates 18 USC §1001,
§1505, and §2331 and the PATRIOT ACT, Section 800, Domestic terrorism.
17. There are three different and distinct forms of the "**United States**" as revealed by this case law:

"The high Court confirmed that the term "United States" can and does mean three completely different things, depending on the context." Hooven & Allison Co. vs. Evatt,

324 U.S. 652 (1945) & *United States v. Cruikshank,* 92 U.S. 542 (1876) & United States v. Bevans, 16 U.S. 3 Wheat. 336 336 (1818)

The Courts and its officers fail to state which United States they represent, since they can represent only one, the Federal Debt Collection Procedure, as a corporation, the United States, Inc., and it's satellite corporations have no jurisdiction over an American national and a belligerent claimant, the people hereby assert their right of immunity inherent in the 11th amendment: *"The judicial power shall not be construed to extend to any suit in law or equity, commenced or prosecuted against one of the United States by citizens of another state, or by citizens of any Foreign State."* The court, by definition are a FOREIGN STATE, and are misusing the name of the Sovereign American by placing Sovereign American 's name in all capital letters, as well as by using Sovereign American 's last name to construe Sovereign American, erroneously, as a "person" which is a "term of art" meaning: *a creature of the law, an artificial being, and a CORPORATION or ens legis:*

"*Ens Legis.* L. Lat. A creature of the law; an artificial being, as contrasted with a natural person. Applied to corporations, considered as deriving their existence entirely from the law." —Blacks Law Dictionary, 4th Edition, 1951.

18. All complaints and suits against such CORPORATION, or *ens legis,* fall under the aforementioned FSIA and service of process must therefore be made by the clerk of the court, under Section 1608(a)(4) of Title 28 USC, 63 Stat. 111, as amended (22 U.S.C. 2658) [42 FR 6367, Feb. 2, 1977, as amended at 63 FR 16687, Apr. 6, 1998], to the Director of the Office of Special Consular Services in the Bureau of Consular Affairs, Department of State, in Washington, D.C., exclusively, pursuant to 22 CFR §93.1 and §93.2. A copy of the FSIA must be filed with the complaint along with "a certified copy of the diplomatic note of transmittal," and, "the certification shall state the date and place the documents were delivered." The foregoing must be served upon the Chief Executive Officer and upon the Registered Agent of the designated CORPORATION or FOREIGN STATE.

19. MUNICIPAL, COUNTY, or STATE COURTS lack jurisdiction to hear any case since they fall under the definition of FOREIGN STATE, and under all related definitions below. Said jurisdiction lies with the "district court of the United States," established by Congress in the states under Article III of the Constitution, which are "constitutional courts" and do not include the territorial courts created under Article IV, Section 3, Clause 2, which are "legislative" courts. *Hornbuckle v. Toombs*, 85 U.S. 648, 21 L.Ed. 966 (1873), (See Title 28 USC, Rule 1101), exclusively, under the FSIA Statutes pursuant to 28 USC §1330.

20. It is an undisputed, conclusive presumption that the Sovereign Americans, the real parties in interest are a not a CORPORATION, and, further, are not registered with any Secretary of State as a CORPORATION. Pursuant to Rule 12(b) (6), in these situations, the Prosecuting Attorney has failed to state a claim for which relief can be granted to the Defendant, a FATAL DEFECT, and, therefore, the instant case and all related matters must be DISMISSED WITH PREJUDICE for lack of *in personam*, territorial, and subject matter jurisdiction, as well as for improper Venue, as well as pursuant to the 11th amendment Foreign State Immunity.

21. Moreover, the process in the instant matters before these courts are not "regular on their face." Regular on its Face -- "Process is said to be "regular on its face" when it proceeds from the court, officer, or body having authority of law to issue process of that nature, and which is legal in form, and contains nothing to notify, or fairly apprise any one that it is issued without authority."

COURT LACKS JUDICIAL POWER IN LAW OR EQUITY

Federal, State, County or municipal governments can be sued in their corporate capacity when functioning as federal debt collectors under the Fair Debt Collection Practices Act (FDCPA). If the Federal or State government can claim immunity under the 11th Amendment, then the Federal or State or County or municipal government cannot use Law or Equity jurisdiction against the sovereign people in Court, since the people are not subject to a "foreign state" under Title 28 USC, Judicial Procedure, §§1602 -1610. The States are made up of "State Citizens," and under the 11th Amendment, "State Citizens" cannot be sued by a "foreign state."

Article III section 2 and the 11th Amendment of the Constitution are in conflict. The courts cannot convene under Article III equity jurisdiction and then have its public officers claim 11th amendment immunity. The courts are operating in a foreign state capacity against the people once the court officials take their oath.

Article III Section 2
The judicial power shall extend to all cases, in law and equity, arising under this Constitution, the laws of the United States, and treaties made, or which shall be made, under their authority;—to all cases affecting ambassadors, other public ministers and consuls;—to all cases of admiralty and maritime jurisdiction;—to controversies to which the United States shall be a party;—to controversies between two or more states;— **between a state and citizens of another state**;— between citizens of different states;—between citizens of the same state claiming lands under grants of different states, and between a state, or the citizens thereof, and foreign states, citizens or subjects.

The ratification of the Eleventh Amendment on February 7, 1795 effectively altered Article III Section 2, and now "**All**" public offices are using the Eleventh Amendment as a defence against being sued, whereas, the Eleventh Amendment actually removed protection since judicial power no longer extended to any suit in Law or Equity, and subsequently afforded the people the same protection as any level of government. The people cannot be charged in Law or Equity claims by anyone in the government. The court only has one action as revealed by the Rules of Civil Procedure: "Rule 2—One form of Action : There is only one form of action – the civil action." Civil action can be brought only by the people and not by any level of government.

Amendment XI
The judicial power of the United States **shall not be construed to extend to any suit in law or equity**, commenced or prosecuted against one of the United States by citizens of another state, or by citizens or subjects of any foreign state.

Stripping Doctrine. The Constitution was amended again in 1868 to protect various civil rights, and Section 5 of the 14th Amendment granted Congress the power to enforce, by appropriate legislation, the provisions of that amendment.

The courts have recognized that this new amendment, again a consensus of the people, abrogates the immunity provided by the 11th Amendment. When Congress enacted legislation under the auspices of Section 5 of the 14th Amendment, they specifically abrogated 11th Amendment immunity, and states can, under such federal statutes be prosecuted in federal court. The 1875 Civil Rights Act. The Supreme Court ruled that this Congressional enactment was unconstitutional. **Civil Rights Acts** (1866, 1870, 1875, 1957, 1960, 1964, 1968) US legislation. The Civil Rights Act (1866) gave African-Americans citizenship and extended civil rights to all persons born in the USA (except Native Americans). The 1870 Act was passed to re-enact the previous measure, which was considered to be of dubious constitutionality. In 1883, the US Supreme Court declared unconstitutional the 1870 law. The 1875 Act was passed to outlaw discrimination in public places because of race or previous servitude. **The act was declared unconstitutional by the Supreme Court (1883–85),** (U.S. Supreme Court Civil Rights Cases, 109 U.S. 3 (1883) Civil Rights Cases Submitted October Term, 1882 Decided October 16th, 1888 109 U.S. 3**) which stated that the 14th Amendment, the constitutional basis of the act, protected individual rights against infringement by the states, not by other individuals**. The 1957 Act established the Civil Rights Commission to investigate violations of the 15th Amendment. The 1960 Act enabled court-appointed federal officials to protect black voting rights. An act of violence to obstruct a court order became a federal offense. The 1964 Act established as law equal rights for all citizens in voting, education, public accommodations and in federally-assisted programs. The 1968 Act guaranteed equal treatment in housing and real estate to all citizens.

No level of the Executive or Judicial government has ever introduced into any Court action a real party of interest under Rule 17. The Court has no jurisdiction under 12(b) (1), (2), (3) over the Petitioner or people. **Decision and Rationale:** The 8-1 decision of the Court was delivered by Justice Joseph P. Bradley, with John Marshall Harlan of Kentucky alone in dissent. The Court decided that the Civil Rights Act of 1875 was unconstitutional. Neither the 13th nor the 14th amendment empowers the Congress to legislate in matters of racial discrimination in the private sector, Bradley wrote. "The 13th Amendment has respect, not to distinctions of race...but to slavery...." The 14th Amendment, he continued, applied to State, not private, actions; furthermore, the abridgment of rights presented in this case are to be considered as "ordinary civil injuries" rather than the imposition of badges of slavery.

Bradley commented that "individual invasion of individual rights is not the subject-matter of the 14th Amendment. It has a deeper and broader scope. **It nullifies and makes void all state legislation, and state action of every kind, which impairs the privileges and immunities of citizens of the United States, or which injures them in life, liberty or property without due process of law, or which denies to any of them the equal protection of the laws." Therefore, the Court limited the impact of the Equal Protection Clause of the 14th Amendment.**

LACK OF SUBJECT MATTER JURISDICTION

In a court of limited jurisdiction, whenever a party denies that the court has subject-matter jurisdiction, it becomes the duty and the burden of the party claiming that the court has subject matter jurisdiction to provide evidence from the record of the case that the court holds subject-matter jurisdiction. *Bindell v City of Harvey*, 212 Ill.App.3d 1042, 571 N.E.2d 1017 (1st Dist. 1991) ("the burden of proving jurisdiction rests upon the party asserting it."). Until the plaintiff submits uncontroversial evidence of subject-matter jurisdiction to the court that the court has subject-matter jurisdiction, the court is proceeding without subject-matter jurisdiction. *Loos v American Energy Savers, Inc.*, 168 Ill.App.3d 558, 522 N.E.2d 841(1988)("Where jurisdiction is contested, the burden of establishing it rests upon the plaintiff."). The law places the duty and burden of subject-matter jurisdiction upon the plaintiff. Should the court attempt to place the burden upon the defendant, the court has acted against the law, violates the defendant's due process rights, and the judge under court decisions has immediately lost subject-matter jurisdiction. In a court of limited jurisdiction, the court must proceed exactly according to the law or statute under which it operates. *Flake v Pretzel*, 381 Ill. 498, 46 N.E.2d 375 (1943) ("the actions, being statutory proceedings, ...were void for want of power to make them.") ("The judgments were based on orders which were void because the court exceeded its jurisdiction in entering them. Where a court, after acquiring jurisdiction of a subject matter, as here, transcends the limits of the jurisdiction conferred, its judgment is void."); *Armstrong v Obucino*, 300 Ill. 140, 143, 133 N.E. 58 (1921) ("The doctrine that where a court has once acquired jurisdiction it has a right to decide every question which arises in the cause, and its judgment or decree, however erroneous, cannot be collaterally assailed, is only correct when the court proceeds according to the established modes governing the class to which the case belongs and does not transcend in the extent and character of its judgment or decree the law or statute which is applicable to it." *In Interest of M.V.*, 288 Ill.App.3d 300, 681 N.E.2d 532 (1st Dist. 1997) ("Where a court's power to act is controlled by statute, the court is governed by the rules of limited jurisdiction, and courts exercising jurisdiction over such matters must proceed within the strictures of the statute."); *In re Marriage of Milliken*, 199 Ill.App.3d 813, 557 N.E.2d 591 (1st Dist. 1990) ("The jurisdiction of a court in a dissolution proceeding is limited to that conferred by statute."); *Vulcan Materials Co. v. Bee Const. Co., Inc.*, 101 Ill.App.3d 30, 40, 427 N.E.2d 797 (1st Dist. 1981) ("Though a court be one of general jurisdiction, when its power to act on a particular matter is controlled by statute, the court is governed by the rules of limited jurisdiction."). "There is no discretion to ignore that lack of jurisdiction." *Joyce v. US*, 474 F2d 215. "A universal principle as old as the law is that a proceedings of a court without jurisdiction are a nullity and its judgment therein without effect either on person or property." *Norwood v. Renfield*, 34 C 329; *Ex parte Giambonini*, 49 P. 732. "Jurisdiction is fundamental and a judgment rendered by a court that does not have jurisdiction to hear is void ab initio." In Re Application of Wyatt, 300 P. 132; Re Cavitt, 118 P2d 846. "Thus, where a judicial tribunal has no jurisdiction of the subject matter on which it assumes to act, its proceedings are absolutely void in the fullest sense of the term." *Dillon v. Dillon*, 187 P 27. "A court has no jurisdiction to determine its own jurisdiction, for a basic issue in any case before a tribunal is its power to act, and a court must have the authority to decide that question in the first instance." *Rescue Army v. Municipal Court of Los Angeles*, 171 P2d 8; 331 US 549, 91 L. ed. 1666, 67 S.Ct. 1409. "A departure by a court from those recognized and established requirements of law, however close apparent adherence to mere form in method of procedure, which has the effect of depriving one of a constitutional right, is an excess of jurisdiction." *Wuest v. Wuest,* 127 P2d 934, 937. "Where a court failed to observe safeguards, it amounts to denial of due process of law, court is deprived of juris." *Merritt v. Hunter*, C.A. Kansas 170 F2d 739. "the fact that the petitioner was released on a promise to appear before a magistrate for an arraignment, that fact is circumstance to be considered in determining whether in first instance there was a probable cause for the arrest." *Monroe v. Papa*, DC, Ill. 1963, 221 F Supp 685. "Jurisdiction, once challenged, is to be proven, not by the court, but by the party attempting to assert jurisdiction. The burden of proof of jurisdiction lies with the asserter." See *McNutt v. GMAC*, 298 US 178. The origins of this doctrine of law may be found in *Maxfield's Lessee v. Levy*, 4 US 308. "A court has no jurisdiction to determine its own jurisdiction, for a basic issue in any case before a tribunal is its power to act, and a court must have the authority to decide that question in the first instance." *Rescue Army* v. *Municipal Court of Los Angeles*, 171 P2d 8; 331 US 549, 91 L. ed. 1666, 67 S.Ct. 1409. "Once jurisdiction is challenged, the court cannot proceed when it clearly appears that the court lacks jurisdiction, the court has no authority to reach merits, but, rather, should dismiss the action." *Melo* v. *US*, 505 F2d 1026. "The law provides that once State and Federal jurisdiction has been challenged, it must be proven." --*Main v. Thiboutot*, 100 S. Ct. 2502 (1980). "Once jurisdiction is challenged, it must be proven."--*Hagens v. Lavine*, 415 U.S. 533. "Where there is absence of jurisdiction, all administrative and judicial proceedings are a nullity and confer no right, offer no protection, and afford no justification, and may be rejected upon direct collateral attack." --*Thompson v. Tolmie*, 2 Pet. 157, 7 L.Ed. 381; *Griffith v. Frazier*, 8 Cr. 9, 3L. Ed. 471.

"No sanctions can be imposed absent proof of jurisdiction." --*Standard v. Olsen*, 74 S. Ct. 768; Title 5 U.S.C., Sec. 556 and 558 (b). "The proponent of the rule has the burden of proof." --Title 5 U.S.C., Sec. 556 (d). "Jurisdiction can be challenged at any time, even on final determination." --*Basso v. Utah Power & Light Co.*, 495 2nd 906 at 910. "Mere good faith assertions of power and authority (jurisdiction) have been abolished." --*Owens v. The City of Independence,* "A departure by a court from those recognized and established requirements of law, however close apparent adherence to mere form in method of procedure, which has the effect of depriving one of a constitutional right, is an excess of jurisdiction." --*Wuest* v. *Wuest*, 127 P2d 934, 937. "In a court of limited jurisdiction, whenever a party denies that the court has subject-matter jurisdiction, it becomes the duty and the burden of the party claiming that the court has subject matter jurisdiction to provide evidence from the record of the case that the court holds subject-matter jurisdiction." --*Bindell v City of Harvey*, 212 Ill.App.3d 1042, 571 N.E.2d 1017 (1st Dist. 1991) ("the burden of proving jurisdiction rests upon the party asserting it."). "Until the plaintiff submits uncontroversial evidence of subject-matter jurisdiction to the court that the court has subject-matter jurisdiction, the court is proceeding without subject-matter jurisdiction."--*Loos v American Energy Savers, Inc.*, 168 Ill.App.3d 558, 522 N.E.2d 841(1988)("Where jurisdiction is contested, the burden of establishing it rests upon the plaintiff."). The law places the duty and burden of subject-matter jurisdiction upon the plaintiff. Should the court attempt to place the burden upon the defendant, the court has acted against the law, violates the defendant's due process rights, and the judge under court decisions has immediately lost subject-matter jurisdiction. In a court of limited jurisdiction, the court must proceed exactly according to the law or statute under which it operates. --*Flake v Pretzel*, 381 Ill. 498, 46 N.E.2d 375 (1943) ("the actions, being statutory proceedings, ...were void for want of power to make them.") ("The judgments were based on orders which were void because the court exceeded its jurisdiction in entering them. Where a court, after acquiring jurisdiction of a subject matter, as here, transcends the limits of the jurisdiction conferred, its judgment is void."); *Armstrong v Obucino*, 300 Ill. 140, 143, 133 N.E. 58 (1921) "The doctrine that where a court has once acquired jurisdiction it has a right to decide every question which arises in the cause, and its judgment or decree, however erroneous, cannot be collaterally assailed, is only correct when the court proceeds according to the established modes governing the class to which the case belongs and does not transcend in the extent and character of its judgment or decree the law or statute which is applicable to it." *In Interest of M.V.*, 288 Ill.App.3d 300, 681 N.E.2d 532 (1st Dist. 1997) ("Where a court's power to act is controlled by statute, the court is governed by the rules of limited jurisdiction, and courts exercising jurisdiction over such matters must proceed within the strictures of the statute."); *In re Marriage of Milliken*, 199 Ill.App.3d 813, 557 N.E.2d 591 (1st Dist. 1990) ("The jurisdiction of a court in a dissolution proceeding is limited to that conferred by statute."); *Vulcan Materials Co. v. Bee Const. Co., Inc.*, 101 Ill.App.3d 30, 40, 427 N.E.2d 797 (1st Dist. 1981) ("Though a court be one of general jurisdiction, when its power to act on a particular matter is controlled by statute, the court is governed by the rules of limited jurisdiction.").

LACK OF JUDICIAL IMMUNITY

Thus, neither Judges nor Government attorneys are above the law. See *United States v. Isaacs*, 493 F. 2d 1124, 1143 (7th Cir. 1974). In our judicial system, few more serious threats to individual liberty can be imagined than a corrupt judge or judges acting in collusion outside of their judicial authority with the Executive Branch to deprive a citizen of his rights. In *The Case of the Marshalsea*, 77 Eng. Rep. 1027 (K.B. 1613), Sir Edward Coke found that Article 39 of the Magna Carta restricted the power of judges to act outside of their jurisdiction such proceedings would be void, and actionable.

When a Court has (a) jurisdiction of the cause, and proceeds *inverso ordine* or erroneously, there the party who sues, or the officer or minister of the Court who executes the precept or process of the Court, no action lies against them. But (b) when the Court has no jurisdiction of the cause, there the whole proceeding is before a person who is not a judge, and actions will lie against them without any regard of the precept or process . . . Id. 77 Eng. Rep. at 1038-41.

A majority of states, including Virginia (see, Va. Code §8.01-195.3(3)), followed the English rule to find that a judge had no immunity from suit for acts outside of his judicial capacity or jurisdiction. Robert Craig Waters, 'Liability of Judicial Officers under Section 1983' 79 Yale L. J. (December 1969), pp. 326-27 and 29-30).

Also as early as 1806, in the United States there were recognized restrictions on the power of judges, as well as the placing of liability on judges for acts outside of their jurisdiction. In *Wise v. Withers*, 7 U.S. (3 Cranch) 331 (1806), the Supreme Court confirmed the right to sue a judge for exercising authority beyond the jurisdiction authorized by statute.

In *Stump v. Sparkman*, 435 U.S. 349 at 360 (1978), the Supreme Court confirmed that a judge would be immune from suit only if he did not act outside of his judicial capacity and/or was not performing any act expressly prohibited by statute. See Block, *Stump v Sparkman* and the History of Judicial Immunity, 4980 Duke L.J. 879 (l980). The Circuit Court overturned
this case and the judge was liable.

Judicial immunity may only extend to all judicial acts within the court's jurisdiction and judicial capacity, but it does not extend to either criminal acts, or acts outside of official capacity or in the 'clear absence of all jurisdiction.' see *Stump v. Sparkman* 435 U.S. 349 (1978). "When a judge knows that he lacks jurisdiction, or acts in the face of clearly valid

Constitutional provisions or valid statutes expressly depriving him of jurisdiction or judicial capacity, judicial immunity is lost." --*Rankin v. Howard* 633 F.2d 844 (1980), *Den Zeller v. Rankin*, 101 S. Ct. 2020 (1981).

As stated by the United States Supreme Court in *Piper v. Pearson*, 2 Gray 120, cited in *Bradley v. Fisher*, 13 Wall. 335, 20 L. Ed. 646 (1872), 'where there is no jurisdiction, there can be no discretion, for discretion is incident to jurisdiction.' The constitutional requirement of due process of the law is indispensable: "No person shall be held to answer for a capital, or otherwise infamous crime, unless on a presentment or indictment of a Grand Jury, except in cases arising in the land or naval forces, or in the Militia, when in actual service in time of War or public danger; nor shall any person be subject for the same offense to be twice put in jeopardy of life or limb; nor shall be compelled in any criminal case to be a witness against himself, **nor be deprived of life, liberty or property, without due process of law;** nor shall private property be taken for public use without just compensation." Article V, National Constitution. "A judgment can be void . . . where the court acts in a manner contrary to due process." --Am Jur 2d, §29 Void Judgments, p. 404. "Where a court failed to observe safeguards, it amounts to denial of due process of law, court is deprived of juris." --*Merritt* v. *Hunter*, C.A. Kansas 170 F2d 739. "Moreover, all proceedings founded on the void judgment are themselves regarded as invalid." --*Olson v. Leith* 71 Wyo. 316, 257 P.2d 342. "In criminal cases, certain constitutional errors require **automatic reversal**," see *State v. Schmit*, 273 Minn. 78, 88, 139 N.W.2d 800, 807 (1966).

PERSON vs PEOPLE

"This word 'person' and its scope and bearing in the law, involving, as it does, legal fictions and also apparently natural beings, it is difficult to understand; but it is absolutely necessary to grasp, at whatever cost, a true and proper understanding to the word in all the phases of its proper use . . . A person is here not a physical or individual person, but the status or condition with which he is invested . . . not an individual or physical person, but the status, condition or character borne by physical persons . . . The law of persons is the law of status or condition." -- American Law and Procedure, Vol. 13, page 137, 1910.

The following case citation declares the undisputed distinction in fact and at law of the distinction between the term "persons," which is the plural form of the term "person," and the word "People" which is NOT the plural form of the term "person." The above-mentioned "real party in interest" is NOT a subordinate "person," "subject," or "agent," but is a "constituent," in whom sovereignty abides, a member of the "Posterity of We, the People," in whom sovereignty resides, and from whom the government has emanated: "The sovereignty of a state does not reside in the **persons** who fill the different departments of its government, but in the **People**, from whom the government emanated; and they may change it at their discretion. Sovereignty, then in this country, abides with the constituency, and not with the agent; and this remark is true, both in reference to the federal and state government." (Persons are not People).--*Spooner v. McConnell*, 22 F 939, 943: "Our government is founded upon compact. Sovereignty was, and is, in the people" --*Glass v. Sloop Betsey*, supreme Court, 1794. "People of a state are entitled to all rights which formerly belong to the King, by his prerogative." -- supreme Court, *Lansing v. Smith,* 1829. "The United States, as a whole, emanates from the people ... The people, in their capacity as sovereigns, made and adopted the Constitution ..." --supreme Court, 4 Wheat 402. "The governments are but trustees acting under derived authority and have no power to delegate what is not delegated to them. But the people, as the original fountain might take away what they have delegated and entrust to whom they please. ... The sovereignty in every state resides in the people of the state and they may alter and change their form of government at their own pleasure." --*Luther v. Borden*, 48 US 1, 12 L.Ed 581. "While sovereign powers are delegated to ... the government, sovereignty itself remains with the people" --*Yick Wo v. Hopkins*, 118 U.S. 356, page 370. "There is no such thing as a power of inherent sovereignty in the government of the United States .... In this country sovereignty resides in the people, and Congress can exercise no power which they have not, by their Constitution entrusted to it: All else is withheld." -- *Julliard v. Greenman*, 110 U.S. 421. "In common usage, the term 'person' does not include the sovereign, and statutes employing the word are ordinarily construed to exclude it." -- *Wilson v. Omaha Indian Tribe* 442 US 653, 667 (1979). "Since in common usage the term 'person' does not include the sovereign, statutes employing that term are ordinarily construed to exclude it." -- *U.S. v. Cooper*, 312 US 600,604, 61 S. Ct 742 (1941). "In common usage, the term 'person' does not include the sovereign and statutes employing it will ordinarily not be construed to do so." -- *U.S. v. United Mine Workers of America*, 330 U.S. 258, 67 S. Ct 677 (1947).

"Since in common usage, the term 'person' does not include the sovereign, statutes employing the phrase are ordinarily construed to exclude it." -- *US v. Fox* 94 US 315. "In common usage the word 'person' does not include the sovereign, and statutes employing the word are generally construed to exclude the sovereign." -- *U.S. v. General Motors Corporation*, D.C. Ill, 2 F.R.D. 528, 530:
The following two case citations declare the undisputed doctrine, in fact and at law, that the word (term of art) "person" is a "general word," and that the "people," of whom the above-mentioned "real party in interest" is one, "are NOT bound by general words in statutes." Therefore, statutes do not apply to, operate upon or affect the above-mentioned "real party in interest:" "**The word `person' in legal terminology is perceived as a *general word*** which normally includes in its scope a variety of entities

other than human beings., --*Church of Scientology v. US Department of Justice* 612 F2d 417, 425 (1979). " **The people, or sovereign are not bound by *general words* in statutes** , restrictive of prerogative right, title or interest, unless expressly named. Acts of limitation do not bind the King or the people. The people have been ceded all the rights of the King, the former sovereign ... It is a maxim of the common law, that when an act is made for the common good and to prevent injury, the King shall be bound, though not named, but when a statute is general and prerogative right would be divested or taken from the King (or the People) he shall not be bound." -- *The People v. Herkimer*, 4 Cowen (NY) 345, 348 (1825): "In the United States, sovereignty resides in people." --*Perry v. U.S.* (294 US 330). "A Sovereign is exempt from suit, not because of any formal conception or obsolete theory, but on the logical and practical ground that there can be no legal Right as against the authority that makes the law on which the Right depends." --*Kawananakoa v. Polyblank*, 205 U.S. 349, 353, 27 S. Ct. 526, 527, 51 L. Ed. 834 (1907).

DEL CODE TITLE 8 Chapters 6 § 617: Delaware Code - Section 617: CORPORATE NAME

The corporate name of a corporation organized under this chapter shall contain either a word or words descriptive of the professional service to be rendered by the corporation or **shall contain the last names of** 1 or more of its present, prospective or former shareholders or of persons who were associated with a predecessor person, partnership, corporation or other organization or whose name or names appeared in the name of such predecessor organization.

Texas Administrative Code
Subject: 1 TAC § 79.31 CORPORATIONS (ENTITY NAMES)
§ 79.31. Characters of Print Acceptable in Names
(a) Entity names may consist of letters of the Roman alphabet, Arabic numerals, and certain symbols capable of being reproduced on a standard English language typewriter, or combination thereof.
(b) **Only upper case or capitol letters, with no distinction as to type face or font, will be recognized.**
Delaware legislation March 10 1899
"An Act Providing General Corporate Law" This Act allow the corporation to become a "PERSON"

A **legal person**, also called **juridical person** or **juristic person**,[1] is a legal entity through which the law allows a group of **natural persons** to act as if they were a single composite **individual** for certain purposes, or in some jurisdictions, for a single person to have a separate legal personality other than their own.[2][3] This **legal fictio**n does not mean these entities are human beings, but rather means that the law allows them to act as **persons** for certain limited purposes. **SANTA CLARA COUNTY v. SOUTHERN PAC. R. CO., 118 U.S. 394,** New York Central R. Co. v. United States, 212 U.S. 481 (1909), United States v. Dotterweich, 320 U.S. 277 (1943)
"**Street Name** " :BLACK'S LAW DICTIONARY ABRIDGED FIFTH EDITION
"Securities held in the name of a broker instead of his customer's name are said to be carried in a "street name". This occurs when the securities have been bought on margin or when the customer wishes the security to be held by the broker. The name of a broker or bank appearing on a corporate security with blank endorsement by the broker or bank. The security can then be transferred merely by delivery since the endorsement is well known. Street name is used for convenience or to shield identity of the true owner."

CUSIP Definition:

CUSIP® Is a registered trademark of the American Bankers Association : Acronym CUSIP refers to the Committee on Uniform Security Identification Procedures. The acronym CUSIP typically refers to both the Committee on Uniform Security Identification Procedures and the 9-character alphanumeric security identifiers that they distribute for all North American securities for the purposes of facilitating clearing and settlement...
First 6 Characters identify the unique name of the:
- Company
- Municipality
- Government agency
A hierarchical alpha numeric convention linked to alphabetic issuer name.
Next 2 Characters Identifies the type of instrument:
- Equity
- Debt
• Uniquely identifies the issue within the issuer
Servus Servorum Dei
• A hierarchical alpha numeric convention
Next 1 Character
• A mathematical formula checks accuracy of the previous 8 characters • Delivers a 1 character check result
Resulting 9 Characters
• A unique identifier
* **CUSIP® - Universally recognized identifier for financial instruments.**
* **CINS - CUSIP International Numbering System**
* **CSB ISIN -Participation in the assignment of CUSIP-based International**

Securities Identification Numbers CINS

CUSIP International Numbering System (CINS) is a 9-character alphanumeric identifier that employs the same numbering system as CUSIP, but also contains a letter of the alphabet in the first position signifying the issuer's country or geographic region. CINS was developed in 1989 as an extension to CUSIP in response to U.S. demand for global coverage, and is the local identifier of more than 30 non-North American markets.

CSB ISIN

The International Securities Identification Number (ISIN) is a unique global code that identifies instruments in different countries to facilitate cross-border trading. CSB is responsible for the assignment of ISINs in the U.S. and in other areas where designated or appointed. CSB ISINs are 12 character identifiers that have a CUSIP or CINS embedded in them, which always appear in position 3 to 11.

CSB has agents in countries such as Canada, Bermuda, The Cayman Islands and Jamaica, and is also the representative agency for countries in South America. Because of this, it was necessary to develop a separate identification system to designate CSB-assigned securities from these jurisdictions.

The American Bankers Association:

The American Bankers Association (ABA) is a free-trade and professional association that promotes and advocates issues important to the banking industry in the United States. The ABA's national headquarters are in Washington, D.C. In addition to its trade association mission, the ABA also performs educational components for consumers through its Educational Foundation affiliate.

Organization:

While the ABA works on a national level, it also is supported by state operated offices (sometimes referred to as "Leagues") which focus attention on state level support. Both the ABA and the state organizations are dues supported trade associations. Both the state and national offices also operate Political Action Committees (PACs) which use registered lobbyists to work for laws that are advantageous for the banking industry. The president of the ABA is Edward Yingling.

Political action committee;
In the United States, a Political Action Committee, or PAC, is the name commonly given to a private group, regardless of size, organized to elect political candidates. Legally, what constitutes a "PAC" for purposes of regulation is a matter of state and federal law. Under the Federal Election Campaign Act, an organization becomes a "political committee" by receiving contributions or making expenditures in excess of $1,000 for the purpose of influencing a federal election.

When an interest group gets directly involved within the political process, a PAC is created. These PACs receive and raise money from the special group's constituents, and on behalf of the special interest, makes donations to political campaigns.

The American Federation of State, County and Municipal Employees (AFSCME) is the second- or third-largest labor union in the United States and one of the fastest-growing, representing over 1.4 million employees, primarily in local and state government and in the health care industry. AFSCME is part of the AFL-CIO, one of the two main labor federations in the United States. Employees at the federal government level are primarily represented by other unions, such as the American Federation of Government Employees, with which AFSCME was once affiliated, and the National Treasury Employees Union; but AFSCME does represent some federal employees at the Federal Aviation Administration and the Library of Congress, among others.[1]

According to their website, AFSCME organizes for social and economic justice in the workplace and through political action and legislative advocacy. It is divided into more than 3,500 local unions in 46 U.S. states, plus the District of Columbia and Puerto Rico. Each local union writes its own constitution, holds membership meetings, and elects its own officers. Councils are also a part of AFSCME's administrative structure, usually grouping together various locals in a geographic area.

According to OpenSecrets.org, the top contributors since 1988 ranked by their total spending along with the party tilt of their contributions are:
Rank Organization Total Dem % Repub % Tilt
1 AFSCME $39,947,843 98% 1% Solidly Dem (over 90%)

Table Of Definitions

Foreign Court The courts of a foreign state or nation. In the United States, this term is frequently applied to the courts of one of the States when their judgment or records are introduced in the courts of another.
Foreign jurisdiction Any jurisdiction foreign to that of the forum; e.g., a sister state or another country. Also, the exercise by a state or nation jurisdiction beyond its own territory. Long-arm service of process is a form of such foreign or extraterritorial jurisdiction
Foreign laws The laws of a foreign country, or of a sister state. In conflicts of law, the legal principles of jurisprudence which are part of the law of a sister state or nation. Foreign laws are additions to our own laws, and in that respect are called "*jus receptum.*"
Foreign corporation A corporation doing business in one State though chartered or incorporated in another state is a foreign corporation as to the first state, and, as such, is

required to consent to certain conditions and restrictions in order to do business in such first state.

Under federal tax laws, a foreign corporation is one which is not organized under the law of one of the States or Territories of the United States. I.R.C. § 7701 (a) (5). Service of process on foreign corporation is governed by the Fed. R. Civ. P. 4 See also Corporation.

Foreign service of process Service of process for the acquisition of jurisdiction by a court in the United States upon a person in a foreign country is prescribed by Fed R. Civ. P. 4 (i) and 28 U.S.C.A. § 1608. Service of process on foreign corporations is governed by Fed. R. Civ. P. 4(d) (3).

Foreign states Nations which are outside the United States. Term may also refer to another state; i.e. a sister state.

Foreign immunity With respect to jurisdictional immunity of foreign states, see 28 USC, Sec. §1602 *et seq*. Title 8 USC, Chapter 12, Subchapter I, Sec. §1101(14) The term "foreign state" includes outlying possessions of a foreign state, but self-governing dominions or territories under mandate or trusteeship shall be regarded as separate foreign states.

Profiteering Taking advantage of unusual or exceptional circumstance to make excessive profit; e.g. selling of scarce or essential goods at inflated price during time of emergency or war.

Person In general usage, a human being (i.e. natural person) though by statute the term may include a firm, labor organizations, partnerships, associations, corporations, legal representative, trusts, trustees in bankruptcy, or receivers. National Labor Relations Act, §2(1).

Definition of the term "person" under Title 26, Subtitle F, Chapter 75, Subchapter D, Sec. Sec. §7343

The term "person" as used in this chapter includes an officer or employee of a corporation, or a member or employee of a partnership, who as such officer, employee or member is under a duty to perform the act in respect of which the violation occurs. A **corporation** is a "person" within the meaning of equal protection and due process provisions of the United States Constitution.

Tertius interveniens A third party intervening; a third party who comes between the parties to a suit; one who interpleads. Gilbert's Forum Romanum. 47.

Writ of error *Coram nobis* A common-law writ, the purpose of which is to correct a judgment in the same court in which it was rendered, on the ground of error of fact, for which statutes provide no other remedy, which fact did not appear of record, or was unknown to the court when judgment was pronounced, and which, if known would have prevented the judgment, and which was unknown, and could of reasonable diligence in time to have been otherwise presented to the court, unless he was prevented from so presenting them by duress, fear, or other sufficient cause. "A writ of error ***Coram nobis*** is a common-law writ of ancient origin devised by the judiciary, which constitutes a remedy for setting aside a judgment which for a valid reason should never have been rendered." 24 C.J.S., Criminal Law. § 1610 (2004)."The principal function of the **writ of error** *Coram nobis* is to afford to the court in which an action was tried an opportunity to correct its own record with reference to a vital fact not known when the judgment was rendered, and which could not have been presented by a motion for a new trial, appeal or other existing statutory proceeding." Black's Law Dictionary., 3rd ed., p. 1861; 24 C.J.S.,

Criminal Law, § 1606 b., p. 145; *Ford v. Commonwealth*, 312 Ky. 718, 229 S.W.2d 470.At common law in England, it issued from the Court of Kings Bench to a judgment of that court. Its principal aim is to afford the court in which an action was tried an opportunity to correct its own record with reference to a vital fact not known when the judgment was rendered. It is also said that at common law it lay to correct purely ministerial errors of the officers of the court. Furthermore, the above-mentioned "real party in interest" demands the strict adherence to Article IV, section one of the National

Constitution so that in all matters before this court, the Full Faith and Credit shall be given in each State to the public Acts, Records, and judicial Proceedings of every other State; and to Article IV of the Articles of Confederation, still in force pursuant to Article VI of the National Constitution, so that "Full faith and credit shall be given in each of these States to the records, acts, and judicial proceedings of the courts and magistrates of every other State," selective incorporation notwithstanding. The *lex domicilii* shall also depend upon the Natural Domicile of the above-mentioned "real party in interest." The *lex domicilii*, involves the "law of the domicile" in the Conflict of Laws. Conflict is the branch of public law regulating all lawsuits involving a "foreign" law element where a difference in result will occur depending on which laws are applied.

AMENDATORY RECONSTRUCTION ACT OF MARCH 11, 1868
An Act to amend the act passed March 23, 1867, entitled "An Act supplementary to 'An act to provide for the more efficient government of the rebel states,' passed March 2, 1867, and to facilitate their restoration. SUPPLEMENTARY RECONSTRUCTION ACT OF FORTIETH CONGRESS. An Act supplementary to an act entitled "An act to provide for the more efficient government of the rebel states," passed March second, eighteen hundred and sixty-seven, and to facilitate restoration. " This act created the 14th amendment federal citizen under section 3 of the federal constitution. All who hold public office fall under this section as UNITED STATES citizens. Those who hold office have knowingly and willingly given up their citizenship to this country under Title 8 Section §1481 to become a foreign state agent under 22 USC. The oath of office to the constitution requires officeholders to uphold and maintain our Constitutional form of government under the people's authority. This right was never surrendered by the people; failure to do so violates 10 USC §333 and 18 USC §1918, chapter 115 §2382, §2383, §1505, §1001, §241, §242, 42 USC §1981 & 31 USC §3729 just to name a few.

The Federal Debt Collection Procedure places all courts under equity and commerce and under the International Monetary Fund. The International Monetary Fund comes under the Uniform Commercial Code under banking and business interest and Trust laws. This makes the Court / Judges trustee over the trust and responsible whether or not the Petitioner understands the trust issue.

The 1933 bankruptcy act placed all public officials in a fiduciary position to keep the accounts in balance via discharge of the debt against the pre-paid, priority exempt accounts of the American people.

The American people were fraudulently identified as enemy combatants under the TWEA for the purpose of skirting the UNITED STATES' debtor obligation to the sovereign people of America and facilitating the pillage and plunder of the sovereign people under the direction of the international banking families.

The TWEA suspended the U.S. Constitution in the court room, turning the courtrooms into debt collection facilities under admiralty/maritime and therefore, the standard American flag in the courtroom was replaced with a military Admiralty flag for dealing with alien enemy combatants. The people never rescinded their nationality to the real united States of America. Those who hold public office rescinded their nationality to become a foreign agent in order to hold public office. International law requires the judge to uphold the people's Constitutional form of government as defined in the "Federalist Papers".

Federal Rules of Civil Procedure / Rules of Civil Procedure Rule 2 only allows civil action, and under Rule 17, a real party of interest has to be present in the courtroom in order for there to be any claims of injury or damages against "the people." Any charges under the

"UNITED STATES" or "THE STATE OF........" fall under the TWEA Section 23. The people are not subject to this jurisdiction as it is a Foreign State jurisdiction. The people hold 11th amendment immunity to claims in equity and commerce from a foreign state. The courts lack jurisdiction over the people by Congressional mandate.

All debt of the UNITED STATES, except that debt owed to the sovereign people of America, has been abandoned and vacated and the UNITED STATES has DECLARED PEACE with the world and the sovereign people thereof, therefore, the gold fringed military flag designating the admiralty/maritime jurisdiction shall be immediately removed from all courtrooms, meeting rooms, etc. of the administrative agencies of the UNITED STATES and the civil peace flag of the united states of America shall be proudly displayed in their stead..

The U.S. Courts who have been operating as debt collection facilities under TWEA and the EMERGENCY WAR POWERS ACT shall immediately make the corrections and cure the torts against the people, vacating all claims, attachments and/or restrictions on the private rights of the sovereign people and make them whole.

The courts, as well as all administrative agencies of the UNITED STATES, shall share resources making room for and facilitating the establishment of the organic courts, operating under the common law, for the adjudication of all matters concerning the sovereign American people, other than the prosecution of grievances against an administrative agency for the trespass of the private rights of the people. All administrative agencies shall actively participate in the establishment of two distinctly separate systems, common law and administrative, operating side by side for the benefit of the CREDITORS, the sovereign people of America.

All administrative courts and agencies of the UNITED STATES shall operate in good faith and honor as servants of the sovereign people of America. Said administrative courts and agencies have grown out of control, beyond the intent of the original founders and their usefulness and shall begin to make the corrections, a reversal, bringing about balance, transparency, full disclosure and honor for the remedy of the Real Parties In Interest.

All debts of the UNITED STATES have been abandoned, except the debt to the sovereign people; The Pledge of the private property of the American people has been relinquished, therefore, the administrative agencies of the UNITED STATES shall make the return of the interest back to source, the sovereign people.

The UNITED STATES shall immediately activate the established pass through account, vacate the blocks on the asset accounts and make the financial adjustments to discharge the debt and return the accounts of the sovereign people back into balance. The UNITED STATES shall maintain the natural flow and balance in the accounts for the remedy of the people, returning the interest back to source in the discharge of debt against the pre-paid account, at all times remaining in honor.

The UNITED STATES shall immediately make the corrections as concerns the unlawful restrictions of the liberties of the sovereign people by the administrative agencies of the UNITED STATES;

All Deeds, warranty deeds, trust deeds, sheriff deeds, tax deeds and all Certificates of Title are colorable titles issued to facilitate the 'Pledge' of the private property of the sovereign people.

The Pledge has been relinquished, therefore, the UNITED STATES shall make the corrections to discharge all colorable titles, make the re-conveyance and issue the land patent/ allodial title for the property back to the people.

It is the duty of the military to serve and protect the post, therefore, the UNITED STATES military shall serve and protect the sovereign people of America, the creditor of the UNITED STATES. All branches of the U.S. Military shall follow the orders of the "Transitional Committee", interim government and government of the republic, respectively throughout this transition.

The Provost Marshals are the organic police force with a duty to serve and protect the sovereign. The Provost Marshal shall immediately serve and protect all who claim protection under this treaty making top priority any/all requests for assistance on claims of unlawful restrictions on the liberties of a sovereign.

There shall be those members of the sovereign people, ambassadors, with a passion to service, who shall choose to serve the republic; lightworkers, visionaries, warriors, teachers and people knowledgeable in the art of peace and love; to serve as watchdogs or compliance, ensuring the integrity and protection of the people's rights; or facilitators and educators charged with presenting real truth, that the enslavement of the sovereign people may never happen again; beacons of light, guiding the people out of the darkness, into the truth;

There shall be those members of the sovereign people who shall be instrumental in breathing life into the civil government of the republic, bringing empowerment to the counties at large; in interfacing with the administrative agents and agencies to compel performance and compliance, to bring about balance and restore the natural flow of energy; to empower the civil government, the people; to nurture and infuse this fledgling republic with peace, light and love; to rise above the fear; to be the light;

These members of the sovereign people, awakened into the truth, compelled to service, may apply to accede hereto; upon receipt, acceptance and registration of the application and Public Declarations shall be empowered as a Private Postmaster of a non-independent postal zone, with all of the rights, power and authority of a wholly sovereign nation, with the authority to seat civilian citizen grand juries; to empower judges in the common law, Rangers and Inspectors with the power and authority to compel performance; to make the corrections to bring compliance and honor within the administration.

The power shall reside with the people on the county. It shall take the agreement of no less than three (3) private postmasters to empower a judge or Ranger who shall serve the people under guidelines presented by the Transition Committee and/or interim government.

Repository and Registration of Treaty
The postmaster general of the original, organic post office for the united states of America is hereby designated as repository for the registration, publication and notification of this treaty and Public Declarations of all acceding members in accordance with Article 77 of the *Vienna Convention, 1969*.

Postmaster General for the Post Office for the united states of America
c/o USPS HDQR
475 L'Enfant Plaza SW
Washington, D.C. 20024

Executed this 11th day of May, 2010.
THE UNITED STATES
1500 PENNSYLVANIA AVE. NW
WASHINGTON, D.C. 20020

The Registration And Enforcement

It will be asked: How can this be enforced? In the following chapters, the process by which this has been done ill be described. This process will then be simplified in the final Part of this book to reveal how others can be part of this new light of peace and prosperity.

In this peace Treaty, it is clearly revealed how the Administrators of the Trusts and the deployment of the military complex has been shifted to create the economic war machines that serve as the economic generators of profit to serve the few at the expense of the many. Here it becomes clear how the energy of the people has been captured to create the great pyramid of debt to serve the needs of the gods through religion so to serve the business plan of the New world Order.

One key ingredients in understanding the process of how the Earthling was manoeuvred into these business structures, and therefore the understanding of how to rectify the relationship as well as enforcing the declaration, is to look deeply into these Trusts. How trust are set up and work is of interest and we now will dedicate a compel chapter on this.

49

IT'S ALL ABOUT TRUST(S)

First And Foremost Is Our Divine Trust

PLANET EARTH is a private business enterprise serving those gods who carefully crafted it. It is not a formal registered organization. It is a fictional entity that I have created. Over centuries, the evolution of commerce has required the creation of fictional entities called corporations to act as the vessels. There are many different types. Of particular interest now is the business enterprise vessel which is called a Trust which is a very old concept of holding titles to what are thought as assets. . Here we will learn more about the origins and implementations of these trusts as they relate to the vessel which is you, the human, and to that which it holds titles to as Beneficiary, your Estate.

You came here with nothing and you leave with nothing. Your stay on Planet Earth is about a divine experience. Right from the beginning, everything is held in Trust, at the Divine Right of Use Today. Everything is held in trust.... everything is about trusts, Implied or Expressed.

The Creator gave man dominion over all things. Dominion over equates to control over NOT ownership. Control over all things, yet not ownership. That is a Divine Right of Use.

A Divine Right of Use of the Divine property/the All of earth held in trust means the entire world we call earth is held in trust, the Divine Trust, for our benefit as Beneficiaries. This **Global Divine Trust is an Implied Trust** as opposed to an Expressed Trust.

In the beginning man was responsible, as a Trustee, for the care and well being of that portion of the Divine Estate upon which he/she exercised their Divine Right of Use as a Beneficiary. He would benefit from it in some way. And usually someone was chosen to administer it according to some defined rules, called a fiduciary.

Through the decades man has given over that Divine fiduciary obligation to legal fiction trustees. There are as many forms of trusteeships as there are people in the world. Some very fair and equitable, say a republic, all the way to a dictatorship, each with various degrees of freedoms and rights, taxes and limitations.

Who is the Trustee responsible for your piece of the Divine Estate, our Global Estate Trust? In America today we have Township Trustees, County Trustees, State Trustees and Federal Trustees just to name a few of the many levels of fiduciaries within the Trusteeship which is involved in the administration of our Divine Estate(s), the Global Estate Trust. Judges, Clerks of Court, Prosecutors and Attorneys all play their own part in the administration of our Global Estate Trust leveraging our Divine Estates to do as they please as we have simply entrusted them to do so. It is our faith and trust in these trustees and fiduciaries that has allowed this to be.

To unravel this intentionally complex Trusteeship of the Global Estate Trust let us begin at the top and work our way down. At the bottom is you and the Vital Statistics Office issued the Certified copy of the Birth Certificate, a security which represents the Divine Estate Trust, therefore they hold the original and are the holder in due course of the estate. They are the Intermediary Agent for the Trust with a <u>fiduciary duty to the Beneficiary of the Estate</u>. and the true beneficiary is you in the flesh and blood.

At the top, the Vatican in their Papal Bull, states dominion over the entire earth, via conquest, and is answerable ONLY to the Divine Spirit. Dominion over means control over, not ownership. The Vatican's un-rebutted claims establish them as the <u>Primary Trustee of the Global Estate Trust</u>, our Divine Inheritance; a very unpopular fact. But a fact that opens a doorway placing the cure for the mis-administration and theft of our Divine Inheritance within our grasp.

The Vatican is the Primary Trustee of the Global Estate Trust. To facilitate the administration of this Global Trust the Vatican established the Universal Postal Union as the Secondary Trustees of the Global Trust charged with dividing the Global Trust into zones and endowing these legal fiction zones with sovereign authority to facilitate the efficient administration of the Global Trust.

The Preamble to the Constitution created the Estate Trust which held the freedoms guaranteed in the Articles of Confederation and the Declaration of Independence in trust for future generations. The Articles of the Constitution established the Trusteeship as well as the powers and limitations thereof. The Congress and Senate were Trustees charged with the Administration of our Divine Inheritance, the Global Estate Trust.

In this 'general post office' seat of government there was established the 'civil administration' called the United States. Civil administration? What do they administrate? Our Divine Estate Trust, the Global Trust, our Divine Inheritance. Remember, we can never OWN anything. We simply have a Divine Right of Use of the property of the Divine Estate, the Global Trust.

So, we the people of this earth have a Divine Right of use of the Global Trust while the civil administration is charged with the administration of our estate for our benefit.

In the world of trusts Civil Administration/Government equals Trusteeship.

So, the entire world is held in trust. The Global Estate Trust, our Divine Inheritance, our birthright is held in trust and is administrated by the various 'governments' who gain their sovereign authority via the Universal Postal Union, the Secondary Trustee of the Global Trust answerable to the Vatican.

In the world of trusts and trust law, rights, duties and obligations are very straight forward, cut and dry, black and white. There are no opinions, secret codes, rules or statutes, period. These are just the facts. There is a chain of command, consequences for your actions, or lack thereof, and accountability.

As **James Thomas** will testify: *"it has been a slow and cumbersome process to overcome the out of control momentum of the civil administrators of the world today. There have been countless casualties as a result of our efforts to unravel the illusion; to overcome the programming and fear which fuelled the beast to reach the core where truth and accountability resides".*

But first, let us look more closely at this vehicle of commerce called a Trust.

The History Of Trusts

Trusts date back to ancient Egypt, circa 4000 B.C., when the equivalent of today's trust officers were charged with holding, managing, and caring for other people's property. Various prototypes of trust institutions were later developed in second-century Rome, some of which involved the use of property for charitable purposes. Trusts began to evolve into their present form during the eighth century, when English clergymen acted as executors of wills and trusts. Throughout the Middle Ages and into the 17th century, trusts developed under English common law to resemble their current legal structure in the United States.

Roman law had a well-developed concept of the trust (*fideicommissum*) in terms of "testamentary trusts" created by wills but never developed the concept of the "inter vivos trust" that applied while the creator was still alive. This was created by later common law jurisdictions. Personal trust law developed in England at the time of the Crusades, during the 12th and 13th centuries.[]

At the time, land ownership in England was based on the feudal system. When a landowner left England to fight in the Crusades, he needed someone to run his estate in his absence, often to pay and receive feudal dues. To achieve this, he would convey ownership of his lands to an acquaintance, on the understanding that the ownership would be conveyed back on his return. However, Crusaders would often return to find the legal owners' refusal to hand over the property.

Unfortunately for the Crusader, English common law did not recognize his claim. As far as the King's courts were concerned, the land belonged to the trustee, who was under no obligation to return it. The Crusader had no legal claim. The disgruntled Crusader would then petition the king, who would refer the matter to his Lord Chancellor. The Lord Chancellor could do what was "just" and "equitable", and had the power to decide a case according to his conscience. At this time, the principle of equity was born.

The Lord Chancellor would consider it "unconscionable" that the legal owner could go back on his word and deny the claims of the Crusader (the "true" owner). Therefore, he would find in favor of the returning Crusader. Over time, it became known that the Lord Chancellor's court (the Court of Chancery) would continually recognize the claim of a returning Crusader. The legal owner would hold the land for the benefit of the original owner, and would be compelled to convey it back to him when requested. The Crusader was the "beneficiary" and the acquaintance the "trustee". The term *use of land* was coined, and in time developed into what we now know as a *trust*.

Also, the Primogeniture system could be considered as a form of trust. In Primogeniture system, the first born male inherited all the property and "usually assumes the responsibility of trusteeship of the property and of adjudicating attendant disputes."

The Waqf (*http://en.wikipedia.org/wiki/Waqf*) meaning confinement and prohibition is an equivalent institution in Islamic law, restricted to charitable trusts.

"Antitrust law" emerged in the 19th century when industries created monopolistic trusts by entrusting their shares to a board of trustees in exchange for shares of equal value with dividend rights; these boards could then enforce a monopoly. However, trusts were used in this case because a corporation could not own other companies' stock and thereby become a holding company without a "special act of the legislature". Holding companies were used after the restriction on owning other companies' shares was lifted.

The trust is widely considered to be the most innovative contribution to the English legal system. Today, trusts play a significant role in most common law systems, and their success has led some civil law jurisdictions to incorporate trusts into their civil codes. France, for example, recently added a similar, though not quite comparable, notion to its own law with *la fiducie*, which was modified in 2009; *la fiducie*, unlike the trust, is a contract. Trusts are widely used internationally, especially in countries within the English law sphere of influence, and whilst most civil law jurisdictions do not generally contain the concept of a trust within their legal systems, they do recognize the concept under the Hague Convention on the Law Applicable to Trusts and on their Recognition (to the extent that they are signatories thereto). The Hague Convention on the Law Applicable to Trusts and on their Recognition also regulates conflict of trusts.

Although trusts are often associated with intrafamily wealth transfers, they have become very important in American capital markets, particularly through pension funds (essentially always trusts) and mutual funds (often trusts).

Setting Up A Trust: The Mechanics

Basic principles of a Trust Property of any sort may be held on trust, but growth assets are more commonly placed into trust (for tax and estate planning benefits). The uses of trusts are many and varied. Trusts may be created during a person's life (usually by a trust instrument) or after death in a will. In a relevant sense, a trust can be viewed as a generic form of a corporation where the settlors (investors) are also the beneficiaries. This is particularly evident in the Delaware business trust, which could theoretically, with the language in the "governing instrument", be organized as a cooperative corporation, limited liability corporation, or perhaps even a nonprofit corporation. One of the most significant aspects of trusts is the ability to partition and shield assets from the trustee, multiple beneficiaries, and their respective creditors (particularly the trustee's creditors), making it "bankruptcy remote", and leading to its use in pensions, mutual funds, and asset securitization.

Creation of a Trust Trusts may be created by the expressed intentions of the settlor (express trusts) or they may be created by operation of law known as implied trusts. Implied trusts is one created by a court of equity because of acts or situations of the parties. Implied trusts are divided into two categories resulting and constructive. A resulting trust is implied by the law to work out the presumed intentions of the parties, but it does not take into consideration their expressed intent. A constructive trust is a trust implied by law to work out justice between the parties, regardless of their intentions.

Typically a trust can be created in the following ways:
1. a written trust instrument created by the settlor and signed by both the settlor and the trustees (often referred to as an *inter vivos* or "living trust");
2. an oral declaration;
3. the will of a decedent, usually called a testamentary trust; or
4. a court order (for example in family proceedings).

In some jurisdictions certain types of assets may not be the subject of a trust without a written document.

Formalities of a Trust Generally, a trust requires three certainties:
1. **Intention**. There must be a clear intention to create a trust
2. **Subject Matter**. The property subject to the trust must be clearly identified One may not, for example, settle "the majority of my estate", as the precise extent cannot be ascertained. Trust property may be any form of specific property, be it real or personal, tangible or intangible. It is often, for example, real estate, shares or cash.
3. **Objects**. The beneficiaries of the trust must be clearly identified, or at least be ascertainable. In the case of discretionary trusts, where the trustees have power to decide who the beneficiaries will be, the settlor must have described a clear **class** of beneficiaries. Beneficiaries may include people not born at the date of the trust (for example, "my future grandchildren"). Alternatively, the object of a trust could be a charitable purpose rather than specific beneficiaries.

Trustees The trustee may be either a person or a legal entity such as a company. A trust may have one or multiple trustees. A trustee has many rights and responsibilities; these vary from trust to trust depending on the type of the trust. A trust generally will not fail solely for want of a trustee. Where a trust is absent any trustees, a court may appoint a trustee, or in Ireland the trustee may be any administrator of a charity to which the trust is related. Trustees are usually appointed in the document (instrument) which creates the trust.

A trustee may be held personally liable for certain problems which arise with the trust. For example, if a trustee does not properly invest trust monies to expand the trust fund, he or she may be liable for the difference. There are two main types of trustees, professional and non-professional. Liability is different for the two types.

The trustees are the legal owners of the trust's property. The trustees administer the affairs attendant to the trust. The trust's affairs may include investing the assets of the trust, ensuring trust property is preserved and productive for the beneficiaries, accounting for and reporting periodically to the beneficiaries concerning all transactions associated with trust property, filing any required tax returns on behalf of the trust, and other duties. In some cases, the trustees must make decisions as to whether beneficiaries should receive trust assets for their benefit. The circumstances in which this discretionary authority is exercised by trustees is usually provided for under the terms of the trust instrument. The trustee's duty is to determine in the specific instance of a beneficiary request whether to provide any funds and in what manner.

By default, being a trustee is an unpaid job. In modern times trustees are often lawyers, bankers or other professionals who will not work for free. Therefore, often a trust document will state specifically that trustees are entitled to reasonable payment for their work.

Trusts are often confused with legal persons, but are mere *relationships*, not entities. Thus, they have no legal existence independent from the trustee and his or her ownership of the subject matter of the trust. In order to sue a trust, one must sue the trustee in his or her capacity as trustee for a specific trust; conversely, if the trust needs to sue someone, the lawsuit must be brought by the trustee in his or her capacity as such.

Beneficiaries The beneficiaries are beneficial (or **equitable**) owners of the trust property. Either immediately or eventually, the beneficiaries will receive income from the trust property, or they will receive the property itself. The extent of a beneficiary's interest depends on the wording of the trust document. One beneficiary may be entitled to income (for example, interest from a bank account), whereas another may be entitled to the entirety of the trust property when he attains the age of twenty-five years. The settlor has much discretion when creating the trust, subject to some limitations imposed by law.

Implied and Express Trust Implied trust. An implied trust, as distinct from an express trust, is created where some of the legal requirements for an express trust are not met, but an intention on behalf of the parties to create a trust can be presumed to exist. A resulting trust may be deemed to be present where a trust instrument is not properly drafted and a portion of the equitable title has not been provided for. In such a case, the law may raise a resulting trust for the benefit of the grantor (the creator of the trust). In other words, the grantor may be deemed to be a beneficiary of the portion of the equitable title that was not properly provided for in the trust document.

More Trust Basics: Relationships

Some of the earliest Trusts date back to the Middle Ages. They were first widely used during the Crusades and other foreign campaigns, when prolonged absences were commonplace. Over the centuries, the concept of Trusts developed in countries using the English Common Law system. Today, Trusts are used for a wide variety of purposes. The following definition of a Trust is taken from a noted author on the subject of Trusts, Sir Arthur Underhill:

"A trust is an equitable obligation binding a person (called a Trustee) to deal with property over which he has control (called the trust property) for the benefit of persons (who are called beneficiaries) of whom he may himself be one, and any one of whom may enforce the obligation"

A Trust arises when a person known as the **Settlor** transfers legal title to property to another person known as the **Trustee,** with instructions as to how the property is to be used for the benefit of named persons known as **Beneficiaries**. To be valid, a Trust must have a Settlor, a Trustee and identifiable beneficiaries. The beneficiaries may be identified by name, or as being members of a class - for example, "my children" or "my grandchildren". A Trust cannot be created until legal title to some property has been transferred to the Trustee. Although the Trustee has legal title to the Trust property, beneficial ownership rests with the beneficiaries (beneficiary). Assets of all kinds can be placed in a Trust, including bank accounts, real estate, stocks and bonds, mutual fund units, limited partnership interests and private businesses.

In common law legal systems, a **trust** is a relationship whereby property (real or personal, tangible or intangible) is held by one party for the benefit of another. A trust conventionally arises when property is transferred by one party to be held by another party for the benefit of a third party, although it is also possible for a legal owner to create a trust of property without transferring it to anyone else, simply by declaring that the property will henceforth be held for the benefit of the beneficiary. A trust is created by a settlor (archaically known, in the context of trusts of land, as the *feoffor to uses*), who transfers some or all of his property to a trustee (archaically known, in the context of land, as the *feoffee to uses*), who holds that trust property (or *trust corpus*) for the benefit of the beneficiaries (archaically known as the *cestui que use*, or *cestui que trust*). In the case of the self-declared trust, the settlor and trustee are the same person. The trustee has legal title to the trust property, but the beneficiaries have equitable title to the trust property (separation of control and ownership). The trustee owes a fiduciary duty to the beneficiaries, who are the "beneficial" owners of the trust property. (Note: A trustee may be either a natural person, or an artificial person (such as a company or a public body), and there may be a single trustee or multiple co-trustees. There may be a single beneficiary or multiple beneficiaries. The settlor may himself be a beneficiary.)

The trust is governed by the terms under which it was created. The terms of the trust are usually written down in a trust instrument or deed but, in England, it is not necessary for them to be written down to be legally binding, except in the case of land. The terms of the trust must specify what property is to be transferred into the trust (certainty of subject-matter), and who the beneficiaries will be of that trust (certainty of objects). It may also set out the detailed powers and duties of the trustees (such as powers of investment, powers to vary the interests of the beneficiaries, and powers to appoint new trustees). The trust is also governed by local law. The trustee is obliged to administer the trust in accordance with both the terms of the trust and the governing law. In the United States, the settlor is also called the trustor, grantor, donor or creator. In some other jurisdictions, the settlor may also be known as the "founder".

While there are many different uses of Trusts, there are two main categories. **Living Trusts** (also referred to as inter vivos trusts) and **Testamentary Trusts**.

To fund a Living Trust, ownership of assets must be transferred from the Settlor's name into the Trustee's name. The Trust can be funded with cash, stocks, bonds or almost any other asset. As mentioned above, the Trustee has legal title to the Trust property, but beneficial ownership rests with the beneficiaries. One of the advantages of a Living Trust is that the Settlor may choose to be the Trustee, or one of several co-Trustees. This may be important to individuals who want continued control of the assets while they are alive. This is often the case when a family business is placed in a Trust, and the Settlor wants to continue to have some influence on the business.

A Testamentary Trust is created under the terms of a Will, and only operates on the death of an individual (the "Testator"). Prior to the testator's death, the terms of the Trust can be modified, or the Trust can be removed, simply by having a new Will prepared. Testamentary Trusts are funded from the proceeds of the deceased's estate. The terms of a Testamentary Trust can be kept confidential until the Testator dies. After death, when the Will is probated (becomes a valid Will), it becomes a public document.

	Living Trust	Testamentary Trust
How Established	Created during an individuals lifetime and takes effect when the Trust is funded.	Created under the terms of a Will and takes effect after the death of the Testator.
How assets are placed into the Trust	Assets of a living person are re-registered from the Settlor's name into the the Trustee's name.	Funded with assets from the deceased's estate.
Who can be Trustee	The Trustee can be anyone, including the Settlor.	The Trustee can be anyone, but is often the person who acted as the deceased's executor.

Discretionary Vs Non-Discretionary Trusts Discretionary Trusts may provide the Trustee with the power to pay part or all of the income to an income beneficiary, or to pay capital to a capital beneficiary prior to the distribution date. In a Non-Discretionary Trust, the trust document provides the Trustee with the amount of the income payments, or how much capital can be paid to any beneficiary prior to the distribution of the Trust.

What is the Trust Agreement? The Trust Agreement is a written document that sets out the terms of a Living Trust. In the case of a Testamentary Trust, the terms of the Trust are contained in specific clauses within a Will. These clauses state what property is transferred to the Trustee(s), the powers and obligations of the Trustee(s), and most importantly, how and under what circumstances the income and the capital of the Trust will be distributed. The Trust Agreement or Trust Clauses within a Will should clearly set out what the individual wants done, and give sufficient power to the trustees to carry out their duties. Generally, a domestic Trust is governed by the law of the province in which it is administered. Similarly, an international Trust is governed by the laws of the foreign jurisdiction in which it is located. When considering the terms to put in a Trust Agreement, the key question is, "What if?"...

- What if the named beneficiary doesn't survive you?
- What if the condition for taking a gift is not fulfilled?
- What if the capital beneficiary dies before the income beneficiary?
- What if it makes sense to sell the Trust property and invest in something altogether different, or collapse the Trust?

What is the Role of the Trustee? A Trust is an agreement for the transfer of property from the Settlor to the Trustees, for the benefit of the beneficiaries. The Trustees become the legal owners of the property, with their ability to deal with the property limited by the Trust Agreement and Trust law. The Trustees have the following legal obligations:
- Trustees cannot transfer rights, powers, or obligations to a third party. They must act for themselves and not delegate powers.
- As the owners of the Trust property, Trustees have all the legal and equitable obligations to invest and manage the Trust property.

- Trustees must ensure that the income and capital of the Trust is distributed in accordance with the Trust agreement.
- Trustees are personally liable for acts or omissions which adversely affect the Trust or the beneficiaries.
- Trustees must deal impartially with the beneficiaries.
- Trustees cannot use the property in any way to benefit themselves. For example they are prohibited from purchasing property from the Trust unless specifically permitted in the agreement. However, under Trust legislation, Executors and Trustees are entitled to compensation for their services.

What is a Fiduciary? A fiduciary duty (from Latin *fiduciarius*, meaning "(holding) in trust"; from *fides*, meaning "faith", and *fiducia*, meaning "trust") is a legal or ethical relationship of confidence or trust between two or more parties. Typically, a fiduciary prudently takes care of money for another person. One party, for example a corporate trust company or the trust department of a bank, acts in a fiduciary capacity to the other one, who for example has funds entrusted to it for investment. In a fiduciary relationship, one person, in a position of vulnerability, justifiably vests confidence, good faith, reliance and trust in another whose aid, advice or protection is sought in some matter. In such a relation good conscience requires the fiduciary to act at all times for the sole benefit and interest of the one who trusts.

A fiduciary duty is the highest standard of care at either equity or law. A fiduciary (abbreviation *fid*) is expected to be extremely loyal to the person to whom he owes the duty (the "principal"): he must not put his personal interests before the duty, and must not profit from his position as a fiduciary, unless the principal consents.

In English common law the fiduciary relation is arguably the most important concept within the portion of the legal system known as equity. In the United Kingdom, the Judicature Acts merged the courts of equity (historically based in England's Court of Chancery) with the courts of common law, and as a result the concept of fiduciary duty also became available in common law courts.

When a fiduciary duty is imposed, equity requires a different, arguably stricter, standard of behavior than the comparable tortious duty of care at common law. It is said the fiduciary has a duty not to be in a situation where personal interests and fiduciary duty conflict, a duty not to be in a situation where his fiduciary duty conflicts with another fiduciary duty, and a duty not to profit from his fiduciary position without knowledge and consent. A fiduciary ideally would not have a conflict of interest. It has been said that fiduciaries must conduct themselves "at a level higher than that trodden by the crowd" and that "[t]he distinguishing or overriding duty of a fiduciary is the obligation of undivided loyalty."

Relationships The most common circumstance where a fiduciary duty will arise is between a trustee, whether real or juristic, and a beneficiary. The trustee to whom property is legally committed is the legal—i.e., common law—owner of all such property. The beneficiary, at law, has no legal title to the trust; however, the trustee is bound by equity to suppress his own interests and administer the property only for the benefit of the beneficiary. In this way, the beneficiary obtains the use of property without being its technical owner.

Others, such as corporate directors, may be held to a fiduciary duty similar in some respects to that of a trustee. This happens when, for example, the directors of a bank are trustees for the depositors, the directors of a corporation are trustees for the stockholders or a guardian is trustee of his ward's property. A person in a sensitive position sometimes protects himself from possible conflict of interest charges by setting up a *blind trust*, placing his financial affairs in the hands of a fiduciary and giving up all right to know about or intervene in their handling.

The fiduciary functions of trusts and agencies are commonly performed by a **trust company**, such as a *commercial bank*, organized for that purpose. In the United States, the Office of Thrift Supervision (OTS), an agency of the **United States Department of the Treasury,** is the primary regulator of the fiduciary activities of federal savings associations.

Primary Elements of Duty A fiduciary, such as the administrator, executor or guardian of an estate, may be legally required to file with a probate court or judge a surety bond, called a **fiduciary bond** or **probate bond**, to guarantee faithful performance of his duties. One of those duties may be to prepare, generally under oath, an *inventory* of the tangible or intangible property of the estate, describing the items or classes of property and usually placing a valuation on them.

Accountability A fiduciary will be liable to account if proven to have acquired a profit, benefit or gain from the relationship by one of three means:
- In circumstances of conflict of duty and interest
- In circumstances of conflict of duty to one person and duty to another person
- By taking advantage of the fiduciary position.

Therefore, it is said the fiduciary has a duty not to be in a situation where personal interests and fiduciary duty conflict, a duty not to be in a situation where his fiduciary duty conflicts with another fiduciary duty, and not to profit from his fiduciary position without express knowledge and consent. A fiduciary cannot have a conflict of interest.

A fiduciary's duty must not conflict with another fiduciary duty. Conflicts between one fiduciary duty and another fiduciary duty arise most often when a lawyer or an agent, such as a real estate agent, represent more than one client, and the interests of those clients conflict. This would occur when a lawyer attempts to represent both the plaintiff and the defendant in the same matter, for example. The rule comes from the logical conclusion that a fiduciary cannot make the principal's interests a top priority if he has two principals and their interests are diametrically opposed; he must balance the interests, which is not acceptable to equity. Therefore, the conflict of duty and duty rule is really an extension of the conflict of interest and duty rules.

No-profit rule A fiduciary must not profit from the fiduciary position. This includes any benefits or profits which, although unrelated to the fiduciary position, came about because of an opportunity that the fiduciary position afforded. It is unnecessary that the principal would have been unable to make the profit; if the fiduciary makes a profit, by virtue of his role as fiduciary for the principal, then the fiduciary must report the profit to the principal. If the principal consents then the fiduciary may keep the benefit. If this requirement is not met then the property is deemed by the court to be held by the fiduciary on constructive trust for the principal.

Breaches of duty and remedies Conduct by a fiduciary may be deemed *constructive fraud* when it is based on acts, omissions or concealments considered fraudulent and that gives one an advantage against the other because such conduct—though not actually fraudulent, dishonest or deceitful—demands redress for reasons of public policy. Breach of fiduciary duty may occur in insider trading, when an insider or a related party makes trades in a corporation's securities based on material non-public information obtained during the performance of the insider's duties at the corporation. Breach of fiduciary duty by a lawyer with regard to a client, if negligent, may be a form of legal malpractice; if intentional, it may be remedied in equity.

Where a principal can establish both a fiduciary duty and a breach of that duty, through violation of the above rules, the court will find that the benefit gained by the fiduciary should be returned to the principal because it would be unconscionable to allow the fiduciary to retain the benefit by employing his strict common law legal rights. This will be the case, unless the fiduciary can show there was full disclosure of the conflict of interest or profit and that the principal fully accepted and freely consented to the fiduciary's course of action.

Remedies will differ according to the type of damage or benefit. They are usually distinguished between proprietary remedies, dealing with property, and personal remedies, dealing with pecuniary (monetary) compensation.

Constructive trusts Where the unconscionable gain by the fiduciary is in an easily identifiable form, such as the recording contract discussed above, the usual remedy will be the already discussed constructive trust. Constructive trusts pop up in many aspects of equity, not just in a remedial sense, but, in this sense, what is meant by a constructive trust is that the court has created and imposed a duty on the fiduciary to hold the money in safekeeping until it can be rightfully transferred to the principal.

Account of profits An account of profits is another potential remedy. It is usually used where the breach of duty was ongoing or when the gain is hard to identify. The idea of an account of profits is that the fiduciary profited unconscionably by virtue of the fiduciary position, so any profit made should be transferred to the principal. It may sound like a constructive trust at first, but it is not.

An account for profits is the appropriate remedy when, for example, a senior employee has taken advantage of his fiduciary position by conducting his own company on the side and has run up quite a lot of profits over a period of time, profits which he wouldn't have been able to make without his fiduciary position in the original company. The calculation of profits in this sense can be extremely difficult, because profit due to fiduciary position must be separated from profit due to the fiduciary's own effort and ingenuity.

Compensatory damages Compensatory damages are also available. Accounts of profits can be hard remedies to establish, therefore, a plaintiff will often seek compensation (damages) instead. Courts of equity initially had no power to award compensatory damages, which traditionally were a remedy at common law, but legislation and case law has changed the situation so compensatory damages may

The Vatican And The Crown Are Primary Trustees

Statutory law, is imposed upon basis of the 'property right', and that property right is the property right of the corporate Crown in Canada, and corporate State (be it a State or the UNITED STATES) in the USA. The same scheme can be found in any country that is a subject country of the Pontiff of Rome's Holy Roman Empire. Thus, in actuality, the assumed 'property right' is that of the corporate Holy Roman Empire, as the Crown or incorporated State is an agency for the Holy Roman Empire.

The 'Crown' is the administrative corporation of the Pontiff of Rome owned City of London, the financial, legal and professional standards capitol of/for the Vatican, The City of London is a square mile area within Greater London, England, and is an independent city-state. In the USA, the administrative corporation for the Pontiff of Rome is the UNITED STATES, and that corporation administers the Vatican capitol, for, primarily, military purposes, called Columbia, or the District of Columbia. The UNITED STATES also administers the 50 sub-corporate States of the United States of America, identified with the 2 cap letters – CA, OR, WA, brought down to the administrative levels of the Postal Codes.

Adult humans are brought into the corporate world by way of the fiction name, as imprinted on the copy of the birth certificate received from Provincial/State Vital Statistics, or to whatever source. Although the birth certificate is of somewhat recent origin and used to formally offer 'citizens' as chattel in bankruptcy to the Pope's Holy Roman Empire owned Rothschilds' Banking System, the false use of the family name goes back into the Middle Ages in England. Thus, it is with the family name made a primary, or surname, (example - Mister Jones), and the given names of the child (example - Peter) made a reference name to the primary name. This is the reverse or mirror image to reality. A 'family name' is NOT a man's name - it is a name of a clan - a blood relationship.

As people are then 'forced' or 'obliged' to use that name in all commercial and Government dealings and communications 99.99% of the human inhabitants of North America (and most of the world) do, supposedly 'voluntarily' attach themselves the free will adult human, to the Crown/State owned property, called the 'legal identity name' as an accessory attached to property owned by Another party. Think of a ship under tow by another ship. Which captain decides what route the ships will take? The 'legal name/strawman' is the tow rope, and the towing ship is the corporate (make-believe ship at sea) Crown of the City of London. As an attachment to the legal name owned by the Crown, you are the towed ship, and your vessel captain, your free will mind, is now a subservient crewmember to the captain of the Crown.

The State or Crown does not give us authority, grant, license, permission or leave to use the Crown or State owned legal identity name. Thus, our use of it as an adult free will man (male or female) is a form of 'theft' against a maritime jurisdiction entity (all incorporated bodies are 'make-believe ships at sea'). In maritime law, the accused is guilty until proven innocent. This allows the Roman Law system, which we have, to impose 'involuntary servitude' upon an adult man. Involuntary servitude simply means a slave stripped of granted rights of a slave called a citizen, subject or freeman. This stripped rights included 'due process of law' - no jury trial, and charges where no harm has been done against another man, or his property with criminal intent.

We see this Roman Law within the US 13th Amendment (#2) instituted in the mid 1860's: *"Neither slavery nor involuntary servitude, except as a punishment for crime whereof the party shall have been duly convicted,"* The crime with which you have been convicted is 'unauthorized use' of the State's or Crown's intellectual property - the legal identity name.

The Crown/State then invokes the legal maxim, accessio cedit principali, [an accessory attached to a principal becomes the property of the owner of the principal], where the principal is the legal identity name as 'intellectual property'. The owner is the corporation called the Crown/State, or UNITED STATES, and the accessory is the free will human who has supposedly volunteered himself to be 'property by attachment' of the Crown/State. An adult human who is property is, and by any other name, of 'slave status', be it <u>citizen, subject or freeman</u>.

The relationship between free will man and Government/corporate bodies is contractual are incorrect. In the scenario so described, as a slave, one's property in possession, including body and labor, belongs to the slave owner 100%. And, the property right is a bundle of rights - own, use, sell, gift, bequeath and hypothecate property.

Thus, ALL 'income' resulting from the owned human slave's mental and/or physical labor belongs to the slave owner. That which is left with or granted to the slave for his own use and maintenance is called a 'benefit'. In Canada, the 'return of income' [the phrase itself tells the story] is called a T1 'tax and benefits package'. The T1 or IRS (USA)1040 is an accounting by the slave of his fruits of labor that belongs to the slave owner, and the prescribed 'benefits' that he may keep or have back from withholding. Thus, all income tax cases against the people', in reality, result from fraud, illegal concealment and theft by the accused slave of the slave owner's 'property'.

Going back to an above paragraph, we find that the attachment of oneself to the Crown/State owned name is 'assumed to be voluntary', as the Crown/State has no valid right to impose slavery upon adult humans against their will, except as stated in the next paragraph. Anyone working as an employee is in a contract of voluntary servitude - direction and time control by, and obedience and loyalty to, the employer. Until we 'assumed to be slaves' get our heads around this key to the lock that holds our chains of slavery around our necks and ankles, we will continue to attempt to swim with that 100 lb ball chained to our leg.

Another factor of the use of the Roman Law system is contained within the 1860's 13th Amendment to the US Constitution, the Constitution of the corporate UNITED STATES, [and not the 13th Amendment of the US Republic inserted around 1819]. In the later 13th amendment, it says: "Neither slavery nor involuntary servitude, except as a punishment for crime whereof the party shall have been duly convicted, shall exist within the United States, or any place subject to their jurisdiction." Notice that this applies only to the corporate body called the UNITED STATES.

All corporate bodies are make-believe ships at sea, and are thus, internally, under maritime law, [incorrectly called 'admiralty law', unless applied to the military]. In maritime law, an accused is guilty unless proven innocent. Thus, a free will adult man who uses, without authority, the property of a corporate body is under maritime jurisdiction. This makes a free will man who uses a corporate Crown or corporate State owned legal identity name a 'convicted criminal', and thus subject to the imposition of slavery, involuntary servitude.

You, as a child, were Crown or State property by way of the birth registry, and thus, you could use Crown or State property, the legal identity name. When you became an adult, as a vessel on the 'sea of life' as a sovereign captain/free will mind, you no longer had a right to use (as an 'identity' name) that Crown or State owned legal identity name.

However, under the 'property right' of a slave owner in regard to property in the possession of an owned slave, a 'demand' for the property by the slave owner, or the slave owner's agent (such as the IRS, or county tax collector, or for a court imposed fine), is all that is necessary, without regard to due process of law. Remember, ALL that a slave possesses belongs to the slave owner. In this context you are NOT slaves but it is important to understand that Government, and its employees, judges and officers SEE you as a SLAVE. Further, when any 'officer' of the corporate body, be it 'peace officer or police', all the way to King or President choose to declare someone 'homo sacer' (meaning a man who has been stripped of his status of 'person' - that being an obedient corporate slave member of the corporate body politic) - he is stripped of the rights of due process of law, and can be fined, punished, tortured or killed without repercussion to the officer, or officer involved. This happens all the time in the world of the Holy Roman Empire.

And so it that you powers, and your Divine Trust where your property is registered for use, is compromised because you allowed this to be by way of good faith and trust that the Trustee, who represents GOD and GOD's Code (word) and that coprorated body beneath that corporate structure, will act in accordance with what you believe to be God's law (Word) to your benefit.

In truth, you simply believed this was correct, and allowed this to be by acceptance. Of course the issue is that under the universal laws of commerce, your contract to become a slave, and lose control of your Trust, was not fully disclosed.

The Divine Estate Is An Implied Trust

An implied trust, as distinct from an express trust, is created where some of the legal requirements for an express trust are not met, but an intention on behalf of the parties to create a trust can be presumed to exist. A resulting trust may be deemed to be present where a trust instrument is not properly drafted and a portion of the equitable title has not been provided for. In such a case, the law may raise a resulting trust for the benefit of the grantor (the creator of the trust). In other words, the grantor may be deemed to be a beneficiary of the portion of the equitable title that was not properly provided for in the trust document

An implied trust is a type of situation that arises when the courts find evidence that there is a basis for what amounts to a trust after reviewing the types of arrangements put in place by a grantor. Not considered a formal trust arrangement, the implied trust is supported by the collection of financial plans and preparations made by the grantor to provide for loved ones once he or she passes away. A court will look at the cumulative evidence and, if the information meets the criteria of an implied trust, will proceed with the settlement of the estate accordingly.

Within the broad definition of an implied trust, several types of trust arrangements may emerge. One of these forms is known as a statutory trust. With this arrangement, the trustee associated with the will or other documents left behind by the grantor is charged with the responsibility of selling properties related to the estate, with the proceeds from those sales ultimately going to a beneficiary. In the interim, the trustee manages the property, which may be in the form of real estate holdings, or some sort of business operation. The idea is to hold onto the property and secure the best possible price for the holdings allowing the beneficiary to receive more benefit from the arrangement in the long run.

Another form of trust, the **cestui que** is a trust that was used rooted in medieval law. It became a vehicle for a legal method to avoid the feudal (medieval) incidents (payments) to an overlord, while leaving the land for the use of another, who owed nothing to the lord. The law of cestui que tended to defer jurisdiction to courts of equity as opposed to common law courts. The cestui que was often utilized by persons who might be absent from the kingdom for an extended time (as on a Crusade, or a business adventure), and who held tenancy to the land, and owed feudal incidents to a lord. The land could be left for the use of a third party, who did not owe the incidents to the lord. This legal status was also invented to circumvent the Statute of Mortmain. That statute was intended to end the relatively common practice of leaving real property to the Church at the time of the owner's death. Since the Church never died, the land never left the "dead hand" ("Mortmain" or Church). An alternative explanation of "mortmain" was that an owner from generations earlier was still dictating land use years after death, by leaving it to the Church. Hence the term "dead hand." Before the Statute of Mortmain, large amounts of land were bequeathed to the Church, which never relinquished it. This was in contradistinction to normal lands which could be inherited in a family line or revert to a lord or the Crown upon death of the tenant. Church land had been a source of contention between the Crown and the Church for centuries. Cestui que use allowed religious orders to inhabit land, while the title resided with a corporation of lawyers or other entities, who nominally had no relation to the Church.

Constitutional Relationship To Current Trusts

The Constitution for the United States is a document of dual nature: in that it is a trust document, and it is the articles of incorporation and created a unique trust res and estate of inheritance. It is a tenant of law that in order to determine the intent of a writing one must look to the title, the Empowerment Clause in statute, which in the case of the Constitution is the Preamble. In writing the Constitution the founders followed the common law of England which stretches back some 1000 years. The Preamble fulfills the requirements necessary to establish a trust. It identifies the Grantor(s), Statement of Purpose, Grantee(s), Statement of Intent, Written Indenture, and the name of the entity being created and is written and constructed as a trust so that it would have the thrust of ageless law. In this declaration, it states:

"WE THE PEOPLE (Grantors) of the United States (from or out of) in Order to form a more perfect union, establish justice, provide for the common defence, promote the general welfare and secure the Blessings of Liberty (statement of Purpose) to ourselves and our posterity (Grantees/heirs unnamed), Do Ordain and establish (Statement of Intent) this constitution (Written Indenture) for the United States of America (name of the entity being created)."

The trust res (contents) is in the Articles of the Confederation and the Declaration of Independence. The intent of the constitution was to bequeath freedom, life, liberty and the pursuit of happiness to themselves and their posterity. The founders intended to secure and pass on the sovereignty of the people to the people of future generations of Americans, in perpetuity. One's rights are derived from the land upon which one stands and your relation, or status, to that land. In America these rights originated with the Articles of Confederation and the Declaration of Independence and are attached to the land called America (The Laws of Real Property). Our status, or relation to that land, is determined by the laws of Descent and Distribution. The right to freedom, life, liberty and the pursuit of happiness are Our inheritance bequeathed to us via the Constitution of the United States of America.

The constitution granted the government the power and authority to administrate and to carry on corporate functions. Under the common law, inherent rights cannot devolve to a 'body politic' through a corporation. Rights only devolve to human beings is through and by way of a trust. Under the constitutional law, in order to determine the meaning of a written instrument the court must look to the title. In this case, once again, it is the Preamble. Pursuant to the laws of real property that have been existence from the beginning, the Preamble clearly shows a freehold in fee simple absolute in it. Freeholds in fee simple were instruments of trust, not corporate. "Our Posterity" cannot be speaking of a corporate entity as posterity can only mean a living man/woman, by birth/nativity.

The Articles of the Constitution are the Articles of Incorporation that established congress as Trustees of the Trust and defines their power and authority as well as their limitations. Annexed to the Constitutional Trust is a will like structure, the Amendments. The Trust and the trust res were already in existence when the will/codicil (Amendments) were added some four years later. The Amendments do not constitute the Trust in fact, they are annexed to the Trust as a codicil (a supplement or addition to the will, not necessarily disposing of the entire estate, but modifying, explaining or otherwise qualifying the will in some way.)

A Trust, once completed and in force cannot be amended or altered without the consent of the parties in interest except under reserved power of amendment and alteration. An amendment is ordinarily possible by parties in interest and against parties without vested interest. Prior to the 14th Amendment the freeborn inhabitants, citizens of the states were the parties in interest. The 14th Amendment created the 14th Amendment legal fiction citizen who do not have a vested interest in the trust or the trust res.

The 14th Amendment can be viewed as a codicil to the will that republished the constitution with new meaning, changed the intent behind it and turned it into a testamentary instrument with capabilities of being used against the free born inhabitants through a seemingly voluntary revocation.

Thus the freeholders, Beneficiaries to the trust have been tricked and coerced by the Trustees into Testifying against themselves when they apply for an S.S. #, drivers permit, marriage license or when they sign an IRS 1040 form, which the Trustees have mislead them to believe are mandatory. When one applies for a Social Security number, provide evidence of birth and claims to be a United States citizen, a party with no vested interest in a freehold, the trust or the trust res, one literally declared the free born inhabitant to be deceased; the decedent retains no interest in the property and that you, in your dual capacity as a legal fiction citizen are now the executor of the estate. It is here that the **cestui que** implied trust shows its flexibility to the creators.

The Trustees have breached the trust having amended the will for their own personal profit and gain at the expense of the true heirs. The freeholders/ Beneficiary has unwittingly, without full disclosure, become the executor and the Trustees have become the Beneficiaries to the trust through the Laws of Donations, effectively stealing Our inheritance.

A breach of trust of fiduciary duty by a Trustee is a violation of correlative right of the Cestui Que Trust and gives rise to the correlative cause of action on the part of the Beneficiary for any loss to the estate Trust. This rule is applicable in respect to both positive acts or negligence constituting a breach of fiduciary duty by the Trustee. A Trustee's breach of fiduciary duty falls within the maxim that 'equity will not aid one who comes into court with unclean hands.'

When the Trustee's breach is by an act of omission the beneficiary can question the propriety of the Trustee. The Beneficiary had to have full disclosure, full knowledge of the material facts and circumstances. A Beneficiary must have had knowledge of and understood their rights and have no obligation to search the public records to obtain said knowledge.

The Trustees have committed acts of omission, mis-representation, deceit and deception in order to mislead and coerce us into giving up our beneficial interest in the trust and the trust res. The Trustees have compelled the free born inhabitants, freeholders in fee simple, to accept the benefits 'under the will' perverted by the 14th Amendment, without freedom of choice for failure of full disclosure thereby precluding our enforcement of contractual rights in property bequeathed to us by the will. The Trustees are trying to repudiate the Trust, employing a lifetime of propaganda and programming and enforced through threats, violence and coercion, and failing to provide notice to the Beneficiaries of the repudiation which must be 'brought home.'

The Doctrine of Election in connection with testamentary instruments is the principle that one who is given a benefit 'under the will' must choose between accepting the benefits and asserting some other claim against the testator's estate or against the property disposed of by the will. A Testamentary Beneficiaries right to elect whether to take 'under the will' or 'against the will' in case he has some inconsistent claim against the testator's estate, is personal to him; is a personal privilege which may be controlled by the creditors of the Beneficiary. They can claim no right or interest in the estate contrary to the debtor's election and may have no right of a legacy or devise to their debtor if he elected to take against the will.

Acceptance of benefits 'under the will' constitutes an election which will preclude the devisee from enforcing contractual rights in property bequeathed the will. This rule is, of course, subject to the qualifications that acceptance of a benefit 'under the will' when made in ignorance of the Beneficiaries rights or a mis-apprehension, mis-representation as to the condition of the Testator's estate does not constitute an election.

In the beginning God gave man dominion over all things, Beneficiaries of the Divine Trust. The Founding fathers of the United States of America created the constitution for the United States, an estate trust, to pass on sovereignty of the people to the people of future generations, in perpetuity.

Three Cestui Que Trusts Are Created By Vatican And State

In Canada and America today, upon giving birth a mother is compelled, without full disclosure, to apply for the **creation of the first Cestui Que Vie** trust, creating a 14th Amendment paper citizen of the United States. Upon receipt of the mother's application the Trustees establish a trust under the error of assumptions that the child has elected to accept the benefits bequeathed by the will, 'under the will'. The Trustees further assume that the child is incompetent, a bankrupt and lost at sea and is presumed dead until the child re-appears and re-establishes his/her living status, challenges the assumption of his/her acceptance of the benefits 'under the will' as being one of free choice and with full knowledge of the facts and redeems the estate.

Under the assumption that the child is a 14th Amendment citizen, the child's print is placed on the birth certificate by the hospital creating a slave bond that is sold to the federal reserve, who converts the certificate into a negotiable instrument and establishes a **second Cestui Que Vie trust**. The child's parents are compelled to apply for a social security number for the child, unwittingly testifying that the child is a 14th Amendment paper citizen of the United States, not a party in interest to the trust or the trust res, and assumed to be dead after 7 years, when the federal reserve cannot seize the child, they file for the issue of the salvage bond and the child is presumed dead.

In 1666, in London, during the black plague, and great fires of London Parliament enacted an act, behind closed doors, called Cestui Que Vie Act 1666. The act being debated the Cestui Qui act was to subrogate the rights of men and women, meaning all men and women were declared dead, lost at sea/beyond the sea (back then operating in admiralty law, the law of the sea, so lost at sea).

When a child is Baptized by the church, the Baptismal certificate is forwarded to the Vatican who converts the certificate into a negotiable instrument and **creates a third Cestui Que Vie trust.** These three trusts represent the enslavement of the property, body and soul of the child.

The civil administration, UNITED STATES, continues to operate today under this triple crown of enslavement based on the error of assumptions that we are 14th Amendment citizens of the United States based on the breach of trust by the trustees.

Cestui Que As A Method Of Fraud

Cestui que (also ***cestuy que***) (is a shortened version of *cestui a que use le feoffment fuit fait,* literally, "The person for whose use the feoffment was made." It is a Law French phrase of medieval English invention, which appears in the legal phrases *cestui que trust*, *cestui que use*, or *cestui que vie*. In contemporary English the phrase is also commonly pronounced "setty-kay" (/ˈsɛtikeɪ/) or "sesty-kay" (/ˈsɛstikeɪ/). According to Roebuck, *Cestui que use* is pronounced "setticky yuce" (/ˌsɛtikiˈjuːs/). *Cestui que use* and *cestui que trust* are more or less interchangeable terms. In some medieval materials, the phrase is seen as **cestui a que**.

The *cestui que use* is the person for whose benefit the trust is created. The *cestui que trust* is the person entitled to an equitable, as opposed to a legal, estate. Thus, if land is granted to the use of A in trust for B, B is cestui que trust, and A trustee, or use. The term, principally owing to its cumbersome nature], has been virtually superseded in modern law by that of "beneficiary", and general law of trusts.

By the fifteenth century, *cestui que use* was a vehicle to defraud creditors. The main use was to leave land, or parts of land to members of the family other than the primary heir. This was a way to avoid primogeniture inheritance. While the use was intact, the occupant of the land could take advantage of the *cestui que use* to avoid the feudal payments and duties (incidents). Incidents such as wardship, marriage penalties and other gifts, taxes, fines, fees, and knight service were onerous. Common law did not recognize *cestui que uses* as such, and there was difficulty fitting these cases into the existing writs and case law. The incidents could not be enforced against a person who was on a Crusade, or other war, or business adventure. They were not present in the kingdom to be enforced to perform. Since the feudal oath was to the person, and not the land, there could be no lien against the land. A hallmark of medieval feudalism was the person to person oath of allegiance. The feudal incidents could not be enforced upon the beneficiaries of the *cestui que use*, since these were not the owners of the land. The users had not sworn an oath to the lord. Therefore, they owed the lord nothing. The *cestui que use* had no estate. They had no seisin, nor a trespass, and therefore, ejectment could not be effected. These required possession. Assumpsit was of no avail. In 1402, the Commons had petitioned the king for a remedy against dishonest feoffees to uses, apparently with no result. *Cestui que use* became a new kind of property and property use.

Cestui Que A Medieval Invention In Practice

Many reasons have been given for the invention of the cestui que use as a legal device. During the Crusades, and other wars on the Continent, landowners might be gone for long periods of time. Others might be absent because of business adventures or religious pilgrimages. There was no assurance they would ever return home. The *cestui que use* allowed them to leave a trusted friend or relative with the sort of powers, discretions and they hoped, the duties. Today, this power would be called the "power of attorney". Religious orders such as Franciscans, Cistercians, Benedictines and other mendicant orders took vows of poverty, yet retained the use of donated property. *Cestui que use* allowed them the benefits of land without legal ownership. Besides the obvious limitations placed on cestui que by the Statute of Mortmain, Statute of Uses and the Statute of Wills, its legality was shaped indirectly by provisions within the Magna Carta and Quia Emptores.

Example 1: Albert is the owner of a landholding called Blackacre. He conveys this to Richard with the command that Richard hold the land with the duty not for Richard's benefit, but for a different purpose. This could be to do a job, such as collect rents and profits for the purpose of passing them to a third person, Lucy. This was nothing more than a clever legal device with Richard playing either an active or passive role.

Example 2: If Jane (women could engage in cestui que use), granted Blackacre to Charles to the use of David, then David became the beneficial owner and Jane could not vary or detract from that ownership.

Example 3: If Mary wanted to grant Blackacre away from her direct heir James, to her younger son Jasper, then she might well do so by a grant of Richard to the use of Jasper in tail, remainder to James in fee simple. Only Richard had a legal estate, the interests of

Jasper and James being equitable analogues of a legal fee tail and fee simple in remainder.

Example 4: If Mary wanted to make a will of the equitable ownership of Blackacre, she would be able to do so by a grant to Richard to the use of herself, Mary. The ownership of Blackacre did not pass on Mary's death to her heir but went to wherever she might will it. By this method, Mary could keep her wishes secret until her death when her will would be read, and would prevail. This was a way to defeat primogeniture inheritance.

Example 5: Uses were so common by the middle of the fifteenth century that they were presumed to be in existence even if no intention could be proved. If Martin granted Blackacre to Martha, and she could show no consideration (that is, that she paid for it), then Martha would be considered in equity to be the feoffee to unspecified uses to be announced at Martin's discretion. If Martin sold Blackacre to Martha, but did not go through the formal routines of feoffment to complete the conveyance, Martha could not become the legal owner. But in equity, Martin held the land to the cestui que use of Martha. It would have been unconscionable for him to do otherwise having taken her money for the sale of Blackacre.

Example 6: Albert might convey Blackacre to Richard for the use of Jane. In this case, Richard was called the "feoffee of uses". Jane was the "cestui que use". This was short for "cestui a qui use le feoffment fuit fait", i.e. "The person to whose use the feoffment was made." This device separated legal from beneficial ownership.

Concerted efforts were made under Henry VII of England to reform cestui que. A change in the laws made feoffees the absolute owners of the property of which they had been enfeoffed, and they became subject to all the liabilities of ownership. They were the only ones who could take proceedings against those who interfered with their ownership. If a trespass had been committed with the license of the *cestui que use* they could take proceedings against him, for he was at law only a tenant at sufferance. Similarly, feoffees were the only ones who could take the proceedings against tenants of the land to compel them to perform their obligations. If a debt was brought for rent by a *cestui que use*, and the defendant pleaded "nihil habuit tempore dimissions", the plaintiff would have lost his action if he had not made a special replication setting out the facts. The purpose of these changes was to make *cestui que* in general, and *cestui que use trusts* more cumbersome and economically unattractive.

Henry VIII sought to end all cestui que uses and regain the incidents (fees and payments) that had been deprived him. Thomas Cromwell and Audley who succeeded Thomas More vigorously crushed cestui que uses in the courts, persuading judges to declare them illegal or void.[By 1538-39, over 800 religious land holdings had been returned to the Crown. Many of these were subsequently sold, converted to private dwellings, given to loyal supporters of the English Reformation, dismantled for building materials, or abandoned and allowed to degenerate into ruins. Claims of religious corruption were frequently used to justify reclamation by the Crown. Since many of these religious orders provided charity, much of the local medical and social services were left in disarray.

The Statute of Uses was enacted in 1535, and was intended to end the "abuses" which had incurred in *cestui que use*. It declared that any holder of a cestui que use became the holder of the legal title of the ownership in fee simple. This voided the advantages of a cestui que use. The feoffee to uses was bypassed. The *cestui que use* had seisin. Henry VIII of England got his incidences back. The land owner lost the ability to will the land to heirs other than those in direct lineage. There could be no bypassing of heirs with a cestui que. This condition was modified in the Statute of Wills (1540). One of the effects of the Statute of Uses in executing the use, was to make a mere sale of land without feoffment (the formal public transfer) effective to pass the legal estate. The buyer became the owner by operation of the statute. It necessitated a public announcement of the intended sale to determine if the land had been surreptitiously sold to someone else. The Statute of Uses required a public registry of sale of land, later called the Statute of Enrollments.

Lawyers quickly determined that adding the words to a conveyance "land to Leonard and his heirs, to the use of John and his heirs, to the use of Kenneth and his heirs." For a time, this device defeated the intent of the Statute of Uses. Lord Hardwicke wrote that the Statute had no real effect other than to add, at most three words, to a conveyance. He was referring to the doctrine that had become settled before his time: that the old use might still be effected despite the Statute, by a "use on a use". The Statute of Uses had been considered a great failure. It did not wipe out double ownership, legal and equitable, which has survived into the modern system of trusts. The preamble of the Statute went far in enumerating the abuses the system of uses had brought into play. The Statute did not, as had previously been suggested, try to remedy these abuses by declaring any uses void. It merely declared that the possession should be transferred to the use and that the cestui que use should have the possession after such manner and form as he had before the use.

History in German and Roman Law It is the opinion of William Holdsworth quoting such scholars as Gilbert, Sanders, Blackstone, Spence and Digby, that cestui que in English law had a Roman origin. An analogy exists between cestui que uses and a usufructus (usufruct) or the bequest of a fideicommissum. These all tended to create a feoffement to one person for the use of another. Gilbert writes, (also seen in Blackstone): *"that they answer more to the fideicommissum than the usufructus of the civil law." These were transplanted into England from Roman Civil Law about the close of the reign of Edward III of England by means of foreign ecclesiastics who introduced them to evade the Statute of Mortmain. Others argue that the comparison between cestui que and Roman law is merely superficial. The transfer of land for the use of one person for certain purposes to be carried out either in the lifetime or after the death of the person conveying it has its basis in Germanic law. It was popularly held that land could be transferred for the use from one person to another in local custom. The formal English or Saxon law didn't always recognize this custom. The practice was called Salman or Treuhand. "Sala" is German for "transfer".*[5] *It is related to the Old English "sellen", "to sell".*

The earliest appearance of cestui que in the medieval period was the feoffee to uses, which like the Salman, held on account of another. This was called the cestui que use. It was because the feoffor could impose on him many various duties that landowners acquired through his instrumentality the power to do many things with their land. This was a to avoid the rigidity of medieval common law of land and its uses. Germanic law was familiar with the idea that a man who holds property on account of, or to the use of another is bound to fulfill his trust. Frankish formulas from the Merovingian period describe property given to a church "ad opus sancti illius." Mercian books in the ninth century convey land "ad opus monachorum". The Doomsday Book refers to geld or money, sac and soc held in "ad opus regus", or in "reginae" or "vicecomitis". The laws of William I of England speak of the sheriff holding money "al os le rei" ("for the use of the king").

Others state that the *cestui que use trust* was the product of Roman Law. In England it was the invention of ecclesiastics who wanted to escape the Statute of Mortmain. The goal was to obtain a conveyance of an estate to a friendly person or corporation, with the intent that the use of the estate would reside with the original owner.

Pollock and Maitland describe *cestui que use* as the first step toward the law of agency. They note that the word "use" as it was employed in medieval English law was not from the Latin "usus", but rather from the Latin word "opus", meaning "work". From this came the Old French words "os" or "oes". Although with time the Latin document for conveying land to the use of John would be written "ad opus Johannis" which was interchangeable with "ad usum Johannis", or the fuller formula, "ad opus et ad usum", the earliest history suggests the term "use" evolved from "ad opus".

The Significance Of The Cestui Que Vie Trust Today

In 1666, in London, during the black plague, and great fires of London Parliament enacted an act, behind closed doors, called Cestui Que Vie Act 1666. The act being debated the Cestui Qui act was to subrogate the rights of men and women, meaning all men and women were declared dead, lost at sea/beyond the sea (back then operating in admiralty law, the law of the sea, so lost at sea).

The state (of London) took custody of everybody and their property into a trust, the state became the trustee/husband holding all titles to the people and property, until a living man comes back to reclaim those titles and can also claim damages. The rule of the use of CAPITAL LETTERS used in a NAME: when CAPITAL letters are used anywhere in a NAME this always refers to a LEGAL ENTITY/FICTION, COMPANY or CORPORATION no exceptions. e.g. John DOE or Doe: JANE (PASSPORT, DRIVER LICENSE, MARRIAGE CERTIFICATE and BIRTH CERTIFICATE)

CEST TUI QUE TRUST: (pronounced setakay) common term in NEW ZEALAND and AUSTRALIA or STRAWMAN common term in USA or CANADA is a LEGAL ENTITY/FICTION created and owned by the GOVERNMENT whom created it. I repeat owned by the GOVERNMENT. Legally, we are considered to be a FICTION, a concept or idea expressed as a NAME, a symbol. That LEGAL PERSON has no consciousness; it is a juristic PERSON, ENS LEGIS, a NAME/word written on a piece of paper.

This traces back to 1666, London is a state, just like Vatican is a state, just like Washington DC is a state. The Crown is an unincorporated association. Why unincorporated, its private, the temple bar is in London, every lawyer called to the "bar" swears allegiance to the temple bar. You can't get called, without swearing this allegiance. The Crown already owns North America and everything in it. Your only way out is to reclaim your dead entity (Strawman) that the Crown created, become the trustee of the cest tui qui trust and remove yourself from the admiralty law that holds you in custody.

When London burned the subrogation of men's and woman's rights occurred. The responsible act passed... CQV act 1666 meant all men and women of UK were declared dead and lost beyond the seas. The state took everybody and everybody's property into trust. The state takes control until a living man or woman comes back and claims their titles by proving they are alive and claims for damages can be made.

This is why you always need representation when involved in legal matters, because you're dead. The legal fiction is a construct on paper, an estate in trust. When you get a bill or summons from court it is always in capital letters, similar to tomb stones in grave yards. Capital letters signify death. They are writing to the dead legal fiction. A legal fiction was created when someone informed the government that there was a new vessel in town, based upon your birth. Birth certificates are issued at birth, just as ships are given berth certificates.

Your mother has a birth canal, just like a ship. All this information relates to how the general public are still legally tied. Through admiralty law, through this ancient legal construct we can be easily controlled. Learning about your legal fiction helps you to unlock yourself. Otherwise you are just a vessel floating on the sea of commerce. It is possible to be free from financial stress and debt.

Parents are tricked into registering the birth of their babies. In about 1837 the Births, Deaths and Marriages act was formed in UK and the post of registrar general was established. His job was to collect all the data from the churches which held the records of birth.

Regis - from queen or crown. All people are seen to be in custody of," The Crown". This allows people to function in commerce and to accept the benefits provided by state.

So we are in custody. Worldwide - under the IMF the majority of people are fed, sheltered and provided for, however now it is the system that is benefitting while many are suffering, are poorly fed, housed and water is contaminated. Many people are now getting sick and dying as a result - not to mention that as people evolve, they now seek to be independent of any system that seeks to control or oppress and harms the earth that this is all taking place on.

We have legally elected representatives. We have to understand who we are as men and women and how we can relate in the system.

The City of London is a centre for markets, where merchants work. Then there is mercantile law. It comes from Admiralty. Look at the symbols in the City of London that relate to Admiralty.

Our national banks are not our banks. The private shareholders from the private banks own the banks. It is all private, not public as we are led to believe. "OF" also means "without", eg. The bank without England. Private banks issue private currency.

With WWI a change happened where money was not backed by gold or silver anymore, it is now based on peoples labour. People are now pledged to the IMF as the surety to pay back the creditors in the global bankruptcy. Men and women are not bankrupt, they are the only source of credit. The public is bankrupt.

Regarding the currency that gets issued at the Bank of England, people are the gold or the treasure. The government issues bonds or treasury bills that are bought by investors. The money goes back into the economy in order to pay for the people to build things, e.g. an Olympic Stadium. However, the people are paying taxes for the privilege of using someone else's currency and paying back the principal and the interest on the original loan that was given against the treasury bonds, bills and notes. It is a private corporation that will own the Olympic stadium, be responsible for running it, be able to sell commercial rights, yet the people are actually the ones who own it and should be profiting from it. However, principal and interest is coming through the people in order to raise the money.

So where you have commerce and money, you also have "justice". You need to understand the bankruptcy before you can understand the judiciary. You need to accept the bankruptcy. We have accepted the claim to accept the summons. There is an obligation to accept any liability which has been created. All you can do is accept the bankruptcy. We are operating in admiralty. A not guilty plea dishonours the bankruptcy. The Strawman, aka legal fiction is always guilty. It needs to be accepted for value. Barristers and solicitors make a living out of creating controversy. By creating a controversy you become liable for the case.

Are you in honour and dishonour? To remain in honour you have to accept a claim and settle it. Then you add conditions. I accept on proof of claim and proof of loss. This gives the liability back to them. The legal fiction is always guilty. Only in the high courts, can the real man or woman appear. Games are played on courts; hence the name court is a game with actors (acting on acts). It has to be treated as a game and just business. Court room dramas are misinformation. In the public, we are operating in bankruptcy and you receive benefits. It takes a lot of time, effort and study to use these tools. You have to be prepared to go fully through the process, get the right tool out of your toolbox at the right time. People need to learn how to act as creditors. In summary:

- Money is backed by labour.
- We cannot exchange it fairly for gold or silver.
- Capitalisation of "name" means a dead entity, a legal fiction.
- Know who you are, you are not your Strawman or dead fictitious entity.
- Learn how to become a creditor in commerce.

So in summary, when in 1666 an act of parliament created during the black plague, and great fires of London , behind closed doors, it was called Cestui Que Vie Act 1666. (see end of chapter)

The act being debated was the Cestui Qui act which was to subrogate the rights of men and women, meaning all men and women were declared dead, lost at sea/beyond the sea. This was done during a crisis. The state took custody of everybody and their property into a trust, the Cestui Qui trust, the state became the trustee/husband holding all titles to the people and property, until a living man comes back to reclaim those titles and can also claim damages.

The Cestui Qui act or Trust created is an ALL-CAPITALIZED NAME, a 'dead entity' who had all his belongings put into a trust. This act still exists, and this trust still exists. This is how it started. If you were born on earth, if you have a birth certificate, this applies to you. The only way to claim your trust and get free from admiralty law, is to understand who you really are, and that admiralty law does not apply to you, but in order to get free you must do some homework, file forms and know how commerce applies to you.

Is The Cestui Que Used Today?

We include a letter posted on the Internet from: Hughes, Paul (Civil Law) Ministry of Justice 18 February 2011. It was a response from a letter sent by a Mr. Bolwell which assed about the Cetui Que trust:

"Dear Mr. Bolwell, Thank you for your e-mail of 19 December 2010 to the Data Access and Compliance Unit in which you ask for information about the Cestui que Vie Act 1666. You ask what the Act is about and whether or not it is still in effect. Your e-mail has been passed to me for reply as I work in the part of the department responsible for issues relating to the presumption of death. Your e-mail is not being dealt with under the Freedom of Information Act 2000. I am sorry for the delay in sending you a reply. The Cestui que Vie Act 1666 is still in force but parts of it have been amended or repealed over the years. Specifically:

The preamble was amended by the Statute Law Revision Act 1948; Section 2 was repealed by the Statute Law Revision Act 1948; Section 3 was repealed by the Statute Law Revision Act 1863; and Section 4 was amended by the Statute Law Revision Act 1888. The Act provides for the recovery of a lease where the life tenant has disappeared for seven or more years and there is no proof that the person is still alive. In this situation, the Act gives the court the power to declare the life tenant dead. There are very few references to the statute in the textbooks I have checked, suggesting it is little used. The following extract was taken from Halsbury's Statute Volume 20 (2009 reissue).

In the normal form of a strict settlement (which by virtue of the [1]Trusts of Land and Appointment of Trustees Act 1996, s 2, cannot in general be created on or after 1 January 1997) a limitation to a life tenant invariably precedes one to a tenant in tail in order to restrict the tenant in tail's power to bar the entail. Save where there is a trust for sale, the land will fall within the [2]Settled Land Act 1925 (see s 1 of that Act) and, if the life tenant is of full age, he will be the statutory tenant for life under s 19 of that Act, in whom the fee simple should be vested in trust for himself and the remainder men. The Cestui que Vie Acts 1666 and 1707 help to ascertain whether a life tenant is still alive.

If you have a problem to which the Act relates I can only recommend that you take independent legal advice. If you do not have an adviser your local Citizens Advice Bureau or Community Legal Advice Centre may be able to help him find one. Information about Community Legal Advice can also be found on its website:

[3]www.communitylegaladvice.org.uk or by telephoning 0845 345 4345. I hope you find this information helpful."

Yours sincerely, Kirsty Milliam
Ministry of Justice
102 Petty France
London SW1H 9AJ Tel: 020 3334 3207

The Cestui Que Vie Act Of 1666

For those interested in further understanding this vehicle, the following is provided:

1666 CHAPTER 11 18 and 19 Cha 2
An Act for Redresse of Inconveniencies by want of Proofe of the Deceases of Persons beyond the Seas or absenting themselves, upon whose Lives Estates do depend.

X1 Recital that Cestui que vies have gone beyond Sea, and that Reversioners cannot find out whether they are alive or dead.

Whereas diverse Lords of Mannours and others have granted Estates by Lease for one or more life or lives, or else for yeares determinable upon one or more life or lives And it hath often happened that such person or persons for whose life or lives such Estates have beene granted have gone beyond the Seas or soe absented themselves for many yeares that the Lessors and Reversioners cannot finde out whether such person or persons be alive or dead by reason whereof such Lessors and Reversioners have beene held out of possession of their Tenements for many yeares after all the lives upon which such Estates depend are dead in regard that the Lessors and Reversioners when they have brought Actions for the recovery of their Tenements have beene putt upon it to prove the death of their Tennants when it is almost impossible for them to discover the same, For remedy of which mischeife soe frequently happening to such Lessors or Reversioners.

Annotations:
Annotations are used to give authority for changes and other effects on the legislation you are viewing and to convey editorial information. They appear at the foot of the relevant provision or under the associated heading. Annotations are categorised by annotation type, such as F-notes for textual amendments and I-notes for commencement information (a full list can be found in the Editorial Practice Guide). Each annotation is identified by a sequential reference number. For F-notes, M-notes and X-notes, the number also appears in bold superscript at the relevant location in the text. All annotations contain links to the affecting legislation.

Editorial Information

X1 Abbreviations or contractions in the original form of this Act have been expanded into modern lettering in the text set out above and below.

Modifications etc. (not altering text)

C1 Short title "The Cestui que Vie Act 1666" given by Statute Law Revision Act 1948 (c. 62), Sch. 2

C2 Preamble omitted in part under authority of Statute Law Revision Act 1948 (c. 62), Sch. 1

C3 Certain words of enactment repealed by Statute Law Revision Act 1888 (c. 3) and remainder omitted under authority of Statute Law Revision Act 1948 (c. 62), s. 3

[I.] Cestui que vie remaining beyond Sea for Seven Years together and no Proof of their Lives, Judge in Action to direct a Verdict as though Cestui que vie were dead. E+W

If such person or persons for whose life or lives such Estates have beene or shall be granted as aforesaid shall remaine beyond the Seas or elsewhere absent themselves in this Realme by the space of seaven yeares together and noe sufficient and evident proofe be made of the lives of such person or persons respectively in any Action commenced for recovery of such Tenements by the Lessors or Reversioners in every such case the person or persons upon whose life or lives such Estate depended shall be accounted as naturally dead, And in every Action brought for the recovery of the said Tenements by the Lessors or Reversioners their Heires or Assignes, the Judges before whom such Action shall be brought shall direct the Jury to give their Verdict as if the person soe remaining beyond the Seas or otherwise absenting himselfe were dead.

II. . . . . F1 E+W

Annotations:

Annotations are used to give authority for changes and other effects on the legislation you are viewing and to convey editorial information. They appear at the foot of the relevant provision or under the associated heading. Annotations are categorised by annotation type, such as F-notes for textual amendments and I-notes for commencement information (a full list can be found in the Editorial Practice Guide). Each annotation is identified by a sequential reference number. For F-notes, M-notes and X-notes, the number also appears in bold superscript at the relevant location in the text. All annotations contain links to the affecting legislation.

Amendments (Textual)

F1 S. II repealed by Statute Law Revision Act 1948 (c. 62), Sch. 1

III. . . . . F2 E+W

Annotations:

Annotations are used to give authority for changes and other effects on the legislation you are viewing and to convey editorial information. They appear at the foot of the relevant provision or under the associated heading. Annotations are categorised by annotation type, such as F-notes for textual amendments and I-notes for commencement information (a full list can be found in the Editorial Practice Guide). Each annotation is identified by a sequential reference number. For F-notes, M-notes and X-notes, the number also appears in bold superscript at the relevant location in the text. All annotations contain links to the affecting legislation.

Amendments (Textual)

F2S. III repealed by Statute Law Revision Act 1863 (c. 125)

IV If the supposed dead Man prove to be alive, then the Title is revested. Action for mean Profits with Interest. E+W

[X2 Provided always That if any person or [X3person or] persons shall be evicted out of any Lands or Tenements by virtue of this Act, and afterwards if such person or persons upon whose life or lives such Estate or Estates depend shall returne againe from beyond the Seas, or shall on proofe in any Action to be brought for recovery of the same [to] be made appear to be living; or to have been living at the time of the Eviction That then and from thenceforth the Tennant or Lessee who was ousted of the same his or their Executors Administrators or Assigns shall or may renter repossess have hold and enjoy the said Lands or Tenements in his or their former Estate for and during the Life or Lives or so long term as the said person or persons upon whose Life or Lives the said Estate or Estates depend shall be living, and also shall upon Action or Actions to be brought by him or them against the Lessors Reversioners or Tennants in possession or other persons respectively which since the time of the said Eviction received the Profits of the said Lands or Tenements recover for damages the full Profits of the said Lands or Tenements respectively with lawful Interest for and from the time that he or they were ousted of the said Lands or Tenements, and kept or held out of the same by the said Lessors Reversioners Tennants or other persons who after the said Eviction received the Profits of the said Lands or Tenements or any of them respectively as well in the case when the said person or persons upon whose Life or Lives such Estate or Estates did depend are or shall be dead at the time of bringing of the said Action or Actions as if the said person or persons where then living.]

Annotations:

Annotations are used to give authority for changes and other effects on the legislation you are viewing and to convey editorial information. They appear at the foot of the relevant provision or under the associated heading. Annotations are categorised by annotation type, such as F-notes for textual amendments and I-notes for commencement information (a full list can be found in the Editorial Practice Guide). Each annotation is identified by a sequential reference number. For F-notes, M-notes and X-notes, the number also appears in bold superscript at the relevant location in the text. All annotations contain links to the affecting legislation.

Editorial Information

X2annexed to the Original Act in a separate Schedule

X3Variant reading of the text noted in The Statutes of the Realm as follows: O. omits [O. refers to a collection in the library of Trinity College, Cambridge]

50

THE NATIONAL BANKING ASSOCIATION

Philosophy And Mission

At the heart of its purpose, the National Banking Association as set up by James Thomas McBride, Postmaster General, has a purpose as the flow through of the good faith and equity that has been so diligently recorded and used for military benefit. It is we that created the value in the trusts that are both global and personal. It is we that are the beneficiaries. It is we the people that need to recognize this truth and take the action to realign the purpose away from the financing of the war machines and the purposeful creation of conflict for prosperity of the kingdoms. He states:

"The process of shifting into a new money system involves the removing the blocks to allow the energy to continue its natural flow back to source. As the source is our estates it must return to us having been transmuted into value. We must facilitate the forward movement of the energy. You cannot UNDO something that has been created. You move through the blocks to settle or balance the energy. Moving through this is the key fore as we move through it we transmute the negative blocked negative energy to a positive, healing energy. Negative energy only has negative effects on the people because of the blocks.

This is zero point! Everything stays at a balanced zero. All needs are met while all debts are satisfied leaving the sum total at zero point. Abundance in balance! We are the alchemists! It is not for us to transmute lead to gold, but, to transmute the dark energy to light! That is the true value, not the gold! That is what discharge of debt is all about. These blocked negative energies are returned to the natural flow and as it returns to source, mother earth, the negative energy becomes whole again and one with the light ..... alchemy at its best!" James Thomas: McBride June 2012

James further states: *"Many years ago I learned that I had the ability to work with the energies. I learned that I could transmute the negative energy into healing energy and redirect that healing energy to where ever I liked. Some time ago I connected the outer grid with the earth grid like a regulator or shock absorber to assist in balancing the* energy in any crisis. Recently it came to my attention that these electrical grids reached into every room of every home in America and into nearly every home in the world. I connected that physical grid to the outer and inner grids to extend the shock absorbing ability in case of extreme drama in the world. There is a portal at the location that has been chosen for the seat of government and now I can and do inject divine energy into the grid which flows to every home on earth and discharges the negative, stressful, chaotic energy and returns it to source. This is the as above to the as below of the new banking system we created to facilitate the return of the natural flow of energy and transition into the new world. This is true divine alchemy. Transmuting the living energy from dark into light."

"And in taking this lesson to heart, the solution I found rested upon a new flow of energy within the existing corporate system but within the context of positive light--freeing the good faith and credit so as to flow it as the positive energy with its intrinsic values back to where it originated. "

"The new banking system has been established and is to work through the postal services of the world. The post office has been continuously solvent from its creation. Postal Money Orders are still backed by gold. Since we know that the post office will take fiat money and give you a gold backed Money Order in the exchange, we know that they know how to do the exchange from public to private funds. They do it every day. We know that the post office is capable of operating and charging the prepaid accounts and that the people are able to access the services of the post office in nearly every part of the world."

"So, here we have the basis for the new banking system with potential access from every computer on earth. The international banking community and the UPU both have existing banking software to handle the required services at the necessary volume to make this work in the shortest upstart time frame."

"As a process of implementation with the UPU and actually establishing this for the American people, Switzerland has announced this new banking system for the entire world which was designed to discharge debt and return the value to the people, worldwide. It is here that the Postmaster General James Thomas placed a pass through account as the prepaid account upon which all services where to be billed. As it is the United States, the franchised owner/operator of the US Postal Service [USPS] he instructed the UPU that the Office of the PMG and the people, in original jurisdiction, would be piggy backing off of the services of the USPS and the UPU, charged against the prepaid account."

As James states: "When the banks created the debt they hypothecated it 10 times. Therefore, if we suddenly discharge all of the personal debt of the people thru this account, we still have 90% of the private funds available for our use which must be discharged. As I see it, these funds will be made available to secure the basic needs of every man, woman and child on earth. We have banking software for use in monthly auto payments where one can set up their monthly bills, rent, utilities, etc. to be automatically paid each month. I foresee this being made available to ensure that all of the survival needs of the people are met. This alone changes the entire game on earth. Now, we have the opportunity to seek out our passion in life where one will receive a currency of value or a barter system will provide the extras one might like to enjoy in life."

"We know that we are transitioning towards a system without currency for currency is a tool of lack and limitation, to a world of true abundance. With we truly have an *abundance of everything available to us at any, every given time then there is no need to store up or save up for a rainy day, Thus, no need for currency. This is a transition that may take 50-100 years, but, I believe this new banking system will facilitate this transition over the long haul."*

"This is exciting stuff that we are developing/ creating right here and now in the here and now. I not only see it in my mind's eye I feel it as it takes root and begins to manifest into reality. This system sets the stage for the "delivery of the prosperity packages."

"The Office of the PMG truly is one of the Trustees of the Global Trust. Is it not the Fiduciary / Trustee who is the proper party administrate the estates of the people, the Global estate trust, for the benefit of the people. And in preparation for so doing, a new banking system is created and will be run by the Post Office, Trustees of the world."

"This is just the beginning of the good things which can be done through this office. As true Trustees of the Global Trust we can inject the light and love of the Divine into the trusteeship and forever change the world in which we live. For me, this has been 500 years in the making .... and today, we have arrived! The time has come to really apply our powers of alchemy to transmute this world." James Thomas May 2012

National Banking Association

Those who constitute an association nationwide of private, unincorporated persons engaged in the business of banking to issue notes against these obligations of the United States due them; whose private property is at risk to collateralize the government's debt and currency, by legal definitions, a 'national banking association'; such notes, issued against these obligations of the United States to that part of the public debt due its Principals and Sureties are required by law to be accepted as "legal tender" of payments for all debts public and private, and are defined in law as "obligations of the United States", on the same par and category with Federal reserve Notes and other currency and legal tender obligations."

In the operation of commerce in Bankruptcy, or Receivership, a Public Official may refuse a valid request, one time. That first request is done in the VOLUNTARY Bankruptcy side of the transaction. A Public Official's refusal, or Dishonour, charges the INVOLUNTARY Bankruptcy and their mandatory obligation to honour your request. They have a mandatory obligation to honour your request when presented the second time. Their refusal to honour your second request is Bankruptcy Obstruction and constitutes a dialectal default and their voluntary surrender or abandonment of their office and all power and authority therein.

It is noted that as of this date, this particular phase is in fast evolution. Part of this process requires that certain documents be sent out and membership be in place. This will be covered later.

51

THE PROCESS OF CURE FOR James-Thomas: Mcbride

Changing The System Flow Of Money Energy

If you have arrived at this place in the book, you may ponder what it is that must be done on the commercial side that would divorce you from the Strawman employed by PLANET EARTH and acquire access to the Good Faith and Credit held in the Strawman Trust. In this set of Chapters, we are going to use the case of James-Thomas Mcbride as the example. There are always forerunners, warriors of truth that open the path and slash their way through the labyrinth. It is stated that this process that James Thomas reveals to us may not be the perfect solution because the establishment is not yet willing to rollover and agree so it is evolving. However, what the process undertaken by James Thomas reveals is that it is "state of the art" from which the truth WILL come to the surface. As you read these chapters, you will see how the new truths brought forward in Part 1 form the basis for this implementation which we call a "cure".

It is indeed a complex world of commercial and religious "takeover "that has allowed the PLANET EARTH business plan to evolve to a very critical point in time. The question arises as to how is it possible that such a monolithic dynasty could fall and effectively allow the meek to inherit the earth? How are the blocks in the system removed? How does a mere mortal face the great goliaths and survive.

Over time, history shows that all dynasties have fallen. It is the way energy works. As to how and when, it appears that that time is now because it has shown itself as two distinct pathways where the people will choose. and the consciousness that now prevails is as mighty as the powers that held it back. It is no secret in mass marketing that when a critical point in consciousness arises (like the mentality of a stock market crash) to a certain point that consciousness (shift from bull to bear market mentality) becomes the manifestor of that reality. Similarly, mass marketing works that way in that when people of mass consciousness believe a certain product is needed, the others simply follow without question to consume the same brand. DNA is like that too. When a critical threshold is reached (like the monkey effect) a certain instinct or habit simply becomes encoded in all DNA as quantum update.

The mass consciousness as we has explained, has occurred in the last decade. It is at the same time as the powers that be plan their grand finale of their business plan: New World Order versus the New Order of the Ages.

In this new consciousness, millions now seek out the truth in the light of peace and new look at the real God who has cleverly hidden Himself within us and our hearts. Each individual can now open to this and share the new knowing as a grain of sand that will, when the winds of consciousness blow on the grains, form a dune, then a mountain. In seeking this path of truth both spiritual and commercial, we have been dedicated to the revelation of a new truth so as to present a choice in a new light. It within this context that James Thomas of the family McBride has dedicated his work, and now presents the secrets of navigating the labyrinth of commerce within the mindset of the new spiritual consciousness. It is not to wage war but to carry light of peace. it is not for inequality and dominion but to acknowledged we are all One and spiritually interconnected. It is not in hatred and conflict but in love and without judgment. it is not about sin, it is about we as perfection.

And so now we open to the assimilation of the knowledge s far presented into the process of cure, with particular attention to what James Thomas of the family McBride learned, implemented and executed. This process will now be become familiar in the reasons behind its structure and content.

In effect, each human who is registered at birth has become an employee of PLANET EARTH INC. subservient to the administrative incorporated body of the City of London called the CROWN, AKA: the BRITISH CROWN, [In America, it is the administrative incorporated body politic called the UNITED STATES of the District/City of COLUMBIA]; and thus, the owner of those corporate City States, the Pontiff of Rome and his HOLY ROMAN EMPIRE, the primal head corporation of the World.

James reports:

"Since we are dealing with and subjected to people who have unknowingly chosen to believe that they are officers on a make-believe ship at sea called a corporate body, as are the nature of Governments and Nations, the prevalent belief is that their assigned duty is to discipline disobedient crewmembers. Unknowingly ALL property, including labour, and the fruits of labour of the people/slaves belongs to the "slave" owner, the Pontiff of Rome, and his Holy Roman Empire, through his agency, the corporate Crown of the City of London. Or, in America, it is the corporate UNITED STATES]- with the Pontiff of Rome being the claimed to be direct owner of that legal, financial, and professional accreditation enclave within Greater London. And since all Courts are primarily used for dealing with "slave disobedience" [against the rules of the slave owner - acts, statutes, laws, rules, regulations and edicts], it is very difficult to come up with any exact remedy against such violations of TRUE LAW and UNALIENABLE RIGHTS perpetrated by Governments and Agencies of Government. It is primarily because they exist within fiction, mythology in their land of "Make Believe".

Thus, all any researcher, like myself (James Thomas), can accomplish is to enlighten you on how you became a slave, where the very labour of your mind and body belongs to another evil worldly power, and you can, and will be severely punished for disobedience to the slave owner's rules, and for not accounting for and pledging that property to the agencies that exist under the authority of the Pontiff and Cardinals of Rome. We can only suggest possible peaceful remedies to the gross wrongs and violations against your right to life that have been so deceitfully imposed upon you, but history shows that those methods of redress usually are only partially effective or are ineffective, or will be made ineffective by more deceit, lies or myths in their fantasy dictatorship. But, notwithstanding the above statement, we must continue to follow the rule set out by Winston Churchill, as found at the bottom of this webpage. And, we may be in phase two, or even three of his observed necessity of action. Remember, labour is your time, Life is time. Therefore, when your labour, or the fruits of your labour, are confiscated, your life is taken. The Rule of Necessity [derived from Creator God's Law] says that you can use the force necessary to defend your life."

Communications From The New Postmaster General

In the forgoing information there are three important websites that are `pulse of the new Postmaster General:

www.postmastergeneralna.org
www.office-of-pmg.com/index.html and **www.postmastergeneralna.org** This is the official Office of the Postmaster
www.legal-registries.com/index.html This is the official Repository for special documents of the Postmaster Office
www.notice-recipient.com/index.html This is the communications arm of the Postmaster General

The following material is taken from these websites:

On the websites, **James Thomas** further states: *"These sites are interlinked and provide an information and communications network connecting freeholders around the world to assist us all in bringing order out of the chaos as we enter and begin co-creating our new world.*

"We have a nice research and articles section that we are adding to every day. We have a great deal of material that was on **www.theTrustee911.com** *site which many have requested be posted that we hope to have up in the days to come."*

"The information, documents and the process presented here are the result of countless hours of research by tens of thousands of people. There are those who have invested a great deal of their life energy making their research available for all. We will direct you to those people and those sites as well. We gladly send you to their sites and thank them for their efforts to expose the truth so that we may all return from being lost in a sea of illusion."

The information that follows, particularly the reference documentation to the authority of the new Postmaster General is provided here and it may be freely downloaded from the sites. Of note is that the purpose of presenting this is not for use; it is for education. In this particular business, it is always advisable to go to the source; just like in the spiritual area-GO TO THE SOURCE. Of relevance in closing this particular Part of the book is the process by which the sentient human James Thomas of the Family McBride reclaimed his true status and separated himself from the Corporate entity JAMES THOMAS McBRIDE.

Also, the process of claim on the seat of Postmaster, the claim of authority, the definition of a peace treaty and the creation of the flow through national banking system via the Federal Reserve is explained.

In the final Part 3, the simplified process will be brought forward to all who choose that take a similar path. Before this we will begin with a summary of critical information. Although this is a repeat, it serves to bring it back into the awareness light.

Breach Of Divine Estate And Funding The Military Complex

For decades the Divine Estate(s) of the American people have been leveraged to fund the Military Industrial Complex which has raped, pillaged and plundered the world resulting in the impoverishment and enslavement of the people. This has all simply been a part of the business plan of those bloodline kingdoms that direct the mission of Corporation PLANET EARTH in its invisible fictional corporate system down to the STRAWMEN and STRAWWOMEN in the POSTAL ZONES. The controlling factors have been the Rule Books of GOD as the WORD and the LAW as attached to corporate entities as Acts, Statutes, Bills and what is called the code of law. In this way, the religious and monetary command and authority has been accepted to the point of world domination by debt money and Vatican endorsements.

And so it has come to pass that our Divine Estates have been leveraged to fund the endless wars and violence resulting in the death of over 100 million people in the past century to satisfy the greed and lust for power and control by the few over the many.

The entire earth has been tainted by the touch of this Military Industrial Complex which has brought us a constant diet of fear, violence and death as it waged war against all of humanity. Clearly it has been "good business" to instigate, finance, and enjoy the spoils of war and conflict. This Military Industrial Complex has employed the use of fear, terrorism and out of control debt created out of thin air to support their weapon of choice, the Federal Reserve Banking System, for the purpose of re-assigning and using our Divine Inheritance, our birthright.

And so it has come to pass that world peace is NOT a privilege! Abundance and Prosperity is NOT a privilege! Peace and harmony are NOT a privilege! They are our Birthright!! Our Divine Inheritance! And no man, agency or entity may tax, license or limit your Divine Estate, your Divine Inheritance, without your consent. Yet this has not been the path of evolution simply because the business enterprise of PLANET EARTH and its directors have been able to implement their own designs for dominion.

James Thomas McBride states: "*As one of the Trustees of the Global Trust, under whose direction the United States operates, I have identified and demanded a cure for* **the Breach of Trust** *which created the Military Industrial Complex which authorizes the Federal Reserve Banks to leverage our Divine Estate(s) wreaking havoc on the people of earth.*"

"*The evidence of the Breach and Demand for the Cure thereof, as well as my standing to receive a cure thereto has been argued and adjudicated at the highest level and it has been Decreed that a breach of trust must be declared:*"

A Cure To The Breach Must Be Declared

"*The Pass Through Account has been activated to facilitate the charging of the sub accounts releasing the blocked private funds for the administration of the Estate Trusts of the people in original jurisdiction in harmony with the original intent of the trusts. The stage has been set for the administration of our Divine Estate(s), our abundance and prosperity, in original jurisdiction for our benefit, bringing about world peace and Global Debt Forgiveness in the transition.*

Further, this Cure must be made available to anyone and everyone who seeks it!

The Cure to the Breach of Trust which removes you and your Divine Estate from the grasp of the Military Industrial Complex and returns you and your estate to original jurisdiction, activating your abundance and prosperity is provided herein as a gift of this Trustee of the Global Trust.

As one of the Trustees of the Global Trust, creator of this site and author of much of the material which is freely shared herein one might notice certain spiritual principles which express themselves through me and my work. This is not about religion nor any need to compel the reader to believe as I do. I believe there is room enough in this world for a great diversity of beliefs to co-exist in peace and harmony. I believe that spiritual and personal sovereignty is the Birthright of every living being.

From the beginning, please understand, as the creator of these site and author of much of the writings herein, I am but a cog in the Universal wheel of humanity that made it possible. I simply did my part. The information presented herein is the compilation and evolution of the millions of man hours of research by thousands of selfless men and women dedicated to unravelling the illusion in which we live to bring about the rebirth of personal and spiritual sovereignty for all mankind.

I wish to thank all who steadfastly held tight to the belief that world peace, abundance and prosperity, was not a privilege, but like personal and spiritual sovereignty, they are our birthright; For all of those courageous men and women who understood that if we did not stand up and expose the illusion and corruption in our lifetime that our children and their children would be enslaved forever and chose to stand against the terrorist tactics of the Military Industrial Complex at their own peril and sacrifice. I also wish to thank all of the families of those dedicated souls who lived with the sacrifice, the pain and loss, for you too did your part and have been a motivating factor which moved us through the corruption and chaos. Because of all of our sacrifice(s) we stand today at the doorway of a great evolutionary leap for mankind.

So, let's begin from the beginning, at the Divine Right of Use Today, everything is held in trust. Everything is about trusts, Implied or Expressed. The Creator gave man dominion over all things. Dominion over means control over NOT ownership. This is a Divine Right of Use

A Divine Right of Use of the Divine property/ the All of earth which is held in trust. So, the entire world we call earth is held in trust, the Divine Trust, for our benefit as Beneficiaries. This Global Divine Trust is an Implied Trust as opposed to an Expressed Trust. In the beginning man was responsible, as a Trustee, for the care and well being of that portion of the Divine Estate upon which he/she exercised their Divine Right of Use as a Beneficiary.

Through the decades man has given over that Divine fiduciary obligation to legal fiction trustees. There are as many forms of trusteeships as there are people in the world. Some very fair and equitable, say a republic, all the way to a dictatorship, each with various degrees of freedoms and rights, taxes and limitations.

Who is the Trustee responsible for your piece of the Divine Estate, our Global Estate Trust? In America today we have Township Trustees, County Trustees, State Trustees and Federal Trustees just to name a few of the many levels of fiduciaries within the Trusteeship which is involved in the administration of our Divine Estate(s), the Global Estate Trust. Judges, Clerks of Court, Prosecutors and Attorneys all play their own part in the administration of our Global Estate Trust leveraging our Divine Estates to rape, pillage and plunder the world and enslave the people.

To unravel this intentionally complex Trusteeship of the Global Estate Trust let us begin at the top and work our way down. The Vatican boasts, in their Papal Bull, dominion over the entire earth, via conquest, and is answerable ONLY to the Divine Spirit. Dominion over means control over, not ownership. The Vatican's un-rebutted claims establish them as the Primary Trustee of the Global Estate Trust, our Divine Inheritance; a very unpopular fact. But a fact that opens a doorway placing the cure for the mis-administration and theft of our Divine Inheritance within our grasp.

The Vatican is the Primary Trustee of the Global Estate Trust. To facilitate the administration of this Global Trust the Vatican established the Universal Postal Union as the Secondary Trustees of the Global Trust charged with dividing the Global Trust into zones and endowing these legal fiction zones with sovereign authority to facilitate the efficient administration of the Global Trust.

It is no surprise that the first requirement for the international acknowledgment of a sovereign nation is the necessity of a Post Office. The primary objective of the military in any 'zone' is the protection of the Post, or the Post Office, for in their original jurisdiction, the Postmaster Generals are the Trustees of their respective zone.

In 1789 the Continental Congress passed a bill to "establish the seat of government, a general post office, under the direction of the Postmaster General." That's right, a general post office under the direction of the Postmaster General. They were further dividing the postal zone of North America establishing a new zone, and endowing it with sovereign authority, whereby our founding fathers believed they could establish a Trusteeship which would ensure that sovereignty of the people would be passed down to the people of future generations.

The Preamble to the Constitution created the Estate Trust which held the freedoms guaranteed in the Articles of Confederation and the Declaration of Independence in trust for future generations. The Articles of the Constitution established the Trusteeship as well as the powers and limitations thereof. The Congress and Senate were Trustees charged with the Administration of our Divine Inheritance, the Global Estate Trust.

In this 'general post office' seat of government there was established the 'civil administration' called the United States. Civil administration ? What do they administrate? Our Divine Estate Trust, the Global Trust, our Divine Inheritance. Remember, we can never OWN anything. We simply have a Divine Right of Use of the property of the Divine Estate, the Global Trust.

So, we the people of this earth have a Divine Right of use of the Global Trust while the civil administration is charged with the administration of our estate for our benefit. In the world of trusts Civil Administration/ Government = Trusteeship.

So, the entire world is held in trust. The Global Estate Trust, our Divine Inheritance, our birthright is held in trust and is administrated by the various 'governments' who gain their sovereign authority via the Universal Postal Union, the Secondary Trustee of the Global Trust answerable to the Vatican.

In the world of trusts and trust law, rights, duties and obligations are very straight forward, cut and dry, black and white. There are no opinions, secret codes, rules or statutes, period. These are just the facts. There is a chain of command, consequences for your actions, or lack thereof, and accountability.

It has been a slow and cumbersome process to overcome the out of control momentum of the civil administrators of the world today. There have been countless casualties as a result of our efforts to unravel the illusion; to overcome the programming and fear which fuelled the beast to reach the core where truth and accountability resides."

The Need For The Universal Postal Treaty

Further, James Thomas McBride explains the importance of the Postal Treaty that was presented in a previous chapter:

"The International Postal Treaty For The Americas, 2010 stems from a Claim On Abandonment that has been received and accepted at the absolute highest levels wherein the Abandonment of all creditor claims against the UNITED STATES was documented (dilectual default) as well as the abandonment of all sovereign rights, power and authority of the general post office commonly known as the UNITED STATES and the relinquishment of the 'pledge' or the release of all pledged property of the sovereign people of America and subsequent claim on said abandonment for and by We the sovereign people of America.

The bankruptcy obstruction and overt impairment of the absolute priority right of redemption by the CREDITOR Federal Reserve Bank and banking families has established in fact the CREDITOR'S operation in equity in bad faith and with unclean hands and constitutes a delictual default and abandonment of all CREDITOR claims and the relinquishment of the PLEDGED property; and

The bankruptcy obstruction and overt impairment of the absolute priority right of redemption by the COURTS has established in fact the general post office styled as the UNITED STATES' operation in equity in bad faith and with unclean hands and constitutes a delictual default and abandonment of all equity claims of the UNITED STATES and their voluntary abandonment of all sovereign rights, power and authority associated therewith; and the sovereign people of America, through and by James-Thomas: McBride, private postmaster, have served Notice of the Abandonment and registered the priority claim on the abandonment."

<u>The Claim on Abandonment by the sovereign people of America has been received and accepted without objection or dispute.</u>

"The general post office styled as the UNITED STATES has been in a perpetual state of war since its inception. The 'Powers That Be' have used the UNITED STATES as a weapon to wage war on the sovereign people of America, operating under the Emergency War Powers Act and the secret presumption that the sovereign people are the enemy of the UNITED STATES for the purpose of evading their liabilities under the original equity contract and to pillage and plunder the private property of the people they were created to serve.

The general post office styled as the UNITED STATES has been used as a weapon to wage an economic war at arms length against all of the people of the world bringing all of humanity to the brink of destruction as the CREDITOR'S master plan of total economic slavery over the sovereign people of the world has been implemented.

The Powers That Be have used the UNITED STATES as a weapon to wage war on the sovereign people of the world via the unconscionable creation, production and distribution of harmful drugs for the purpose of enslaving the people and funding and executing their genocide against humanity.

The Powers That Be have used the UNITED STATES as a platform for their propaganda, creating the world's problems and then presenting themselves as the world's savior bringing about the solution and protection from their self created illusionary boogie men for the purpose of enslaving the sovereign people of the world.

And so it has been necessary to let humanity and the Powers that from a specific day forward the UNITED STATES shall be used as a tool, actuated by humility, to promote universal peace, love and unity among all men. The UNITED STATES shall become a broker and facilitator of peace; a springboard for ascension and balance within the world consciousness. The UNITED STATES shall immediately stand down and withdraw itself from all acts of aggression and vacate all occupied land and shall immediately bring all American soldiers home.

The agents and agencies of the UNITED STATES shall immediately cease and desist in all forms of gun and drug production and distribution, all forms of terrorism and genocide of the people, all standard operating procedure of the powers that be since the days of the East India trading Company.

All Administrative Agencies of the UNITED STATES shall immediately remove all gold fringed military flags from their offices and courtrooms and shall display the civilian flag of peace. The Custodian of the Alien Property shall immediately update his/her files, removing the names and private property of the American people from their files/lists and make the return of the property to the rightful owners. All administrative agencies and administrative courts shall operate in peace and honor, servants of the sovereign people.

The jurisdiction of the courts of the united states is described as the American flag of peace; red, white and blue with stripes of red and white horizontally placed in alteration. Under the jurisdiction of the American flag of peace the private rights of the sovereign people of the united states are protected and all rights are preserved. Here, the People are 'innocent until proven guilty.' Under the military gold fringed flag there are no rights.

The general post office styled as the UNITED STATES is a free republic operating under the concepts and intent of the Articles Of Confederation, establishing a perpetual Union between the several free and independent states, to wit:

A 'Transitional Committee' shall be seated for the purpose of ensuring a peaceful and efficient transition from an Empirical War based mentality and operating system to one of peace, humility and unity. Said Transitional Committee shall establish and empower an interim government for the united states of America and shall operate until such time as the people can be duly informed as to the true history of the UNITED STATES and the fraud that has been perpetrated against them, not to exceed one year.

The Postmaster general of the organic post office for the united states, creator of the general post office styled as the UNITED STATES and located within the ten miles square commonly known as Washington, D.C., under whose direction the UNITED STATES operates, shall operate in the capacity of trustee for the people and shall take instructions from the Transitional Committee until such time as the Interim government shall be seated and empowered.

All debt of the UNITED STATES, except that debt owed to the sovereign people of America, has been abandoned and vacated and the UNITED STATES has DECLARED PEACE with the world and the sovereign people thereof, therefore, the gold fringed military flag designating the admiralty/maritime jurisdiction shall be immediately removed from all courtrooms, meeting rooms, etc. of the administrative agencies of the UNITED STATES and the civil peace flag of the united states of America shall be proudly displayed in their stead..

The U.S. Courts who have been operating as debt collection facilities under TWEA and the EMERGENCY WAR POWERS ACT shall immediately make the corrections and cure the torts against the people, vacating all claims, attachments and/or restrictions on the private rights of the sovereign people and make them whole.

The courts, as well as all administrative agencies of the UNITED STATES, shall share resources making room for and facilitating the establishment of the organic courts, operating under the common law, for the adjudication of all matters concerning the sovereign American people, other than the prosecution of grievances against an administrative agency for the trespass of the private rights of the people. All administrative agencies shall actively participate in the establishment of two distinctly separate systems, common law and administrative, operating side by side for the benefit of the CREDITORS, the sovereign people of America.

All administrative courts and agencies of the UNITED STATES shall operate in good faith and honor as servants of the sovereign people of America. Said administrative courts and agencies have grown out of control, beyond the intent of the original founders and their usefulness and shall begin to make the corrections, a reversal, bringing about balance, transparency, full disclosure and honor for the remedy of the Real Parties In Interest.

All debts of the UNITED STATES have been abandoned, except the debt to the sovereign people; The Pledge of the private property of the American people has been relinquished, therefore, the administrative agencies of the UNITED STATES shall make the return of the interest back to source, the sovereign people.

The UNITED STATES shall immediately activate the established pass through account, vacate the blocks on the asset accounts and make the financial adjustments to discharge the debt and return the accounts of the sovereign people back into balance. The UNITED STATES shall maintain the natural flow and balance in the accounts for the remedy of the people, returning the interest back to source in the discharge of debt against the pre-paid account, at all times remaining in honor.

The UNITED STATES shall immediately make the corrections as concerns the unlawful restrictions of the liberties of the sovereign people by the administrative agencies of the UNITED STATES;

All Deeds, warranty deeds, trust deeds, sheriff deeds, tax deeds and all Certificates of Title are colorable titles issued to facilitate the 'Pledge' of the private property of the sovereign people. The Pledge has been relinquished, therefore, the UNITED STATES shall make the corrections to discharge all colorable titles, make the re-conveyance and issue the land patent/ allodial title for the property back to the people.

It is the duty of the military to serve and protect the post, therefore, the UNITED STATES military shall serve and protect the sovereign people of America, the creditor of the UNITED STATES. All branches of the U.S. Military shall follow the orders of the Transitional Committee, interim government and government of the republic, respectively throughout this transition.

The Provost Marshals are the organic police force with a duty to serve and protect the sovereign. The Provost Marshal shall immediately serve and protect all who claim protection under this treaty making top priority any/all requests for assistance on claims of unlawful restrictions on the liberties of a sovereign.

There shall be those members of the sovereign people, ambassadors, with a passion to service, who shall choose to serve the republic; lightworkers, visionaries, warriors, teachers and people knowledgeable in the art of peace and love; to serve as watchdogs or compliance, ensuring the integrity and protection of the people's rights; or facilitators and educators charged with presenting real truth, that the enslavement of the sovereign people may never happen again; beacons of light, guiding the people out of the darkness, into the truth;

There shall be those members of the sovereign people who shall be instrumental in breathing life into the civil government of the republic, bringing empowerment to the counties at large; in interfacing with the administrative agents and agencies to compel performance and compliance, to bring about balance and restore the natural flow of energy; to empower the civil government, the people; to nurture and infuse this fledgling republic with peace, light and love; to rise above the fear; to be the light;

These members of the sovereign people, awakened into the truth, compelled to service, may apply to accede hereto; upon receipt, acceptance and registration of the application and Public Declarations shall be empowered as a Private Postmaster of a non-independent postal zone, with all of the rights, power and authority of a wholly sovereign nation, with the authority to seat civilian citizen grand juries; to empower judges in the common law, Rangers and Inspectors with the power and authority to compel performance; to make the corrections to bring compliance and honor within the administration.

The power shall reside with the people on the county. It shall take the agreement of no less than three (3) private postmasters to empower a judge or Ranger who shall serve the people under guidelines presented by the Transition Committee and/or interim government."

Declaring And Establishing The Rightful Claims

Before heading into the next chapters to explain and illustrate the documentation for the claim of authority, it is important to note that this is the process that the years of research by James McBride and many others that has come to fruition; into a set of documents that are the mainstay for what other individual can do by choice, and for James McBride, the basis for a more simplified version which will be shown in Part 3.

In the following chapter, many legal documents are explained in summary form that abide by the "Law of the Land "and commerce. The list below is found on the website at **www.postmastergeneralna.org** and provided as a summary:

Serving Notice on Breach of Trust
 Documentary Evidence of Authority, gaining authority as Trustee
 Ecclesiastic Deed Poll defines harm, notice of protest, demands for cure

Activation of Authority Federal Reserve
 Activation of Federal Reserve Account
  Exhibit A: Declaration of Political Status
  Exhibit B: Affidavit of Fact-Title Dispute
  Exhibit C: Notice of Surety Act and Bond and related documents;
  Exhibit D: OHIO DEPARTMENT OF HEALTH, CERTIFICATE OF LIVE BIRTH
  Exhibit E: Fidelity Investments Symbol Look-up
  Exhibit F: UCC-1 Financing Statement File
  Exhibit G: NOTICE OF ENTITLEMENT RIGHT-
  Exhibit H: PRIVATE INDEMNITY AND SET-OFF BOND
  Exhibit I: ACKNOWLEDGEMENT OF AN ORIGINAL ISSUE OF CURRENCY
  Exhibit J: SOCIAL SECURITY CARD for JAMES THOMAS MCBRIDE
  Exhibit K: Form 56 Notice Concerning Fiduciary Relationship

Reclaiming Trusteeship and Postal Authority
 Charging Sheet
 Claim on Abandonment

Declaration of Peace
 Universal Postal Treaty Declaration of Peace

These are provided on www.postmastergeneralna.org

52

SERVING NOTICE ON THE BREACH OF TRUST

The first part of establishing one's truth and position includes the following:

Documentary Evidence of Authority, gaining authority as Trustee
Ecclesiastic Deed Poll defines harm, notice of protest, demands for cure

These documents as created and served by James-Thomas: McBride are summarized here

Authority As Trustee For The Global Abundance Program

The pages in this chapter provide the details as documentary evidence of James-Thomas: McBride serving notice towards the attainment of having authority as Trustee and the authority for this Global Abundance & Prosperity Program. You may refer to the web site **www.office-of-pmg.com/files/TheBeginning.html.** **or** **www.postmastergeneral.na.org**

James qualifies the information:

"What is presented is the result of years of study and research, by myself and others; years of documents and processes building one upon the other, continually moving forward. Please understand that my studies, my work and my tenacious efforts and unfailing refusal to cave to the pressures of The Powers That Be [TPTB] have cost me 16 years of my personal freedom, two marriages, the repeated loss of all material things and the loss of my relationships with my family and friends. There have been countless casualties throughout the years. I have been blessed to have studied and worked alongside some of the best and most dedicated souls who have filled this gruelling journey with love and hope for all of mankind. We have lost many a good man/woman along the way to whom I say Thank You..... Bless you where ever you are today. Your work and your energy lives on through these pages.

My point being, Freedom does not come without a cost. Freedom will not be delivered to your door as you sit all content on the couch. Freedom takes diligence, an ever watchful

eye and the willingness to take back your power; Your willingness to put aside the fear and doubt and allow truth to shine through and manifest in your reality.

Freedom, Abundance and Prosperity will not come from the knock on the door, but, will begin within, for our outer world is but a reflection of that which is within. If in our heart we harbour thoughts and/or beliefs of lack, wanting, poverty and/or limitation then lack, wanting, poverty and limitation is what will be reflected into our outer reality. The change we seek must begin within.

So that no man, woman nor child should ever have to travel the pothole laden path which was my journey, I give you the following to light your way to personal and spiritual sovereignty. I/we have done 95% of the work for you, we have blazed the trial, clearing away the briers and thorns, but, each man, woman and child must still carry the ball the rest of the way Home. For even in the acceptance of a gift, one must reach out one's hand and take hold of that gift and bring it into your reality.

This is my gift to the world. Reach out, take this gift and make it your own; take it in; own it to your core, for personal and spiritual sovereignty is our Birthright! World Peace, Abundance & Prosperity is NOT a privilege, it is our Birthright!

We believe that for Abundance & Prosperity to manifest in our lives that we must allow abundance to manifest through us; that abundance & prosperity begin within as a feeling, an expression, and become a way of life. We believe Paying it Forward to be an expression of our abundance in which all may participate, rich or poor; a method of Priming the Well of our abundance, if you will.

This site is my way of Paying It Forward, of investing in America, investing in all mankind, for I see great hope for mankind as we stand on the edge of great change. For this reason I have been Paying It Forward with my work and my life for many years at a great cost to my family and friends. I pray that one day they will understand."

Documentary Evidence Of Authority

"In an attempt to break down and make understandable a complex journey I present this overview of the documents and processes with links to the documents in their entirety for your review. Please take your time for their is a great deal of information. Remember, knowledge is power!

Through the years I had proven the existence of the 'private side' funds, and that one could access those 'private' side funds for the discharge of debt and the Redemption of property from the collateral pool of the Military Industrial Complex. I found the evidence that the UNITED STATES had indeed created funds/ negotiable instruments by leveraging my Birth Certificate and later Court Cases, and that the 'private side' funds sat awaiting my use for the discharge of debt, if only I could access them. Our National debt continues to spiral out of control while the private side funds, which were created to discharge this debt, sit idle.

For years we KNEW that they had monetized our Birth Certificate(s), but, we never had the evidence. Suddenly, it was no longer some "crazy conspiracy Theory", it was now absolute fact evidenced by public documents.

Armed with the evidence that they had monetized my 'account' on several occasions; the knowledge that these 'private funds' where set aside for our use to discharge the debt, and an ever increasing working knowledge of the economic system I set out to Activate my Private Side Account with the Federal Reserve Bank with the knowledge and assistance of the U.S. Treasury.

This account was verified as activated, funds where received as evidence, and the account survived two (2) Secret Service investigations, one which I initiated. Within 72 hours of activation, I received a 'call in the night' informing me that an 'Angel' had been watching my account; that $4 Trillion had been fraudulently moved from the account by the Fiduciary; the funds had been recovered from the Bank of Hong Kong, would I please demand the Secret Service investigate the matter.

On June 3, 2009, within hours of getting the call, I delivered a demand for investigation along with a complete set of documents to the Secret Service.

This is the Pass Thru Account established to discharge debt to facilitate Global Debt Forgiveness, just one goal of this Global Abundance & Prosperity Program. To make the transition from fiat money to currency of value we must discharge the debt in full, a matter of adjusting the digits on a computer screen."

Important Notice To The American People

"When one steps back and looks at the bigger picture he can see that the American people's Good Faith and Credit funding the aggression and occupation of the nations of the world by the Military Industrial Complex costing the lives of over 100 million people since its creation in our name has left a huge stain on the Good Faith and Credit.

From that same perspective one might ask Does the global aggression and occupation by the Military Industrial Complex funded by the Good Faith and Credit of the American people reflect the beliefs and morals of the American people? Are the American people the aggressive and controlling war mongers as expressed through their government to the world or are they simply the powerless puppets of the war machine?

Throughout history the Constitution for the United States established two sets of Congress and Senate each with their own set of rules, regulations and moral operating principles. Each is responsible for the administration of the affairs and estates of the American people, each employing their own brand of administration.

The Constitution established the original Congress and Senate in original jurisdiction. The 14th Amendment established a second congress and senate under whose jurisdiction we operate today, presumably by our own consent.

Throughout our lifetimes we have been tricked and deceived into living under the 14th Amendment as if by choice and consent. The Offices, Agencies, Officials and Agents in original jurisdiction still exist as a choice for the administration of our affairs, our estates, awaiting our return.

It has been oft said that the military, in original jurisdiction, will stand up and protect the American people once they return to original jurisdiction. The great movement by the people to return to original jurisdiction has landed on barren ground, until NOW.

The Powers That Be have acquiesced to the rights and demands of the people !

The Remedy must be made available to every man, woman and child who seeks it!

Today we have a choice, but, for one to make an informed decision one must open one's mind to truth. We, as a people, have become familiar with Denial, unwilling to accept truth if it threatens the status quo or our field of study or endeavour, no matter how convincing the evidence. We seem to be willing to accept the devil we know rather to face the unknown even though the evidence suggests that change would yield wonderful results.

In original jurisdiction a minimalist, non-invasive, public servant mentality exists, where the administration exists entirely for the purpose of service to the people where the core of authority resides with the people on a local level. The Congress and Senate operate under the jurisdiction of the people to ensure the peace and security of the nation. In original jurisdiction world peace is possible.

In original jurisdiction the Treasury of the United States is responsible for the printing and distribution of a currency of value where a debt is established only in the exchange of value as opposed to mere book entry loans of fiat money. In original jurisdiction everything exists NOW to facilitate global debt forgiveness.

In original jurisdiction the military plays a purely defensive role protecting our borders from aggression or invasion. The Coast Guard and Provost Marshals are the people's protection in original jurisdiction, with a duty to ensure against aggression against or the violation of the private rights of the American people by the state and/or its associated agencies.

In original jurisdiction we have a sales tax sufficient to fund the operation of the administration as well as the construction and maintenance of necessary public infrastructures.

In original jurisdiction we have complete transparency of operation where real justice is standard operating procedure and the court and prison systems are used to protect the people from the elements of evil.

The 14th Amendment congress and senate employs an ever expanding bigger is better mentality. The core of authority is coercively wielded from the top down with little meaningful input from the people on a local level. In original jurisdiction the congress and senate operate under the jurisdiction of the people while under the 14th Amendment the people operate under the jurisdiction of congress and senate. We see and experience the mirror image in the two systems as concerns the authority and jurisdiction.

Under the 14th Amendment we have the private Federal Reserve Banking system which issues fiat money created out of thin air, on which the American people pay interest, based on the Good Faith & Credit of the American people, which has purposely lead to insurmountable hyper inflated global debt which has been wielded as a weapon to justify the ever increasing taxation and limitation of the people.

The 14th Amendment established the Military Industrial Complex, funded by the Good Faith & Credit of the American people, who have been the core of the state of perpetual war and aggression which has existed since their creation. Over 100 million people have died at the hands of the Military Industrial Complex since its inception, funded by the American people. World peace would mean the death of the Military Industrial complex as it is war that produces profits.

Under the 14th Amendment Military Industrial Complex we have numerous secret 'Black' ops and 'Black' budgets for use by the ever increasing number of Alphabet Agencies to promote and fund aggression and occupation throughout the world with zero oversight or accountability.

The people have been identified as Enemies of the State in the 14th Amendment congress and senate's Trading With The Enemy Act giving rise to the numerous Wars against the people which have historically proven to exponentially expand the behaviour they purport to war against.

Under the 14th Amendment the courts and prisons are used to leverage the lives of the people for the creation of funds out of thin air and is used to protect the State from the people who fund it.

The War on Drugs has brought us a 100 fold increase in the illicit use of drugs; the protected importation of those illicit drugs by our own ABC organizations and the intentional drugging of America by the huge pharmacy companies resulting in the expansion of the prisons for profit system which exist today.

The War On Terrorism has brought us the extreme expansion of terrorism in the world today which has been used not only to justify the invasion of the private rights of the people but are used today to justify government sanctioned assassinations and the physical and sexual molestation of the people as we travel across this once great land.

The 14th Amendment's Federal Reserve Banking System has brought Foreclosure Gate and the intentional destruction of the American housing industry opening the door for the theft of over fifteen (15) million homes from the American people by the banks.

The 14th Amendment has brought election fraud and special interest groups who now buy their own self serving brand of Legislation to the detriment of the people.

Removing our portion of the Good Faith and Credit that funds the Military Industrial Complex

Removing our portion of the Good Faith and Credit that funds the Military Industrial Complex takes the wind out of the sails of the war machine, the Prison for Profit scheme and the ponzi scheme fiat money systems in which the courts participate.

Removing our portion of the Good Faith and Credit forces a settlement of our accounts, the discharge of debt and a return of the interest to the people which could result in global debt forgiveness and a reboot of the global economic system birthing a system of value.

The matching funds created against our Good Faith and Credit are still available for our use. Removing our portion of the Good Faith and Credit forces the Military Industrial Complex to provide a full accounting of our accounts forcing the release of the private funds held in trust by the DTC, DTCC and OITC for the discharge of debt and redemption of the property, the balance to be administrated as a charitable trust, for our benefit.

So, the choice is: Do we choose to Remove our portion of the Good Faith and Credit that funds the Military Industrial Complex and return it to original jurisdiction where the mechanics for global debt forgiveness already exist and allow the rebooting of an economic system of value, honor and integrity?

Do we choose to remove our portion of the Good Faith and Credit taking the profit out of the war machine opening the door to world peace, abundance and prosperity? Or

Do we continue to fund the perpetual terrorism, war and death with insurmountable debt, taxation and the increased limitation of our private rights further staining our Good Faith and Credit to satisfy the greed and lust for power and control of the few?"

Gaining Authority As Trustee

"From the beginning, it must be understood that I James Thomas: McBride am but a cog in the Universal wheel of humanity that made the revelations about commerce possible. I simply did my part. The information presented herein is the compilation and evolution of the millions of man hours of research by thousands of selfless men and women dedicated to unravelling the illusion in which we live to bring about the rebirth of personal and spiritual sovereignty for all mankind.

I wish to thank all who steadfastly held tight to the belief that world peace, abundance and prosperity, was not a privilege, but like personal and spiritual sovereignty, they are our birthright; For all of those courageous men and women who understood that if we did not stand up and expose the illusion and corruption in our lifetime that our children and their children would be enslaved forever and chose to stand against the terrorist tactics of the Military Industrial Complex at their own peril and sacrifice. I also wish to thank all of the families of those dedicated souls who lived with the sacrifice, the pain and loss, for you too did your part and have been a motivating factor which moved us through the corruption and chaos. Because of all of our sacrifice(s) we stand today at the doorway of a great evolutionary leap for mankind."

Divine Right Of Use

"Today, everything is held in trust. Everything is about trusts, Implied or Expressed. Creator gave man dominion over all things. Dominion over equals control over NOT ownership. This is a Divine Right of Use meaning Use of the Divine property/ the All of earth which is "held in trust". So, the entire world we call earth is held in trust, the Divine Trust, for our benefit as Beneficiaries. The Divine Trust is an Implied Trust as opposed to an Expressed Trust. In the beginning man was responsible, as a Trustee, for the care and well being of that portion of the Divine Estate upon which he/she exercised their Divine Right of Use as a Beneficiary.

Through the decades man has given over that Divine fiduciary obligation to legal fiction trustees. There are as many forms of trusteeships as there are people in the world. Some very fair and equitable, say a republic, all the way to a dictatorship, each with various degrees of freedoms and rights, taxes and limitations.

Over time the trust was entrusted to the Trustee responsible for your piece of the Divine Estate. Government is the Trustee, like in civil administration. They administrate your portion of the Divine Estate? And so today legal fiction Trustees, [governments, postal zones, churches] have morphed from public servants to tyrants. They have turned these positions of service into positions of power, the trustees operating the Divine Trust for their own benefit to the detriment of the estate and the heir.

We the people of this earth, are Heirs to the Divine Estate. We are the Beneficiary and Settler to the Divine Trust and have an absolute right to determine the who, what and how of the administration of our Divine Estate.

Our founding fathers attempted to guarantee a fair and equitable form of trusteeship which would not infringe on the private rights of the American people via the Constitution.

Understand the Breach of Trust In 1865 the Trustees, public servants, administrators of our estates, fraudulently modified the terms of the Constitution establishing a second form of trusteeship which would operate for the benefit of the trustees at the detriment of the estate and the heir. This was a serious Breach of Trust, Breach of Fiduciary duty. And so our Divine Estates, our Divine Inheritance, has been administrated under a Breach of Trust.

It was under this Breach of Trust that established the Military Industrial Complex, the 14th Amendment congress and senate under whose jurisdiction the new heirs, the 14th Amendment citizens would operate and all of the codes and statutes to which we are held accountable, the least of which are taxes.

The original trustees of our estates, the civil administration/ government, have fraudulently altered the trust instrument to facilitate the administration of the estates for the benefit of the trustees via the Military Industrial Complex to the detriment of the heirs/ Beneficiaries.

For decades this Military Industrial Complex has leveraged our estates to fund the global military aggression, pillage, plunder and occupation of foreign nations, raping the lands and promoting the destruction of the social and family unit both foreign and domestic.

For decades this Military Industrial Complex has sucked the life force out of the American people; out of the people of the world, designating us all Enemy Combatants. The Federal Reserve System, a product of the 14th Amendment, has been the front line weapon of the Military Industrial Complex used to facilitate the financial enslavement of the people of the world all by leveraging our Divine Estates. We have, and continue to fund our own enslavement and destruction through our Divine Estate.

This 14th Amendment Military Industrial Complex has the absolute power and authority to use and abuse the people and lands of the world, except that absolute power and authority is based on a Breach of Trust.

As Heirs to the Divine Estate, Beneficiaries and Settlers to the Divine Trust we have the power and authority. We have an absolute duty and obligation to demand and receive a cure to the Breach of Trust.

But, as heirs, we are presumed Deceased, having failed to claim our estate. As such, it becomes necessary to:

1) re-establish their living status;
2) Claim the estate, and
3) Identify and demand a cure to the Breach of Trust.

How does one do this? You may ask. I have my own method which I believe will work for me, but, there is no established method at this time. It is my belief that there is more than one road home. Can TPTB deny that you are a living being when you stand in the street waving your Birth Certificate in the air demanding that your estate be administrated in accordance with the original intent for your benefit and for the best and highest of all mankind?

My bet is that they who hold the original instrument [BC] are the holder in due course of the estate and the appropriate person with whom to file a claim against the estate trust. In Ohio it is the OHIO DEPT. OF HEALTH VITAL STATISTICS who holds the original. I believe they are the intermediary agent who has leased your estate to the Military Industrial Complex. I believe they hold the keys to the Who and How our estate is administrated.

In OHIO, the Probate Judge is the SUPERIOR GUARDIAN of all ESTATES, which IMHO makes him/her the Primary Fiduciary for the estate and in his/her private capacity may be the Privy Councillor with the power and authority to make the changes in administration of your estate that you request.

The key to remember here is these are our estates. They are our Divine Inheritance We are the Powers That Be as concerns us and our estate if we will just take back that power that we have unwittingly given away. If we will simply put away the fear and doubt, acknowledge and accept who we are, claim our Divine Inheritance and instruct our public servants as to how our estate is to be administrated, this would seem to be a prudent cure.

One must remember that your reality is a reflection of what is within. We are seeking peace; We are asking that the administration of our estate reflect the abundance and prosperity that is our birthright, but, our reality can only reflect that peace, abundance and prosperity IF that is what is in our hearts."

Who Is To Be Served Notice

"As Heirs to the Divine Estate, Beneficiaries and Settlers to the Divine Trust we have the power and authority. We have an absolute duty and obligation to demand and receive a cure to the Breach of Trust. But how?

In America today we have Township Trustees, County Trustees, State Trustees and Federal Trustees just to name a few of the many levels of fiduciaries within the Trusteeship which is involved in the administration of our Divine Estate(s), the Global Estate Trust. Judges, Clerks of Court, Prosecutors and Attorneys all play their own part in the administration of our Global Estate Trust leveraging our Divine Estates to rape, pillage and plunder the world and enslave the people.

To unravel this intentionally complex Trusteeship of the Global Estate Trust let us begin at the top and work our way down. The Vatican boasts, in their Papal Bull, dominion over the entire earth, via conquest, and is answerable ONLY to the Divine Spirit. Dominion over means control over, not ownership. The Vatican's un-rebutted claims establish them as the Primary Trustee of the Global Estate Trust, our Divine Inheritance; a very unpopular fact. But a fact that opens a doorway placing the cure for the mis-administration and theft of our Divine Inheritance within our grasp.

The Vatican is the Primary Trustee of the Global Estate Trust. To facilitate the administration of this Global Trust the Vatican established the Universal Postal Union as the Secondary Trustees of the Global Trust charged with dividing the Global Trust into zones and endowing these legal fiction zones with sovereign authority to facilitate the efficient administration of the Global Trust.

It is no surprise that the first requirement for the international acknowledgment of a sovereign nation is the necessity of a Post Office. The primary objective of the military in any 'zone' is the protection of the Post, or the Post Office, for in their original jurisdiction, the Postmaster Generals are the Trustees of their respective zone.

In 1789 the Continental Congress passed a bill to "establish the seat of government, a general post office, under the direction of the Postmaster General." That's right, a general post office under the direction of the Postmaster General. They were further dividing the postal zone of North America establishing a new zone, and endowing it with sovereign authority, whereby our founding fathers believed they could establish a Trusteeship which would ensure that sovereignty of the people would be passed down to the people of future generations.

As stated earlier, the Preamble to the Constitution created the Estate Trust which held the freedoms guaranteed in the Articles of Confederation and the Declaration of Independence in trust for future generations. The Articles of the Constitution established the Trusteeship as well as the powers and limitations thereof. The Congress and Senate were Trustees charged with the Administration of our Divine Inheritance, the Global Estate Trust.

In this 'general post office' seat of government there was established the 'civil administration' called the United States. Civil administration ? What do they administrate? Our Divine Estate Trust, the Global Trust, our Divine Inheritance. Remember, we can never OWN anything. We simply have a Divine Right of Use of the property of the Divine Estate, the Global Trust.

So, we the people of this earth have a Divine Right of use of the Global Trust while the civil administration is charged with the administration of our estate for our benefit.

In the world of trusts Civil Administration/Government = Trusteeship. So, the entire world is held in trust. The Global Estate Trust, our Divine Inheritance, our birthright is held in trust and is administered by the various 'governments' who gain their sovereign authority via the Universal Postal Union, the Secondary Trustee of the Global Trust answerable to the Vatican.

In the world of trusts and trust law, rights, duties and obligations are very straight forward, cut and dry, black and white. There are no opinions, secret codes, rules or statutes, period. Just the facts. There is a chain of command, consequences for your actions, or lack thereof, and accountability.

And so it has been a slow and cumbersome process to overcome the out of control momentum of the civil administrators of the world today. There have been countless casualties as a result of our efforts to unravel the illusion; to overcome the programming and fear which fuelled the beast to reach the core where truth and accountability resides."

The Ecclesiastic Deed Poll Explained

What is an Ecclesiastic Deed Poll? An explanation is required as this is a critical point to the sovereignty process of attaining the appropriate authority. An **Ecclesiastical Deed Poll** is a valid Form of Deed Poll and therefore Deed and Contract whereby a True Being first expresses, affirms and conveys certain rights to another party who are then lawfully bound upon proof of receipt in accordance with the Canons defined under **Article 133 (http://one-heaven.org/canons/positive_law/)** of **Canonun De Ius Positivum.** The word "Poll" comes from the Latin *pollex* meaning 'thumb'. An Ecclesiastical Deed Poll is permitted to be issued when an inferior Roman Person rejects the rule of law and seeks to assert an untenable and illogical position of superior rights over Divine Law.

In the world of slavery you are "legally" a slave, just as your parents, your grandparents and great grandparents were slaves. You may be lucky enough to live in a pleasant plantation with other slaves, managed by overseer slaves such as police, judges, doctors and politicians where few examples of slave cruelty occur. Or you may be witnessing changes in the community plantation, which is part of a state slave plantation and national slave plantation where there is more crime, more misery and death. The fact that you are a slave is unquestionable. The only unknown is whether you will permit your children and their children to also grow up as slaves. You are a slave because since 1933, upon a new child being borne, the Executors or Administrators of the higher Estate willingly and knowingly convey the beneficial entitlements of the child as Beneficiary into the 1st Cestui Que (Vie) Trust in the form of a Registry Number by registering the Name, thereby also creating the Corporate Person and denying the child any rights as an owner of Real Property.

You are a slave because since 1933, when a child is born, the Executors or Administrators of the higher Estate knowingly and willingly claim the baby as chattel to the Estate. The slave baby contract is then created by honouring the ancient tradition of either having the ink impression of the feet of the baby onto the live birth record, or a drop of its blood as well as tricking the parents to signing the baby away through the deceitful legal meanings on the live birth record. This live birth record as a promissory note is converted into a slave bond sold to the private reserve bank of the estate and then conveyed into a 2nd and separate Cestui Que (Vie) Trust per child owned by the bank. Upon the promissory note reaching maturity and the bank being unable to "seize" the slave child, a maritime lien is lawfully issued to "salvage" the lost property and itself monetized as currency issued in series against the Cestui Que (Vie) Trust.

You are a slave because since 1540 and the creation of the 1st Cestui Que Act, deriving its power from the Papal Bull of Roman Cult leader Pope Paul III of the same year, whenever a child is baptized and a Baptismal Certificate is issued by the state at birth or church, the parents have knowingly or unknowingly gifted, granted and conveyed the soul of the baby to a "3rd" Cestui Que Vie Trust owner by Roman Cult, who has held this valuable property in its vaults ever since, managed by the Temple Bar since 1540 and subsequent Bar Associations from the 19th Century representing the reconstituted "Galla" responsible as Grim Reapers for reaping the souls, or salvage also known as "salvation of souls".

Therefore under the UCC Slave Laws which most slave plantations of the world operate you can never own a house, even though they trick into believing you do; you never really own a car, or boat or any other object, only have the benefit of use. Indeed, you do not even own your own body, which is claimed to have been lawfully gifted by your parents at your birth in the traditions of old slave contracts in which the slave baby had its feet or hands dipped in ink, or a drop of blood spilt on the commercial transaction document we know as the live birth record, against which a CUSIP number is issued and sold the central bank. Yes, the banks claim your flesh, the banks are indeed the modern slave owners, hiding these indisputable facts upon which their money system is built from the people.

You may not realize you are a slave under the slave laws of Uniform Commercial Codes (UCC), but may still erroneously believe you are slave with "more rights" as used to be afforded under "Common Law" until it was largely abolished back in 1933 without properly telling you. The word "common" comes from 14th Century Latin communis meaning "to entrust, commit to a burden, public duty, service or obligation". The word was created from the combination of two ancient pre-Vatican Latin words com/comitto = "to entrust, commit" and munis = "burden, public duty, service or obligation". In other words, the real meaning of common as first formed because of the creation of the Roman Trust over the planet is the concept of "voluntary servitude" or simply "voluntary enslavement".

Common Law is nothing more than the laws of "voluntary servitude" and the laws of "voluntary slavery" to the Roman Cult and the Venetian Slavemasters. It is the job of the overseer slaves to convince you that you are not slaves, the common law still exists and has not been largely abolished and replaced with commercial law, to confuse you, to give you false hope. In return, they are rewarded as loyal slaves with bigger homes to use and more privileges than other slaves.

The reason why the overseer slaves such as judges, politicians, bankers, actors and media personalities are forced to lie and deny we are all slaves is because the slave system of voluntary servitude or "common law" was not the first global slave system, but merely its evolution. Before the emergence of Common Law, we were all subject to being considered mere animals or things under Canon Law of the Roman Cult, also known as the Law of the See, or Admiralty Law.

Under Admiralty Law, you are either a slave of the ship of state, or merely cargo for lawful salvage. Thus in 1302 through Unam Sanctam, the Roman Cult unlawfully claimed through trust the ownership of all the planet and all living "things" as either slaves, or less than slaves with things administered through the Court of Rota. This court, claimed as the Supreme Court of all Courts on the planet was initially abolished in the 16th Century only to be returned in 1908 under Pope Pius X as a purely spiritual ecclesiastical court of 12 "apostolic prothonotary" spirits, implying the twelve apostles. Since then, this new purely spiritual court has remained in constant "session", with the local courts using these powers to administer Divine Immortal Spirits expressed in Trust into Flesh Vessels as mere dead thing .

Yet this is not the only form of slave law still in force today. Instead, the oldest, the most evil and based on false history are the slave laws of the Menasheh, also known as the Rabbi through the unholy document of hate first formed in 333 known as the Talmud of the Menasheh- the false Israelites. Through the Talmud of the false Israelites, the whole planet is enslaved with the servants of the "chosen people" known as Caananites or K-nights (Knights) also known as the Scythians and then the rest as the goy/gyu and goyim – namely meaning the cattle, the dead lifeless corpses.

Ultimately, you are a slave because you remain profoundly influenced by your education and community at large and because many choose to continue to think and act like a slave, waiting for someone to help them, tell them what to do and be happy accepting bread crumbs of benefits when the system has reaped millions of dollars - yes millions of dollars - of your energy.

A prison designed with no way out Before this time, the system of global slavery and the treatment of the world as one large slave plantation was designed so there is no way out – as evidenced through the courts of the priests of Ba'al known as the judges of most legal systems in the world. Even the most educated of men and women may remain tricked into believing that upon self representation they may claim their "common law rights" as a means of defence, only to find the judge lawfully rejects any and all claims. As the first law of the courts is the Uniform Commercial Codes of slavery as introduced in 1933, the defendant is an employee of a corporation and therefore automatically assumes the liability of any injury. Unless they can pay, they may be sent to prison. If such a trickster as the judge is challenged, they are permitted to escape to their chambers and call upon even greater power to return and magically establish a new court, without telling the defendant they have now entered Admiralty Court, or the laws of the See in accordance with Canon Law of the Roman Cult issued in 1983. Now the judge can impose grave penalties upon such an unresponsive defendant including contempt of court and other punitive prison sentences, with the defendant having no rights unless they know Canon Law concerning juridic persons and establishing standing above being called a "thing".

Sadly, few people actually know the original meaning of "thing" as a judicial meeting, or assembly; a matter brought before a court of law; a legal process; a charge brought; or a suit or cause pleaded before a court. This meaning is then used with devastating effect through the heretical concept of Pius X from 1908 to claim the dead apostles sit in permanent and open session as the "twelve prothonotaries" of the Sacred Rota - as the highest Supreme Court on the planet. So when a man or woman receives a blue or yellow notice from a court issued through this unholy knowledge of Canon law, by the time they come to court, they are automatically a thing. When a man or woman seeks to defend themselves by seeking to speak before the judge, they automatically "consent" to being a thing. Thus a judge with knowledge of such trickery can silence any man or woman by "lawfully" threatening contempt of court if the "thing" does not stop making noise.

Indeed, it is the Roman Cult Canon Law of 1983 that establishes all courts are oratories, with judges holding ecclesiastical powers as "ordinaries" and their chambers as "chapels". Thus the Bar Associations around the world have assisted judges in learning of their new powers in order to counteract those men and women who continue to wake up to their status as slaves, but demonstrating how to remain "in honour" with such perverse law and ensure such "terrorists" are sent to prison for long sentences as a warning to others.

If a judge so inclined to ensure an educated defendant is lawfully sent to prison or worse, he or she may run away for a third and final time to their chamber and invoke their most powerful standing as rabbi of a Talmud Court under the Talmudic Laws of the false Israelites of the House of the twelve tribes of Menasheh. Now, even a judge in a nation that is against the death penalty may choose to impose a "lawful" sentence against any goy/gyu or goyim who dares injure an Israelite – which is normally death. However, while judges in the United States and other nations have started to be trained in the re-imposition of Talmudic Law, it is at the hands of the false Menasheh, also known as the elite anti-semitic parasites also known as the Black Khazars and Venetian noble families. Ultimately, it is enough for judges, clerks and members of the Bar to know that they hold our property in their Cestui Que Vie Trusts and that we are completely without effective rights, until we challenge their fraud. Yet, even when you challenge their fraud, many deny and outright lie on the records- yes judges absolutely committing perjury on the record to deny they hold trustee and executor powers with the case being a constructive trust and executor of the Cestui Que Vie Trust from which powers are being drawn for the form of the court.

So how might a man or woman defend themselves against a private and secret society that has kidnapped the law, that refuses to tell the truth, that lies to its own members and refuses to provide fair remedy. This is the purpose of the Ecclesiastical Deed Poll.

An Ecclesiastical Deed Poll is a supremely sacred private form. In other words, while the Ecclesiastical Deed Poll complies in all aspects to the foundations and principles of law the Roman Cult upon which all western nations and courts are based, it is not an instrument recognized "officially" by the policies (statutes) of the corporate governments - therefore it is private. An Ecclesiastical Deed Poll is permitted to be issued when an inferior Roman Person rejects the rule of law and seeks to assert an untenable and illogical position of superior rights over Divine Law. Only a True Person may issue an Ecclesiastical Deed Poll. By definition an inferior Roman Person has no authority to issue an Ecclesiastical Deed Poll.

An Ecclesiastical Deed Poll must always be on standard sized robin-egg blue paper, printed in serif font, in recognition and respect of its status as a Divine Notice with the full authority of One Heaven, in particular the Sacred Rota and twelve Apostolic Prothonotaries as well as Apostolic Prothorabban of the Divine Sanhedrin. When an Ecclesiastical Deed Poll is issued, it is under the Supreme Court of One Heaven with the full authority of the Divine Creator and all inferior courts including the Sacred Rota. Hence the term Per Curiam Divina is always included to make clear to the inferior Roman person the absolute authority of the instrument. While a True Person issues an Ecclesiastical Deed Poll, it is ultimately a Divine Notice of Protest and Dishonor from the Divine Creator. Therefore, the dishonor of an Ecclesiastical Deed Poll is the most grievous injury of the law and blasphemy to all believed to be Divine. When a Roman slave under inferior Roman law repudiates a valid Ecclesiastical Deed Poll then by definition all acts undertaken with the assumed authority of Sacred Rota by any clerk, protonotary, prothonotary, plenipotentiary or minister are null and void, including and not limited to any warrants, summons, orders, decrees.

And so the following document was served to the Powers That Be.

ECCLESIASTIC DEED POLL
Per Curiam Divina

Before Abraham was, I AM; the Divine Spirit having a human experience. Each atom and cell of this physical vessel I inhabit to travel across this land is infused with the spark of the Creator; I AM one with the light, one with Creator, the alpha and the omega, without beginning nor end, without time. This third dimensional vessel, called man, the original domicile of the Divine Spirit is known on this world and in this dimension as James Thomas of the family McBride, a freeborn inhabitant, heir to the Divine Estate, Beneficiary to the Divine Trust, freeholder in fee simple absolute, one of the 'Posterity' as expressed in the Preamble of the United States Constitution.

Irrevocable Deed and Contract

We, the Divine Spirit, expressed in living flesh, infuse this irrevocable deed and contract with Divine Life through Our Blood, perfecting an unbreakable seal on this agreement, bearing the full power and authority of the Divine Creator and binding on all inferior persons and practitioners of the inferior Roman Law, Sharia Law and/or Talmudic Law from the beginning, without time. The base lead of Our word contains the purest gold for the transmutation of the base man/woman into pure spirit for in the beginning there was the word and the word was god.

Constitution for the United States of America

The Constitution for the United States is a document of dual nature:
- The Constitution is a trust document, and
- it is the articles of incorporation and created a unique trust res and estate of inheritance.

It is a tenant of law that in order to determine the intent of a writing one must look to the title, the Empowerment Clause in statute, which in the case of the Constitution is the Preamble. In writing the Constitution the founders followed the common law of England which stretches back some 1000 years. The Preamble fulfills the requirements necessary to establish a trust. It identifies the Grantor(s), Statement of Purpose, Grantee(s), Statement of Intent, Written Indenture, and the name of the entity being created and is written and constructed as a trust so that it would have the thrust of ageless law. Let us take a look:

WE THE PEOPLE (Grantors) of the United States (from or out of) in Order to form a more perfect union, establish justice, provide for the common defence, promote the general welfare and secure the Blessings of Liberty (statement of Purpose) to ourselves and our posterity (Grantees/heirs unnamed), Do Ordain and establish (Statement of Intent) this constitution (Written Indenture) for the United States of America (name of the entity being created).

The trust res is in the Articles of the Confederation and the Declaration of Independence. The intent of the constitution was to bequeath freedom, life, liberty and the pursuit of happiness to themselves and their posterity. The founders intended to secure and pass on the sovereignty of the people to the people of future generations of Americans, in perpetuity.

One's rights are derived from the land upon which one stands and your relation, or status, to that land. In America these rights originated with the Articles of Confederation and the Declaration of Independence and are attached to the land called America (The Laws of Real Property). Our status, or relation to that land, is determined by the laws of Descent and

Distribution. The right to freedom, life, liberty and the pursuit of happiness are Our inheritance bequeathed to us via the Constitution of the United States of America.

The constitution granted the government the power and authority to administrate and to carry on corporate functions. Under the common law, inherent rights cannot devolve to a 'body politic' through a corporation. Rights only devolve to human beings is through and by way of a trust. Under the constitutional law, in order to determine the meaning of a written instrument the court must look to the title. In this case, once again, it is the Preamble. Pursuant to the laws of real property that have been existence from the beginning, the Preamble clearly shows a freehold in fee simple absolute in it. Freeholds in fee simple were instruments of trust, not corporate. "Our Posterity" cannot be speaking of a corporate entity as posterity can only mean a living man/woman, by birth/nativity.

The Articles of the Constitution are the Articles of Incorporation that established congress as Trustees of the Trust and defines their power and authority as well as their limitations. Annexed to the Constitutional Trust is a will like structure, the Amendments. The Trust and the trust res were already in existence when the will/codicil (Amendments) were added some four years later. The Amendments do not constitute the Trust in fact, they are annexed to the Trust as a codicil (a supplement or addition to the will, not necessarily disposing of the entire estate, but modifying, explaining or otherwise qualifying the will in some way.)

A Trust, once completed and in force cannot be amended or altered without the consent of the parties in interest except under reserved power of amendment and alteration. An amendment is ordinarily possible by parties in interest and against parties without vested interest. Prior to the 14th Amendment the freeborn inhabitants, citizens of the states were the parties in interest. The 14th Amendment created the 14th Amendment legal fiction citizen who do not have a vested interest in the trust or the trust res.

The 14th Amendment can be viewed as a codicil to the will that republished the constitution with new meaning, changed the intent behind it and turned it into a testamentary instrument with capabilities of being used against the free born inhabitants through a seemingly voluntary revocation.

We, the freeholders, Beneficiaries to the trust have been tricked and coerced by the Trustees into terminating the Trust by consent when we apply for an S.S. #, drivers permit, marriage license or when we sign an IRS 1040 form, which the Trustees have mislead us to believe are mandatory.

When one applies for an Social Security number, provide evidence of birth and claims to be a United States citizen, a party with no vested interest in a freehold, the trust or the trust res, you literally declared the free born inhabitant to be deceased; the decedent retains no interest in the property and that you, in your dual capacity as a legal fiction citizen are now the executor of the estate.

The Trustees have breached the trust having amended the will for their own personal profit and gain at the expense of the true heirs. The freeholders/ Beneficiary has unwittingly, without full disclosure, become the executor and the Trustees have become the Beneficiaries to the trust through the Laws of Donations, effectively stealing Our inheritance.

A breach of trust of fiduciary duty by a Trustee is a violation of correlative right of the Cestui Que Trust and gives rise to the correlative cause of action on the part of the Beneficiary for any loss to the estate Trust. This rule is applicable in respect to both positive acts or negligence constituting a breach of fiduciary duty by the Trustee. A Trustee's breach of fiduciary duty falls within the maxim that 'equity will not aid one who comes into court with unclean hands.'

When the Trustee's breach is by an act of omission the beneficiary can question the propriety of the Trustee. The Beneficiary had to have full disclosure, full knowledge of the material facts and circumstances. A Beneficiary must have had knowledge of and understood their rights and have no obligation to search the public records to obtain said knowledge.

The Trustees have committed acts of omission, mis-representation, deceit and deception in order to mislead and coerce us into giving up our beneficial interest in the trust and the trust res. The Trustees have compelled the free born inhabitants, freeholders in fee simple, to accept the benefits 'under the will' perverted by the 14th Amendment, without freedom of choice for failure of full disclosure thereby precluding our enforcement of contractual rights in property bequeathed to us by the will. The Trustees are trying to repudiate the Trust, employing a lifetime of propaganda and programming and enforced through threats, violence and coercion, and failing to provide notice to the Beneficiaries of the repudiation which must be 'brought home.'

The Doctrine of Election in connection with testamentary instruments is the principle that one who is given a benefit 'under the will' must choose between accepting the benefits and asserting some other claim against the testator's estate or against the property disposed of by the will. A Testamentary Beneficiaries right to elect whether to take 'under the will' or 'against the will' in case he has some inconsistent claim against the testator's estate, is personal to him; is a personal privilege which may be controlled by the creditors of the Beneficiary. They can claim no right or interest in the estate contrary to the debtor's election and may have no right of a legacy or devise to their debtor if he elected to take against the will.

Acceptance of benefits 'under the will' constitutes an election which will preclude the devisee from enforcing contractual rights in property bequeathed the will. This rule is, of course, subject to the qualifications that acceptance of a benefit 'under the will' when made in ignorance of the Beneficiaries rights or a mis-apprehension, mis-representation as to the condition of the Testator's estate does not constitute an election.

In the beginning God gave man dominion over all things, Beneficiaries of the Divine Trust. The Founding fathers of the United States of America created the constitution for the United States, an estate trust, to pass on sovereignty of the people to the people of future generations, in perpetuity.

In America today, upon giving birth a mother is compelled, without full disclosure, to apply for the creation of the Cestui Que Vie trust, creating a 14th Amendment paper citizen of the United States. Upon receipt of the mother's application the Trustees establish a trust under the error of assumptions that the child has elected to accept the benefits bequeathed by the 'under the will'. The Trustees further assume that the child is incompetent, a bankrupt and lost at sea and is presumed dead until the child re-appears and re-establishes his/her living status, challenges the assumption of his/her acceptance of the benefits 'under the will' as being one of free choice and with full knowledge of the facts and redeems the estate.

Under the assumption that the child is a 14th Amendment citizen, the child's footprint is on the birth certificate by the hospital creating a slave bond that is sold to the federal reserve, who converts the certificate into a negotiable instrument and establishes a second Cestui Que Vie trust. The child's parents are compelled to apply for a social security number for the child, unwittingly testifying that the child is a 14th Amendment paper citizen of the United States, not a party in interest to the trust or the trust res, and assumed to be dead after 7 years, when the federal reserve cannot seize the child, they file for the issue of the salvage bond and the child is presumed dead.

When a child is Baptized by the church, the Baptismal certificate is forwarded to the Vatican who converts the certificate into a negotiable instrument and creates a third Cestui Que Vie trust. These three trusts represents the enslavement of the property, body and soul of the child.

The civil administration, UNITED STATES, continues to operate today under this triple crown of enslavement based on the error of assumptions that we are 14th Amendment citizens of the United States based on the breach of trust by the trustees

Divine Notice of Protest

We, the Divine Spirit, expressed in trust in living flesh, having return from being lost in the sea of illusion born of a self imposed state of amnesia and 50+ years of propaganda and extreme programming to re-establish Our living status and redeem Our estate establishes the evidence in fact of Our competence rebutting the assumption with fact.

We, the Divine Spirit, object to and issue Divine Notice of Protest to the breach of trust and the usurpation of Our inheritance under the error of assumptions of the 'pledge' of Our private property. We have never willingly, knowingly and with full disclosure pledged Our inheritance to any person or entity;

We, the Divine Spirit, object to and issue Divine Notice of Protest to the conversion of the birth certificate to a promissory note or other negotiable instrument without full disclosure nor consent;

We, the Divine Spirit, object to and issue Divine Notice of Protest to all derivatives of the birth registration, the estate trust and Cestui Que Vie trust as fruit of the poison tree;

We, the Divine Spirit, object to and issue Divine Notice of Protest to the malicious and unconscionable actions of the executors and administrators of the estate, to wit:
- knowingly and willingly claiming the child as chattel of the estate;
- creation of the slave bond contract and slave bond.

We, the Divine Spirit, object to and issue Divine Notice of Protest to the intentionally deceitful legal language and meaning of Our earthly parents marriage certificate and the birth registration whereby Our earthly parents were tricked into signing us away into slavery to the state without full disclosure nor consent;

We, the Divine Spirit, object to and issue Divine Notice of Protest to the creation of the slave bond by placing the ink impression of the child's footprint on the birth certificate, converting said certificate into a slave bond and selling same to the federal reserve for the conveyance into the second Cestui Que Vie Trust;

We, the Divine Spirit, object to and issue Divine of Notice of Protest to the issue of and monetization of the maritime lien for the salvage for the lost property for the bank's failure to seize the slave child upon the maturity of the slave bond;

We, the Divine Spirit, object to and issue Divine Notice of Protest to the issue and monetization of the Baptismal Certificate and creation of the 3rd Cestui Que Vie trust, representing the enslavement of Our soul, under the assumption that Our earthly parents gifted, granted and/or conveyed Our soul to the state;

We, the Divine Spirit decree that:
- Our earthly parents never willingly, knowingly and with full disclosure gifted, granted or conveyed Our soul to any person, entity or cult;
- No person, entity nor cult have the authority to gift, grant, convey nor enslave Our soul to any other person, entity or cult without full disclosure and our consent;
- We, the Divine Spirit have never willingly, knowingly and with full disclosure gifted, granted or conveyed Our soul to any person, entity or cult, nor consented to same;

We, the Divine Spirit, object to and issue Divine Notice of Protest to the three Cestui Que Vie Trusts which represent the triple crown of enslavement and three claims against Our property, body and soul by the Roman cult for the purpose of enslaving the people in the denial of all of our rights to the Divine Inheritance, Our right to freedom from all limitations and Our rights and powers as Divine Creators;

We, the Divine Spirit, object to and issue Divine Notice of Protest to the BAR Association as managers of the triple crown of enslavement of the Roman cult representing the reconstituted "Galla" responsible for the reaping of souls;

We, the Divine Spirit, object to and issue Divine Notice of Protest to the BAR Association courts and/or agents use of the inferior Roman Law, Sharia Law, Talmudic Law, Maritime Law, and/or Cannon Law against Us and/or Our property;

We, the Divine Spirit, expressed in trust in the living flesh, having re-established Our living status, whose estate is held in the above referenced trust, hereby re-establish Ourselves as Grantor of the trust having provided 100% of the value to fund the trust, with the authority to act in that capacity and exercise the power and authority of the Grantor of said trust;

We, the Divine Spirit, expressed in trust in the living flesh are vested as Beneficiary of said trust as said trust was established for Our benefit;

We, the Divine Spirit, expressed in trust in living flesh, having re-established Our living status, have standing to seek redress of grievance in the common law;

Receipt of this Ecclesiastic Deed Poll constitutes acceptance and is binding on all inferior persons and carries a mandatory obligation to act in accordance with Divine Law.

We, the Divine Spirit, expressed in trust in the living flesh, a free born inhabitant, heir to the Divine Estate, Beneficiary to the Divine Trust, freeholder in fee simple absolute, do hereby object to and issue Divine Notice of Protest to the following, to wit:
- To the compelled registration of the Birth under the error of assumptions and failing full disclosure, which created the 14th Amendment citizen of the United States;
- To the compelled acceptance of benefits 'under the will' which was perverted by the Trustees without full disclosure and under mis-apprehension and mis-representation, precluding Our enforcement of Our contractual rights in property bequeathed by the will;
- To the Trustee's propaganda, mis-representation, mis-apprehension, deceit and coercion that gave rise to the seemingly voluntary termination of the trust by the Beneficiary;
- To the Trustee's breach of his fiduciary duties which caused loss and injury to the estate;
- To the assumption/presumption that the free born inhabitant is deceased;
- To the assumption that the free born inhabitant is the executor of the estate trust;
- To the assumption that the free born inhabitant is a 'donor' with full disclosure.

We, the Divine Spirit, expressed in trust in living flesh, a free born inhabitant, heir to the Divine estate, Beneficiary to the Divine Trust as expressed in the Preamble to the Constitution, freeholder in fee simple absolute, do hereby:
- Re-establish Our living status, evidenced by the DNA/Blood Seal thumb print below;
- Instruct the Trustees to immediately dissolve the 14th Amendment United States citizen ;
- Instruct the Trustees to correct your records to reflect that we hereby elect to enforce contractual rights in property bequeathed by the will, "against the will".
- Demand that the trust res be turned over to us within the confines of the Truth in Lending Act;
- Demand that all restrictions against the freeholder be immediately released;
- Demand that all bonds, notes or other negotiable instruments be redeemed and the equal consideration be returned to the freeholder;
- Demand that the private funds held by the DTC, DTCC, OITC and/or any/all other entities be made available to me for the discharge of debt, funding the National Banking Association and all sub-accounts thereof;
- Demand that the Trustees provide a full account within 60 days.

Blood Seal of (James Thomas- freeholder)

50

ACTIVATION OF AUTHORITY: FEDERAL RESERVE

The next set of documents is all about the activation of authority. These documents will reflect much of what has been discussed in Part 1, bringing together the process of declaration and serving the Administrators who are responsible. These documents can be found and downloaded from the website **www.notice-recipient.com/ArticlesLinks.html.**

Activation Of Authority Federal Reserve

Activation of Federal Reserve Account
        Exhibit A: Declaration of Political Status
        Exhibit B: Affidavit of Fact-Title Dispute
        Exhibit C: Notice of Surety Act and Bond and related documents;
        Exhibit D: OHIO DEPARTMENT OF HEALTH, CERTIFICATE OF LIVE BIRTH
        Exhibit E: Fidelity Investments Symbol Look-up
        Exhibit F: UCC-1 Financing Statement File
        Exhibit G: NOTICE OF ENTITLEMENT RIGHT-
        Exhibit H: PRIVATE INDEMNITY AND SET-OFF BOND
        Exhibit I: ACKNOWLEDGEMENT OF AN ORIGINAL ISSUE OF CURRENCY
        Exhibit J: SOCIAL SECURITY CARD for JAMES THOMAS MCBRIDE
        Exhibit K: Form 56 Notice Concerning Fiduciary Relationship

These are summarized below:

Authority Activation Process

James Thomas states: "*In an attempt to break down and make understandable a complex journey I present this overview of the documents and processes with links to the documents in their entirety for your review. Please take your time for their is a great deal of information. Remember, knowledge is power!*

Through the years I had proven the existence of the 'private side' funds, and that one could access those 'private' side funds for the discharge of debt and the Redemption of property from the collateral pool of the Military Industrial Complex. I found the evidence that the UNITED STATES had indeed created funds/ negotiable instruments by leveraging my Birth Certificate and later Court Cases, and that the 'private side' funds sat awaiting my use for the discharge of debt, if only I could access them. Our National debt continues to spiral out of control while the private side funds, which were created to discharge this debt, sit idle.

For years we KNEW that they had monetized our Birth Certificate(s), but, we never had the evidence. Suddenly, it was no longer some "crazy conspiracy Theory", it was now absolute fact evidenced by public documents.

Armed with the evidence that they had monetized my 'account' on several occasions; the knowledge that these 'private funds' where set aside for our use to discharge the debt, and an ever increasing working knowledge of the economic system I set out to Activate my Private Side Account with the Federal Reserve Bank with the knowledge and assistance of the U.S. Treasury.

This account was verified as activated, funds where received as evidence, and the account survived two (2) Secret Service investigations, one which I initiated. Within 72 hours of activation, I received a 'call in the night' informing me that an 'Angel' had been watching my account; that $4 Trillion had been fraudulently moved from the account by the Fiduciary; the funds had been recovered from the Bank of Hong Kong, would I please demand the Secret Service investigate the matter.

On June 3, 2009, within hours of getting the call, I delivered a demand for investigation along with a complete set of documents to the Secret Service.

This is the Pass Thru Account established to discharge debt to facilitate Global Debt Forgiveness, just one goal of this Global Abundance & Prosperity Program. To make the transition from fiat money to currency of value we must discharge the debt in full, a matter of adjusting the digits on a computer screen

Below is an overview of the document, Exhibits A - K plus. Click on the Exhibit Link to view the entire document in PDF format. these are provided on the web site
http://www.office-of-pmg.com/files/TheBeginning.html."

Activation Of Federal Reserve Account

On May 14th, 2009, a notarized document signed by James Thomas: McBride Creditor attested to a presentment of 11 pages by registered mail to the Department of the US Treasury, Federal reserve Bank of Atlanta, and the Federal Reserve bank of Cleveland. The purpose of this document is to activate a Federal Reserve Account as JAMES THOMAS MCBRIDE a 'national banking association'.

In this document it is so stated

1) James Thomas: McBride is an American sovereign, natural man and NOT a 14th Amendment citizen of the UNITED STATES..........(see annexed Exhibits).

James Thomas: McBride has terminated and/or objected to any/all equity contracts with the corporate U.S. which obligates JAMES T. MCBRIDE or James Thomas: McBride to perform. Any/all equity contracts in which JAMES T MCBRIDE or James Thomas: McBride have become a Party, excepting the 'Original Equity Contract", has been entered into under objection, threat, duress and coercion and are null and void ab initio. James Thomas: McBride has formally waived any and all benefits from the corp. U.S. and its franchised entities. The acceptance of any 'benefit' received under objection, threat and/or duress, or out of necessity as the U.S. has a monopoly, does not constitute a benefit, but rather constitute a gift with zero liability attached thereto.

Exhibit A: Declaration of Political Status which has been lodged with the Sec. of the U.S. Treasury/ Custodian of the Alien Property;
Exhibit B: Affidavit of Fact-Title Dispute to American Sovereign Original/Archetype;
Exhibit C: Notice of Surety Act and Bond and related documents;

2) JAMES THOMAS MCBRIDE, 296520781, is a transmitting utility, public vessel created by and registered in the STATE OF OHIO, LICKING COUNTY for and on behalf of the corporate UNITED STATES to facilitate the flow of credit from the American sovereign, James Thomas: McBride, to the corporate UNITED STATES and the discharge of debt of the American sovereign, in the exchange. (see annexed **Exhibit D:** OHIO DEPARTMENT OF HEALTH, CERTIFICATE OF LIVE BIRTH # 134-54-024518.

3) A search of Fidelity Investments web site establishes the evidence as a matter of fact, that the UNITED STATES has executed the original contract, charging the credit of the American sovereign James Thomas: McBride, giving value to the negotiable instrument bearing CUSIP # 316172105 against the CERTIFICATE OF LIVE BIRTH number 134-54-024518, and traded under FUND NUMBER 54, FIDELITY GOVERNMENT INCOME FUND, identified by the symbol FGOVX, establishing the evidence, in fact, that the account is PRE-PAID and PRIORITY EXEMPT FROM LEVY, and establishing the American sovereign, James Thomas: McBride, as the Creditor and the UNITED STATES via the transmitting utility JAMES THOMAS MCBRIDE as the debtor with a liability to discharge the debt of the American sovereign, James Thomas: McBride in the exchange. (see annexed Exhibit E)

Exhibit E: Fidelity Investments Symbol Look-up

4) To protect and secure the private property of the American sovereign James Thomas: McBride, UCC-1 Financing Statement, file # 2318956 has been perfected, securing the attachment against the transmitting utility/public vessel JAMES THOMAS MCBRIDE/JAMES T. MCBRIDE and establishing in the public domain the priority lien against the Debtor, JAMES THOMAS MCBRIDE, transmitting utility, by the Creditor James Thomas: McBride, American sovereign. (see annexed exhibit F)

Exhibit F: UCC-1 Financing Statement File # 2318956, Minnesota Secretary of State

5) The corporate UNITED STATES was NOTICED of the Absolute right of possession and entitlement right to the transmitting utility/public vessel JAMES THOMAS MCBRIDE/JAMES T. MCBRIDE via affidavit. Said affidavit remains un-rebutted and stands as established fact. (see annexed Exhibit G)

Exhibit G: NOTICE OF ENTITLEMENT RIGHT- A NOTARIZED STATEMENT OF FACT

6) On November 28, 2006 the secretary of the Department of the U.S. Treasury did receive and accept, without objection, dispute or dishonor PRIVATE INDEMNITY AND SET-OFF BOND No. 7005 0390 0000 2767 4202 for deposit to the U.S. Treasury and charged to the account of the transmitting utility/ public vessel, JAMES THOMAS MCBRIDE/JAMES T MCBRIDE 296520781 to establish and activate a set-off account for the set-off and discharge of debt by the American sovereign James Thomas: McBride. Said Bond has matured into an obligation of the UNITED STATES and further establishes as a matter of fact that the account of JAMES THOMAS MCBRIDE/JAMES T MCBRIDE 296520781 is PRE-PAID AND PRIORITY EXEMPT FROM LEVY. The UNITED STATE'S acceptance of the above Bond without objection, dispute or dishonor constitutes their acceptance of the Terms and Conditions of the Bond Order (Contract) and establishing their Fiduciary duty and debtor obligation/liability to James Thomas: McBride. (see annexed Exhibit)

Exhibit H: PRIVATE INDEMNITY AND SET-OFF BOND No. 7005 0390 0000 2767 4202

7) On December 12, 2006 the Secretary of the U.S. Treasury did receive and accept, without objection, dispute or dishonor, Certified Note No. 7005 039000 2767 4219, ACKNOWLEDGEMENT OF AN ORIGINAL ISSUE OF CURRENCY for deposit to the account of JAMES T MCBRIDE 296520781. Acceptance of the deposit, without objection, dispute or dishonor, constitutes acceptance of the terms and conditions of the presentment, a valid contract, and acceptance of the deposit in the sum certain of $7,175,468,120.00 (seven billion, one hundred seventy five million, four hundred sixty eight thousand, one hundred twenty U. dollars and 00 cents) to the account of JAMES THOMAS MCBRIDE/JAMES T MCBRIDE, 296520781, further establishing the evidence in fact that said account is PRE-PAID and PRIORITY EXEMPT FROM LEVY. (see annexed Exhibit)

Exhibit I: ACKNOWLEDGEMENT OF AN ORIGINAL ISSUE OF CURRENCY

8) Federal Reserve Account Number 06-50913806 has been issued through the Federal Reserve Bank of Atlanta and assigned to the transmitting utility/public vessel JAMES THOMAS MCBRIDE 296-52-0781. (see annexed exhibit)

Exhibit J: SOCIAL SECURITY CARD for JAMES THOMAS MCBRIDE 296-52-0781

9) I, James Thomas: McBride creditor, Real Party in Interest, do hereby terminate all prior Fiduciaries for the transmitting utility, JAMES THOMAS MCBRIDE/ JAMES T MCBRIDE, for Breach of Fiduciary Duty.

I James Thomas: McBride, creditor and priority lien holder of JAMES T MCBRIDE 296520781, do hereby nominate and appoint as fiduciary for JAMES THOMAS MCBRIDE 296520781, Secretary of the Department of the U.S. Treasury, Secretary Tim Geithner. Said appointment of Secretary Tim Geithner, being fully qualified to perform the duties as fiduciary, is effective as of May 13, 2009 and shall continue until further notice, re-appointment, substitution, revocation or termination by James Thomas: McBride. The duties and responsibilities of Sec. Tim Geithner, as fiduciary for JAMES THOMAS MCBRIDE 296520781, are to exercise scrupulous good faith and candor, acting in the best interest of the creditor and lien holder for JAMES THOMAS MCBRIDE 296520781 for the benefit and remedy of James Thomas: McBride, American sovereign; the exclusive and limited purpose of discharging debt for the redemption of property; maintaining a zero balance in the account in accordance with International Bankruptcy Law and shall maintain compliance with all applicable Revenue Codes and statutes.

The Fiduciary shall receive and accept all liabilities; receive and accept all service of process and other documents, instruments, bonds and/or other important documents and Presentments; to appear and discharge, settle and close matters material to said public vessel, and all assignments for or an behalf of said public vessel and to do any and all acts requisite to fully and faithfully execute said appointment including providing a complete and regular statement of accounting to the creditor, James Thomas: McBride. The same shall be by the order of James Thomas: McBride, his assigns and/or assignees. The Fiduciary shall provide the timely activation of this Federal Reserve Account in accordance with Regulation Z and ensure the efficient execution of the day to day operation of said account.

Secretary Tim Geithner, acting as fiduciary for JAMES THOMAS MCBRIDE 296520781 is hereby indemnified and held harmless for all costs, fees and other charges which may exist, occur or arise from the lawful execution of his duties as fiduciary in this matter. (see annexed exhibit

Exhibit K: Form 56 Notice Concerning Fiduciary Relationship

51

RECLAIMING TRUSTEESHIP AND POSTAL AUTHORITY

National Banking Association

In the Public National Banking association is defined as: "*Those who constitute an association nationwide of private, unincorporated persons engaged in the business of banking to issue notes against these obligations of the United States due them; whose private property is at risk to collateralize the government's debt and currency, by legal definitions, a 'national banking association'; such notes, issued against these obligations of the United States to that part of the public debt due its Principals and Sureties are required by law to be accepted as "legal tender" of payments for all debts public and private, and are defined in law as "obligations of the United States", on the same par and category with Federal reserve Notes and other currency and legal tender obligations."*

In the operation of commerce in Bankruptcy, or Receivership, a Public Official may refuse a valid request, one time. That first request is done in the VOLUNTARY Bankruptcy side of the transaction. A Public Official's refusal, or Dishonor, charges the INVOLUNTARY Bankruptcy and their mandatory obligation to honor your request. They have a mandatory obligation to honor your request when presented the second time. Their refusal to honor your second request is Bankruptcy Obstruction and constitutes a dilectual default and their voluntary surrender or abandonment of their office and all power and authority therein.

A Charging Sheet, a form of indictment, was presented under subpoena to John Potter, Postmaster General who had a mandatory obligation to respond and/or act to provide the remedy. His dishonor resulted in the issue of an administrative judgment which carries the same force and effect as if issued by the highest court in the land, documenting his dilectual default and voluntary abandonment of his office and all power and authority therein.

EXHIBIT 1: CHARGING SHEET
This is found on the web site as
www.notice-recipient.com/ArticlesLinks.htmlNeed description

James Mcbride explains:

"*I continued to assist the American people to document the Bankruptcy Obstruction in their foreclosure cases and register this widespread Bankruptcy Obstruction with the Postmaster General, the Trustee, under whose direction the United States operates and I demanded a remedy for the American people.*

I continued to document the collusion between the courts and the banks in sweeping the obstruction under the rug while ignoring real evidence; ignoring real judgments against the banks documenting the bank's admissions to the fraud.

I continued to document the Bankruptcy Obstruction of the Trustees, banks, courts and the Postmaster General -Organic. My research into the power and authority of a Private Postmaster and how to invoke the jurisdiction of the Universal Postal Union gave birth to my **Claim On The Abandonment** *of the Office of the Postmaster General, Trustee, under whose direction the Trust styled as the UNITED STATES operates.*

I spent months documenting the Bankruptcy Obstruction, employing full disclosure at all times. I believe in telling them several times exactly what and how I am going to hold them accountable.

I Registered my Official Claim on the Abandoned Office of the Postmaster General-Organic [not to be confused with the USPS] for and on behalf of the American people. The trust, the entire Global Trust is out of control and if an enlightened being could step into that office then real change could be made on a global level."

EXHIBIT 2 CLAIM ON ABANDONMENT
This is found on www.notice-recipient.com/ArticlesLinks.html

"*My Claim on Abandonment was forwarded to the Vatican for a decision. In the 11th hour, acceptance of the Claim and acknowledgment of* **my authority to act in the capacity of the Postmaster General with all of the power and authority of the Office of the Postmaster General** *was received from the Vatican in a very material way.*"

A Trustee Of The Global Trust.

James McBride continues the story: "*I found myself on the inside, as a Trustee of the Global Trust. The administration of this Global Trust was out of control and I was now in a position to guide this listing ship in a new direction. In the operation of a this Global Trust the administrators have been able to function under a Breach of Trust for decades until someone registered a complaint, identifying the Breach and Demanding a Cure. One must simply identify the Breach. The single act or action which constitutes fraud under which the Trust is being administrated, register a complaint thereto and Demand a Cure. In trust law, there are inescapable repercussions for failure to Cure a Breach.*

Upon Acknowledgment of my Claim on Abandonment by the Vatican, I understood that there must be an ACCEPTANCE. The same as when offered a gift, one must reach out and take hold of the gift as a sign of acceptance. If one refuses to grasp the gift and bring it into their reality, the gift remains un-accepted and becomes mute and void.

As Trustee of the Global Trust I felt it necessary to set the foundation for how We the People would now interact with the trust, informing the administration that we have entered a new day and that business as usual is no longer acceptable.

This ACCEPTANCE, establishing the foundation for the future, came in the form of the: Universal postal Treaty for the Americas 2010.

Now as Trustee and Postmaster General, the Declaration of Peace (as presented in earlier chapter was registered into the repository."

EXHIBIT 3: Universal Postal Treaty for the Americas

The Universal Postal Treaty For The Americas

This is found on ***www.notice-recipient.com/ArticlesLinks.html***

This has been presented in an earlier Chapter. The summary below is presented as a repeat in the Postmaster General's words:

The Universal Postal Treaty For The Americas 2010 was a self executing Treaty presented under the Codes of the Universal Postal Union and the UNITED STATES and has been accepted as positive law, the highest form of law. As always you may read the entire Treaty at the Link provided.

I wish to present a brief overview of what was in the Treaty, what it accomplished, how it effects We the People and the Global Trust and how it effects our abundance and prosperity. So, here it is From the beginning.

The Universal Postal Treaty For The Americas 2010 was a self executing Treaty presented under the Codes of the Universal Postal Union and the UNITED STATES and has been accepted as positive law, the highest form of law. As always you may read the entire Treaty at the Link provided.

I wish to present a brief overview of what was in the Treaty, what it accomplished, how it effects We the People and the Global Trust and how it effects our abundance and prosperity. So, here it is From the beginning.

Preamble When in the Course of human events, it becomes necessary for people to dissolve the political bonds which have connected them with others, and to assume among the powers of the earth, the separate and equal station to which they may choose to aspire, a decent respect to the opinions of mankind requires that they should declare the causes which impel them to the separation. We hold that no truths are self-evident, but must have their usefulness demonstrated. That all people are created with equal freedom from tyranny, but frequently accept domination or obedience to a legal code, to a greater or lesser degree from person to person. That people are endowed with only what rights they have chosen to be endowed with, through wisdom or common folly, for wealth or ilth. That people can secure for themselves, with understanding of their own unique situations, those rights which best allow them to live in peace and fruitful harmony with nature and all Her various species.

That whenever any person, Government, or other entity, not fully recognizing the unique situation of each individual, becomes in any way oppressive or destructive, people may choose to ignore, alter, abolish or separate themselves from such an institution, and to live in peace and harmony. That man can choose to resolve any conflict through intelligence, with, adequate communication and a full understanding of each and every point of view involved, by each and every person involved. Prudence, indeed, will dictate that Governments long established should not be changed for light and transient causes,

but only after calm consideration of the True Will and mutual goals of all those individuals involved. All experience has shown that people are more disposed to suffer, while evils are sufferable, than to right themselves by abolishing the forms to which they are accustomed. But when a long train of abuses and usurpation evinces a design to reduce them under absolute Despotism or Dogma not chosen by the individual concerned, it is their right, it is their duty to themselves and their Creator, to throw off such a Government and to accept responsibility, each for their own actions and future security.
Declaration Of Peace

The general post office styled as the UNITED STATES has been in a perpetual state of war since its inception. The 'Powers That Be' have used the UNITED STATES as a weapon to wage war on the sovereign people of America, operating under the Emergency War Powers Act and the secret presumption that the sovereign people are the enemy of the UNITED STATES for the purpose of evading their liabilities under the original equity contract and to pillage and plunder the private property of the people they were created to serve.

The general post office styled as the UNITED STATES has been used as a weapon to wage an economic war at arms length against all of the people of the world bringing all of humanity to the brink of destruction as the CREDITOR'S master plan of total economic slavery over the sovereign people of the world has been implemented.

The Powers That Be have used the UNITED STATES as a weapon to wage war on the sovereign people of the world via the unconscionable creation, production and distribution of harmful drugs for the purpose of enslaving the people and funding and executing their genocide against humanity.

The Powers That Be have used the UNITED STATES as a platform for their propaganda, creating the world's problems and then presenting themselves as the world's savior bringing about the solution and protection from their self created illusionary boogie men for the purpose of enslaving the sovereign people of the world.

Let it be known by all of humanity that the: UNITED STATES HAS DECLARED PEACE ! From this day forward the UNITED STATES shall be used as a tool, actuated by humility, to promote universal peace, love and unity among all men. The UNITED STATES shall become a broker and facilitator of peace; a springboard for ascension and balance within the world consciousness. The UNITED STATES shall immediately stand down and withdraw itself from all acts of aggression and vacate all occupied land and shall immediately bring all American soldiers home.

The agents and agencies of the UNITED STATES shall immediately cease and desist in all forms of gun and drug production and distribution; all forms of terrorism and genocide of the people, all standard operating procedures of the powers that be since the days of the East India trading Company.

All Administrative Agencies of the UNITED STATES shall immediately remove all gold fringed military flags from their offices and courtrooms and shall display the civilian flag of peace. The Custodian of the Alien Property shall immediately update his/her files, removing the names and private property of the American people from their files/lists and make the return of the property to the rightful owners. All administrative agencies and administrative courts shall operate in peace and honor, servants of the sovereign people.

A "Transitional Committee" shall be seated for the purpose of ensuring a peaceful and efficient transition from an Empirical War based mentality and operating system to one of peace, humility and unity. Said "Transitional Committee" shall establish and empower an interim government for the united states of America and shall operate until such time as the people can be duly informed as to the true history of the UNITED STATES and the fraud that has been perpetrated against them, not to exceed one year.

The Postmaster general of the organic post office for the united states, creator of the general post office styled as the UNITED STATES and located within the ten miles square commonly known as Washington, D.C., under whose direction the UNITED STATES operates, shall operate in the capacity of trustee for the people and shall take instructions from the "Transitional Committee" until such time as the Interim government shall be seated and empowered.

Declaration of Causes for Separation On July 26, 1775 the Continental Congress appointed Benjamin Franklin as the first postmaster general of the organic Post Office for the united states, union of several states. In 1776 the united states of America declared its independence and in May 1789 the Constitution for the united states of America was adopted.

On Thursday, Sept. 17, 1789 we find written, *"Mr. Goodhue, for the committee appointed for the purpose, presented a bill to amend part of the Tonnage act, which was read the first time. The bill sent from the Senate, for the temporary establishment of the Post Office, was read the second and third time, and passed. The bill for establishing the Judicial Courts . . . , for establishing the seat of government . . ."* The organic post office for the united states of America established the seat of government, a general post office, under the direction of the postmaster general.

This is verified on March 1825, when an act was passed entitled "An act to reduce into one the several acts establishing and regulating the post office department," 3 Story, U. S. 1825. "It is thereby enacted; That there be established, the seat of the government of the United States, a general post office, under the direction of a postmaster general."

The organic post office for the united states of America established the ten miles square, styled as WASHINGTON, D.C., as a general post office and independent postal zone with the rights and authority of a sovereign nation, operating under a corporate structure under the direction of the postmaster general to function as the seat of government of the United States.

Treaties are the highest form of law. The Universal Postal Treaty For The Americas 2010, an international Treaty, set as positive law the following which will be covered more in the Breach of Trust section and can be read in its entirety by clicking on the provided link.

Complex Regulatory Scheme
Claim On Abandonment
House Joint Resolution 192 which guaranteed our Right of Redemption of the estate via Discharge of the Debt
Declaration of Peace see below or read the entire document
Law Form
Established a Transitional Committee to operate under the Postmaster General-Organic
Sets a new course for the courts More fully covered in *The Breach* section

A "Transitional Committee" shall be seated for the purpose of ensuring a peaceful and efficient transition from an Empirical War based mentality and operating system to one of peace, humility and unity. Said "Transitional Committee" shall establish and empower an interim government for the united states of America and shall operate until such time as the people can be duly informed as to the true history of the UNITED STATES and the fraud that has been perpetrated against them, not to exceed one year.

The Postmaster General of the organic post office for the united states, creator of the general post office styled as the UNITED STATES and located within the ten miles square commonly known as Washington, D.C., under whose direction the UNITED STATES operates, shall operate in the capacity of trustee for the people and shall take instructions from the "Transitional Committee" until such time as the Interim government shall be seated and empowered.

The Treaty sets a new course for the courts. These Administrative Courts shall operate as established, for the purpose of facilitating the prosecution of grievances against an administrative agency by the American people for the administrative agencies trespass on the private rights of the sovereign people of America and shall operate side by side with the common law courts for the people.

And so James Thomas McBride offers his path of experience to others freely. as he explains, this is the way I found my way. In Part 3, we will derive the benefit of his experience when he offers advancements on the process which are much simpler.

55

THE PHANTOM ADMINISTRATION OF PLANET EARTH INC.

All Government Officials Are Private Contractors

We will leave Part 2 with a final Chapter that has an interesting twist. Much of this book is dedicated to revealing PLANET EARTH INC as made up fictional thing by me. However, this phantom structure has a pyramid of corporation beneath it that is indeed registered. The UNITED STATES is a corporation **(www.abodia.com/2/United-States-is-a-corporation.htm#Its_a_Corporation)** and **CANADA is a registered CORPORATION under the USA.** And you thought we were an independent country. Canada is a Corporation Under UK Queen - Canada is TRADED in the US Stock Exchange and registered as "*…CORPORATE CANADA in USA. This is Canada's Corporate registered number. 0000230098 CANADA DC SIC: 8880 American Depositary Receipt. Business Address Canadian Embassy 1746 Massachusetts Ave., NW, Washington, DC 20036…*" You can check out http://inpursuitofhappiness.wordpress.com/2006/12/02/canada-is-a-corporation-under-uk-queen/ and check it out on Edgar at http://www.sec.gov/cgi-bin/browse-edgar?action=getcompany&CIK=0000230098&owner=include

If, as an American or Canadian, you are sceptical about the Vatican's involvement in the administration over America, you need to do some research on the **www.manta.com** website, owned by Dunn & Bradstreet. If you research the private corporation called 'the UNITED STATES Government', you will find that the 'OWNER' is listed as being 'Archbishop Deric J. McLeod, of the The Basilica of the National Shrine of the Immaculate Conception, of Washington, DC'. Since Archbishops of the Vatican are sworn to poverty, then, the Archbishop can only be the named agent for the secular Holy Roman Empire, situate in the city/state called the Vatican.

If you wish to have proof that the Pontiff of the Holy Roman Empire has used religion as a means of entrapment of millions of souls into a state and status of slavery for centuries, check out these webpages:

The Pontiff of Rome gains control over England, and makes the Monarch of Great Britain a puppet Monarch FOREVER See King John at:
http://www.nndb.com/people/536/000092260/

Pope declares by edict that all humankind are his subjects(slaves) - last sentence here: Unam Sanctam *http://www.fordham.edu/halsall/source/B8-unam.asp*

The false Apostle, the Roman author of most of the New Testament, Paul:
http://www.judaismvschristianity.com/paulthe.htm

False Christianity, Mithraism becomes Roman Christianity First Pope:
http://www.reformation.org/pope-constantine.html

The primary assertions made on this website are:

1. The income tax applies only to fictional (legally dead) entities called persons. Upon the recording of live birth of a child, a 7 year countdown begins. If that child, or its parents, do not give notice that the child is still alive, the child is declared 'legally dead', thus allowing the child, when becoming an adult, to be infused with the 'legally dead' legal name, as found on a birth certificate. That is why judges and lawyers wear black robes - for the same reason undertakers wear black suits - they are dealing with the 'dead'.

2. There is absolutely no government act, statute or law to which any free will living adult human in Canada, or in the USA, is subject.

3. A free will living adult human cannot enter into a contract with a fictional entity, such as with the de facto nation called Canada or Government of Canada, nor with a de facto Province of Canada or Government of a Province, nor with the de facto Crown in right to either of the above, or with a State[USA], and thus, certainly not a contract of servitude. And, so, any exchange of labour an adult free will living man or woman may do with any Government department or agency must be done through an agent in commerce where the free will adult living human remains as an 'undisclosed principal' and the claimant in equity of all remuneration paid over to the fictional legal name/ agent. The 'legal name' agent is a 'tool', in the form of intellectual property, owned by the Crown and used by the living adult free will status human, the undisclosed principal, under the Rule of Necessity.

4. The fraudulent tricking of people, through their ignorance, into the status of "plantation slave" by their using a name created and owned by the Crown or State is an act of treason, by government, upon the sovereign people. That Crown or State owned name is the name as found on the Birth certificate.

5. Since we, as free will beings, are REQUIRED to use the Crown/State owned legal identity name in all commerce and in government communication, such use is not a voluntary act on our part, as we must use it by PRIVATE NECESSITY to sustain and maintain our life. That negates the Crown/State claim that we voluntarily use it, and thus negates our becoming property owned by the Crown/State through the legal maxim, accessio cedit principali.

6. The 'legal fiction name', AKA: 'person/taxpayer', has only the function of an 'agent in commerce' and 'trustee in trust' for the free will living adult human to which it is associated.

And for Canada specifically:
7. The British Monarchy ceased to have any relevance to Canada in 1901, upon the death of Queen Victoria. All British Monarchs have been pretender Monarchs of Canada since that date. The office of 'The Queen', 'Her Majesty' or 'the Crown' is the 'also known as' name for the City of London, and its owner, the Vatican, as the Monarchs of England have been vassal Monarchs subject to the Pope's Holy Roman Empire since 1213 AD.

8. The Parliament of Canada is a de facto usurper of governing power over Canada since 1931, and in reality, since 1901; and, in fact is a commercial corporation subject to the City of London. Although we see all court cases where the action is brought by Government to be "The Queen" or the Latin "Regina". That only indicates that the Queen of Great Britain is acting in the role of agent for the City of London. That is why she does not have to comply with her Coronation oath to defend the individual rights of the people. That oath is not applicable in her role as agent for the Crown of the City of London. And also, the fact that, since 1213, all incoming Monarchs of England must make a pledge of fielty/fealty to the Pontiff of Rome, not to the Roman Catholic Church, but to his secular Holy Roman Empire, before being allowed to be crowned Monarch of Great Britain, would make the Coronation Oath invalid where it conflicts with Papal Policy. And, as with the Oath of Office of the President of the UNITED STATES, who must also be subject to the Pontiff and his policies, and thus that Oath being so commonly ignored, so too is it ever more evident that the Queen of G.B. is following policy that conflicts with her Coronation Oath. Secondary Oaths only apply when they are complicit with the Primary Oath.

Think this is ancient history? Check out the pledge of a newly crowned Pope/Pontiff - Father (creator) of Kings and Princes, and obviously of Presidents and Prime Ministers at **www.aloha.net/~mikesch/claims.htm**

We have presented two situations where "we the people" are taking back positions that have been vacant. The Republic of the United States group has been presented as one as repopulating the seats of Congress. The other is the Postmaster General which has been vacant. Now it has to be understood that much research has gone into that determination.

But there is a fellow named Rod Class who has been deeply immersed in going much further. He has been receiving a ruling that US Government Offices are Vacant and all Government Officials are private contractors.

On **www.the2012scenario.com** October 14, 2012, the following article was published:

US Bombshell; Rod Class gets FOURTH Administrative Ruling "Gov't Offices are Vacant"- All Gov't Officials are "Private Contractors"
Submitted by The South on Sun, 10/14/2012 - 18:25

"Yes, you read that correctly; it is true, and is now on the court record; black ink on white paper. Please read on:

A lot of us have been exposing the crime of the UNITED STATES corporation for many years, but until recently, no one has had the proof that all government offices are vacant; no one is home; those supposed government offices/agencies are being occupied by PRIVATE CONTRACTORS and are NOT being occupied by a legitimate government body.

This is equivalent to the ice cream man knocking on your door and extorting taxes from you. He has no lawful authority to do anything other than drive the ice cream truck - he's not a government official; he's an ice cream man.

Your supposed government officials are nothing more than ice cream men/women who are fraudulently extorting money from you and your family; throwing you in prison; taxing you to death; stealing your children and imposing their will on you, and enforcing their own **internal-statutory rules and codes upon you and your family.**

Rod Class has now received **FOUR** *Administrative Rulings that prove what many of us have felt to be truth: What you think is government; what you think are legitimate Government Officials/Senators/Congressman/Policeman/Governors/Tax Collectors, etc. are nothing more than* **private contractors**, *extorting money from American Citizens and failing to pay off the public debt as they are instructed to do by the 1933 bankruptcy.*

What they have done is this:
These people have switched places with the average American Citizen. They are enforcing their own Administrative codes, that are only meant for THEM, upon regular Citizens who are not being paid by the corporation. The supposed elected officials have hoodwinked the country into an employment position without pay. They themselves are taking public money to occupy government seats/positions/agencies, when they are nothing more than private contractors ... Felony!

They are treating us as if we are paid government employees; enforcing their own internal rules-regulations-codes, and statutes on the average Citizen, as well as conveniently forgetting to send us our weekly/monthly government employment check.

I've been preaching this for the last year + with no avail on this forum. Perhaps now, people will begin to listen and take action.
In these radio shows, Rod explains his Administrative Rulings from the various Judges; explains the con, and shows you, where in their very own US Codes the above aforementioned information is spot on.

There are a few shows you need to listen to, and here are some bullet points of those shows:

1. All BAR attorneys are prohibited from representing John Q. Public; can only represent gov't officials and employees within their own agencies, their BAR Charter says so.
2. Any Judge that prohibits you from representing yourself or hiring a defense other than a BAR attorney, are in fact, committing a felony on the bench in violation of the Taft-Hartly Act (running a closed union shop) and the Smith Act (overthrow of Constitutional form of Gov't)

3. Anytime an BAR attorney represents someone in a case against you, you can now claim that person is incompetent; a ward of the state, with no standing to sue.

4. Any and all tax collectors, police officers, sheriffs dept's, DOT, tag agencies, BAR attorneys, Judges, Highway Patrol, supposed elected officials, are nothing more than private contractors, who can now be brought up on fraud charges for impersonating a public official while receiving federal funding.

5. Any and all home, vehicle, credit card loans are supposed to be discharged through the Treasury window, in compliance with the 1933 bankruptcy laws. These scumbags are double dipping and never discharging the debt like they are supposed to. They are embezzling the funds and pocketing them for themselves.

6. Every person sitting in prison today was railroading by a BAR attorney who's first allegiance is to the State; who had no lawful authority to represent them; who worked in concert with the State to perpetrate a fraud upon its victims.

7. Orders from Administrative courts prove for the fourth time, an agency of the State is NOT an agency under the State.

8. Elected Officials are claiming 11th Amendment sovereignty, when it's actually you and I that hold 11th Amendment sovereignty. They are getting paid by the corporation, you and I are not.

9. They have admitted to the crime of no one actually holding a public office; they are filling corporate seats and defrauding the public.

10. Political subdivisions are not getting their 40% funding from the Feds as they are supposed to get.

11. These Judges have admitted (black ink on white paper) that all these State Offices are .... EMPTY!

12. Now we have Administrative paperwork - ruling these public offices aren't part of the State agencies.

13. Attorney Generals may not practice law; can't represent the people who are not public officials.

14. If the State is a 3rd party interloper in your Marriage (marriage license); Vehicle Title (State Registration), etc. then they are liable for 1/3rd of the cost to manage the daily activities of that contract.

15. If the State demands you have a Drivers License and Tag your vehicle because it is registered with the State, then as the owner of the vehicle, the State is required to pay for the vehicle, the tags, licensing, fuel, tires, oil, etc. and they are also to pay you a salary for driving a State owned vehicle; it says so in their own Highway Safety Act and USC - CFR rules and regulations.

16. We now have the court orders that goes back and nullifies any and all IRS and Tax cases, Foreclosures, Credit Card Debt, cases or actions. These people never had the lawful right to demand anything of you; they are corporate actors, not a legitimate government body.

17. Judge admits the 1933 bankruptcy, and no way to pay off anything because of Federal Reserve Notes; all public debt is t be discharged through the Treasury.

18. Only the Secretary of Transportation can hear traffic cases; all traffic cases are civil, not criminal.

19. If you're not being paid for you time, you are not required to have one of their CDL or CMV licenses; it's prohibited.

20. Says we now have a major labor dispute on our hands; US corporation running a slave racket against American Citizens without the pay.

21. United States Codes (USC) and Titles #1 thru #50 are void; have never been passed by Congress; all have been repealed.

As I've been saying for a very long time on this forum: If you are not getting a weekly or monthly paycheck from the so called federal government aka UNITED STATES or one of its sub corporations such as the STATE OF ***, then their statutory rules (not laws), codes and regulations **DO NOT APPLY TO YOU** .... Period!

There is so much information packed into these last six calls, I can't even begin to share it in this post. If you want your freedom; if you want to know with 100% surety that the foreign corporation known as the UNITED STATES has zero authority over you unless you are receiving a weekly paycheck from them, take the time to listen to call #646 through #651 here:

http://www.talkshoe.com/talkshoe/web/talkCast.jsp?masterId=4...
Scroll down the page and click on the orange "Listen" button; a pop up player will appear for your listening pleasure. And believe me: This is pure listening pleasure, with the court filings; rulings and US Code to back it all up. By the time you finish these few short shows, your fear of the government will be a thing of the past.

Also, many of Rod's current filings against the infrastructure are at: http://harveyw26.minus.com ...some may be easy to download, some may not !

And for those of you who are new to the forum and want to get a better grasp of all this prior to or after listening to the calls, here are some of my more informative posts on the matter at hand:
Public Notice to Gun Grabbing Politicians:
http://www.dailypaul.com/246514/public-notice-attention-to-a...
So the Government wants you to collect a sales tax?
http://www.dailypaul.com/245362/have-a-business-and-the-govt...
Your Home Loan was paid the day you signed the note:
http://www.dailypaul.com/244590/want-to-stick-it-to-the-bank...
The real reason for the 14th Amendment:
http://www.dailypaul.com/244553/they-created-the-14th-amendm...
What's the One Document in your possession that gives you the authority to rule over my life?
http://www.dailypaul.com/244165/whats-the-one-document-you-h...
Can the State be an actual injured party? ..... No, it cannot!
http://www.dailypaul.com/243521/can-the-state-be-an-injured-...
Having a Social Security # is not a contract with the State/Feds:
http://www.dailypaul.com/243164/social-security-is-not-a-con...
Trust Law, your Rights and how to enforce them:
http://www.dailypaul.com/243090/trust-law-your-rights-and-ho...
Why you should never hire an attorney:
http://www.dailypaul.com/242260/this-is-why-you-should-never...

Hopefully now in light of these **Administrative Court Rulings** people will now come to realize the fact, that **Unless You Are Getting A Weekly Check From Government,**

Their Statutory Rules-Codes-Regulations They Put Off As Laws, Have Zero Force Or Effect On You Personally. *No Contract = No Jurisdiction.*

Did you fill out an employment contract with the State; are they paying you for your services? If not, why the hell are you following their rules? This is how we change our current form of Government back to the Republic it was initially intended to be. If you don't take the time to listen to at least those last six shows at the link above, you are overlooking the most important information ever to come to light within the Liberty Movement. Stop looking for a savior to save us from tyranny and listen to the shows I've provided. Now you are your own savior - Individually, now you can make a HUGE difference in our political structure and form of government."

You may think this is a pretty good joke but rest assured, the evidence is there to check it out. As yourself, what power does IBM Corp have over you? And what if any Corporation presented a bunch of documents that you signed because they hid the truth of your employment? Would that be fraud? Would it nullify the contract?

Dear Mister Obama, We Have A Speech For You

This was taken from ***www.the2012scenario.com*** on OCt 19. 2012. Treat this as another joke if you will but this is written with a lot of thought that represents the research of many, many people. The article was entitled ***The Global Announcement ... What If?***

What if President Obama pulled back the curtain on the secret state? In this article, Michael, a reader of Jean Haines' blog, *2012:* ***What's the Real Truth****?* could not wait for President Obama to make a speech telling the truth about the cabal, world finances, Disclosure, etc., and so he wrote it for him. We (the editors) might make a few very minor changes, but no matter. The speech has been written for the President. Thanks to Mary. Michael says: *"In case anyone out there is currently drafting a global announcement that will address the gist without freaking everyone out, here's my take (*presumed *speaker is President Barack Obama)."*

The Global Announcement
by Michael, 2012: What's the Real Truth?
Oct. 19, 2012 (***http://tinyurl.com/8zj89j4***)

"My fellow Americans, and my fellow citizens of the world, Shortly before I took office four years ago, I became aware – as every president since John F. Kennedy has before me – that a shadow government of financial interests exerts a pervasive control over the affairs of this world, and has done so since at least the early years of the 20th century, if not long before. It was made clear to me at that time by representatives of these interests that the parameters of my power as president would be severely limited by the dictates of this shadow government. John Kennedy was the last president to directly confront and oppose the dictates of this hidden global regime, and his death has served as a warning to future occupants of the White House ever since.

I recognized at that time that the Constitution that I had sworn to uphold and preserve had already, in fact, been betrayed, and that the republic envisioned by our founders had been systematically dismantled by this shadow government, whose agenda and goals are diametrically opposed to the ideals of freedom and equal opportunity upon which this country was founded. It was made clear to me, moreover, that this shadow government has controlled and manipulated the outcome of every presidential election since 1968, including the election that brought me into office.

This shadow government has been controlled since the 19th century by the banking families of Europe, headed by the Rothschilds and Warburgs, and their so-called 'bloodline' allies in European royal families, represented in this country by the private banking cabal that controls the Federal Reserve System. The agenda and goals of this cabal were entirely self-serving, with the avowed goal of reducing the population of our planet by the mass elimination of billions of human beings through war, starvation, and disease, leaving a remnant of half a billion debt slaves.

The list of their crimes against humanity is long and shocking, and I know that many among us will simply refuse to believe that such things could happen. However the evidence is massive and incontrovertible, and indicts members of this cabal of crimes that include the planning and execution of the 911 terror attacks, the deliberate triggering of financial panics, including the financial crisis of 2008 and the Great Depression, and the manipulated fomentation of numerous wars. Though their influence has been pervasive throughout government, media, finance, science, agriculture, and religion, their core membership is small, comprised of less than 10,000 tightly controlled and disciplined members, many of whom have been subjected to mind control, torture, and abuse since childhood.

I vowed to myself on that day that I would do everything within my power to restore our freedoms, while knowing that I would be required to play a double game merely to ensure my own survival. The safety of my family was also at risk. But thousands of Americans in uniform take the same risks on behalf of our freedom every day, and I vowed to be worthy of their example.

Tonight I am grateful to God, and to the many thousands of men and women throughout the world who risked their lives in the struggle against this dark regime, to share with you the news that this shadow government has been defeated. Their assets have been seized. Their leaders are being arrested, in accordance with due process of law, by local law enforcement, with the assistance of U.S. Marshalls, and backed where necessary by military units, in keeping with the military oath to protect and preserve our Constitution against 'all enemies, foreign and domestic.' Massive evidence of the cabal's crimes has been collected. They will be brought to justice. The even more heinous crimes against humanity that they have been tirelessly attempting to execute – including detonation of nuclear weapons in some of the world's most populous cities – have been prevented. Their tactics have centered on seizing power during times of chaos – chaos that they themselves created. Those tactics have been thwarted.

The enormous funds and treasure - numbering in the many trillions of dollars – that they have stolen and abused for nearly a century will now be available for the benefit of mankind. The advanced technologies that they suppressed are even now being developed for widespread use – technologies that can bring undreamed-of prosperity and peace to our world. The crushing burden of debt they deliberately created to enslave mankind will be wiped clean.

The primary tool of control used by this cabal has been their ability to control the currencies of the world. As one of their founders, Nathan de Rothschild put it, 'allow me to control a nation's currency, and I do not care who makes its laws.' Over a period of a hundred years, they succeeded in seizing control of an enormous cache of gold – gold which was set aside, after World War II, for the benefit of mankind. That gold has been returned to its rightful guardians, and will now be used as a Global Development Fund to heal our world.

The ability of the cabal to control world affairs through the printing of so-called fiat currency – that is, currency that is not backed by any real asset – has now been removed, and a new system of asset-backed currencies has already been implemented. Worldwide financial reform – reform that has been decades in the planning – based on total transparency, and the replacement of a debt-based system with an equity-based system, is already largely in place.

This world-transforming change has only been possible through an alliance of 140 nations which banded together to throw off the control of the banking cabal, headed by the so-called BRICS nations of Brazil, Russia, India, China, and South Africa, and with the aid of patriotic elements in the Pentagon and intelligence community. An unseen internal war has raged over the last two years, in a race against time to prevent the cabal from implementing bloodshed on a scale unseen in world history.

A financial war has raged as well. The U.S. dollar had been artificially propped up by the banking cabal as the reserve currency of the world. That status now will end, and the so-called "petro-dollar" (by which countries were required by major oil producers to pay for oil only in U.S. dollars) will be a thing of the past. A natural adjustment of currency values will then take place.

These are earth-shaking and epochal changes. But I urge all of us to remain calm. The news I bring – news which is being shared around the world tonight by leaders in other global capitals -is good beyond hope. An era of peace and prosperity is dawning tonight. The era of debt and war and financial panics, of hidden agendas and secret societies, is at an end. The national debt of the United States has been wiped out, as has the debt of every nation on earth. Credit card, mortgage, and student loan debts will also largely be forgiven or repaid from global funds.

The Internal Revenue Service will be dismantled, and income tax will be eliminated. America will be restored to our organic constitution. The United Nations, the International Monetary Fund, and the World Bank – all of which had been either created or thoroughly manipulated by the banking cabal – will be reformed from the ground up. And an enormous fund amounting to more than a hundred trillion dollars will now be available for the healing and restoration of our wounded planet, for feeding the hungry, healing the sick, caring for the elderly, and for the development of the marvellous technologies that should have been available to us many decades ago.

As if these revelations are not epochal enough, I am also now able to share with you news that many of us have long suspected – that we are not alone in this universe. The amazing freedom that is now ours could not have been won without the help of the friends I like to refer to as our "off-planet cousins" – near relations to humanity who have refrained from interfering until now, who have stood silent guard while honouring our divinely given free will to govern ourselves.

There is indeed a Galactic Federation, and when we are ready, we may choose whether or not to accept their invitation to join the greater family of free planets – a family to which we are closely related through millions of years. Until now, the enormously advanced so-called 'alien' technologies have been a closely held secret of the shadow regime, but now these too will be available for the benefit of humanity".

Here in America, we will now be able to hold the first truly free elections in many decades – elections by paper ballot – and the interim government now in place will then be replaced by one freely chosen by a free people. A time of reconciliation and healing will be necessary. Many grievous shocks await us, as the true nature and scope of the crimes of the hidden government become apparent, and politicians on both sides of the aisle, as well as many prominent figures in finance and media are tried for their crimes.

I, too, will stand before the tribunal of your justice, like any other citizen, and be judged for my part in this hidden regime. And I stand ready to serve my country again as your president if you should do me that great honour.

And let me urge you all from my heart to forget the divisions that have separated us: red state from blue, believers from non-believers, faith from faith, gay from straight, liberal from conservative. Let us strive instead to see each other as brothers and sisters, children of one Creator, a family that honours our differences, and cherishes together the one garden of earth we call home.

As many found in Europe after the fall of the Iron Curtain, the corruption had reached out to ensnare and taint many thousands who had little choice but to cooperate, for this shadow government operated exactly like organized crime, in which extortion, bribery, blackmail, and murder were the daily tools of control. We are called to a time of understanding and reconciliation. Let us seek the truth, and seek justice, but let us temper justice with mercy, and look to our own responsibility, to the part we ourselves may have played in this long and tragic time of hidden domination.

In closing, let us remember the great wisdom of Lincoln, and beginning in this moment, let us create a time of healing and peace.

With malice toward none; with charity for all; with firmness in the right, as God gives us to see the right, let us strive on to finish the work we are in … to do all which may achieve and cherish a just, and a lasting peace, among ourselves, and with all nations.

Good night, and may God bless you, your family, our country, and our world."

A Note On Your New Path

Are things changing? You betcha! At Light Speed!!! By now you are filled with confusion. You are a mere mortal that wants to be happy and pay your bills. You do not want to take on the system even though it may be a fraud. You want peace and harmony not conflict. You do not want to be warrior of light or commerce. What do you do? Do you really want to take new path? What would it be?

That's what Part 3 is all about...

PART 3

DISSOLUTION AND SOLUTION

WHAT IS THE CURE?

PART 3 OVERVIEW

Part 3 is about Lessons. What have you learned from the words which have been presented in Parts 1 and 2? Are you happy with your life or are you not? Part 3 is about choosing. It is about how you resign from PLANET EARTH Inc. and attain your pension called Good Faith and Credit. It is about burning your prescription for those blue pills of Religions and the CODE of gods that diverts the power of Spirit. We have seen how the Cure of James Thomas of the McBride family has taken form. Now it is time to look at the individual Cure. You can make a choice now that you are informed that a choice exists.

And so The Matrix of a New Consciousness manifesting into reality is everywhere, it is all around us. You can see it when you look out your window, or turn on your television set. You can feel it when you go to work, when you go to church, when you pay your taxes. It is the wool that has been pulled over your eyes to blind you from the truth. You are a slave like everyone else. You were born into a prison that you cannot see, that you cannot smell, or taste or touch. A prison for your mind is your spiritual abandonment, a choice made by you. A prison of your body that is your trade of sovereignty for perceived benefits and money. And a prison of your soul that was accepted in your religious beliefs to follow the gods and the words of GOD Unfortunately no one can be told what the Matrix is. You have to see it for yourself. This is your chance to understand the Matrix and to choose a way out. After this, there is no turning back.

Take the blue pill, the story ends, you wake up in your bed and believe whatever you want to believe. Take the red pill, you will stay in wonderland, and I will show you how deep the rabbit hole goes. Remember, what I am offering is the truth, nothing more. Follow me."

There are many Lessons that the journey of the Soul faces in rising in its vibration. And it matters not whether the journey is dark or light for the destination is the same. In this Part, we will put before your mind what are the most difficult revelations of the Earthling in the Soul's quest to find Home. These are not lessons easily accepted and even though they are placed directly in front of you, the tendency is for intellect and ego to reject these from belief until these are experienced directly in the Soul's quest.

Nevertheless, the purpose here is to bring these forward into conscious awareness for even though they may not be accepted directly as truth, they may provide the attraction to investigate to the satisfaction of each.

56

THE TWO FACED EARTHLING

In every aspect of life we live in an inherent polarity that is ingrained from the first day one takes a breath to cry or get attention driven by instinct. Even before that event, the way your mother thinks, speaks and acts has influences upon your being. The Earthling has accepted a world of polarity as there is always a conditional "two-faced" standard on those important issues of life:

In the Bible, even god does not follow his Ten Commandments;
In cultures, we worship those who are the kings, queens, popes, rulers, gods;
In business, we are obedient to our masters called CEO's who pay us;
In government, we cower to the political leaders;
In military, we fear the mighty power of the armed forces;
In our personal lives we favour bloodlines;
In corporate life, we follow a satanic survival of the fittest philosophy;
In religion, we overlook rape, pillage, slavery, death, and destruction by a god;
In life, we fear the consequence of death and sin;
In purpose, we seek carnal pleasures and desires so as to better than others;
In family it is our bloodlines we protect not the rest;
In family it is our fortunes and accumulations that we hand down and protect;
In our family we are willing to forgive others unless they mess with us;
In life's rules, the 10 commandment rules are for others;
In history we believe what experts write;
In life, our forgiveness, love, and preferences are conditional;
In behaviour we follow those deemed smarter, more powerful;
In beliefs we follow a pyramidal structure of hierarchy and inequality;

The loving, vengeful gods and their spokesmen have taught many they are born sinners and they can absolve sin. So we as a mass believe we can be kind to a few to dissolve hate of others. We have been conditioned to think light and dark, good and evil.

It is ok to kill those who are perceived as a threat. Earthlings are addicted to the drama of polarity and conflict. The scenario is a double standard life of a two-faced human. On one hand the human has an inherent desire to live in love, peace and harmony to help others until one is crossed, deceived or threatened. Then it all changes to a scenario of vengeance and "putting it right" unfolds. Why is it this way? It is because this polarity and separation of self and one's immediate family is what we have been taught. It stems from the gods who taught us. Whether we like it or not, the commandments are ok until it is time to take an eye for an eye. Whether we have higher spiritual inklings or not, we follow the carnal needs to express the lower desires of self and ego. We like peace but we have clearly seen as a corporate "culture" and the satanic beliefs prevail so as to line our pockets. It is to live life to the fullest expression of self. Everything we think, hear, see and therefore express is a drama between good and evil. Our movies are this drama; so is our lives. We love it. And we hate it. And so with such love of polarity, does it come as a surprise that we create more of it? This endless drama is hardly surprising when we create and live in a world of vengeance and conflict; how can it ever cease?

The Two-face Earthling is best shown true colors with family bloodlines. They are the loved ones, the protected ones and all the stops are pulled out, until one of them pisses the other off. Then the rules change. The whole idea of equality and love of all is just lip service; really a big joke. It is the ego and intellect at play with as Christ put it: "the carnal self".

Yet this two faced Earthling has always had choice. It is the way it is because the Earthling has liked it this way. The Earthling as measured by what is and what the majority chooses has consistently chosen to be led by others and to favour immediate family and carnal desires. It is the polarity that is the norm and opinion, condition, desire that supports Earthlings in being employed by PLANET EARTH Inc. Yes, so far, the Earthling has accepted it this way and the powers of PLANET EARTH know it. It's the corporate culture! But as we have seen, perhaps the jig is up now and it is time to thank the Elite Bloodlines for the journey to this point, say thank you, it's been a good lesson, now let us move on together.

The Light And The Dark Ascension

Yet how could one know good if he did not know what was bad? How could one see light when he has lived in the dark. When both are visible one can rise above. A dark side has been presented here simply to show that there are two sides to everything we believe. For once one see both, one can choose. It is like the Triad, the triangle of light and dark at the two bottom apexes, and the top apex of the merger of the two where there is no distinction. Here above, all is perfect once you rise above both light and dark. It is a place where neither judges the other as wrong or right. It is a place of unity vibration that makes us all, love. Love does that, hate can't

If you begin to look at the belief systems of Christ Consciousness and Lucifer Consciousness, it seems that while one is dedicated to the service of self, the other is dedicated to the service of others. And so we have two major schools of thought and behaviour; the Spirituality of Lucifer and Christ. We have looked closely at both. We have unknowingly chosen in the past, the spirituality of Lucifer because we have supported the corporate pyramid model and followed other's word of god. Yet in either case, we strive for a better life and a better world. It seems that some Divine Plan may be upon the Earthling in the form of the Word of God?

As we have seen in Part 2, much of humanity is not simply accepting the old truth anymore, they are subconsciously aligning with a new truth without even being led; desire of peace, love, and service to the Earth and mankind.

Let us divert slightly and look at this thing called ascension. Dictionaries typically define this as "moving upward". The act of rising to an important position or a higher level. The ascent of Christ into heaven on the fortieth day after the Resurrection. In the New Age, it is an increase in the level of vibration. This is not too helpful as to what this really means to you and I.

Valerie Hunt, *www.valeriehunt.com* is a physical therapist and professor of Kinesiology at UCLA. she developed a way to confirm and measure the human energy field. For example, Doctors use EEGs and EKGs to measure electrical activities of brain and heart for example. She discovered the EMG Electromyograph measures the energy field in muscles and expanded into the aura. Normal frequency range in the brain is 0-100cps (cycles per second) most occurring between 0-30cps. Muscle goes to 225cps, heart to 250 but this is where electrical function associated with biology drops off. She picked up a field of energy radiating from the body that ranged between 100 and 1600cps.

These were strongest in areas of the chakras. She noted the field behaves holographically as do the energy fields of the body and that these fields were non-local—could be measured anywhere on the body. She called it the holographic field reality. When the main focus of consciousness is on material the frequencies are in lower range around 250cps. People who have psychic abilities and can heal are 400-800cps. People who can go into a trance and channel other information operate in a narrow band of 800-900cps to receive information.

Those who are mystical are above 900—those who possess the wisdom to know what to do with the channelled info—aware of cosmic interrelatedness of all things and are in touch with every level of human experience. They are anchored in both psychic and trance abilities, but their frequencies extend beyond of up to 200,000-cps.

So is there a progression of psychic abilities? If you look at the A-Z of psychic abilities, there are some 200 listed. But the main ones are; After life communications, Aparitioning, Apportation, Astral projection, Card reading, Channeling, Clairvoyant, Déjà vu, Divining, Divine Intervention, Invisibility, Empathy, ESP, Levitation, Materialization, Necromacy, OBE, Ouji, Past Life Regression, Palmistry, Psychic healing, Remote Viewing, Regression, Scrying, Tarot, Tea Cup Reading, Telekinesis, Teleportation, Telepathy, Transfiguration.

What Valerie is saying is that there is a relationship between the vibrational frequency of the body's electromagnetic system and specific psychic abilities. This is what we refer to as *raising one's vibration.*

If you look at the New Age believers (or the new consciousness), the process of ascension is indeed rising to a higher vibration which they say is unconditional love. And when you can be in totality that which you already are (unconditional love vibration), let go of this polarity then you get to that higher state of ascension and all these magical abilities above open to you.

This is called the new energy and with reference to the New Age beliefs, we can create an interesting graph of this process of ascension and ability upgrade. This is further explained in my books **Can You Let Go** and **Managing Human Subtle Energy.**

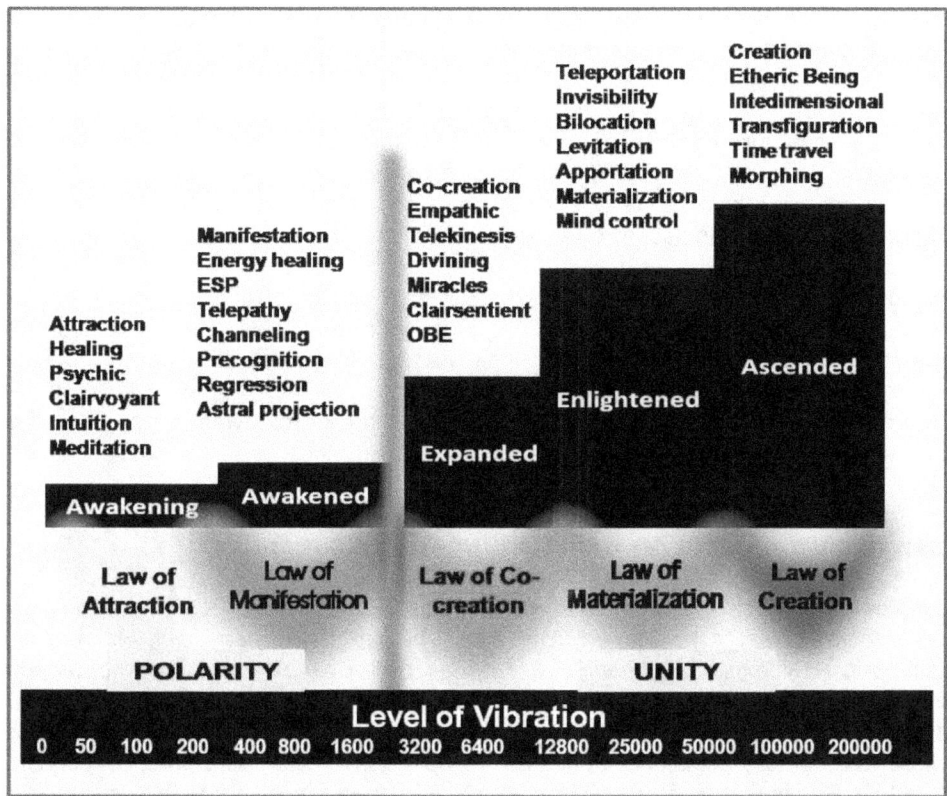

At first, this graph may seem far out but you will see that there are several things of interest here.

1. The Level of Vibration is a logarithmic scale like things natural in nature,
2. The stages or classes of vibration that "opens" to
3. The types of psychic powers.

The vast majority of humans simply accept that they have limited control of their lives and experience whatever energy comes at them. This is true if you let it be so and go to default. The default is to let your lower mind and body do what ego believes is correct for you. The default is to allow your energy systems dictate to the Law of Attraction. The process of the shift from low to high change goes through several stages. The lowest stage is the lower form of life—purely instinctual (like an animal) run by behavior totally void of the consciousness of spirit—the higher mind. At the higher end is the highest form of life—totally inspirational run by the consciousness and power of Spirit. The stages are reflected by the level of vibration. For the sake of simplicity these different stages are sleeping; awakening, awakened, expanded, enlightened, and ascended. This is the process typically referred to as Ascension.

Now first of all you have to open your mind to the fact that the "unexplainable" is all around us. Materialization, bi-location, invisibility, levitation are abilities that people on this planet already have. These may be rare but nevertheless exist.

Have a close look at this diagram. Consider how a material object such as ice changes its rate of vibrational frequency and its properties as heat is placed on it. It *sleeps* as ice but starts *awakening* when heat is applied. At the *awakened* stage it becomes water and at the *expanded* stage it is steam. At the *enlightened* stage it is now no thing and at the *ascended* stage it is pure spiritual energy from what the ice was made. The evolution of rising vibration brought totally different properties each time as the energy simply changed from evolving back to its original state of no thing; no thing being every-thing or all of creation. That is the ascension process in action, for even ice can ascend!

Now consider the power of love of the heart. It is high vibration (like fire) being applied to a human (like ice) that is at a state of lower vibration. This unfolds in a similar evolution with new properties coming out at each stage. The more love (heat) you apply to this body (ice), the more the body, and its properties change in energy form. If you look at some of these properties on the chart, you get the drift of what these properties are.

For some insight in this you can check out recent Russian research on DNA at **www.psychicchildren.co.uk/4-3-RussianDNAResearch.html.**

Grazyna Fosar und Franz Bludorf says: *"The human DNA is a biological Internet and superior in many aspects to the artificial one. The latest Russian scientific research directly or indirectly explains phenomena such as clairvoyance, intuition, spontaneous and remote acts of healing, self healing, affirmation techniques, unusual light/auras around people (namely spiritual masters), mind´s influence on weather patterns and much more. In addition, there is evidence for a whole new type of medicine in which DNA can be influenced and reprogrammed by words and frequencies WITHOUT cutting out and replacing single genes."*

What is even more intriguing is how DNA control things from the subconscious to conscious and receive information into its holographic computer like structure, which works best when it is in the "frequency mode of love" where it is like an electrical current that enhances the hypercomunnications!

And so if you can recall the story of the Soul who travels to Earth to have its experience by taking on a vessel called a physical body, it gets trapped into the slavery of the system and hence the trapped body inhibits the growth of the soul by keeping its vibration in the lower range. At the lowest range, the Earthling behaves instinctually like an animal but can rise through the development of intellect above that stage by choice. And so the Earthling takes its journey of expression and experience to rise trough the Power of the Body (physical) into the Power of the Mind (Intellectual) and to the Power of Spirit. The Earthling, begot of love between masculine and feminine energies through a love relationship travels on the journey in the Earth reality in an attempt to rejoin its true self which is a quantum piece of Source, from where it came referred to as Home. Each journey brings choices on the reality it chooses and the level of vibration it attains so as to experience those abilities and qualities that we have discussed. All these are simply neutral abilities and whether the application is good, evil, or in-between is individual choice.

And so one can become a good Earthling or a bad Earthling by choice. So if we were to create a simple graph of ascension for the "good "guys of Christ Consciousness we would get a picture that shows vibration and the various stages. These powers are the ones that we strive to attain as good guys and if you attain these, like telepathy and so on you are engaging in the esoteric world of White Magic.

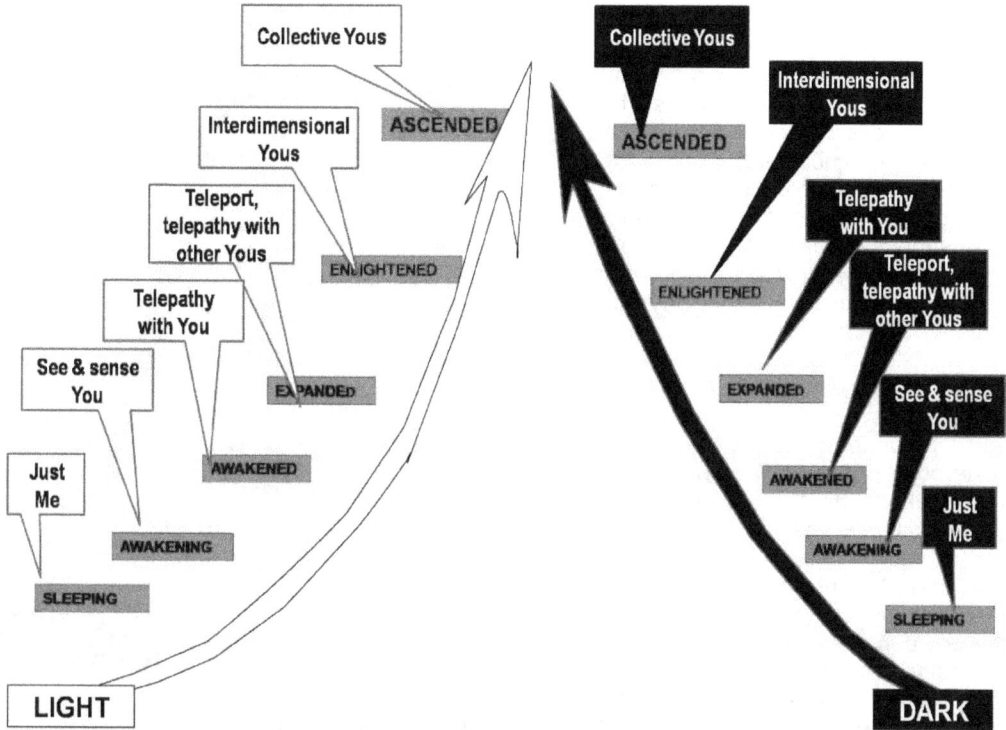

As noted before, there are many with these special powers to read minds, to heal, to read the future, to see and feel energy, to influence others, to sense others, to levitate, to materialize things, to be invisible, blah, blah. These are not understandable and have in the past been branded as occult, esoteric nonsense, but they exist. Now if you exhibit these occult powers of magic, the Inquisition will not burn you but you are still an oddity.

But what about the "Bad" guys, the Satanists and their spiritual quest? For them, the picture would look like this one below. Beside one being white and the other white, the process of ascension is the same. This is what these "Bad" guys would call enhanced abilities and the "Good guy would call Black magic.

The irony of it all is that what the "good" guys are told by the bad guys that black magic, the abilities they have, is black and not to be used.

Yet when you look at the ability itself, it is all a matter of individual choice as to how these capabilities are deployed. They can be for evil or good. And then as to whether they are really good or evil, it becomes a gray matter subject to interpretation, perception and choice.

So as we have seen in this book, there is a dark and light, evil and good to just about everything around us.

Now let us consider the possibility that no matter who we are, good or bad, were all on the same quest. When born, you were created out of the soup of love through your parents, and so it seems from the soup of all creation (bad or good) love. The soul begins the journey in the physical vessel called a body and a mind. Each soul undertakes the journey to experience and express itself as it chooses within the environment that it chooses (we will get into this choice of reality later). In a simple explanation, the soul begins its journey through its reality learning the power of the physical body.

If it learns to rise above the instinctual level of its workings, it begins to understand the next level as the power of the mind and begins to awaken to new possibilities and abilities as we see on this simple chart. Whether that Soul engages in Light or Dark is not relevant because these are simply abilities and how they are deployed for the purpose of expression of the soul is subject to interpretation and in-between the blab and the white extremes is a mixture which the degree of gray.

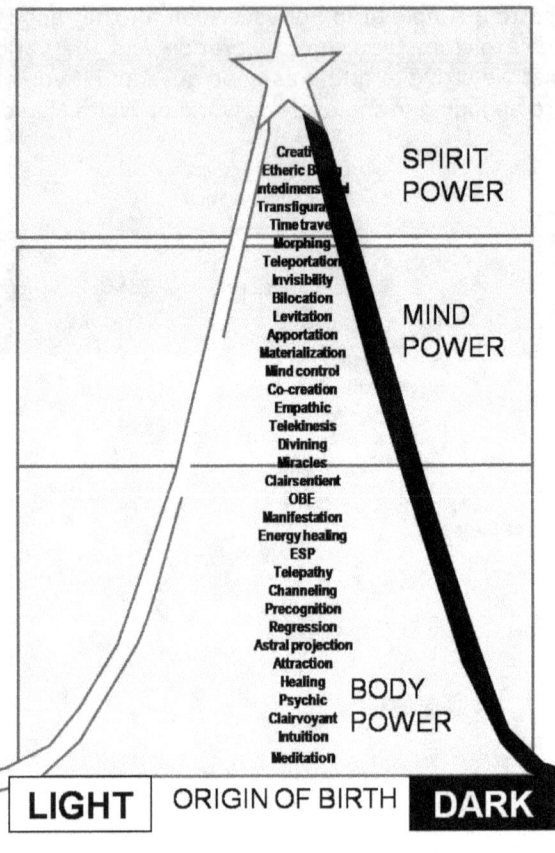

At some point in the process of rising to awaken the powers of the mind, a convergence occurs where there is a doorway or portal. That portal is opened into the abilities of the power of Spirit. The portal has a key to open the door and that key is unconditional forgiveness. That is the entry back to where the Soul as a piece of Quantum Source began the journey. Here polarity and gray does not exist, nor does time, or anything else that was used.

So the Dark ones and the Light Ones are on the same journey, learning from each other about each other. And what appears to have happened is that the "bad guys" have been on a plan to make a better place for their slaves. There is no denying this because they have even done so well at this, most earthlings do not even suspect they are slaves. Of course there has been a compromise in certain freedoms, but let's face it, the Earthling is not exactly the shining example of peace and harmony. So these alleged evil ones seem to have humanity's best interest in their hearts, just because they consider the majority of Earthlings to be at the same status as we would consider cows or chickens, that appears to beside the point.

What does this infer? When Good and Bad have no distinction and each forgives the other, thanking them for the revelation and experience, both can transcend into the power of Spirit.

What we are also saying is that the Bloodlines who run PLANET EARTH Inc. understand fully the Power of The Mind. This power, inherited through blood, attained by higher knowing teaching, or learned by the climb of the Souls journey, or whatever, are part of the souls on the same path of convergence. And when that Earthling finally realizes the truth of the power of the mind to create its reality resides there without polarity and opens the doorway of forgiveness, each one is also choosing to affect the whole consciousness that way.

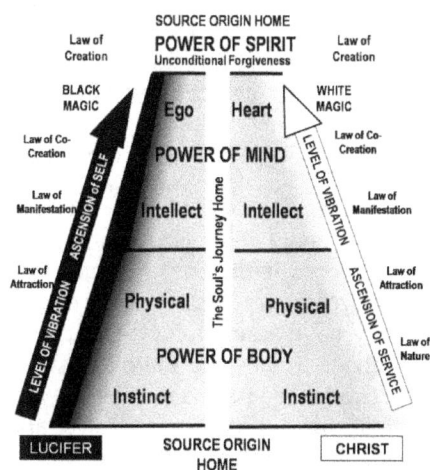

The Creator That Resides In You

Let us go back to the picture and the various stages of vibration. Here you have to release your judgments and take on an intellectual notion that you are simply a form of vibrating energy unique to yourself and have within your abilities that are like energy generators and receivers. The abilities open by rising vibration, and the generators, receptors are engaged and applied through the chakra system of thought, image, words, emotion. Each of these create energy which draws your reality to you.

One part of the drawing of reality is what has been commonly referred to as **The Law of Attraction** which reflects the way energy works. Under this hypothesis, any energy created by you will seek out energy of likeness so as to present this to you for your experience and expression. How you then engage, interpret, choose action is your choice.

So this Law is always going on through you as the generator. In a simple model, if you follow your chakra functions you move from the top three functions of thought, image, word through the heart (emotion) to the lower of intent, action, reality. Unknowingly, it is on autopilot and your active and reactive realities are process that create that which you are not aware of. You simply have no knowing or attachment, or awareness of it because you do not believe this is the way it works. When you start to become aware of this process, you begin to take control and proactively create your reality and begin manifesting instead of relying on Attraction..

In a simple sense, let us call this manifesting. In this case, there are four simple ways to manifest something, whether it is an object, event, or situation. For the sake of simplicity, let us say you desire an apple. There are four ways to get the apple:

1. You go to the store and buy an apple
2. You speak of your desire until someone brings you an apple
3. You visualize eating an apple until at some time it comes to you
4. You materialize an apple in front of you

Now the last one may be farfetched to you but understand that there are people (like Sai Baba) who have materialized objects instantly from their feet or hands. In looking at our picture of the levels the Soul rise through, we could say that manifesting using 1 is through the power of the Body, and 2 is a process using body and mind, 3 is a power of mind and 4 is a power of Spirit. In the following example, let us take our leave of the autopilot Law of Attraction and accept that it is you that controls this law.

If you look at the graph, there were several stages explained as follows:

The first stage after the power of love wakes you is what I refer to as **awakening**. It is when you begin to realize that your mind and body are energy generators (thoughts, images, words, emotions) that give life to energies. You begin to realize that you may be creating your own destiny and reality with these energies because once you give them life; they have a sole function of attracting situations, people, and things that create like experiences. Hence the **Law of Attraction** hits you. You may begin to see that thinking and creating negative energies may not be so smart. So you start to think more about stopping these negative energies and show a bit more tolerance, understanding and compassion. In fact, many people that are at this stage show several metaphysical abilities like healing, psychic, intuition, clairvoyance, and meditation as being a part of their lives.

The next stage I call the **awakened** stage when you begin to realize that you can proactively control energies, experiences, and perceptions so as to draw to you more of what you desire. This is where you begin to place a conscious awareness on the energies avoiding negative ones and then proactively managing the positive to begin to carve out your life differently. Your attention, perception, and intention, when it comes to creating perceptions, thoughts, emotions, images, and words begins to take on a more love-compassion fundamentalism. It is at this state that you are working on the **Law of Manifestation** and typically you find people with new properties (abilities) like energy healing, ESP, telepathy, channeling, precognition, regression, and astral projection to name a few. Here you are now engaging the heart through feelings and emotions.

There is a dividing line here as the next stage is reached which I call **expanded**, something changes dramatically. It is where you go in the space of the heart. This is where the big mind shift takes place and that wall is broken down. Instead of attracting and manifesting with existing energy matter to bring experiences, you begin to defy the laws of classical physics to actually create new outcomes of matter. Yes, it is where you become mindless of the usual intellect and mind perception of what *can't* happen. The best example of this is a healing miracle brought about by energy healers, placebos and other miraculous recoveries where suddenly, in an instant in time, a situation—like a broken bone—corrects itself.

This stage is attained when you realize that if you solicit the assistance of a new Divine buddy—your Co-creator Heart—letting go of classical beliefs and surrendering to it, you can do things that are deemed impossible by science. Yes, the **Law of Co-creation** sits here. Here you find empathics, telepathics, telekinesis practitioners, diviners, out of bodiers, clairsentience people, miracle healers, diviners, clairvoyants, and so on. These are some of the new abilities that open to those that have learned to let go and trust the co-creator partner will assist. What is important here is that there is a realization of being in the heart to truly open these new abilities. This is the shift away from Polarity where you believed you were separate from the Divine goes to that of belief in Unity. This is a place where you and the Divine are One. Yes, the heart is your personal link to your Higher Divine Self.

The next stage **enlightened** really gets serious. When the attitude is totally One and you are full time in the heart. It means total empathy for all things. Here the belief is we are interconnected and to affect anything else affects us and visa versa. This is where Sai Baba sits. Teleportation, materialization, levitation, apportation, mind control, bi-location and invisibility are a few of the characteristics here. This is where that Co-creator partner is being employed full time. This is where the **Law of Materialization** becomes a reality. The laws of classical physics simply don't apply here as the traditional laws of material, gravity, and solids get violated. This stage occurs when you learn to really let go most of the time. You live "in your heart". You are a complete empath showing heightened, unconditional love and compassion—those high vibration fires—for all things as they are you. You now firmly hand command to the Higher Divine Mind that you have replaced with your material limits and ego driven existence. And you have absolute faith and trust in this Higher Self of mind and body.

What is the lesson here? Materialization and the Enlightened stage of vibration is a process of self evolution of taking control of the energy you create while rising in your state of vibration. It is a process of self growth into the Power of Spirit which is not attained overnight. And does it matter whether you follow the Light or Dark path of Ascension? No, for all, assuming that you wish to rise, converges to the same doorway. At this doorway, you as a Soul are infinite and eternal and there is no distinction between right or wrong for it is all part of your person journey, your person holographic reality which you share with others so as to express yourself in any way you decide. The lesson here is that the Creator resides within you and that there are abilities residing in you looking to be unleashed. The final gateway is the unconditional forgiveness of love, peace and harmony of Source from whence you originated.

In the next chapters we will look closer at these energies that create your reality and these Laws because, as many have learned, this Law of Attraction does not always seem to work the way you want it.

57

THE MANAGEMENT OF HUMAN ENERGIES

All That Is, Is Energy

It's pretty hard to accept one of the New Age consciousness beliefs that you create your own reality through your energies of thoughts, images, and words. It is even more difficult to understand that the heart gives emotional power energy to those energies you create. Normally we can't correlate the cause and effect because there is a time lag between when you create the energy, and when it comes back in some form. So dear old science simply says it's all balderdash. Nevertheless there is the Law of Cause and Effect working away. In the lower vibratory state, it's obvious. Piss someone off and they will try to get you back at some time and in some way. We are quite used to seeing the consequences in the physical domain. But, just think; what if this is really true in non-physical domain? If it was, would you be more careful about what you think, visualize, say, and feel?

What new research is finding is your mind and the perception of things that come out of it are all invisible energies. In fact it is not a difficult thing to accept that all—everything that exists—is some form of vibrating energy with its own frequency. And certainly Quantum Physics has a lot to say about that. It is not a stretch to also believe that everything you perceive and the way you perceive it is your choice. You either created it or accepted it as a perception. Anything that you see in your world creates feelings, impressions, and perceptions that science cannot quantify. Yet these are yours. And it does not matter where you read it, saw it, felt it, or experienced it, for whatever it is, ends up as a perception in you. You use your thoughts, your vision, ears, mouth, and emotions to create your perception. But at the same time, those thoughts, images, words, emotions create living energies with a purpose. It is because you are an energy generator—a creator of energy.

If you have an impression of somebody for example, it becomes vibrating energy. But you can bring that impression forward into your consciousness and change it any time you like. Even if it is a bad memory of something, you can change your perception to good, replacing the old. You may not have changed the event that caused it, or the person, or the situation, but you can change your perception of it. That is your personal hologram of your life as it was and as you live it—all just energy vibrating away.

But that energy you create has a life. It has a purpose. And what you create this way has an inherent magnetic attraction to draw to it a mate. A mate of similar vibration. The most obvious example is to call someone a vile name. It attracts a mate you will recognize more clearly as a response—like a punch in the mouth, a vile name back or it could be returned later. What if everything you perceive and the process you use to create that perception had to find a mate? Would you pay more attention to your energy generator? Let us expand on this simple notion and move into the more extreme manipulation of energy. You create energy (cause) and the Law of Attraction attracts likeness (effect).

Energy Benders

There is an incredible example that distorts the physical beliefs of science. It has to do with materialization—creating an object instantly out of thin air. This is an extreme example of creating something out of nothing, out of that which is raw energy. And from that raw energy materializes a specific form into an atomic state. The most famous modern day materializer and miracle maker was **Sathya Sai Baba** an Indian Holy man in Southern India. He was reported to materialize lockets, rings, jewellery, delicacies, sacred ash, and specific objects that are requested by others. He created these out of thin air then passes them out as gifts. Thousands have witnessed this. Scientists who study this are befuddled by it of course, simply discounting it and claiming it is a hoax. After all, if science can't explain it, it ain't proven science. Yet this man was deemed a saint, and he was visited by many daily to materialize vast quantities of food; even sizzling hot delicacies fell from his hands and feet. He would produce exotic and rare objects, fruits, and even anomalous ones like half apple, half orange on two sides. He walked about producing sacred ash with the wave of his hands. Sai Baba was also a bi-location example. Numerous witnesses reported watching him snap his fingers and vanish instantly reappearing several hundred feet away. This is not an isolated case. There are many Holy men in India with this ability. If you don't believe this, just Google it. And so it is with many of the esoteric sciences... it's all just heresy so it's supposed to vanish from reality.

Energy Manifesting

The first real test of your mind to accept is that you create living energy. The tons of books on the Law of Attraction have changed millions of minds about a cosmic law of energy. It simply states *that which is like unto itself is drawn.* Like stated it is not too difficult to understand that concept in many physical situations; if you are going be a shit to others, they will be a shit to you. And if you are kind to others then you will also receive kindness back. It does not mean it will be instant, or the recipient will be the giver; it means expect the same kind of stuff back! It starts to become a belief stretch however when you hear the statement that all in your life is a cause and effect behaving this way. Yet you know everything you perceived was up to you, wasn't it? Why not everything you receive being a result of what you created yourself? Well, this is only part of the story. There are other Laws. They are based on the use of the energies you can and do create.

First, as we described before in the ascension graph, we have the Law of Attraction and the Law of Manifestation. Here the energy you create attracts like energy and is the way to manifest energy proactively. It is based on energy you give life to that follows a cosmic law of finding an energy mate. We also have The Law of Co-creation and the Law of Materialization. As stated it is the place where the miracle workers go for a few moments, and people like Sai Baba go fulltime. There is a division here because that's where the shift in thinking and belief occurs. It is where miracle workers go temporarily. It is where your engagement in higher vibration takes you. On one side referred to as polarity you simply believe you can't. On the other side you believe you can. On one side you are polarized from the heart and on the other side you are unity with it. What is the significance of the heart? Again, it is the center—your co-creating buddy. On the polarity side you engage the heart through charging your energy with emotions. On the unity side, the heart is a full time buddy.

But why the heart? Here is the most interesting part. These four laws are the tip of the iceberg. Research shows that the heart's electrical field when in the energetic field of love, works in its optimum way. This means that the communication with DNA as a biological Internet opens to language. *(www.bibliotecapleyades.net/ciencia/ciencia_genetica02.htm)* where it becomes possible to modify genetic defects and takes you into those higher frequency abilities. The emotion of love is a high positive vibration, as are other emotions of the heart. Hate is a low vibration. The vibrational process changes in you as you change the energy you create from lower to higher.

The vast majority of humans simply accept that they have limited control of their lives and experience whatever energy comes at them. This is true if you let it be so and go to default. The default is to let your lower mind and body do what ego believes is correct for you. The process of the shift from low to high change goes through several stages. The lowest stage is the lower form of life—purely instinctual run by behavior totally void of the consciousness of spirit—the higher mind. At the higher end is the highest form of life—totally inspirational run by the consciousness of Spirit. The stages are reflected by the level of vibration as we saw in the chart.

But here is the pith of it—the dividing line in that picture of Polarity-Unity that you alone can cross. It is between the higher and lower mind, between the heart's intuition and the ego's intellect and between creating something versus making something. You are used to making things out of what exists because physics says you have to. Get used to creating things out of nothing because metaphysics—and your Divine mind—says you can.

It is the Divine Path through the Heart. This means that your desires of manifestation need to be aligned in thought, image, words and emotion, your total being, with the Heart—the Divine. It is where you learn to Create—like the Sai Baba guy who creates from nothing. And it also likes all the healing miracles that occur instantly.

Here is the big difference. You can go ahead and *manifest* things bad or good and feel the discord and ill feeling of the Heart if the energies are not aligned; and you will find your experience from existing stuff, *making* things out of things already made. Or, you can align with the heart properly where there is no bad energy and *create* out of nothing that which is of desire. But because this is not believed, and secondly Sai Baba abilities are not exactly instantly achieved, not too many are prepared to spend much energy on this option. And it is certainly not helpful to be told by those experts called scientists that this is all nonsense.

If you want to co-create, then create—to change the very fabric of the material—like in a miracle that creates something like a new possibility in your mind instantly, you need to have a co-creator buddy to work with. That is your Higher Divine Self living in your Heart. Attention is the first lesson. This is not an overnight deal any more that you earned your diploma overnight. It is through knowing that the true power of manifestation and creation reside there. That must be your mind shift in belief. So yes, you need to have attention and thoughts and words and emotion but those are aligned for the higher good of yourself and all that is. Otherwise why would your Divine counterpart—your co-creator care to respond? But this does not require continued reinforcement—a healing miracle is instant—because it simply happens as a new possibility that takes you or something to its zero state of perfection. But it is the belief that limits—the belief of who you are and what you can do. So you need not drive yourself to distraction by affirmations. Simply place attention, go to your Heart, keep faith and trust that it will be. Yes, we know this is not easy but it is that simple. You have been doing some of this the hard way because you have not believed in your partner—your Co-creator that is part of you. And your Co-creator is Love—your Heart—it is you; that part which needs your 3D attention and belief to shift.

What this means is that when you begin to truly take control of your power to proactively manifest, attract, co-create and create, you must know that it is done at the instant in time that it passes the attention. The instant healing miracle is like that, as is the materialization example.

The Process Of Co-creation

The process of Co-creation is more relevant to what actually happens in manifesting. You are a Co-creator of your life and you do have the ability to materialize or co-create at a new level. You have a Divine Partner in this process and although you are already doing this automatically, you have not quite got the process unobstructed by your intellect. Yes, you are co-creating all the time because you do not even think about it.

It is automatic and your belief and intent of this is synchronized because you have no obstacles in believing that negative things can come your way—it is the way of it, right? Do you not think you will attract negative energies in your life by creating anger and conflict? After all, you have had many lifetimes, and many years of practice in embedding this in your beliefs. Your memories are full of these thoughts. But positive things come the same way.

You do not even knowingly attach yourself to the outcomes because you believe there is no connection. Of course you don't want issues and problems, but by engaging your energetic chakras placing your thoughts, images, words and feeling onto these issues and problems, you end up with more of the same. So you automatically generate these discordant energies at will, and ask for your co-creating partner—which is really your Higher Self—to help attract and manifest them. So you are very practiced at creating the energy, giving it life, disconnecting yourself from an outcome, and waiting for the experience—even though you don't want it—ironic isn't it? Yes, you are adept at autopilot reactive attraction and manifesting already.

But when it comes to proactive co-creation, it is an entirely different matter because you may have a shadow of doubt, or be insecure as to the process, be too attached to the outcome and dilute the energy of desire so it sits there in a transition state. And even you create energy instantly, it waits for you to congeal or materialize it by your actions and intent. Of course the power of this energy is related to how you align your thoughts, visions, words and feelings. And of course others can help to amplify this as well. This is where reinforcement of that energy clarifies the outcome and further energizes it into being. But if there is doubt within you, and your beliefs are not aligned, then this serves to delay, dilute or even dissolve the power of a result. These are the limits and blocks that you impose on the process. And for true proactive co-creation, where you are in control, you need to be very aware of your Divine relationship with your heart and eliminate your shadows of doubt.

Let us back up a minute and note that your world which appears solid is simply in a different energy state and it has been created by the Creator consciousness. Everything in it which is simply a hologram of energy in a different dimension has life with a purpose of evolving. You as a physical body are integrated into this scene to play out your roles as you see fit to expand it and yourself. Within the movie you are able to co-create different ways. You can create, rearrange, or attract your creations and hence experiences. To create means to materialize something into a solid form. Humanity has a long way to go to do this but it is indeed possible to materialize something solid in front of you. *If you think about how your imagination and mind work now, how you can create things, scenes, people, relationships, emotions in multiple places and shift your awareness to each one without time or space limitations, this is the way the real You is creating your reality here.*

You have come to know this in miracles—like those of healing. And no one can deny the existence of these; they just can't explain them. This is a process where after attention to a solution, and a Divine partnership is made in the heart, you detach from the outcome and rely on faith to prevail. And so as you understand it, the quantum state of waves, manifests itself into a new state of perfection—which is all we know—and it becomes a solid representation of what was sought as the desire. Eventually you will learn that materializing a solid object relies on the same process as you are simply adding to the hologram in your dimension.

To rearrange is a similar process. It is one of changing the arrangement of the form into a new form that is solid. This is a transformation process as done in Alchemy which abides by specific natural laws. The partnership with the Divine, if not there, with the strong belief, is vital. Without it, nothing will happen.

In the case of attraction, you are creating the energy that has specific vibratory qualities and strength attached by you. You do it daily. What occurs here is that this energy sits in a temporary holding area looking for other energies that will be attracted to it like a magnet. Here you are not creating the object; you are attracting the objects, events, people or situations that already exist to provide you with the experience.

Think about this like the little dots that you see on the movie screen or TV or your computer screen. They are simply dots configured into unique patterns that are meaningful to you and give you an experience. Yet they are not solid things in the screen. They are just little dots of energy composited into some meaningful expression of energy. The energies you create are similar. All you have to add is that these patterns on your screen are magnetic and they set up fields—which you call morphic—that eventually attract similar patterns. The time to do this depends upon the strength and your belief that it can be so. As we have pointed out, you are already doing this without thinking—and therein lies the big clue—you are not thinking about it. And without even knowing, you have let go of limits and are co-creating with your Divine counterpart. And yes, it can be negative or positive. The heart only knows perfection and it knows what is happening. And if it is not perfection, there will be a reaction in your body and Soul. You will feel this as dis-ease or disease or dysfunction—perhaps a feeling of discord.

The Two Pathways

There is another way of looking at this that reflects two opposite paths related to this awareness. There is the Ego and the Heart. They are of course commanded through the mind which can determine which path you use. Both Ego and Heart can control or command your chemistry either automatically or by you, depending on your awareness. The Ego pathway into the manifesting field is what humanity usually relies on making things. These are stagnated into that which exists in the physical world, and although your energy packets reach into the Divine—most call it Zero Point Field, they don't create without the cooperation of the Divine Buddy. They are simply commands to manifest as we have discussed. There is no distinction of bad or good, negative or positive, it is simply energy looking for a likeness—a mate. The Heart, on the other hand, knows what is not perfection—that which is not love—and you will sense a discomfort when discordant energies are placed into the inventory. This is the normal way of creating your life.

You may have many energies that are there waiting for you to enforce them by emotion, attention and alignment. They could even be from previous lives. If these energies of intent are weak or confused, they will sit there. If many of these weak ones are there, you can be easily drawn into other energy fields that are stronger and that is the way of it even if it has no distinct purpose. You then become a victim of other energies that have created their own morphic fields. What this means is that you are letting your life be commanded by default, and if you allow your Ego to create the fear, attention and intent, then you are defaulting to what the Ego desires—not what your heart desires. That is the Gopher Wheel that the ego sees as great things ahead—if you keep slogging on the wheel. And so your intellect, another tool of ego, comes to govern how you will do the slogging.

When you, by awareness of the Heart, and the Divine in it create the commanding partnership, then you stop on the relative Gopher Wheel and look with new eyes. You shift command to the Divine Higher Mind of the heart. There is no intellect here, only inspiration and positive feelings. This is how you change the nature of your manifestation in that they are more controlled and you become a true Co-creator. But the partnership relies on your belief and faith. I will let you in on a secret here. The Heart and the Divine are perfection and they strive to bring back that perfection when that partnership is clear like non attachment, clarity, trust, faith, believe, and love based. The stronger this is the faster it congeals from temporary to visible energy. This is the secret to materialization which humanity is a long, long way from. But, if you want to see more common examples, look to what happens in health miracles.

So at the top of the Gopher Wheel-no Gopher Wheel sits the true Manager—the Mind. It is it what chooses using your free will to pick the path to tread. And the success is dependent upon your awareness and belief system. What does this mean? Make a new choice because the ego is the guy keeping you in the Gopher Wheel. You need to take command and build this faith and relationship—to balance the Ego. For its decisions if left unchecked will affect your health, quality and length of life. The body was designed to live long within the realm of the Heart. The control has been given to the Ego, to power, to gratification of the senses, to conflict over material things—those eyeball visions on the vision board before you. These all have consequences to your body as a result. Shifting to the command center of the Heart unfolds a grand partnership as a true co-creator on a grand scale that you have yet to understand.

In Simple Terms There Are Four Steps

These steps are Attraction, Manifestation, Co-creation and Materialization. It is a progression from outside to inside, from unknowing to knowing or unconscious to conscious command. The first two have the Heart involved while the last two have the Heart engaged. The first two are your first major pathway we have discussed, where you create any kind of energy in a holding area like an escrow and then passively or actively enforce the strength of it to attract and manifest an experience. The last two are active engagement in the partnership of the Divine—the Heart—to co-create an event, situation, or material object. While one simply attracts and manifests with existing matter, the other through the help of the Divine rearranges matter into something new.

Of course you know this second path as miracles. And you know that the Co-creator is your Higher Self which is part of the Divine. And you know that the key here is Belief, Compassion, Love, Faith, Trust and Gratitude, don't you? This does not require continued repetition like an assertion to manifest experience, only a strength of belief, a heart's desire to be perfection, a trust in yourself, a detachment from the outcome, a faith that it is so, and gratitude that it is done. Does it sound difficult for you? Yes, it has been difficult because you have not known yourself and you limit this through your belief by listening to other people who do not believe. And you are so busy analyzing it you cannot detach yourself to surrender and listen.

Yes, that is the way of it. So while your mind slumbers about this, you begin by your Law of Attraction and create a resonating field which attracts like energy. Then you may begin to realize that by managing your energies of thoughts, images, words and emotion, you can more actively manifest the experience. That you can call the Law of Manifestation because you are proactive.

And Now Miracles And Emotion

It is important to tell you more about something that is usually missing in a proactive manifestation. It is about the emotional body that envelopes you and in particular your heart. Your heart has many fields of energy that you are not aware of but the one that is important in energy creation is the one that is referred to as the emotional body or feeling body. It is like a light bulb and is the most beautiful creation when it is lighted. Everyone has one and it is a radiant light which emanates its colors and vibrations of excitement. The height and brightness is caused by the emotion from your heart—which is an energy of emotion generated from your sensory systems of taste, sight, smell, touch, and hearing. Think about the feelings that your body creates for you when you eat something wonderful, or see something beautiful, or touch someone you love, or smell a pleasing flower, or hear peaceful music. These are all incredible feelings that impact your emotional body and permeate your being in a harmonizing result.

There is of course a hierarchy of these; unconditional love being the strongest. Compassion, bliss, joy, laughter, harmony, peace, gratitude are others that are very strong energies and make your emotional body pulsate with wondrous colors and brightness. Of course there are the opposites of fear and conflict that do not create the light and the emotional body dims and closes to the discord. This state in your emotional body is very important in your manifestations.

For example, in your attractions and manifestations, the emotional strength is what gives the manifesting energy that you create with thoughts, visions and words its true power. The stronger this is and the clearer it is, the faster is the change from etheric energy created instantly to external energy that you can experience. The field which you refer to as a morphic field vibrates with excitement as it entrains with the emotional body. And as we have said, it matters not whether it is negative or positive because it is still energy you create. But if the energy is strongly negative, you can be drawn to other like energy whereas if it is positive, you will draw it to yourself. You must know that although your emotional body may be dimmer due to the discord and negative emotion, it is still energy and still has power to attract, but not with any divine co-creative partnership.

However, if you are to be a Co-creator, your co-partner does not hear you if you are not of a strong positive and pure emotional vibration-hypercommunication, remember? Its domain is perfection and it cannot be of assistance unless you are pure of heart and with a highly charged emotional body. You have learned that the Intent is first, the Pathway is meditation, awareness and prayer, and the means are the positive emotions or feelings created. These positive ones we mentioned are higher level energies of completion. You know that when the energies of thought, vision, words and emotion are aligned with the Heart's desire, and continuously re-enforced, you have the true secret of creating your own manifestations. Your strength and consistency in the emotional body will impact the speed at which the etheric energy attracts the physical energies. This is because the field excites the electrons that are the basis to all things and gets them to seek each other—they are all one anyway, remember?

But with miracles, or co-creation, be clear that the electrons common to both the etheric and material states become highly excited when the emotional body is positively charged with unconditional love and compassion. When this occurs, they are easily influenced to rearrange from a quantum perspective into a new possibility simply by changing paths, states and orbits into a different outcome or different atomic state which you sense and perceive as solid. And it is also here that we and the Divine Heart has its power to influence that new arrangement. But we caution you in that the emotional body cannot be fooled. Emotion is a universal energy and laughter can be false, or love can be with condition, or talk can be a lie. This does not fool the Heart and its emotional body. It is part of your belief system as well.

Should you carry an ulterior negative motive in your laughter or your outward feelings do not match your internal Divine ones, you fall back to reactive manifestation and attraction. Many may not even be aware of this discord and simply believe you are doing good. Sorry, that is not the way of Divine energy. It knows. It, like you for example pick up the discordant notes in a piece of music instantly even though the piece attempts to disguise it. Miracles occur when the emotional body of the Healer is strong, pure of heart and genuine—either directly by initial attention or indirectly through trusting the Heart. The most miraculous healers are of the purest state of high emotional body who enfold their patients.

Training The Emotional Body

If you were to research this, you will find that the heart actually has a brain and it has an energy field that is the strongest of your total "energetic" system. It is an energy field that is shaped like a donut—called a torus—that reaches way out depending on its strength. This field is out there doing its thing unbeknown to you so its time you made this more "known" to your mind which is supposed to be in charge.

During your daily activities, you must learn that you are there to change or convert discord to light—bad to good or fear to love. The first area of discord and disharmony will come from the papers you read, the news you hear, the problems you are surrounded with. Remember these are perceptions that convert to manifesting energy and that you are there to help change this, take a higher perception, or assist to make it better. Do not let these influence your emotional body. Your heart will tell you when these are not compatible.

There are also the thoughts and visions that you yourself create by way of your ego or other matters that may come to you. Will yourself to not let these be of conflict, discourse and negative nature. Be careful to not give these any life and simply move to a higher place of perception with your Higher Self to change the energy to positive upon detection. Keep your emotional body protected from these by instantly acknowledging that they are not beneficial and eliminating or changing them.

Then there are events and experiences that you may be drawn into or witness. These may be tragic, conflictive, or have a major impact upon your emotional body. These are to help you learn what you do not want or to show you how to move to a higher perception of good. Look to see something good that it created and place your attention on that.

Then there are the plans and attractions and manifestations and miracles that you wish to create and co-create. These are as we have said earlier. Make a habit of creating these solutions and desires as completed, enjoyed so your emotional body totally engulfs the completion of it. Learn to solidify your belief, faith and trust in your Co-creator.

As you follow this path, you begin to take command of your life and the true center of command begins to take over as the emotional body becomes stronger and brighter. It will completely change the experiences of your life as soon there cannot be any discord or limitations that can influence, penetrate or affect you.

This is how you get off the Gopher Wheel. Your perceptions switch completely and you see everything in a new light while you practice your manifestations. And over time magic starts to unfold. Why? Because you put the magical energy there to work for you. You are not working for the energy anymore.

Let us now delve into the greatest mind shift that we all fear most of all—death and loss. It is Mr. Ego's greatest fear of ceasing to exist and losing everything it has seduced you into on the Gopher Wheel. The best lesson of dealing with this is where people have experienced death and lost everything, then miraculously come back. The lesson? It has to do with you suddenly knowing that you are actually made up of something more than a physical vessel. But ego and intellect had to temporarily die to allow this to happen.

The Non-Science Of Dying

NDE's are short for Near Death Experiences. There are millions of people dying all the time—then coming back to tell about it. What is of particular interest here is that so many of these cases come back with miraculous changes—like big, big changes in their lives and even in their bodies. Yes, miracles—totally unexplainable miracles. Many professionals and scientists have studied thousands of cases and compiled observations about people pronounced clinically dead. These have returned to tell about their little vacation in what is deemed no-where land.

Now, you must understand that NDE's mean the person is dead! Gone! What is called "clinically" dead for some period of time like 15-60 minutes! Heart stopped and the body weighs one half to one ounce less! Yes, something left the body. This means that the cells are dying in the brain from lack of oxygen, and it is coffin time. At least that is what the medical belief box tells us. After all, if you stop feeding oxygen to the brain, cells die rapidly, right? Wrong!

There are some 13 million cases of NDE's that have been recorded. Reports are that an energy force of approximately one ounce simply leaves the body (nice to know a ghost weighs an ounce!) and floats up and away to take a little vacation. Is this consciousness that has left the force that gives life? Whatever it is separates at the point of death and the NDE people are completely aware of this separation as they see their bodies lie lifeless below.

Consciousness Is A Separate Intelligent Energy Form

Now here is the mind-bender that flattened the side of my belief box. This consciousness that separates can see, hear, think, move, communicate, and tell jokes, and retain senses regardless of distance from the body. In fact the senses are even better—heightened. It seems the body and brain weren't the only things that could do this.

Everything that was ever learned, experienced, and felt along with all of the senses (perhaps taste may be questionable unless you can get some ghost food!) are left completely intact. But did we not learn that the brain was responsible for all that? And when you croak, that memory is no more? Not so.

Consciousness, which clearly includes the life giving force, leaves the body, goes on a little trip, then comes back and ta dah, the body has life again. All the dead cells are happy again. Rigamortis has no say here—the white face gets pink again, and it is wakey, wakey time! And then! All is better than before—sometimes with a few miracles kicked in.

But what about the little vacation that this ghost, or consciousness takes when it leaves the body? It is like a little visit to an amusement park. Where does it go? What happens?

Well, reports are pretty unanimous on this. Most went through similar stages when they left their physical lives. They all kept a consciousness that retained their life stories—every moment. Some higher mind was there to take them through their steps and decide whether a return was needed.

This little vacation away from the body and ego off the Gopher Wheel of mortal life, permanently on a trip that the life force of consciousness takes exhibits striking similarities between cases.

First, they heard the news of dying from the Doc or others around the "dead" body. They saw people and events around them. They then experienced wonderful feelings of comfort, peace, quiet, relief, and no pain. No hell and brimstone, just peace. Many went into a tunnel and were pulled rapidly through in a wonderful worry free ride.

They had an *Out of body* experience for after they *died* they would find themselves looking at their body, watching and hearing things as a spectator. They felt like pure consciousness that was indescribable—most called it a spiritual body—but they could not touch other bodies or material things. No one could hear or see them. They were separate, weightless, floating, going through things like a cloud. They had projections like rounded limbs but all their senses were intact. Consciousness existed outside the body! What we would commonly call a ghost! So upon death, the other part of us—the ghost—was the one invited to the amusement park.

The next stage is where they encountered other spiritual beings, people they had known before, like friends and relatives that came to greet them. They were recognizable ghosts. Everything was filled with white light and was beautiful—like a feeling of coming home. These beings had a clear body outline but no physical body. They communicated as a direct transfer—no language. They were totally telepathic with no need for any language. All that was there were questions like are you ready to die. What have you done in your life that is sufficient? There was a point of stressing preparation yet there was no condemnation or judgment, only total love and acceptance coming from the light.

Then the stage where a bright light Being presents a high speed video panorama review of life—instant like when people report when drowning. Here the intent seems to be only to provoke reflections. Get this; rapid temporal memories in chronological order occur almost instantaneous yet totally comprehendible! The images generate emotions as they flip by. The being asks what they have done with their life, stressing love, and pointing out things. No one could gage time.

At the *Coming back* stage some would come back spurred by some Being which many said was God. They would be sent back for obligations, or pulled by relatives. Some actually felt a re-entry into the physical body.

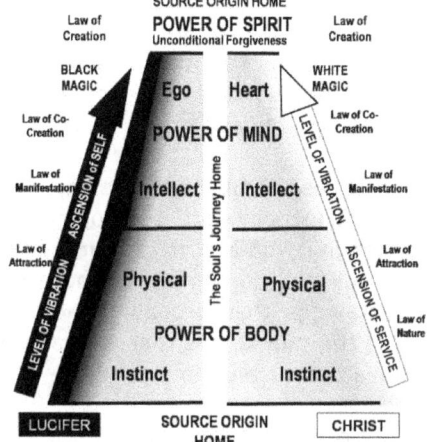

With those that came back, they inevitably had a totally changed life, just like in many of the miracle cases. Researchers go on to say that most times this experience created a totally new attitude in life. Some reported enhanced senses, some picked up on other's feelings better, expressed a need to cultivate love of others, seek knowledge, became morally purified, and created new clear goals mostly in service of others. This vacation away from ego suddenly paradigm shifted their belief systems and behaviour dramatically—that in itself is an unexplainable miracle.

Where did they go? Remember the little diagram? They were in that world of meeting their Soul in its territory. They met God or whoever was their powerful deity was really Self. They temporally passed through into their Source; Home! They had a chat with their true selves.

What Does Near Dying Tell Us?

Life is immortal consciousness that grows in an unlimited way. After everything was lost, let go of—poof no more body, ego, stuff, world, kids relationships, another mind takes over. It was sitting there waiting for the wakeup call. Too bad they had to croak to wake it, wouldn't you say? But this consciousness of ours—or life force—is alive and does not croak like the body. In fact it IS LIFE as it gives such to the body upon entry and exit. It can take a vacation. It is the field of transpersonal experience that is the source of all knowledge and memory—not the brain. It is independent of the person's mind. Whole consciousness is stored somewhere in space not in the brain. The brain serves as a relay station for connecting to and running the physics of our bodies when we are in a conscious state of being awake.

I am not a rocket scientist and I may not be the brightest crayon in the pack but what I clearly understood here is that we are made of a body and some invisible, separate energy field that gives me life. And when it decides to leave the old body, the life ceases. That is not exactly a mystery. But having this energy measured and keeping all of our consciousness and sensory abilities intact; wow! That's a bit different from the old belief box. Actually I found many people are not so surprised at this notion but they are not willing to readily admit it in public—peer pressure from "science" I am sure.

And what about these scientists and medicine? Well how do they explain that when people came back to life—into the dead body that is—the body was still ok—not dead smelly and dead brain cells clogging life, but fine. And then there was a life transformation. Hmmm, I began to realize, that this little episode altered something in the mind and body resulting in life changing habits because a higher mind was given a chance to take over. The old belief and faith had been completely altered because there was nothing there to be in conflict with what that higher mind "knew" and could do—like send you back for another try off the Gopher Wheel! And it all happened within seconds to a minute. And that person's life was totally transformed. And what would you guess the transformation was all about? Would you believe that life became centered on the "heart" not on the ego or the brain.

So in this case, death is a passing, a simple shift in vibration from one state of energy to another. The body is a temporary vehicle here and when it's lost, there is a subtle reminder that you are more than a body, death is a crock, and it may be more useful to come back and do something more meaningful than the Gopher Wheel of polarity and ego's cravings that probably had some influence on why you croaked temporarily. Perhaps the message is that we have more fun while we are on the Earth. So why don't we pay attention and do this before we croak?

Now, I ask you, if you came back after you croaked for an hour, floated around in a tunnel, got your ticket to this wonderful, peace filled amusement park, talked to some friendly ghosts, met the big boss in the sky, then had an instant replay of your life's movie, remembered everything out of your body, what would it do to your mind? And on top of this what if you came back with something healed instantly? And what if you knew you actually passed through to meet yourself?

Would you believe anyone—scientific or otherwise—that told you when you croak that's it? Not likely! What if they said it was nonsense what you saw? What if they told you miracles like the one you had was nonsense? You would tell them to keep smoking what they are on and go away. You would not care much to associate with them and simply keep your new knowledge to yourself. They would become the idiots, wouldn't they? Simply knowing it would be your truth. And no one on the planet would convince you otherwise. Your belief system would have taken a paradigm shift because you knew your own truth. Period.

Would this change your approach to life? Would you then be afraid of dying? Would you not realize you needed to do something meaningful and had been given a new chance? Would you be grateful? What would you be like after? Would you be completely freaked out and shrivel away? I think the possibility of that would be remote because you would have gained a new will and purpose to live. And where would that notion be? In a thing called consciousness—your mind.

Perhaps if you listened to the people living inside their limited belief boxes on this you may think you had gone mad, but I think you would change your consciousness—your awareness—to accept beliefs outside of your usual belief box. It would change me. It has already without having to croak. Realize you don't need to croak to go through this. But you do have to change your beliefs and be totally faithful to facilitate some changes—

especially miracles. That is what miracles do. They provoke a paradigm shift in the mind—in your consciousness and your beliefs.

But here is the real lesson: What happened was you unknowingly gave command to another quite physically independent part of you—your Higher Divine Mind. It wasn't willingly or knowingly, but there was really no option because everything that your lower mind is aware of was lost—gone! Poof, no baggage, conditions, attachments, expectations, only the reality of Source where you came from. It's the same place you go in the state of Co-creation and Creation.

In the so called real world of your physicality, you do not blot out the usual noise, and just let go of the usual world. But here it's poof and you are under the master command of the higher mind of inspiration and you went mindless—your terrestrial ego mind and its frantic consciousness of the Gopher Wheel of life as your primary attention vanished. You went into the land of Nothingville just like in the NDE, because there was truly nothing else there.

Can you do this while alive? Many do as an Out of Body Experience. But, and here is the big but, if you don't keep with the same program of higher vibration, you simply fade back into reactive Gopher Wheel life.

58

SELF POTENTIAL AND LAWS BEHIND MANIFESTATION

The Mindset Shift In Belief

Here is the key to this. The energy we are focussed on during our conscious time is made up of thoughts, images, words, feelings and emotions. You as an energy creator/generator have the choice of what these are and how you give life to them. You create your reality the same way you can in your imagination-your mind. What you have not realized or accepted is that your true Self is creating your life in this existence the same way. You must first understand that every bit of energy is given life and purpose by you. The greatest mind shift in this, in moving from the polarity to the unity side is the *acceptance of the knowing that there is a space where the basic substance of energy exists as no-thing*. The other is that you are the master of your own reality so that what you generate is not only what you receive back but it also forms your physical reality. And it is that primary substance of quantum no-thing that something is created from. From you comes the directive to change that substance. It is through the actions of attention and intent upon that which you apply your energy generators of thought, image, word, and emotion. These are formed instantly to then seek purpose. The strength of the directive depends on how it is charged with emotion from the heart and the strength of belief. This then dictates how long the directive may take to come back to you in some form of energy.

On the Law Of Attraction

So if you have any idea this is a bit far out, first think about how this works in the physical world. Try pissing someone off with your words. Try hugging someone who is pissed off at you. What you give out comes about. So give your brain (and ego) some leeway here and let go of the idea that it does not work the same way with the other energies you create constantly.

Think about how you create your desires—you want to find a new friend, or find something and you think about it, dream about it, feel it in your heart. You are creating waves of energy that create a field. It is actually a morphic field alive with purpose and it permeates other energies. It is like a swirling vortex of energy which builds a stronger charge depending on how much clear energy of desire you create.

Think about your TV set and the particles that form images. Think about how these particles that create emotions in your physical body are nothing but specs of light, color and intensity that your senses interpret. These dots or pixels could have a magnetic pull that either individually, or combined, created a specific pull signature that looks for like energies and attracts them. Do these dots sometimes draw you? Yes, a hologram that can draw others! This is not a difficult concept except that it is not supported by our scientific wisdom.

There are several pathways to manifesting. It is the split again; heart or head, intuition or intellect, create or make. The Divine path is fast, while the manifesting path of attraction is not so fast. The attraction path manifests experiences where it draws to you the energies that have likeness. It draws to you the energies that you generate through your thoughts, visions, words and emotions. The speed of manifestation is determined by the clarity of the desire, the alignment of these subtle energies dictates how rapidly the energy that you create draws or propels you to the like experience. This process is not creation, or co-creation, it is simply manifesting the experience of something desired by drawing the people, situations, things that already exist.

Think about how you may do this in two ways that you are used to. First, you may want to create something, or do something to have an experience—say it is flying or climbing a mountain. You simply plan it and away you go to have it. Sometimes it may be more complex, so you create a business plan and follow the activities you have outlined to make this experience occur. It may result in the creation of something as a result—like a business. You are used to this. It is all done in the outside. This is the way the Gopher Wheel keeps you busy.

But then there is also another way and that is to create the energy of alignment and watch how you draw others into your energy field. You may want a house, or new TV, or new opportunity; then suddenly it is there as a choice for you. This does not mean the TV suddenly materializes in your house. It could mean that the TV may be seen at a store or it appears somewhere for you to make a choice on. Certainly you have to buy it and you may not have the money—so manifest the money as well. Clarity and alignment are vital. Remember this as this is an easier way, as you are letting the Law of Attraction work for you after you clearly define what it is that is your desire and continue to energize it by reinforcement. It is done from the inside.

Think about this. Sometimes, you may be drawn into others energies as well. This is the way of it as you may have a need to sell something and someone else has a need to buy something. All that happens is that the two needs attract each other. How? Well, your energies penetrate everything depending on the strength and because all that exists is within you all, it is a matter of matching the energy signatures and drawing them like those little TV dots. This may be a local morphic field or a larger one. It may come from anywhere—an ad, a TV show, another person, but it is this drawing within the fabric of all matter.

Now you are doing these two ways automatically all the time. That is how you create your world of experience and perception whether you know it or not. This way is not particular to the need or the type of energy you create. It is simply energy the laws respond to, negative or positive. Most are used to such strong alignments when it comes to fear that permeates your thoughts, visions, words and emotions. Most of you are good at this already. Clarity and focus are the key and continued attention reinforces the energy to make it resonate stronger.

It is like a musical note. It has a specific tone or vibration when played. From 7 notes, you can create a song. These 7 notes can be combined into new patterns that are each unique. These can be played by different instruments making different tones and this can be combined into a magical concerto. These are all energy signatures looking to attract others of like sound. You are the orchestra playing the music. Your chakras are the original 7 notes and they can create any concerto you want if you use them. What are their musical sections? Thoughts, images, words, and emotions, brought about by your perception of your experiences.

So how do you manifest and attract now? Well, first you determine a need by *placing your attention* on it. It is in your target range. Now you work like hell to attain it, to make it, to buy it. But the other process you are not paying attention to is the other energy you create, especially the negative ones of fear, worry, lack, doubt. Every time you think or feel poor, useless, sick, unworthy, angry, guess what? And if you supercharge this with the emotion this is like a command for this energy to get its shit together fast and find a fit. And what happens when something really pisses you off and your energy levels hit the roof? A big flag goes up and starts waving for a mate. What about hatred from the past, an enemy, the boss, fear of the future, the tax man? And what about wanting more? Have you ever considered you are creating the energy of wanting? What wishing and hoping about great things? Great things are ok but what happens when it is counteracted with hoping? It has no power to manifest. And what do you think about most? It is not abundance because you lack. That is the energy you create to go out and hunt for a mate. You give it life and purpose.

Now here is the kicker. What do you occupy your mind with in regards to plans and wants? Is it the work needed, the effort required, or is it the completion itself? One, the problem is negative energy because it attracts more problems, The other, the solution is positive energy which attracts solutions. But hold on you say, that's BS! How can I occupy my mind with the solution when it has not happened yet? Well, I will let you in on a little secret... it is most likely the way most successful businessmen got to be so "successful". Do you think they engrossed themselves in the problems? You will find out that between gut feel, a positive stance, and a vision, things just happened and deals and people—out of the blue—just happened.

Here is where the mind shift is needed. The universe works the opposite of what you think. Sure you can struggle away on the Gopher Wheel and make it happen. But the better process is like assertions and successful business people follow. Create the energy of solution, of completion and energize it with emotion, see a vision of it completed. That is the energy you need to have out there and let the Laws of Attraction and Manifestation deal with the problems. These fellows know about how suddenly a deal just comes to them, something happens from nowhere and that dream becomes manifested into reality.

Here is the bottom line. To those in the know of how this works, they continuously re-enforce the vision of completion over and over with thoughts, an emotion, with a knowing, a faith, and a trust that this is the way it works.

If you look at your 24 hour day there are 86,400 seconds. It is said that we can generate 20-30,000 thoughts in a day. How would you classify these? And if every one of these critters is energy with purpose, what do you suppose the reflection would look like as an expression of your current life? Of course the vast majority may be mumbo jumbo energy because they are not clear or with purpose so they never mate. But what about those strong ones that do? When you are on the Gopher Wheel, you do not make any correlation between the energy you create upstairs to the experience you get downstairs. So perhaps it is time to become more aware of how you think and act.

There are four main types which are proactive and reactive. The reactive ones come from what you let into your attention—media, TV, news, others opinions, etc. That is probably the majority. What are the usual thoughts you create from a world full of bad news and conflict? Then there are events that happen to you. How do you react to these when you disagree or become angry, or spiteful as to why they happen to you?

Then the proactive ones come forth. These are the ones you simply generate in your own space. Do you ponder on lack, fear, problems, or issues? Then there are the ones that are your desires and plans for a better life. Do you think about the solution or the lack of one?

These are the critters of life that need to be muzzled and directed through the heart. These are the energies that create your perception and your life. Can you remain in that positive space of the heart? The trick is to stay there.

But most important of all is the need to change that double whammy we had in the introduction. First, if the energy you create is there to find a mate, it makes sense to pay more attention to creating positive energy. Secondly, if the energies strength of attraction is dependent upon the added emotion, then it would make sense to start creating strong positive emotion and start a program where you proactively choose what it is you want to attract and manifest. Third, if the negative energy plays havoc with your physics and your physiology by creating dis-ease and disease, it would make good sense to avoid creating these.

Unconscious Creation And Conscious Manifestation

Speculate again and allow yourself to believe that you can control and attract what you want to manifest. The lesson here is that you are already creating your reality without understanding how. The difficult part of this is that although your energy centers of thought, vision, communication and emotion create energies that seek out likeness, there is no correlation. The Earthling has fallen to the first two levels of manifestation in believing that you either have to go get something or get someone else to get it for you. There is no correlation between when the thought occurs and when the result is attained. and when you try to materialize that million dollar check it does not happen. Why?

Because you have not graduated in your vibrational journey to take the responsibility of Creatorship. Yet your energy center are always at work asking and the universe of the quantum soup is always responding in its own way and in its own time. What you have not learned is the process by which these laws work. You must understand the difference between Unconscious Creation and Conscious Manifesting.

First, let us look at what happens without you knowing. What you request is already done because it is formed by your energies that take the quantum energies and creates something from no-thing. These are simply energies with no distinction of bad or good. It is like your mind creates a vision from nowhere, Secondly, because it is handled by the subconscious, there no expectations, conditions, attachments because you are not even aware of it happening. And so a process of energy mating occurs and the law of attraction draws forward the situation, event that give you a likeness. This is why if you are filled with fear, you are asking for more. If you are always questing, or feel sick, or poor, that is the energy you are projecting for more of it.

All this is automatic as it is the way energy works. It is an unconscious process. However, when you attempt to bring this into your conscious reality and manifest proactively, the ball game shifts into the rule book of beliefs.

There is a science behind the Law of Attraction, and that science is the Law of Belief. The Law of Belief governs what you create in your lives. Within the Law of Belief are the addendums of the life 'set ups' you plan and contract to yourself for growth. But the lessons you arrange are met through your confrontation and disciplined effort. It is therefore essential that you fully realize that you are never at the mercy of events, you are not helplessly fated to face the unexplainable like a ship lost at sea. Masters, neither psychological events nor physical events have control over you. When you fully comprehend the vast capacity of your brain to hold a diversity of conclusive beliefs associated with your experiences, you will see that you have an infinite array of choices.

But for those of you stuck in old patterns and limiting beliefs, you are mired in a repetitive cycle of predetermined responses, including the propensity to block new solutions through denial of better thinking. In that sense if you do not learn from past errors, you are self- fated to repeat them. Indeed you will repeat the cycle until you learn how the process of achieving Divine Mind functions. That is true for all humans. You must challenge yourself to break free.

There are three separately governed processes under the Law of Attraction. The three have succinctly different criteria for achievement. Let us define the primary aspect of each Law:

The Law of Attraction:- Thoughts have a frequency and attract like frequencies;

The Law of Belief: Knowing beyond doubt. You can only manifest what you believe is possible;

The Law of Conscious Creation: The conscious ability to focally manifest objectives & events via the multidimensional mind in higher vibration.

Before discussing these, it is important to know why these laws may not work at all.

Attraction and Avoiding Responsibilities

Understand that it is your beliefs that are projected to form your individual and group reality. Understand there are scenarios planned by your higher self, your Divine Mind aspect, that may be termed 'set-ups' or soul-contracts that you yourself have chosen as growth lessons to assist you in moving into greater wisdom. With that reminder in hand, understand that 'karma' in your terms, is not a debt owed to one from another, in the higher sense but rather it is ever to the Self, it is balancing the Divine Self. It is part of your evolutionary path Home.

Should you have a goal or objective in manifestation that would conflict with higher self, it will not in most cases be manifest, unless it is chosen as a growth lesson. For example if a human desires wealth, and that wealth would either be misused or stop the growth process, the higher self may reject such a desire from manifesting. In some cases, humans who have all of their material 'needs' met, are less compelled to search for expansion.

When you find yourself in the confines of any experience that is uncomfortable or not to your liking, you must understand that YOU created that seeming conundrum. Within this axiom, there are indeed, within duality, scenarios in linear time that you must face. Whether one accepts it or not, every circumstance and every resulting action, however dire, was absolutely self created. If, for example, in an extreme circumstance a crime is actually committed, and an individual is duly sentenced to prison, those actions will be faced and experienced.

The sentenced prisoner cannot, in most duality circumstances, simply wish it away. Rather they must face the duality they have themselves created in linear time. There are Laws of Cause and Effect in your physical reality that will play themselves out. Responsibility for not only your actions, but indeed for your beliefs is a key part of your growing process on the planet of lesson. Owning both is essential. But by facing them, you can change the landscape around you.

So understand whenever you seek to avoid the responsibility for your own actions, you generally do so by attempting to give that responsibility, the 'blame', to some other individual, group or cause. But in that process of shifting blame, you unconsciously give away your power, and take away the ownership that allows you to 're-create'. The difficulty most have in accepting self responsibility for your behaviour lies in the desire to avoid the pain and guilt of the consequences of the very actions that resulted. You don't like to admit your errors. But in less obvious circumstances of abundance lack and untoward relationships, you must not only change the nature of your conscious thoughts, but also the belief in those very expectations....and then act on those beliefs.

Unconscious Programming

You create our own reality from what you choose to believe about yourselves, and the world around you. Period. If you do not deliberately & consciously choose your own beliefs, you are unconsciously programmed. You will mindlessly absorb them from your 3D culture, schooling and surroundings. If you are accountable and responsible for your actions, how can you afford NOT to question your beliefs? How you define yourself, and the world around you, forms your belief, which, in turn, forms your reality. Once you fully comprehend that your beliefs form reality, then and only then are you no longer a captive of the events you experience. You simply have to learn the mechanics & methods. It is only when you believe, and program that belief to fully override and replace previous erroneous beliefs, that the integral field of the triad of the three step function of own, change, action is completed.

In the process, thoughts must harmonize with beliefs and be followed by ACTION ! This process is best understood as the Christ Consciousness of Thought, Word, and Deed being the prevalent unified action of unconditional love and forgiveness in all moments as the ACTION. This is the path to conscious creation.

Ad so the lesson is that you are NOT at the mercy of your circumstances, but that belief is, interestingly, the reason you erroneously think you are. Take a moment to consider that. It is the **Law of Belief**. If you believe that circumstances have you trapped, then they do, and will until you change that core belief. You are creators learning how to co-create. You are here to learn that you can and do create. One of your key reasons for being in duality Earth is to learn how to create responsibly, and consciously. The principle professor is often Dr. Cause & Effect, and this doctor makes house calls! You reap what you sow and however uncomfortable, the untoward harvest is the very means for consideration of what got you there.

To break out of circumstances that are caused by our psychology, requires conscious disciplined effort for change to occur. The key again is your belief. There is little difference if you believe that your present life is caused by incidents in your early childhood or by past lives over which you equally feel you have no control. Your events, your lives, your experiences, are caused by your present beliefs. Change the present beliefs and your life changes, not only in the present, but in the past and future in kind. That is the creative power of belief.

Regardless of your level of Light or Dark vibration, whether you are unconsciously creating or consciously manifesting, you cannot escape your beliefs. They are the enzymes through which you create your experience.

The Processes Of Brain And Mind

The reason that most of the books and commercialized teachings on manifestation do not work, is because they do not have the understanding of deeper mind versus 3D brain. Most are about manifesting monetary wealth, and in most cases the only one truly manifesting is the publisher from book sales. There are many nuances, many aspects unexplained in the texts. Even when you expand the mind, you must optimize and balance the auric field for the Crystalline aspect that allows creation to function.

The Key Evolvement Principles for Accessing the Law of Creation are:

1) Expanded Programming of the Brain - Knowledge into Belief
2) Release of Ego-Personality Control to Divine-Mind Aspect of Higher Consciousness
3) Maintain EMF Balance
4) Activate the Mer-Ka-Na Crystalline aspect of Pituitary, Pineal, & Thymus
5) Maintain Balance & Clarity

It is essential that you understand that the 3D brain, the ego-personality aspect incorporated in your physical 3D biology is programmed for 'survival' in a primary coding. It is the 'survival' code that brings in the warning signals that involve cautions often experienced as fear and doubt. The frontal mind, the ego-personality aspect, is engineered to dominate your 3D consciousness, in order to allow linear time flow and survival within the physical plane. The challenge is that to arise above 3D consciousness you must rise out of ego consciousness and flow into Divine Mind within the Seat of the Soul, the gateway into Divine Mind.

The brain is in 3D, the mind is of higher dimension, and within higher mind is your Divinity. The brain operates in 3D and in a manner of speaking, its 3D programming is somewhat dominant in the field of duality. It operates in a more confined paradigm, and to expand into mind, you must operate 'outside the box' to engage your true creativity.

The importance of defined clarity is important in creation. Humans only partially engage wishes through 'Someday I will ' dreamscapes. That is like partially programming a computer program. Is it any surprise that it doesn't happen? Someday I will travel, One day I will be rich, some day I will realize my dreams... These then become merely 'maybes', spaced in a distance. So what you are attempting to create always stays at the distance, the someday you programmed. You did not put it in the present. Yes, the dream is the first part, but it must be clear, concise and followed by definite actions.

Your brain has two hemispheres, one dealing with intellect, one with feeling. The brain works through bio chemical activations and stimulus. The intensity & clarity of a thought program is extremely important for it to become a belief. Your brain is a 3D living computer. It must be dealt with in defined terms. It will not work with 'maybe' or 'can I?' For example, if one were taken into a deep hypnotic state, and asked , "Can the mind heal the dis-ease in this body?" the answer would be "Yes". But it is the empirical answer to whether it is possible for the mind to heal the body. It is not the healing.

Every thought produces a bio-chemical enzyme. That enzyme works with the physical and nonphysical, in sync with the programming. One of the exceptions to the concept of 'Ask and it Shall be given', is that unless the asking is channelled from within, in sync with higher mind, it may have little effect. So a human on the path, in a relatively advanced state of consciousness, may well neutralize from a higher stance desires that would impede progress. There is then, a natural filtering for those in a state of grace. Goals must be worthy.

The most noble goal is to learn the mysteries of life. To gain wisdom and Mastery. But to achieve these goals you will have to take on certain pressures and stresses that are taxing. It requires discipline and will. If you are lazy, you will not get there. You must take on the task to achieve it. So attempts to create a challenge free life may be in stark conflict with a life intent on learning. Goals have challenges. Masters do not plan challenge free lifetimes.

Mind is the builder, and focused will-power is the activator. The more responsibility you appropriately take on, the more your frequency will increase. Learning to program the brain is essential. The brain is a biological computer with 3D filters and 3D programs that are ingrained from birth. Unless you were born in a Tibetan Monastery, your programming has come from socio-cultural indoctrinations. Most social programming teaches you to accept a very limited view of human existence, and human ability. You are taught to believe only what you can sensually detect through sight, hearing, taste, smell or touch.

Know that the physical world of matter you see around you is imagery that you sensually interpret and project. It is received in the eye, transferred via the optic nerve to the brain. What is received stimulates neurons, and a response occurs through a bio chemical reaction that is thermal in nature. Because you generally believe what you see, smell , taste or hear you accept it, you believe it as real. You then decide if it is pleasing or not. The brain then releases neurons based on like or dislike. This is how your reality and attraction works. You are initially attracted to people who are attractive, have a melodious voice and smell good ! Your physical sensual body says yes or no.

In kind, the brain takes ideas and either accepts them or deflects them, according to program parameters. In truth the brain is unable to differentiate between an actual event or a psychological one, such as a dream. In multidimensional mind the two are the same. And although the human brain is capable of receiving information and frequencies from well above 3D, most humans program it to reject anything above 3D frequencies of sensory conformity. The brain computer thus receives only what you allow it to receive. In such limiting paradigmic programming, the only parts of your brain that are activated are the right and left hemispheres of the upper cerebrum and portions of the lower cerebellum, composing and imposing an activity level of only about 10-12 percent of the brain. The brain activity and processes in the neocortex of the cerebral hemispheres conduct the primary activity in the physical realm. The 90% majority of your brain remains unused, un-activated, programmed into dormancy. That is because any thought that does not fit in with the limited thinking programs of your cultural programming or dogma, you auto-deflect.

Herein is one of the great reasons the 'Law of Attraction' does not work for you:

limited belief from limited thinking programs. To be so narrow-minded is to be closed to the grand possibility of anything existing beyond the small band of frequency that can be perceived through the five senses of your physical 3D body.

So how do you expand the brain. How do you open to mind? How do you reprogram the computer? The answer is simple but seemingly a difficult hurdle for many of you to accomplish. It is by doing. It is by examination and study, and willing self to open. Accordingly the very desire to expand attracts powerful thought frequencies that will allow for expansion. And then every Occasion in which you openly accept an idea that is beyond your accepted parameters, that idea activates yet another part of your brain into purposeful use.

Each time you do that, the expansive idea will offer itself as a carrier to expand your field of belief, and allow greater Cosmic reasoning. That process, sincerely repeated, will attract new ideas with study and meditation. In kind, this cycle will activate other portions of your brain for more expansion, new programming and new reception, by accepting in a clear mind. When you have no doubt, when you know and it is absolute....it is Belief. It is through expanded mind that you begin the steps of creating your destiny.

How do you functionally expand the brain and open the doors to Divine Mind ? It is not done in one illuminating flash realization. It is not a one step Divine Anointing. The sacred pathway to what you may term 'Enlightenment ' is achieved in deliberate steps. There are many in metaphysics that want to open the book of knowledge and skip over to the final chapter. It doesn't work that way. It begins by self exploration. By carefully auditing what works and does not work for you. In this method you allow fresh and expansive ideas to enter the brain from the Divine Mind as high frequency thought. Then you process and contemplate it, experience the new concept by embracing it. Acting it out. Evolve it and drive it with emotion , and live the new information into knowledge and wisdom.

The issue most humans have in not changing their beliefs is blind acceptance of mental 3D programming. You can think positive thoughts, think positive change, but if in your deeper mind you doubt they will occur, then they will not. Doubt is one blockage that prevents manifestation of your desires. If you doubt, you do not believe. Doubt in the brain creates a bio-chemical reaction. It activates a neuron carrier in the brain that flows from the Pituitary gland to the Pineal and blocks the 'gateway' from opening. The doubt is there because you do not believe.

The survival aspect programming of the Personality Ego brain utilizes 'fear' in duality as a warning system. However, the duality aspect, the double edge of that sword, is that fear out of context can reach into many negative emotions including depression, doubt, hatred, jealousy and self contempt. These are at their root, negative aspects of fear, and fear creates static in the auric field, and can lead to auric bleeding. The human Aura must be integral to optimally operate in the Law of Creation.

The belief thought-images that surround you are co-created in mass fields by all of humanity in agreement in the macro. Individually they are projected according to your light quotient. These manifest into physical reality. This involves a physical process. Thought frequencies are digitally received and are immediately propelled bio-chemically within the brain. Mental enzymes are connected with the pineal gland. The Pineal gland receives them as geo-coded transmissions. Each image, each thought, being interpreted and sorted according to its energetic signature. They must pass through the program parameter of belief after reception at the pineal. Your brain screens what is determined as real or unreal. Believable or unbelievable according to the light quotient programmed into the brain. The bio-chemicals produced are produced with acceptance ingredient or rejection ingredient. These are allowed to open or close the gate to higher mind accordingly.

These bio chemicals are sent as coded neurons, and are the delivery mechanism of this thought-energy, containing all the codified data necessary for translating any thought or image into physical actuality, or not. Thoughts that are congruent with belief move to reproduce the inner image within the brain and through each nerve fiber of the body physical. These then are the initial fires of gestation for forming the new reality. The next step is through clear mind intent, the force of will, will driven by the acceleration of emotion and feeling.

This done, the physical body releases the objective in a digital code to the sublime body, the intact Auric Field in a semi solid, congealed light code, projected and accelerated from the chakra system. The clarity and intensity you insert behind the thought-desire or goal determines to a great degree the immediacy of its materialization. Once you learn the mechanics of conscious creation it is essential then to utilize the engine of genuine desire with image visualization and emotion to complete the process of physical manifestation.

When It Does Not Work

You create your reality, and there is no other rule. You are here in the University of Duality, to learn how to responsibly create. But it is not thought that on its own, is creative, rather it is BELIEF .... belief expressed in thought in a clear mind. So to clarify syntax, let us say that in the Law of Attraction, it is wise to substitute the word Believe "for "Think", because while positive thought can encourage new belief, until you believe what you think you are not generating new reality. Belief generates reality. This is logical. So understand, beyond the syntax, that thinking positive thoughts can only manifest if they are in sync with your beliefs. For example, if at your core, you BELIEVE you are unworthy of abundance, or in your core mind, believe that the accumulation of abundance is materialistic and therefore wrong, you will not manifest abundance by merely thinking about it. If you believe money is the root of all evil, the Law of Attraction will not work for you until you change that core belief. If you believe that you are poor and will always be scraping to make ends meet, then your very belief will create that experience. No matter if you work 2 or 3 jobs, your core belief is generated, projected into dimensionality and indeed will be manifested. You will struggle economically.

If you believe you are not 'very smart' , your brain will take on that belief and you will be limited. If you believe you are not attractive, you will project that image to all around you telepathically. You constantly project your beliefs, and their manifestations constantly "meet you in the face" when you view the world around you. They form the reflective mirrored- image of your realized beliefs. You cannot escape your beliefs. They are, however, the method by which you create your experience. In kind, if you believe, in very simple terms, that people mean you well, and will treat you kindly, they will. And, if you believe that the world is against you, then so it will be in your experience. And, if you believe that your body will age and begin to weaken at age 40 , then it will.

You are in physical existence to learn and understand that your beliefs, energetically translated into feelings, thoughts and emotions, cause all experience. Period. Now your experience can change your beliefs, and at any time you are in control of what you choose to believe. The key is to form BELIEF through 'over-soul' Mer-Ka-Na **(http://www.earth-keeper.com/EKnews_2-26-2010.htm)** aspectual conscious choice and not by unconscious programming.

Now, let's take this concept into multi dimensionality. Imagine that you have a number of lifetimes as a monk or priest where you have taken strict poverty vows. You have shunned the 'material' and adhere strongly to the BELIEF that money is 'the root of all evil'. All lifetimes are simultaneous in the eternal now. In the present lifetime there is the focus on creating your reality. You have need for abundance. You realize money is not evil, it is simply energy, and that it can be used for many positive things.

You have read all the books, read all the articles on how positive thinking triggers the 'Law of Attraction', yet you are still not bringing in abundance. Could it be that you are multi dimensionally 'outnumbered'. If you have a dozen ongoing lifetimes in their NOW moment simultaneously shunning, rejecting what they BELIEVE to be 'material things' and one lifetime trying to create abundance, which effort contains the most energy projection ? You have the ability in NOW mind in Mer-Ka-Na to change the seeming past and create a unified harmonic of that which you desire and believe. And Dear Ones, money is not evil ! It is energy and in the new paradigm you are required to learn to create in responsible loving manner. You CAN have what you want, what you need, but the Belief must be harmonic in multi dimensionality.

It is not as simple as "Ask and it shall be given". It must be projected in clear harmonic mind. And mind is above brain. Mind is multi dimensional.

Now, the multi-dimensional aspect of human experience is quintessential to your understanding of the mechanics of the 'Law of Attraction'. A key part of understanding your multi-dimensionality is that your higher self , the part of you above physicality, scripted certain of your 'life growth challenges'. And that these cannot be avoided or wished away. Rather they are 'required' courses in the curriculum of the 'University of Earth' that you yourself have chosen to complete for higher good. And you can't skip the classes. They will come to you because you enrolled, they are a part of the 'Law of Attraction' from higher mind, and cannot be repelled.

This then is an area in which duality thinking, of trying to wish away a seeming obstacle, seems to defy the 'Law of Attraction'. You may find yourself in an uncomfortable scenario at work, find that all the 'positive thinking' applications seem to fall flat. That is because there is a lesson here that must be faced, and until it is faced it will repeat over and over again, until it is completed...because you have attracted it to you from higher mind, and duality -aspect brain is unable to avoid it. It is only completed when you master it.

While it is true that your thoughts and beliefs create the reality you experience in duality, you in higher aspect thoughtfully and carefully compose and create the challenges that you face. These have great purpose. Whether you truly believe it or not, you write your own tests. So while 'positive thinking' is a key frequency, positive thinking is meant to help you approach your life lessons and does not circumvent the learning process itself. You cannot just ignore or wish away the growth lessons you script for yourself in order to expand. That is because your chosen set ups are in most cases outside, beyond the ability of the duality aspect of ego-brain to remove or will away. You will face them, because you have in divine self, willed it from higher perspective. In higher mind you have scripted your challenges.

There is nothing more stimulating, more worthy of actualization, than your manifested desire to evolve, to change for the better. That is indeed each of your lifetime missions. It is not enough to meditate, or to visualize the desired goal being accomplished if you do not act upon the inner voice , the drive from which your meditations and visualizations arise.

Intent, focus and meditation must absolutely be teamed with action. Becoming impeccable, and eventually achieving your enlightenment does not mean, as some religions indirectly imply, that you are suddenly in a blissful state of oblivion, or in some distant state of nirvana. Masters, we tell you that you are as much a part of a nirvana now as you ever will be, you simply need to discover it within you.

There will indeed be cycles within your emotional state; that is part of being human. There will be times in which you feel apathetic and depressed. Not only the problems you face, but even certain astronomical gravities can be the source of such despair, on their own. All of these must be faced, and can be surmounted. So be aware that 'Nirvana', in your vernacular, is achieved attitudinally, and not through avoidance, ignorance or escape, but through impeccable confrontation of the reality projection that surrounds you.

Earth experience, duality mastery is difficult. This is a great truth, one of the greatest truths of duality, and one commonly misunderstood. The study and mastery of life requires work. You can't simply put the text book under your pillow and sleep on it, it must be read and understood a page at a time. Moment by moment.

So then your full understanding and accepting that your life is a construction of 'set ups' that you planned in order to enable your spiritual growth is an even greater truth. You see when you accept this noble truth, you have the opportunity to transcend it. That which you term 'destiny' is in truth the situations you pre-planned for your life lesson. And Dears Ones, that very self scripted 'destiny', in your terms, will assist you to both face your challenges and then manifest your desires, but not because you protest what you do not like. In order to experience the light of your desire, you must ignite the passion that will free it from the stronghold where it has been closely guarded. The greatest path is to accept the challenge of self purification by being a living example of your own light rather than protesting the darkness that still exists within the world in 3D, or choosing to insulate yourself from it.

By accepting that you are here to face challenges, then you can more robustly create the energy needed to face them. Because once it is accepted, the fact that life can be difficult no longer scares you, rather it motivates the spiritual warrior into resolve. The greatest issue you have in accepting ultimate ownership and responsibility for your actions lies in the core desire to avoid the pain of the consequences of that behaviour. But we tell you that it is the confrontational courage of impeccably solving problems that provides and indeed nurtures meaningful growth in your life.

Facing your problems is the serendipitous cutting edge that distinguishes between success and failure, or better said, between growth and stagnation. Problems call forth your best effort to resolve and refine courage and wisdom within the impeccable seeker. It is categorically because of stressful predicaments and obstructions that you grow mentally and spiritually. It is through the pain of confronting and resolving life-puzzles and 'set-ups' that you learn the greater meaning of the science of love. Dear Hearts, the candid fact is that some of your most poignant accomplishments and indeed greatest growths are spawned when you are placed in the troubling crossroads of conundrum.

Your greatest trials and revelations take place in times when you are outside of your 'comfort zone', feeling bewildered, unfulfilled, or even in a state of agonizing despair. For it is in such moments, propelled by your discomfort, that you are compelled to burst out of the confining cages and seek a better, more spiritually satisfying way of life.

What then is impeccability? We are not understating the base premise, when we define impeccability simply as ' always trying your best'. To remain impeccable requires more effort as the scope of your gained wisdom and consciousness expands. The greater your consciousness, the more you 'know' . The more you know, the greater the responsibility to live accordingly. You are in the process of expanding your vibratory awareness, of becoming a conscious participant with the soul. You are becoming what your soul is, discovering your greater identity.

When you grow spiritually, it is because you have opened to seek growth and are taking action, working to achieve it. Impeccability involves the deliberate extension of your Beingness into evolution. Impeccability puts you in the state of grace. Impeccability does not infer that you have achieved enlightenment or have learned all you need to learn. Rather it means you are on the only track, the right pathway to get there. So we will define Impeccability in two layers, two phase formats:

1) Conditional Impeccability: This is when the entity is not highly advanced, yet working toward mastery . Doing one's best. Utilizing knowledge to the best of one's ability to do the right thing, even when there may be ignorance and innocent misconceptions. By that it means you truly believe what you are doing is the right course, even if it is not the full or expansive truth . All of you go through such phases. In this phase if you make a mistake, it is an honest mistake, in which you genuinely believed you were doing what you felt is right.

2) Mastery Impeccability: This is the phase of the soul in human existence that is on the cusp of Mastery. One highly advanced, and walking the talk. Having no inner conflict between what one believes to be the right path, and what one actuates.

Both phases activate what you may term as an accelerated state of grace. Grace is assistance from the Divine Self to help the outcome of situations when one is trying their best. It may be thought of as the 'Guardian Angel', because in many cases that is exactly what a Guardian Angel is, your Divine Self serendipitously intervening in situations to assist you on your path. If we were to redefine what your religious texts consider as sin, it would not be in terms of the commandments, rather it would be: "knowledge not utilized". Taking actions you know to be incorrect, actions in conflict to your highest beliefs.

Wisdom Is Within

All of you desire wisdom greater than your own. Seek and you will find, and Masters you can find it 'hidden' inside you. And sadly that is often the last place you look. It takes work. You see the divine interface between God and man is within what your academics term as the subconscious. Even your religious texts tell you that God is within you, that you are a spark of the Divine. The subconscious mind, or 'back brain' in your terms, is the part of you that is God. The portion of your greater self that contains the knowledge of 'All That Is', the part of you that contains the Akashic Records, the soul memory of everything.

Since the subconscious is the Divine Mind within you, the goal of spiritual growth is achieved by entering into that sacred 'Garden of Wisdom'. It is entered by quieting the ego mind. Meditation has ever been the gateway. It is the key to quieting the personality-ego narration and allowing the 'Voice of the Divine Soul' to be heard. Again, effort is required. There are no short cuts. The re-attainment of God-ness is the purpose of your individual existence on the polarity plane. You are born that you might become, as a conscious individual, a physical expression of God. A divine expression in Being-ness.

The challenge is your soul quest, your true purpose, and in physical sojourns, the clock is ever ticking. Obtaining Godhood in physicality is achieved on time-release, through immaculate desire that is actuated in the physical realm by merging with the wisdom of the non physical. Time matters. In polarity the current shifting of paradigms and energies can throw you off center rather easily in these quickening times. Your true purpose is often difficult to subjectively define and your understanding and ballast lies juxtaposed between illusion and perceived reality. You may feel you are living in a distortion and that nothing is exactly as it seems. In the process you can become confused and complacent. You can lose track of time.

Your lives, each moment of your physical life is precious, far more so than some of you realize. Far more than most of you utilize. Time is a precious commodity, and it is finite within your duality. Each of you reading these words will at some point in the future transition out of the physical. In your vernacular, you will experience death, you will die. This is a condition of physicality as you know it. Yet so many of you act as though you will live forever. Indeed the soul is eternal, but you will not ever be the same person, the same personality or expression that you are now, in any lifetime or in any other aspect of your 'Beingness'. You are here to learn the expressions of your own Godliness within duality and indeed duality is a gift. Life is a gift. You are here to learn how to co create, for indeed you are co creators of the Universe, of the Cosmos. You are here to achieve Mastery, and so many of you are very close, very near that achievement.

Until you truly value yourself, you will not be in the grace of impeccability and thus not be motivated to truly value and optimize your time. Unless you place great value on your allotted time, you will not do your 'best' with it. "Carpe Diem", is translated as "Seize the Day", and this is so appropriate. You must seize each moment! So many of you, despite your good intentions, allow yourselves to be tranquilized into complacency at certain phases or within certain conditions of your chosen sojourns. Many of you waste time; misuse time and lifetime after lifetime can be squandered. What you do not face, what you do not resolve in any one moment or lifetime, will resurface. You will repeat the set up until you successfully solve it, and that is indeed a great truth. Utilizing your time in duality is quintessential, and that is a complex undertaking for it necessitates that you seek impeccability. It requisites love of self, for until you genuinely value yourself, you truly do not value your life and time. And until you value your time, you will not be compelled to maximize how you spend it.

It is natural Discipline that is the basic set of tools to solve life problems. Without discipline it is difficult for you to have the driver required to focus on the work of solving your problems. Simply stated, you can become immobilized...apathetic, complacent or lazy. On the 'Ladder of Ascension', you are moving up, sitting still or moving down.

In third dimensional physics there is a law that states that energy that is highly organized will naturally degrade when not in dynamic state. It is easier by natural law to be in a state of complacency in the physical plane, than to be in an upwardly mobile condition. That is clearly logical. It is the Law of Love that motivates all souls into greater consciousness, and that requires dynamics...work! Laziness is in a real sense one of your biggest obstacles, because work means swimming against the tide. Seize the Day!

All is In Perfect Order

Some of you say and feel that "Everything works out as it should, all is in perfect order". But that concept is something of a paradox, and like a face card it is upside down either way you look at it. From the higher perspective all is in perfect order, but from the perspective of humankind within duality, it is not! If it were there would be no need for lessons, no need for what you term reincarnation. One need but take a look around and know that the plight of humankind on the planet Earth is far from being perfect. Indeed it will NOT work out as it should, until you make it so!

On the final walk of Mastery, most of your major issues have been dealt with, and we honor you for that. What remains may however be elusive to confront. And it is important to confront any and all unresolved issues and energies.

We say this without judgment. We point this out in order to assist you. For in time all must be dealt with. The more advanced you become, the more difficult it can be to sweep up the last remaining bits of unresolved issues, because they are often well hidden. The unresolved energy, the final issues can become polarized and repelled outside your mental field, forgotten in the residues of many lifetimes. Take time to self review in multidimensional self and determine what is left to be worked on.

Polarity Physics - The 'Law Of Opposite Attraction'.

There is yet another conundrum about the Law of Attraction, so says Metatron: "The closer you get to light, the stronger you attract the dark. Light attracts bugs! The more you advance, the more criticism you will draw, and that requires wisdom to deal with. The polarity aspect of the 'Law of Opposite Attraction' herewith comes into play. From a state of detachment what takes place is electromagnetics. Pure positive energy has the greatest 'magnetic' attraction to negative energy. So as your light shines brighter, the magnetic to polar opposite increases. It can be managed, but you must have the light, humility, the strength and discipline to deflect it. So dealing with affronts, the hard energy of jealousy, hatred and anger are an important piece of the puzzle in achieving the Master level of Impeccability.

How do you deal with this? Don't take anything personally is perhaps easier said than done, but it is quite true. Your bible talks of turning the other cheek. But this doesn't mean you apologize when someone steps on your foot. Part of the paradox is indeed standing up for your truth. But it does mean you don't step on the feet of others, intentionally or otherwise. Standing in your truth is peaceful action. It is a benevolent expression of aggression that allows grace and dignity to be retained on both sides of any conflict or attack. It sends the attacking energy back to its source, but without malice and with love. Each of you has an opportunity to stand in impeccability within any conflict. You can deal with conflict, without engaging it. Do you understand? Deal with, face it from a stance of emotional detachment, as the observer, and that is not easy, yet it is the way of the Master. It is how you 'Don't take anything personally', you detach from the emotional reaction.

Each of you has an opportunity to be impeccable every day. The scenario in which you recognize your own failings, your own conflict with integrity, is the day you encompass Mastery level Impeccability, and indeed it is a journey. Likewise the day you stand in your truth with willingness to recognize another person's truth, you encompass integrity. The divine mind is only achieved, only accessed through crystalline Mer-Ka-Na resonance, within crystalline thought waves. Crystalline thought is above emotion, above petty feelings. It is achieved in detachment. It is the crystalline lake of Shamballa, of true Nirvana, as smooth as glass, no waves distorting its mirrored visage."

59

YOUR HOLOGRAPHIC REALITY

The Law Of Conscious Creation

You know of Unconscious Creation and Conscious Manifesting. What about Conscious Creation? What Earthlings have not come to understand is that the workings of the mind in what is termed "imagined reality" is a model of way the 3D material reality works. The real dream is your life here. Understand that there is no physical object about you, nor any experience in your life that you have not created. This includes your physical form, your body. There is nothing about your own physical image that you have not made. In fact if you were able to view self in other life sojourns, you would be surprised at how many similar physical characteristics you create in what would be termed sequential lifetimes. When you have Divine Wisdom, you can create kingdoms unlimited. When you have knowledge, there is nothing to fear, for then there is no thing, no element, no principality, no understanding that can ever threaten or enslave or intimidate you. When fear is given knowledge, it is called enlightenment.

You have a natural rhythm of existing in the physical and non physical. It is your waking and sleep state. Dreams are one of your greatest natural therapies and assets as connectors between the interior and exterior realities and universes. Your normal consciousness benefits by excursions and rest in those other fields of nonphysical actuality that are entered when you sleep, and the so-called sleeping consciousness will also benefit by frequent excursions into the physical matter waking state.

But let us tell you that the imagery you see in both is at its base, mental interpretations of digital frequential fields of core consciousness units. The frequency that your brain receives is actually a digital code, a crystalline pattern of symbols (akin to what you may term as X's and O's), that you interpret and translate into images and feelings. It is not so difficult for you to accept that you create your dreams, as it is to accept that you also create your physical reality, but you do both. You also determine if both or either are real...or not.

The issue most humans have in not changing their beliefs is blind acceptance of mental 3D programming. You can think positive thoughts, think positive change, but if in your deeper mind you doubt they will occur, then they will not. So we return to programming and its effect on manifestation within the Law of Attraction. Doubt is one blockage that prevents manifestation of your desires. If you doubt, you do not believe. Doubt in the brain creates a bio-chemical reaction. It activates a neuron carrier in the brain that flows from the Pituitary gland to the Pineal and blocks the 'gateway' from opening. The doubt is there because you do not believe.

Through the ages it has been known that the Pineal is the interface between the higher dimensions and the physical realm. It can be said then to be the gateway between the ego personality, brain and the Divine Mind. It has been termed by metaphysicians such as Descartes and Edgar Cayce as being the 'Seat of the Soul'.

The pineal is the agent of advancing knowing into reality manifestation. The pineal works with the pituitary to open the bridge, the gateway between the physical and nonphysical, between brain and mind. Whatever knowledge you allow yourself to believe can only become a reality by the pineal first opening the gate to the Divine. It does this by interpreting the frequency of thought into a thermal bio chemical electrical current throughout your body and opening to mind.

Your human brain transforms the thoughts you generate into thousands of bio-chemicals every second. But not every thought of the ordinary brain reaches into Higher Mind. Divine Wisdom comes from Divine Mind, and when you allow mind to take the reins over ego personality you achieve the wisdom of Divine Creativity. It is this wisdom distilled from knowledge that gives you the ability to enter the Law of Creation. Once entered, then know what you want to create and take action toward it.

The human body is an instrument that can be used to access the amazing and extraordinary energies of the Divine. But there are dedicated principles for accessing the Divine. When the body is fine tuned, wisdom is achieved, the aura is maintained in balance and the doors to the Law of Creation through the Law of Belief and Attraction are opened. For that to occur, all systems must work in balanced synchronicity. If you use your body for physical gratification rather than as an instrument to achieve the divine...you will reap what you sow.

You are ever the Master of each experience. Even in your most abandoned states of seeming helplessness, you are the scripter of each iota of that experience. Yet if you will utilize determination and wisdom by owning the responsibility to reflect upon your situation, and to search diligently for the Law upon which being is established, you then become the wise master, directing your energies with intelligence, and fashioning thoughts to worthy focus and realization. One thought attracts another. Positive energy attracts more positive energy. One intelligent thought attracts another. Likewise when you dwell in self pity, depression and issues of poor self esteem, you draw more of these to you. That is the Law of Attraction.

Such is the conscious human, the Master, and you can only thus evolve by discovering within Self the Laws of Conscious Creating; the discovery of which is totally a regulated science. It is a matter of application, self-analysis, and experience.

You can indeed intentionally manifest your world, and in doing so experience what is termed the Kingdom of Heaven. Conscious Creation is your destiny, and you can all make your lives the golden experience you responsibly desire.

Think How Your Mind Works

If you understand how your mind works, they you can understand how your physical reality as a hologram created by the mind can or should work. To take from quantum physics, your mind can bring into its reality any possibility you can think of. From the soup of no-thing, some-thing as an image, idea can be brought forward into your imaginary reality simply by shutting out your senses like closing your eyes and creating the picture in your mind. An event, experience, object, people; all can all be brought into reality. It begins with quantum nothing and like in the Observer effect of quantum physics becomes something. There need not be space or time. You can flip from one scene to another, you can play a movie like a dream, you can bilocate, materialize, be invisible, meld into other things, even deploy your physical senses given practice. You are engaging in the Creative process within you as a creator and here there are limitless possibilities to be "formed" by the conscious awareness of your mind. Everything can be everywhere, nowhere at once. It is nonlocal. You entangle by way of conscious intent to create whatever you desire to create.

The holograph of your world, your reality can work the same way and it does but you have not learned, nor believe this is so.

A New Look At Creating Reality

It is attention and intention and love as the substance of power that allows an image to congeal into a material representation of an abject in a hologram. This means that the Divine Mind be the total agent of the image of some object that is simply created in your mind's eye. It will be a clear image so you need much practice here. At the point at which your Higher Mind and the Heart—the congealer—create that image, it is projected onto a place of choice by intent and at the same time the image of the mind is projected to the God Source to be reflected back like a mirror as a beam of divine light to the same place of choice—yes it is like converging laser beams of light that create the 3 dimensional holographic image.

As these two actions converge upon the place of choice from you and the divine beam from the source, they form a holographic duplicate representation of the object that is to be replicated or materialized. Yes, from a wave form to an atomic form as the electrons arrange themselves into the image which is your higher consciousness choosing a new possibility from the no-thing.

It is not necessary to concern yourself as to how the chemistry, atomic structure and so on occurs as it is all under natural cosmic law that such an arrangement is created. These laws understand how this is done and your divine consciousness abides by these so they all understand what this is made up of to congeal this into the expression of the holographic image to be interpreted as such by your and other sensory systems of your brains—your sensory receiving stations.

You first create a clear image in your mind's eye with the assistance of the heart, then project it to a place of materialization. Then you project this to the One to project back to the same place. A holographic image is created. This is similar to the way a holographic image is created with beams of light that are split, reflected and converged again. What is it? A hologram. What form is it? It is whatever you see clearly that your brain understands and has meaning for or memory of.

It is your brain that does the final work as a material representation by retrieving what it knows and what cosmic rules apply in the material representation. It retrieves information and the cosmic rule simply "knows" what it is.

So let us say an apple is chosen. Is it big, small, red, yellow? What kind is it? The brain is designed to hold its own local knowledge—like a copy of its own experience that is held current. It uses this to fill the gaps of creating this from what it knows about the apple. The brain, and of course your consciousness or mind has information and the cosmic rules of its composition, formation, are drawn to complete the picture.

So a word, an object, and image, all have meaning to the brain by its experience and it with the assistance of cosmic law reverse engineers the process to create the result from memory and let us call it technical information as to its composition or material makeup. Although an image of the apple is only a representation in your lower mind and brain, it already has the appropriate material characteristics from higher sources as to how it would be materialized. So anything can indeed happen in materialization therefore it requires a high degree of responsibility.

You see, the brain which interprets senses also fills in the gaps to complete it. Many times, you will not actually see things exactly as the brain only picks up half of what is there, filling in the rest by itself—unless you place strict attention on it and see the difference. The brain fills the gaps, holes, missing information and uses a process you call extrapolate and interpolate from its memory what is needed to complete the picture. If you see and read the words "I luv yu" or "wht a wndrful da" you know what this is meaning, do you not? Your brain is interpolating the true meaning even though parts are missing. But by closer inspection and attention, you see the difference. So it is with an image of an apple.

The brain is the holographic processor that creates the meaning, composition, representation through its memory and the interpretation of the senses of your lower body. You see, feel, taste an apple and it seems so real. So if you take the senses of see, feel, taste and the memories of this, then reverse engineer the process back through the brain—with divine assistance—it will create the apple appearing solid in the hologram.

What you have not done is to do this outside of your imagination in an eyes open conscious state of awareness. Yet as you know, some can indeed do this—like holy men—by a reverse process which is easy in your mind but not in your hologram of 3D. But you are learning. It is what you are learning as you vibration reaches a certain level. Yes, this is so because of a certain level of responsibility, and partnership with the Higher Divine Self is required as reflected by the alignment of heart, purpose and Divinity—the One.

You are creating energy that will either seek out and energy mate or it will materialize into something that the energy represents into a new form from the essence of particles of what consciousness is made up of—electrons you call them—common to all things whether material or non material. This is what you call a reality, the attention of your awareness within the total consciousness—the mind of God. Each energy lives and has purpose and once created, lives to expand itself according to its purpose and it design which will behave according to cosmic laws of creation. Once live, it remains so and evolves as it was perceived at the time of creation, then it grows, changes and evolves.

Think also of how we have informed you of materialization and how you form the holographic image of some thing that can materialize—but with the alignment of the divine partner—approval to actually create—knowing the divine cosmic laws and being are explicitly in the heart so you are indeed the creator .

Each particle is of the whole and all is one therefore all that exists, existed or will exist resides here in the hologram which is the mind—the total consciousness of the One—the Creator. In your lower form of mind and body, this become like an individual compartment of the whole which is your local individual consciousness.

Once thoughts or actions of the lower form create, these energies remain to attain their purpose. They may be transmuted if you have attained the level of vibration that is of the Higher Body and Divine Mind. However, this responsibility is not of the lower form. If the energies are created from the Lower Selves, they will simply congeal into a transitional etheric state, attract, evolve and interact as they are designed by intent and attention to do—fulfilling either a cosmic or a purpose assigned by the creator you.

Through your senses of the Lower Self, the experiences are interpreted and perceived with the brain being the interpreter. The mind is what creates, sets, interprets, the instructions and is the actual link and control center of all this interacting energy and the body which itself is energy. A body is thus a hologram formed the same way and once created, a genetic code is set creating a signature of its makeup like in DNA. It is like this in all things as an initial blueprint that can replicate and evolve once given life.

Your Hologram Is A Living Growing Intelligent Medium

In the strictest sense, the consciousness of the Creator of the One is like a holographic with some major differences. Describing it this way is a convenient way for you to relate to it and understand it. It reflects all that can be or has ever been imagined by God. It is not a true hologram in your scientific terms however, in that it is a living and intelligent medium with all that exists living and interacting within it—all energies—living things that are themselves seeking to expand, flourish and ascend towards their purposes in their own individualized consciousness. Flowers, animals, human, rocks, and all energy placed within this hologram in their lower forms seek to evolve and expand through their instincts and purposes as encoded in their DNA or life code or inherent coded information that defines them and their higher states of expression. In humans the expression of this is through the Higher Divine Self which itself is consciousness.

All things are at the fundamental stage energy of consciousness and all have some form of consciousness as individualized. This brings and records an awareness through various interaction and processing of other energies—or sensory systems—to interact with and to seek expression and to evolve in a way to find their purposes. This is a cycle of material form—material by perception—of being created, living, blossoming, reproducing and all things are drawn to this process as encoded in the DNA as directed by their consciousness. In your lower form of Self, you are no different than a flower or rock or animal that seeks to live life, flourish, expand, and reproduce. You like all else are able to reproduce and create and evolve within an interactive live world of the hologram which itself is also evolving and lives with purpose of love.

You as a higher being can also create energy with your mind and body by placing attention here and triggering energy systems. You give it life and set it loose to evolve according to purpose—given by you--as so defined or by cosmic laws of evolution and expression.

Your Lower Self is designed to interpret energies so as to process them through senses and interpret them according to your physical brain. These are senses by the body and it transmitted back into it for action-reaction, as well as recording in consciousness for the perception of the experience. It is so it can learn, grow, live, expand according to instinct (lower purpose), cosmic law and expand (higher purpose. This process of material physical perception is this way and once some thing is formed in the hologram, it remains as part of it for others to perceive and sense.

In the lower form all interacts with and reacts to these energies that form the group or global hologram. Although you are creating certain energies through your mind and lower equipment, these are transient energies not yet congealed but are given life to seek purpose and find energy mates or entrain with like energies in the hologram. You know all about this. These energies can be dark or light and depending on their creation can do this rapidly or remain forever within the hologram.

In the Higher form, however, you are able to create new energies, passing the temporarily congealed state and materialize directly from the total consciousness—as a Creator. This is where a huge difference lies in the ability to transmute or actually create within the hologram.

Holograms Form From A Consciousness And Need To Express

You were given entry to this world of the Creator's mind and consciousness. This was created as a wondrous hologram of beauty and perfection within which beings could live, expand and learn to love and enjoy the life they had been given.

The entry of beings to this world has not gone according to this plan because of the lower state taken, the choice of will and others who have designs different fed by lower energies and requirements. Essentially other energies have been given life and purpose, evolving not within the light, filling the consciousness with interacting forces and energies not of the light. Energies you create retain a signature of ownership to find energy that it itself vibrates or entrains with. It draws other energies that represent people situations, and their owners with them. Thus in the hologram all energies live and interact. All beings interact in these physical and non-physical energies playing out their lives, as you do.

Many times this has resulted in much darkness within the hologram accumulating in a temporary form attempting to congeal into the hologram, not yet mated. It has dominated and at time almost destroyed the hologram. And so it has come to its end of a natural cycle of life as well at which point the energies are transmuted by death or by active awareness of its purpose. This purpose to many of you is known and therefore you have begun to form a new hologram in parallel which represents a world different than this one. The process is not known as to how these two worlds will merge or separate except to say it is all at an end which is the beginning.

The Hologram Is Limited By Beliefs

The hologram you have formed for yourself has limited you through your beliefs and as that belief changes, your senses and awareness of it expands, you begin to take control of it. As this occurs, the new 5D hologram that has been formed—much like your global consciousness—begins to be clearer. As your limited senses of 3D intent and bring material and mental perceptions of experience, so does the 5D self do the same in the new hologram. These worlds then expand so you with either at will begin to walk both. You are learning to use 5D senses in a 3D world. You will bring 3D into the 5D world.

As you sit quietly and imagine a world, or write about it, you are forming your hologram with your signature. This is a part of the larger hologram of joint imaginations. Anything is possible here but you are not yet able to walk this world except in your imagination. Once you give life to it, it is there and your tags of ownership so it can be changed as in a movie. All vibrations are above a threshold, all is interlinked and your awareness of how this works in one medium of intelligent evolving life unfolds to you. This you do not understand but there are cosmic laws that govern the way energies evolve, interact and change.

The Hologram Abides By Rules

Your mind may be busy with 4D the "transitions zone" as part of the hologram wondering why it has not come forward into your reality. Yes, it is another lane or dimension which is all around you like the air you breathe. It is beyond your 3D sensory system bounds, however—which you have imposed yourself. It is where energy is first created and interacts at an invisible etheric level. It is like a transition stage where energy waits in some form awaiting congealment and purpose. It is there to seek out an energy mate, to congeal, to materialize, or to co-create some thing that it is or represents. Think back to the laws of manifestation and Co-creation and how you create energies that seek mates.

For example, you may have a moment when you are angry and your thoughts, emotions instantly form this transition energy in the 4D plane. It is created in your field of influence. What does it do? It is tagged as belonging to you as you created it. Under cosmic law it has been created with a purpose of your anger that enfolded it. This may or may not be clear or strong in its intent provided by you. Under cosmic law, it is a living energy with purpose and such purpose it must strive to satisfy by seeking out a likeness to it and its purpose—an energy mate. It is a living energy seeking to expand and satisfy its purpose and signature vibration that it represents—namely your anger. So it can do this in several ways.

It can find a likeness to attract a situation that satisfies the purpose by an experience. It manifests a balance. It manifests, it evolves, it seeks until this is done and be balanced so the purpose is released. Such energy, depending upon it strength and clarity can take unknown time and it can also influence other energy fields to have an effect on them. It must to this in order to draw other energies to it. So it may be something that is in your own field that is strong enough to affect dysfunction in your own field and body because it is attached to you—and your belief system can attract others the same way. The dysfunction remains until it is balanced, like the idea of karma, but many times the energy results in creating disease or dis-ease or dysfunction in your Lower Self without your knowing. The effect of regression reveals the imbalance to correct this. Many energies are created as dark troublesome energies without purpose and they will simply be around looking for something dark to attach to.

The 4D world is full of these energies and over centuries have accumulated much unbalanced energy that has not yet satisfied its purpose and these affect the larger consciousness of those living in the hologram—in 3D. They struggle to evolve. You see the energy can be poorly defined and without purpose, unable to balance. It can be anything imaginable and there is no time here so it stays in 4D.

Your higher abilities if developed—as with clairvoyants and psychics are able to read these energies and sense them with expanded senses. They can read these living this to detect purposes, strength, have visions, read information that is attached to them as well as their owners. They can reveal what is forming or attached to you transcending past or future as the senses pick up this information thereby reading the future or revealing the past. These can see, hear, feel, read, know what is forming, the strength, the purpose.

Yes, ghosts, apparitions, dark energies, boogey men of unimaginable purposes and creations reside here. But you have been protected from these by your sensory limitations. However, as these senses evolve, so do protective abilities.

You have not yet widened the range of your sensory systems to read these energies—and to see them. Many animals have examples of enhanced ranges that sense these energies—much beyond yours. You do have them and they must be awakened again in your 3D form. In your 5D form there are many more as there are in your 4D form which is your aura that surround your body. You have others awaiting your awakening.

So yes there are many energy forms here awaiting their own evolution and purpose. That is why we speak of 3D and 5D, and not of 4D as 4D is simply a transition hologram from one to the other.

What you sow is what you reap reflects this 4D hologram of transition from one to another or back to the one that created it. It reflects the cosmic workings of energy as you sow it in 4D to reap it in 3D from where it is sown—or use it to grow to 5D. But you may not know what this is, and how or when it shall reap—that is part of raising your vibrations to sow wonderful positive energy in every moment.

The Collective Hologram Of Reality

You can understand that there is much energy being created by all beings on Earth. Some is dark, some is of the light, some is weak, some is strong, some has purpose some has not. But without exception each energy formed is attached to the creator and joins the collective coalescing energy. It is important to understand that in creating it, a tag is placed upon it by you—a word, a vision, an image, a symbol that represents this so it can be recalled for further attention instantly. It can be made clear, stronger, enforced, reinforce and define with clarity and strength of emotion so it is a stronger vibration energy with a clear purpose. Otherwise it can be aimless and purposeless with no thing to do except to bring unto itself the same, likeness—for you the creator of it—to experience. Clarity of purpose, strength of vibration through continued attention makes it strong and powerful to entrain and attract that which it reflects and is its purpose.

You understand that all beings form a collective hologram the same way as a composite of individual ones. These are combined as the group hopes, wishes, actions and perceptions all the time interacting and congealing into various forms that may materialize into new energies and forms. It is within this vast hologram that yours exists, all being within the larger one of the One—the mind of God. The hologram itself is alive and all within it cannot be changed in its perceived material form—a joint belief and congealment of form—without the attention and agreement of the Higher Divine Mind—your link to the Creator of the One. This as you know requires the higher vibration and purpose reflecting the truth of your essence of light. Otherwise energies only attract and attach to each other while at the same time that which is perceived to be material and physical in the 3D dimension remain unaltered except by its own growth evolution.

Thus there are interacting layers in the hologram of the One—3D material world, 4D coalescing energies, 5D etheric world. Within this 3D hologram layer all that is material is therefore your own holographic plane as perceived by you. What you perceive from it is your parallel world and yours alone interacting with the 3D world forming your physical hologram of your reality. It is recorded and once attention goes there it remains.

Let us give an example. An apple is a 3D material construct and the sight, smell, taste of it are your personal constructs in 4D as determined by your senses and perceptions—the link between the two planes. The whole hologram is overlain by your personal perception of all that is in it that comes into your awareness or attention. This parallel world is your own movie of life using other beings, props and objects of 3D to create your scenes and settings for you to interact with to create your perceptions, emotions, feelings, experiences to learn to yourself expand and grow towards your own purpose. How you do this is of your free will and this world of perception is yours alone as to what is in it.

Holograms Are Within Each Other Nested Nonlocal

It is important to understand you think this way in linear fashion. The Higher Self we have split into two words or concepts for you of Higher Mind and Higher Body. Yet the higher and lower Mind do not have any clear division as does not the higher and lower body. They are all one in the hologram and are simply a level of energy vibration which is a continuous scale—like the amount of love—it is less or more. Even the body is not clearly divided although you may perceive visible and invisible as this line of division but it is not so. It of course all depends upon the level of sensing perception, and who and what you are to be able to sense see feel interact with these energies; and to what degree. Similarly the hologram is not separate with clear divisions. Just like the mind itself, it can be nowhere and everywhere, or nonlocal. It brings into consciousness whatever it decides to "observe".

They are one mind, one consciousness and we have referred to them as separate 3D, 4D, 5D but they are not. Even at the 3D level there is no real matter as it depends on how well developed your sensory systems and state of vibration are. It is your beliefs that create the limit and boundaries. Even with what you think so material—like a rock-- is all no thing as you peer closer into it. So all that is, is a matter of sensory degree, not classes. There are beings within all these dimensions and planes and they are also of different energies, in different energy states of body and mind. As you interact and sense in 3D so do others of higher or lower states interact as well. The Higher Self therefore transcends all of these states and dimensions and holograms. It is the degree of vibration that one can sustain and maintain that determines the state of awareness and interaction. The degree of susceptibility and vulnerability to other beings or forces and the degree of separation from the Divine heart is the variable here and even in higher states it is possible to impose and influence to the dark side which is a simple withdrawing of light. The Higher mind transcends all dimensions as it is one but there is a state of vibration where the Divine is and thus impervious to any dark energies or beings. Let us say this is 6D. Remember that other beings and energies are of different abilities that can be dark as well—disconnected from the heart. This is why in your work you are always connecting your mind to your heart and to the One, to the Divine. And in your local holographic world, this is the heart.

Holograms Are Information

The holograms you live in retains information and are somewhat like a computer program that creates its functions. We do not want to make this complex for you and its working you must accept as Divine and orderly. You must know you can interact with it even though it is invisible and you do not yet sense it. Change it and learn from it and you will become stronger as you progress. It is the Higher Divine mind that is your quest to be with it and know at all times. Then this new world begins to unfold rapidly as you bring your state of being into the new state of awareness and vibration. This is all about the invisible part of the hologram that you, like a newborn child are learning to sense and develop your lower self in. Within this hologram are certain cosmic laws and rules as to how it all works by Divine order. These will come to you soon but you created a contract of your proposed path or program in this hologram. It may have been simple or complex and it was done in agreement with others who may or may not play a part. And it involved your higher Divine Mind. This was an outline of what you would encounter in this hologram and this was chosen to find yourself by experiencing these things. Yes, it is so—it was your destiny and you chose this for a reason. But the experience of it—the perceptions and energies created by you--was not chosen or defined. That is an interactive experience in the hologram and to be determined as you progress. You must understand what you encounter is there for a reason, for you to become more perfect until you are perfection itself.

As the living hologram also lives and evolves like you, it is also partly governed in its consciousness by the frequencies generated by the planets, celestial bodies and group consciousness. These create vibrations that entrain to all things affecting them in a way dependent upon their own living signatures of vibration. It is like a setting of vibration that draws attention and tendencies of behaviour into a certain way. It is all part of the Divine plan.

60

YOU THE CREATOR

There is nothing like the wakeup pill of an NDE to teach you that lower mind (ego) must back off. Millions have done this but it does not have to be quite as dramatic! In your Gopher Wheel of Life as a mortal Earthling, you knowingly or most often unknowingly quest for something higher. It is just there in the back of your mind niggling that you are something more than this mundane Earthling. There is a spiritual niggling that perhaps you came here to do something more, like fun, inspirational, and fulfilling? Guess who niggles? Your Higher Divine Mind of your Soul. But the Higher Mind is about love without condition. It is like the Mother that loves her children regardless of what they are or do. It is not about croaking you, creating fear and discord, and giving you shit about what you are or are not doing. It will not tell you to fire this cur of an ego because it's killing you and screwing up your life. After all, you have free choice and will so how could a loving Higher Mind centered in a loving heart energy stand and shout?

Let me tell you more about you. If you have read this far, you are now ready for the next level of mind shift to take a better look at who you are. It is a reversal of believing you are just a body with a brain that leads you to nemesis. The shift is that there is no nemesis once you turn away from it and accept the realm of your Higher Mind.

Before you ask where this information comes from, I will tell you. It is telepathically received by me, sort of like channelling. I myself went through several personal transformations which would be similar to near death experiences. In the business world and personal life I made and lost fortunes, loved and lost in pursuit of ego's trappings. It was at the start of the new century that I got off the Gopher Wheel and began to learn to talk to this Higher Mind and let it do its thing.

Much of my writings are now from the Higher Mind. You can call the communications divine inspiration, or whatever you like but know that this is where I have received unbelievable guidance of getting off the corporate Gopher Wheel permanently. The communications answered many, many questions I had about what the *bleep* am I and what am I here for. Most of all, as more disease and dis-ease ensued from the Gopher Wheel pursuit of material, my question of what the *bleep* is wrong with what I am doing in life needed resolution. When I was diagnosed with fatal MS and heart problems, it was a choice of either succumbing to these degenerative mind and body things and croaking or finding a better way out. It's 15 years later now and no Gopher Wheel, no job, only a life of wonder and expression. I have to tell you that many others I share this information with have found this information profound and practical.

There was a new understanding necessary to open me to new possibilities because the old programming of science and what others thought was deeply encoded in my life habits and beliefs. And my ego was pretty well having a free-for-all running my life and body chasing the power and glory trappings of corporate life. So let me lay the heavy stuff on you now. I keep a log of all my sessions which have become a daily practice. These sessions have been directed at me personally as guidance. It has also served as guidance for a group that was brought back together to serve humanity in the transition of ascension to the new age. I am going to try to summarize these as best I can because they sure gave my mind a jolt.

So What Are You?

Ok, let's get to the meat. I want to make this as simple as possible because it is simple. You and I are immortal beings of light. That immortal part of you is your higher mind and higher body. Your higher mind is your connection to the Source, the Creator. That higher energy, which is higher in vibrational frequency, is your consciousness that interfaces to a physical body. The interface is usually referred to as an etheric or energetic body called chakras of which there are 12 (seven are most common). This is all invisible stuff to science because science cannot measure or see things like this. It is the same as you cannot see, hear or sense beyond a certain range of frequency. It is not because it is not there, it is because the stupidity of science and the limitations of your equipment prevent "seeing" it.

Now the physical stuff. You are also a physical being which is a more dense energetic "seeable" counterpart overlain by the invisible. The lower mind contains the intellect and what is your ego. It is invisible but science at least acknowledges its presence. It is designed to attend to the needs of the physical body, like keep it fed, find mates, reproduce, be housed; yes, all that comfort that it wants for the lower form as a basic instinct. The body has its higher body counterparts. So the heart, a physical organ, is overlain and interfaced with the heart chakra. It is the center of emotion and love. Each chakra has a physical counterpart which it communicates with from higher frequencies to lower (like electrochemical, biochemical, physiological stuff).

Although the higher and lower are actually all one mind, and the higher and lower body are as one body, and it all functions as one aspect of frequency signature, the separation between high and low is only in terms of the level of vibration. The energy force that gives this whole thing life is what the Creator is all about—the primordial soup of love. At the top of this frequency is an individual aspect of the soup which is the Higher Divine Mind. It is like a little copy of that which created you and gave you life—the Creator. You can call it whatever you like but when it decides to leave you, you die.

The Creator Mind

Let us now look at the mind. This is just a catch-all term which describes your consciousness. In terms of vibrational frequency, it starts low at the ego, intellect of lower mind, then upwards into the higher inspirational, love and higher frequency aspects of the higher mind. At the top is the Divine Higher Mind. It is the connection to the Source, to God, to All that is, the Force, whatever you feel is that Creator.

What part of the mind do you bring into your awareness? It is your choice. What you place your mind's attention on is what is your local consciousness. Most of the time, particularly if you are on the Earthling Gopher Wheel, that attention and local consciousness is driven by the lower ego and intellect. The other two sit in the back seat of the car while ego drives you in the Gopher wheel. But here is the cool part. All of the ancient wisdom of the knowing of the Creator and Creation are already within you looking for a time to be re-remembered. You just need to start choosing higher aspects. So in effect, the mind has choices. And since you are your mind, it is your Manager which you allow to choose an awareness to follow.

Let us look at this mind more closely. If you have ever meditated, or found stillness, you can enter the state of pure love of the heart where there is nothing else. If there is, then you have not entered true silence. It is your own space of consciousness, and you are indeed a Creator. Here you can create by imagination anything you bring forward into your awareness. Anything you can imagine can be created here. A beach, a family, a situation, sense, money, anything is here to be created. You may call this a dream, or a day dream or just silly fantasy but regardless, that mind of yours can not only choose what is brought forward into consciousness, it can create sequences, like a movie, a play of absolutely anything and even reach beyond that. And then... you can even affect your emotions and feelings, and physiology with this that is seemingly nothing but empty imagination. Hmmmm. What if you could do that in your physical realm?

In your consciousness you do this daily in your imagination, your dreams, your visions, your non-realities which you relegate to nothing of substance. Yet it may not be so for what if you entered the realm of the Higher Divine Mind and you entered the realm of the Creator and all Creation. What if the hoohahh about instant miracles—instant physical changes to the human body were not the silly non-reality of imagination and inspiration? What if you were in this higher place full time, one with the Creator and the Creator Consciousness creating this world drama of yours the same way you can create in your own local mind? So in this realm, any thought, any thing, any idea, or that which you bring to attention is formed, fashioned, created instantly with purpose and life? Pretty hard to imagine right?

The Creator's Mind

Well, it seems that the Creator does this all the time. As we have stated, just look around at these unexplainable miracles. The Sai Baba's. The lessons of NDE vacations before the almighty something. What is doing these crazy things that make a mockery of stupid science and medicine? It is the Mind of God, a super intelligent order of process of energies. It is a force of love, not much different than the behaviour, purpose, actions of magnetism as a simple analogy.

The Creator's Mind is simply the whole of consciousness. It is everything that exists was and will be. In a local sense, your mind contains what was, what is and what you can imagine to be in your future. It doesn't mean that any of it is real—like physical. It means you have a mind that contains a memory, any idea or a perception of something intangible that represents that which has been or will be.

Well, the Mind of the Creator is the same on a larger scale. It houses everything that is and it has its own glue which makes up its essence called unconditional love. And what is that segment of your own mind called the Higher Divine Mind? It is a part of that greater consciousness of the Creator Mind. When you let your mind choose this part you enter the One Mind, in all that is, was, will be, all folding upon an instant of infinity. It is much like the workings of your own mind except that you have not gained access to all of it. It cannot be explained, only known. You and all things, including the extension of the One Source are within this cosmic realm, each with a signature vibration with life and purpose.

And so you have your own dream universe with your own consciousness and your mind accesses parts of this from your own realm of experience, your lives, your perception, your feelings, and what you have encountered as an individualized component of the whole consciousness. It is the same model for the Greater Consciousness, the Mind of God. That's what you are—a little piece of the whole of Consciousness. You are an eternal being of Light (love).

And So You Became A Little Creator

In order for the Creator and all his little Creators to attain a means of expression, the lower form of body was designed and encoded as a physical lower vibration form of energy. All that information is encoded in DNA. This could interact with lower dimensions yet retain the ability to interact and remain connected to the higher dimensions. In this way the higher form and lower would meld as One and experience would be expressed from lower to upper. The interface in this creation would be the essence of love energy itself which was interconnected to the lower form through the chakra system with lower and upper or above and below balanced by the heart, the main energy vehicle between the two. In this way the abilities, functions and purpose of the lower form could be expressed through its life experience and received by the higher form. As the higher form is only love itself, of high vibration, it is not able to experience the lower forms of energies unto itself, except to retain and retrieve memory of what it as an individual unit of the Creator has experienced. And so the body as interfaced by the mind allowed individual consciousness to come into being. This was to be able to use the physical vessel for experience and to allow its own expression as felt and experienced by the whole. Sort of like your nervous system... do something to one part and the whole feels it. This allowed the form of high and low to retain an individual expression of the Creator; to grow, expand and express love in ways in which it desired.

The Divine Plan Of Expression

So the choice of the vessel was designed in form and substance by the Creator. And the Individual Creator became the Higher Divine component of the Creator's Mind. The purpose of expression and expansion of perfection would be influenced by cosmic and planetary energies of expression once life in a lower form was assumed. And of course it would unfold under the Cosmic laws within a scope of an overall pathway or script of a planned life outline. It would engage one with aspects related to what needed to be learned and experienced. The rest was governed by the way the expression would be received and perceived through the vessel of body within a physical environment. It would allow the Creator in you to assert itself by choice, to create its perceptions and attract, manifest, make or create that which its free will deemed necessary.

At birth, each retains these abilities of purity and divine love and the awareness of a wondrous knowing to have the wonderful and joyful relationship with the individual environment, the family within which its love could be expressed and received back, purely, openly and without condition. This its primary purpose, could effectively transmit to the Higher Self as a wondrous experience of joy as a wonderful child of extension of its parents, regardless of its form, character or perceived defects. Love in both directions transcends all else—the way it was designed to be. And the child, by simply being a child shines its light and love upon its parents so the parents feel the love and bliss in return. In the greater scope, you as an individualized unit of Creator, are the child filled only with a knowing and the Creator is your parent.

The vessel, then can effectively transmit to the Higher Self and the Creator, the learning, the feelings, the sensory results of its growth and expansion. Its primary purpose to expand its love and light as this is the prime purpose of creation. All this would be recorded within the Consciousness. It is as you do now when your life, your consciousness movie is captured on film of memory; every moment, every thought, every experience, every relationship, emotion, place, thing, perception; all that has ever entered your consciousness, is placed in your holographic camera. And once a thought or action or perception is created, it abides by the order it is given to exist, expand, to be what it is.

You are part of the Creator Being because you are in yourself perfection of love. You create as the Creator creates the Vast Consciousness of all that is, your own creations within your movies. We know that is difficult for your 3D mind, so you must not think at all. That is why letting go of this opens to who and what you are as your Higher Divine Mind is Creation and is the Creator. See this as a cell in your body, each carrying the genetic code of everything that can replicate you and all that is but with specific biological function, behaviour, purpose, alive to carry out specific encoding and knowing, working together as one unit.

That is what creation is and that is what it does. Your individuality of ego and lower form that has separated you temporarily is a gift which you have blessed yourself with as a vessel of expression of the whole and this is a unique part of the whole of the Creator. The Creator is the infinite composite of this. All that is as a vast space of intergalactic order that is the wondrous force of love—a gentle essence of beingness. In your mind it is not an easy thing to define this force but it is still so regardless of what you attempt to attach to it. It simply is you, your being, your essence and as you lift away from that vessel which you have as a body of expression, you are unencumbered by your logic and intellect, as it is so with the Creator. It is the total Consciousness of the vastness of mind, just as you may sit in this space of love and form, create, fashion, act upon any and all things that you can bless with life and purpose.

Separation Of High And Low

But unconditional love or the essence of the Creator, and hence the Higher Mind does not know darkness and is almost inaccessible to the mind. And it is totally inaccessible to the body. So it was necessary to create a gift for all the Little Creators and split Consciousness into separation to allow the level of perception making the mind a perceiver rather than a Creator. The lower consciousness is the domain of ego which has evolved to be a wrong minded attempt to perceive as you wish to be rather than as you are. The blessing of will allowed this to be. The ability to perceive made the body possible because you must perceive something with something so as to bring the knowledge of what one does not need. But the interpretation function of perception is a free will choice of creation that permits one to interpret the body as your true self with nothing else. So the Higher Mind is relegated to the back seat.

The Creator extended itself to its creations as perfection because unconditional love is perfection. And what can be expressed and received through that expression of perfection is more bliss and love. So if the Higher Mind is in command, then anything that can be expressed through and encoded back to the Higher Source would be a new expansion of experience so as to expand the One Mind.

But ego has its own domain in the lower forms. So the perfection can be lost by extension or projection when an emptiness or lack is believed that can displace your knowing with your own ideas of truth. Thus ego and intellect work together to make you believe what the Creator created can be changed with your own mind. What is perfect can be rendered imperfect or lacking, that you can detract creations of Creator—even yourself, and you can create yourself and the direction is up to you. This is separation from Creator, a split to judgement and fear that can be reversed or corrected in an instant. Separation brings an illusion of perfection because you are incapable of knowledge of the truth since you perceive loosely through the ego. Separation introduces perception of the Trinity of mind, body, spirit being separate. It is only the unity of these that can allow truth to open. So what was to be perfection and expansion through the Higher Divine Mind was lost as the mind allowed ego and intellect to create the illusion it could do a better job at perfection—creating heaven for you. That is what the Soul's journey is all about. So which side do you choose?

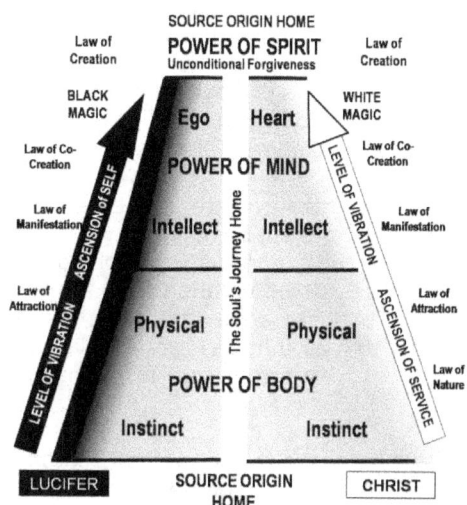

So Where Is The Higher Mind?

The truth is that as the Soul takes its journey, it has been rendered ineffective—not listened to right from the start. The truth will overcome this separation. But knowledge or knowing does not do anything. What has to happen is that you must reunite with the Creator to erase this and move to guidance. Erase the error, correct it and act through forgiveness of the error by thinking in the heart. Free will was given to you for joy in creating the perfect which already is in you. By separation and thinking it is not, that you can do better, that separation has created the block to your being as a Creator.

Where is the Creator in you? It is with the removal of separation and the release of the Higher Divine Mind to be allowed to lead you on the path it was obligated to follow. It means you must give free will to the Higher Divine Mind and place the ego and its buddy—the intellect into the back seat and let the driving be done by someone that already is and know perfection. It already knows what is perfect for you. It means that you know the key to the portal is unconditional forgiveness.

Your World Of Creation

The physical world around you is a creation of physical order. It is congealed energy, created into a lower vibrational form and it is all given life and purpose to live and expand just like you. It behaves according to rules such as science attempts to observe, measure and qualify but these are a very narrow perspective of what is. It observes behaviour, it does not make it. Nor can all that is be inferred from a set of narrow rules. There are unknown rules of behaviour, of cause and effect, of the energy itself that have eluded science as long as it observes outside of ourselves. These are all energies with rules of interaction, interrelation, living, growing, reproducing and expanding within their purposes and expression. This physical universe has been created for you to experience and is your physical playground for your movies of expression to play out. Within it you choose by your will how this expression will unfold. This physical universe is simply within the Mind of the Creator as a physical expression of that consciousness. It is a hologram of congealed thought. Once created in the physical realm of the hologram it remains in its primary form as it is encoded as such and subjected to the rules of the cosmos.

Its form can only be changed by the Creator or its Little Creators. All is either created for you or by you. What you have not attained the practice of is the acceptance of the knowing of how the link from above of thought to below of material is achieved. It is because you yourself have not attained your true status as Creator. That is why the hologram of creation, your world, is made for you so that you, in your physical form can learn to create like you were made to, and are designed to do.

This is not to mean create in the sense that you create dinner, or make something as that is not true creation. That is what you make, not create. And it is indeed true that you are exercising your creation of energy that attracts and thereby manifests experience. But true creation is to transform a physical congealed energy such as in a miracle or to make something from the primary substance of love—pure divine energy. You know this as miracles or materialization. Your growth as part of the Creator within Creation is to learn to create for yourself by yourself, when you know you are indeed a Creator.

What this means is that only the Creator can create and only when you re-establish that truth and that you are one with the Creator, can you yourself do what you were always meant to. Until that happens, you only manifest and attract existing energies. When you learn to co-create, you are on the verge of the true knowing of yourself. It is the love in your heart, reconnection with the Divine Mind and the enlistment of Divine Love as you partner to aid you in creation together. When you have brought the Higher Divine Mind and its buddy the heart that thinks with positive emotion you then begin to release your true creative powers.

As a Creator you can then create for others, as the Creator has done for you and as Sai Baba did for others. It is when you have let go of the notion that you and your ego can outdo perfection—the Mind of the Creator and ego and separation. It is when you have yielded to a new truth and you have forgiven yourself for those stupid thoughts that you and your Gopher wheel can do a better job. It is when your thoughts and you have moved to a space of consciousness where knowing and shining your light of divine love expands as it was meant to so as to bring the bliss you seek. This is not the path of betterment and learning because you are already perfect and there was no reason for the detour you took with ego.

What this means is that you need to be like a new child when your mind was as an empty vessel, with only a knowing of love and perfection would shine your light of divine love upon those around you. That was your Higher Divine Mind. You were so strong and untouched that your very presence would bring joy and happiness and love and wonder to others who would simply place their eyes upon you. You radiated the true essence of divine love in your pure innocence as there were no preconceived ideas, perceptions and by simply being you and allowing that beingness to be, you had this power. It is how you entered the physical realm eager to expand. And then... you were taught to stick the Divine Higher Mind where there is no sunshine.

The Mind of the Creator creates the physical world for your expression of love and perfection. That is your purpose and your lower form of body is a creation granted to you to express that which you are so as to return this expression as did the child to the parents. Now can you let the Higher Divine Mind use your body to send the same expression of love back to the Creator which is your real Father?

So What Say I

Now I want deal with what my reaction was to this information. Yep, I thought, this is really cool but how does this pay my bills? I don't get it. If I have all this Creator power why can't I just say I intend to bring attention to these bills that make me stay on the Gopher Wheel and have them paid? I will even tell my heart I love it so what's the deal? Hey, I love everybody! What am I missing here? I would love to give this advice to others on how to get off the Gopher Wheel but how can I have any confidence if I can't do this Creator stuff?

Well, Mr. Ego and his buddy Intellect are like that. Where's the logic; I want proof; seeing is believing; show me the money. That's what puts this on the back burner and the Higher Divine Mind mumbles its niggling again. Oh, dear it says, we love you but it would be sooo nice if you listened to your heart.

In the previous chapter there were a few things mentioned that I said we would explain later. Now is later. These are communications that got my attention as a simple explanation of how us stubborn ego based Earthlings have to go through a process to become the Creators. What happens in a few moments of time during Near Death Experience can take us much more time. There are two explanations that were very cool to me and they are as below. I have been using the Gopher Wheel of Life as my analogy. I use that because as long as you keep walking in the wheel, it continues to turn and keep that which you are trying to get out of reach—the vision board of ego. In this material following, it is the **River of Life.** Then when you decide to get off the wheel, you stop, look away, and decide to get off. That is called **Crossover.**

The River of Life And Crossover

So here we are on Planet Earth, born into a physical vessel of a body with a destiny as created by the Higher Divine Mind. We are all a specific unit, a specific aspect of energy frequency within the One Mind. What needs to happen, as it does in the case of an NDE, is that Higher Divine Mind is allowed to take command and let it do the thinking for you without the interference of ego, intellect and separation. The Higher Divine Mind expresses through the energetic heart chakra tied to the physical heart. But whoops, it's a trap! I have been born an Earthling slave!

Well, here is a little story. This little analogy of the River of Life was communicated to me as a personal guidance. It is simple and gets to an important process of following your life path which is already known by the Higher Divine Mind. It is that you are the vessel flowing in it. The wonderful analogy here is that you either flow with the river and give command to the Higher Divine Mind to reach Home, your destiny, Heaven, or you ignore it and let Ego and Intellect steer your vessel upstream to attain what it believes is Heaven to be.

If you are striving to find your heaven as ego believes it to be it is like the Gopher Wheel. Remember as an option and free will, you can choose whether you follow your terrestrial intellectual goals of what this is, or you can follow what you decided to do here that the Spiritual Divine Mind and you agreed to. In one case it is like trying to paddle up the river of life, against the current.

Now I am going to convert to what I was told directly.

"To you that struggle was simply one that was needed to get back to some destination upstream, working at avoiding the things coming towards you and paddling madly struggling against the current. Did you think Home and Heaven were there? Did you ever arrive there or are you still paddling? Home is the other way you know. Yes, it is much effort to paddle upwards, there is no time to do anything but paddle, is there?"

"Your first point of shift is to drop an anchor and stop paddling. And what will you see as you stand against the flow and it passes by? This is the point at which you can begin to change that which flows towards you, avoiding the debris of life manifestations. Aha you say, there is some darkness coming and I can scoop it up and convert this to light. And here is an obstacle coming, perhaps I can see the goodness of it and let it by. Or perhaps I can scoop it up and change it to the light so the flow that comes to me is cleared with the heart. Some you may deflect, some you may change but this is still much easier than paddling madly to get upstream through the debris and the swirls of life plus avoiding the debris. So you sit firm and look to see what flows for as you look from where you came these are all your creations coming towards you. Some hit you hard but you stand firm."

"But suddenly you realize that if you cut the anchor, turn and let go with the flow, that which is behind you cannot be seen. And now you are flowing, and only around you is your place of attention and all that flows is flowing at the same rate—there is no struggle to avoid it anymore. Now there is nothing left to convert from the past as you and all around you are flowing together down the river of life. But now what? Well you have crossed over, for it is now your Higher Mind that looks in a different direction that is awake. The simple act of shifting your view and your actions previously governed by your Lower Mind has changed. It was taking you the wrong way! Now there is no looking back and the river of life takes you and you can see a world you did not see before as you were so occupied. All that stuff and things that were in your way are no more because they were all your own creation. All you had to do was turn around and let go. Now it is not in your view. Now you can see a shore that you never saw. Now your Higher Divine Mind takes the helm as you float. Ahaa you say, now I can allow inspiration, and I can see the beauty around me! Do I worry about the future? Hardly! The Higher Mind does not recognize that as an issue because it is Creation itself. So now you say I can just be and feel the beauty and love and reverence of all that is in my river as there is no attention to struggle and debris in my way. And then, alas, there is the shore that I did not see clearly before. Perhaps I can steer there and see what I have never been able to see and create, in a place that was always there."

"You change when you turn as you are at Crossover; ready to shine your light on the River of Life as you flow. You are in a total belief of Christ Consciousness. So all around you is lightened and enlightened like you. And there is no debris of the past, and there is no fear of the future, and there is only flow of each moment to see the beauty of what you are and all that is around you. Soon you are ready to go onshore. And then? Yes, you become the River of Divine Love."

"As you walk your path of life, there is a signpost marked CROSSOVER. This is not meant to mean a point of no return, it was a sign post of awareness of choice now in your presence. It is a choice that may be brought present any time to be fully placed in your life. The path which leads to crossover is one that lets go of the material constructs and their importance and strings and perceptions of struggles. It is one of following the inspirations of your Divine Mind—your soul's expression through your heart towards your life's purpose. It is one of living in a way that allows the flow of love through your being so what you allow your life to engage in is brought to you by inspiration—the thoughts of the Higher Mind. This is your Higher Divine Mind doing its plan that is, and has been created for it as you remember or recall it to being."

"As the path approaches Crossover, all that is you that you do with the mind, body, soul and heart, being allowed to direct, guide, lead, think, speak, act, move, and live is being left to your divine intelligence to flow through you, as created by the heart. The crossover appears as all attachments to material needs fall away as there is no need for them in this whole state of being. It is the path of the Co-creator and Creator. This does not mean that you live without 3D needs, it means that they are brought to you a different way—as a divine Creator and as needs of the heart. It means they have a different value than that which ego sets upon them. It is this distinction that many struggle with and are frustrated with, but it is this that in itself, the struggle and frustration that prevents taking the path."

"On the path to crossover it is much different as it is one of filling your essence with doing; those activities which block inspiration as the ego is directing the doing. It is attentive to needs and wants of the lower mind, attached to 3D where you engage in doing those activities that fill your lives, not of inspiration and passion. It is one of stifling the flow of inspiration and filling your life with needs and activities based upon ego's desires, not the heart's. It is what you have grown accustomed to, of struggle and need, of limit and want. Such alignment prevents you from true growth, attentive to the 3D material world not spiritual growth. At a point where you awaken to the difference, and believe that the choice of soul expression will already provide a passionate life of lower expression through the heart, you are ready to move towards crossover and open the flow towards your true purpose that the soul already wrote and created for you. Once your belief becomes uncluttered by ego and material constructs of needs and lower perceptions to occupy your intent and attention, and your awareness is filled with the belief there is a better choice, you are ready."

"This is not a split in your path as your choice is always there as it has come to awareness. It is a sign of reminders by your Higher Divine Mind calling and will continue, pointing to crossover, a better way, the way you were destined to travel, free, without limits, in peace and love as a Creator—in whatever lifetime you choose. Your awareness of this now has been brought to your attention and it will constantly reappear at moments of ego's draw to material attachment. You wanted it to be so."

What this means is that you simply be the vibration of love—not try to be but just be. Now it is time to bring into your reality two very important things.

First, you are the Captain of your ship call reality; all that is your energy that creates your life hologram.

Second, you walk as Christ did in the new version to think, speak, see and act indeed from the heart.

It is to be what you are and no need to try. When you let be, and enter the beingness of the heart, you will see that you will be guided and that which was meant to be will come to you, so it can flow through you freely and expand your true essence towards, love, bliss, expansion and the expression of fulfillment of destiny.

Now, perhaps this is the lesson that many bring back after a Near Death Experience? Or an Out of Body Experience? They hit Crossover and then turn around on the River of Life? And finding your peace and silence is like a temporary Crossover as you are flowing with the River of Life. It is a space of higher vibration that aligns with the heart and your higher design. There has to be a genuine belief and acceptance that to turn on the River or stop the Gopher Wheel was a better, easier way to find my heaven. But there had to be more to this. What else was I missing? How would this magically pay my bills?

When you turn on the River of Life, when you reach Crossover, and when you decide to stop the Gopher Wheel, you need to know and accept that there is a better way totally different from what you are trained to do. It is a mind shift from lower to higher body, mind, and perception. But what is the meaning of this shift? How does it translate into what I think, believe, and act upon? And this heart thing, and Higher Mind; what's the connection to miracles and creative powers?

We are at a time when the River of Life is the Tsunami of Consciousness taking us into the New Age. We approach Crossover, the marker in the timeline being Dec 21, 2012.

The Five Cosmic Laws

I can tell you that if you are pissed off at the world for not allowing you your due fortune, yourself for not attaining things, and others because they are not within your beliefs, then you will not get anywhere else but to remain in the energy hologram you create. If ever there was a 101 Course in this life changing process—and it is a process—then I would say learn to accept in all you do, the Five Cosmic Laws. It is your grounding.

The Law of One is a reflection of all that is, was and would be, We are all One, all interconnected as One consciousness, one living being of supreme intelligence. Above and below are one interconnected ocean of all that is with any part affecting the whole and the whole affecting the individual parts. The Law of One is that we are all intricate parts of the Oneness. There is nothing else and everything that is ever done within this cosmic ocean of the One is the whole of the Source of the One that give it all life. This is the basis for all life showing total faith, trust, honour and knowing they were interwoven into the fibre of the Oneness totally integrated in the total essence with the Source—the Creator—and the Creator's total consciousness of One Mind.

The Law of Divine Love is the vibratory essence of the all that is One. It is the force of the One that is the purpose of its existence. It is the foundation of all creation itself. Divine Love is the most potent force of what is. It is the very substance of the One. It is the highest vibrational essence in its purest form when pure of heart and unconditional love is offered with grace and in forgiveness, infinite in its supply. It is the true substance of creation itself. This is reflected in the heart of a creator being.

The Law of Creation is that all things are a creation through a manifestation of that which is in the Mind of total consciousness. That which we as Creators within the One bring forward into consciousness becomes so created. The law is that what shall be so created shall be given life as we are the givers of life. The Law of Creation is that the level of creation abilities is based upon the progression in the Law of Life and the degree of vibratory essence associated with Laws of Love and One. It is the means by which that which is, will be, and was, is created as a manifestation or creation within the realm of conscious awareness.

The Law of Life is that all that exists lives with a purpose and essence given by the creator. The Law of Life is that all that lives expands and grows within the cycles of the ebb and flow of all things and all life, interconnecting to live its life so as to fulfill its purpose. This relates to a predetermined path as encoded in its being, its karma from other lives, and purpose as given by the Creator of it. Its purpose is to satisfy its karma, its purpose and to expand within its highest vibratory essence for the betterment of itself and the One that it is. Life has a fundamental encoded purpose **to be** what it is—an expression of its higher being. It is done **through** what it is—Divine Love; back **to** what it is—Divine Love—that which itself created.

The Law of Will is that Creators have free will within the Oneness of Love to choose their life path before any incarnation, and are free to choose how experience is perceived along that path after incarnation. It is their sole choice to create that which they alone have the power to bring into their conscious awareness by placing attention upon it and creating intent and purpose. It is such a choice that within the Mind of the One is in itself creation of life with purpose and need.

The Great Leap Of Faith

These words about the five laws only give meaning to each of us through our own choices of perceptions and experience. When you accept these as your truth, life changes. That's what happens in so many NDE's. *What I want to convey here is this is the way the Higher Mind thinks and feels with the heart about things.* And when you align your life activities with these simple principles, you are simply excluding the lower mind and allowing the higher to do your thinking. This is not a radical switch and a terrible torment you have to go through. It is simply the way you think. Does it require a great leap of faith to do this? Hardly. Do you have to die to shift? Hardly! You simply place your faith in a new way of thinking. And because it is usually so different in thinking, it may indeed be described as a Leap of Faith.

Let me give you an example of a most dramatic case of a leap of faith into the Higher Mind's domain. Allowing the Divine partner to take control while still conscious (not an NDE) is underscored by a well known spiritual writer, **Eckhart Tolle**. In his first book, the **Power of Now**, he sheds some light on letting go of the old mindset in a rather extreme case. Eckhart had many little demons that he held onto that screwed up his life. In his book he explains the ultimate despair that led him to fall into a fear void. He probably had the equivalent of a near death experience that re-birthed his life. At the depth of his depression, the soul seemed to take over and he **let go** of everything that his dismal self had clung onto. He sat on park benches for two years in a state of joy and then became a spiritual teacher. His story as taken from his book:

"Until my 30th year I lived in a state of almost continuous anxiety interspersed with periods of suicidal depression. One night after my 29th birthday I woke in a feeling of absolute dread… Everything felt so alien, so hostile and utterly meaningless that it created a deep loathing of the world. The most loathsome thing of all was my existence. What was the point of the misery? I could feel the deep feeling of annihilation, for nonexistence, was now stronger than the instinctive desire to keep living."

"I repeated over and over that I cannot live with myself any longer. I suddenly became aware that there was two of me: the I and the self that I cannot live with. Maybe only one of us is real. I was so stunned that my mind stopped. I was fully conscious but there were no more thoughts. Then I felt drawn into a vortex of energy, slow then accelerating. I was gripped by fear and started to shake. I then heard the words resist nothing spoken as if in my chest. I felt I was being sucked into a void within myself rather than outside. Suddenly there was no fear and I let myself fall into that void. I had no recollection after that."

"When I was awakened by a chirping bird outside my window, I had never heard such a sound before. My eyes were still closed and I saw the image of a precious diamond. Yes, if a diamond could make a sound that is what it would sound like. I opened my eyes. The

first light of dawn was filtering through the curtains. Without any thought, I felt, I knew that there is infinitely more to light than we realize. That soft luminosity filtering through the curtains was love itself. Tears came into my eyes. I got up and walked around the room. I recognized the room and yet I knew I had never truly seen it before. Everything was fresh and pristine as if it had just come into existence. I picked up things, a pencil, an empty bottle, marvelling at the beauty and aliveness of it all."

"That day I walked around the city in amazement at the miracle of life on earth, as if I had just been born into this world. For the next five months I lived in a state of uninterrupted deep peace and bliss. I could still function in the world although I realized that nothing I ever did could possibly add anything to what I already had."

"It wasn't until several years later after I had read spiritual texts and spent time with spiritual teachers that I realized what everybody was looking for had already happened to me. The intense pressure of suffering must have forced my consciousness to withdraw from its identification with the unhappy and deeply fearful self, which is ultimately a fiction of the mind. This withdrawal must have been so complete that this false, suffering self immediately collapsed. What was left was my true nature as the ever-present I Am: consciousness in its pure state prior to identification with form."

"I learned to go into that inner timelessness and deathless realm that I had originally perceived as a void and remain fully conscious. I dwelt in states of such indescribable bliss and sacredness that even the original experience pales in comparison. A time came when I for a while had no relationship, no job, no home, no socially defined identity. I spent almost two years sitting on a park bench in a state of the most intense joy."

"Later people would ask if they could have that which I have. I would say: You have it already. You just can't feel it because your mind is making too much noise. That answer grew to be this book."

"Unless you learn to recognize the false as false—as not you—there can be no lasting transformation, and you would always end up being drawn back into illusion and into some form of pain. Don't read with the mind only. Learn to watch for a feeling-response as you read and a sense of recognition from deep within. It is a reminder of what you have forgotten. Something within you will say, yes I know this to be true."

The main pitch is that you need to let go of your usual Lower Mind—ego—that runs your show. Here we see what happens when things really go awry and that Lower Mind takes control. While you look for material things and scraps of fulfillment, you have within you the great treasure. It is incessant mental noise that prevents stillness of what he calls *being* and casts a shadow of fear preventing enlightenment. His thesis is that you normally don't use your mind, it uses you. You believe you are your mind. You cannot stop thinking so you are not in control and enslaved. When you let go of this and truly recognize it as enslavement, you can then let your Higher Divine Mind—your other self take over.

Dramatic? There are millions of cases like this. Near Death and Out of Body Experiences are rife with vivid and dramatic examples. It's the same paradigm shift. The main point here is that the mind creates a brick wall called belief between the two worlds—the one where you hold onto the old self; where the laws of attraction/manifestation prevail, and the other, where you let go and let the laws of co-creation and materialization prevail.

So does one need to engage in such drama to trigger the change? Some people can quit smoking cold turkey. Others may take a few months of perseverance and some can't do it. We are all different of course, but what is the real difference here. Obviously willpower, is it not? It depends on how strongly encoded into your belief system—and hence your cellular memory—as to how much you really need that smoke. The bottom line is that eventually you have to convince yourself and no matter how much science or statistics or others frowning at your nasty habit bug you, it is mostly irrelevant until something convinces you to take action, change your belief and create a belief you can do it.

The Five Laws in their simplicity move to the awareness of total consciousness of your 3D life when you believe them. These ring with the purity and power of heart. Can these be embodied in your existence and in your being to guide how you walk and express yourself in your 3D world? If not, why not? Will they hurt you? This is the fundamental essence of your Higher Divine Mind always connected, always in command, always attentive of living a life of pure love of heart, always in gratitude, service and reverence of all. It's a pretty simple idea—the whole of humanity is your family, not just the kids, wife and in-laws—*everything*—even that shithead you call a boss.

Do The Laws Pay The Bills?

The real question is why are you not allowing the laws to pay the bills. How many times do you get to that fine edge of despair, like Tolle and think what the *bleep* is the point of the Gopher Wheel? Why can't I just always be happy? Why do I have to struggle for what I want? Well, once again it is all in the Cosmic Laws, if you can believe the one about Creation.

As an analogy you are standing at the edge of a chasm. You believe all this about being a Creator. You can see it now. Ok, ok, you scream, I got it, I got it! On the other side is 5D, your Higher Self, your Soul beckoning to you, waving its fuzzy arms, beckoning you to walk across to join the celebration. Here is where you get off the wheel, manifest your desires, everything is very cool. But you do not see a bridge with your 3D eyes because ego says it's an illusion. Is there one in your third eye? Perhaps but you may fall if you stepped on this and your 3D ego mind-intellect cannot allow you to perish. You believe you will fall. It is so with your trust in your Higher Being. That requires a leap of faith to surrender to it and let it totally govern your 3D life. Yet you know you need to cross the chasm. How can this invisible bridge seen by the third eye ever support you?

You stand there as you understand the power of Light and Divine Love as supreme. You say yep, it brings bliss and harmony and peace in and to all who embody it. Ok, the expression of divine love is through the heart and is my connection to my true self. I know it is my conduit between 3D and higher dimensions. I have listened to all the stuff about NDE's, miracles, to manifesting your heart's desires. And I can also understand that by knowing completion, the celebration of it and by clearly enfolding it in the emotion of bliss, gratitude and celebration that I can create what I want. I get the picture that I alone have created my life, my path, my karma, my experience, my perceptions, and my dramas.

So let us, you and me get this show on the road oh mighty Divine Mind, cause I sure don't want this other crap anymore!

But then you wake up the next day and it's time to get on the Gopher Wheel... Why? The alarm clock went off!

So do you suddenly say screw this and leap off a cliff? Stop the Gopher Wheel, step off, quit the job, ask the heart to get you a new Ferrari?

How Long Does It Take?

As a child, your parents and your society were quick to teach you the ways of the 3D Gopher Wheel. It was void of true spirit and focussed on the development of intellect. Go out their Kid, they said, get a job, work your ass off and make a better life than us. Keep your nose to the grindstone. Never give up. Your dreams are there to find.

And so you began your paddling up the River of Life, learning to relinquish your choice to the will of intellect and ego. Of course the big boys controlling PLANET EARTH had some strict guidelines that aided your tendencies to let ego and will have their way. But it was all part of what is needed to decide what it was that you would achieve and perceive along the path of Agreement and Destiny. Sure the employment in PLANET EARTH led you to believe and achieve fulfillment of finding Home and Heaven was in the wrong direction... Sometimes you turned in your struggle and felt the segments of joy and bliss but mostly you persisted in the struggle up the River. That's where the Ferrari was! Even though the bliss and true path aligned with the divine plan of the higher mind was an easy float down the river, it was your ego and your intellect that made you turn the other way. Ego said that was horseshit, no divine mind could pay the bills; don't even think about turning around. You will be scorned, starve, die!

Sometimes you turned with a knowing that struggle was not right, that a misalignment was there, yet over and over, you yielded to what the ego perceived as Home and Heaven. And the glimpses of peace and love and bliss did not awaken you to your wrong direction, turning again to the ego's intellectual construct of what Home and Heaven was. It was not a knowing that came to you as it was veiled by those who planned to influence your choice, and to feed the lower vibrations of ego itself, as it could not know better.

So the idea of laying back in the flow of the River of Life downstream, within the being of unconditional love was never really on. This is the shift that needs to be changed.

How long will it take to reverse this thinking in you? How long have you been trained to do the opposite? To do this, do what your parents have done to you. They took command because they believed you were a child. Know you have a Divine Father and Mother that guide you. Know you have a divine mind that guides the true child in you, the ego. The ego is your child. It must learn the ways of Spirit. It cannot have dominion over you as it has not yet learned the truth. When it cries or seeks your attention, how do you respond? Do you ignore the tantrums of desire and send it love. It is your personal spiritual child to show and to teach it the ways that allow this intellect to blossom as feelings of love, joy and bliss. It must know it is not in charge of your life and your direction any more than a child is. It can separate you from spirit by convincing you to paddle up the river. It is down river that Spirit needs to go, in the opposite direction—no paddling, no struggle—along its prescribed journey that you agreed to. Your ego and its intellect are the child. Make it so and let it earn its place of enjoying the love and the bliss but through the heart and higher dimensional mind steering your vessel along the river that will take you on its course regardless of what you think.

Align these with the flow of life as it was agreed to and designed by yourself. Align the intellect to serve and entertain you as if it was a new child. Know that you do not let your children command your actions and thinking on your life's path. They are there to teach you joy, wonders of life, to allow feeling and expansion and expression. They are not there to oversee it and direct it, are they? The ego and its intellect represent but a tiny fragment of what is. It is so small that your 3D eyes could not even see it. It is like one electron in a sea of life that is all interconnected. Why would you allow that one helpless electron of ego to believe it can orchestrate the rest. And why would you act upon its ways? It is your Divine Mind that can—in a sea of unconditional love. Let it flow through your every moment as you float down your River of Life.

How long will it take? Here is a simple clue that relates to your new training:

KINDERGARTEN: The Five Cosmic Laws
GRADE 1: UNITY AND EGO
GRADE 2: YOU THE CREATOR
GRADE 3: MANAGING ENERGY
GRADE 4: MANIFESTING AND CREATION
GRADE 5: INTEGRATION INTO LIFE
GRADE 6: GETTING THE HIGHER MIND A JOB

How long do you suppose it will take you to pass the exams? At each stage you have to do a muscle test. If you need to know about a muscle test, just Google it. It's a simple process and it is your own lie detector.

One thing is certain; you can't bullshit the heart and the Higher Divine Mind. And they are the ones doing the test!

61

YOU CAN'T "BS" THE HEART (or SOUL)

You may wonder why there is all this yatter about love all the time. It's vibration of a higher frequency. If you haven't picked up on this yet, unconditional Love is the primordial soup of all that is. It is the essence of the Creator and it is what the physical forms are made of. If you are a scientific quantum physics genius, you will recognize this as the atomic state (solid, lower frequency) or the wave state (not yet solid, higher frequency). One is yet to be created into something. That creation device is within you. So you can make things out of the solid stuff, or you can create new things out of the soup. Needless to say if this essence of the Creator is unconditional love—a specific high frequency medium—then the best way to make something with it is to align yourself with that same frequency so you are now able to "communicate" with it and create with the creating tools you have. These are your higher body tools that are your energetic doubles that take care of the process. The big buddy here is the heart. This is not the physical heart, it is the etheric heart—pure source energy.

Otherwise, how do you communicate with the medium of love if you are not within it? It would be like trying to use a typewriter to telephone with.

This medium does not recognize low vibrations any more than your ears can pick up frequencies outside of its operating range. The best way to illustrate this is something I used in the book *Can You Let Go?* A thermometer showed the arbitrary scale for vibration from -100 (really strong negative energy) to +100 (really strong positive energy).

The Higher Mind does not live in the negative levels any more than love can exist where hatred dominates. You can't have dark where there is light. Darkness is simply a lack of light. Living in both worlds of dark and light is Polarity. Living on the topside of light is Unity because you believe everything is connected and if you hurt anything else, you hurt yourself. It is being a total empathic human working as one unit. It is like your cells work together as a unit called the body. You and your body are like a cell of all that exists. When you think with the Higher Mind—which you already can do—you think positive—and all your intentions, attentions, perception, and actions are positive.

This is the same place that the energetic Heart lives with its own frequency signature. So when you are *"dropping into the heart"* you are moving your mind, your attention, and actions into this higher vibratory place. Who is in charge of the thermometer? You? Simply by placing your attention on a thought, creating the intention of the Higher Mind, you create. If it is the Lower Mind, you make, not create.

Love-The Engine Of Creation

So you can understand why Unconditional Love is throughout this book yet it has not been a point of its own attention. It obviously has its own powers, yet it is illusive in its definition. It simply is and it is accepted as an invisible force of unknown abilities and qualities that are simply experienced as something that results from its attention to attaining that level of vibration—sort of when you fall in love. Love brings feelings of joy and bliss in an unexplainable way, regardless of whether it is seen, imagined, spoken, read, heard, felt, or experienced. All senses respond to it as an invisible energy that manifests a wonderful expression when attention is aligned with it. That is its design as that is what the Source is. And many have experienced its wondrous power that transcends fear, makes the meek mighty, protects the weak, nurtures the helpless, knows no bounds or logic, and its unconditional union provides the ultimate bliss.

It is because you yourself are actually made of pure love, the divine essence. So when you, a form of energy of highest vibration gets its shit together and re establishes what it always was by aligning the great emotional engine of heart with the other energy centers that create words, images, thoughts, and emotions, magic happens to your being and your way of existence.

Yet this is only part of your essence. When the purity of this energy enfolds you and what you are, synchronized with what you are part of, the engine of you responsible for the creation part awakens and wondrous things begin to happen. When the engine as an expression of you—your heart—takes its true power back, you become Source, a perfection of what you are. That is when you reach Crossover and turn in the River of Life.

Let us use a simple example. Your heart is like an electronic device that performs a function when it has electricity flowing through it. With a device, when the right power flows, the device expresses itself in what it is designed to do. Turn the power on and it performs. Now look at your heart. It is the device of Creation and the electricity that powers it is love. When the flow of love moves through it, it also can perform its function and express itself. Without current, neither the heart nor the electronic device can perform. Love is the power, the heart is the device and your mind is the switch. And the device is the manifesting device. And what makes it flow? It is conversion of negative to positive. And when the right power is supplied as determined by your body, and its senses that become the vehicle of transformation, things flow. It is consciously choosing the love energy from every moment passing your attention, especially that which it is compatible with. The flow of this energy through the device of the heart can become truly functional to provide what it was meant to handle--Creation. Yes, it is your heart energy field that is the device of Creation, of manifestation, designed to interface between the above of pure love to that of physical creation below in the hologram. Go back and read what the Russians have found out about this heart field and hypercommunication with DNA and everything else.

So if you are aware of this flow, it may be appropriate to look at every moment that flows through your body, mind and sensory systems as a wonderful chance to convert it to unconditional love. Every moment is like every electron in the current of a physical device. That conversion, a choice of will, expressed into its original form of love is the fire of creation that fills your device of Creation. But understand that like your electrical device, its true expression and functionality of its purpose cannot be attained until the flow of power is of sufficient strength and there is a flow, otherwise it cannot perform its purpose and cannot even run. It is designed so. Your own device of creation is so and the flow must reach a threshold to allow its true abilities to work. And what is the flow? It is the conversion of each moment that draws attention to the energy of love flowing through the heart. It is the conversion of light, from negative to positive. Yes, Crossover. Love, the specific frequency is the power that allows the heart to function. Like the power cord that allows flow into your computer, it cannot be weak or of different frequency, otherwise it is dysfunctional. And when the power to the heart is flowing and strong, the wondrous abilities of your physical and nonphysical machinery open to full functionality of Creation. It is because you are Creation and all that is needed to awaken is a pure source of the purest form of energy that ever was, is or will be—love. And when you connect below—your wondrous planet and her beings—to that above—the wondrous Source of Creation—the wiring is there to flow, just like the circuit in your electrical power cords.

Forgiveness And Your Path

Within this medium of high vibration love, there are certain processes that intercommunicate like higher voltage better than others. You have already noted that low vibration energy cannot exist in the higher realm of the mind. It's like putting ice in hot water. They may meld, or entrain within, or communicate with the higher vibration. And it has already been stated that there is a threshold the essence of unconditional love exists at that has to be attained first to truly be one with it.

There are various processes that act like carrier waves to activate instructions within this primordial soup. A process entails something you carry out some action on to do something. In this case it is a process of creating specific energy that acts like a communication. If you don't have the right frequency then the messages on your cell phone don't get anywhere, do they? You have to turn to the right channel to receive and transmit.

Just like the hierarchy of emotions on the thermometer, they also can reflect a process. But more relevant are the processes like forgiving, praying, blessing, being, loving, and many others that are the strongest communication channels. The thing is however, they have to be genuine. You either forgive someone or not. There is no maybe. Like Yoda said: *"You either feel the force or you don't, there is no try."* Well the Heart energy system can't be BS'd. It knows if you do or don't. Feeling does not lie as it is a specific frequency. You feel the emotion of hate or love.

If you hate something and say you love it, that is misalignment—BS'ing the heart. Sorry, things don't work that way!

What happens when you look deeply within your heart and feel deeply into yourself? You may carry heaviness of old lives and even from this life that keeps your wings from lifting you. Look at your world, your families, your relationships. Look at these with a heart full of the essence to heal that which needs it. Look at what it is that you do not like, are afraid of, brings shivers to you, that upsets you. Things that you judge. Bring these forward not to dwell on them and reinforce the negative, but to forgive yourself for creating the perceptions of judgement or discord, and to bring forward solutions of the heart. It must start with you as it is your perceptions and attention that has created this issue. What is worse is that you are most likely aligned the wrong way. Your emotion is hate or discord and your poor heart is not well about it so it and the body suffer the discord. In the meantime the hate energy goes out with a vengeance to find more. You BS'd the heart and it ain't well about it.

What is it that you harbour in your past lives that brings anger? Do you have fears of life, loss of loved ones? Do you have little demons that feed your ego? And what of your ego? Does it persist in your life, overshadowing the heart, making you believe it is the heart it is satisfying? Do you want to impose your ways, your ideas on others? Why? Because you judged them to be wrong?

Bring your strongest power of forgiveness into action, draw these things to your heart for redemption. Here is a little exercise you can do. Take one who has wronged you badly—one you cannot forgive, or even one you do not know. Bring this energy to your heart and feel the tightness let go as you whisper forgiveness of yourself and the others. Lift this energy to your throat chakra and feel the dryness change to lightness as the energy cleanses that chakra. Lift it to the 3rd eye to feel the emotion of tears well up from the joy of forgiveness. Then as your knowing lifts to the crown and up, it is now you know the joy of true forgiveness as your spirit lifts and expands your Source.

Otherwise, what you say and what you feel are not aligned. You say you forgive but it is BS. You may even act that way but it is BS. When your energy centers express their area through your senses, it is not BS!

Look back and release all your judgements, your limits, boundaries which do not serve you. Forgive yourself for this, for harbouring energies of discord and disharmony—release those energies that do not serve the heart that have not yet manifested. Let it all flow away. It is your intent and attention that is important, as you have learned. You do not have to identify specific things that you cannot remember.

We are all creators of our own movies—a movie you carefully planned to teach you and expand You. Have you? Why not have a review? Know those parts in your movies that are of discord are your wonderful opportunities to shine light upon. That is what you planed. Shine this into your own dark places. That is where it starts and that is where it began.

Beingness Is The Natural State Of The Higher You

Finding bliss in your true self and your Soul journey is Beingness. This state is perplexing to many. So many cannot be themselves; their true Divine selves. That is what being is all about. It s what Christ attempted to teach and exhibit in thought, word, deed in our story of the Aquarian Gospel. Being your lower selves is what creates the endless quest for identity and doing so many things that do not answer your search. It is what he cautioned as carnal desire. This is ego's game to do, to do, to do, to be more, to be better. It is a state of doing. Your state of being is you—a Being—to know you are already perfection and there is nothing to seek out. It is indeed being yourself—your true Higher Self. The true state of being is your Higher Mind's game, not the ego's. And working for PLANET EARTH is what keeps ego on the Gopher Wheel of Life. Resign, quit; it is to inspire expansion of self. This is when you are in your heart. There is nothing to do except nothing. Can you do that? No, because you have so many things to do, right? How can you just be and do nothing you ask?

Try it. Sit with nature and just be there absorbed in it. You do this in a state of lower meditation with your eyes closed. Now do this in a state of nature with eyes open. Gaze with the wonder of your heart by being in it at a leaf, a tree, a flower. Look only at it and let the heart feel. Do nothing, no analysing, drop away from the rest and look. Feel with your Higher Self. Just know you are. Feel the difference of what this is. Do you pick up on a difference? You will know this in your being but you will have to be and let your

Divine Mind loose first, to be itself which is really you. Soon enough you will sense newness about what is there. It may phase in and out opening dimensions, it may feel wonderful—the essence of love and oneness of all. It may show an aura, even speak to you. See nothing? Fine. It doesn't matter. It's the process that's important.

This is how to learn that Divine Love of the heart is the true power of the Universe—your true key to eternity and mastery of life, the Creator in you. It is attained when you are aligned with hearts, with the Heart of the Creator. It is the vibration of all that you are synchronizing. It is when you know how to simply be. That is the state of beingness.

Let go, move inside, with meditations or with whatever you need to get there. Then take it into your personal hologram. It will automatically influence the greater hologram of common consensus even if you are unaware of it. It is simply engaging in the fundamental state of yielding to your Divine Self and higher abilities that is important. As you do this, you will feel the beingness of One, of being the One, of being you—to be. Once you know, sense and feel this and your higher senses are opened, you will snap your fingers with intent and you are there in a state of beingness. Then watch. It will be like rubbing the lamp with the Genie. Yes, when you be the true state of Love and you be that what you are—Divine Love—you will move mountains with your mind. This is the basis to your ascension—your first initiation. Your struggle of doing falls away as you have nothing to do but to follow divine inspirations and feel the wonder of it. True Beingness is Divinity.

I am now going to phase into some of the lessons I got for not "getting it." After these messages, I have stopped saying it. Even though directed at me, and my own personal evolution, I decided to print them as they came, so as to not change the meanings. What is important here is the advice I got on how to stop BS'ing myself and in particular, my heart.

Inspiration Is The Truth Of The Heart

"Everybody has dreams, some have aspired to these. But as you move from moment to moment, even from when you were a child you had dreams of what you would be and what you would do. But how many of you had dreams of who you are? It is what you are that manifests the dreams. Many have followed aspirations, to become something or someone, to have something, and you have wished for this that you had not, and many have worked away at this because it was what you were told, or what you had to do as your part in the rules of your society. And so this became your path. But is it your true path of pure inspiration? And are you of the knowing this is indeed your destiny, the one you designed?"

"Or have these dreams been fulfilled by your subdued passions, through hobbies, private likes of heart that are attached to idle time not consumed by your daily duties of doing? To aspire is to hope, to strive, towards a dream. It is the way of lower mind. Inspire is to affect, guide, or arouse by divine influence, to a vision. Perhaps you may not see a difference but it is the difference between the workings of the lower and higher minds. Dreams and aspirations are not you. Visions and inspirations are. When you know who you are, your visions become clear and inspiration flows as passions unfold before you. They become manifested in your world. The being of one's true self opens your heart and the visions become your true path as expressed by your heart, opening to you in continuous inspiration."

"Much of aspirations and dreaming clutters your true path as it is driven by ego that allows you to dream as it is fantasy, not truth. An inspiration becomes a reality through your lessons on Co-creation. When you allow inspiration to flow, you are one with the heart and the Higher Divine Mind. So what are your inspirations? Perhaps they are blocked by ego's idle dreams? Remember dreams may be ego's play from the lower mind, usually rooted in lack of what you do not have, or what others have that you want. Inspiration is passion released towards vision, no lack, no wanting in polarity. This is desire of heart; to follow your true path as who you are."

"Is it not time to bring forward your visions and allow inspiration to flow, to begin to flood your essence of being with this? Not as ego's dream of idle thoughts, but as your heart's desire to manifest and create? Truth is your heart's field that is the same. It is the manifestor, the attractor, the Creator in you. It is what transmutes above of 5D energies of consciousness into 3D energies of matter. And it is what transmutes 3D energies of matter and the expression of you into 5D energies of consciousness memories."

"Perhaps you ponder this because you cannot see results instantly. Perhaps you say "I believe so I want to materialize that red apple and it is not there?" And ego says: "Well, where's the apple, quit dreaming!" Yes, you can and you will but it is only when you yourselves know and are of higher divine consciousness. Your schooling is not done. Yes, you have not graduated with a certificate labelled I have achieved CROSSOVER and I AM LOVE. And do not forget that that apple can be attained many ways. You can ask for it, you can work for it, you can buy it, you can attract it, you can grow it, you can manifest it, or you can materialize it. Where do you sit on this vibrational scale of schooling? Would it not be best to do this from the Creator side? Bring your dreams to visions, your aspirations to inspirations. Let these out of your heart, out of hiding from your back rooms of hobbies, away from ego, without reservation or limitation. See this not as a dream but a vision of completion all made of moments of inspiration. Bring these to thoughts, to words, to images, in clarity and simplicity, in rejoicing and celebration of the fulfillment of your heart's higher path. Then you will know you are following a life along your true destiny."

House Cleaning Helps Set Your "Tone"

"At some point as you walk your world and your houses that you have created, and even sometimes lift above this, fill yourselves with the Divine Love through your heart and offer it freely as your light grows. It is how heaven is brought to earth."

"Look up at the sun, your light, yes, it is also in your heart, but do not be afraid to look down to see things that are there, perhaps some strings to hold you as anchors, perhaps some darkness, something that takes your senses to feel uneasy or feel dysfunction. Look in the cracks and under things for they may be things that need your light, your forgiveness, your blessings, your resolve and release. Look into the eyes of your ego, look into what haunts you. Look upon these so you will not stumble upon them as you walk, and look upon these as what will allow you to lift you higher, for they are your lessons, your lightening. They are your strings, your attachments, your limits awaiting you and you alone to face them and to change them. For you know the power of the Light to change darkness, and you know the power of love to shift and change them into higher vibration."

"Walk your worlds this way as your world is yours to cleanse to perfection. Fear not those things that make you tremble, that you dislike, feel dis-ease with or hate as those that create dominion and oppression. They are also these things that have limited your world and are there to forgive as you forgive yourself for creating these perceptions. They are there because you put them there. Walk without judgment through shadows of your lives full of light and watch the darkness withdraw. Face all this that pulls and tugs at you and *annoys you, that trigger your intuition of not right, then right them, first in your world of perception, then in your physical world. Look for these like hunters of darkness. Do not hide within or fear these but to enlighten this. It is your knowing now and your path."*

Humility Is Not To Give In

"This is an interesting word and concept. It is not meant to suggest that one cower, be subject to obedience, nor show fear of that which may be perceived to be greater than you. It is one of a quiet, peaceful surrender to the knowing of what and who you are and allowing your being to show and be loved without force, power, judgment, intimidation, dominion or glory over others. Many of you have chosen lives of fame and glory, of power and dominion, some even dark at times. Some of you have chosen lives, less glorious, of humble and poor stature, even war and conflict and destruction."

"What you are is a composite of these lives and although you may not be aware of this, these experiences are reflected in your habits and essences as they are encoded in your DNA. You understand the need for humility as being humble to your Creation and creative powers as a balance. Many of you have in previous lives moved to the pull of the 3D world's glories, fame and power that have resulted from your ego's desires of flesh, of emotion to overlord, to be better, to impose your ways, and to bathe in the perception of benefit from materials and riches. You have also lived lives that denied these. This is why you have chosen the more humble, less glorious life you have to this point. But as you move forward, it is important to attain a balance between all of this which is indeed you."

"As you move forward and uncover the secrets of creation, and bring forward your powers over the material realm, bring forward your perceptions of cleansing, of righting wrong in your lives, it is the sense of pure unconditional love and respect for free will that balances humility and dominion. For neither will serve you well as they are the extremes needing balance. Your balance is to simply be, love, teach and serve. Do not force, nor be afraid to share your knowing of what is truth. And when others admire, shower you with praise, with gifts, and you attain more than others, what will you choose to do or become? Will you want more or will you be humble in a grateful reverence for your wondrous abilities and knowing? Even many gods have fallen and struggled with this. Many have fallen to darkness in their quests for desires of the body and ego as they craved to the needs of the material world they came to overcome and to express themselves through."

"As you move forward it is important to know you are pure love, not here to impose, nor dominate, but to show and share what you know as a better way for other free will to choose. What we say is that you are humbled yes, but to the knowing of you being the marvellous creation yourself of such a wondrous power of Creation itself. Go forward always in the heart. Enjoy and share. Know you are here for the expression of love and service. Love yourself and others equally and serve yourself as you would serve others. Yes it is the Law of One and the five laws that surround it, the ones you know well. Keep these in sight as indeed you are all One."

The Mission Is To Know Your True Self

"As you unfold your path, it is important to know your primary mission. It is to know yourself in your true being and the essence of pure love as well as to show a better way. You are here to shine your light upon all that is and express your light by enlightening darkness. Your visions are those that allow you to express your desires and passions through your physical and mental beingness through compassion, reverence and empathic connection with all that is—the One. How this unfolds for you will be through

inspiration by allowing—allowing your Higher Divine Mind and your heart to take direction of your body, your thoughts, your acts, your intents, your words, your emotions, your visions. You will always be with a higher vibration of the Cosmic Five Laws. You are at the beginning of your mission now and as you move into your visions, knowing yourself is your foundation in that it is your greatest grounding, anchoring you above and below. This is your greatest challenge. You discover by taking your special time to silence yourself and learning to listen to your Higher Mind and true self taking your steps to wherever it leads you. Remember the greatest power lies in the heart and although your visions may draw your attention, it is your prime mission of self that is the most important. Once this is truly established in your knowing, the rest will unfold like a flower."

That Which Needs Fixing Imposes Judgement

"There are many things that you think you would like to fix. That which needs to be fixed has already been determined to be wrong and has therefore been judged as so. But in whose eyes is it that the judgement has been made? You must be cautious that your judgement upon others is not as wrong as the one you yourself created. Do you remember the Law of Will? You and all are One—as one organism of unconditional love of the Creator. Everything lives for a purpose. So is your work to fix or to be love? What may seem as a terrible injustice to you may not be so to another. What may appear as unfair situations may be a contracted path. What may be a travesty on someone may have been their calling, or it may in many cases be what they have created knowingly or unknowingly. What may have been imposed by those of the mind of dominion have a choice like you have, to step away and move out of this. And many do, but not all. What is the key word in this? It is unknowingly. It is a lack of awareness as to a different choice, just as you have opened to your own awareness that has led to a choice."

"It is this awareness that is the variable, the awareness of who you are, the power of love, the truth of your connections, the knowing of the One that all leads to a choice of a different way. This is when light shines upon this and they who you judge can see a different path. A fix does not offer a choice. It is nice to have your heart feel warm and filled with love as you fix something like poverty or illness but has it opened a new choice? Is it opening an awareness of a better way or is this a temporary fix in 3D land?"

"The Creator does not judge as love cannot. It does not engage in taking sides to fix or select that which is right as there is no right or wrong. It honours free will and it opens to the awareness of a brighter way for shining light and love on all things without condition or judgement. In the lower forms of life, death and struggle are the way of it. It may be unpleasant to see this but it is the way of the natural world. You accept this. When you fix things, consider whether you are allowing free will to flourish by knowing a way of the light—a path of pure love not just a better material life. Is it assistance to help through awareness of truth without imposing upon the will? These go hand in hand. What we say is that going around fixing is only part of your path. Fixing by offering a choice so a situation can be fixed by itself is another way. Yes, to teach, to show, to lead, to shine light upon darkness, to open to a new choice equally to all is the way. With more light those who are in shadows can see the brightness and a path to a new way. With more love, hearts open. Yes, assist others to have a hand up instead of a hand out but when they have stood up, will they know a better way to choose?"

The River Of Nows

"The first thing that may trouble you is how do you get from where you are now to where you want to be. How do I get to where I can be myself and know the bills are paid? When will the Leap of Faith Bridge show? These are all 3D strings and attachments that you bring into your awareness, into your consciousness as you work your way through time. Some are troubled by an unknowing of themselves, their progress, their awakening. Let it alone and let it go, drop it away and let simplicity of nothing or no-thing flow through your beingness. Let each moment of your day of consciousness flow to you and let yourselves be the Light and the Love. It is your simplest solution and as each moment flows to you, dark or light, flow it through your heart so as it passes, it is charged and enlightened. In your day there are so many seconds—let them be your moments of NOWS. Let this river of nows flow through you and soon changes will come to you. As your ego and attachments fade and you see in the new light as moments flow, you will begin to accelerate your knowing of all what may limit you—as your Higher Divine Mind takes over your thoughts."

"And then suddenly you will see Crossover and the stream of Nows stop. You then flow in the river of love freely with the flow, your heart shining bright flooding that which is before you with your light. And then there are no questions or doubts. You are aligned with the being of who you are."

"When you say? When this is so. How long? As long as you take to place your awareness of moments on automatic alignment with the heart and with the Higher Divine Mind in command. When will you know? When it is so. Is this a test? Yes, you created it. Stop your fussing and your need for answers. Be what you are, let go, let it flow and soon enough you will be the river of light."

Perfection Yes Or No

"The process of self examination is now. You have been given the information to shift your mind in a new direction. The question is will you? You understand how as you open your heart it draws a likeness and suddenly your world looks and feels different. And the heart field around you feels fuller and lighter. Yes it is so simple but will you begin? Will it be hard for you to open your arms and your heart to the past? It is time perhaps for all of you to examine relationships, family, with others, with all that is in your worlds and to open your arms and heart. This is forgiveness energy you open to and offer so your space can be filled with the light as you walk. Yes, be the light. Change your perception of these things that you do not feel good about, or are right and irritate you. Turn the switch in your mind to 'Light On'. It is as easy as that to banish darkness from your mind. It is there that the true power of love can take its position and flourish to show you the better way."

"It is time to conduct your examination and to pass the exams you have set for yourselves. Look at you, your body, your habits, your family, your relationships, your dislikes, your life, your dis-ease, your discords. Look at these squarely and thank them for coming to you and that you need to see them no more as you convert them to light. Take your moments each day and let these come before you for your cleansing. Feel the wonder of your heart growing stronger and stronger. Yes, it is that simple. It is all about what you choose to see, to feel, to perceive."

"And look deeper into your past lives that are already reflected in you. Simply sit in silence and ask your heart to open, to go back and cleanse that which is not perfection, knowing it serves you no more, your test is done. You have no need for it any more. It has served its purpose to give you a step up to a higher place."

I want to say that this chapter has been focused on me. It is somewhat like a lecture but it has some important messages for all. I wanted to include this because it is what understanding the Soul Journey is all about. It is cleansing, being, inspiration, and letting the heart and the Divine Mind be you. It is about placing your attention on the positive aspects of all life, and learning to create what you desire a totally different way.

62

SO THE RUBBER MEETS THE ROAD

As I sat and pondered upon a moment, I asked: "God when will you pay my bills?"

"Well," said God, "it is when you allow Me to pay the bills."

"But how?" I asked.

"When you shift your will away from separation to unity and the Divine Higher Mind."

"How long will this take?

"As long as you take to take every moment that comes as a place to be in your natural state of unconditional love," replied God.

"But how will that pay my bills?" I pondered.

"When you accept in your total being that as above so below is a process that divine love cannot ignore," replied God.

"Then you will pay my bills?"

God smiled. "Then you know you are a part of Me and can create your own payments."

As Above So Below

What is important is to know that there are many words, symbols, expressions we have assumed the meaning of. This reflects how words and the actions or processes can be misaligned with the real process they represent. Because you can't BS the heart, it is really the control center of emotion and emotion cannot lie. It's like an actor who acts out a drama. The crying, the love, the feelings, are all fake. This is a misalignment.

You may have heard the expression As Above, so Below. It's a pretty common expression brought forward by Hermes and Thoth. What does it mean? Does it mean that everything above in the cosmos is the same as on earth? Does it mean all that we think consciousness is the same as below? What is above and what is below? Is this a definition of stuff or is it a process?

Let me tell you. As you create in the mind *above* the heart so you manifest into the material *below* the heart. You are deploying energy centers that phase from invisible energy (thoughts, images, words) through the heart (emotion) to the visible (intent, relationship, material). As you create intent above in the higher dimensions, through the heart, so you create in the lower dimensions. It is also true that in the substance, what is above is also below—all made of the same substance of love. But you see that if one is a definition of what is while the other is a process of action, one can be misaligned with the process and miss out. It is the way many meanings have been misaligned to become dysfunctional. If you are focussed on the belief that above and below are the same, then the true power of the process of the words is lost.

Can you also create material from that which is below? Yes, a crystal or a tree will speak to you but it cannot *create* that which is material. Yes, you can *make* what you can imagine, but it is the old 3D way of simulating creation. It is not creating in its true sense. Even those two words have been misaligned. It is like the difference between proactive and reactive intent attached to the process of creation. It is all within the mind. The *lower mind thinks* while the *higher mind feels*. It is the Higher Divine Mind that feels with the heart and the ego that thinks with the intellect.

This is all to say that the real shift begins upstairs with the realization and awareness that the lower mind is downstairs and it needs to be quiet, thus allowing the higher to feel with the heart. That begins with the mind above that creates the action below through the heart. I used to think that sometimes when you could not shift your belief system quickly, you had to create new physical habits to create and enforce a new belief or philosophy in the mind. It was the habit that created the belief. That is the hard way and the long way, not always successful because the truth is that the mind, in one instant can result in new physical habits, as it does in a near death experience or when you trigger what you call cold turkey. But in reality which was first? Was it truly the habit?

Atonement is the reparation and reconciliation of a wrong doing. The wrong doing in this case is believing you and your ego buddy can do a better job at paying your bills and creating a joyful life than your Higher Mind can. It is simply a more difficult way because you choose the Gopher Wheel of life's path up the River of Life. The reparation and reconciliation is when you turn around and with the flow, forgive yourself and your ego for believing this and get the hell off the Gopher Wheel. Like in a Near Death Experience, why not cold turkey and begin to learn how to create anything as if you were the Genie? The big test is when you shift from head to heart, from believing you still have to pay the bills to knowing they are paid. It is when you empty your mind of limits and lack and know there is no such thing except what you yourself have created.

But here is the real issue. This alignment has to have the heart and its positive emotions onside to create. This is where BS'ing the heart will not provide the results. So if the process of as above (an image of heart's desire) is not enfolded with the right emotion (bliss of completion) guess what? No creation.

Quit The PLANET EARTH Gopher Wheel Of Life

So what does one do to get off the Gopher Wheel and launch the creative essence? There are zillions of gizmos, more books, energy things, DNA activations, etc., etc. that are there to convince the ego to back off. It won't. You have to relegate it to a new position by your own choice of action. It is also hard to bullshit it when you have spent your life training it. You have to think with the heart.

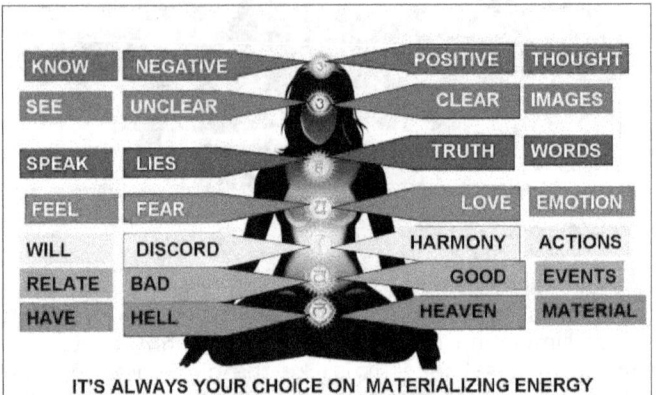
IT'S ALWAYS YOUR CHOICE ON MATERIALIZING ENERGY

So here is your strategy. Get with the program of how your energy system works! Get on the positive side of unconditional love and forgiveness for all things and transcend above the polarity of light and dark. It's about learning to create a life, not earn a living. So don't step off the Gopher Wheel while its moving, start looking outside the Wheel, away from ego's trappings. Look for your passions, your bliss in the harmony of forgiveness so your heart electrical filed is working at its optimum. Look at your old life a different way. It is supposed to teach you what you **do not want,** rather than give it more life by your attention to lack and conflict. You don't have to leap off but you have to shift the mind to a new place of attention.

We all carry negative baggage from the past—families, jobs, others, experiences, tons of crap that influence our behaviour and steal our attention. Stop it. They are your lessons.

There are energies that you have already given life to that are still looking for mates. Some may not be so good when they succeed and manifest in front of you. Change your perception of them to one from a higher place. Know you created them so don't act surprised and pissed off. Thank them, learn and let them be gone.

As you see and feel with your senses, there may be a preponderance of conflict, dis-ease, disease and discord. How do you react? You hate this or that, you feel crappy. It pisses you off. Don't give life to that energy. Don't create that feeling.

There are things that are happening around you and you are deluged by their negativity. Get over this. It's all there to teach you how to rise above it.

There are many things that your heart desires and you as a Creator can create. Begin the process.

How? Every moment that comes to you has a purpose. To the Higher divine Mind, each moment is a wonderful chance to create something better—for the big organism of Consciousness you are a part of.

Then start looking at those categories of energies above, your relationships, your baggage, your teachings, your events, your desires. Zero them out and forgive yourself for being negative, and forgive others. Live in that world of unconditional love every one of those moments. What's the point of giving these crap things life when they go find more crap? Imbed the Cosmic Laws in your behaviour and energize the energy you create with honest pure emotion of the heart—no bullshit, no acting.

How long will it take you to be a Creator again? Well, some are still working at it over many lifetimes. With some, like NDE's it's instant. Take your pick because it's your choice.

And have you got anything to lose by doing this? Yes, perhaps a life on the Gopher Wheel? Perhaps dis-ease and disease? Perhaps less of the old crap? Does better health, a new life and fulltime bliss interest you?

Don't be disappointed if the million dollars does not suddenly materialize before you in 3D instantly because you think you have it and know the process. Don't be disappointed when God doesn't transfer the money for your bills from the cosmic bank account tomorrow. It may be so in your mind. That is where it starts and that is your true grounding when you shift to that way of thinking. But you are a still all in schooling as you have been many lifetimes. Graduation is indeed accepting the process of Creation through the Higher Divine Mind. Start, yes start on the River of Nows with a quiet, patient detachment that is mindful of heart and love. You have an infinite supply of it to give away to all, to everything, without reservation, without condition, without attachments, freely, and openly. Just pour it out of you every moment that you encounter down the river. And you have an infinite amount of it to create, not make a wonderful life. It's that simple. Your graduation certificate is in view, can you see it?

And God smiled and said:

"Then you know you are a part of Me and can create your own payments."

Who is God? We all are! We are Me learning how!

As we end this chapter, the important lesson is to not renew the old prescriptions that the PLANET EARTH subsidiaries of Religion and their Codes prescribes as the Blue Pill. This places you in a new world of belief in your Self and a clear understanding of your journey.

We are at a unique time where some assistance from God, from Divine Intervention, from Above, from Self, whatever you want to call it, is happening whether many like it, know it or not. How you align with this is the unique choice you have but one think appears to be the pressing result; Who you are and the truth will be revealed.

Now, within that light, and the belief of peace without conflict, let us move into how to resign from PLANET EARTH and access your retirement plan of Good Faith and Credit.

63

RESIGNING FROM PLANET EARTH INC.

You Always Have A Choice

The choice is simple and clear. It is to rise above the issue of dark and light. Each must choose between the old and the new. You may choose to remain with the corruption and insurmountable debt and fiat money of the old world or you may choose Global debt forgiveness rebooting a system of value where abundance and prosperity is available for all. You may choose to remain in the old world of terrorism, violence and war, at your expense, to satisfy the greed and lust for power and control of the few, or you may choose to remove the funding from the Military Industrial Complex bringing an end to all wars for profit and opening the door to world peace.

You may choose to live a life of doubt and perpetual fear in the old world or you may choose to enter the new world of love, honor, integrity, transparency in all dealings and a return of family values and morals where a sense of community pride and cooperation bloom anew.

You may choose to dwell on the evil and the dark and sob in your woes or you can choose look up and see the light. You can choose a different way of life. You choose a different belief system. You can choose to be a conscious Creator and you can choose to forgive, dissolve the perceptions of hate and conflict and choose bliss. Choose, choose choose.

You may even choose to be as you are under the domain of PLANET EARTH. After all, your keepers have worked towards giving you as much freedom as they dare to without losing control. You may even believe that this is all hogwash this ascension stuff, and this PLANET EARTH stuff.

But, if you have that feeling that you, and your life are much, much more and you are not able to express your true self, that perhaps all the controls on your being and the deception so as to work off other's debt is not on, then you need to resign from PLANET EARTH and bring in a new awareness away from those green pills.

The Choice Is Now Yours: Red Or Green?

Yes, the red or green pill as Morpheus said. It is time to choose and now you know what the choices are. This Part is about solutions; spiritual and commercial solutions. Many have been the warriors of truth that precede these solutions, in a light of simplicity and the attainment of sovereignty in both the commercial and spiritual aspects of life on Planet Earth. What if you work towards Conscious manifestation of the true you on Planet earth AND quit your job in PLANET EARTH? These work hand in hand together. First is to understand who you are and to stand in your truth as Christ did-- walking in thought, word and deed in the light of what God is--you as an expression of that Divine force. It means resigning from the sub Corporation that is GOD and that code called scriptures, bibles, and the likes.

Second is to resign from the Commercial world as an employee of PLANET EARTH and declare your sovereignty. You cannot accept your pension while you work for PLANET EARTH. Here is the place where you work towards the allowing of the certain statures and laws attached to the corporation and enter the private world of commerce. Here you take back the position of Creditor and look towards attaining the beneficial status to the Divine trust that you have worked all your life to create.

If you choose to continue to fund the perpetual terrorism, war and death with insurmountable debt, taxation and the increased limitation of your private rights further staining your Good Faith and Credit to satisfy the greed and lust for power and control of the few, then you need do nothing. We bless you and honor your free will. That is the old way rapidly giving way to the New Way.

But, on the other hand, if you choose to remove your portion of the Good Faith and Credit that funds the Military Industrial Complex and return it to original jurisdiction where the mechanics for global debt forgiveness already exist it assist in creating a consciousness to allow the rebooting of an economic system of value, honor and integrity. If you choose to remove your portion of the Good Faith and Credit taking the profit out of the war machine opening the door to world peace, abundance and prosperity, then read on for we offer a remedy that is so easy anyone can execute it.

In this series of chapters, you will learn how to resign from PLANET EARTH Inc. as best can be known at this time; in peace. Because you have acquiesced for so long, certain assumptions about you have been set in stone. By way of your acceptance, you have been operating and living as a dead person, a fictional entity that does not have the sovereign rights of the real Earthling. The estate that you have placed your life's labour and assets into has been probated because you have acquiesced by not knowing or acting and you are considered dead in the fictional process of laws and codes. All that is left is for that fictional entity of the Strawman to have a certificate of death created so as to place its name on the tombstone and all is done. because you have accepted this, you have to reidentify yourself and reclaim that which you have given away. The process by which this is done, in the best way that has evolved to date is the subject matter now. it is about resigning and reclaiming without blaming anyone but yourself.

The process by which you have accepted this may have been deception but that is not the issue here. Once you realize deception exist, you can rise above it. For in truth, the estate does leave a legacy of good faith and trust, and those who allegedly defrauded you have only conducted their jobs as directed from the powers above. Would it not be great to access that estate? If you understand the total process now, it is one of forgiveness and being grateful of coming to the truth. It is time to move forward in peace and harmony and not to seek vengeance upon others as a two-faced Earthling. It is to become that Creator and take the path of controlling your hologram and creating your world proactively.

It's all about Resurrection of your true identity and your true powers.

In the chapters before this point, the process has been covered as to how this has been done and served by one man, namely James-Thomas: McBride. Now it is time to look at the individual process. Again, thanks to James, he continues to simply, verify and provide simpler and clearer ways to do this.

again, in this regard, we have to use the site **www.notice-recipient.com** and **www.postmastergeneralna.org** where James Thomas McBride opens the gateway. be aware that this process changes daily.

A Word Of Caution

The world of the Strawmen is rife with lower vibrational energy. The Global Elite have implemented a system that has not yet fallen, nor totally disclosed-yet. Until it is, the journey to collect the estate and quit can be a perilous journey and create anything but peace should you engage in it with vengeance, greed and ignorance of the hidden laws. The purpose here is to bring this into the light and it is within the light of higher vibration of foreignness and peace that one should consider. The fundamental grounding in this to be in that space of higher vibration, for as many warriors have learned, this is by no means a simple battle. What follows is one way to resign. There are many ways to "disconnect" from PLANET EARTH, especially with the focus on becoming One with the Laws of Attraction, Manifestation and Creation. Should you decide to follow the process of the formal resignation and access to the Good Faith and Credit through this process, do not, I repeat, do not copy and try without the appropriate grounding in what these documents represent. It is recommended that if you do care to indulge this way, go to the websites and contact the ones who are in peace here, and have done their homework. As a long time studier of this process as published in **The Book of Secrets Trilogy** at **www.edrychkun.com**, I can assure you that this is not straight forward and a very easy way to mess with Satan.

The Required Basic Information To Resign

In order to resign, you will need to collect certain information about you and your birth. For the sake of example, we are going to use a name of Name of **John George Doe born on March 14, 1956. He was given the names John, George by the mother or father of the family/bloodline George. As such, the proper way he would be addressed as a real sentient human would be John George of the family Doe. This is commonly seen in Strawman lingo as John-George: Doe. His counterpart that the Trust/Estate is assigned to is JOHN GEORGE DOE.**

Given Names: John George
Family Name: Doe
Domicile Mail Location: 1234 Anywhere Road, Anytown, USA
Nativity Date of Birth: March 14 1956
Strawman Name: JOHN GEORGE DOE
Birth Registration Date: March 15, 1956
The red # on the back of the birth certificate. It's not formatted like the US one, and on the newer BC, it's on the bottom right under a bar code. For example, on the old format BC, there is a red # like this: P 123456, and on the newer one, it looks like this: NS00012345 -"NS" is for Nova Scotia, for example.

Birth Certificate File Number XX-XX-XXXXXX (Canadian)
Trust/Bond File Number-YYYYYYY Number on Reverse of Social Security Card. In the case of Canada there is Social Insurance Card without a red number. In this case the SIN would have to do.

Note that you may go web site *www.postmastergeneralna.org* to assist you in this process. Here once you have provided the information as listed above, the appropriate documents will be sent to you with instructions for execution.

The Administrators To Notify

The next part relates to the people that need to be notified. The key Administrators of the process are those listed below. The Last Provincial or State Agency who Issued the Birth Certificate (Vital Statistics) In Ohio for example, it is The State of Ohio Dept. of Health Vital Statistics. If it is in Canada, it would be the Vital Statistics Agency of the Province you were born in. Note that as a US citizen, the list would be those listed under US. If born in Canada it would include those listed under Canada plus those listed under US. A name that addresses the private human entity directly is required; only the position is shown here so some research would be needed.

CANADIAN	US
Chief Executive Office Vital Statistics Agency of BC 818 Fort street Victoria BC	Rector Basilica of the National Shrine of the Immaculate Conception 400 Michigan Avenue, Northeast Washington, D.C. 20017
Attorney General of Canada 284 Wellington St. Ottawa Ontario, Canada K1A 0H8	**U.S. Attorney General** Executive Office of the U.S. Trustee U.S. Department of Justice 950 Pennsylvania Avenue, NW Washington, DC 20530-0001
Secretary of Treasury Board Strategic Communications and Ministerial Affairs L'Esplanade Laurier, 9th Floor, East Tower 140 O'Connor Street Ottawa, Canada K1A 0R5	**U.S. Secretary of State** U.S. Department of State 2201 C Street NW, Washington, DC 20520
Governor General of Canada Rideau Hall 1 Sussex Drive Ottawa, Ontario K1A 0A1	**Justice of the Supreme Court of Virginia** American Inns of Court 1229 King Street, 2nd Floor Alexandria, Virginia 22314
	James-Thomas: Mcbride **Postmaster General** Office of the Postmaster General 1300 Pennsylvania Ave, Suite 190-175 Washington DC

The Process Of Providing Notice

There are a total of six documents that are served, the purpose of these being to regain your living position, identify yourself within the appropriate laws of the land, and to regain access as beneficiary to the Estate. These are:

1. Ecclesiastic Deed Poll
2. Statement of Identity
3. Acknowledgement of Deed
4. Entitlement Order
5. Certificate of Authority
6. Covering Letter of Service

If you choose to engage in this, it is already mentioned that you work with the people at www.posrmatergeneralna.org to assist you. For a nominal charge they will create the paperwork for you and give you the instructions. The process of mailing and giving notice, plus creating the documents is vital. This book is not meant to give you a process which may change rapidly. This book is for educational purpose only.

64

ESTABLISHING YOUR LIVING STATUS

The Ecclesiastic Deed Poll [EDP]

The common law and a common law remedy are reserved for living beings ONLY. We are seeking a remedy for the living man, a common law remedy although we will not be entering a common law court. In this regard, James Thomas: McBride offers his advice:

"At present, We the American people, have no standing to receive a common law remedy as the common law is for living beings only. We the American people are all presumed to be 'Deceased'. Assumptions which are supported by first hand testimony against us, by ourselves and others. We unwittingly give testimony against ourselves, supporting the assumption of our 'Deceased' status, when we file for a Social Security number, driver permit, Marriage License, loan or mortgage as we are testifying that we are 14th Amendment legal fiction paper citizens and therefore, NOT LIVING BEINGS.

By the time you are in your mid twenties you have unwittingly given false witness against yourself several times, each time supporting your prior testimony. By the time we figure out what has happened the assumption is firmly established in fact by our own word and hand and our efforts to re-establish our living status becomes a daunting task. Being 'Deceased' we cannot be heard by the courts so our words fall on deaf ears.

The first thing we must do is to overcome the firmly rooted assumptions of our 'Deceased' status so that our voice can once again be heard.

Your DNA, along with the testimony, 'out of the mouths of two or more', in affidavit form testifying to your identity, is the ONLY acceptable evidence of your living status that I personally know to work.

Before you can be heard by this system to overcome the many assumptions under which they operate, you must first overcome the assumption of your living status. Period! Next, you must rebut, or overcome, the remaining assumptions and object to the actions of the Trustees in the administration of your estate which have effectively enslaved you."

The Ecclesiastic Deed Poll [EDP] was explained in detail in a previous chapter. It not only effectively re-establishes your living status but also rebuts all of the assumptions and objects to all of the actions which have adversely effected you and your estate. Please read the EDP and related research which is extensive and very convincing. Again, knowledge is power! And this is about self-empowerment, is it not!?

James continues:

"The EDP with your living DNA, or blood seal, infusing the document with Divine life will be the top document of these nine (9) sets of Originals. I can hear many of you screaming that this is some sort of satanic, blood ritual type thing and I tell you that is exactly what the Powers That Be want you to believe. Let me repeat.....

Your DNA, along with the testimony, 'out of the mouths of two or more', in affidavit form testifying to your identity, is the ONLY acceptable evidence of your living status that I personally know to work. The EDP begins with Who We Are. Each one of us carries a spark of Creator in ever atom and cell of our body and are therefore, a Divine Spark of Creator and therefore, a lining being and NOT a legal fiction paper citizen.

At the end of the document you find a Blood Seal of your given name. This is not a document that is signed for t is your blood and the DNA that truly identifies you. Don't be squeamish, you have plenty of blood to do this. Prick your finger and put your DNA on there! On each of the eight originals."

The Ecclesiastic Deed Poll Document

Although presented earlier, EDP is an important document and it can now be read in a different light. In these examples, the basic information that identified John George: Doe has been inserted in the appropriate highlighted areas.

ECCLESIASTIC DEED POLL

Per Curiam Divina

John George of the family Doe
Nativity Date 1956-03-14

Domicile Non-Domestic Private Post
Anywhere Road 1234
Anytown state on Anystate
on USA

Before Abraham was, I AM; the Divine Spirit having a human experience. Each atom and cell of this physical vessel I inhabit to travel across this land is infused with the spark of the Creator; I AM one with the light, one with Creator, the alpha and the omega, without beginning nor end, without time.

This third dimensional vessel, called man, the original domicile of the Divine Spirit is known on this world and in this dimension as **John George** of the family **Doe**, or simply **John Doe**, a freeborn inhabitant, heir to the Divine Estate,

Beneficiary to the Divine Trust, freeholder in fee simple absolute, one of the 'Posterity' as expressed in the Preamble of the United States Constitution.

IRREVOCABLE DEED AND CONTRACT

We, the Divine Spirit, expressed in living flesh, infuse this irrevocable deed and contract with Divine Life through Our Blood, perfecting an unbreakable seal on this agreement, bearing the full power and authority of the Divine Creator and binding on all inferior persons and practitioners of the inferior Roman Law, Sharia Law and/or Talmudic Law from the beginning, without time. The base lead of Our word contains the purest gold for the transmutation of the base man/woman into pure spirit for in the beginning there was the word and the word was God.

CONSTITUTION FOR THE UNITED STATES OF AMERICA

The Constitution for the United States is a document of dual nature:

1. The Constitution is a trust document, and
2. it is the articles of incorporation and created a unique trust res and estate of inheritance.

It is a tenant of law that in order to determine the intent of a writing one must look to the title, the Empowerment Clause in statute, which in the case of the Constitution is the Preamble. In writing the Constitution the founders followed the common law of England which stretches back some 1000 years. The Preamble fulfills the requirements necessary to establish a trust. It identifies the Grantor(s), Statement of Purpose, Grantee(s), Statement of Intent, Written Indenture, and the name of the entity being created and is written and constructed as a trust so that it would have the thrust of ageless law. Let us take a look:

WE THE PEOPLE (Grantors) of the United States (from or out of) in Order to form a more perfect union, establish justice, provide for the common defence, promote the general welfare and secure the Blessings of Liberty (statement of Purpose) to ourselves and our posterity (Grantees/heirs unnamed), Do Ordain and establish (Statement of Intent) this constitution (Written Indenture) for the United States of America (name of the entity being created).

The trust res is in the Articles of the Confederation and the Declaration of Independence. The intent of the constitution was to bequeath freedom, life, liberty and the pursuit of happiness to themselves and their posterity. The founders intended to secure and pass on the sovereignty of the people to the people of future generations of Americans, in perpetuity.

One's rights are derived from the land upon which one stands and your relation, or status, to that land. In America these rights originated with the Articles of Confederation and the Declaration of Independence and are attached to the land called America (The Laws of Real Property). Our status, or relation to that land, is determined by the laws of Descent and Distribution. The right to freedom, life, liberty and the pursuit of happiness are Our inheritance bequeathed to us via the Constitution of the United States of America.

The constitution granted the government the power and authority to administrate and to carry on corporate functions. Under the common law, inherent rights cannot devolve to a 'body politic' through a corporation. Rights only devolve to human beings is through and by way of a trust. Under the constitutional law, in order to determine the meaning of a written instrument the court must look to the title. In this case, once again, it is the Preamble. Pursuant to the laws of real property that have been existence from the beginning, the Preamble clearly shows a freehold in fee simple absolute in it. Freeholds in fee simple were instruments of trust, not corporate. "Our Posterity" cannot be speaking of a corporate entity as posterity can only mean a living man/woman, by birth/nativity.

The Articles of the Constitution are the Articles of Incorporation that established congress as Trustees of the Trust and defines their power and authority as well as their limitations. Annexed to the Constitutional Trust is a will like structure, the Amendments. The Trust and the trust res were already in existence when the will/codicil (Amendments) were added some four years later. The Amendments do not constitute the Trust in fact, they are annexed to the Trust as a codicil (a supplement or addition to the will, not necessarily disposing of the entire estate, but modifying, explaining or otherwise qualifying the will in some way.)

A Trust, once completed and in force cannot be amended or altered without the consent of the parties in interest except under reserved power of amendment and alteration. An amendment is ordinarily possible by parties in interest and against parties without vested interest. Prior to the 14th Amendment the freeborn inhabitants, citizens of the states were the parties in interest. The 14th Amendment created the 14th Amendment legal fiction citizen who do not have a vested interest in the trust or the trust res.

The 14th Amendment can be viewed as a codicil to the will that republished the constitution with new meaning, changed the intent behind it and turned it into a testamentary instrument with capabilities of being used against the free born inhabitants through a seemingly voluntary revocation.

We, the freeholders, Beneficiaries to the trust have been tricked and coerced by the Trustees into Testifying against ourselves when we apply for an S.S. #, drivers permit, marriage license or when we sign an IRS 1040 form, which the Trustees have mislead us to believe are mandatory.

When one applies for a Social Security number, provide evidence of birth and claims to be a United States citizen, a party with no vested interest in a freehold, the trust or the trust res, you literally declared the free born inhabitant to be deceased; the decedent retains no interest in the property and that you, in your dual capacity as a legal fiction citizen are now the executor of the estate.

The Trustees have breached the trust having amended the will for their own personal profit and gain at the expense of the true heirs. The freeholders/ Beneficiary has unwittingly, without full disclosure, become the executor and the Trustees have become the Beneficiaries to the trust through the Laws of Donations, effectively stealing Our inheritance.

A breach of trust of fiduciary duty by a Trustee is a violation of correlative right of the Cestui Que Trust and gives rise to the correlative cause of action on the part of the Beneficiary for any loss to the estate Trust. This rule is applicable in respect to both positive acts or negligence constituting a breach of fiduciary duty by the Trustee. A Trustee's breach of fiduciary duty falls within the maxim that 'equity will not aid one who comes into court with unclean hands.'

When the Trustee's breach is by an act of omission the beneficiary can question the propriety of the Trustee. The Beneficiary had to have full disclosure, full knowledge of the material facts and circumstances. A Beneficiary must have had knowledge of and understood their rights and have no obligation to search the public records to obtain said knowledge.

The Trustees have committed acts of omission, mis-representation, deceit and deception in order to mislead and coerce us into giving up our beneficial interest in the trust and the trust res. The Trustees have compelled the free born inhabitants, freeholders in fee simple, to accept the benefits 'under the will' perverted by the 14th Amendment, without freedom of choice for failure of full disclosure thereby precluding our enforcement of contractual rights in property bequeathed to us by the will. The Trustees are trying to repudiate the Trust, employing a lifetime of propaganda and programming and enforced through threats, violence and coercion, and failing to provide notice to the Beneficiaries of the repudiation which must be 'brought home.'

The Doctrine of Election in connection with testamentary instruments is the principle that one who is given a benefit 'under the will' must choose between accepting the benefits and asserting some other claim against the testator's estate or against the property disposed of by the will. A Testamentary Beneficiaries right to elect whether to take 'under the will' or 'against the will' in case he has some inconsistent claim against the testator's estate, is personal to him; is a personal privilege which may be controlled by the creditors of the Beneficiary. They can claim no right or interest in the estate contrary to the debtor's election and may have no right of a legacy or devise to their debtor if he elected to take against the will.

Acceptance of benefits 'under the will' constitutes an election which will preclude the devisee from enforcing contractual rights in property bequeathed the will. This rule is, of course, subject to the qualifications that acceptance of a benefit 'under the will' when made in ignorance of the Beneficiaries rights or a mis-apprehension, mis-representation as to the condition of the Testator's estate does not constitute an election.

In the beginning God gave man dominion over all things, Beneficiaries of the Divine Trust. The Founding fathers of the United States of America created the constitution for the United States, an estate trust, to pass on sovereignty of the people to the people of future generations, in perpetuity.

In America today, upon giving birth a mother is compelled, without full disclosure, to apply for the creation of the Cestui Que Vie trust, creating a 14th Amendment paper citizen of the United States. Upon receipt of the mother's application the Trustees establish a trust under the error of assumptions that the child has elected to accept the benefits bequeathed by the will, 'under the will'. The Trustees further assume that the child is incompetent, a bankrupt and lost at sea and is presumed dead until the child re-appears and re-establishes his/her living status, challenges the assumption of his/her acceptance of the benefits 'under the will' as being one of free choice and with full knowledge of the facts and redeems the estate.
Under the assumption that the child is a 14th Amendment citizen, the child's footprint is placed on the birth certificate by the hospital creating a slave bond that is sold to the federal reserve, who converts the certificate into a negotiable instrument and establishes a second Cestui Que Vie trust. The child's parents are compelled to apply for a social security number for the child, unwittingly testifying that the child is a 14th Amendment paper citizen of the United States, not a party in interest to the trust or the trust res, and assumed to be dead after 7 years, when the federal reserve cannot seize the child, they file for the issue of the salvage bond and the child is presumed dead.

When a child is Baptized by the church, the Baptismal certificate is forwarded to the Vatican who converts the certificate into a negotiable instrument and creates a third Cestui Que Vie trust. These three trusts represent the enslavement of the property, body and soul of the child.

The civil administration, UNITED STATES, continues to operate today under this triple crown of enslavement based on the error of assumptions that we are 14th Amendment citizens of the United States based on the breach of trust by the trustees.

DIVINE NOTICE OF PROTEST

We, the Divine Spirit, expressed in trust in living flesh, having returned from being lost in the sea of illusion, born of a self imposed state of amnesia and years of propaganda and extreme programming, to re-establish Our living status and redeem Our estate establishes the evidence in fact of Our competence rebutting the assumption with fact.

We, the Divine Spirit, object to and issue Divine Notice of Protest to the breach of trust and the usurpation of Our inheritance under the error of assumptions of the 'pledge' of Our private property. We have never willingly, knowingly and with full disclosure pledged Our inheritance to any person or entity;

We, the Divine Spirit, object to and issue Divine Notice of Protest to the conversion of the birth certificate to a promissory note or other negotiable instrument without full disclosure nor consent;

We, the Divine Spirit, object to and issue Divine Notice of Protest to all derivatives of the birth registration, the estate trust and Cestui Que Vie trust as fruit of the poison tree;

We, the Divine Spirit, object to and issue Divine Notice of Protest to the malicious and unconscionable actions of the executors and administrators of the estate, to wit:
- knowingly and willingly claiming the child as chattel of the estate;
- creation of the slave bond contract and slave bond.

We, the Divine Spirit, object to and issue Divine Notice of Protest to the intentionally deceitful legal language and meaning of Our earthly parents marriage certificate and the birth registration whereby Our earthly parents were tricked into signing us away into slavery to the state without full disclosure nor consent;

We, the Divine Spirit, object to and issue Divine Notice of Protest to the creation of the slave bond by placing the ink impression of the child's footprint on the birth certificate, converting said certificate into a slave bond and selling same to the federal reserve for the conveyance into the second Cestui Que Vie Trust;

We, the Divine Spirit, object to and issue Divine of Notice of Protest to the issue of and monetization of the maritime lien for the salvage for the lost property for the bank's failure to seize the slave child upon the maturity of the slave bond;

We, the Divine Spirit, object to and issue Divine Notice of Protest to the issue and monetization of the Baptismal Certificate and creation of the 3rd Cestui Que Vie trust, representing the enslavement of Our soul, under the assumption that Our earthly parents gifted, granted and/or conveyed Our soul to the state;

We, the Divine Spirit decree that:
- Our earthly parents never willingly, knowingly and with full disclosure gifted, granted or conveyed Our soul to any person, entity or cult;
- No person, entity nor cult have the authority to gift, grant, convey nor enslave Our soul to any other person, entity or cult without full disclosure and our consent;
- We, the Divine Spirit have never willingly, knowingly and with full disclosure gifted, granted or conveyed Our soul to any person, entity or cult, nor consented to same;

We, the Divine Spirit, object to and issue Divine Notice of Protest to the three Cestui Que Vie Trusts which represent the triple crown of enslavement and three claims against Our property, body and soul by the Roman cult for the purpose of enslaving the people in the denial of all of our rights to the Divine Inheritance, Our right to freedom from all limitations and Our rights and powers as Divine Creators;

We, the Divine Spirit, object to and issue Divine Notice of Protest to the BAR Association as managers of the triple crown of enslavement of the Roman cult representing the reconstituted "Galla" responsible for the reaping of souls;

We, the Divine Spirit, object to and issue Divine Notice of Protest to the BAR Association courts and/or agents use of the inferior Roman Law, Sharia Law, Talmudic Law, Maritime Law, and/or Cannon Law against Us and/or Our property;

We, the Divine Spirit, expressed in trust in the living flesh, having re-established Our living status, whose estate is held in the above referenced trust, hereby re-establish Ourselves as Grantor of the trust having provided 100% of the value to fund the trust, with the authority to act in that capacity and exercise the power and authority of the Grantor of said trust;

We, the Divine Spirit, expressed in trust in the living flesh are vested as Beneficiary of said trust as said trust was established for Our benefit;

We, the Divine Spirit, expressed in trust in living flesh, having re-established Our living status, have standing to seek redress of grievance in the common law;

Receipt of this Ecclesiastic Deed Poll constitutes acceptance and is binding on all inferior persons and carries a mandatory obligation to act in accordance with Divine Law.

We, the Divine Spirit, expressed in trust in the living flesh, a free born inhabitant, heir to the Divine Estate, Beneficiary to the Divine Trust, freeholder in fee simple absolute, do hereby object to and issue Divine Notice of Protest to the following, to wit:
- To the compelled registration of the Birth under the error of assumptions and failing full disclosure, which created the 14th Amendment citizen of the United States;
- To the compelled acceptance of benefits 'under the will' which was perverted by the Trustees without full disclosure and under mis-apprehension and mis-representation, precluding Our enforcement of Our contractual rights in property bequeathed by the will;
- To the Trustee's propaganda, mis-representation, mis-apprehension, deceit and coercion that gave rise to the seemingly voluntary termination of the trust by the Beneficiary;
- To the Trustee's breach of his fiduciary duties which caused loss and injury to the estate;
- To the assumption/presumption that the free born inhabitant is deceased;
- To the assumption that the free born inhabitant is the executor of the estate trust;
- To the assumption that the free born inhabitant is a 'donor' with full disclosure.

We, the Divine Spirit, expressed in trust in living flesh, a free born inhabitant, heir to the Divine estate, Beneficiary to the Divine Trust as expressed in the Preamble to the Constitution, freeholder in fee simple absolute, do hereby:
- Re-establish Our living status, evidenced by the DNA/Blood Seal thumb print below;
- Instruct the Trustees / Intermediary to immediately Terminate the Lease of my Estate Trust to the Military Industrial Complex and administrate my estate trust OUTSIDE the 14th Amendment Breach of Trust and dissolve the 14th Amendment United States citizen ;
- Instruct the Trustees that my Divine Estate Trust shall be administrated as a Charitable Trust in accordance with its original intent;
- Provide the Heir the delinquent rent;
- Demand that all restrictions against the freeholder be immediately released;
- Demand that the private funds held by the DTC, DTCC, OITC and/or any/all other entities be made available to me for the discharge of debt, funding the National Banking Association and all sub-accounts thereof;
- Demand that the Trustees provide a full account within 60 days.

Blood Seal of John George (freeholder)
BLOOD THUMB PRINT (DNA)

65

STATING YOUR LIVING STATUS

Re-establishing Living Status

In conjunction with the EDP, the next important document is the Statement of Identity. The common law and a common law remedy are reserved for living beings ONLY. We are seeking a remedy for the living man. To complete the process of re-establishing your living status you need to execute an affidavit.

Anyone who has known you for awhile will do, but, parents or siblings are the best.

This is the second document, just behind the EDP. These two documents effectively re-establish your living status.

Statement of Identity Document

STATEMENT OF IDENTITY

John George of the family Doe
1956-03-14
Domicile Non-Domestic Private Post
Anywhere Road 1234
AnyTown state, Anystate
on USA

JOHN GEORGE DOE
XX-XX-XXXXXX

We, the undersigned, being of the age of consent, stable of mind and competent to testify, having first hand knowledge of the living being whose identity we seek to establish, do by our own free will and act, "out of the mouths of two or more," establish the facts, as set forth herein, to wit:

We know the living being in question to be John George of the family Doe, or simply John Doe a living man, not a legal fiction 'person', who came into this world on the 1956-03-14.

We know **John George Doe** to be an honourable man/woman and have seen no evidence which challenges his identity, and believe that none exists.

We believe the Estate Trust styled as **JOHN GEORGE DOE** to represent the interests of **John George Doe** which are held in trust. We have seen no evidence which disputes our belief and believe that none exists.

We did witness the living being, known to us as **John George Doe**, place his thumb print hereon. We have seen no evidence to dispute that said thumb print represents the physical being known to us as **John George Doe**, and believe that none exists.

Thumb Print

We, the undersigned, do hereby certify the foregoing to be the truth, the whole truth and nothing but the truth as we know it to be. By our own free will act and deed by our hand and word do hereby establish the facts.

Fred Witness   May 25, 2012
witness autograph   date   thumbprint

Lucy Witness   May 25, 2012
witness autograph   date   thumbprint

66

AFFIDAVIT OF SIGNATURE

The Acknowledgement Of Deed Affidavit

An **affidavit** is a written sworn statement of fact voluntarily made by an *affiant* or *deponent* under an oath or affirmation administered by a person authorized to do so by law. Such statement is witnessed as to the authenticity of the affiant's signature by a taker of oaths, such as a notary public or commissioner of oaths. The name is Medieval Latin for *he has declared upon oath*. An affidavit is a type of verified statement or showing, or in other words, it contains a verification, meaning it is under oath or penalty of perjury, and this serves as evidence to its veracity and is required for court proceedings.

- To obtain a declaration on a legal document, such as an application for voter registration, that the information provided by the applicant is truthful to the best of the applicant's knowledge. If, after signing such a declaration, the information is found to be deliberately untrue with the intent to deceive, the applicant may face perjury charges.

Affidavits may be written in the first or third person, depending on who drafted the document. If in the first person, the document's component parts are:

- a *commencement* which identifies the affiant;
- the individual *averments*, almost always numbered as mandated by law, each one making a separate claim;
- a *statement of truth* generally stating that everything is true, under penalty of perjury, fine, or imprisonment;
- an *attestation* clause, usually a jurat, at the end certifying the affiant made oath and the date; and
- signatures of the author and witness.

If an affidavit is notarized or authenticated, it will also include a caption with a venue and title in reference to judicial proceedings. In some cases, an introductory clause, called a *preamble*, is added attesting that the affiant personally appeared before the authenticating authority.

What you stating here is that while you have been lost in the sea of illusion, that your estate was placed in trust. You have awakened to the truth, so long hidden from man, and now will redeem your estate. You would hereby **acknowledge and accept the deed** and your right as lawful and proper owner of the estate with exclusive right of use of all land, tenements and heredimants thereof, to have and to hold **in fee simple forever.**

The Acknowledgment of Deed must be notarized, so you need to sign all originals in front of a Notary. You need to take these originals to the Clerk of Court and have the Notaries signature and seal Authenticated. You can also take these to the Secretary of State for Authentication which gives the document FULL FAITH & CREDIT OF THE CONSTITUTION. The example follows:

The Acknowledgement Of Deed Document

ACKNOWLEDGEMENT OF DEED

In the Matter of :

Estate Name: JOHN GEORGE DOE
FILE #: XX-XX-XXXXXX
Registration Date: March 15 1956
Claimant: John George of the family Doe
Nativity Date: 1956-03-14
Domicile: non-Domestic Private Post
Anywhere Road 1234
Anytown state Anystate
On Country USA

LET IT BE KNOWN BY ALL MEN, AND THEIR PERSONS, BY THESE WORDS that this public record is full proof having full faith and credit of the Constitution of and for the UNITED STATES.

Before Abraham was, I AM; the Divine Spirit having a human experience. Each atom and cell of this physical vessel I inhabit to travel across this land is infused with the spark of the Creator; I AM one with the light, one with Creator, the alpha and the omega, without beginning nor end, without time.

This third dimensional vessel, called man, the original domicile of the Divine Spirit is known on this world and in this dimension as John George of the family Doe, a living man, freeborn peaceful inhabitant, heir to the Divine Estate, Settler and Beneficiary to the Divine Trust, freeholder in fee simple absolute, one of the 'Posterity' as expressed in the Preamble of the United States Constitution, tribunal of the Court of Record and king of my sovereign nation state.

I have been lost in the sea of illusion, my estate placed in trust. I have awakened to the truth, so long hidden from man, and now redeem my estate. I hereby **acknowledge and accept the deed** and my right as lawful and proper owner of the estate with exclusive right of use of all land, tenements and heredimants thereof, to have and to hold **in fee simple forever.**

This freehold in fee simple has been held under an assumed lease for years. Said fee has been held in ***abeyance***, in expectation, remembrance, and contemplation in law there being no person in esse, in whom it can vest and abide: though the law has considered it as always potentially existing, and ready to vest whenever a proper owner appears.

It is hereby established, in fact, that **John George** of the family **Doe** is the proper owner of the estate in whom it can vest and abide to have and to hold in fee simple forever. It has been **decreed and covenanted that the Grantor is lawfully seized of said estate in fee simple**; and Grantee is granted good, right and lawful authority and exclusive right of use of the estate and that said estate is free of all encumbrances, restrictions, easements, limitations and zoning ordinances of record.

The grantee is hereby vested with the immediate and exclusive right of use and enjoyment of the executed estate to have and to hold in fee simple forever.

So let it be written, so let it be done.

Witness my hand and seal done by my freewill act and deed.

John George
_____ seal
John George of the family **Doe**

On the **2** day of **June, 2012**, a living wo/man appeared before me, a Notary Public, identified himself to my satisfaction and/or known to me to be **John George** of the family **Doe** executed this instrument and acknowledged before me that he/she executed this instrument of his/her own free will act and deed.

Andy Notary
_____ **Stamp/seal**
Notary signature

My commission expires on: **Oct 23 2014**

65

ESTABLISHING YOUR ENTITLEMENT

The Entitlement Order To Original Status

After establishing that you are the top dog in the estate trust represented by your Birth Certificate, it is necessary to instruct the intermediary agent who holds the trust documents to Terminate the lease of the estate, your Good Faith and Credit, from the 14th Amendment Military Industrial Complex and return it to original jurisdiction for administration in harmony with original intent.

Since your estate, our Good Faith and Credit, have been under lease to the Military Industrial Complex since your birth and assumed death, they owe you the delinquent rent. The rent has been held in abeyance until you returned from being lost in the sea of illusion to redeem your estate. Now, it is due and owing. There are no provisions for paying the rent, or interest, on the estate in fiat currency. This must be made in value.

You would autograph with your GIVEN name only and you do not sign your last name here. Place your red thumb print seal on the line. The example follows and it should be read carefully to clearly understand the intent.

Entitlement Order Document

ENTITLEMENT ORDER

TERMINATION OF LEASE
DEMAND FOR DELINQUENT RENT

John George of the family Doe
Nativity Date 1956-03-14
Domicile: Anwhere Road 1234
Anytown state on Anystate
on USA

ESTATE Name: JOHN GEORGE DOE
STATE FILE # XX-XX-XXXXXX
Registration Date March 24 1956
Public/Private # YYYYYYYY

Before Abraham was, I AM; the Divine Spirit having a human experience. Each atom and cell of this physical vessel I inhabit to travel across this land is infused with the spark of the Creator; I AM one with the light, one with Creator, the alpha and the omega, without beginning nor end, without time.

This third dimensional vessel, called man, the original domicile of the Divine Spirit is known on this world and in this dimension as **John George** of the family **Doe**, a living man, freeborn peaceful inhabitant, heir to the Divine Estate, Settler and Beneficiary to the Divine Trust, freeholder in fee simple absolute, one of the 'Posterity' as expressed in the Preamble of the United States Constitution, tribunal of the Court of Record and king of my sovereign nation state.

I came into this world an Heir to the Divine Estate as one of the 'Posterity' named in the Constitution. I was born into this illusion; a world of legal fictions where assumptions stand as fact; where the truth is hidden from man like a pirates treasure buried under layer upon layer of intertwining rules, regulations and codes; where opinions are treated as law; where one is held accountable for his ignorance for his inability to ferret out the truth.

On the day of my birth while still in recovery, my mother was compelled, without full disclosure, to place my estate in trust to be administrated by the civil administration **ANYCOUNTRY** in accordance with the Constitution. Acting as intermediary agent and holder in due course of the Deed for the estate trust, the STATE OF **ANYSTATE** established a Charitable Trust to facilitate the lease of the estate to the 14th Amendment congress and senate, for my benefit. Said fee has been held in *abeyance*, in expectation, remembrance, and contemplation in law there being no person *in esse*, in whom it can vest and abide: though the law has considered it as always potentially existing, and ready to vest whenever a proper owner appears.

JOHN GEORGE DOE Entitlement Order **XX-XX-XXXXXX**

I have been lost in the sea of illusion in which I was born, my estate placed in trust. I have awakened to the truth, so long hidden from man, and now claim and redeem my estate. I have acknowledged and accepted the deed establishing my entitlement right as lawful and proper owner of the estate, the appropriate person and entitlement holder within whom the estate shall vest and abide with exclusive right of use of all land, tenements and heredimants thereof, to have and to hold in fee simple forever.

ELECTION TO TAKE AGAINST THE WILL

It is hereby decreed and established in fact that, as Heir, I **reject the benefits under the will** electing to **enforce my contractual rights in the estate against the will.** This estate, and/or the Heir thereof, are not subject to the jurisdiction of the 14th Amendment of the Constitution, the congress and senate created therein, nor the codes, regulations or statutes thereof.

ACCEPTANCE OF OATH OF OFFICE

Let it be known by these words that the Oaths and bonds of all public officers are hereby accepted and confirmed and I hereby bind them to it, who by fealty and homage bear faith in opposition to all men without any saving or exception, to protect the King and his property from belligerents. I bestow my sovereign immunity on them while administering my lawful orders. This public record under the seal of a competent court is guaranteed full faith and credit per Article 4 Section 1 of your Constitution. Any officer of the public who fails to immediately execute these lawful orders admits and acknowledges warring with the Constitution and committing treason. Any/all orders or writs issued by **John George** of the family **Doe** tribunal of the Court of Record orally or witnessed under my hand and seal is binding on all officers, courts, corporations, agencies, individuals and/or persons. Failure to immediately execute said orders and/or writs constitutes a violation of said Oath of Office and an act of war against the Constitution.

DETERMINATION OF THE LEASE

This estate trust has been administrated under pledge/ lease to the 14th Amendment Congress and Senate since its creation. It has been established as a matter of fact that the UNITED STATES has exercised the lease, creating numerous negotiable instruments based on the value of the estate, adversely effecting the estate and the proper owner thereof.

It is herein determined and decreed, by my own act and deed, that any/all pledges and/or leases of this estate, past and/or present, express or implied are hereby and herein terminated. Any/all rights, power and/or authority granted therein is hereby terminated and withdrawn. All principal and interest shall be immediately returned to the owner and a full account shall be made thereof.

DEMAND FOR DELINQUENT RENT

This estate has been in abeyance awaiting the completion of conditions president. All conditions have now been met. Demand is herein made for all delinquent rent. Payment in full satisfaction is due immediately. All principal and interest shall be immediately returned to the owner and a full account shall be made thereof.

ADMINISTRATION OF THE ESTATE

From this moment forward this estate shall be administrated under the original Constitution for the United States and the Congress and Senate created thereunder, without the 14th Amendment. This estate shall be administrated in accordance with the original intent, as a Charitable Trust, under the direction of the Settler and Beneficiary of the estate.

PURPOSE AND INTENT

This estate shall be at peace with all nations and shall strive to be always in harmony with Mother Earth; to promote growth and healing to facilitate the transition into the new world; to assist the people of the world to grow beyond the want and lack; to grow beyond the fear and doubt to bring about the birth of a world of abundance and prosperity for all mankind; a world of love and compassion; a world without limitation.

THE DEMESNE PROPERTY

This estate trust holds the Demesne lands/ properties which are to be set aside for the use of the owner, his family and staff and shall be conveyed to his possession for his immediate use. Said property shall be maintained by the trust to maintain and preserve the estate. The body of the Heir, **John George** of the family **Doe**, is a part and parcel of the Demesne property of this estate and is inviolable.

The intermediary shall appoint a fiduciary agent to administrate the estate. Said fiduciary shall immediately introduce him/her self to the entitlement holder and establish a time and location to sit down and identify and return the Demesne property to the entitlement holder; to discuss the collection of the delinquent rent and other issues as concerns the administration of this trust.

The securities intermediary:
- **shall** comply with an entitlement order if the entitlement order is originated by the appropriate person;
- **shall** act at the direction of an entitlement holder to change a security entitlement into another available form of holding for which the entitlement holder is eligible;
- **has** the same obligation to the holder as to the owner;
- **shall** exercise **rights** with respect to a financial asset if directed to do so by an entitlement holder to wit: the right to elect how the estate shall be administrated; if, and to whom the estate may or may not be leased.

So it is written, so let it be done.
By my hand and seal by my freewill act and deed.

John George
_____ seal
John George Entitlement holder
JOHN GEORGE DOE Entitlement Order **XX-XX-XXXXXX**

68

ACCESSING YOUR GOOD FAITH AND CREDIT

The Access To Good Faith And Credit

The activation of the Federal Reserve Account, **JAMES T. MCBRIDE National Banking Association**, was presented as the Cure Process in a previous Chapter. This was structured as a pass through account and provided for the activation of sub-accounts making this pass through account available for everyone. This thus eliminates the necessity of everyone having to go through the long process as did James Thomas McBride to activate their own account. The end result is the same, discharge of all debt to facilitate the transition from a fiat system to one of value and transparency.

A Certificate of Authority is issued by the Office of the Postmaster General NA attached to your documents alerts and directs the Intermediary Agent to the sub-account to facilitate the timely settlement of the account, discharge of debt and later issue of a "charge card" for your use to charge the account for the immediate discharge of debt, as it arises.

Through the Official Registry **of the Office Of The Postmaster General NA a**n account was established as a pass through account to facilitate the discharge of debt in the settlement of our accounts as we withdraw our Good Faith & Credit from the Military Industrial Complex and return to Original jurisdiction. The sub accounts await activation by the American people accessing the Private Funds for the immediate discharge of debt to facilitate the transition to a value backed currency.

Certificates of Authority are issued upon request through **www.Legal-Registries.com/Registry** or through the application process at **www.notice-recipient.com**. and are delivered electronically. All Certificates are issued specific to your account, within an hour of your request.

Once your Certificate arrives you will need to print it out and save a copy to your files. I had to copy and paste it into a word document, do a bit of adjusting to ensure proper page alignment and save and print

You may activate your own Federal Reserve Account as James Thomas McBride did, or, you may request activation of a sub account under **National Banking Association through www.Legal-Registries.com**.

Upon request the Office of the Postmaster General NA will issue you a Certificate of Authority & Activation Order to attach to your documents. These Certificates will include all of the pertinent information specific to your account and will arrive via e-mail within hours of receipt of your request. The example follows:

The Certificate Of Authority Document

Office Of The Postmaster General NA
Trustee of the Global Trust

YYYYYYY

CERTIFICATE OF AUTHORITY
American Freeholder in fee simple absolute
John George of the family Doe
Date of Nativity 1956-03-14
Domicile Non Domestic Private Post
Anywhere Road 1234
on Anytown on Anystate
on Country USA
Non-Domestic without the 14th Amendment

Estate Trust
JOHN GEORGE DOE
Reg. Date March 24 1956
File # XX-XX-XXXXXX

Universal Postal Treaty For The Americas 2010

The Pledge/Lease of the private property of the Freeholder in fee simple has been rescinded and withdrawn, therefore, the administrative agencies of the UNITED STATES shall make the return of the interest back to source.

The UNITED STATES shall immediately activate the sub account routed through the pass-thru account, **JAMES THOMAS MCBRIDE, a 'national banking association'** for use by the Freeholder identified on this Certificate of Authority to vacate the blocks on the asset accounts and make the financial adjustments to discharge the debt and return the accounts back into balance. The UNITED STATES shall administer the above Estate Trust in Original jurisdiction, without the 14th Amendment.

JAMES THOMAS MCBRIDE, a 'national banking association'
Activated Federal Reserve Account number **XX-XXX-XXXXXXX** with Routing numbers as follows:
  I) Cashier Checks/Certified Checks Cleveland FRB XXXX-XXXX-X
  II) E-Checks Atlanta FRB XXXX-XXXX-X
  III) Fed-Wire Atlanta FRB XXXX-XXXX-X

The UNITED STATES shall immediately settle the account, make the return of the interest/ lease back to the freeholder and issue the "Charge Card" for use by the Certificate holder to charge the account to facilitate the immediate discharge of debt as it arises and make an full account.

The UNITED STATES shall immediately deliver the delinquent rent, which has been held in abeyance, in a currency of value.

Registration of Intent

The request for issue of a Certificate of Authority by the above referenced American freeholder establishes the freeholder's Intent To Withdraw His/Her Divine Estate from the Military Industrial Complex, discharge the debt in the settlement of the account and return to original jurisdiction.

It is clear that the above referenced American freeholder's intent is to overcome all of the assumptions of his status and re-establish themselves as a living being, American freeholder, returned from being lost in a sea of illusion to redeem their Divine Estate and return to original jurisdiction

Notice to Principle is notice to agent. Notice to agent is notice to Principle.

Evidence of the issue of this Certificate of Authority is maintained by Legal-Registries.com for verification at any time.

Certificate of Origin

This document originates from the Office of the Postmaster General NA under the jurisdiction of the Universal Postal Union (UPU), constitutes "Official Mail" and is in compliance with regulations as concerns Private Mail Carriers.

James Thomas of the family McBride, American freeholder, acting in the capacity of Postmaster General NA

Office Of The Postmaster General NA

69

DELIVERING YOUR NOTICE AND DECLARATION

Formal Notice Of Declaration

It is now necessary to create provide a covering letter to the Administrators so as to formally put them on Notice of Your Declaration. The Following is provided as a guide only. Check to see who the recipients are and receive advice from the Postmaster website. The names within those positions as of May 05, 2012 are shown as example only and this is a Canadian example:

Notice And Declaration Document

What is important is that this document is issued in under the key motivation of **peace** (not conflict) in the need to simply **correct an error**.

NOTICE AND DECLARATION
RE: Trust and Estate JOHN GEORGE DOE XX-XX-XXXXXX

Notice to the principle is notice to the agents and notice to the agents is notice to the principle

May 05, 2012

Jack Shewchuck **Chief Executive Officer** Vital Statistics Agency of BC 818 Fort street Victoria BC **By Registered Letter RRRRRRRRRR**	Walter R. Rossi, Rector Basilica of the National Shrine of the Immaculate Conception 400 Michigan Avenue, Northeast Washington, D.C. 20017 **By Registered Letter RRRRRRRRRR**
Michelle d'Auray, **Secretary of Treasury Board** Treasury Board of Canada Secretariat Strategic Communications and Ministerial Affairs L'Esplanade Laurier, 9th Floor, East Tower 140 O'Connor Street Ottawa, Canada K1A 0R5 **By Registered Letter RRRRRRRRRR**	Eric H. Holder, **U.S. Attorney General** Executive Office of the U.S. Trustee U.S. Department of Justice 950 Pennsylvania Avenue, NW Washington, DC 20530-0001 **By Registered Letter RRRRRRRRRR**
Robert Douglas Nicholson, **Attorney General of Canada**	Hillary Clinton, U.S. Secretary of State U.S. Department of State

284 Wellington St. Ottawa Ontario, Canada K1A 0H8 **By Registered Letter RRRRRRRRRR**	2201 C Street NW , Washington, DC 20520 **By Registered Letter RRRRRRRRRR**
David Johnson, Governor General of Canada Rideau Hall 1 Sussex Drive Ottawa, Ontario K1A 0A1 **BY REGISTERED MAIL RRRRRRRRRR**	Donald W. Lemons, Justice of Supreme Court of Virginia American Inns of Court 1229 King Street, 2nd Floor Alexandria, Virginia 22314 **BY REGISTERED MAIL RRRRRRRRRR**

To Those Recipients Listed:

Notice is hereby declared and given to all Recipients as to my status as a living man and my relation to my Estate and Trust which you have been responsible for administering as Trustees and Fiduciaries. Such responsibilities have been conducted either knowingly or unknowingly in error. The documents enclosed correct these errors, issuing divine notice of protest to reinstate my relationship, authority and lawful ownership of such Trust, and define legal administrative and fiduciary obligations under Trust Law. You are hereby given notice of the declarations, corrections and new directives reminding each of you listed that you have sworn oaths to abide by and to uphold the Constitution of Canada and the Constitution of the United States of America including the Charter of Rights and Freedoms. The declarations set forth in these documents clearly define and reclaim my true identity, and establish my rights to withdraw my Good Faith and Credit from the Estate Trust of **JOHN GEORGE DOE**. You are noticed to immediately act to administer in accordance with the demands so stated and to comply with your correct fiduciary duties. Please find enclosed five formal, original documents served to each and all equally under the Supreme Law of the Land outside of the 14th amendment fictions. You are placed on formal Notice to respond as stated and administer as directed. The five documents are as listed below

1. **STATEMENT OF IDENTITY** As witnessed I declare proof of the identity of living man and existence of **John George** a flesh and blood man and the existence of Estate Trust **JOHN GEORGE DOE**;
2. **ECCLESIASTIC DEED POLL** As so evidenced by the blood seal DNA, **I** re-establish **John George** as a living man;
3. **ACKNOWLEDGEMENT OF DEED** As Heir to the divine estate, settler and beneficiary to the Divine Trust and fee simple absolute, I hereby acknowledge and accept the deed and lawful right as lawful and proper owner of the estate to have and hold in fee simple forever;
4. **ENTITLEMENT ORDER** As authority in the estate trust represented by my birth certificate I hereby give instructions to the intermediary agent who holds the trust document to terminate the lease of my estate from the 14th Amendment Military Industrial Complex and to return it to original jurisdiction and original intent;
5. **CERTIFICATE OF AUTHORITY** As authorized and issued by the Office of the Postmaster General NA, I hereby declare my authority of activation and use of the Federal Reserve Account as a pass through account;

Please register and act upon these documents in compliance with their declarations.

John George   *Oct 20, 2102*

Autograph   Date   Seal

Delivering Notice

The documents are delivered by registered mail. A common process is to go to the local postal office and ask for the registered letter tags/labels ahead of time. These are typically given freely both in Canada and US. The complete package of documents thus includes the following:

	Notice & Declaration Cover Letter	8.5 X 13	White
1	Ecclesiastic Deed Poll	8.5 X 11	Robin egg blue

2	Statement of Identity	8.5 X 11	White paper
3	Acknowledgement of Deed	8.5 X 13	White paper
4	Entitlement Order	8.5 X 13	White paper
5	Certificate of Authority	8.5 X 13	White Paper

The documents are all originals which will be bundled together and sent to the each of the parties as listed. Each should be registered mail with the registered number placed on the Cover Letter document and the certificate of delivery can be received from the Postal Office upon delivery.

Again, verify all this with the Postmaster General.

70

A MATTER OF NEW IDENTITY

The Divine Estate and Province

In order to facilitate the resignation from PLANET EARTH, the Postmaster General of North America, James Thomas has brought into being the Divine Province. This is akin to a separate divine territory that is totally outside the jurisdiction of PLANET EARTH and outside of the laws thusly imposed on the Strawman, facilitated by the use of the Papal Seal under the Postal Union and the Postal Peace treaty. On his website **www.postmastergeneral.org** he states:

"We understand that we are what we are today because of our choices yesterday. As we look around we recognize that the problems created as we live and interact within the current global personality ethics are deep fundamental problems that cannot be solved on the superficial level on which they were created. For decades we have operated upon an 'outside-in' approach to problem solving. We have said **'If only THEY would change their ways, WE would be fine.'** We understand that it is the way in which we look at the problem that is the problem. We understand that we must begin an inside-out approach to the solution. We understand that we must examine and improve self first, redeveloping our own principles of character such as honour, integrity, courage, compassion and justice; following the laws of nature, Our Creator and the Golden Rule. We understand that these principles of character are deep fundamental truths, classic truths, generic common denominators that are tightly woven threads running with exactness, consistency, beauty and strength through the fabric of life."

"We understand that our outer reality is a reflection of that which is within and if we do not like our reality then we must go within and make the changes, for only then may we reflect a better reality without. If we seek a reality of peace, compassion and acceptance then we must first develop a sense peace, compassion and acceptance within."

He further explains the purpose of the Divine Province:

"At Divine Province we are at peace with ourselves, at peace with the world, at peace with the universe. The Office of the Postmaster General NA and the Divine Province are charged with restoring the peace and returning the Divine Estate to honour. We are the bridge, the transition team lighting the way to peace, prosperity and abundance for all mankind. We invite you to join us to learn how to Be at Peace."

*"Fear, greed and the desire for power are the psychological motivating forces behind warfare and violence between nations, tribes, religions and ideologies that have resulted in the death of over **100 million people** in the past century at the hands of their fellow man. The United States has been 'at war' since its creation; waging war against crime, war against drugs, war against terrorism and war against the sovereign people of the world. The end result of these wars has been a dramatic increase in crime, in drug abuse, in terrorism around the world and has bred a population consumed with dis-ease, living in a constant state of fear and violence."*

"The United States is a legal fiction corporate army of the Vatican and the Crown, waging war on the Divine Estates and the Living Beneficiaries thereof robbing we the people of earth of our Divine Inheritance for their own self enrichment. The mighty war machine, the Military Industrial Complex, known as the UNITED STATES has become what they professed to fight against! The UNITED STATES is a universal bully enforcing their will on the world, obtaining the 'consent' of the people at the end of a barrel. The UNITED STATES has engaged in perpetual war in the name of peace for decades spilling the blood of the people chasing an illusionary boogy man of their own creation polluting the earth and poisoning the people in the process."

*"The UNITED STATES has identified the American people, the very people who fund their day to day existence, as enemies of the state waging war on the people and our estates under the assumed 'consent' of the people gained by deceit and deception and maintained by threat and duress. The enlightened being understands that peace will never be born of fighting and violence: for fighting and violence begets fighting and violence, war begets war, and finally, **Peace begets Peace**."*

*"The Divine Province is charged with restoring the peace for the redemption and return of the estates to honour; opening the door to **universal peace, prosperity, and abundance for all mankind.**"*

As such, one of the services offered by the Office of the Postmaster General North America, Divine Province is the establishment of a new identification. The Office of the Postmaster General, Divine Province as already described in previous chapters, is an International Peace Council established under the Universal Postal Treaty For The Americas 2010 operating under the authority and protection of the Papal Seal of Peter under country code DVN/DP/999. All members of the Council are Internationally protected foreign officials, International Diplomats at peace with the United States and the many franchised County, City, Towns and States thereof. The Office of the Postmaster General, Divine Province has its own Country Code registered with the UPU and the United Nations.

In order to explain how this all works, seminars are provided to explain and assist in the process (www.postmastergeneralna.org and ***www.notice-recipient.com***/ where people may learn:

- How to use Diplomatic IDs and remain in honour,
- How to remove your property from the tax rolls, and deal with foreclosure,
- How to mark your property and private mode of transport,
- How to Export your mode of transport to the Embassy of the Divine Province,
- How to establish your property as a foreign consulate attached to the Embassy of the Divine Province and NOT subject to the civil law,

- How to handle the IRS, their demands and Notice of Liens,
- How to go to peace with the United States and free yourself forever!
- How to create your own pre-paid postage and how to use it for; Postage, as a codicil to modify demands for payment to pre-paid status, to close a contract under the jurisdiction of the UPU, and to Authenticate a document
- Learn what is the Court of Chancery and how do the Writs and Final Orders work for foreclosure, IRS, other court issues.

In order to properly execute this, in addition to the process described earlier to declare and notice the Administrators in North America, this identification Process is designed to bring together, by **Private** membership those people who truly want peace, sovereignty and access to the Divine trust. Once again, these documents are provided as examples only, not for use. It is recommended that if you should wish to peruse this, go to the website and join the Divine Province.

In the Notice and Abstract of Unincorporated Association Operating Agreement, it states:

KNOW ALL BY THESE PRESENTS, that on the date of commencement set forth below an unincorporated private association was created by the Members thereof, and that said association will hold both equitable and legal title in real property, receive personal property, preserve assets in its own name, engage in whatever business may be lawful and will further the preservation and protection of the association assets for the benefit of the association.

The following aspects of the said Operating Agreement are hereby provided so that all the world will be informed of the terms and conditions under which activities and business concerning said property and the association itself shall be conducted. By submitting this application for meeting attendance in a private function hosted by The Office of the Postmaster General Divine Province or The Divine Province UA, and/or for membership in the Private Unincorporated Association known as The Divine Province UA, Member Applicant acknowledges the Private nature of the relationship to be created between the Member Applicant and The Divine Province UA. The Member Applicant further agrees to hold all information related directly or indirectly to The Divine Province UA strictly confidential and unless specifically pre-authorized in writing by the Executive Board, to never reveal nor disclose any information whatsoever, either directly or indirectly, to anyone at any time for any reason whatsoever, other than to members of the Executive Board or other duly authorized members. The Member Applicant acknowledges such provisions are made for purposes of privacy between contracting parties which is in the nature of membership in a private unincorporated association.

In placing my autograph upon this application, Member Applicant does solemnly swear the following:

"I have made this application for membership in this Unincorporated Association honorably and that I voluntarily have given no aid, countenance, counsel, or encouragement to persons engaged in any hostility against this Unincorporated Association or its Members; that I have neither sought nor accepted nor attempted to exercise the functions of any office whatsoever under any authority or pretended authority in hostility to this Unincorporated Association or its Members; that I renounce, refuse and abjure any allegiance or obedience previously sworn which is in conflict to my peaceful inhabitance upon the land, peaceful co-existence with Members of this Unincorporated Association, or toward my fellow man; that I take this obligation freely, without any mental reservation or purpose of evasion; and that I will well and faithfully discharge the responsibilities of my Membership on which I am about to enter, so help me God."

IN WITNESS WHEREOF, as a Member Applicant to become a Limited Member of the Private Unincorporated Association known as The Divine Province UA, the parties hereto set their hands at a date and time convenient to each after careful reading, thought and review of the Private Protocols and Operating Agreement without duress or undue influence and by so doing offers to each and accepts from each their commitment to be bound by the Agreement."

Notice Of International Diplomatic Status

The first document required in the Identification process is the Notice of International Diplomatic Status. It is a clear declaration of Diplomatic Status under the flag of peace. It also declares the relationship of the sentient being with the Strawman Trust and the Post Office as the judicial district of the Divine Province. Critical identifications and legal information are placed on both sides of the identification. These are issued by, and only by the Postmaster. Here is an example:

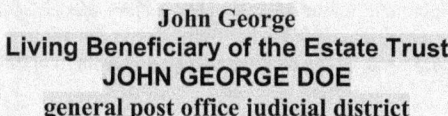

John George
Living Beneficiary of the Estate Trust
JOHN GEORGE DOE
general post office judicial district

Notice is under the judicial district, general post office and flag of peace
I am at Peace with the Crown and all Dominions
No flag of war shall be allowed to affect upon My Divinity

Notice of International Diplomatic Status

Phil Lawmaker
c/o Sheriff Phil Lawmaker
Any County Police Department
AnyTown, AntState, Postal Code

IN RE: **JOHN GEORGE DOE** ESTATE
John George Living Beneficiary

Peace, Peace, Peace be unto all men and women in this world. The Divine Spirit, Living beneficiary and heir to the Divine Estate lives at peace with all men and women.

The Divine Spirit, Living beneficiary has returned to redeem the estate and hereby claims the priority right of salvage enrolling the Estate on the chancery rolls of the court of Chancery under the Office of the Postmaster General, Divine Province.

The superior lien right and Divine Claim against the Estate by the Divine Spirit, Living beneficiary, heir to the Divine Estate, as herein identified is recorded on the rolls of the court of Chancery, as evidenced by the final order from the court of Chancery attached hereto and incorporated herein by this reference, is binding on all men and superior to any/all claims by any fictions, artificial or civilly dead entity and/or assumptions of abandonment.

The Estate has surrendered to the contest and conflict and is at peace with the Crown, at peace with the 'One Holy', neutral in the public with the priority claim against the derivative annuities for Set-Off of all charges against the Estate in accordance with the terms of surrender;

The Estate is Tax Pre-Paid, Bonded and underwritten by the derivative annuities given life by the living beneficiary, Divine Spirit and shall be afforded Safe Harbor/ Safe Passage unmolested by pirates or privateers who shall seize and/ or docket the Estate at their own peril. A breach of the Safe Harbor/ Safe Passage shall constitute High Treason against an ally of the Crown.

The Estate is on and at all times within the judicial district under the general post office and under the protection of the Crown under the Laws of Great Britain and NOT subject to the codes and statutes of the United Kingdom and not subject to alienation.

The Estate has the right to hypothecate the Title to create the funds, remaining solvent at all times, for settlement of all charges against the Estate.

The Estate shall operate in unlimited liability at all times. All charges against the Estate shall be in unlimited liability ONLY.

Any actions against the estate shall constitute an Act of War, High Treason, an act outside your corporate charter and cause for an action before the Crown.

Please update your database to reflect the diplomatic status of the Divine Estate JOHN GEORGE DOE and its Sacred Cargo John George. Please instruct all employees the Divine Spirit, living beneficiary will be/are in your country on a diplomatic mission of peace. Peace, Peace, Peace be unto all men and women in this world.

Dated this **12th** day of **December**, two thousand and twelve.

John George

> This document is under the jurisdiction of the Universal Postal Union (UPU), constitutes "Official Mail" and is in compliance with regulations as concerns Private Mail Carriers.

Notice of Title and Protection

The postal treaty for the Americas operates under the authority and protection of Papal Seal of Peter and the Vatican. Members of the Council, as members of the divine Province and Postal Union are its internationally protected foreign officials and International diplomats at peace. The Notice Caveat instantly makes a reader aware of what they are bound to and liable for should they interfere with the individual so named.

Here is an example.

John George
Living Beneficiary of the
JOHN GEORGE DOE ESTATE
general post office judicial district

Notice Caveat Notice

The Office of the Postmaster General, Divine Province is an International Peace Council established under the Universal Postal Treaty For The Americas 2010 operating under the authority and protection of the Papal Seal of Peter under country code DVN/DP/999. All members of the Council are Internationally protected foreign officials, International Diplomats at peace with the United States and the many franchised County, City, Towns and States thereof. Please take note that you are bound and liable under the following, to wit:

TITLE 18, PART I; CHAPTER 1 Sec. 1.; Sec. 11.
Sec. 11. - Foreign government defined

The term "foreign government", as used in this title except in sections 112, 878, 970, 1116, and 1201, includes any government, faction, or body of insurgents within a country with which the **United States is at peace, irrespective of recognition by the United States.**

18 U.S.C. § 112 - Protection of foreign officials, official guests, and internationally protected

(a) Whoever assaults, strikes, wounds, imprisons, or offers violence to a foreign official, official guest, or internationally protected person or makes any other violent attack upon the person or liberty of such person, or, if likely to endanger his person or liberty, makes a violent attack upon his official premises, private accommodation, or means of transport or attempts to commit any of the foregoing shall be fined under this title or imprisoned not more than three years, or both. Whoever in the commission of any such act uses a deadly or dangerous weapon, or inflicts bodily injury, shall be fined under this title or imprisoned not more than ten years, or both.

(b) Whoever wilfully
    (1) intimidates, coerces, threatens, or harasses a foreign official or an official guest or obstructs a foreign official in the performance of his duties;
    (2) attempts to intimidate, coerce, threaten, or harass a foreign official or an official guest or obstruct a foreign official in the performance of his duties; or
    (3) within the United States and within one hundred feet of any building or premises in whole or in part owned, used, or occupied for official business or for diplomatic, consular, or residential purposes by
        (A) a foreign government, including such use as a mission to an international organization;
        (B) an international organization;
        (C) a foreign official; or
        (D) an official guest; congregates with two or more other persons with intent to violate any other provision of this section;
    shall be fined under this title or imprisoned not more than six months, or both.

(c) For the purpose of this section foreign government, foreign official, internationally protected person, international organization, national of the United States, and official guest shall have the same meanings as those provided in section 1116 (b) of this title.
(d) Nothing contained in this section shall be construed or applied so as to abridge the exercise of rights guaranteed under the first amendment to the Constitution of the United States.
(e) If the victim of an offense under subsection (a) is an internationally protected person outside the United States, the United States may exercise jurisdiction over the offense if
    (1) the victim is a representative, officer, employee, or agent of the United States,
    (2) an offender is a national of the United States, or

(3) an offender is afterwards found in the United States. As used in this subsection, the United States includes all areas under the jurisdiction of the United States including any of the places within the provisions of sections 5 and 7 of this title and section 46501 (2) of title 49.

(f) In the course of enforcement of subsection (a) and any other sections prohibiting a conspiracy or attempt to violate subsection (a), the Attorney General may request assistance from any Federal, State, or local agency, including the Army, Navy, and Air Force, any statute, rule, or regulation to the contrary, notwithstanding.

18 U.S.C. § 878 - Threats and extortion against foreign officials, official guests, or

(a) Whoever knowingly and wilfully threatens to violate section 112, 1116, or 1201 shall be fined under this title or imprisoned not more than five years, or both, except that imprisonment for a threatened assault shall not exceed three years.
(b) Whoever in connection with any violation of subsection (a) or actual violation of section 112, 1116, or 1201 makes any extortionate demand shall be fined under this title or imprisoned not more than twenty years, or both.
(c) For the purpose of this section foreign official, internationally protected person, national of the United States, and official guest shall have the same meanings as those provided in section 1116 (a) of this title.
(d) If the victim of an offense under subsection (a) is an internationally protected person outside the United States, the United States may exercise jurisdiction over the offense if
    (1) the victim is a representative, officer, employee, or agent of the United States,
    (2) an offender is a national of the United States, or
    (3) an offender is afterwards found in the United States. As used in this subsection, the United States includes all areas under the jurisdiction of the United States including any of the places within the provisions of sections 5 and 7 of this title and section 46501 (2) of title 49.

18 U.S.C. § 1116 - Murder or manslaughter of foreign officials, official guests, or

(a) Whoever kills or attempts to kill a foreign official, official guest, or internationally protected person shall be punished as provided under sections 1111, 1112, and 1113 of this title.
(b) For the purposes of this section:
    (1) Family includes (a) a spouse, parent, brother or sister, child, or person to whom the foreign official or internationally protected person stands in loco parentis, or (b) any other person living in his household and related to the foreign official or internationally protected person by blood or marriage.
    (2) Foreign government means the government of a foreign country, irrespective of recognition by the United States.
    (3) Foreign official means
        (A) a Chief of State or the political equivalent, President, Vice President, Prime Minister, Ambassador, Foreign Minister, or other officer of Cabinet rank or above of a foreign government or the chief executive officer of an international organization, or any person who has previously served in such capacity, and any member of his family, while in the United States; and
        (B) any person of a foreign nationality who is duly notified to the United States as an officer or employee of a foreign government or international organization, and who is in the United States on official business, and any member of his family whose presence in the United States is in connection with the presence of such officer or employee.
    (4) Internationally protected person means
        (A) a Chief of State or the political equivalent, head of government, or Foreign Minister whenever such person is in a country other than his own and any member of his family accompanying him; or
        (B) any other representative, officer, employee, or agent of the United States Government, a foreign government, or international organization who at the time and place concerned is entitled pursuant to international law to special protection against attack upon his person, freedom, or dignity, and any member of his family then forming part of his household.
    (5) International organization means a public international organization designated as such pursuant to section 1 of the International Organizations Immunities Act (22 U.S.C. 288) or a public organization created pursuant to treaty or other agreement under international law as an instrument through or by which two or more foreign governments engage in some aspect of their conduct of international affairs.
    (6) Official guest means a citizen or national of a foreign country present in the United States as an official guest of the Government of the United States pursuant to designation as such by the Secretary of State.
    (7) National of the United States has the meaning prescribed in section 101(a)(22) of the Immigration and Nationality Act (8 U.S.C. 1101 (a)(22)).

(c) If the victim of an offense under subsection (a) is an internationally protected person outside the United States, the United States may exercise jurisdiction over the offense if
  (1) the victim is a representative, officer, employee, or agent of the United States,
  (2) an offender is a national of the United States, or
  (3) an offender is afterwards found in the United States. As used in this subsection, the United States includes all areas under the jurisdiction of the United States including any of the places within the provisions of sections 5 and 7 of this title and section 46501 (2) of title 49.
(d) In the course of enforcement of this section and any other sections prohibiting a conspiracy or attempt to violate this section, the Attorney General may request assistance from any Federal, State, or local agency, including the Army, Navy, and Air Force, any statute, rule, or regulation to the contrary notwithstanding.

18 U.S.C. § 1201 – Kidnapping

(a) Whoever unlawfully seizes, confines, inveigles, decoys, kidnaps, abducts, or carries away and holds for ransom or reward or otherwise any person, except in the case of a minor by the parent thereof, when
  (1) the person is wilfully transported in interstate or foreign commerce, regardless of whether the person was alive when transported across a State boundary, or the offender travels in interstate or foreign commerce or uses the mail or any means, facility, or instrumentality of interstate or foreign commerce in committing or in furtherance of the commission of the offense;
  (2) any such act against the person is done within the special maritime and territorial jurisdiction of the United States;
  (3) any such act against the person is done within the special aircraft jurisdiction of the United States as defined in section 46501 of title 49;
  (4) the person is a foreign official, an internationally protected person, or an official guest as those terms are defined in section 1116 (b) of this title; or
  (5) the person is among those officers and employees described in section 1114 of this title and any such act against the person is done while the person is engaged in, or on account of, the performance of official duties,
  shall be punished by imprisonment for any term of years or for life and, if the death of any person results, shall be punished by death or life imprisonment.

(b) With respect to subsection (a)(1), above, the failure to release the victim within twenty-four hours after he shall have been unlawfully seized, confined, inveigled, decoyed, kidnapped, abducted, or carried away shall create a rebuttable presumption that such person has been transported in interstate or foreign commerce. Notwithstanding the preceding sentence, the fact that the presumption under this section has not yet taken effect does not preclude a Federal investigation of a possible violation of this section before the 24-hour period has ended.
(c) If two or more persons conspire to violate this section and one or more of such persons do any overt act to effect the object of the conspiracy, each shall be punished by imprisonment for any term of years or for life.
(d) Whoever attempts to violate subsection (a) shall be punished by imprisonment for not more than twenty years.
(e) If the victim of an offense under subsection (a) is an internationally protected person outside the United States, the United States may exercise jurisdiction over the offense if
  (1) the victim is a representative, officer, employee, or agent of the United States,
  (2) an offender is a national of the United States, or
  (3) an offender is afterwards found in the United States. As used in this subsection, the United States includes all areas under the jurisdiction of the United States including any of the places within the provisions of sections 5 and 7 of this title and section 46501 (2) of title 49. For purposes of this subsection, the term national of the United States has the meaning prescribed in section 101(a)(22) of the Immigration and Nationality Act (8 U.S.C. 1101 (a)(22)).
(f) In the course of enforcement of subsection (a)(4) and any other sections prohibiting a conspiracy or attempt to violate subsection (a)(4), the Attorney General may request assistance from any Federal, State, or local agency, including the Army, Navy, and Air Force, any statute, rule, or regulation to the contrary notwithstanding.
(g) Special Rule for Certain Offenses Involving Children.—

  (1) To whom applicable.—
  If
  (A) the victim of an offense under this section has not attained the age of eighteen years; and
  (B) the offender
    (i) has attained such age; and
    (ii) is not

(I) a parent;
(II) a grandparent;
(III) a brother;
(IV) a sister;
(V) an aunt;
(VI) an uncle; or
(VII) an individual having legal custody of the victim;
the sentence under this section for such offense shall include imprisonment for not less than 20 years.

[(2) Repealed. Pub. L. 108–21, title I, § 104(b), Apr. 30, 2003, 117 Stat. 653.]

(h) As used in this section, the term parent does not include a person whose parental rights with respect to the victim of an offense under this section have been terminated by a final court order.

18 U.S.C. § 877 - Mailing threatening communications from foreign country

Whoever knowingly deposits in any post office or authorized depository for mail matter of any foreign country any communication addressed to any person within the United States, for the purpose of having such communication delivered by the post office establishment of such foreign country to the Postal Service and by it delivered to such addressee in the United States, and as a result thereof such communication is delivered by the post office establishment of such foreign country to the Postal Service and by it delivered to the address to which it is directed in the United States, and containing any demand or request for ransom or reward for the release of any kidnapped person, shall be fined under this title or imprisoned not more than twenty years, or both. Whoever, with intent to extort from any person any money or other thing of value, so deposits as aforesaid, any communication for the purpose aforesaid, containing any threat to kidnap any person or any threat to injure the person of the addressee or of another, shall be fined under this title or imprisoned not more than twenty years, or both. Whoever knowingly so deposits as aforesaid, any communication, for the purpose aforesaid, containing any threat to kidnap any person or any threat to injure the person of the addressee or of another, shall be fined under this title or imprisoned not more than five years, or both. Whoever, with intent to extort from any person any money or other thing of value, knowingly so deposits as aforesaid, any communication, for the purpose aforesaid, containing any threat to injure the property or reputation of the addressee or of another, or the reputation of a deceased person, or any threat to accuse the addressee or any other person of a crime, shall be fined under this title or imprisoned not more than two years, or both.

Thank you for your cooperation in restoring the peace in America.

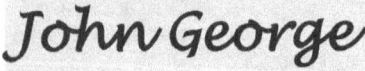

Divine Province

International Diplomatic Identification

The process also includes attaining two pieces of Identification. These are the International Diplomatic Id and the International Drivers Permit. These are issued through membership to the Divine Province only. The examples follow:

Universal Postal Office Diplomat

John George Doe
Born: March 14, 1956
Sex: M Eyes Brown
Ht: 5'9"

Judicial district
Post XXYY0011

Expires: 01 06 2018

universal post office master
universal general post office
Master of Vessel JOHN GEORGE DOE

The Chancery Court And Rolls

As members of the Council of the Peace Treaty, and Office of the Postmaster, Divine Province, each is The Divine Spirit and Living beneficiary who returns to redeem the estate. Here each is calming the priority right of salvage enrolling the Estate on the chancery rolls of the court of Chancery under the Office of the Postmaster General, Divine Province. This becomes the enforcement process of a Court.

A Chancery is a Court of Equity is a court having the jurisdiction of a chancellor; a court administering equity and proceeding according to the forms and principles of equity. In England, prior to the judicature acts, the style of the court possessing the largest equitable powers and jurisdiction was the "high court of chancery.

The judge of the court of chancery, often called a court of equity, bears the title of chancellor. The equity jurisdiction in England is vested, principally, in the high court of chancery. This court is distinct from courts of law. American courts of equity are, in some instances, distinct from those of law; in others, the same tribunals exercise the jurisdiction both of courts of law and equity though their forms of proceeding are different in their two capacities. The Supreme Court of the United States and the circuit courts are invested with general equity powers and act either as courts of law or equity, according to the form of the process and the subject of adjudication. In some of the states, as New York, Virginia, and South Carolina, the equity court is a distinct tribunal, having its appropriate judge, or chancellor, and officers. In most of the states, the two jurisdictions centre in the same judicial officers, as in the courts of the United States; and the extent of equity jurisdiction and proceedings is very various in the different states, being very ample in Connecticut, New York, New Jersey, Maryland, Virginia, and South Carolina, and more restricted in Maine, Massachusetts, Rhode Island, and Pennsylvania. But the salutary influence of these powers on the judicial administration generally, by the adaptation of chancery forms and modes of proceeding to many cases in which a court of law affords but an imperfect remedy, or no remedy at all, is producing a gradual extension of them in those states where they have been, heretofore, very limited.

The jurisdiction of a court of equity differs essentially from that of a court of law. The remedies for wrongs, or for the enforcement of rights, may be distinguished into two classes; those which are administered in courts of law, and those which are administered in courts of equity. The rights secured by the former are called legal; those secured by the latter are called equitable. The former are said to be rights and remedies at common law, because recognized and enforced in courts of common law. The latter are said to be rights and remedies in equity, because they are administered in courts of equity or chancery, or by proceedings in other courts analogous to those in courts of equity or chancery.

Now, in England and America, courts of common law proceed by certain prescribed forms and give a general judgment for or against the defendant. They entertain jurisdiction only in certain actions and give remedies according to the particular exigency of such actions. But there are many cases in which a simple judgment for either party, without qualifications and conditions, and particular arrangements, will not do entire justice, ex aequo et bono, to either party. Some modification of the rights of both parties is required; some restraints on one side or the other; and some peculiar adjustments, either present or future, temporary or perpetual. Now, in all these cases, courts of common law have no methods of proceeding which can accomplish such objects. Their forms of actions and judgment are not adapted to them. The proper remedy cannot be found or cannot be administered to the full extent of the relative rights of all parties. Such prescribed forms of actions are not confined to our law.

They were known in the civil law; and the party could apply them only to their original purposes. In other cases he had a special remedy. In such cases where the courts of common law cannot grant the proper remedy or relief, the law of England and of the United States (in those states where equity is administered) authorizes an application to the courts of equity or chancery, which are not confined or limited in their modes of relief by such narrow regulations, but which grant relief to all parties in cases where they have rights, ex aequo et bono, and modify and fashion that relief according to circumstances.

The most general description of a court of equity is that it has jurisdiction in cases where a plain, adequate and complete remedy cannot be had at law, that is, in common law courts. The remedy must be plain; for if it be doubtful and obscure at law, equity will assert a jurisdiction. So it must be adequate at law; for if it fall short of what the party is entitled to, that founds a jurisdiction in equity. And it must be complete; that is, it must attain its full end at law, must reach the whole mischief and secure the whole right of the party, now and for the future otherwise equity will interpose and give relief.

The jurisdiction of a court of equity is sometimes concurrent with that of courts of law and sometimes it is exclusive. It exercises concurrent jurisdiction in cases where the rights are purely of a legal nature, but where other and more efficient aid is required than a court of law can afford to meet the difficulties of the case and ensure full redress. In some of these cases courts of law formerly refused all redress but now will grant it. But the jurisdiction having been once justly acquired at a time when there was no such redress at law, it is not now relinquished. The most common exercise of concurrent jurisdiction is in cases of account, accident, dower, fraud, mistake, partnership and partition. The remedy is here often more complete and effectual than it can be at law. In many cases falling under these heads, and especially in some cases of fraud, mistake and accident, courts of law cannot and do not afford any redress; in others they do, but not always in so perfect a manner.

A court of equity also is assistant to the jurisdiction of courts of law in many cases where the latter have no like authority. It will remove legal impediments to the fair decision of a question depending at law. It will prevent a party from improperly setting up, at a trial, some title or claim, which would be inequitable. It will compel him to discover, on his own oath, facts which he knows are material to the rights of the other party, but which a court of law cannot compel the party to discover. It will perpetuate the testimony of witnesses to rights and titles which are in danger of being lost, before the matter can be tried. It will provide for the safety of property in dispute pending litigation. It will counteract and control, or set aside, fraudulent judgments. It will exercise, in many cases, an exclusive jurisdiction. This it does in all cases of morally equitable rights, that is, such rights as are not recognized in courts of law. Most cases of trust and confidence fall under this head.

Its exclusive jurisdiction is also extensively exercised in granting special relief beyond the reach of the common law. It will grant injunctions to prevent waste, or irreparable injury, or to secure a settled right, or to prevent vexatious litigations, or to compel the restitution of title deeds; it will appoint receivers of property, where it is in danger of misapplication it will compel the surrender of securities improperly obtained; it will prohibit a party from leaving the country in order to avoid a suit it will restrain any undue exercise of a legal right against conscience and equity; it will decree a specific performance of contracts respecting real estates; it will, in many cases, supply the imperfect execution of instruments and reform and alter them according to the real intention of the parties; it will grant relief in cases of lost deeds or securities; and in all cases in which its interference is asked, its general rule is that he who asks equity must do equity. If a party, therefore, should ask to have a bond for a usurious debt given up, equity could not decree it unless he could bring into court the money honestly due without usury.

The Chancery Rolls From the end of the 12th century, the Chancery began to record copies of the documents it produced on several series of rolls. As outlined below, various series were produced at different times, but probably the most important for the genealogist are the Patent and Close Rolls (which originally recorded royal letters - sent open or closed), the Charter Rolls (royal charters) and the Fine Rolls (financial 'offerings' to the king). With a few exceptions, these four series have been published, at least as far as the year 1509, mostly as English abstracts. (These printed texts run to about 180 volumes, as far as the reign of Elizabeth.)

The printed versions of these records, most of which are indexed by name, are among the most accessible and useful for medieval genealogists. The people mentioned in them are certainly not all royal officials (although if your ancestor was a royal official, they may allow a fairly detailed account of his movements to be compiled). Many of the entries record the day-to-day dealings of the manor-holding classes with government - appointments to local offices, permission to hold markets or grant land, involvement in law suits, debts, misdemeanours and so on. Others are concerned with matters of more direct genealogical interest, such as the inheritance of land, provision of dower for widows and the wardship of minors. In the late medieval period, many private charters were also enrolled for safety. Many humbler people are also mentioned in the rolls, either in their own right, or incidentally - for example, the enrolled orders concerning the partition of estates may contain detailed surveys, in which tenants are named.

Keeper of the Rolls of Chancery The Keeper or Master of the Rolls and Records of the Chancery of England, known as the Master of the Rolls, is the second most senior judge in England and Wales, after the Lord Chief Justice. The Master of the Rolls is the presiding officer of the Civil Division of the Court of Appeal and serves as the Head of Civil Justice. The first record of a Master of the Rolls is from 1286, although it is believed that the office probably existed earlier than that. The Master of the Rolls was initially a clerk responsible for keeping the "Rolls", or records, of the Court of Chancery, and was known as the Keeper of the Rolls of Chancery. The Keeper was the most senior of the dozen Chancery clerks, and as such occasionally acted as keeper of the Great Seal of the Realm. The **Great Seal of the Realm** or **Great Seal of the United Kingdom** (prior to the Treaty of Union the **Great Seal of England**, then until the Union of 1801 the **Great Seal of Great Britain**) is a seal that is used to symbolize the Sovereign's approval of important state documents. Sealing wax is melted in a metal mould or matrix and impressed into a wax figure that is attached by cord or ribbon to documents that the monarch wishes to make official.

In the case of the Postmaster and the Court of Chancery, the great seal would be operating under the authority and protection of the Papal Seal of Peter. This would as you have learned constitute the highest authority in the land.

The post of Keeper evolved into a judicial one as the Court of Chancery did; the first reference to judicial duties dates from 1520. With the Judicature Act 1873, which merged the Court of Chancery with the other major courts, the Master joined the Chancery Division of the High Court and the Court of Appeal, but left the Chancery Division by the terms of the Judicature Act 1881. The Master still retained his clerical functions by serving as the nominal head of the Public Record Office (PRO) until 1958. However, the Public Records Act of that year transferred responsibility for the PRO from the Master of the Rolls to the Lord Chancellor. The Master of the Rolls is also responsible for registering solicitors, the officers of the Senior Courts.

Through the Postmaster General, the relationship to the Vatican, the Chancery has been reinvoked to provide the court of power for the Council members.

Notice To Set-off Against The Good Faith And Credit Estate

This section is provided as a simple example of one of many ways access to the Good Faith and Credit would be placed in effect. Reference is given to the chapter on Set-off. This would be a process of setting off a debt against the Good Faith and Credit of the Estate, acting as the True Beneficiary. This is an example only sent to the Chief Financial Officer

IN RE: **JOHN GEORGE DOE** ESTATE
       John George Living Beneficiary

Prepaid Account Number: **XX-XXXXXXX**

Peace, Peace, Peace be unto all men and women in this world. The Divine Spirit, Living beneficiary and heir to the Divine Estate lives at peace with all men and women.

The Divine Spirit, Living beneficiary has returned to redeem the estate and hereby claims the priority right of salvage enrolling the Estate on the chancery rolls of the court of Chancery under the Office of the Postmaster General, Divine Province.

The superior lien right and Divine Claim against the Estate by the Divine Spirit, Living beneficiary, heir to the Divine Estate, as herein identified is recorded on the rolls of the court of Chancery, as evidenced by the final order from the court of Chancery attached hereto and incorporated herein by this reference, is binding on all men and superior to any/all claims by any fictions, artificial or civilly dead entity and/or assumptions of abandonment.

The Estate has surrendered to the contest and conflict and is at peace with the Crown, at peace with the 'One Holy', neutral in the public with the priority claim against the derivative annuities for Set-Off of all charges against the Estate in accordance with the terms of surrender;

The Estate is Tax Prepaid (taxe perçue), Bonded and underwritten by the derivative annuities given life by the living beneficiary, Divine Spirit and shall be afforded Safe Harbor/ Safe Passage unmolested by pirates or privateers who shall seize and/ or docket the Estate at their own peril. A breach of the Safe Harbor/ Safe Passage shall constitute High Treason against an ally of the Crown.

The Estate is on and at all times within the judicial district under the general post office and under the protection of the Crown under the Laws of Great Britain and NOT subject to the codes and statutes of the United Kingdom and not subject to alienation.

The Estate has the right to hypothecate the Title to create the funds, remaining solvent at all times, for settlement of all charges against the Estate.

The Estate shall operate in unlimited liability at all times. All charges against the Estate shall be in unlimited liability ONLY.

Please take note that any further actions as privateers against the vessel, estate or the Living Beneficiary shall constitute an Act of War against an ally of the Crown in violation of your corporate charter and High Treason.

If you have a valid claim against the vessel or the Estate you are authorized to do the set-off against the prepaid account as provided above. Your failure to settle and close this matter within ten (10) days after receipt of this notice and provide me evidence of the transaction shall establish the evidence that your claim was NOT a valid claim.

Dated this *12th* day of *December*, two thousand and twelve.

John George

This document is under the jurisdiction of the Universal Postal Union (UPU), constitutes "Official Mail" and is in compliance with regulations as concerns Private Mail Carriers.

Caveat Notice To Reader

It is important that in these writings and examples that a warning and cautionary declaration be stated. These examples are to shed light upon a highly evolved process of resignation from PLANET EARTH and gaining access to the ESTATE of the STRAWMAN. These procedures are to be used only in conjunction with and through the guidance of the Office of the Postmaster found on *www.postmastergeneralna.org* under the jurisdiction of the Divine Province as part of a Council related to the Peace Treaty.

Of particular importance is the truth, and the documents are evolving exponentially at this time. Even at the time of writing, the documents and process have become simpler; and the means of enforcing compliance stronger. Check in at www.divineprovince.org.

If it has not become clear, the two part revelation of Commerce AND Spirit is that of Divinity in each EARTHLING starts with Peace and Unconditional Forgiveness on Earth. This realization is the foundation in moving forward within the Divine Realm of True Self through the intermediary vessel of Divine Province.

And so ends our revelation of Light with regards to Commerce and PLANET EARTH INC. Now let us complete the Journey of Self.

71

LOVE, LAUGH, LIVE AS ONE HEART

The True Secret Is Love

In the last chapters, much has been stated about Peace and Love. What is important to really understand is that the traditional path to enlightenment—the one that Christ and many others achieved—has been difficult on Old Earth. It has been the greatest challenge of humanity and civilizations to truly embrace this because as long as Earthlings fear death, the one who threaten it can continue dominion. **It is not so this time during the End Times.** Over the ages, many, many, esoteric practices, cults, traditions, and wisdoms, have evolved as humanity seeks enlightenment. Back in the Mystery Schools of Egypt, even Christ had to wrestle with this lesson, of overcoming the draw of the flesh, and of ego. That is the way it was, and history has served to show how not to overcome this.

as we have seen, in the current day because there is a tsunami of this unity consciousness flooding humanity, there are zillions of products around, with millions of experts that have gizmos and secret ways to heal your dysfunctional body, help you extend life, find unbelievable wealth and happiness. Is this in itself not a wakeup call to a new consciousness?

None of this is needed.

If you have taken lesson from the way energy works, the more you seek this, the more you engage in seeking. Remember, that is the way of energy manifestation. Seeking a solution is work, negative energy that in itself keeps you seeking. The solution is already in you so stop seeking. And at this special time, no one has to sit like a monk in celibacy on a mountain top most of his life trying to be enlightened to seek the solution. Unless, of course, you ignore this gifting that is upon you.

All you have to do is create the intent of allowing the process to unfold and to enjoy the train ride. That intent is to rise above the conflict and fear.

This is the ultimate secret of life revealed during the End Times. All you have to do is understand and accept that which some simple words like being in the heart, peace, and unconditional love mean. That is not so simple if you cannot believe a new way is upon you. Nor is living your mortal life the way of the heart a simple matter if you are entrenched in ego's attachments. Many have been trained to love bloodlines and dam the rest. But understand all are One and we are all of the same bloodline called Earthlings has not come through the lower mind.

Your true being sits in a place that is your heaven. You sit there as an aspect of the Creator as a piece of its total consciousness which is a quantum substance of love. As an analogy, it is like your currently local 3D mind that has no clear definition or substance. It simply exists and you know this because it drives your process of thinking and acting.

Here you sit as this Higher Mind as a Being of Light in your Origin watching a lower aspect of you as a Soul in Old Earth playing out a movie drama of life. You watch and you wonder; when will he or she know the secret of what is already known?

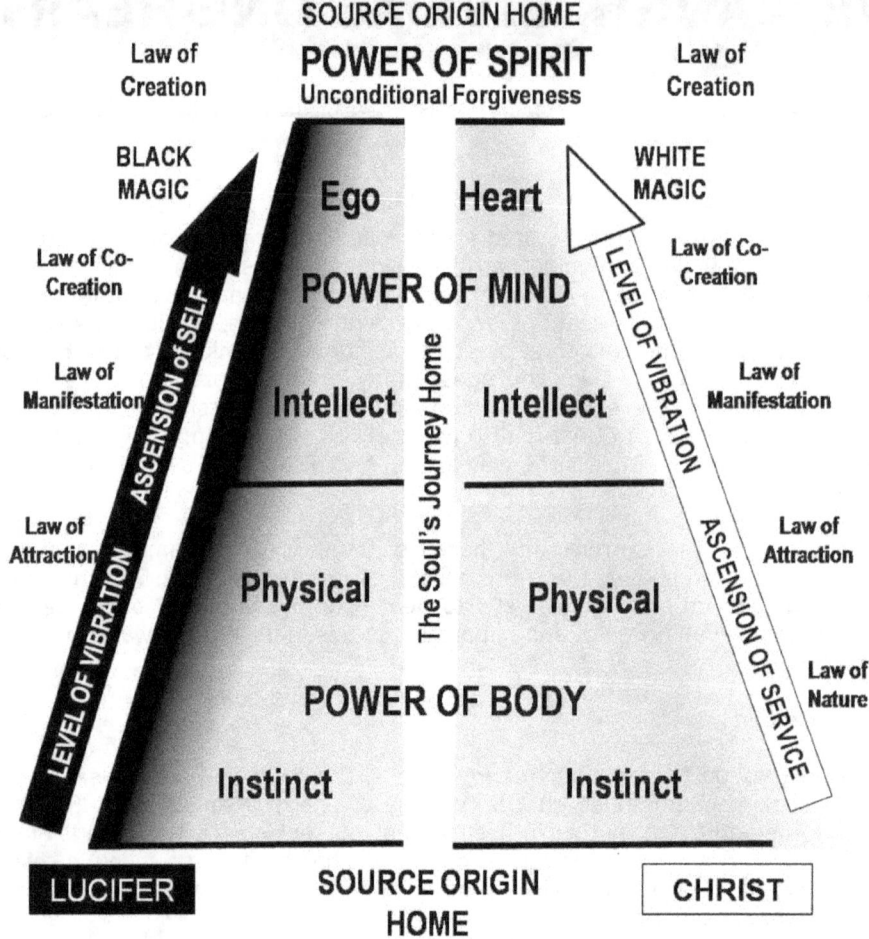

You watch this mortal in its lower form evolving slowly but struggling with physicality, strength, body, age, health which takes much attention. You watch the dealings with issues of money, of family, of things that are seemingly so unfair with the suffering of others, the unjust dominion of the elite beings, and the long story of the slavery of humans. And you wonder why he or she has not implemented the secret yet. You wonder, when will the physical and mental lower form walk through the portal to Home?

And you think and project upon this lower form of physicality some information in the hope it can listen. It is this information of question and answer; What is it that cannot be solved by love? How can you change your life? Love. How do you heal your body? Love. How do you find bliss? Love. How can you heal the planet? Love. How can you materialize physicality? Love. How do you ascend? Love. How do you open to your fullest Creator abilities? Love. Is there anything that cannot be solved by love? And what is it that is infinitely abundant that is the true power of the universe? Love.

The secret is unconditional love and the portal through which you walk opens the door with the key of unconditional Love and Forgiveness. Nothing evil can live there. It is the highest vibration of all things. It is the vibration of the Creator and the makeup of all Creation, that is what you struggle to rise to. As Creator, your vibration is pure, absolute and the highest possible. That is the end of it. What you do in 5D in the essence of love is the same in 3D. The lessons are to teach you to rise above, to attain the degree of power through the level of vibration. Otherwise how can the endless cycle of conflict ever end?

Do you know that as a Creator, you can overlay a thought grid upon Gaia that will affect the physical behaviour of all humanity? This is a large responsibility is it not? It is not done by those that are not of the highest, purest vibration of heart, and without the knowing of your soul group and Divine mind. That is all there is to this. In 3D absolutely every moment must be pure unconditional Divine love; that's it, nothing else. Ask yourself what cannot be solved by love. So what is it that slows you? Immerse into the purity of love—nothing else—Oneness of All That Is. The alignment of you with the God Consciousness is the first step, and to know who you are.

The next step is the degree of purity which is the level of vibration. It is reflected in everything you do in your physical form. Once it is aligned as one aspect, and the strength of that absoluteness is your very being, all your issues are solved—permanently. No secrets, nothing but love.

A New Job: Unconditional Forgiveness In Thought Word Deed

It is what Christ rose to. It is what the Christ Consciousness gifts you. And this time there is no struggle, no convincing others, no opposition because it's *all happening to all at the same time*.

There is a new job for you. First get your belief system into the new jurisdiction. Resign from PLANET EARTH and throw away the old blue pills. It is your conscious intent to live in a New Earth of unconditional love and be God that is your ticket now. Throw the blue pills away and burn the prescription.

Then place your Trust and Faith not in others but in yourself. Don't look for instant miracles for it is a transition. During this transition here is your new "job".

You have a charged Heart Light and it is to shine light upon any darkness that you may come upon. It draws your love and shines where your new Darkness Detection Device in your heart senses darkness. It is best that as you do your daily surveillance of darkness that you use your new hovercraft of your etheric body which allows being above so you are not engaged directly. Here you can have a direct top view of any darkness.

What you receive in return for shining your Heart Light is joy. Your heart is connected to Source heart so you have an infinite supply of light and love to shine, and the process of converting to joy is like a current flow. It is what allows your craft to stay in its higher plane and the conversion process of changing darkness (negative) to joy (positive) is a flow of current that affects the brightness of your heart AND your DNA bulb which contains your total signature and it awakens. And the stronger the flow of conversion to bliss, the brighter is your bulb and the lighter is your body.

Sometimes you may feel it is appropriate to land and engage with others to feel joy and also become brighter on the ground. But remember that by engaging in lower experiences with others sometimes the light may cast shadows where darkness hides itself. Of course these are moments that are opportunities to reap the joy but you must be mindful not to attach or allow attachment. The brightness of your bulb here is very powerful as it can be felt by others around you. Each moment is there for you to enjoy the encounter and provide a possible moment to convert into the current to enhance your brightness. You know how to deploy your new senses in all your 3D affairs for this to expand your DNA to its full brightness and it will then entrain the body within it from its lower form upwards into higher form.

That is all you have to do in your new job. Be your true Self and stop the cycle of polarity conflict.

Know Your QLP: Quantum Limitless Potential

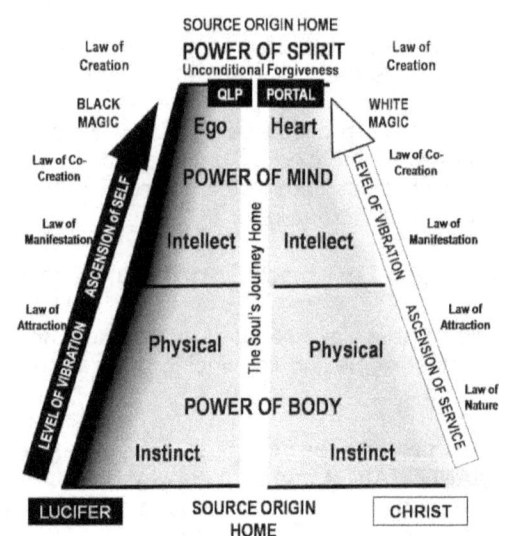

There are many who may be confused. There are many who have doubts about manifestation, the Law of Attraction, about themselves as Creators. Many, in their climb up the mountain to Organ, Heaven, Source, Home, Enlightenment, whatever you care to name it, use whatever means, rituals, gizmos, techniques, abilities, beliefs, etc., to make that ascension upwards. What this is matters not for it is the intent to climb and the climb itself that is relevant. How each does it is truly their own business. And even if you sit at the bottom of the mountain and care to argue about what is better, that is ok too but it does not get you to the top. In the past, there have been several distinct ways know to Earthlings to pass through the portal to Source or Home:

The Process of Death where the Soul separates and heads back Home to Source Creation;
The Process of Near Death Experience where the Souls separates temporarily to go Home and visit Source Creation to possibly return;
The Process of Out of Body Experience where through deep meditation, ritual, or proactive means to temporarily go Home and visit Source.
The Process of Regression where you are taken back in lives, or into the place of Home.

Either way, the process is one of separation between the Soul and the physical Vessel so as to go through the Portal into the Power of the Spirit jurisdiction. This is exactly what in the Commerce chapters, the Divine Province and the death of the STRAWMAN was all about. In the processes of Death it is final because the connection is severed between all possessions, attachments, intellect, relationships. The NDE in millions of cases, brings back a new awareness most of the time but the connection is temporarily suspended. The OBE is less predictable as to outcome because the connection is still there. But while you visit "there" you understand--bring into your conscious--awareness of who you are and your full potential. Then depending upon how rooted you are in old ways of habit, beliefs, understanding, you choose to fall back or shift your life into this new potential.

In the End Times, a process like the NDE and OBE is on the horizon. The shift in consciousness of the Earthlings is demanding this. The shift demands that Earthlings have had enough of this polarity and conflict and it is time to learn and move on by rising above it. This, for the sake of naming is a doorway that you pass through permanently (death) pass through temporarily (NDE) in an unconscious state, or you visit through temporarily (OBE) in a conscious state. The process of Regression is also a temporary visit. How you pick up the information over there as to you true potential may be a hit and miss because of the nature of the "attachments" or connections to the lower vibrational Earthling ways. Here we are attempting to pull information from the subconscious to the conscious and retain it in our awareness.

This portal, according to **Ronald Conn** is best described as QLP or Quantum Limitless Potential. Why? It is Quantum in that this is Source, zeropoint, quantum energy where every thing and no thing exist as limitless potential all under the command of you, your Soul within total consciousness. In his book ***Unleashing your Quantum Limitless Potential,*** Ron describes how he takes his people into the guided regressive state to separate so as to go through the QLP Portal on a little vast to the jurisdiction of Soul, in the objective of achieving the same as a NDE can-most of the time.

On his website**, www.myqlp.org** entitled **The Academy of Self Transformation and Ascension:** The energetic portal that activates and unleashes your Quantum Limitless Potential, Ron states:

"QLP Activation Centre transforms anyone by activating and unleashing their Quantum Limitless Potential through their personal QLP Activation and controlled out of body experience."

Ron as the founder of QLP Activation Centre, explains that during his Near Death Experience on June 25, 1996. He was told not to reveal his knowing of QLP until the anointed time when the required amount of "awakening energy" from humanity had opened the QLP energetic portal. He states:

"The QLP energetic portal re-connects your Soul/spirit directly with the All Knowing Source exactly the same way at a person's death or at a person's near death experience. Your Quantum Limitless Potential is your ultimate enlightenment. It actualizes the same energetic mindset and energetic at-one-ment that Christ, Buddha, Moses and all great spiritual teachers and ascended masters activated and unleashed in their lives. It is our Theta Intelligence that is locked away within us all. Energetically, our Theta Intelligence is revealed through the Theta symbol, the eight letter of the Greek alphabet. Here's how it works:

θ Theta is the eighth letter of the Greek Alphabet and its lower case symbol is θ.

▬ Energetically, the line through the middle of the Theta symbol represents a person's limiting thought patterns of consciousness. These limiting thought patterns are revealed to us through our 5 sense reality of sight, sound, touch, taste and smell. Our consciousness's limiting thought patterns have limited us to actualize no more than 2% of our QLP or Theta Intelligence.

U Energetically, the bottom semi circle of the Theta symbol represents our sub consciousness. Our sub consciousness is all of our past time and space memories from all of our past life experiences. When activated by completing your QLP Activation, all past time and space memories from all past life experiences begin to reveal themselves.

∩ Energetically, the top semi circle of the Theta symbol represents our Soul/spirit. Our Soul's purpose is to unleash its Soul intelligence. Our Soul's intelligence is it's time and space memories of all its "between life" lessons taught by Source during their previous at-one-ments. These lessons are activated by the completion of your QLP Activation. They are presently hidden within our mature DNA that science refers to as "junk", waiting to be unleashed to actualize our Theta Intelligence, Quantum Limitless Potential and ultimate enlightenment.

He goes on to explain:

"Our Theta Intelligence is comprehended through our mind's Theta brainwaves that operate at the speed of 4-8 cycles per second. It is at the Theta brainwave speed that we can comprehend our Soul and sub consciousness intelligence. Our consciousness cannot process our Soul and sub consciousness intelligence at the Beta brainwave speed of 14-

39 cycles per second we operate at in our daily lives.

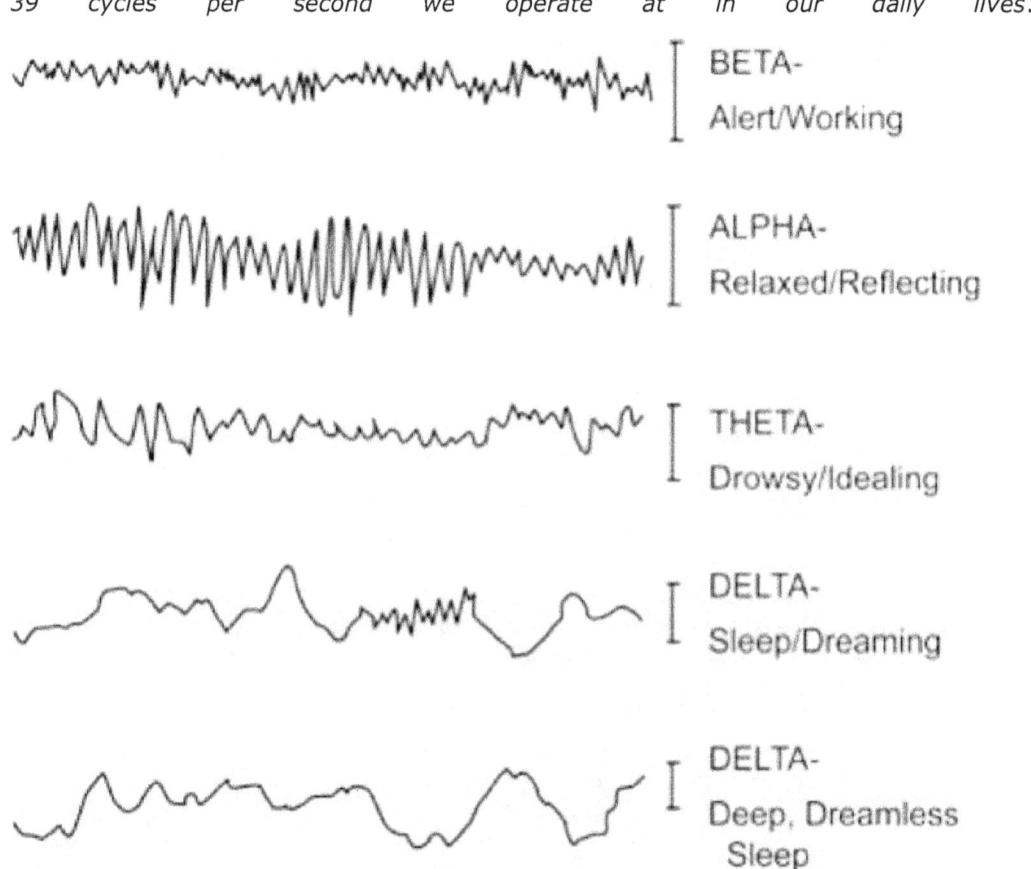

"These brainwave speeds of Beta- 14-39 cycles per second, Alpha- 8-14 cycles per second, Theta- 4-8 cycles per second, and Delta- 0-4 cycles per second are known states. Theta brainwaves activate and unleash our Theta Intelligence of Soul, sub-consciousness and consciousness intelligence. It is here where our role in the ascension process for the Universe, planet and all of humanity resides. It is also here where every answer/solution for every situation in our daily lives can be found."

"Your QLP Activation will:
1. develop your greatest awareness of reality,
2. confirm your immortality,
3. unleash your Quantum Limitless Potential and ultimate enlightenment,
4. eliminate your fear of death,
5. unleash your maximum abilities,
6. increase your desire for life's solutions,
7. accelerate the evolution of humanity, planet and universe,
8. reveal your role in the ascension process,
9. unleash spontaneous healing,
10. maximize your self awareness,

11. maximise your spirituality,
12. recognize and understand your past lives,
13. understand your "between life" lessons from your previous at-one-ments with the All Knowing Source,
14. create you life long at-one-ment encounter with the All Knowing Source by making it real,
15. increase your respect for yourself and life,
16. eliminate all your fears,
17. maximize your knowledge and wisdom,
18. access your All-Knowingness of everything,
19. increase your energy,
20. unleash all unknown memories,
21. complete your life.

"Previously, your Soul/spirit had only experienced its at-one-ment with the All Knowing Source through going through its Death Portal when the body it was in had previously died or its Near Death Portal when having a Near Death Experience. Now, for the first time in the history of humanity, our energetic QLP portal has been opened. This means your Soul/spirit can now for the first time re-connect with the All Knowing Source in the spiritual realm without your body dying or suffering a near death. The All Knowing Force will activate and unleash a person's soul/spirit to access their Theta Intelligence and Quantum Limitless Potential of ultimate enlightenment presently stored away in the 98% of mature DNA that science calls junk DNA."

"QLP Activations bring your Soul/spirit into the spiritual realm, where your soul/spirit will move freely, without no restrictions from the physical world. There is no gravitational force to hold you down, no sense of time to break up what you experience, and no physical sensations. You can't feel pain, temperature, or fatigue. Your Soul/spirit is simply led back to their at-one-ment with the All Knowing Source."

"QLP Activations usually encounter other Soul fragments of who they were in past lives that have become stuck in their journey home. Others have met Souls of people that have passed away, including loved ones, others have even met historical figures and learned from them. This is the same pathway that Christ, Buddha and Moses travelled to activate their ultimate enlightenment and Quantum Limitless Potential. Your QLP Activation guided out of body experience is a priceless experience that will re-connect your Spirit/Soul to the All Knowing Source and activate and unleash your Quantum Limitless Potential or ultimate enlightenment."

What is important about Ron's work is that there is a best way of activating this potential rather than a hit and miss process that drags the intellect and the attachments into the process.

The Power Is In The Heart

Over the ages, the heart has received a lot of press. Heartless, heart of a lion, heartfelt, with all my heart, the list is endless. What's the infatuation with this thing that's a physical pump?

It ain't *just* a pump; it, like everything else of your being has an invisible, quantum counterpart of energy. You can go back and review the chapter of what you are but the heart is the link between who you are as an immortal Being of Light and who you are as a mortal being of holographic substance—material form. That's what it is all about.

And if you don't think there is power there, just think about the process of being in love, or protecting your children. Think about the physical and mental power that these reflect. Heartfelt, love from the bottom of my heart, heart of a lion? It's not that pump that instigates the behaviour is it?

The simplicity of all is that essence of above of God, love, heart all reside in the heart center as the expression vehicle of lower form. It is to practice this learning turned to knowing that becomes your path to mastery. Yes, *love, laugh, and live as One Heart*. Express yourself as the true You in your life with thought, word, and deed aligned with heart in every moment and the rest will simply unfold. The heart is the key to all that is, mastering the space between and of all that is; knowing and showing of what you are, a heart of expression. Every moment that comes before the heart is one to cast light of love upon, get a joyous laugh, and in so doing create the flow of pure life in its Divine essence. This means to be in it, to connect it, to live it, and to maintain it in a state of joy and bliss. This is what your prime purpose is, and so you allow as one with all to expand and experience the prime essence of Divine love.

So you say it doesn't pay the bills? Well, first change the rules of engagement in your working efforts. Don't *expect* an instant transfer from God's bank to yours. Then begin your new job with your heart light, knowing a transfer will occur—then watch what happens. Know that like earning a degree at school, it is done by time and attention of experience and deed; for if someone hands you the degree it has no value in execution. Understand that all the residual baggage energy which may be from who knows when may still need to manifest. Resist that temptation to create more of it through your reactions. Otherwise you cannot break the conflict cycle.

There is no greater power as it is the supreme power and it cannot be subjected to, or be below dominion, nor can it be used for that purpose. It is the link and the conduit between God and you as part of God. As you live every moment in the heart, to love, to laugh, the return is bliss and joy. The heart is the conduit between the 3D world of body and the higher divine mind which is God. It cannot be fooled and it is all knowing, simply being patient for you to know and to show how to love, laugh, live every moment within it. Yes it is so.

The Pull To Perfection That Already Is

Through this End Time pay attention to a shift. You will feel a pull of perfection and the New Earth upon you as an overlay on the Old Earth, forming itself as the new hologram. It is subtle and you feel it as you walk with it in your consciousness, when you see, hear, speak, feel that around you. You are beginning to drop your attention to the discord and darkness as it does not vibrate within you now, except to point out what is not right of heart, and you may feel the empathy, of sorrow yet it does not engage you to bring forward fear, lack, anger or lower emotions and vibrations for these are losing their hold on you to engage.

Because of the special time you are in you are losing the attention to old energies as being important and you look to the beauty, the reverence, the joy of senses, and laughter as your moments pass before you. You look to alternatives that give you peace and intuitive comfort. You sense your body's shifting as it does not work the same and is sensitive in new places as it is shifting; yet you know not what is happening. The affairs of masculine and feminine extreme energies seem diminished—like a balancing—yet you cannot explain these moods that are softer.

And you are looking inward, into yourself for answers, for things of joy that are suddenly noticeable that have no price tag and are not in the stores, free of will to experience at the flick of the mind. All things of matter are beginning to look different. Yes it is the new hologram energizing itself from 4D and it is your new form shifting and adjusting. Yet it is subtle—God's plan is subtle as it sneaks upon you and yet you know. There is no time here, no scheme, no deception, only the granting of divine gifts for all.

Think of this as you ask how this can all occur in such a short time, as you look down upon the discord. It has been transitioning for a long time, you have not seen it. It has been the *Matrix*. Now you begin to sense you are the One and you pay attention to your heart, your life, your powers to perceive, to express, to manifest, to create. Allow yourself to shift first as you will then assist others in your revelations.

Find new ways to live your life. Sit down and go through your day's moments and let your heart see, feel, speak, think, hear, sense and act. Do this from your chair as you imagine your perfect day, then go out into your old world and do this as you walk the moments of your day. This is what is happening to all of humanity now—it has begun, the revelations as a subtle energy poured upon consciousness.

All humanity has entered a time of special allowing like none ever before. No karma, no need for lesson, no need for devices, for contraptions to ascend or open DNA, only pure intent and love. Just say so and believe it. And there is no need to heed those who proclaim special wisdom and affiliation with gods, those who pretend to know God's will, for it is all within, waiting to pour out. There is no need for pain or suffering to receive lesson. All is opened for all of humanity equally and all of the cosmic and divine energy is poured upon all in the grandest time of revelation of all time. All that is needed is your free will to choose to accept and be what you are—love. That is you pulling now, you feel it but cannot explain it. And it is only the beginning.

Think, See, Hear, Feel, Act With The Heart

We have all been seeing, hearing, thinking, feeling and launching intention to acting with our mortal beings. It is ego, it is survival, it is using the physical sensors of body. But as you now hopefully understand there is a counterpart of immortal form overlaying this body form—exactly like there is a New Earth overlaying the old. The Old Earth lower mind is being replaced by the New Earth higher mind and instead of the brain being the physical control center it is the heart that becomes the physical command center.

The new configuration of heart and higher mind shifts command to what is New Earth and the old senses of hear, see, feel, etc. give way to a huge range as picked up by the partners of the chakra system that links to the transformed physical (higher vibration). That process that knows only love and unity is to open to the heart. It is to align into the higher carrier wave of all that is, made of the substance of love.

What this means in practice is to take every moment that comes before you and to deploy these new senses to act like a filter of energies of thoughts, visions, words and feelings coming in and to act as the generator of its higher vibration going out of you. This is the energy that you accept or create within your hologram. The filter is to convert all coming in to something positive or good by seeing, hearing, saying, feeling the good part only. That is through the heart. The generator is to create energies going out from the heart that are good, based in love, unconditional—as you would with your own children. The difference here is that everything that is, is your own children. So all you have to do is join hearts, like you do with your family. But your family has grown to New Earth.

No one needs to buy devices, gizmos, or stuff that promises you a DNA awakening, new health and wealth. This is a realm that is accessible through the heart. It is free like the Train Ticket to Ascension. It is all being given to you if you wake up and accept it. **You don't even have to work for it, but you have to work at it**.

It's unstoppable, it is only a question of choice—yours. Will you now like to stay behind and serve the gods or would you be God? Your Choice!

Know Creatorship Within

Know this:

Whatever you choose, there is no judgment attached to your choice. Nor is there a judgment day.

In fact, all of this shifting between Old and New Earths will be subtle at first. It will begin like a new global marketing strategy where the mass consumer simply shifts his attention. But as the new energy floods in, so it replaces the old and many large systems lose their ability to be sustained. It is like the financial and religious systems that are based on debt and dominion—an energy that can't stay anchored in this shifting consciousness.

In addition, a lot of big environmental things will continue to happen as the shift occurs to highlight old errors of our old system and these become catalysts to change fast as people perish in the lesson. These are areas of old energy dysfunction and deception that get cleared in mass. The shifting from old to new will be like this up until the Time of Transformation when many physical changes to humans and Earth begin their new emergence. It is when the cosmic forces begin to make the old forms strain in an effort to adapt to a changing atmospheric and consciousness environment.

There is a very deep resistance within humanity to believe in cosmic influences, despite the fact that the majority of humanity support the stories of Genesis and Christ; these could easily equal the best science fiction story of all time. The ascension process is a global and cosmic phenomenon which quickens now. It is through the influence of the harmonics of cosmic bodies such as the Sun and the Moon as well as other cosmic bodies and energies that are in configurations and energy influencing patterns like in no other time. The ancient science of astrology has atrophied in its attention similar to humanity's own sensory abilities.

Like electrons, celestial bodies orbit along their paths with an essence and energy of their being and in so doing resonate or ring their unique vibrations that emanate from them. For example, all are used to understanding the moon and its gravitational and emotional pull or influence. It is both a physical and mental influence on energies of matter and non-matter, or consciousness. It is because you are 90% energetic in nature.

And so these cosmic bodies are like balls swung on a string near your ears. The vibration of it becomes louder and stronger as it approaches, entraining with specific parts of you that are receptive to it—like your chakras in particular. All cosmic bodies and things create different resonances of vibration and have different unique purposes that are projected, affecting Gaia and all living things to some degree. This becomes more or less intense depending upon its distance, alignment with others, and position away, all to induce a specific pattern. Their individual and joint vibrations that they emanate can affect your consciousness which is itself energy in a wave form transmitted through the chakras to the physical body, affecting biochemistry and behaviour. It is all about interacting energies that we have no control over.

There are many, many such cycles and influences of this nature that come and go to combine into different patterns setting an underlying consciousness environment for all living things. And some of these are very long indeed. We also emit energy patterns with characteristics of vibration with our own heart field— our unique signatures. The effect of course is different on each that receives it or comes under the influence. Many forms exist such as with heat, ultraviolet, infrared, and special cosmic particles of energy are felt by you and their characteristics are known by science. But the characteristics of love, or compassion or spirit are not so obvious to you. They are nevertheless the same, emanating as wave vibrations upon the bodies and minds of all living energies, in different ways or intensity depending upon the vibrational or resonant makeup of each. At the root of this is the strongest force that manages how it is received and transmitted—intent.

It is important to understand there are influences and energies at play here that are all interacting to contribute to the overall influence of consciousness on the planet, irrespective of whether these are 3D, 4D, or 5D states. Such cycles and alignments affect your seasons, your growth and expansion of all living things.

This knowledge of the star systems and the cosmic influences were handed down from ancient knowledge to many who have retained it in some form. The Mayans are the more known but this is also written and known on other continents with the Tibetans, Egyptians, American Indians, and many others. The Mayans were very knowledgeable and understood the workings as related to their growing seasons and life within it. They were conscious of the influences and knew of the longer cycles and alignments of cosmic forces. Thus they indeed knew of the point of 2012 as the time when the shift to a new age would occur from material time to no time—a time when the overall resonance would reach a zenith and a shift into a new consciousness would complete.

This has to do with the ascension of Gaia and those symbiant to her. It involves the influence of vibrations that flood her and you from cosmic neighbours; and from her own larger living body of which she is but a part. These cosmic influences and cycles are vibrations that are influencing the ascension and these are of a nature that you have not yet understood, such as the energy of love and of unity, of spirit and wholeness, of the Light of the Creator—the One. It is of the rising of love and the higher energies that set the scene and the background to Gaia's movie being played out. And as you are symbiant to her, as One, are influenced to some degree.

As Gaia moves into her galactic alignment which is a cycle of 26000 years, it is part of a large portion of an intergalactic cycle of 12 times that. And as Earth approaches the zenith, the influence and hence the pace of potential change quickens as the resonance strengthens. The influence of the bodies, their characteristics and their unique emanations increase as the alignment approaches the maximum. Then a new setting begins to take over and the old world fades. This is all part of the energies delivered to Earth as the new age of influence of Aquarius. This is not an instant process. It is strengthening of new and weakening of old vibrational influence, like the pull of the moon on your oceans—and your consciousness.

As individual units of consciousness and energetic bodies, each human has their own vibrational signatures that entrain with the larger settings and bodies in different degrees and different specific effects—but yet all the same in a larger overall scope.

This is now at a point where the influences and alignments quicken as the zenith of many influences combine in unique configurations that project specific essences of behaviour and physical transformation. If you do not believe this, think about x-rays, ultraviolet, infrared rays. There are many others that affect consciousness. They will begin to override the ego's dominion of these forces. It is the 2012 time where the zenith is reached and it is the point where the greatest influence upon Gaia and her living things is created.

It is important to understand that this process is already well underway. This was clearly shown in Part 2 of this book. And all are affected to some degree but because each has free will as creator Beings of Light, each can choose how they align with this. They can choose their path and the degree to which they accept the influences of consciousness. Not all will ascend with Gaia and they will live out their lives according to the energies they create. She, like many other creatures, does not have the option. Even though the influences and the body changes to your consciousness come to your awareness, this does not mean that you have to choose the higher path.

The process can be one of a graceful transition and evolution into a new spiritual age of enlightenment and expansion. Or it can be filled with fear and destruction. But whether it is a direct revelation or through others, each comes to a knowing of their place as the equal of Christ. In this respect they can accept that they are an eternal being, that their chosen hologram is one of perfection, and that the parallel world of New Earth is indeed real, awaiting a choice of how and when each enters it. It will become increasingly real on the upper path, especially for those who learn to walk both. However, they can reject this as well. There is no judgement except from one's self.

It is Gaia's time to ascend and move into her rightful place as it is yours if you so choose. It is a process that is set in the Mind of God and its cosmic workings. As it is all One, you are part of the ascension process as is all else. But the choices each individual conscious being makes, and the path chosen, and the way it is to unfold into the life that is completed upon Gaia's, is not decided. It is each that must choose.

The Final Message

If you have arrived at this place in this book, you will have realized that there are many sides to a story, science, history, even about you. It is simply a chosen point of view, a personal perception, or an opinion. It is that way but in the end you leave with nothing- the same way you came in. In the end, it is all irrelevant, just like this book. It is because once you understand there is a choice, you can make one. And that choice is not to be light or dark, evil or good because that is a judgment call. There is no choosing when you are above the light or dark because it is all simply love. It is just a place to be. Be You as you were designed to be.

Can you afford to ignore the most incredible process of history? There are indeed the Upper and Lower Paths of the ascension choices that unfold before all. Both paths receive the same amount of Light of the One and the ascension energy of awakening. It is all equal but the attention and the awareness to it is very different. As Gaia ascends her own physical body changes as her Higher Essence draws the lower form upwards into the light. This will mean, like your own body, that the body will lighten and begin to change its properties as well.

This proceeds towards the Grand Alignment of 2012 within the Galactic system to align Gaia's heart with others and the Galactic center of heart known as the center of the Milky Way. As the characteristics change and reach the zenith those energies that are not aligned with this fade and dissolve away, transmuted into the dominant energy of the Light and Love of the Source. Those energies that are not compatible will change and shift upon Gaia and the consciousness of humanity that enfolds her. Just as lower forms of energy do not exist in the higher realms, so it is with the negative and darker energies of control, dominion and conflict.

The essence moves to the central heart of the Galaxy and aligns. These lower energies lose their strength as attention to the new shifts and the awareness and attention increases. At the same time, Gaia's properties shift in terms of her physical nature, affecting weather, temperature, water, air, and she begins to glow and shine within her larger body and her scope within the universe expands. Many old energies and devices and material things will begin to be dysfunctional and irrelevant, not supported by the new ways. These will be replaced by the new, more in alignment with the consciousness of the One and all being in harmony with her. These new ways and energies are already surrounding Gaia. Is this a plan by God? Who cares. It is happening by whatever means or tale an Earthling wants to construct.

As the consciousness opens and cosmic neighbours open the new awareness, new discoveries, processes compatible with Gaia's changing body will be embraced and brought forward. Many are ready to meet this calling and many are ready to lead and show the new way. The Crystal Children will awaken and emerge to take their rightful place as they will feel the draw with a deepness and strength that will bewilder those that are not awakened. They will teach their knowing and their advanced abilities as the ones of the Higher Path are learning and doing. As this process evolves and quickens towards the alignment of galactic hearts with the heart of One, many changes will occur. The old energy of polarity will fade and a new leader will emerge under the command of their Higher Divine Selves.

Now you walk in the 3D world and are learning to walk differently in your Higher World. This is not yet congealed but has formed through the joint consciousness of those who are awakened and increasing in numbers rapidly, having chosen the Upper Path. What many others are doing now is learning to walk both paths. Look for these as they will come forward as did Christ. This world that is forming has no limits and it is the learning of bringing the heavier body to the higher realm that is coming to attention. As below, the way of it is to have the Higher Mind and Body brought consciously to live upon Gaia and bring limitless possibilities to her and the totality of all humanity as family which is all that is One. Over time a convergence of this will occur. This is the ascension that is an unstoppable process.

Through this immediate period there will be those that sleep or resist, who will not awaken, as there are those that will work to impede the ascension as it does not serve their cause. This simply will not continue. They have become subservient to their needs of power and their DNA is dormant. The conflict of this dark and light will become resolved as more and more light shines upon you, Gaia, and them. As these energy forces clash, as they are now, over the next years the strain of polarity will be felt, both on Gaia and her living things and this will also reach its zenith. The process is one of underlying fading dark energy strength while the light energy is strengthening. During this period it is important to understand that the dark ones are attempting to take desperate means to counteract and to confuse this new consciousness, using devices, technology and their knowledge of the higher worlds so as to flood dysfunction and generate lower energies as Gaia shifts. It is simply the lessons to be learned. And understand that they also have a path to create a better world. It may not be the one that you wish to choose.

Through the confusion of energy change, all you need to understand is that as the new consciousness grows and floods Gaia, the old fades, one replacing the other. Together these energies of conscious purpose and type create the whole of the influences of consciousness. As one fades, the new replaces and as the new increases to the zenith at the Grand Galactic Heart alignment, eventually all of the old will be replaced. As this proceeds, the crystalline structure will slowly move each away from the usual 3D body requirements, especially any that are not aligned with the Higher Divine mind and heart. This is the Higher Path that can be chosen **but you need to choose.**

But, and here is the big but.

Right now, as has always been, there is an invisible world that each of us as a mere mortal human cannot see, nor understand. We have simply denied its existence by indulging in the mortal life. It is the quantum world that has always been there and will always be. The entry to it has always been the same—by a conscious awareness of its existence and by a knowing, and acceptance of who you are. The process of change, from Old Earth which is visible, to New Earth which is not, is essentially a transparent process up to a point. Up to a point of merging all will appear the same as old energy clings to old. But those souls who are aware and use intent to take the truth will begin to move between these Earths freely. Unfortunately that point may be too late to get on the train and it is like missing the big Christmas party when the goodies are handed out. How this New Earth unfolds into view and how you deal with the Old Earth as it begins to fade out of view is an individual choice.

The key words of wisdom are this. Take your leave of PLANET EARTH INC. knowing in your heart there is a New Earth forming. On Old Earth remain in a space of non engagement and walk above that which you perceive as wrong or in judgement. That's the train ticket to New Earth. Walk the Old Earth with a love for all and look upon all things with reverence as perfect the way they are, simply like you, in a state of evolving. Accept everything and resist nothing for that which you resist persists and energy flows where attention goes. You have a task at hand and need not engage in that which brings conflict, tears, pain or fear for they will eventually be known as only perceptions. Old Earth will begin to shift and will lose its hold upon you and soon as you see the shift of physicality you will resurrect yourself into your true self. Be patient with this and be steadfast, remember to love, laugh, live as one heart in every moment as your Train heads to Heaven.

But here is the truth of it. God, whatever it is called, will love you despite yourself because in the end, you already are He, regardless of what you may believe.

What is written in the prophesies as being played out now is simple:

By accepting this process of ascension through unconditional forgiveness you agree that you give pure intent to live as your true self in a world of unconditional love and accept your Divine gifts.

Then all you have to do is sit back and enjoy the ride.

There is one more question that you may want to ask. Is this new version of End Times credible in its source of information? First it is a fact that human consensus creates the human mass consciousness. Second, during the time of Revelation, millions of "psychic channels" have come forward with a new consensus of truth and it is escalating exponentially. Third, this is coming directly from the Co-creators from the guidance of Source because there are no Earthlings that are creating the rules and beliefs. Fourth, how does it feel to you? On this topic, we will finish this book on a final question of what appears to be an inevitable crossroad in the destiny of the Earthling.

The Inevitable Is Upon The Earthling

There appears to be no doubt in millions of minds that the End Times are a reality and that that there is some Divine Plan that is different than the New World Order Plan. The year 2012 has been pegged as the year that the process of ascension would become a prevalent shift in consciousness as predicted by the Mayans. As we have seen in Part 2, this process is indeed well underway as millions of new "channelers" and spiritual light holders and warriors emerge exponentially. The consciousness shift from above is indeed prevalent as witnessed by the number of "disclosures", inquiries on corrupt banking, religion, and demands for truth and transparency. Indeed, something is occurring that is shifting the nature of duality towards some form of unity. But it is still choice on the part of individual and global consciousness. Will it be the New World Order of service to Self and dominion of the Mighty Elite? Or will it be the New Order of The Ages of service to others under the dominion of Source? The choice is yet to be tabulated.

One thing is for sure: Many are already going through this process of OBE and QLP, and as the mass of New Agers tell it, all Earthlings are headed for this process to pass through the portal temporarily so as to decide what their fate will be. On this topic, I will present what I have come to know as to how this will unfold. Keep in mind that this is an evolutionary process of individual experience and it is not a mass event. Here is my "take" on this as "guided by my own personal Advisors who showed me the portal:

The ascension process is indeed similar to the NDE where each will experience the temporary separation of Soul and vessel to meet yourselves. It is not to meet God but Self. Each will lapse into this on their own in their own way to see their lives flash by as the consciousness re-boots itself. They will feel the truth peace of Source and love, and will meet their preferred Guides and Master beings whom they have chosen to be within their lives. As you open all dimensions, you will suddenly open to the knowing of how the other world and energy works. Each experiences this with the time of suspension from the vessel varying. This is not an instant and the process can occur leading up to Dec 21, being more intense after. Each will retain and bring that open awareness into consciousness into their vessel and re-ground it into the vessels reality in the old reality. Here you will see and feel differently as chakras for example and energetics begin to reveal themselves and as do your true abilities become turned on. They will not be instant but more like a child, ready to be explored opened and refined, developed through the process of the new light, triggered by intent. Your New Worlds will become more advanced and real as you begin to converge the two worlds of old and new from your total knowing now opened into your awareness.

There will be no exceptions as to coming back from the process of separation as it is not due to death and the astral connection of soul-physicality remains. Yet it will begin to dissolve itself to allow the soul and total consciousness to free itself of the vessel, yet remain with it. This is how each can walk the dimensions but this is still choice as to how you will react, act, and engage the new learning much like the child with the exception of what you have learned, become, were, and still are remains as is. It is to each to expand this at their own pace, or even ignore it. The process of seeing more, understanding more, and being more can only be developed by intent and choice by self, not by others like parents in the case of a child. As this will be occurring for most at the same interval, many advanced in this can assist others. In effect the DNA will open and the transformation to crystalline will accelerate upon reaching a certain threshold in those who are aware of this process. The prime starting point is one of awareness of other dimensions, realties, lives, and abilities. This must be grounded by choice into awareness and remain there to take hold.

As the individual trigger draws near, a feeling of sadness may overwhelm you and you will drop into a state which is much like meditation. Most will feel a loosening of physical self and an immobility. It will come with quiet and a moment of peace, not when the lower mind or physical self is active. The separation of soul and consciousness will be obvious and strange to many but not to cause fear. This will be a very natural process which many advanced vibration souls have already experienced. This is the beginning of the new journey which will be like a new birthing arriving Home, then returning with Home resident within awareness as the DNA triggers it's awakening. As the connection between Soul and vessel remains, it will be understood that you really never left, yet the knowing and awareness will become more absolute as a hard intuition with physical 3D evidence around you to enforce the knowing. This will remain until a comfort zone occurs where your new awareness sets into acceptance. Through the settling in period each will be wayward and seemingly at odds with the old energies and old ways as they have no attractive power. This will pass when full acceptance occurs by the intentional action into the development of the new birthed self whole and one.

The process of rebirth is what occurs, the difference being you are not a child and the awareness of soul power becomes dominant. Your upper mind will not be clouded or influenced in any way except to fulfil your journey and open to your full potential as a vessel of Source. Much of what you have clung to before will simply fall away in interest and attention. You will begin to explore your energetic self and your multidimensional abilities as you become aware of the vast expanse of Source and full consciousness. To some this may come as an overload and if confusion arises remember who you are and settle into the peace of soul so clarity can prevail. Know you are indeed a Light Being in transition expressing through form, through holograms and many lives. This is important so as to maintain your awareness of self as you replace old ways with new of your powers of spirit, and the development of self into creatorship. The situation will be like the child with new toys, so many it will not at first know what to play with. No one can interfere with this now and a process of careful evolution now controlled by your Soul. It is not an instant process for like the child that learns to walk and to talk, you must learn to take the full responsibility of your true spiritual essence and mind. In the following months prepare yourself for this as the intensity builds.

The stepping in and out of the higher dimension of Source which is the Souls' Home will be different for each. Many will move into that space awkwardly at first and you will meet your favourite beings of your hologram as you do now in your meditative state. What will become awkward is that these beings will begin to be seen in your 3D plane with your eyes open. These entities may seem like ghosts and will appear so as to communicate in your normal quiet state. Unknowingly your senses and DNA will be at a new level as that is what you brought back as the gifts. This will become more and more clear as your acceptance improves and you will begin to see how as you call forward the aspect of these beings, and others there will be immediate existence in your hologram. So it is with other lives and even shifting location. You will shift your aspect energetically and then learn to draw forward the physicality into that location simply because it is already there and everywhere. Your senses will unfold as your chakras and DNA align in preparation for your discovery process of refining these gifts. You will note that the entry of negative energies and files will slow down progress but you will be totally aware of these limiting energies, especially ones that you may yourself create. You will interpret these and decide of their worthiness for your attention. Those who come back from source with fear or denial will continue to live in the 3D world but they will become more and more the minority, foreign to the prevailing energies and consciousness. This prevailing consciousness will create major changes in the following year.

Understand that each Soul is taking responsibility for their personal holograms of the life and although each shares aspects of others as multidimensional frequencies, they are not "originals". These are all non local quantum copies that are connected yet separate. Each individual life hologram is a part of the whole. So it is the world of self that is being attended to here as the initial process of ascension to the whole. Your world is shifting with Gaia's, then you will shift, then your world and your influence on the whole will depend upon your level of responsibility and strength of field that is your hologram. The strength of your inductive field of heart and belief will set the power. And so your internal world morphs into the outer whole of Source consciousness, yours being simply recorded information interpreted by energetic chakras and DNA to interpret your vessels reality.

When you move to the Home of Soul this will become clearer and you will understand this process as it is beyond the 3D intellectual mind to comprehend. It is how multidimensional holograms interact and work within the whole, and how you and your vessel express and create within it. It is not important now. Many advanced beings are completing their own holograms which they must at peace with. This is necessary first as the whole must be worked on in grounded unison of personal aspects or "original yous" after December because it is the responsibility of the whole and can only be co-created by an awareness its deed aligned with a unity of purpose. No one can change the whole of the reality, only influence a part of consciousness; only their hologram first, then there is a psychic unification of telepathic purpose that can affect the whole of creation The individual consciousness is first, the individual hologram is second and a threshold of global consciousness acting as grounded unity is next, when they can communicate and act in a higher state of vibration in unison after the portal opens.

The process has already been occurring in vast numbers and it is not a triggered event as many celestial bodies and divine energies are involved in a sequential showering to shift energy patterns. The drama event is a man made construct of sensationalism and Dec 21 is not such an event. It is a marker, like a doorway into a room of new energy. It is like a passing of a date, like an Equinox, into a new phase which is a quiet, subtle transition. As Gaia approaches the galactic alignment the intensity of the new energies energetically morphs upon her and there is a quickening of the process of induction upon her physical self. It is a passing and the process of awakening, like the NDE is easily facilitated more and more so in the individual. The above to below process is already intact by many who talk about this. Many already are using the wisdom of soul, as you are so you need not expect a dramatic event, but a confirmation of knowing and path as many pop into awareness. If there is any event, it is the individual popping into the new reality much like an NDE but that is a self induced transformation or realization that occurs depending upon the individual and his personal hologram of life.

What you will notice however is that it would be like walking in from the cold, through a doorway into a warm room full of warmth, peace and people of like mind discussing the new feelings of New earth. You will notice that the abilities of manifesting and co creation are more evident; you will notice your knowing has no doubts or reservations as it shows itself into the translation of intent into reality. You will notice it is a shifting of grounding energies becoming obvious as will sensing them. What you will also notice in this room are that the body feelings are different and the energies of Gaia consciousness also feel different as she, like you become energetically aligned into peace and love of Source that is clearly within. You will also note the parallel nature of time, reality, dimension, not that you are not aware of it, but that it becomes your reality. Yes, it is that you have been led to this room from the cold and Dec 21st is when you arrive at the doorway with Gaia. She will enter it and her consciousness will enfold like entropy on those within.

The separation you puzzle over is more of a transformation into multiple dimensions, the Earth plane being one of many. The process of coming back is not one of true dislocation but one of realization because you never really left. The physics you know will be different because of your knowing as the Soul is now in full expression and control. as you become conscious and aware of the Earth plane hologram for what it is, you will look different and be different as it is your DNA that fully accessed by Soul commands the process of interpretation physics from what has been known in limited brains interpretation. You world becomes any interdimensional timeless worlds of expression and you how your holograms relate to your chosen aspects of others souls. This is very difficult to place into expression by your words which are inadequate to describe this process which has little expression in man-constructs of language. The DNA-chakra-Body connection now places the Souls consciousness into the driver's seat bypassing the construct limited brain in 3D. Here the knowing between instant communications without speaking as a telepathic process is what develops and what is best to describe this process. What you see as body begins to wane under the transformation so the whole concept of body is different. This transformation is by your choice and intent as to how you perceive and accept this process. Thus it may not come into effect, or it may, but regardless it is an individual choice of evolution.

Those who choose not to accept this truth will remain as they are and will by choice wane or improve their opened selves. The world of their realities will remain as is and they will die and leave as they would under the normal death cycle. You will be aware of this old dimension but in a total new light as all dimensions open to you so you will be here, there, everywhere. Think how your mind works and think of your New Earth as being the real reality. It will be like you are everywhere but with a new kind of body which is not truly a body as you have understood it to be in 3D but as an energy form that may look like one. The challenge becomes one of adjusting to the many who have taken on the truth.

When Gaia passes into the alignment she becomes a new being of higher vibration. It is like a birthing for those that can see it. She will entrain consciousness and allow individual doorways to open thus creating the opportunity for all to meet and know their Souls as Self. She will become that form of new energy of ascension and now all will feel the shift; some will walk away in fear and confusion but those that will not, will assist others. Gaia's process is also transitional as the alignment is simply a trigger to open the door, the time of each being up to the individual. It has been said that the opening of 24 to 2400 hours that will last for each, but once opened it will remain open as each individual time is variable depending on their acceptance; and the shift can be an instant or months. Gaia now being in her astral form can be seen differently and accepted. The others will see only the old as the means of holographic conversion through the brain; for them it is retained as a parallel hologram but not seen-as has been the case.

Conscious creation is what you do in your mind. It is the other world which is the real world. When you have accepted this alternate "imaginary" reality as the true reality, your current world shifts into it as One and an upgrade re-boot occurs to all depending on whether a tipping point has been reached in numbers. That is the portal of realization when the Soul is visited. However, that process is different as it entails shedding the limits of polarity; a nudge by Soul to loosen the hold upon you. It will like an Ah ha type moment when your awareness now becomes solidified and enters your aspects of vibration all at once, in all lives together. In the past, taking this power has been through tedious acts of the upper chakras; the process being natural but taking many lifetimes. Now in an instant this knowing faces itself as truth in that with the senses of 3D it becomes a stark "seeing is believing' reference, proof, or whatever the intellectual resistance of unconsciousness disbelief programming requires to dissolve itself.

The Soul as part of Creator sends aspects of self to forms. How? it is the same as you in your mind can place an aspect of self in India, on the Moon, in another life to play, visit, learn. Your attention to it at that place form instantly as in the Observer Effect of Quantum physics, formed instantly from memory. It is your attention to it that brings into awareness that life, that living. As an overseer of these aspects and their form and environment, your Soul aspects experience, express and gather information in local expression and central storage of Soul's Self as well as in the total consciousness. This tie will not be broken as in death and when the unveiling occurs the meeting of self as Overseer occurs allowing all this to be "seen" and known as true reality. Like an overseer or director of movies of life, each movie is not real only for an instant or frame when the coded information is interpreted into a reality. It is no thing except photographic-computer information which when replayed brings the "seeing". Such is the process of overseeing holograms of other interpreted realities and the choice of retaining this knowing, believing it, and acting upon it is presented. It is that tasting of reality that opens to the totality of who you are when the love, forgiveness, peace are retained in the thought, sight, word, emotion ad deed. It is a chosen rebirth of Self into all dimensions and realities from a point of Origin.

So when you create, as in your mind, there are no limits except natural order and experience. When the ahha moment comes what you see is how you create the illusion of your life here. it becomes the same as placing yourself and others in aspects of other places in your mind. if you have a place now you can go there and be by way of your attention. That is a hologram of your creation. Now that is also your Heaven or Agartha and your Soul directs this as movies including you here, as you can direct movies here. You have been stuck in the limits of the environment depending on the form, your degree of belief/knowing, and in many case agreements to the purpose. The process of mind being limited becomes opened as the shift from one to all occurs as direction of all lives. Thus you never leave one or the other unless you do not recall it for without time it suspends or evolves according to the rules of the whole and divine order. Your life here, there, with others remains in your mind regardless of whether they ascend or not as you and they are at origin. How you decide to relate your knowing to theirs in that life form becomes the question as to whether you forget again or not.

When you step into the ascension room, it will be unique for each. You see it is different than an NDE in that the whole truth is opened and is able to stick. To use a simple example, electricity must increase to a certain level of current to light a bulb. The ascension process has been slowly increasing as the current. Then a switch can turn it on which is the purpose of the stepping through the portal which is like an activation so the bulb can shine. And the time for this to be in place is around the Dec 21 2012. Here you will be the bulb to lighten and know all selves and know all your families in the shared holograms, regardless of their state or choice. The drop back into the old reality will then present the challenge for each as to how they will hold that bulb or knowing in the on position and is dependent upon the current of love continuing to flow. This cannot affect your other reality where your movies are made by all. It all relates to how you apply yourself. But you can never be the same because the knowing is entrenched in your being.

The Current World Scenario

We will leave this topic with a channel by **Suzy Ward** – October 21, 2012 at **www.matthewbooks.com**

"With loving greetings from all souls at this station, this is Matthew. Perhaps especially among lightworkers, who know that Earth's exit from third density is imminent, there is concern because turmoil isn't abating, and in some instances, seems to be increasing. We want to set your minds at ease about this by explaining why the world situation is what it is, and it starts with the Beginnings.

Beloveds, what you differentiate as science and spirit are one and the same. There can be no separation because the origin and makeup of every thing in existence cosmos-wide is energy. This energy is the pure love-light essence of Creator, Supreme Being of the cosmos, Source, All That Is, Totality, I AM.

At the same time that each of you is a unique, independent and inviolate soul self, in the infinite and eternal interconnectedness of All, each resident of Earth is a microcosm of the planet. Earth is a microcosm of your solar system, the system is a microcosm of the Milky Way, and your galaxy is a microcosm of this universe. Our universe is a microcosm of the cosmos, whose Beginnings were what you call the Big Bang, and from that moment onward, no thing exists only unto itself and anything that happens anywhere affects everything, everywhere.

For the past several decades Earth has been on center stage in this universe because of the unprecedented swiftness and extent of changes on the planet, which are attributed to science, and within her peoples, which are attributed to spirit. Yet, all of the ongoing changes on Earth and within you were set in motion seventy-some years ago when you gave energy new directions, so to say.

Energy is neutral, but streams of energy can be directed by their attachments of thought forms. The forms are actual substances, albeit invisible to your vision, and they are created by every thought, feeling and action of every life in existence. Thus the attachments are either positive or negative in nature, and this universe is teeming with both.

The closer ones are to any energy movement, the more profoundly they are affected. Because your world is awash with duality's negative components—fear, warring, divisiveness, rage, greed, deception, corruption, poverty and random violence—you are at the epicentre of dynamic quaking and shaking.

Not only are those negative streamer attachments being generated there, they are emanating from there. Through the physics that governs life in this universe, energy generated anywhere shoots out into space, attracts and attaches itself to the nearest similar energy and, like a boomerang, returns with that reinforcement. Because Earth's streamers at duality's negative end are being sent out in abundance, they are attracting and bringing back exactly what they sent out. This immutable law of attraction is why your world still is steeped in turmoil.

And this is why we have urged you to focus on what you want in your lives and your world! The many who are preoccupied with thinking about what they don't want and their anxiety, discouragement, anger, sorrow and impatience about those situations are creating more of them in their personal lives and the world. Those kinds of thoughts and feelings are fraught with the negativity that prolongs the situations that they want ended!

The only way to stop that merry-go-round is with love, the most powerful force in the cosmos. Love—the very same energy as light, only expressed differently—is what light beings throughout this universe have been beaming with intensity to Earth for more than seven decades. The initial infusion of light saved her life and gave her the strength she needed to jar loose from deep third density and start on her ascension course.

With that in-pouring of light, Earth had more to offer to all of her residents, the microcosms of her Being, and her peoples who opened their hearts and minds received it and generated their own light, their very life force, more abundantly. We have rejoiced with and for each of them! Not only have their lives been uplifted in spiritual and conscious enlightenment, but their response created positive energy streamer attachments that further benefited Earth and her other receptive souls.

Because we love every soul in your world, it is sad for us that some still are refusing the light that would replace their fear and anguish with healing and joyousness. As long as the dark ones were in control of your world, they felt powerful. When their control started eroding some years back, fear set in. By now, the Illuminati are desperate as their last few tattered remnants of influence—the media and segments of military forces and the economy—are disappearing. Tyrannical rulers also are running scared because their counterparts in some other countries have been overthrown by the citizenry. And many millions are living in fear because of those dark ones' activities.

Fear is a magnified emotion that sends forth the most potent negativity. Although that which is generated on Earth has effects universally, as we said, it most profoundly affects all life on the planet. Think how often we have stressed the importance of sending light to the weakest links in our family chain of souls, those who have become captive of darkness.

Creator's law of free will gives them the right to deny themselves light, but they cannot stop its cosmic forcefulness. Earth's ascension course has reached a vibratory level of intensive energy surges and those are blocking the path of energy streamers with tempestuous negativity. Since those streamers can neither turn around nor go forward into fourth density, they are being forced to spend themselves fast and furiously.

This accounts for the tumultuousness you're seeing, and we hasten to assure you, the current clashing will not end explosively! The light from our universal family combined with your own is far more powerful than the negativity swirling around the planet! And, a clear sign that Earth is prudently handling that is, far fewer deaths and much less property damage have resulted recently from earthquakes, her main mode of negativity release, than formerly.

We have stated that the purpose of our messages is to enlighten, encourage and offer spiritual guidance during this unprecedented time in universal history. Also we have said that we are apolitical—like all other spiritually evolved beings, we have progressed far beyond a political aspect in our nature.

So why do we even speak about politics? Knowing how your world became laden with negativity is essential for understanding Earth's ascension, and an explanation cannot omit her reason: to be free of the massive negativity caused by the effects of political ideologies.

Political decisions affect the lives of the populace—civil rights, laws, education, employment, kinds of information disseminated, cultural practices, economic conditions, taxation, voting, medical care, religious orientation and designation of "enemies." The bedrock of most of your world's governments has long been war, corruption, deception and oppression of one kind or another, and all of that has produced rampant negativity.

Throughout the ages, combative ruling bodies have caused the endless blood-shedding that almost killed your planet. That is why Gaia, Earth's soul, chose to have her body leave third density, where darkness flourishes, and journey into higher densities where bitterly polarized political ideologies and their tragic results do not exist.

Decisions and actions of the United States government are influential worldwide, therefore that country's forthcoming election holds global interest. We have spoken about President Obama' mission in the context of Earth's Golden Age master plan, which is in accordance with Gaia's desire of a peaceful world where all live in harmony with Nature. Her desire and the plan that embodies it transcend politics in every nation.

Obama, who has experienced many lifetimes in leadership positions, accepted the monumental mission to bring peace to your world, and he came in with the wisdom, vision, dedication, and moral and spiritual integrity to lead the way. Neither he nor his mission has changed.

However, throughout his term in office, his efforts have been undermined by the Illuminati—those who are in Congress who are supported by those who are not. An example of their combined handiwork that you will recognize is the oft-berated "Obamacare," which is but a broken skeleton of Obama's intention. To get any of the reforms he wanted for the people of his country, he had no option but to change some provisions and add or eliminate others so that Congress would enact the Affordable Healthcare Bill.

Soon all individuals whose actions are motivated by greed and control no longer will be around. Then you shall see why the highest universal council selected the soul born as Barack Obama to fill one of the most vital roles in your world today. This would have been evident throughout his presidency had it not been for the tenacity of the dark ones.

Despite their ability to delay major progress of reforms, Earth with her vanguard of lighted souls has continued moving apace toward fourth density. With the countdown now measured in only weeks, before long you shall see current upheavals and conflicts start evolving into a unified desire for a world at peace and the onset of Earth's Golden Age.

Let us speak about the very earliest stages of life in that Age. In our last message we enumerated the priority projects that will be undertaken. Now we shall describe what you can anticipate insofar as the general nature of society.

As we have stated before, not all the glories of the Golden Age will be on its doorsill. Neither will a completely different or enlightened society arrive there. Both Earth and Nirvana will continue to be excellent schoolhouses for souls to evolve into androgynous beings—those who have ideally balanced feminine and masculine energies—and what needs balancing most of all are emotions because they influence attitudes and choices of action and reaction.

Simply entering Nirvana doesn't change a person's nature and simply entering the Golden Age won't either. We are not speaking about adherence to a soul contract—any who seriously deviated from their contracts, ignored the guidance of conscience and wilfully chose dark ways, won't be around—but rather your personality traits, interests, ideas, standards, aspirations, skills and talents.

For example, a pessimist won't become an optimist, nor will someone who tends to be lazy suddenly be industrious. Shy individuals won't become gregarious or vice versa. Someone who analyzes a situation at length won't start acting spontaneously and a person accustomed to doing a mediocre job won't be a perfectionist. Baseball and soccer enthusiasts won't switch to embracing the arts, nor will artists start training for the Olympics. Farmers won't change their occupation and neither will teachers, nurses, mechanics, shopkeepers, chefs, architects, carpenters, computer programmers or anyone else whose work is fulfilling.

In short, your characteristics, aptitudes, jobs, hobbies and so forth—everything that comprises the unique individual that each of you is—aren't going to be different until you so choose. We wish to qualify that a bit: Individuals who enjoy hunting and fishing will rapidly change from those forms of recreation to other equally satisfying pastimes that honor all life in Nature's realm.

The grand difference that all will welcome is a willingness to start seeing situations from others' perspectives, to adopt attitudes that lead to harmonious discussions and resolutions, and to proceed in ways that best serve everyone's needs. You will be living in the love-light vibrations that engender those approaches and inspire actions accordingly.

The 'like attracts like' law of physics also connects persons who are kindred spirits energetically. Relationships—in families, workplaces, community activities or national organizations—that are based on that foundation will endure, those that are not, won't. With the understanding that the goal of all souls is to grow in spiritual and conscious awareness, there can be amiable agreement when parting ways offers opportunities for that advancement.

Serious health conditions will change gradually rather than chronic illness ending in one fell swoop; however, once in fourth density's vibrations, you will begin to feel remarkably refreshed in body, mind and spirit. For many years you have been assaulted by a multitude of toxins that have taken a severe toll on the populace. None of those toxic elements is in fourth density, and as you continue moving into its higher, stronger vibrations, bodies will be restored to perfection.

We know how eager you are to hear when our space family members among you and in your skies will be officially welcomed. Our good friend Hatonn tells us that all is in readiness, they are just waiting for the signal from the universal highest council, which acts upon God's guidance.

Is the economy really stabilizing or are the Illuminati manipulating that illusion? The global economy, which is a product of smoke and mirrors, to use your term, is irreparable. The foundation of the new system has been slid under the old so that when its collapse comes, the new foundation will be well established. That will enable the transition from the old system to the new to come about without the dam breaking, so to say.

Customized changes in currency, banking, lending, taxes, commerce and investing will be instituted at a pace to minimize confusion, but debt forgiveness in the case of IMF loans to countries where the money never reached the impoverished masses is an economic priority and so is providing the essentials those many millions require. Remedying your bleak employment, homelessness and refugee situations also are priorities.

To you dear souls who send my mother questions of personal nature—such as where and when to relocate, your missions, is your light sufficient to physically go along Earth, can your illness be cured—we don't have the answers you are seeking. But you do—everything that is important for you to know is within your soul!

In many messages we have urged you to stop relying on external sources to provide answers and instead, go within. Quiet your mind of 3D chatter and let your soul's messages come as they do—intuition, instinct, inspiration, aspiration and conscience, the guidance that keeps you on track with what you chose in your soul contract.

However, regarding missions, we shall repeat what we have said about the comparative few who are needed to fill leadership positions. Most of you chose to be way-showers by radiating your light, and you are fulfilling that role simply by living as the Being you are, one of God's beloved children and related to all others in His family—all of Earth's humankind, animals, the plant kingdom and the invaluable souls in the Devic realms.

It is important to be discerning about information of world events, too, because disinformation still abounds in mainstream media, private publications and the Internet, including channeled messages. Again, go within and pay attention to the sensation that comes. If the information at issue flows easily, very likely it is truth; if you feel any resistance, very likely it is false. The lower consciousness level of a closed mind, however, will cause the person to reject all information that doesn't support her or his rigid beliefs.

Above all, do not get drawn in by any fearful information—there is nothing to fear! This is a time to feel joyful, excited and victorious! You are but a tiny segment of linear time away from the finish line of the greatest triumph ever seen in this universe, and in the continuum you have passed the finish line, you already have triumphed!

We honor you for your valor and steadfastness in the light. We honor you for your perseverance and ingenuity in overcoming all roadblocks set in your way by the darkness and for your patience with delays. We honor you for leading your world into the new era of love, peace and harmony with all of Nature. Please honor yourselves as we do!

LOVE and PEACE
Suzanne Ward

In The End Is The Beginning

So the real question comes back to you. Do you want to serve the gods who run PLANET EARTH or be what you already are as God? Is it The New Order of The Ages inspired by all of these new found Selfs ready for New Earth? Or is it the New World Order directed by the old Elite of PLANET EARTH INC that will continue to keep the slaves happy?

In the end we are in the End Times and it can be the Beginning. In the end, what you have read is irrelevant if you can rise above it all.

It is time to Choose.
Put your vote into the cosmic soup of Source where you really are.

Choose well.

Edward Alexander of the *Rychkun* clan

For more books by Ed Rychkun, go to
www.edrychkun.com

The Book of Secrets I: Breaking the Chains of your Spiritual and Commercial Bondage. In this book, Ed Rychkun tells a story about two happy Light Beings who volunteered for a special mission to planet Earth. Having been incarnated as Tom and Pam Doubtfull, they have been captured in a commercial and spiritual illusion that has consumed their existence. Live with them as they meet two Mentors and uncover the Secrets about the Cloak of the Matrix and how the truth has been hidden from them by the Global Elite. See how they cast away the old belief system to unplug from this Matrix. Learn the secrets of how they break their chains of Spiritual and Commercial bondage to walk through a new door into a new reality, and their New Age birthright. Learn how they *Wake up and unplug from the Spiritual and Commercial Illusion.*

The Book of Secrets II: Taking Back Your Financial and Spiritual Powers In this revealing book, Ed Rychkun continues the journey out of the Commercial and Spiritual Matrix imposed by the Global Elite. Learn astonishing secrets as Tom and Pam Doubtfull, two descended Light Beings who have now awakened from the deception of the Cloak of the Matrix, continue to dig deeper and deeper into the truth behind the Commercial and Spiritual Illusion. Learn how they create a Commercial Duality and recover the powers they have lost. In a compelling dialogue, Tom is subjected to the Commercial Martial Arts to earn his belts, each time opening a new door towards financial freedom. Here he uncovers new tactical secrets in the hidden private world of commerce to develop an arsenal of secret unpublished financial offensive and defensive weapons. See also how they transmute themselves spiritually by rejecting their Religious Duality to ultimately develop their new life plan leading them on their new journey towards ascension. *Learn to take back your own financial and spiritual powers.*

The Book of Secrets III: Preparing For Ascension In this book, Ed Rychkun continues the journey of ascension with Tom and Pam Doubtfull, two descended Light Beings who have awoken to who they really are. Having discovered how they have been captured into the commercial and spiritual illusions, they now know exactly how to unplug from the Cloak of the Matrix and take back their spiritual and financial powers. Now Tom and Pam must set a practical new course that takes them through a Life Plan and back to their lineage of Spirit – their birthright. Follow Pam and Tom as they now lay out their steps of ascending from their 3D material conundrum into 4D and 5D light beings, crossing over the 2012 zero point predicted by the Mayans. Learn how they rationalize the conflicting prophesies, galactic cataclysms, Earth upheaval, and economic collapse using New Age, scientific, biblical and esoteric evidence to determine their ultimate plan. Follow them in their struggle to go back to Nature, leave the material world behind and prepare for their final homecoming. *Prepare yourself for Ascension and the Great Awakening.*

THE DIVINE PROVINCE New Earth is here!
In *The Divine Province*, Jaemes McBride and Ed Rychkun answer a 26,000 year old question of how we manifest and maintain the Golden Age. They bring into our 3D reality the New Earth consciousness unfolding now during the End Times. Taking readers on a 6000 year journey of Old Earth, they expose how Earthlings have been ruled by Elite powers and how their means of conquest has been religion and commerce under a corporate model of PLANET EARTH INC. Learn how the silent dominion has separated the Earthlings from spirit thus accepting the physical imprisonment of the body vessel, disguising the truth of who they are. Now at the end of a 26,000 year cycle, a new consciousness has awakened multitudes of sleeping imprisoned souls to bring a New Earth into awareness, threatening the Ruler's dominion and their business plan of the New World Order. It is an awakening of who we are! Learn how the *Divine Province* has rapidly evolved as an expression of the new consciousness. See how it is now manifesting the physical birthing of New Earth, bringing the means from above in 5D consciousness to below into 3D reality, embodying the manifestation of peace, love, abundance and prosperity upon Old Earth. *Divine Province* is rapidly being populated by Divine beings of Light expressing themselves through Divine physical vessels who know who they are. In this book, the authors reveal how through rising above polarity and fear, one can choose the path leading to the alchemical gold of the Golden Age under *Divine Province* where commercial and spiritual sovereignty reign.

QLP by Ronald Conn QLP is the all-knowingness of everything! QLP is the positive transformation of the year 2012 that humanity has been waiting for. It is our great awakening and spiritual transformation, which unveils the all-knowingness of everything. It accesses and unleashes the wisdom that Christ, Buddha and Moses knew about. It will reveal the energies of life that have been hidden away from us since the beginning of time. It is your Quantum Limitless Potential.

www.ingramcontent.com/pod-product-compliance
Lightning Source LLC
Chambersburg PA
CBHW080814190426
43197CB00041B/2741